Employee Relations Management

Thank you for choosing a SAGE product!
If you have any comment, observation or feedback,
I would like to personally hear from you.

Please write to me at **contactceo@sagepub.in**

Vivek Mehra, Managing Director and CEO, SAGE India.

Bulk Sales

SAGE India offers special discounts
for bulk institutional purchases.

For queries/orders/inspection copy requests,
write to **textbooksales@sagepub.in**

Publishing

Would you like to publish a textbook with SAGE?
Please send your proposal to **publishtextbook@sagepub.in**

Subscribe to our mailing list

Write to **marketing@sagepub.in**

This book is also available as an e-book.

Employee Relations Management

Text and Cases

D. P. Sahoo

*Faculty, Institute of Management Technology,
Ghaziabad, Delhi NCR, India*

Los Angeles | London | New Delhi
Singapore | Washington DC | Melbourne

First published in 2020 by

SAGE Publications India Pvt Ltd
B1/I-1 Mohan Cooperative Industrial Area
Mathura Road, New Delhi 110 044, India
www.sagepub.in

SAGE Publications Inc
2455 Teller Road
Thousand Oaks, California 91320, USA

SAGE Publications Ltd
1 Oliver's Yard, 55 City Road
London EC1Y 1SP, United Kingdom

SAGE Publications Asia-Pacific Pte Ltd
18 Cross Street #10-10/11/12
China Square Central
Singapore 048423

Published by Vivek Mehra for SAGE Publications India Pvt Ltd. Typeset in 10/12 pt Cambria by AG Infographics, Delhi.

Library of Congress Cataloging-in-Publication Data Available

ISBN: 978-93-532-8707-8 (PB)

SAGE Team: Amit Kumar, Indrani Dutta, Ankit Verma, Sonam Rana and Kanika Mathur

Contents

Part 5: **Industrial Relations in Emerging Industries and Impacts of International Bodies on Industrial and Employee Relations in India**

Detailed Contents

List of Figures

List of Tables

List of Abbreviations

AEW	Association of Engineering Workers
AI	Artificial intelligence
AICCTU	All India Central Council of Trade Unions
AIRF	All India Railwaymen's Federation
AITUC	All India Trade Union Congress
ALC	Additional labour commissioner
BALCO	Bharat Aluminium Corporation
BDRWU	Bengal Dooars Railway Workers Union
BEL	Bharat Electronics Limited
BEML	Bharat Earth Movers Limited
BHEL	Bharat Heavy Electricals Limited
BIC	British India Corporation
BIRA	Bombay Industrial Relations Act
BMHA	Bombay Mill Hands Association
BMS	Bharatiya Mazdoor Sangh
BPCL	Bharat Petroleum Corporation Ltd
BSL	Bharat Seats Limited
BSWU	Bharat Seats Workers Union
CIS	Occupational Safety and Health Information Centre
CITU	Centre of Indian Trade Unions
CPI	Communist Party of India
CPI(M)	Communist Party of India (Marxist)
CPI(ML)	Communist Party of India (Marxist–Leninist)
CTU	Central trade union
CTUO	Central trade union organization
DA	Dearness allowance
DCA	Department of Company Affairs
DLC	Deputy labour commissioner
EGEU	Engineering and General Employees Union
EM	Emerging markets
EML	Eastern Medikit Ltd
EOI	Export-oriented industries

EPF	Employee Provident Fund
EPFO	Employees' Provident Fund Organisation
EPL	Eastern Press Ltd
ESI	Employees State Insurance
ESMA	Essential Services Maintenance Act
ESOP	Employee stock option plan
F.I.T.E	Forum for IT Employees
FDI	Foreign direct investment
FY	Fiscal year
GDP	Gross domestic product
GRC	Grievance Redressal Committee
GVA	Gross value added
HAL	Hindustan Aeronautics Limited
HMIEU	Hyundai Motor India Employees' Union
HMIL	Hyundai Motor India Limited
HMKP	Hind Mazdoor Kisan Panchayat
HMS	Hind Mazdoor Sabha
HMSI	Honda Motorcycle and Scooter India
HMT	Hindustan Machine Tools
HP	Hewlett Packard
HR	Human resources
HRD	Human resource development
HRM	Human resource management
IBA	Indian Banks' Association
ICC	Internal complaints committee
ICLR	International Commission for Labor Rights
ID Act	Industrial Disputes Act, 1947
IFFTU	Indian Federation of Free Trade Unions
IFL	Indian Federation of Labour
IISCO	Indian Iron and Steel Company
ILC	International Labour Conference
ILO	International Labour Organization
IMF	International Monetary Fund
IMT	Institute of Management Technology
INTUC	Indian National Trade Union Congress
IR	Industrial relations
IRC	Industrial relations climate
ISI	Import substitution industrialization
IT	Information technology
ITES	Information technology enabled service
ITI	Indian telephone industries
JAF	Joint Action Front
JBW	Jivraj Bidi Works
JCM	Joint consultative machinery
JMC	Joint Management Council

JUSCO	Jamshedpur Utility and Services Company
KKPKP	Kagad Kach Patra Kashtakari Panchayat
LFPR	Labour force participation rate
LO	Labour officer
LPF	Labour Progressive Federation
LPG model	Liberalization, privatization and globalization
MEM	Mazdoor Ekta Manch
MGNREGA	Mahatma Gandhi National Rural Employment Guarantee Act
MRF	Madras Rubber Factory
MRFUWU	Madras Rubber Factory United Workers Union
MSEU	Maruti Suzuki Employees' Union
MSIL	Maruti Suzuki India Ltd
MSWU	Maruti Suzuki Workers Union
MUL	Maruti Udyog Limited
NAB	National Apex Body
NAPB	National Arbitration Promotion Board
NDLF	New Democratic Labour Front
NeGP	National e-Governance Plan
NFITU	National Front of Indian Trade Unions
NFL	National Federation of Labour
NGO	Non-government organization
NIP	New Industrial Policy
NJCS	National Joint Committee for the Steel Industry
NSDC	National Skill Development Corporation
NSSO	National Sample Survey Organization
NTC	National Textiles Corporation
NTUF	National Trade Unions Federation
NWU	Nestle Workers Union
ONGC	Oil and Natural Gas Corporation Limited
PIACT	International Programme for the Improvement of Working Conditions and Environment
PMC	Pune Municipal Corporation
PMKVY	Pradhan Mantri Kaushal Vikas Yojana
PNM	Permanent Negotiating Machinery
PSB	Public Sector Banks
PSU	Public sector undertaking
RMMS	Rashtriya Mill Mazdoor Sangh
RSS	Rashtriya Swayamsevak Sangh
RTUC	Red Trade Union Congress
SAIL	Steel Authority of India Ltd
SEU	Siemens Employees Union
SEWA	Self Employed Women's Association
SWU	Siemens Workers Union
TLA	Textile Labour Association
TUCC	Trade Unions Co-ordination Centre

UNITES	Union for Information Technology and Enabled Services
UTUC	United Trade Union Congress
UTUC-LS	United Trade Union Centre (Lenin Sarani)
VBWU	Volvo Bus Workers' Union
VDA	Variable dearness allowance
VRS	Voluntary retirement scheme
WPM	Workers' participation in management

Preface

It is accepted that industrial relations (IR) culture is undergoing a paradigm shift. Nowadays, the incidences of long-duration strike or lockout in the factories, gheraos by workers and resorting to violent activities while on job are being less heard of. The cordial relations approach of the trade unions with their efforts to understand the reason behind the management's initiatives and act accordingly is replacing the traditional trade union approach of claiming, demanding and agitating without reasons. The young generations are less or not interested in joining trade unions and are rather more inclined towards the management, who have successfully generated a competitive culture in the jobs. In certain industries such as information technology (IT) and information technology enabled services (ITES), the young employees find it risky to join any trade union since the same may have deteriorating relationship with the employers. Employees are adopting the new human resource policies which support better pay for higher efficiency and productivity. These new practices have a different impact on IR. There is an emerging trend of declining employment in the manufacturing sector, low trade union activity in sunrise sectors, decentralized collective bargaining and development of management's direct communication with and involvement of workers. This is the major restructuring happening in IR.

On the other hand, the millennials nowadays are known for redefining 'what work means to them'. In addition to their ambitious drive for achieving career objectives, they also value their personal and family time. There are various factors relating to economy, technology and human relations which are responsible for these changes. This has greatly impacted the labour market. Understanding issues related to people either at the individual or group level vis-à-vis managements is important and also relevant in the context of both unionized and non-unionized situations. The study of 'employment relations' redefines IR covering all aspects of relations between employees and employers/managements encompassing both unionized and non-unionized contexts. It is often debated that the subject IR is no more relevant in the present industrial context. But as long as people are needed in industry and business, IR will remain an area of concern as well as influence in affecting the performance of organizations. IR will continue as the foundation of human resource management (HRM) as long as the employer and the employee are connected through the contract of employment. The subject of IR formulates various conceptual formulations involving the employer, the employee and the government within the industrial context related to the discipline for the purpose of governance of contractual relations. The dynamics of 'terms of employment' between the employer and the employee brings them together.

The textbook *Employee Relations Management: Text and Cases* has been written to make the subject of 'IR' interesting and covers the course curriculum of the post-graduate standard. The book would be equally useful for the students and the practitioners of IR. The contents are relevant to the present industrial contexts, written with the objective to acquaint the contemporary state of situation in the industries. The book has 12 chapters and the subject is organized in five parts. The topics covered under the various parts are as follows.

Part 1	Concept and the industrial relations framework, evaluation and the present trend linking to the industries	Chapter 1 Industrial Relations, Concept and Theories Chapter 2 Emerging Trend of Industrial Relations in India
Part 2	Focuses on the emerging shifts in industrial relations in organizations	Chapter 3 Industrial Relations: The New Prospective
Part 3	Focuses on the growth and development of trade unions in India, the structure of trade unions and their positions including the changing trends in the trade union movement	Chapter 4 Trade unions: Theory and the Growth of Trade Unions in India Chapter 5 Trade Union Structure and Management
Part 4	Focuses on the administrative aspects of industrial relations including labour, administrating the impacts of the changing labour market on industrial relations	Chapter 6 Collective Bargaining Chapter 7 Industrial Disputes and Grievance Redressal Mechanism Chapter 8 The Indian Labour Market Chapter 9 Managing Discipline in Industries and Disciplinary Procedure Chapter 10 Workers' Participation in Management
Part 5	Deals with industrial relations in some emerging specific industries using knowledge workers. It also covers external impacts of international bodies influencing the industrial relations and the employee relations in India	Chapter 11 Industrial Relations in IT and ITES Organizations Chapter 12 International Labour Organization

Chapter 1 discusses the concept of IR and the approaches to understand the same. The 'industrial relations climate (IRC)' and linking the same to 'industrial relations system (IRS)' have also been covered under this chapter. The chapter also covers the factors causing adverse IRC and the approaches of the trade unions to the changing IRC in India.

Chapter 2 focuses on the changing trend of IR in India. It also includes the impact on globalization on the liberalized economy, thereby on the industrial relations.

Chapter 3 discusses the emerging trend of industrial relations in India under Part 2. The chapter also covers impact of the economic, social and political aspects on IRS. Aspects such as the declining of labour power in the era of globalization and the changing power balance due to increased mobility of capital have also been covered. The chapter concludes with IR for a knowledge economy followed by a working concept on IR.

Discussions have been made on the concept of trade union, the need for a trade union in an organization, the roles and objectives of trade unions and the history of trade union movement in India under Chapter 4.

Chapter 5 covers the impact of industrialization on trade unions, politics and trade unions, militancy approach of trade unions, outside leadership of trade unions, recognition of trade union and finally, the Trade Unions Act, 1926.

Part 4 focuses on the administrative aspects of IR including labour administration and the impacts of the changing labour market on IR. There are four chapters (Chapters 6, 7, 8 and 9) under which discussions have been made on 'collective bargaining, industrial disputes and grievance redressal mechanism, the Indian labour market and managing discipline in industries'. This part broadly includes the administrative aspects of labour in changing industrial context and IRC.

Part 5 deals with IR in some emerging specific industries, that is, IT and ITES using knowledge workers. The approach to manage IR in such sectors have been felt to be different from the traditional manufacturing industrial set-ups. It also covers external impacts of international bodies like International Labour Organization (ILO), influencing the IR and employee relations in India.

All efforts have been made to keep the book handy and cover subjects which are relevant to the present and emerging concepts of 'employee relations'.

Acknowledgments

This book is the outcome of my three and a half decades of experience in various organizations in the manufacturing sector—power sector, sugar mills, pulp and paper, and car components; ITES organization; and service sectors such as schools and management institutes. Over this long period, as a faculty and researcher, a corporate trainer, consultant and advisor to corporates, and a practising IR and HR professional, I gained deep insight into the subject through hands-on experience of strategizing, leading and managing the industrial relations (IR) scenarios for various managements and organizations. I am deeply indebted to numerous professionals and seniors/gurus I came across while working in various organizations since 1981—to name a few, Mr Salil Dutta and Mr Molay Sengupta of Garden Reach Shipbuilders and Engineers Ltd, Mr S. P. Srivastav and Mr S. P. Dubey of British India Corporation (BIC), Mr R. C. Banerjee of The Durgapur Projects Ltd and Mr S. Y. Siddiqui of Maruti Suzuki India Ltd (MSIL).

I thank my academic guru and professor, Dr B. N. Ghosh for contributing to this work. I am also thankful to my colleague Dr A. K. Kodwani of IIM, Indore for his contribution.

I am indebted to Dr Atish Chattopadhyay, the then Director, Institute of Management Technology (IMT), who is presently the Director of IFIM Business School, Bangalore. He encouraged and extended all necessary help for working on this book.

I wish to thank Dr Akhtar Hussain, Librarian, IMT, Ghaziabad, for assisting in tracing and providing various publications in different journals, which helped me a lot in this work.

About the Author

D. P. Sahoo, a doctorate in economics and postgraduate diploma holder in industrial relations (IR) and personal management, is currently Associate Professor in HR and OB at the Institute of Management Technology, Ghaziabad (since 2012).

He has worked in various industries including the sugar factories of BIC, power sector (The Durgapur Projects Ltd, Durgapur), paper mills of Ballarpur Industries (BILT), an ITES organization (TechBooks) presently known as Aptara, The Doon School and joint ventures of Maruti (Bharat Seats Limited [BSL] and Machino Plastics). He has more than three decades of corporate experience in people management and managing IR.

He has been a very strong negotiator and represented the management in the Bihar Sugar Mill Wage Board, successfully completed long-due settlements in the sugar units of BIC, in the paper mills of BILT, BSL (a joint venture of Maruti), and settled various IR issues while working at The Durgapur Projects Ltd. Dr Sahoo with his hands-on experience in IR has managed critical labour problems, including strikes, gheraos, workers' demonstrations, agitations, lockouts and has also handled retrenchment cases.

His PhD was on 'Misconduct of Employees in Industries'. This study was conducted by him in the industrial belt of Durgapur and Asansol, which is considered as a zone of adverse IR.

The academic life of Dr D. P. Sahoo began in the year 1987, when he was offered to teach 'Labour Laws' in Burdwan University. He has taught in various management institutes and universities including Kurukshetra University (1998–2000); Sharda University, Greater Noida; Asia Pacific Institute of Management, New Delhi (May 2003–September 2004), and has also worked as a visiting faculty in various management institutes.

Dr Sahoo has headed the HR functions in various organizations including state government undertakings. He had the advantage of bringing to the classroom his experience of professional life. He also worked as a consultant to various organizations, both in the areas of IR and strategic human resources, and conducted various management development programmes for executives of PSUs and private sectors.

PART

1

Concept and the Industrial Relations Framework, Evaluation and the Present Trend

1

Industrial Relations, Concept and Theories

After reading this chapter, you will be able to:

☐ Understand the meaning of industrial relations and its scope
☐ Understand the various actors in industrial relations
☐ Gain clarity on the key concepts and theoretical perspectives of industrial relations
☐ Identify constituents of the industrial relations system
☐ Comprehend the industrial relations climate
☐ Recognize the changing trend in industrial relations

C.1.1. Case for Discussion   The Dilemma

Sanjay Singh returned to his chamber after a long discussion with the general manager of the unit. The general manager instructed Sanjay, the APO, to suspend Mr Rajat Chawhan, a senior operator of the boiler plant, against whom an enquiry was pending. The allegation against Mr Chawhan was disobedience of the instructions of the management. Before Sanjay had taken his seat, for planning and executing the instructions of the general manager, Mr Laxmi Prasad, the general secretary of the registered trade union, stepped into the APO's chamber. He asked the whereabouts of Mr S. P. Dubey, the Head HR, who was incidentally on leave. On learning that Mr Dubey was on leave, Mr Prasad, in a commanding voice, instructed to Mr Sanjay that management should not take any steps against Mr Chawhan without holding a proper enquiry. Mr Laxmi Prasad further threatened that if any steps were taken by the management, the workers will immediately go for stoppage of the works.

Sanjay was in a dilemma. After completing his MBA, he had joined the BIC Group of Sugar Mills as the APO and was posted at Chakia, which was about 45 km away from Mazaffarpur, Bihar. Sugar factories were normally set up in small towns and were dependent on the sugar cane (the raw materials) grown in the area. The workers were mostly from the nearby villages, located at the close vicinity of the factory.

The labour union named 'Champaran Chini Mill Mazdoor Sangh' was a registered trade union under the Trade Unions Act, 1926, and was the only labour union in the unit. The labour union had a very strong bargaining power and its leaders, representing the members of the office-bearers, commanded almost 100 per cent support of its members.

The factory was located in a small town, so almost everyone in the organization knew each other. A small incident happening inside the factory often used to become the talk of the town and produce a wave of effect in the small town. This naturally had a strong impact on the management. So the management considered every demand made by the labour union with caution. The strategy of the management was not to throw away any of the suggestions proposed, or demands raised or expectations of the labour union, since it was deemed to be the voice of the people at large. The labour union's office-bearers also had no scope to act beyond the expectations of their members, since for them to support any issue without the support of the workers meant losing the support of the people, which the office-bearers could hardly choose to do.

Sanjay who was new to the organization was in a dilemma. He was not able to take a call on 'the justified step for him to go for'. He had learnt in his institution that maintaining amicable relationship with the union helps in terms of maintaining good industrial relations (IR). The procedure of taking a disciplinary action presupposes a preliminary enquiry. So on one hand, conceptually, Sanjay was eager to follow the due process of taking a disciplinary action against Mr Chauhan, as per the standing orders of the company, on the other hand, there was a pressure from the general manager of the company to immediately suspend Mr Chawhan.

Mr Chawhan had been working for more than 22 years and never had any track record of any disobedience of the lawful and reasonable orders of the management. He had all through been an employee of choice of his bosses and was known for possessing the skills of his trade. He was also known for maintaining a good relationship and behaviour with supervisors and his co-workers. So while Sanjay was not interested in initiating a hasty disciplinary procedure, the instruction of the general manager of the unit was compelling him to initiate the disciplinary action.

IR to Sanjay implied 'the complex human relationships which emerge in the work situations' between the management and the workers. It is the 'sensational', 'dynamic' and 'cause and effect' relationships generating both 'cooperation and conflict' out of 'collectivism' of the two groups, that is, the management and the workers.

Sanjay pondered for solutions. The general manager had his own logic, which was founded on the principles of discipline and the organization's interest. Laxmi Prasad, the union leader, had his own logic founded on the procedure and the process (of disciplinary procedure). Sanjay, the APO, can hardly defy the instructions of the general manager.

Will convincing Mr Laxmi Prasad serve the purpose? Should Sanjay convince the general manager for having the preliminary (fact-finding) enquiry before proceeding to suspend Mr Chawhan? Should Sanjay convince Mr Chawhan that suspension pending enquiry is not a disciplinary action?

Sanjay realized, while dealing with such sensitive labour issues as a part of managing IR, one should not only be ready to get his hands dirty, but stay prepared to get his hands burnt.

Case Questions

1. Why Sanjay Singh feels that 'while dealing with such sensitive labour issues as a part of managing IR, one should not only be ready to get his hands dirty, but stay prepared to get his hands burnt'?
2. What would you have done in this context?

1.1. Introduction to IR

1.1.1. The Grounding of IR

The term 'industrial relations' is used to express the nature of relationship between two classes, that is, the employees and the employers, in an industry or an organization. The traditional relationship of master and servant, which was more at the individual and personal levels, redefined itself in the industrial context in the form of relationship of the groups (employer and employees). The owners of the means of production, for mass production, needed to relate with working class for their gainful ends. This resulted in the emergence of a complex relationship, involving 'a contract of employment, clearly defining the terms of the contract', 'an expectation for the wages/salary', 'an appropriate working condition, that is, not costing on the health and safety of the working class' and 'a work life which recognizes the dignity of labour'. The series of employer's and employee's (at times termed as master and the servant) behaviours emerging out of the contract of employment, between the employer and the employees, controlled by the sets of governing rules of employment, define this relationship. The following is an all-inclusive framework, which sets the platform to determine the 'IR' in an organization:

1. A binding contract of employment on the parties (the employer/management and the employees/workers).
2. Production or rendering of services in the predefined areas/activities.
3. The product or services for a customer or a group of customers as the end user.
4. The activities are performed in a defined process.
5. Some gainful ends to the parties (the employer/management and the employees/workers), or rendering of some social services to the society at large or a part of the society.

In the present context, IR may appear to be a complex machinery of corporate governance. A keen observation would make one realize that it is a complex set of interconnected factors, emerging from the organizational context at work involving the employer and the employees, within a set of guiding norms, and any malfunction in its working could throw the entire organizational machinery into a chaotic state. In short, IR concerns itself principally with problems of group relationships (the employees and the employer as groups). A good IR climate is not an option anymore for any organization. It is a compulsive necessity for an organization's survival and growth. The plant manager, who is concerned with the day-to-day production and dealing with the working class for achieving the production targets, needs to pursue it for developing relationships congenial to the plant's production interests. The situation can never be a point for argument or debate for making a choice between production *or* relationship; it is rather 'production in a good environment of relationship'. Figure 1.1 provides the conceptual understanding of the term 'relationship' within the conceptual framework of IR.

1.1.2. IR and the Contract of Employment

The 'contract of employment' between the employer and the employees forms the structure and provides the scope for building such *relationships*. The term industrial relationship which is often termed as employment relationship (discussed in the later part of this chapter) implies that the 'contract of employment is the verbal or written, expressed or implied, terms, specifying the conditions under which an individual or a group consents to perform certain duties under the direction and control of the employer in return of some agreed remuneration'. The concept within it encompasses the following:

1. A purpose or objective of the parties
2. A context (the work environment)

Figure 1.1   The Contract of Employment

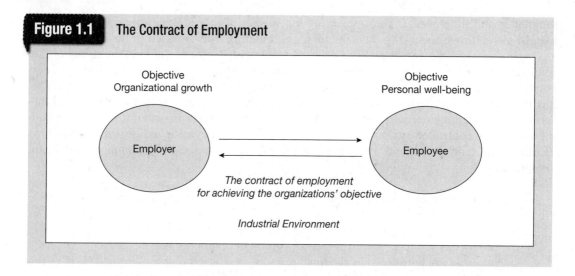

3. Expectations from each other
4. Such expectations are lawful and justified
5. Mutual confidence and trust for each other

The concept 'contract of employment' is as old as the concept of 'industry', within its economic and social objectives. The term explains the legal link between employers and employees, which creates sets of reciprocal rights and obligations between the employer and the employees. The employer's objective is achieving higher 'production', thereby generating 'organizational progress/advancement' and the employees make all efforts to ensure higher flow of individual income thereby ensuring better 'well-being' by way of achieving higher productivity for the organization, thereby creating the bond of this relationship.

With focus on the behaviour of the parties, H. Brewley and J. Forth [1] established that 'employees when treated better contribute better'. It is also observed that whether the treatment is better or not is a function of 'balance of power' between the parties to the contract. H. Brewley and J. Forth point out that 'if the balance of power is in favour of the employees, there is a lower likelihood that they will be subject to adverse treatment, since the costs to the employer of treating employees in a way which reduces their productivity or causes them to seek alternative employment is greater. Conversely, where the balance of power favours the employer, there may be less incentive for the employers to protect their employees against adverse treatment' [1].

The imbalance of power leads to conflict between the parties resulting in employees acting collectively as trade unions or creating scopes for the external parties to represent the views of the employees. The same may turn out to be true for employers through the employers' associations. Thus, the nature of the relationship turns complex, involving different influences and ideologies, making the concept more dynamic. The dynamic aspect of employment relations is well construed from the fact that the relationships are both formal and informal, which are changeable as per context. For example, in a situation where the employer exploits the employees, with time, the employees may oppose such actions of the employer, ultimately the situation may result in conflict between the parties.

C.1.2. Case for Discussion   Workers versus Volvo Management

The workers at the only factory of the Swedish bus manufacturing firm, Volvo, had struck work for around 60 days (starting 2 August 2011). So for 60 days, every regular employee of Volvo had been protesting outside the factory premises against the oppressive management practices adopted by the company.

The strike took place at the works of the Swedish bus manufacturing firm, Volvo, located about 30 kilometres away from Bangalore, because the management had started managing production using a combination of less-experienced trainees, probationers and contract workers hired through the staffing agencies. This resulted in delivery of inferior quality of products, during this period, to the clients who had placed orders with Volvo. On completion of the training period of a batch of trainees and the probationers, they were replaced by a new batch, instead of making these trained trainees and probationers permanent employees in the organization.

The organization, which manufactured for and catered to the luxury segment of a product (each Volvo bus costing between ₹70 lakh and ₹1.2 crore) at a price higher than the market price, focused on higher margins of profit by compressing the labour cost.

The management continued with such an act of using low-cost and low-quality labour, and encashing on their existing brand image. The permanent workers of this well-known firm organized over time to form a labour union, and raised their voice against what they termed as 'an act of continued exploitation of the working class'. The Volvo Bus Workers' Union (VBWU) was registered in October 2009. The VBWU presented its official charter of demands to the management in January 2010.

The share of Azad Builders, who had a 30 per cent minority stake in Volvo India, was bought by Volvo in 2008, making it a fully-owned subsidiary of the Swedish giant. In 2008, the workers were paid a monthly wage of ₹5,500 per month. As the workers continued to demand for higher wages, the management consented to give a salary hike of a measly ₹650 per month in July 2009.

The Spark of Mismanagement

The management called the elected heads of VBWU on 23 April 2010 for a negotiation on the charter of demand of the labour union. The negotiations went on for a long time and came to a conclusion only at 5:30 PM on that day.

Since the factory was located at the outskirts of the town, the company's provided means of transport was the only means of transport for the workers. The nearest town, Hoskote, was about 10 kilometres away from the Volvo factory. There was a lot of curiosity among a section of the workers who were expecting a voluminous wage increase out of the negotiation. So a large number of workers were waiting outside the meeting room to know the results of the negotiation.

The usual timing of the bus departure was 5:40 PM, but Mr Raghuram, Manager, Administration, asked the buses to leave at 5:35 PM since few people had boarded the buses by then. When the workers who were left in the factory learnt that the buses had already left, they demanded the management to recall the buses, which the management refused. The workers gheraoed the management and continued demanding for transportation till the early hours of the next day, which was Saturday, a holiday.

The management, as a disciplinary action, suspended the representatives of the labour union and two other agitating workers. As a protest against the same, on 2 August 2010, the workers went on a strike demanding the wage hike and the reinstatement of their union representatives.

The question in the context emerges whether it was justified for the workers, who are working under a set of contractual relationships, to behave in the manner they behaved? On the other hand, whether the managements' behaviour was justified is equally questionable.

Case Questions

1. Explain whether the worker's behaviour in the context was desirable? Justify.
2. Explain whether the management's action was justifiable?

(Instructor to refer the faculty guide in the companion website for details.)

1.2. The Stakeholders of IR

The stakeholders of IR are not only the employers and the employees. To promote 'balance of power' among these two stakeholders and to encourage against any of these stakeholders having more advantage over the other, leading to dominance over the other, and to facilitate a harmonious relationship between the employer and the employees, there exists a third stakeholder, that is, 'the state/the government'. The structural dynamics of the situation is such that in a highly regulated industrial environment, the state/government is likely to be a dominant player. In the Indian context, for instance, the appropriate government through the provision of law or rules potentially controls over almost every aspect of IR [2].

1.2.1. The Actors of IR

An actor is defined as an individual, a group representing the individuals or an institution that has the capability, through its action, to directly influence the IR process, including the capability to influence the causal powers deployed by other actors in the IR environment. Such influence may be due to some direct or indirect actions arising out of implementation of some institutional norms, including policies, rules and so on. An example of indirect action is when a trade union, not having the legal authority to enact labour legislation, exerts influence on the government to act in a certain way. It is essential for an actor to not only take action for some interest but also have the capacity to take others' actions into consideration and to respond favourably to the expectations, demands or needs.

J. P. Dunlop [7] asserted that an IR system includes three actors. They are as follows:

1. A hierarchy of managers and their representatives in supervision.
2. A hierarchy of workers (non-managerial) and any of their representatives.
3. Specialized government agencies concerned with workers, enterprises and their relationships.

A strategic approach to IR, developed by T. A. Kochan in 1986, elaborated largely on the model of Dunlop's systemic theory which restricts to the three classical actors [3].

In the Indian context, some of the recent industrial trends provide a new look and approach to understand the concept and the roles of the actors. There have been changes in various structures, for example, the structure of production, the business organization(s), the structure of the workers' organization and the systems and the process of interconnectedness between the structures through the intervention of the government's initiatives. The present business environmental contexts in which the Indian investors, employees and government address the issues are more complex and dynamic. The known changes in the context which make it dynamic are globalization and open market concept, new technologies and changes in the working system, changes in both workforce demographics and changes in the socio-economic status of the employees emerging as the neo-human capital/working class. (The actors of IR in the present context have been discussed in the next chapter.)

C.1.3. Case for Discussion   A Case of Government/State Intervention

On 7 January 2009, the employees of ONGC went on a strike, which was called off on 9 January 2009. The reason for the strike was 'demand for higher wages'.

Oil and Natural Gas Corporation Limited (ONGC), an Indian public sector petroleum company, was incorporated on 23 June 1993. The company contributes 77 per cent of India's crude oil production and 81 per cent of India's natural gas production. Indian government holds 74.14 per cent equity stake in this company. ONGC is engaged in exploration and production activities. It is involved in exploring for and exploiting hydrocarbons in 26 sedimentary basins of India. It produces about 30 per cent of India's crude oil requirement.

ONGC suffered a loss of production after officers went on strike in demand for higher pay. During the strike period ONGC's gas output fell by 66 per cent, while its crude oil production declined to 270,000 barrels a day from 350,000 barrels. Production at Indian Oil, the nation's biggest refiner, dropped by about 30 per cent. Indian Oil's plants at Panipat, Mathura and Haldia were badly affected.

The state government invoked the Essential Services Maintenance Act (ESMA) against the officers who went on indefinite strike from 7 January demanding a wage hike along with other demands. But during this period, the ONGC employees passed a resolution 'to face any consequences' and 'more than 2,000 employees in Ahmedabad and 1,650 in the Mehsana division were signatories of this resolution'.

The government took a strong stand and threatened mass arrests under ESMA[1] and NSA.[2] The officers immediately resumed their duties. The ONGC management dismissed 64 officers across the country as a disciplinary action. In the dismissal order, the director, human resources (HR), declared the strike to be illegal, which was as per the existing labour laws.

(The instructor may throw some light on the changing role of the government, which has moved from the role of welfare to a role of organizing business in commercial interests.)

Case Questions

1. Comment on the role of the government in the context.
2. Was it advisable for the government to put pressure on the striking officers to withdraw themselves from striking? Justify.

---

[1] ESMA is an act of the Parliament of India which was established to ensure the delivery of certain services which if obstructed would affect the normal life of the people.

[2] The National Security Act of 1980 is an act of the Indian Parliament promulgated on 23 September 1980 whose purpose is 'to provide for preventive detention in certain cases and for matters connected therewith'. This act empowers the central government and state governments to detain a person to prevent him/her from acting in any manner prejudicial to the security of India.

1.2.2. The Objectives of the Government in IR

It has been accepted worldwide that the state's (government's) objective in intervening in IR is to achieve economic and social goals for the nation. In 2009, while analysing the role of government in shaping employment relations, Hyman highlighted the following roles of the government:

1. An employer
2. A regulator of incomes and prices
3. A manager of the economy
4. A protector of standards and quality of social living
5. A rule maker and legislator
6. A promoter of social citizenship guidelines [4]

In India, the role of the government/state stretches from formulation and control of legislation, designing the macro-economic policies to the role as an employer. It is the economic and the social objectives of the Government of India to control and regulate the relationship between the employer and employees. The economic and the social goals, as accepted by the Indian government, are broadly categorized as follows.

The economic goals

1. Employment generation
2. Economic growth
3. Industrialization
4. Price stability
5. Distribution of wealth and income

The social goals

1. Ensure against labour exploitation
2. Subsistence wages to all workers
3. Pay for skill, competency and individual productivity
4. Minimize conflict between employer and employee

But the Indian government, as a political body and a political institution, had all along been considered as a transient body. With the change in the political party in power at the Centre, the focused drives of the government, which are based more on the ideological beliefs of the political party in power, changes. What has remained common to all political parties coming to power from time to time is that 'the objectives for achieving economic and social ends' continues to be the focus of every government. But with every change in the political party in power, the parties tend to frame their own approach, different from the approach of the earlier political party in power.

1.2.3. The Trade Union and the Employees' Associations

The traditional method of the employees for ensuring that their employers listen and respond to their concerns had been to form groups and make their representatives speak on their behalf. This process ensures them a power to balance against the employer's power of capital. The voice of the employees through their representatives had been instrumental in combating the imbalances of power and unfairness at workplace—claiming fair/reasonable wages, raising the concerns on safety, hygiene, welfare and social recognition. The unity of employees, their negotiation for improvements and betterment in their working environments, employment conditions and social lives were signs of their efforts to countervailing the employer's power against employees.

In the economically advanced countries, trade unionism has assumed roles to make a greater impact on the social, political and economic lives of the working class. Whereas in India, being an agriculture-based economy, the roles of trade unions are mostly restricted to the industrial areas. Being voluntary organization of workers, trade unions in India have left no stone unturned to protect and promote the interest of their members and in addition to the same, they are the instruments for providing proven solutions to mitigate the difference between the employer and the employee as per the expectation of their members, thereby facilitating for balancing and improving the relations between the employer and the employees. The unity of the workers which is represented through trade unions has also been instrumental in bargaining for better wages and working conditions for their members. (The role of trade unions in India has been discussed in the subsequent chapters.)

IC.1.1. INDUSTRIAL CONTEXT FOR DISCUSSION[3]

The Strike Call in Bharat Seats Limited

Bharat Seats Limited (BSL), a joint venture between Maruti Suzuki Ltd and Realans Group of Industries, manufactures seating systems for Maruti Suzuki Ltd and Suzuki Motorcycles. The company is located in Udyog Vihar, Gurgaon, and supplies about 45 per cent of the total seating systems for cars to Maruti Suzuki Ltd and 100 per cent of the seating systems to Suzuki Motorcycles Ltd.

On 27 January 2004, Bharat Seats Workers Union (BSWU) with the support of its members declared through a notice to the management of BSL that they would go for an indefinite strike, in case their long-pending demands raised through a 'charter of demand' are not addressed by 28 January 2004.

On 28 January 2004, in the afternoon, the BSWU issued a statement to its members announcing that the strike action from the following day was called off because the dispute had been resolved following talks with the management of BSL. The office-bearers of BSWU in an announcement to their members stated, 'this success is a testimony to all BSWU members, since their unity as a body against the management of BSL resulted in considering the long-pending demands and the management agreed to initiate negotiation with them from 29 January 2004. Achieving this small milestone was their victory, since the management of BSL was not showing any interest to initiate the discussion on their charter of demand for the last nine months. This is also a great example of what a strong, unified BSWU membership can achieve'.

1.3. IR: The Concept

It has been observed by E. McKenna and N. Beech that 'IR' as a concept was in use before the emergence of the concept of human resource management (HRM), which dealt with interactions between employer (represented by management) and workforce (usually represented by labour

---

[3] The instructor may use this caselet to explain the general practice of the trade unions to represent in a united manner to demonstrate their strength.

unions). It has been also considered that such a relationship as a process involved collective bargaining either at the organization or industry level [5].

The concept has been defined by various authors within the framework of their respective contextual understanding. Dale Yoder [6] and J. T. Dunlop [7] were the few earliest contributors to the thought and defined the concept as follows.

According to Dale Yoder, 'IR is the process of management dealing with one or more unions with a view to negotiate and subsequently administer collective bargaining agreement or labour contract'.

J. T. Dunlop defines IR as 'the complex interrelations among managers, workers and agencies of the governments'.

The above two definitions conclude that there are three dimensions of the concept of IR. They are as follows:

1. The complex interrelations (between labour and management)
2. Negotiation
3. A contract of employment is arrived through collective bargaining agreement

In other words, the concept encompasses within it the collective coexistence of the working class and the management in the industrial context, with their respective bargaining powers to negotiate the terms of contract and its management.

A broader term was contributed by Professor Clegg by defining IR as 'encompassing the rules governing employment, together with the ways in which the rules are made and changed which includes the interpretation of the rules and its administration' [8].

Clegg outlines six different ways of making employment rules. They are as follows:

1. By the law
2. By the employer
3. By the trade union
4. By custom and practice
5. By joint consultation, and above all
6. By joint regulation or collective bargaining between employers and trade unions [9]

The framework provided by Clegg suggests that IR is intrinsically interdisciplinary. It draws elements from economics, law, sociology, psychology, even history and geography for the constitution of the concept. In a broader sense, any knowledge which contributes to the understanding of human behaviour in organizations is relevant, and contributes to the formation of the concept of IR. The concept, in particular, focuses on the collective social relations at work and as such draws on the logics or reasoning from labour laws, labour economics of the country, and the labour and business history of the organization, and uses the industrial sociology or the occupational psychology to explain the IR issues. The concept also sets the ground for clarifying and managing the process of building the relationship between the employer and the employees.

In 1958, John Dunlop explained IR as a system that comprises three sets of actors: (a) a hierarchy of managers and their representatives in supervision, (b) a hierarchy of workers (non-managerial class) and their agents and (c) government agencies including specialized government and other agencies created by the first two actors, who are concerned with workers, enterprises and their relationships.

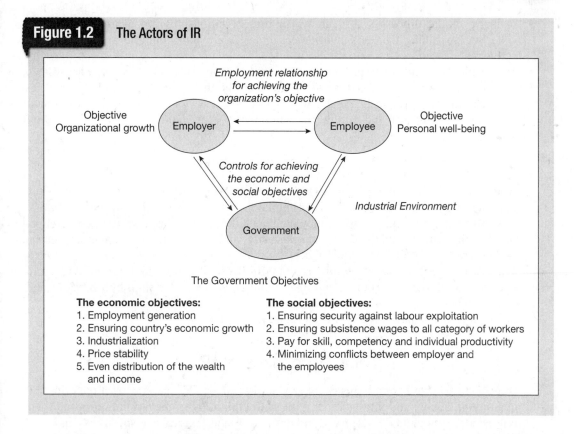

Figure 1.2   The Actors of IR

The Government Objectives

The economic objectives:
1. Employment generation
2. Ensuring country's economic growth
3. Industrialization
4. Price stability
5. Even distribution of the wealth and income

The social objectives:
1. Ensuring security against labour exploitation
2. Ensuring subsistence wages to all category of workers
3. Pay for skill, competency and individual productivity
4. Minimizing conflicts between employer and the employees

He contended that none of these institutions could act in an autonomous fashion. Instead, these institutions are shaped as per their respective contexts which include the market, technological and political contexts.

This is a broad definition that potentially encompasses all actors that engage and seek their respective interests within the employment relationship. The definition is presented graphically in Figure 1.2.

The above definitions imply essentially three rational interventions.

First, IR was conceptually founded on the freedom of association of the working class and collective bargaining between the labour unions and the management, which addresses the balance of power between 'capital' and 'labour'.

Second, the objective of IR is to prevent labour exploitation.

Third, there is a direct impact of the market, social, cultural, legal and government rules and regulations framed from time to time for the parties involved. Such aspects determine and resolve all issues of employment relationship.

IR is essentially (as a concept):

1. Collectivist and pluralist in outlook.
2. Concerned with the relationships which arise at and out of the workplace (i.e., relationships between individual workers/group of workers and their employer; such relationships are promoted and defended by their respective interests).

3. Inclusive of the processes through which these relationships are expressed (such as collective bargaining, worker's involvement in decision-making and grievance and dispute settlement procedures).
4. Management of conflict between employers, workers and trade unions, when it arises.
5. Relationships and processes that are influenced by the government and its agencies (through policies, laws, institutions and programmes, and by the broader political, social, economic, technological and cultural characteristics of each country).

1.3.1. Outcomes of IR

1. **A series of rules which apply to work** (i.e., setting down minimum and other wages set by other norms and terms and conditions of employment for workers, including hours of work, leave, training, termination of employment and the like, as well as issues related to occupational safety and health, social security, and conditions that apply to special categories of workers).
2. **These rules define the roles and responsibilities of the parties, individually and collectively** (through legislation, collective labour agreements, decisions by arbitrators and courts, and enterprise work rules).
   In outcome, the objective is to eradicate exploitation of any form.

1.3.2. Processes of IR

1. Directed to achieve a compromise between 'market forces' (which seek to set the price and quantity of labour) and intervention in the marketplace by employers, workers and their representatives (and by government and its agencies, for political and social reasons).
2. The government in the process establishes various types of rules which govern the employment relationship.

1.4. Approaches to Understand IR

A country's IR system is attributed to the inherent traditions, forming its industrial culture, and the trends of behaviour of the participants/contributors (employer, employees and the government/state) towards the IR system. IR cannot be only a matter of tradition or customs or only a management style. It is the resultant of the mixture of traditions, industrial customs and the sequence of action, reaction and interaction between the parties of the IR system and the government's policies framed with the intent to control the economy.

So all the issues concerning the IR need to be approached on a multi-disciplinary basis consisting the economic, social, psychological or political factors or a combination of any of them. The contributors to the theories of IR have considered such elements of dynamism from time to time for providing a fair understanding of IR systems. The theoretical and conceptual frameworks contributing to IR study the regulation of 'employment relationship' between the employer and employee. Such studies have been done both in collective and individual contexts.

Various theorists from time to time have contributed to the concept of IR, as per their own contextual interpretation on the subject. The theoretical analyses of some such concepts, contributed by theorists from time to time, and considering the identity of their approach, can be broadly classified into 'IR as a social regulation at workplace', 'IR as conflict governance at workplace' and 'IR as a process of rule making at workplace'. The following are the details.

1. **IR as a social regulation at workplace:** Authors have from time to time considered IR as 'a social regulation at workplace'. The same is evident in the writings of the following authors:
    a. Hyman [10] approached the concept as systems contributing to setting the standards for 'social regulation of market forces'.
    b. Cox [11] considered the concept to be 'social regulation of production'.
    c. A similar observation was made by Kelly [12], while he considered the approach of IR as 'class mobilization for social justice'.
    d. The European Industrial Relations Observatory in 2002 [13] explained the concept as 'collective representation and social dialogue'.
    e. Budd considered the concept to be 'the advancement of efficiency, equity and voice in the employment relationship' [14].
2. **IR as conflict governance at workplace:** Theorists have also considered to explain the concept within the framework of governance of conflict between the parties at the workplace. The following are the examples:
    a. Kochan [15] explained the concept as 'managing conflict of interests as pluralist forms of workplace governance'.
    b. Edwards [16] considered 'the employment relationship as structured antagonism at workplace'.
3. **IR as a process of rule making at workplace:** The concept of IR has also been viewed as the process for rule making at the workplace. The following are the examples:
    a. Flanders explained IR as a concept of 'framing the job regulation' [17].
    b. Whereas Bain and Clegg [18] considered the concept as 'the rules governing employment, and the ways in which the rules are changed, interpreted and administered'.
    c. Peter Ackers [19] explained IR to be 'processes and outcomes involving employment relationships'.
    d. E. D. Rose [20] approached to consider the concept as a system of 'determination of substantive and procedural issues at industrial, organizational and workplace levels'.
    e. According to B. E. Kaufman [21], who contributed to the concept in 2010, IR is 'the process of rule making for the workplace'.
    f. Whereas G. Caire, in 1996, followed a mixed approach while explaining that it is a 'process of capitalist production and accumulation and the derived political and social class relations'. In his approach, he combined the sociopolitical aspects to the capitalist production system to explain the concept of IR.

However, the theoretical bases for the above-mentioned points emerge from the following schools of thoughts.

1.4.1. The Unitary Approach

The unitary approach to IR is grounded on the notion that there exists mutual cooperation, interdependence and teamwork between the management and the workers for achieving their shared organizational goals. The concept is based on a set of assumptions that the members of the organization, that is, the management group represented by the managers and the working class and the staff, are driven by a common set of values and objectives, a common purpose of interest. This approach of the group enables them to work in unison towards the accomplishment of shared organizational goals. The conflict between the management and the working class may periodically emerge at the workplace, but such occurrences of conflict are temporary. There is inherently a tendency to cooperate for achieving the interests of the organization that the management and the workers/trade union consider as their common interest for survival.

IC.1.2. INDUSTRIAL CONTEXT FOR DISCUSSION[4]

Goodbye to Strikes and Lockouts in 1998 at Eicher Tractors, Alwar Unit

In 1998, at the Alwar unit of Eicher Tractors, the employees' union surrendered their right to settlement of wages through negotiation. This was a voluntarily taken initiative of the trade union of the unit. The management was free to fix annual remuneration for workers in accordance with the performance norms. Fairness in treatment and adherence to the norms by the management were the only expectations of the workers.

This emerged as a culture in the organization and the productivity increased considerably. In addition to the increased productivity, the motivation level of the workers was high and the level of supervision for getting the job done went down drastically across the organization. There was transparency and open communication resulting in fair treatment from the management and development of mutual trust among the management and the workers.

Source: The Economic Times, 20 March 1998.

1.4.2. The Systems Approach

IR as a system in itself is the approach of this school of thought. For explaining the concept, the following components as elements have been used by the theorists.

- **A group of participants**
  1. Workers and their organizations represented by trade unions or association of workers.
  2. Managers and their organizations represented by bodies of management.
  3. The government and its specialized agencies represented by the machineries and bodies/departments for enactment and implementation of laws, rules and policies.
- **The environment**
  The environment, since it influences the relations between employer and employee, has been considered as a critical constituent, and includes 'the technology', 'work community', 'the product and the market', 'the budgetary constraints that are imposed on the actors', and 'the locus and distribution of power in the society' along with its sub-systems.

[4] Instructor to use this caselet in the context of the theory of unitary approach.

- **The ideology**
  The above participants having their own sets of ideas and beliefs which contribute to their value systems, termed as *ideology*, interact in the environment.
- **The structure**
  The structure constitutes the set of rules and procedures which establishes the interaction between the participants. The structure often takes the shape of 'tools for managing IR' (e.g., collective bargaining procedures, conflict resolutions and grievance settlement practices as adopted by the participants and so on).

All the above participants with their own set of goals and interests interact in their respective industrial context to contribute to the IR systems. The earliest available theory on the system's approach was propounded by Professor John T. Dunlop.

1.4.3. Dunlop's Approach

Professor John T. Dunlop in his book *Industrial Relations Systems* published in 1958 presented an analytical framework to the approach of IR. The framework advocated by him provides tools to analyse and interpret the widest possible range of facts and practices of IR.

His theory explains 'why rules are established in a particular IR system and how and why they change in response to changes affecting the system'. Professor Dunlop defines that an IR system 'at any one time comprises certain actors, contexts and ideology'. These are independent variables of IR. The actors (the participants) as we have seen are (a) the managers and their representatives in supervision representing the 'management', (b) the workers (non-managerial) and their spokesmen represented by trade unions/labour unions and (c) the government and its agencies.

The first two actors are directly related to each other in terms of the contract of employment. The third actor, the government agencies, functionally controls and regulates the relationship between the 'management' and the 'labour unions'. A set of regulations/policies and the statutory norms are designed in the context, which the actors accept to adopt.

The context or the environment, as we have seen above, has a greater importance, since it is the environment in which the actors interact.

The ideology is the beliefs and sentiments held by the actors. Such ideology or a set of beliefs commonly held by the actors helps to bind or to integrate the system together as an entity.

The theory of Professor J. T. Dunlop has been diagrammatically presented in Figure 1.3. The input, process and output model identifies the specific inputs from the environment, which are processed through the interplay of the three actors, and result in the output in the form of 'the rules of the workplace'. In other words, the three actors interact with each other and in this process they negotiate using their economic and political powers to establish a set of rules, which contribute to the output of the IR system.

An ideal IR system requires that the ideologies be sufficiently compatible and consistent so as to permit a common set of ideas and an acceptable role for each actor. An algebraic formula of the above output is provided by the following equation:

$$R = f[A, E, I]$$

Where R is the rules, A is the actors, E is the environmental context and I is the ideology.

Figure 1.3 Dunlop Model

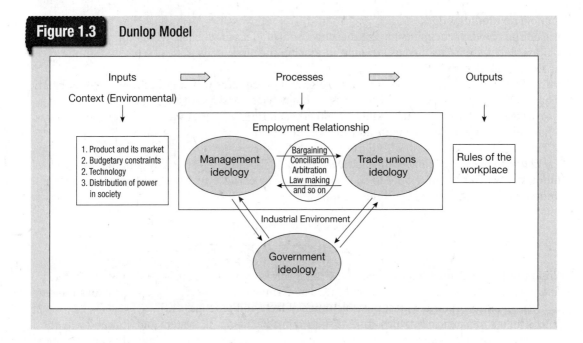

Professor Dunlop opined that the framework of IR is applicable in all the three levels, that is, at the enterprise or plant level, at the national level and at the total economic level, for ensuring its economic development.

1.4.4. Pluralistic Approach

The concept of pluralistic approach is based on the assumption that organizations are *alliance of powerful and divergent sub-groups*. These groups have different competing interests, which are often conflicting to each other's interests. There are needs, which are natural, for mediating to balance the interests of the members/stakeholders of the organization. The organization consists of different stakeholders such as employees, shareholders, consumers' community, managers and government whose interests are conflicting in nature. The inherent notion is that the conflict between the stakeholders is inevitable. Resolution of conflict in such a system is viewed as instrumental for an amicable settlements and harmonious IR. Innovations for growth and well-being of the stakeholders of the organization are the results of the conflict resolution.

Allan Flanders, a British academic, in 1975, contributed to this concept of IR ('the oxford approach to IR'). According to Flanders, 'IR is the study of the institutions of job regulation'. He explains the concept to be *a set of substantive procedural rules, structured to the context which contributes to the IR systems.*

The fundamental assumptions of Flanders are that 'every business enterprise is a social system, where production and distribution are proceeded in a structured pattern of relationships'. The 'institution of job regulation' is categorized by him into two groups, that is, 'the internal employment relations and the external employment relations'. All the frameworks which constitute the internal relationships in an organization were included by him within the internal employment relations. Such factors include code of work-to-rule, wage structure, internal procedure of joint consultation, grievance procedure and so on. The external employment relations included tools which control the relationships between the employer and the employees, for example, collective bargaining, negotiation mechanism and other external processes. A set of *procedural rules* determined as contextual output regulates the external relationships, that is, the behaviour of parties to the collective agreements and negotiation, trade unions and employers' associations; and a set of *substantive rules* regulates the internal relationships, that is, the behaviour of employees and employers as parties to the contracts of employment.

The approach considers *collective bargaining* to be central to the industrial relations system (IRS). The *collective agreement*, which is the result of the collective bargaining process, is contributed internally through the *substantive rules* and externally by the *procedural rules*. Flanders emphasized the following approaches for regulating the relationship between the management and the trade union in an organization.

1. Job regulation through rule making.
2. Involvement of trade union in framing the job regulations.
3. The approach of collective bargaining as an instrument for framing the job regulations.
4. The trade union, which is external to the organization, has economic, social and political purposes.
5. The conflict is contained through institutionalization and regulation of the structure and process of union management relations.

The approach, as a system of IR, gives significant importance to the process of collective bargaining and the institutions of power structures of the stakeholders of the organization.

The pluralistic/oxford approach to IR can be expressed in the form of an equation.

$$r = f(c)$$

Where r stands for the rules governing IRS and c stands for collective bargaining.

IC.1.3. INDUSTRIAL CONTEXT FOR DISCUSSION

The People behind the Wheels[5]

'We also manufacture steel' is the closing caption of the advertisement of Tata Steel. The advertisement of the company indicates the strength of its people, the achievements of its people, the motivational sprit within them, their organized way of achieving their objective and the teamwork which sends the message that nothing is impossible for them. The advertisement links the caption to this people power stating that 'we also manufacture steel'.

The organization is not only conscious of its product quality but also equally conscious of quality of work life it is ensuring to its employees.

[5] This caselet is to be used in explaining the theory of pluralistic approach. The weak collective bargaining of the employees through the trade union lost the grounds for the employees of the town administration.

The development and maintenance of township, where almost 90 per cent of its employees are accommodated with families, are also a concern of the management of Tata Steel. The activity has been entrusted to the Town Administration Department. The employees in the Town Administration Department enjoy the same status and benefits in the organization.

In the year 2004, the management decided to outsource various functions of the Town Administration Department. The management formed a 100 per cent subsidiary of Tata Steel called Jamshedpur Utility and Services Company (JUSCO). The employees of JUSCO were recruited under a different condition of service (different from Tata Steel), which was done to have a control on the labour cost of maintenance.

The workers of the steel plant were not interested in outsourcing such an activity, which they felt would affect the earning of the 'bread and butter' of that section of employees engaged in the town administration. So workers of the Town Administration Department were not prepared for their separation from the department, although they were not losing their jobs. They opposed the company strategy of outsourcing by pressurizing through the Tata Steel Workers' Union.

The trade union assured the employees that it would try its best to prevent the separation. But the management took the benefit of the intra-union rivalries existing in the Tata Steel Workers' Union, which eased the process of formation of JUSCO in 2004. The new leadership of the Tata Steel labour union had taken over the charge in 2002. The union's inability to stick to its commitments and overcome the intra-union rivalries resulted in losing confidence of the people. The office-bearers of the trade union had come in power in 2002. The intra-union rivalry went to the extent that the office-bearers were engaged in legal battles against each other. In the year 2005, the existing trade union lost its registration. A union election was held in 2006 under the direct supervision of district administration and the new body of office-bearers was elected by the people.

1.4.5. Marxist Theory

The Marxian theory is more of *a general theory of society and the class struggle for social changes*. The concept of *class conflict* which was not given importance in the theories of Dunlop and Flanders was conceptualized in the theory of Marx. The approaches of Dunlop and Flanders discussed how 'conflicts are contained and controlled'. These theories overlooked the 'process through which the conflict between the employers and the employees emerges as *disagreements and disputes* in industry'.

The Marxian theory explains 'the process through which disagreements and disputes are generated' in industry. Karl Marx defined a capitalist society to be constituting of the 'haves' and the 'have-nots'. The haves, that is, 'the capitalists or bourgeoisie', are those who own the means of production, and the have-nots, that is, 'the workers or proletariat', are the owners of labour. In society, these two groups, as Marx suggests, are in a constant state of conflict.

The capitalists (investors), as their business objective, constantly endeavour to purchase labour at the lowest possible price, whereas the labour endeavours to sell their labour at the highest possible price. This maximization principle of the parties causes a natural tendency of conflict in the society.

The concept of 'surplus value' as explained by Marx is that 'it is only the labour which creates "surplus value" which is bagged by the capitalist as profit, when the products are sold in the market'.

So the IRS, as per Marx, in a social structure is viewed as a 'class struggle'.

1.4.6. Social Action Theory

German sociologist Max Weber founded the social action theory. The theory views IR from individuals' viewpoints and their motivations to be a part of the organization. Max Weber viewed organizations to be combinations of individual members who are also the actors of IR. The individuals on the other hand are also parts of the society. Such actors of IR have their own goals. The interests of the organization (which is also a part of the society) and the interests of the individual are conflicting, which Max considers to be a normal phenomenon.

The theory of social action is an attempt to analyse 'why the actors behave or do not behave in a particular way' in the organization. Green explained that it is the 'expectations, norms, attitudes, values, experiences, situation and goals of the individuals working in the organizational system' that determine patterns of individual behaviour [22]. Weber's concept of social action emphasizes on 'the mutual orientation' of the actors and their 'understandable motives for their actions' in the organizational context. Such social action may be influenced by the actions of the past, the present and the expected future. The concept presupposes that there exists other individual adopting similar pattern of actions, which implies that there is possibility of 'no social action in isolation'.

Salamon explained the importance of the social action theory in IR. He opined that 'it weakens the fatalism of structural determinism and stresses that the individual retains at least some freedom of action and ability to influence events in the direction that he/she believes to be right or desirable' [23].

The concept of addressing the 'conflicts' has also been considered by other sociologists. According to sociologist G. Margerison, 'conflict is the basic concept that forms the basis of the study of IR'. He emphasized on three types of conflicts which are termed as 'distributive, structural and human relations'; they result from the contextual situations of the work environment. The sources of such conflicts are normally 'the job content', 'the work task and technology' and 'the interaction with factors of production'. These conflicts are resolved through 'collective bargaining, structural analysis of the socio-technical systems and man-management processes'. There will also be a set of conflicts which will emerge from outside the organization and will also be resolved by the internal organizational initiatives of the system.

C.1.4. Case for Discussion   The Case of the Bidi Workers in India

In 2001, about 441,100 people were employed in bidi making in India. Although many bidi manufacturers are large enterprises, 90 per cent of bidi workers work from homes. About 95 per cent of bidi workers are women, and their earnings generally account for 45–50 per cent of their total family income.

The bidi industry is unusual in the 'unorganized' (informal) sector because it is regulated by law. The Beedi Workers Welfare Fund Act, 1976 and the Beedi and Cigar Workers (Conditions of Employment) Act, 1966 aim to protect the interests of bidi workers. Each state of India sets a minimum wage for bidi workers as a piece rate per thousand bidis.

The bidi laws were passed as a result of worker actions, most of which were carried out under the leadership and support from the Self Employed Women's Association (SEWA). SEWA was established in 1972 and in 2012, it had about 13 lakh members in over 14 districts in 10 states of India. It is the largest women's organization in the country. In 2012, its membership included 71,335 bidi workers.

SEWA's interventions in the bidi industry date back to 1978, and in 1981, the Bidi Workers' Organization was established in Ahmedabad. In 1982, SEWA organized a general meeting of 5,000 bidi workers, which was attended by the then finance minister of Gujarat. In 1983, SEWA submitted a report of this meeting to the state government. As a result, the government increased the price paid by factory owners to bidi workers.

SEWA workers then established a cooperative society. The members of the cooperative submitted a memorandum to the labour commissioner of Gujarat detailing their problems. After inspecting the workplaces of the workers, the State Labour Department accepted the demands of the members. Identity cards were issued. A factory owner who had retrenched 200 bidi workers took them back and compensated the workers. He also agreed to give them provident fund benefits.

In 1985, SEWA was invited to be a member of the Gujarat State Advisory Committee on Bidi Workers. The administrative office and health centre provided in bidi welfare legislation were then established in Ahmedabad. From this year onwards, workers and their children could access the services of a range of welfare schemes.

In 1987, the central government approved a project on housing for bidi workers in Ahmedabad. The Housing and Urban Development Corporation provided financial assistance, Ahmedabad Urban Development Authority provided land and the Bidi Workers' Welfare Cooperative provided subsidies. As a result, 110 women bidi workers received houses in 1993.

In 1988, the Gujarat High Court ordered the state provident fund commissioner to carry out an assessment of the provident fund amount payable to the bidi workers. The commissioner arranged a meeting of 37 bidi factory owners and contractors to discuss implementation of the order. SEWA organizers assisted the bidi workers throughout the discussions. After the joint meeting, provident fund payments of ₹497,790 were made to 191 bidi workers.

Based on these achievements, organization of bidi workers spread to other cities in Gujarat. In 1996, interventions spread beyond Gujarat after SEWA submitted a memorandum to the labour minister, welfare minister and finance minister at the central government level. As a result, the central government fixed minimum wages and announced welfare schemes for bidi workers across the country.

In the subsequent years, further similar achievements were won in respect of, among others, increased pay for bidi workers, provident fund payments, housing, access to welfare schemes such as health and bursaries for children, and access to identity cards that allowed access to the various benefits. SEWA also organized savings and credit programmes and health camps for bidi workers.

In many of the activities, SEWA collaborated with both government and employers. The activities undertaken by SEWA when it started organizing bidi workers in West Bengal in 2004 illustrate many aspects of its approach. In West Bengal, together with the labour department of the state government and the Indian Tobacco Corporation, SEWA undertook research on the socio-economic and work conditions of workers from 13 villages. The research resulted in regularization of working hours, uniform wage rates and clarity about the provident fund and benefits under various welfare schemes. More importantly, a local team was formed, and SEWA members were provided with training on the significance of organization, membership, understanding members' problems, their solutions, and planning and monitoring. Three workers from Ahmedabad went to West Bengal to assist with awareness raising and training.

Throughout this time, SEWA guided the workers in bringing an end to the sale–purchase system in which factory owners bought bidis from the workers and no employer–employee relationship existed. In many cases, workers succeeded in achieving an employer–employee relationship, with identity cards issued to workers and service conditions formalized. On this basis, workers then won higher wages, access to a provident fund and maternity benefits among others.

In Madya Pradesh, SEWA's work also resulted in improvement in the situation of the contractors who work as intermediaries between bidi workers and bidi factory owners. Contractors provide raw material to bidi workers in their areas and then collect rolled bidis from bidi workers. It is their role to ensure that bidis received from the workers are of acceptable quality, make the bidis into bundles and then give the bundles to the bidi factory owner, who pays the contractors commission for their services. Since 2005, contractors have formed their own unions and have presented their demands to the bidi factory owners. The most common demand is for regular annual increase in the rate of the commission.

SEWA appreciates that government agencies and government schemes as providing a good base for collective bargaining. The strategy for negotiations is framed within the government rules and regulations. Similarly, projects and schemes announced by the government for workers are used to back up workers' demands.

Case Questions

1. The bidi workers were helped by SEWA for organizing themselves and the upliftment of the socio-economic conditions of the members of SEWA. Justify how the members of SEWA were mutually orientated with high degree of motives for their actions leading to impacts on the organization.
2. Could SEWA establish a link between the individual social backgrounds with the organizational initiatives, thereby establishing the nexus between the organization and the society? How?

1.5. The Constituents of the IRS

The major components of the IRS are as follows:

1. The actors (workers and their organizations, management and government).
2. Contextual or environmental factors (labour and product markets, technology and community or 'the locus and distribution of power in the larger society' [Dunlop's *Industrial Relations Systems*]).
3. Processes for determining the terms and conditions of employment (collective bargaining, legislation, judicial processes and unilateral management decisions among others).
4. Ideology or a minimal set of shared beliefs, such as the actors' mutual acceptance of the legitimacy of other actors and their roles, which enhances system stability.
5. Outcomes including wages and benefits, rules about work relations (e.g., standards for disciplinary action against workers), job satisfaction, employment security, productive efficiency, means of conflict resolution and industrial democracy.

The IR scenario of an organization which the management faces is often characterized by existence of a single trade union or multiple trade unions, no external political interference or a high degree of politicization of trade unions and inter-union rivalry or no union rivalry. The government (state) in a developing country, through its plans (at times five-year plans), undertakes to provide various measures for the promotion of healthy IR between labour and management for securing industrial peace for the development and prosperity of industry, for the growth of a strong and healthy trade unionism in the country, and for the promotion of collective bargaining and raising of productivity through labour and management cooperation. The objectives are harmonious IR, progressive industrialization and economic growth. So the emerging IRS in such economies are a body of rules created to govern the actors at the workplace and work community for maintaining industrial harmony, industrialization and economic growth and social upliftment

Figure 1.4 The Industrial Relations System

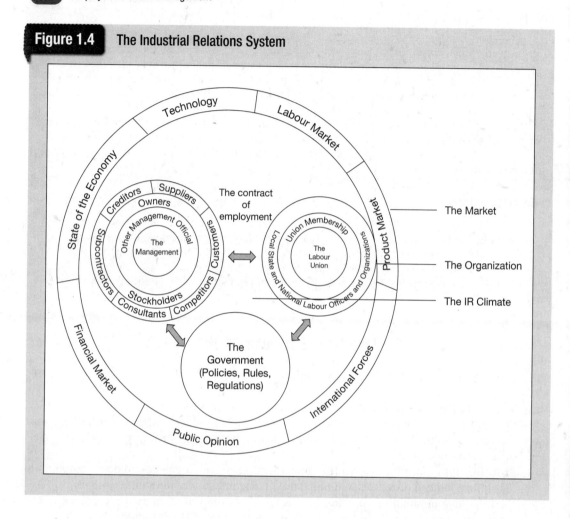

of the members of the society. The process of industrial relation focuses on and is oriented towards managing the conflicts between the actors of IR through various mechanisms which include the collective bargaining procedure, the dispute settling machineries and procedures, recognition and registration of trade unions and the grievance procedure within the institutionalized regulation. The actors of IR in a given context establish the rules for their workplace and work community by first deciding the procedures for establishing rules, followed by constituting the substantive governing rules as well as procedures for implementation and application of the rules in a particular situation. Figure 1.4 represents the IR context in which an organization with the actors of IR functions.

The market contexts which constitute the exogenous factors that impact the functioning of the organization are as follows:

1. International market forces
2. Product market
3. Labour market

4. Technology
5. State of the domestic economy
6. Status of the domestic financial market
7. Domestic public opinion about the organization and its products

The actors of IR in an organization are impacted by the contextual factors that also constitute their own actionable environments. The management's environment includes:

1. Owners and shareholders
2. Customers
3. Suppliers and vendors
4. Creditors
5. Contactors and sub-contactors
6. Competitors
7. Consultants

The labour union's environment is highly impacted by the support of its own members including the supports' strength, the labour union's affiliation with the central trade union (CTU), the ideology and the rules framed by the CTU.

The actors interact within the market context and are controlled by the framework of the rules and procedures set/determined by the government to constitute the IRS.

1.6. Industrial Relations Climate

Industrial relations climate (IRC), according to Dastmalchian, Blyton and Adamson [24], is defined as a subset of organizational climate. It pertains to the norms governing the trade union and management relationship.

The concept of IRC has a nexus with the organizational climate and human resource development (HRD) climate. To understand the concept of IRC, it is essential to understand the concept of organizational climate and HRD climate. Although the terms 'IRC' and 'IR culture' are at times interchangeably used, the concepts 'IRC' and 'IR culture' are different and need to be viewed as different concepts since they explain different set of phenomena. The concept of IRC describes the work environments, whereas IR culture constitutes the contributing factors of the prevailing attitudes of employees in the industrial context (Figure 1.5).

Organizational climate is impacted by its systems which include the organizational task for which it exists within the organizational structure formed with the people at the workplace with the help of the technology. A set of dependent variables, which is perceived in an organization and constitutes the sub-systems, includes norms, feelings, attitudes and a set of attributes that contributes to the organizational climate [25, 26, 27].

A. Dastmalchian [28] observed that organizational climate is affected by a set of causal variables and can potentially influence or get influenced by the end-result variables. The organizational climate therefore refers to set of norms, attitudes, thoughts, feelings and behaviours of the organizational members. As such the concept of organizational culture generally refers to a set of beliefs, norms, expectations and ways of working that are usually generated over a long period of time by a combination of factors and are relatively not so affected by the short-term fluctuations.

Figure 1.5   Industrial Relations Climate

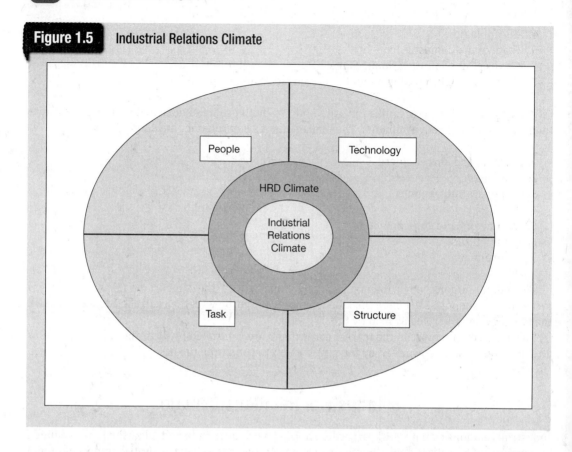

T. V. Rao and E. Abraham [29] in their discussion on HRD climate in the Indian context observed that the HRD climate basically refers to the values, for example, openness, authenticity, trust, collaboration, proactivity, autonomy and confrontation as well as practices such as top management commitment, appraisals, job rotation, supportive personnel policies, training, career planning, feedback and counselling. The concept of HRD climate also refers to the creation of environment where development of individuals and teams gets the highest priority, and HR is considered as the most important resource.

However, A. Dastmalchian [28] considered that IRC is associated with the organization's IR practices forming the atmosphere in the organization. Such characteristic atmosphere as perceived by the members within the organization is regarded as IRC [24].

IRC of a workplace is perceived as the degree of amicable relationship between management and employees. It is seen in terms of how participative, mutually trusting, cooperative and/or respectful they are to each other. Workplace IRC is the outcome of the organizational context and structure, organizational HR policies and the attitudes concerning union–management relations. Every workplace may be characterized as having a particular IRC. The contributors to IRC generally include union–management cooperation, aggression/resistance, apathy, hostility, management's support for trade unions, joint participation, trust, goal identification and power balance maintained by the actors of IR. These dimensions of IRC reflect the perceptions of organizational members. So a workplace IRC generates a set of characteristics leading to an atmosphere in the organization which is perceived by the organizational members and is defined by the degree to which the labour–management relations are cooperative or conflictual, which is reflected in the extent to which relations between management and employees are seen by participants as mutually trusting, respectful and cooperative. In considering climate, the contextual factors and the perceived state of employee–management relationships of a particular workplace are considered.

1.7. Impact of IRC on IRS

The impact of IRC and the outcome or the result of the IR can be explained with the help of the systems model developed by Blyton (1987). Paul Blyton, Ali Dastmalchian and Raymond Adamson followed the systems approach of management to design their model which explains that a set of inputs undergoes the IR processes and influenced by the IRC, they generate IR outcomes as a result. Numerous factors of IRC influence to contribute to the IR outcome. IRC was considered as an intervening variable in the relationship between inputs and outputs, influencing and being influenced by the processes of union–management relations. So both the processes and IRC affect the outcomes.

The model of IRC discusses the outline of how the climate is embedded in a broader set of relationships, involving at inputs level a series of organizational, environmental and IR factors as variables, IR processes, context and climate and various IR outcomes including agreements (on wages and so on), strikes, absenteeism and grievances. Based on the model, different categories of variables are at four different levels—inputs, processes, IRC and outputs. The economic system of any nation contains the product (may be defined through the gross domestic product (GDP) indicating the total value of the products), labour and money markets as well as the nature of macroeconomic conditions which influence IRS through the level of economic activity, for example, inflation, unemployment and interest rates. The factors included under the inputs are classified as follows:

1. Environmental factors
   a. Demographic
   b. Ecological
   c. Economy
   d. Legal
   e. Political values
   f. Social values
   g. Power and politics
   h. Market and competition
   i. Impact of globalization
2. Organizational factors
   a. Organizational size
   b. Ownership
   c. Technology
   d. Nature of business
   e. Decision-making (centralized/participative)
   f. Nature of labour market
   g. Workforce characteristic

Figure 1.6 Impact of IRC

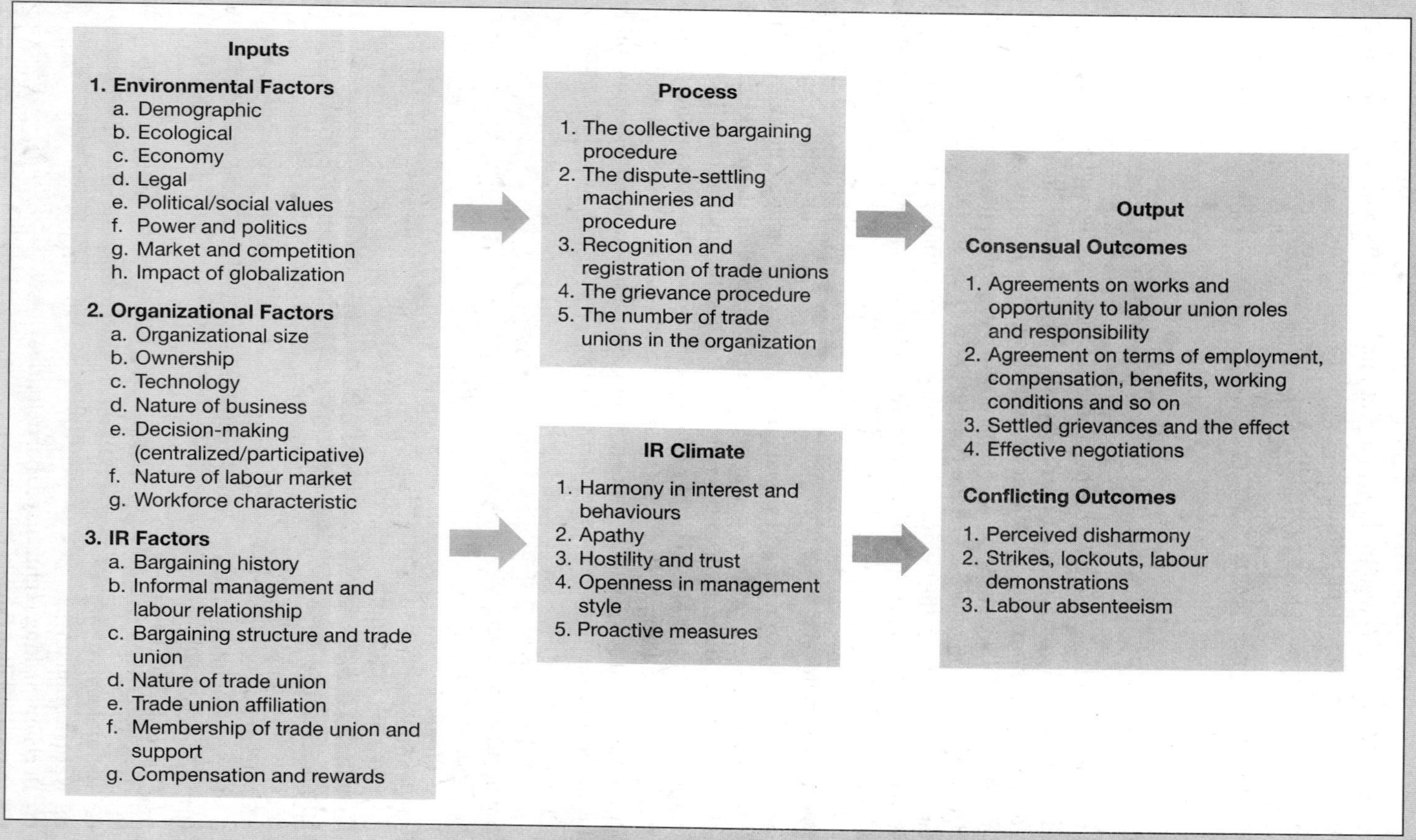

Inputs

1. Environmental Factors
   a. Demographic
   b. Ecological
   c. Economy
   d. Legal
   e. Political/social values
   f. Power and politics
   g. Market and competition
   h. Impact of globalization

2. Organizational Factors
   a. Organizational size
   b. Ownership
   c. Technology
   d. Nature of business
   e. Decision-making
      (centralized/participative)
   f. Nature of labour market
   g. Workforce characteristic

3. IR Factors
   a. Bargaining history
   b. Informal management and
      labour relationship
   c. Bargaining structure and trade
      union
   d. Nature of trade union
   e. Trade union affiliation
   f. Membership of trade union and
      support
   g. Compensation and rewards

Process

1. The collective bargaining
   procedure
2. The dispute-settling
   machineries and
   procedure
3. Recognition and
   registration of trade unions
4. The grievance procedure
5. The number of trade
   unions in the organization

IR Climate

1. Harmony in interest and
   behaviours
2. Apathy
3. Hostility and trust
4. Openness in management
   style
5. Proactive measures

Output

Consensual Outcomes

1. Agreements on works and
   opportunity to labour union roles
   and responsibility
2. Agreement on terms of employment,
   compensation, benefits, working
   conditions and so on
3. Settled grievances and the effect
4. Effective negotiations

Conflicting Outcomes

1. Perceived disharmony
2. Strikes, lockouts, labour
   demonstrations
3. Labour absenteeism

3. IR factors
   a. Bargaining history
   b. Informal management and labour relationship
   c. Bargaining structure and trade union
   d. Nature of trade union
   e. Trade union affiliation
   f. Membership of trade union and support
   g. Compensation and rewards

The IR institutions of an organization, for example, the emergent collective bargaining procedure, the dispute-settling machineries which facilitate the settling process of industrial disputes, the process of registration and recognition of trade union by the government and the grievance-settling machineries including the number of trade unions in the organization contribute to the IR process of an organization.

The inputs to the IR are processed by such IR institutions within IRC to contribute to the outputs which include the consensus outputs and the conflicting outputs. The existing organizational climate also potentially influences the overall organization at the various functional levels within the organization. The IRC of an organization is the contextual and the prevailing IR systems and practices, which are characterized by the atmosphere of IR and the behaviour of the union and management and their relations. The dimensions of IRC reveal the kinds of existing relationship between the union and management which may be harmonious, open, apathetic or hostile.

The consensual outputs include the agreements on works and opportunity of the labour union's roles and responsibilities, and the agreement on the terms of employment, compensation and benefits, working conditions, including the settled grievances, and the effect of effective negotiations between the actors of IR. Whereas the conflicting outputs include the perceived disharmony between the actors, strikes, lockouts, labour demonstrations, labour absenteeism and so on.

C.1.5. Case for Discussion　　IRC in Gurgaon Industrial Belt

A study of the incidence of labour unrests during the period 2005–2012 in Guargaon belt portrays the picture of violence, labour agitations, strikes, lockouts and police actions in the form of arrests and lathi charge to control the mass agitations. The NCR industrial belt witnessed the killing of three executives—Awanish Kumar Dev, Joginder Singh and L. K. Chaudhary—working in different organizations during the years 2005–2012. Can it be presumed that the factors that caused death of these three executives had some common connections? The following are some instances of the extreme cases of labour unrest since 2005 in Gurgaon belt.

1. **Honda Motorcycle and Scooter India (HMSI) Pvt. Ltd's effort to restrict the formation of a labour union:** In December 2004, the workers at HMSI Gurgaon plant demanded for wage increases commensurate with the company's sales growth. The workers' demand was a wage structure at par with the shop-floor workers of Hero Honda. The refusal of the management to the same lured the permanent workers to form a formal registered labour union under the Trade Unions Act of 1926. The union was finally formed in May 2005. The same workers adopted 'go slow' tactics, which ultimately resulted in production losses. The management in its action suspended 50 workers and dismissed four workers' leaders who initiated the formation and registration of the trade

union. In reaction, the labour agitation continued. To bring the agitation to an end, a tripartite agreement, which undertook from the labour union not to go on strike and maintain discipline for productivity, was signed in June 2005. But since the management turned down the demand of the workers to reinstate the 50 suspended workers, the workers withdrew themselves from the agreement of June 2005 and went on a strike on 25 July 2005. During the demonstration, on the same day, the workers turned violent and set some vehicles on fire. The police in its action to restore law and orders adopted stringent measures of lathi charge resulting in injury to around 400 workers, who were a part of about 2,000 agitating employees of the organization.[6]

2. **The labour unrest in Rico for unionization:** There was a pending demand from the workers of Rico for a wage hike of ₹10,000 per year. On 4 August 2009, the workers filed an application for registration of a labour union. In the first week of September 2009, the management learnt about such initiatives of its workers and in reaction the management followed a mixed approach of victimizing, terrorizing, as well as bribing the workers to foil their efforts of unionization. The management in its action suspended 16 workers. This led to a strike called by the workers on 21 September 2009. On the same day, the management closed all the gates of the company and declared a lockout. The management deployed police forces, company's security and hired security to protect the facility and works. The management had filed for an injunction in court prohibiting the workers from gathering outside the gate. On 18 October 2009, the security guards of Rico brutally attacked the workers protesting at the entry gate. A worker named Ajit Yadav received serious head injuries and died in the hospital the same day.

This incident agitated the unions of Gurgaon–Manesar industrial belt. The Joint Trade Union Council of the industrial belt called for a general strike and on 20 October 2009, workers from Sona Koyo Steering Systems, Hero Honda Motors, Bajaj Motors, Lumax Industries, Hema Engineering, AG International and Microtek came out in large numbers to protest against the incident of 18 October 2009.[7]

Finally, on 5 November, a settlement was reached between Rico management and the union. The management agreed to take back nine out of 16 suspended workers but there was no settlement on the workers demand for wage hike.

3. **The labour unrest at Sunbeam:** The Sunbeam management declared lockout on 22 September 2009 over a dispute with its workers over union elections. Sunbeam Auto Ltd is located just adjacent to Rico Auto Ltd. The Sunbeam workers launched a protest demonstration at the entry gate. The management of Sunbeam, a Hero Group company, initially formed a works committee to avoid the formation of a workers' union. But after the workers started the process of formation of a labour union, the management helped a selected group of workers to form another labour union. The Sunbeam Auto Shramik Union was a pro-management labour union and had the government registration under the Trade Unions Act, 1926. On 9 April 2009, the management signed a wage settlement agreement with the office-bearers of the Sunbeam Auto Shramik Union. On 1 June 2009, the newly elected office-bearers of the Sunbeam Auto Sramik Union were accepted and recognized by the management as the sole representative body of its workers and considered them as their negotiating body. In reaction, on 9 June 2009, the workers opposed this and raised a dispute before the labour department claiming that the existing office-bearers of Sunbeam Auto Shramik Union represented only a minority of the workers. In reaction, the management suspended 10 workers and terminated one on the ground of misconduct. Thereafter, the management started compelling the workers to sign a legal declaration stating that the existing office-bearers of the Sunbeam Auto

[6] 'Honda Workers Turn Violent, Cops Go Berserk', *The Indian Express*, 26 July 2005.
[7] http://www.thehindubusinessline.com/todays-paper/labour-unrest-at-gurgaonmanesar-auto-parts-units-continues/article1065794.ece.

Shramik Union were the only representatives of workers. About 250 workers signed the same. To settle the dispute, the management accepted the demands of the union.

While in the fourth week of September 2009, about 2,500 and 1,000 workers of Rico and Sunbeam units, respectively, had gone on strike, about 30,000 workers of auto ancillary of Gurgaon–Manesar belt agitated for around six days. These workers were from major vendors of auto companies such as Maruti Suzuki India Ltd (MSIL), HMSI, Hero Honda, Bajaj Auto and Suzuki Motorcycles Ltd who depend on these vendors for the components used in their manufacturing process. So the auto majors also faced a tough time because of the non-supply of components.[8]

4. **Struggle of Viva Global's workers for minimum wages and unionization in 2010:** The workers of Viva Global, a garment company in Gurgaon, Haryana, demanded revision of minimum wages as per the notification of the state government made in the month of January 2010 and also provision of ID cards, PF and ESI membership cards, salary slip and so on. Since the management did not accept the same, the workers went on a strike for two hours every day with effect from 8 April which continued up to 10 April 2010. On 10 April 2010, one worker was dismissed by the management. The workers, in reaction, protested against this. The management called the police and about 15 workers were taken into custody. The worker's strength was 400 male and 200 female workers. There was no registered labour union, so after this incidence the workers contacted Mazdoor Ekta Manch (MEM)[9] and sought its help in the struggle. Eventually, a labour union was registered in May 2010. The management accepted the demands of the workers after the fifteenth day of their struggle but soon started reducing the workers engaged on contract and finally by 21 August 2010, all the workers hired on contract were out of job. All the permanent workers protested and demanded reinstatement of all the fired contract employees. This was followed by the management declaring a lockout.[10]

5. **MSIL denies union representation:** MSIL, the auto major, got into labour problem during 3 June–21 October 2011. Workers at MSIL, Maneswar unit, agitated for the registration of the Maruti Suzuki Employees' Union (MSEU). The four-and-a-half-month struggle was marked by two strikes sponsored by MSEU, one lockout declared by MSIL, arrest of employees by the police for violating the law and order, dismissal of over 1,000 contract workers and sympathy strikes by thousands of other workers from the industrial belt of Gurgaon and Maneswar. During the course of the strikes and lockout, the management of MSIL dismissed 80 workers and suspended 49 workers including many MSEU leaders. The president, the general secretary and the executive members of MSEU were arrested for various violations of the Indian Penal Code which included rioting and assaulting the officers of the organization. At the initial stage, the Harayana government also denied the application filed by MSEU for registration of union. The mass violence at Maruti Manesar plant on 18 July 2012 caused the death of Awanish Kumar Dev, a senior HR officer, and also caused injury to over 100 others. According to reports, workers armed with iron rods and wooden sticks rioted at the plant attacking managers, smashing equipment and setting the plant on fire. This appeared to be a premeditated attack.[11]

---

[8] 'Labour Unrest at Gurgaon–Manesar Auto Parts Units Continues', *The Hindu BusinessLine*, print edition, 3 October 2009, http://www.thehindubusinessline.com/todays-paper/labour-unrest-at-gurgaonmanesar-auto-parts-units-continues/article1065794.ece

[9] MEM is a platform of workers in Gurgaon. MEM's mission is to build the power of workers and their families, and secure their dignity and rights where they work and live.

[10] 'Viva Global Workers Reach Agreement', http://www.cleanclothes.org/urgent-actions/viva-global-workers-reach-agreement

[11] http://peoplematters.in/articles/maruit-strikes-back-after-13-days, http://m.thehindu.com/opinion/oped/article2490903.ece http://m.thehindu.com/news/national/article2601780, http://ibnlive.in.com/news/strike-at-maruti-plants-declared-illegal-by-govt/192572-3.html]

6. **The labour unrest at Eastern Medikit, Gurgaon:** The workers of Eastern Medikit Ltd (EML), Gurgaon, saw a notice put-up in the five units of EML on 18 May 2012, communicating that the plant is under shutdown. They had never imagined that they would be facing such uncertainty related to their future while working at EML.

EML, established in the year 1988, was manufacturing and exporting medical disposables, disposable needles and surgical needles. The employee strength was 1,200 permanent employees and 400 permanent employees in the supervisory role, and 3,000 contract employees. Since 18 May 2012, the employees were continuously protesting against the company management for abruptly shutting down all the five plants and not paying their salaries and other dues.

The EML management alleged that the workers were not reporting for their duties and were on an 'illegal' strike. On the other hand, the labour union leaders argued that the factory was shut down to compel the employees to leave the organization.

The labour union leaders and the workers complained to the labour department and also took up their issue before the district magistrate to get their problem settled. Families of 1,200 permanent workers had to face dire circumstances due to the closure/lockout declared by the management of EML.

The labour department made efforts to settle the dispute and called conciliation meetings, issued notices to the management and challans for non-compliance of the legal provisions. But the adamantine approach of the management reaped no results. Finally, the labour department made reference of the dispute to the industrial tribunal at Gurgaon.

Case Questions

1. Identify the reasons for the adverse industrial climate in the Gurgaon industrial belt.
2. To understand the factors impacting the IRC of the industrial belt, identify the input under different categories, that is, environmental factors, organizational factors and IR factors.

1.8. The Factors Causing Such Adverse IRC

The climate of IR in the above instances is not conducive to the healthy operation of the organizational business. The contributions to the unhealthy climate have been made by the actors of IR. Conducive climate does not imply that the workers will not have tendencies of collectivism or unionism as envied in the traditional IR context. On the contrary, within the notions of collectivism and unionism the labour unions may show great cohesiveness by subscribing to the ideas and approach of the management. The action framework for the same may be based on certain ideology and beliefs of having greater trust in management which would enable the management to deal with the labour unions fairly and equitably. The situation presupposes a concept of dual commitment of the employees which means that while the employees of an organization are committed to the labour union of which they are members, they are also committed to their works and thus to the business organizations. In other words, the simultaneous coexistence of organizational commitment and ideological commitment towards the labour association to which they sponsor as a member. The workplace may have a particular IRC defined in terms of some degree of relationships between management and employees. Such relationships may be considered as mutually trusting, respectful, cooperative, harmonious and cohesive in their spirit [30]. In other words, workplaces may be characterized as having some 'work climate' defined in terms of the 'norms, attitudes, feelings and behaviours prevalent at the workplace' [28] depicted by the management and the labour unions.

Different workplaces have different IRC. Such an IRC contributes to organizational IR thereby generating a distinctive atmosphere in the organization as perceived by the organizational members. The IRC of an organization depicts the state and quality of union–management relations in an organization. Such IRC as in the Indian context is multidimensional and is impacted by the changing context and concept of IR which is characterized by:

1. The declining number of trade unions (very much evident in the Indian context).
2. Increasing non-union employees at workplaces (diminishing number of membership of trade unions).
3. Emergence of non-politically affiliated associations addressing the issues of the working class (e.g., SEWA).[12]
4. The increased use of direct voice by employees instead of collective voice.
5. The increasing importance assigned to the relationship between workplace practices and organizational performance both by the employees and the employers.

With globalization of the economy, the focus of building a relationship between the labour union and the management are shifting to trusting behaviour for each other generating a network of ties at the local community, national and global levels of economic and social activities. The impact of such factors on the actors of IR is the impact on the interpersonal relations, and on individual's values forming what is called as the 'social capital', as part of the network to which the individual belongs. So the impact of power and influence depends less on personal attributes and more on interactions between people, social life networks, norms and trust. For instance, in the dispute between the labour union and the management in the Maruti case in 2012, the impact of the social factors was highly visible. Similarly, both in the case of Rico and Sunbeam, the pressure created by the supportive labour unions belonging to other nearby organizations in the industrial belt created pressures on both the management of Rico and Sunbeam, as well as on the government for considering the voice and demands of the labour unions. Such phenomenon contributes to the shared objectives of forming the trust and democracy within societies, which ultimately contributes to the formation of the social capital. The example of formation of a social capital is also visible in the case of Viva workers where the permanent employees supported the agitations of the contract labour. Social capital normally involves 'who you know' in your industrial society, which contributes to form the contextual global networked environment. This phenomenon is evident in all the five instances of labour problems discussed above. In other words, organizations are increasingly being viewed as living systems, in which a complex network contributes to a dynamic value to develop trust or distrust, motivation, emotional attachments and feelings of the employees which are the prime contributors to IR culture and thereby influence IRS.

1.9. The Changing IRC and the Approach of the Trade Unions in India

With the massive changing trend in industrialization and the new government initiatives, there have been changes in the practice of IR which caused erosion of traditional IR institutions and thereby the actors have changed their approach to address the issues of IR. The relationship

---

[12] http://www.sewa.org/about_us_history.asp

between employers and employees has undergone a sea change. The institutions which were considered important under IR, for example, settlement of disputes and labour union's attitude as a hostile body to protest against the management, are now disappearing and are replaced by new set of variables explaining the reason behind the phenomenon of the emerging industrial context. This is visible worldwide and with globalization it has impacted the Indian economy. R. Hyman admits that 'the rules which govern the employment relationship, the institutions involved in this process and the power dynamics are among the main agents of regulation' for determining the employee relations [31]. It has been established that there has been serious erosion of the collective and institutionalized forms of regulation which used to contribute to the framework of IR. The factors impacting the changed framework in the Indian context are as follows:

1. Changing importance to collectivism resulting in diminishing levels of unionization among workers, falling levels of collective bargaining coverage, reduced access to high political spheres and authorities among labour.
2. With business taking the shape of global standards, there has been general tendency towards less direct interference of the governmental machinery for regulation of IR, thereby leaving the management and the labour unions to decide the terms at the workplace for managing the relationships and resolving the conflicts.
3. The impact of the globalized market and the multinational culture emerging in various industries creating flexible labour market and industrial culture, for example,
   a. Changes in the working class structure in modern industrialized societies developing in pockets in different parts of the country due to schemes promoted by the central and state governments, for example, Make in India, Digital India, Smart Cities and so on.
   b. Changes in the sectoral preferences of the employees to engage with, that is, more employees are employed in the service sector and proportionately less in the manufacturing sector.
   c. Questions being raised on the propensity of employees to join and remain member of a trade union.
   d. Adhering to ideologies based on political beliefs and the associated institutional values of the political parties are discontinued and replaced by economic interests and activities linking the market and production.
   e. Industrial productivity culture has been established in the Indian industrial societies resulting in substantive changes in work processes and changes in management's attitudes towards labour due to the emergence of new technologies.
   f. The emerging need for a committed workforce due to the international competition emerging from globalization of the economy.

Chapter Summary

1. The management of HR in industry involves a process of getting into a contract with the employees as specified in the terms of employment. The terms of the contract of employment creates conditions for certain relationships to get established between employers and employees.
2. These relationships are termed as IR which due to its inherent complexity and contextually emerging factors generates conflicting atmospheres which are not harmonious for the

functioning of any organization and therefore requires the intervention of the state (government). The three players are termed as the actors of IR.

3. IR refers to the inter-relations between the three main actors—employees and their organizations, the management and the government.
4. The objective of IR is to establish and maintain good and healthy relations between the management and the labour union which is the representative of the workers.
5. The environmental factors influence the IR, which include the existing and emerging economic, institutional and political factors in the region, the social norms and the values of the people of the society, the past history and incidences concerning labour at works.
6. There is a need for a multi-disciplinary approach to study IR since the subject is impacted by socio-economic, psychological, political and other contextual factors of the industrial society.
7. Various theorists from different contextual assumptions attempted to explain the understanding of IR, namely the unitary approach, the systems model of Dunlop, the pluralistic approach, the Marxian theory and the social action approach and so on.
8. The chapter concludes with the concept of IRS and impact of IRC.

Questions

1. Different theorists of the subject of IR provided different definitions. Which definition you feel most appropriately fits to explain the existing context of IR? Justify.
2. Explain the roles of the different actors in the IRS.
3. Suggest how the changed socio-economic and political factors in the Indian context are going to impact the IR in the country.
4. How a harmonious IR can be created in this changing and dynamic industrial context of Indian industries?
5. Develop the conceptual link between the actors of IR and IRC.
6. What, in your opinion, is the future of IR?

Project Work for the Students

1. Identify one recent IR problem and critically examine the roles of different actors. What would be a better solution to the context?
2. What are the major challenges ahead for the actors as per your thinking?

References

1. Brewley H, Forth J. Vulnerability and adverse treatment at work place. Employment Relation Research Series, 112. London: Department of Business Innovation and Skill; 2010.
2. Joseph J. Industrial relations: towards a theory of negotiated connectedness. New Delhi: Response Books; 2004.
3. Kochan TA. A theory of multilateral collective bargaining in city governments. Ind. Labor Relat. Rev. 1974; 27: 525–542.
4. Hyman R. The state in industrial relations. In: Blyton P, Bacon N, Fiorito J, Heery E, editors. The SAGE Handbook of Industrial Relations. London: SAGE Publications; 2009. pp. 258–283.

5. McKenna E, Beech N. Human resource management: a concise analysis. 2nd ed. Harlow: Prentice Hall Pearson; 2008.
6. Yoder D. Personnel management and industrial relations. Englewood Cliffs, NJ: Prentice-Hall; 1938.
7. Dunlop JT. Industrial Relations Systems. New York: Holt Rinehart and Winston; 1958
8. Bain GS, Clegg HA. A strategy for industrial relations research in Great Britain. Br. J. Ind. Relat. March 1974; XII(1): 91–113.
9. Clegg HA. The changing system of industrial relations in Great Britain. Oxford: Blackwell; 1979.
10. Hyman R. Industrial relations in theory and practice. Eur. J. Ind. Relat. 1995; 1(1): 17–46.
11. Cox R. Approaches to the futurology of industrial relations. Bull. Inst. Labour Stud. 1971; 8(8): 139–164.
12. Kelly J. Rethinking industrial relations: mobilization, collectivism, and long waves. London: Routledge; 1998.
13. European Industrial Relations Observatory. Towards a qualitative dialogue in industrial relations. Dublin: EIRO; 2002.
14. Budd J. Employment with a human face: balancing efficiency, equity, and voice. Ithaca, NY: Cornell University Press; 2004.
15. Kochan T. What is distinctive about IR research? In: Whitefield K, Strauss G, editors. Researching the World of Works: Strategies and Methods in Studying IR. New York: Cornell University Press; 1998. pp. 31–49.
16. Edwards P. The employment relationship and the field of industrial relations. In: Edwards P, editor. Industrial Relations: Theory and Practice. 2nd ed. London: Blackwell; 2005. pp. 1–36.
17. Flanders A. Industrial relations: what is wrong with the system? An essay on its theory and future. London: Farber & Farber; 1965.
18. Bain GS, Clegg HA. Strategy for industrial relations research in Great Britain. Br. J. Ind. Relat. 1974; 12(1): 91–113.
19. Ackers P. Reframing employment relations: the case for neo-pluralism. Ind. Relat. J. 2002.
20. Rose ED. Employment relations. 3rd ed. London: Pearson Education; 2008; 33(1): 2–19.
21. Kaufman BE. The theoretical foundation of industrial relations and its implications. Ind. Labour Relat. Rev. 2010; 64(1): 73–108.
22. Green GD. Industrial relations text and case studies. 4th ed. London: Pitman Publishing; 1994.
23. Salamon M. Industrial relations theory and practice. 4th ed. London: Pearson Education; 2000.
24. Dastmalchian A, Blyton P, Adamson R. Industrial relations climate: testing a construct. Journal of Occupational Psychology. 1989; 62: 21–32.
25. Beer M. Organizational climate: a viewpoint from the change agent. Paper presented at American Psychological Association Convention, Washington, DC, September, 197.
26. Payne R, Pugh DS. Organisational structure and climate. In: Dunnette MD, editor. Handbook of Industrial and Organisational Psychology. Chicago, IL: Rand McNally; 1976. 1125–1173.
27. Hellricgel D, Slocum JW. Organizational climate: measure, research and contingencies. Acad. Manage. Res. 1974; 17, 255–280.
28. Dastmalchian A. Environmental characteristics and organizational climate: an exploratory study. J. Manage. Stud. 1986; 23: 609–633.
29. Rao TV, Abraham E. HRD climate in Indian organizations. HRD Newsl. 1985; 2: 9–13.
30. Hammer TH, Currall SC, Stern RN. Worker representation on boards of directors: a study of competing roles. Ind. Labor Relat. Rev. 1991; 44(4): 661–80.
31. Hyman R. An Anglo-European perspective on industrial relations research. Arbetsmarknad & Arbetsliv. 2007; 13(3–4): 29–41.

2

Emerging Trend of Industrial Relations in India

LEARNING OBJECTIVES

After reading this chapter, you will be able to:

☐ Know about the evolution of the IRS in India
☐ Understand why the industrial relation context and the IRS are inter-related
☐ Understand the complexities linked to the development of the IRS in the country
☐ Identify the concerns that need to be addressed by the employer, the government and the trade unions for a harmonious IRS
☐ Understand the paradigm shift in the Indian IRS
☐ Understand how the industrial relation context and the IRS are inter-related

C.2.1. Case for Discussion   Reaching Out to the People

The general manager of HR of one of the units of Liberty Shoes Ltd with two of his colleagues was walking around the shop floors of the unit located at Karnal (Haryana). He went around from one shop to the other, meeting almost all the employees of the organization at their place of work, without discriminating whether they were on contract or permanent employees. Some of the employees talked to him. The discussions were mostly concerning personal problems of these individuals.

The general manager after hearing these employees made a note of certain points and then moved on. He went around the six shops one by one, meeting almost 1,400 employees working there. He also came across the shop floor supervisors, department heads and other officers who also discussed their issues with him.

The supervisors also discussed issues concerning the manpower, skill levels and performance levels of their shop floor employees. The department heads also discussed issues such as organizing a training programmes for skill development of the employees, scheduling workshops on motivational talks, on-the-job training and deputation of the employees for on-the-job training in other units.

Around 10.30 AM, as he reached one of the shops, the hooter announced the tea break. The general manager went to the tea serving area provided for the employees and had a cup of tea with the workers while discussing some of their areas of concern.

This is a routine activity of Mr J. S. Saini, the general manager, HR, which he terms as 'management by walking around'.

The company which fashions footwear and produces an international brand of products, known for their quality, had serious labour problem during the years 2004–2006. The registered trade union agitated for every small issue and frequently called for work stoppages to demonstrate its strength.

Mr Saini, who joined the company as the general manager in December 2006, had tough days initially at Liberty Shoes Ltd as at that time the company was facing a serious labour problem. Work stoppages called by the trade union were frequent, which adversely affected the production. After a series of discussions, conciliation meetings, negotiations and agreements with the trade union, the issues were settled.

With time, a series of proactive policies were introduced in the company. The proactive measures which changed the employee relations were as follows:

1. Employee relations were addressed at a single point of contact, which implied quick redressal of both personal and group issues in the shortest possible time. The grievances and concerns of employees were accorded top priority for their redressal.
2. Regular and scheduled one-to-one meetings, both with the contractual and permanent employees, helped in reducing the distances and the mental blocks between the management and the employees.
3. Open houses were held for each process once every quarter, wherein the top management presented highlights of their performance, policies and answered questions.
4. Reward and recognition (R&R) of high performers became a part of the work life of the employees. Every month R&R schemes of the company awarded performance rewards for individual and group productivities.
5. The company celebrated every small achievements of the employees including the achievements of the members of the family (e.g., good performance of the employees' children, scholarships for meritorious students, social activities done by the housewives and the ladies, and volunteers from the workers' families participating in the company's promotional activities). Various funds had been allocated for such activities in the annual budget of the company.

Mr Saini expressed that:

Because of our proactive policies towards employees, we almost do not face any IR issues. At present the trade union activities have been reduced to zero, and can be said that the union members have taken a back seat. The management addresses all issues directly through regular discussion with the employees. The legacies of settling labour issues through the trade unions have been replaced by the proactive action of settling issues with the workers. The management by walking around in the shop floor has helped me, to bridge the gaps between the workers and the management.

Case Questions

1. What facilitated the turnaround from the 'legacies of settling labour issues through the trade unions to proactive action of the management to settle issues with the workers'?
2. Can there be any other alternative method of reaching out to the employees, reducing the gaps between the management and the workers, thereby reducing IR problems on the shop floor?

2.1. The Trends of IR in India

In the previous chapter, discussions have been made to understand the concept of IR through a structure of relationships between the actors. The three actors, that is, the employer, the employees and the government contributed to the structure of relationships to provide to the concept and the meaning of IR. In this chapter, an attempt has been made to establish the causal link between the outcomes (which are visible in the IR scenario) and the actors.

| Table 2.1 | Industrial Disputes in India (1992–2016) |

Year (Jan–Dec)	Number of		
	Disputes	Workers Involved	Man-days Lost (In '000')
1992	1,714	1,252,225	31,259
1993	1,393	953,867	20,301
1994	1,201	846,429	20,936
1995	1,066	989,695	16,290
1996	1,166	939,304	20,255
1997	1,305	981,267	16,971
1998	1,097	1,255,923	22,062
1999	927	1,310,695	26,767
2000	771	1,416,299	28,763
2001	674	687,778	23,767
2002	579	1,079,434	26,586
2003	552	1,815,945	30,256
2004	477	2,072,221	23,866
2005	456	2,913,601	29,665
2006	430	1,810,346	20,324
2007	369	724,574	27,167
2008	421	1,579,298	17,433
2009	345	1,867,204	17,622
2010	371	1,074,473	23,131
2011	370	734,763	14,456
2012	318	1,307,454	12,937
2013	258	1,838,160	12,645
2014 (Provisional)	287	1,158,770	11,095
2015 (Provisional)	184	627,134	2,919
2016 (Provisional) (Jan–Dec)	77	552,994	1,058

One can hardly overlook the sequence of events in the IR of different companies during the decade 2005–2015. Organizations in India experienced a rising trend in labour unrests both in Indian business houses and in multinationals. Assuming that the statistics are the indicator of the trend of IRC of the country, the figures of the frequency of strikes, lockouts, labour problems causing man-days lost draw the attention for the study (Table 2.1).

In case the statistics are considered as the indicator of the trend of IR, the aforementioned data establishes that the numbers of strikes and lockouts have been drastically reduced in India. During the past two decades there has been a progressive reduction in industrial disputes and the number of man-days lost (on account of strikes and lockouts) (Table 2.2). It is a fact that the

Table 2.2 Industrial Units Affected by Strikes, Lockouts, Man-days Lost During the Period 2013–2016

Items	2013 (Jan to Oct)			2014 (Jan to Oct)			2015 (Jan to Oct)			2016 (Jan to March) (P)		
	Central	State	Total	Central Sphere	State Sphere	Total	Central Sphere	State Sphere	Total	Central Sphere	State Sphere	Total
Industrial units affected by												
(I) Strikes	7	77	84	24	76	100	40	44	84	11	3	14
(II) Lockouts			148		21	21		20	20		1	1
(III) Man-days lost	2,615,816	143,716,177	146,331,993	655,072	1,652,063	2,307,535	439,522	1,225,095	1,668,617	65,145	16,565	81,710
Workers affected as a result of												
(I) Strikes	1,233,040	1,188,711	2,421,751	337,456	23,411	360,867	303,711	23,037	326,748	49,580	900	50,480
(II) Lockouts			60,454		6,395	6,395		5,161	5,161		255	255

concept of 'institutional IR', where violence due to political and the ideological rivalries once dominated, has been replaced by 'logical, value-based agitations for claiming the legal rights'. The industrial scenario of the late 1980s and the early 1990s was dictated by militant trade unionism, with union leaders like Datta Samant heading the list. But over the years, both the trade unions and the management opted for the democratization of workplace by giving increased prominence to 'collective bargaining'. With the emerging trend towards a more matured culture of IR, the pattern of collective bargaining assumed the integrative form where realizing, experiencing, sharing and accommodating for achieving the organizational objective became the focus of the actors of IR.

The employment relations patterns reflect the interplay of three distinct logics of action—the logic of industrial peace, the logic of competition (associated with, but not confined to, globalization) and the logic of employment-income protection.

The government's objective in the post-Independence period was driven by considerations of economic self-reliance. India adopted an advanced import substitution industrialization (ISI) model through a pattern of centrally planned mixed economy [1]. The strategy emphasized the growth and long-term development of heavy capital goods industries managed and controlled by the government, which were based on indigenous technology [2]. Restrictions were placed on the investment and production capacity of the private sectors.

A policy of industrial licensing that regulated the entry of new firms into economic sectors, supported by the policy of imposing import duties, was adopted to ensure the protection of the domestic industry from foreign competition [3]. By the 1990s, that is, after 40 years of adoption of such policy, the economic growth had been rather slow. The economic growth rate during this period was around 2–3 per cent per year. The factors which highly impacted the industrial systems in the country were as follows:

1. The labour legislation was extremely protective of labour.
2. The trade union formation was relatively simple, with any seven persons being able to apply for the registration of a trade union. This caused the formation of multiplicity of unions both at the centre and at the industrial units, though for collective bargaining, a single recognized union was encouraged for all practical purposes [4].
3. The scope for external leadership under the provisions of law provided the scope for a stepping stone to political leadership. Trade union action was therefore often driven by political considerations and was not connected with enterprise problems [5].
4. The multiplicity and constantly competing unions in an enterprise hindered the develop-ment of stable labour–management relationships, resulting in a very high rate of industrial unrest [3].
5. The protection afforded to Indian manufacturers from foreign competition and a guaranteed internal market created huge and inefficient industries that were not able to compete internationally once the economy was liberalized.

So there emerged a need to re-look at the strategic initiative for liberalizing the economy for achieving a faster economic growth rate and economic development. Within the framework of the industrial laws (which controls and regulates the behaviour of the actors of IR), a step to liberalize the economy was taken through appropriate policy decisions of the government in the 1990s.

C.2.2. Case for Discussion   Industrial Relations: Myth and Reality[1]

It was the morning of 18 May 2012. Mr Dhananjay Mittal,[2] the trade union leader at the Eastern Medikit India Ltd (EML), along with some of the workers was reading a notice posted by the management. After reading the notice, everybody had only one question: 'How can it happen?' None of the workers including Dhananjay had ever imagined that they would be landing into such uncertainty regarding their future. They all had been working in the organization for long. (The permanent workers had been in the organization for 15–20 years, as per records.) The notice pasted by the management on the notice board on 18 May 2012 communicated the suspension of all the operations and the shutdown of all the plants located in Gurgaon (now Gurugram),[3] with immediate effect (EML had five plants in Gurgaon, located at Udyog Vihar). Such a deadlock shattered the lives of 1,200 permanent shop floor workers, 3,000 casual workers and 400 managerial staff who were earning their livelihood by working in this organization. Throwing them out from their jobs without notice or information, of any nature whatsoever, was something not expected by anybody in the organization. The question was whether the management's action to shut down the operation of the plants in such an abrupt way, throwing around 4,200 workers out of employment—who were working in different categories in the organization—and vacating the works with no prior notification to the employees, was permitted legally and socially under the 'conditions of employment of the employees' [6–8].

An organization which had been planning for its capacity expansion, with no prelude to the happening of 18 May 2012, going on a process of undeclared stopping of operation in the units of Gurgaon was something beyond the expectations of all who were associated with the organization and its business. On 1 August 2012, the labour union leaders of EML[4] met the district commissioner[5] and threatened to go on an indefinite hunger strike[6] outside his office in case their demands were not met in the next four days [9]. All the workers and the union leaders were totally in doldrums as they found themselves caught in the deadlock situation. They were looking for possible ways to come out from this crisis of uncertainty. The question before the labour union was whether they should agitate to get back their legitimate dues from the EML management or look for possible ways of pressurizing the management to restart all the manufacturing units so that all the workers get their jobs back.

All the manufacturing units of EML had been shut down since 18 May 2012, and the workers had not been getting their salaries since then. The workers submitted a memorandum to the district commissioner in mid-July 2012, requesting his intervention. On 1 August 2012, the district commissioner assured labour union members that he would be arranging a meeting with the owner(s) of EML within the next couple of days to sort out their problems.

The management of EML alleged that because the workers were on strike, the manufacturing operations were all suspended. The question before the Labour Department Haryana, was whether it was a case of lockout declared by the management because the labour union resorted to an illegal

---

[1] The instructor is requested to visit the instructor manual in the companion website for the teaching methodology of this case.

[2] Eastern Medikit Employees' Union leader (name changed).

[3] An Industrial town of Haryana, located in National Capital of Region of Delhi, India.

[4] Established in the year 1988, EML is an ISO 13485 and ISO 9001:2008 certified organization engaged in manufacturing and exporting of medical disposables, disposable needles and surgical needles.

[5] Appropriate authority responsible for handling labour dispute as per the Industrial Dispute Act (ID), 1947.

[6] A hunger strike is a method of non-violent resistance or pressure in which participants fast as an act of political protest or to provoke feelings of guilt in others, usually with the objective to achieve a specific goal, such as a policy change. Most hunger strikers will take liquids but not solid food. (http://en.wikipedia.org/wiki/Hunger_strike)

strike or it was a case of forceful lockout adopted by the management of EML to ultimately close down the manufacturing units in Haryana.

So each of the groups (management, labour union and the Labour Department, Haryana) was faced with different sets of questions/issues to be addressed and was in its respective dilemmas. The office of the district magistrate, the authority for ensuring 'social justice', was also in a 'contextual dilemma' while searching for solutions to the social issue emerging from the situation of a large workforce of about 4,600 jobless employees.

The Organization: Eastern Medikit Limited

EML, a fully owned Indian health care company, was set up in 1988 by Mr Karun Raj Narang, a graduate of the University of California, Berkeley, who owns two patents for catheters with unique design efficiencies. The company was manufacturing and marketing a wide range of international standard disposable medical and surgical devices, such as intravenous sets, catheters and blood bank products. EML had five manufacturing units with around 150,000 square feet of manufacturing space with six class 10,000 square feet clean rooms[7] located at Udyog Vihar, Gurgaon, a few miles from Delhi.[8]

The company had successfully implemented quality management systems, such as ISO 9001:2002, EN 46001, ISO 13485 and European Council directive 93/42/EEC.[9] It had a capacity of manufacturing around 150 million units of finished products per year. Nearly 65 per cent of the total production was exported to more than 57 countries, including Germany, Spain, Italy, Greece, Brazil, Argentina, UAE, South Africa and Malaysia. The vision of the company was to provide high-quality 'health care services' worldwide. The organization maintained high-quality standards, and with time it became a preferred supplier for various clients worldwide [10].

The company was one of the leading manufacturers and service providers of medical disposables, disposable needles and surgical needles with a wide range of similar products.

The Financial Status of EML

During the financial year 2011–2012, the financial situation of the company was very alarming. Reportedly, the company had around INR[10] 30 crore of debt to Punjab National Bank[11] and Union Bank of India.[12] Further, the company had to pay around ₹2.5 crore to the provident fund[13] authorities. The money collected from the employees for the payment of their outstanding loan amount to Gurgaon Gramin Bank was ₹0.6 crore. Outstanding payment for the electricity bill was around ₹0.65 crore. The company also had to pay money to the raw material suppliers. In the year 2011, the labour union alleged that the management had not paid the wages at the increased agreed rates to 1,135 permanent workers (as agreed by the management in the long-term wage settlement with the labour union in the year 2009).

Credit appraisal agency, CARE Ratings, rated EML's bank credit facilities for more than ₹56 crore. The company's net sales in 2009–2010 were ₹131.38 crore with a net profit of ₹22.7 crore. But in 2010–2011, the company incurred a loss of ₹28.4 crore. So CARE downgraded Eastern Medikit's ratings in December 2011 to 'CARE D', indicating that the company had defaulted in the repayment of the

---

[7] Spaces technically equipped for ensuring production of quality products, suitable for medical equipment.
[8] National capital of India.
[9] Different quality standards accepted nationally and internationally, which enhance the product quality.
[10] Indian currency.
[11] Nationalized bank of India.
[12] Nationalized bank of India.
[13] Social security measure in India.

loans to its financers. The rating process took into account the delays in debt servicing by EML, as quoted by the CARE analyst in charge of Eastern Medikit [11].

The organization had recorded reasonable sound business growth till 2010, and as part of the business expansion drive, the management had set up a new plant in Dehradun[14] (Uttarakhand) in the year 2009. The management had explained the reason for setting up the new production centres to the labour union as 'to meet the growing demands of the products in the market'.

The Managements' Action

The senior officers who were involved in the day-to-day functioning and the operational activities had stopped coming to the plants at least a week before the posting of the closure notice of 18 May 2012 on the notice board (the labour union had thought it abnormal, but had not suspected such extreme action from the management). In the course of an interview, the president of the labour union expressed that the management had not declared any lockout or closure officially in the Gurgaon factories. This was to avoid paying lockout/closure compensation to its employees.

The management started operation in the state of Uttarakhand under the name of 'Global Medikit' under a separate registration number. Four production units were commissioned, and by the time the dispute started at the units at Gurgaon, two of these units at Dehradun were made operational for meeting customer requirements. On several occasions, the management had also tried out the process of dismantling some of the machineries at the Gurgaon units and shifting the same to Dehradun. The permanent workers had tried to stop the dismantling and relocation of the machinery, but their efforts had failed.

The Labour Union's Initiatives

To come out of the deadlock created by the management on 18 May 2012, the employees under the leadership of the office bearers of the Eastern Medikit Employees' Union continued their efforts to run all the operations and production of the plants. But the supply of electricity from the state government grid was discontinued from the same day. Attempts were made to continue the production with the help of electricity generated in-house using diesel generators, which continued for three days. But the crisis of raw material and fuel brought the plants to a standstill.

Mr Dhananjay, the president of the EML workers' union, was cornered because the situation normally expected him to initiate steps which protect the interest of workers as well as the management under the legal framework. In course of an interview Mr Dhananjay said, 'The management had set up factories in Dehradun not only to enjoy the benefit of tax holidays,[15] [12] as applicable in the area, announced by the state government of Uttarakhand, but also to reduce the human resource costs'. (The minimum wages in the state of Uttarakhand are less than that in Gurgaon, in the state of Haryana.)

The labour union Eastern Medikit Employees' Union, registered under the Trade Union Act of 1926, was affiliated to the Hind Mazdoor Sabha[16] (HMS), a CTU, which had around 1,378 affiliated labour

[14] One of the growing industrial towns in north India, located in the state of Uttarakhand.
[15] The companies in the two northern hill states, that is, Uttarkhand and Himachal Pradesh, as announced by the Central Government of India are eligible for 10-year tax holiday in case they have commenced operations before March 2010. Such a tax holiday includes exemption to pay exercise duty.
[16] The Hind Mazdoor Sabha (HMS, a Hindi name with approximate meaning 'Workers Assembly of India') is a national trade union in India. It was founded on 29 December 1948 by socialist Forward Bloc followers and independent unionists.

unions. The combined membership of this central labour union was around 5,350,441. HMS not being affiliated to any of the political parties of India functioned as an independent and democratic labour organization. Mr A. D. Nagpal, the general secretary of HMS, wrote to Mr Bhupinder Singh Hooda, the chief minister of Haryana, seeking his personal intervention and requested to direct the management of EML for restarting the operation of the factory. Mr Nagpal was of the opinion that:

> This apathy on the part of management, labor department and local administration may precipitate into a big industrial unrest anytime in the already surcharged industrial atmosphere of the entire Gurgaon belt. There have been instances of such neglect, ignorance, reluctance and rigidity in the past too, and, in some cases, have resulted in serious labour problem. [8]

The workers under the leadership of Eastern Medikit Employees' Union protested against the management's action of abruptly shutting down the plant operations and not paying their salaries. The workers alleged that the management's action of forcefully shutting down the plant without informing them in advance and without taking required approvals from the appropriate government authorities was illegal.[17] The workers also alleged that the management defaulted in paying the provident fund[18] and income tax dues which they had deducted from their salaries. In addition, the company was deducting around ₹4,000[19] per month approximately from those workers' salaries who had taken loans from the Gramin Bank[20] and had not deposited the loan amounts to the bank since January 2012 [13].

The salary for the month of April was not disbursed until 17 May 2012,[21] which was paid on 18 May 2012 with the intervention of the Labour Department. In an effort to come out of this uncertainty and deadlock situation, the labour union leaders of EML met the district magistrate[22] on Wednesday 1 August 2012, and threatened to go on an indefinite hunger strike[19] outside his office in case their demands were not met in the next four days [9, 14, 15].

On 16 September 2012, the workers demonstrated against the management of EML and staged a protest with bare chests [16] (Figure 2.1). The hardships faced by the workers during this period caused the death of two of them. They committed suicide because of their poor financial conditions [17]. Families of all the permanent workers had to face dire circumstances because of the shutdown declared by the management (as claimed by the labour union), and all workers had been rendered jobless and were left with no means to support their families.

Condemning the management of Eastern Medikit, major central labour unions of India, such as Bharatiya Mazdoor Sangh (BMS), Indian National Trade Union Congress (INTUC), Centre of Indian Trade Unions (CITU), All India Trade Union Congress (AITUC), SEWA, HMS and others called all the unions in Haryana to protest against the 'anti-worker attitude' of the management as well as the state government of Haryana. The members of the labour unions of the neighbouring organizations, such as Hero Motors, Honda and Rico, provided external moral support to the workers' agitation against EML[23] [18].

---

[17] ID Act has laid down the procedure for shutting down the operation of a factory.
[18] Social security measure for employees in India.
[19] US$1 ~ ₹60.
[20] One of the local banks.
[21] The Payment of Wages Act, 1936, provides that companies engaging more than 1,000 employees need to pay the wages to its employees by the 10th of the next month.
[22] Appropriate authority responsible for handling the labour dispute as per ID Act, 1947.
[23] Labour unions of the MNCs located in the industrial belt of Gurgaon.

The Initiative of the Government Authorities to Settle the Dispute

After receiving the complaints from the labour union leaders regarding the abrupt shutdown of EML plants and non-payment of wages for the month of April 2012, Labour Department intervened in the matter to release the wages to the workers. Taking cognizance of the management's attitude, the additional labour commissioner[24] (ALC) constituted a committee consisting of the deputy director, assistant director, deputy labour commissioner (DLC) and labour officer (LO) who visited the factory and submitted a report to the government. This committee reported that 1,134 workers were sitting idle and none of the management personnel were available at the factories to run the operations.

Further, to resolve the deadlock, a conciliation[25] meeting was called by the Haryana Labour Department. The promoters of EML had sent their lawyer to represent them in the conciliation meeting. The meeting ended without any result. ALC issued a show cause notice to the management asking for their reply on the issue. Meanwhile, the Haryana Labour Department issued summons to the management personnel alleging that the company had breached the 'terms of a settlement' of 2009 with their workers. The Labour Department filed 29 challans against Mr Mahinder Paul, the occupier, and seven challans against Mr Karun Raj Narang, the director of the company, in the court of the Chief Judicial Magistrate, Gurgaon, for violations under different acts and breach of the agreement with the labour union [19].

The district magistrate, the apex administrative authority of the district, called a meeting on 2 August 2012. Intimations for attending the meeting were sent to the management of EML, the labour union and the authorities of the Labour Department. The workers were expecting a positive outcome from this meeting, but the management did not show any interest and did not participate in the meeting. The labour union representatives were present. Mr Dhananjay, the president of the Eastern Medikit Employees' Union, expressed his disappointment as nobody from the company attended the meeting.

This incidence was followed by an official order issued by the Labour Department (Haryana) on 7 September 2012, ordering the EML management to bring an end to the lockout of all the factories and start operations. The dispute was subsequently referred for adjudication to the Industrial Tribunal[26] located in Gurgaon [20].

In reply to the government's show-cause notice, the management in their representation replied that the workers were not reporting on their duties and were on an illegal strike,[27] and hence they had no other option but to shut down the plant. The management also alleged that workers prevented the release of finished goods worth ₹5 crore million from the factory. All these actions of workers created fear and forced management not to attend the factory.

The Previous Incidences of Labour Unrest in EML and the After Shocks

The deadlock created by the management caused severe hardships to all the employees. One of the workers' wife succumbed to prolonged kidney-related ailment due to the lack of treatment (the family

---

[24] The Labour Department, which is under the control of the state government, is responsible for maintenance industrial peace and harmony, and safeguarding and improving the working conditions of the workers in industries. The department seeks to promote a healthy and positive partnership between the labour, the management and the government.

[25] A process of mediating between the parties to the disputes for the settlement of the labour problems. The provision is laid down under the ID Act, 1947.

[26] Industrial tribunals are constituted under Section 7A of the ID Act, 1947 for the adjudication of industrial disputes relating to any matter, whether specified in the Second or Third Schedule of the Industrial Tribunal.

[27] The concept of 'illegal strike' is provided under Sections 22–24 of the ID Act, 1947.

could not afford the treatment). Mr Tiwari, one of the labour union leaders of the Eastern Medikit Employees' Union, expressed (in course of the interview with the labour union members):

> One of our colleagues, Jagmohan, could not afford treatment for his wife Munni and she died; a 65-year-old mother of another colleague suffered a heart attack when she learned that the management had not attended the scheduled (2 August 2012) conciliation meeting arranged by the Labour Department. We had been running from pillar to post, but nothing happened so far.

'The approach of the management towards the contract labour had never been good', expressed the president of the labour union. The casual workers had to work more hours than the permanent workers and were paid overtime lesser than the permanent workers. The labour union leaders also claimed that their hands use to get smeared with blood because of the needles they manufactured, which was a hazardous job. The management had never looked at it either sympathetically or ensured adequate safety [21].

In another incidence on 18 December 2007, around 3,000 casual workers employed in the five EML factories located at Udyog Vihar, Gurgaon, stopped working during the night shift because the salary for the month of November 2007 was not paid by then. The management called the police to administer the situation. The workers were told to leave the factory premises. But the agitating workers refused to do so and instead made the police officers hear on 'how the management is oppressing them'.

Figure 2.1   Union Members Protesting Against the Shutdown of the Plant

Source: http://faridabadmetro.com/2012/09/18/gurgaon-news-eastern-medikit-employees-protest-against-the-companys-wrongdoings

Case Questions[28]

1. Briefly explain the role of each of the actors of IR played in the case of EML.
2. Identify the factors responsible for the situation in EML.
3. Make a list of the positive and negative aspects of the government's role.
4. Suggest what union/workers should do next and how they can pressurize the management to restart (all) the plants.
5. Do you think labour agitation is the only solution in the context? Justify your answer.
6. How could have such a situation been avoided?
7. What do you foresee for the future? Can the appropriate government initiate any steps for settling this dispute?

2.2. Factors Leading the Present State of IR

The contract of employment between employers and employees within the framework of government regulations is the base of IR in industries. Such contracts, either implicitly or explicitly, result in expectations in the parties to the contract, causing reciprocal behaviours to honour the very objective of the contract. These relationships influence and are also impacted by a wide range of industrial and economic phenomena which include how work is organized, governed and evaluated in the organizations, organizational performance and its contribution to the economy, patterns of investment in various sectors of the economy and their performance, and the dynamics in all these spheres that cause the resultant consequences [28]. In India, all these factors are more controlled by the policies/norms or the rules framed by the government from time to time. The government has all through been a major contributor (directly or indirectly) to the evaluation of IRS in India.

To understand the trend and study the cause of the trend of IR in India, the contextual contributors to the trend during the period starting from post-Independence to the phase of globalization of the Indian economy have been divided into the following two phases:

1. Evolution of the IRS during the period 1947–1991
2. Impact of globalization in the liberalized economy post-1991.

However, the following important developments (prior to 1947) contributed to the evolution of IRS in the post-Independence period in India (the list is illustrative, not exhaustive):

1. 1910s: Conditions of workers deteriorated in the wake of the First World War.
2. 1920s: The Indian Trade Unions Act and the Workmen's Compensation Act were enacted.
3. 1930s: Royal Commission on Labour expressed concern over the conditions of labour.
   1931: In the Karachi Session of Indian National Congress, a resolution was passed to safeguard the interests of workers through legislation and other means.
4. 1940s: First Tripartite Indian Labour Conference under colonial rule was held. Certain key legislations such as the Industrial Employment (Standing Orders) Act, the bill for the regularization of dockworkers employment conditions, the ID Act, the Minimum Wages Act and the Payment of Wages Act were enacted.
5. The Constitution of India introduced provisions which controlled the behaviour of the actors of the IR.

---

[28] The data source for developing the case is secondary.

2.2.1. Evolution of the Indian Industrial System during the Period 1947–1991

Since 1947 (Independence), the Government of India has been playing a crucial role in the industrialization of the country. The government's focus for industrialization was achieved through the five-year plans as well as industrial policies implemented from time to time. Studies by scholars have established, 'The policy goals of the government on industrialization have a strong connect with the IR policy, and thereby are linked to the economic objects of industrialization.' Conceptually, in 1964, Kerr, Dunlop, Harbison and Myers established, 'The Government policies on industrialization and the economic plans highly influenced the IR of the sub-continent [29]. It has also been viewed that in Asia, "the key determinants of IR change with the change in the industrialization strategy" [30] of the nations. Frenkel suggested, 'The level of industrialization of a country influences trade unions thereby IR' [31]. M. Bjorkman, L. Lauridsen and H. Marcussen [32] established in their study, 'Different patterns of industrialization are associated with different kinds of capital-labor relations.'

The approach by the government during the period 1947–1991, considering the uniformity in the objective of the policies implemented, for the maintenance of an effective IRS supporting the industrialization of the nation can be studied under the periods mentioned in the following sections.

2.2.1.1. The Period from 1947 to 1966

The period 1947–1966 includes the First, Second and the Third Five-Year Plans, that is, 1951–1956, 1956–1961 and 1961–1966 respectively.

The Indian economy had been predominantly an agricultural economy till 1947. The First Five-Year Plan (1951–1956) also laid emphasis on agriculture for economic growth. In the Second Five-Year Plan (1956–1961), there was a shift in focus towards heavy industries for the industrialization of the nation, and thereafter this trend continued. With the shift in the economy's dependency from agriculture to industry, the share of the agriculture sector in the GDP declined from 56 per cent in 1950–1951 to 18.20 per cent in 2013–2014. On the other hand, the share of the industrial sector in GDP rose from 15.6 per cent to 24.77 per cent and the share of the services sector in GDP increased from 29 per cent to 57.03 per cent during the same period. The projected average per capita income figure of 2015–2016 was estimated to be ₹93,231. The actual per capita income during the same period was ₹93,293, thereby registering a growth of 7.4 per cent above the financial year 2014–2015, (which was ₹86,879) [33]. Figure 2.2 shows the per capita income growth during the period 2012–2016.

The total population during the period 2015–2016 was estimated to be 133,578,495. Out of this population,

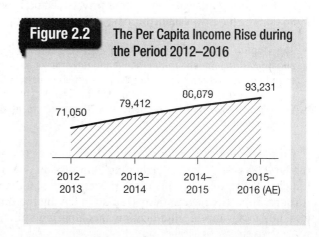

Figure 2.2 The Per Capita Income Rise during the Period 2012–2016

71,050   79,412   86,879   93,231

| 2012–2013 | 2013–2014 | 2014–2015 | 2015–2016 (AE) |

26.7 crore belonged to the middle class (by National Council for Applied Economic Research) and 17.96 crore were living below poverty line.

With India becoming a republic with constitutional provisions to ensure 'justice, liberty and equality', the economic planning emphasized intensively on industrialization, with a focus on the growth of the public sector to attain the commanding heights in the economy. In the first three five-year plans (1951–1956, 1956–1961 and 1961–1966), the approach of the government was focused on generating large employment-intensive public enterprises, mostly in the capital and intermediate goods sectors. The growth and development in these sectors resulted in employment growth in the private corporates, service and transport industries, and the educational sectors. Large private business houses were set up during this period (e.g., Tata Group). Such private organizations also operated in the protected product markets and were made to follow the norms of 'employment maximization' under government pressure. The government not only guided the private sector employers but also controlled the trade union movements in the country. The industrialization strategies and industrial policies followed in India since Independence aimed at both economic development and achieving a faster economic growth rate. But as a practice, the government's approach emphasized more on the regulation aspects than on controlling the developmental aspects of the economy. For example, to protect the domestic industry from foreign competition and to be a self-reliant economy, more emphasis was placed on the implementation of policies of import substitution.

The policy focus of the government during this period can be well categorized under the following:

1. Policy of the government towards foreign participation in industrial initiatives
2. Determination of the relative roles of the public and private sectors
3. Relative emphasis on capital goods over consumer goods
4. Importance of large-scale vis-à-vis small-scale industries
5. Decision on the location of industries considering the economic versus social criteria
6. Concentrated versus broad-based entrepreneurship
7. Licensing policy, procedures, rules and regulations to control industrial activities.

Through the Industrial Policy Resolution of 1948, the government adopted a 'mixed economy' approach for economic development. Majorly investments were made in the public sector, and limited sectors remained open to the private sector. It was in the Industrial Policy Resolution of 1956 that the focus was made for developing a socialist pattern of society. The Resolution put it as:

> The adoption of the socialist pattern of society as the national objective, as well as the need for planned and rapid development, requires that all industries of basic and strategic importance, or in the nature of public utility services, should be in the public sector. Other industries which are essential and require investment on a scale which only the State, in present circumstances, could provide has also to be in the public sector. The state has, therefore, to assume direct responsibility for the future development of industries over a wider area. [34]

On the face of such economic objectives of the government, while framing the objectives for the First Five-Year Plan, the Planning Commission was of the opinion that the best way to settle industrial disputes was to allow the employer and the employees to settle their concerns through bi-partite negotiations instead of having the third party intervention. The Commission was not in favour of adjudication machineries and tribunals. They also laid 'emphasis on improving the working conditions, wages, productivity, and formalizing the process of employment through employment exchange'.

The focus of the government in the Second Five-Year Plan was 'to initiate to secure peace through mutual negotiation, conciliations and voluntary arbitrations'. The Commission wanted the setting up of the wage commissions and wage boards, so it 'laid emphasis on workers' educations, adopting participative management, and skill development for the workers'.

The Second Five-Year plan recommended the following:

1. The avoidance of disputes at all levels between the management and the workers by encouraging mutual negotiations and conciliations.
2. More importance on conflict-preventive measures for achieving industrial peace.
3. An increased association between management and trade unions through the formation of joint councils and a proper demarcation of the functions of workers' committees and trade unions.
4. A need for the avoidance of indiscipline in the industry (for which a Code of Discipline was agreed upon in 1958).
5. Suggested restrictions on the number of outsiders who serve as office bearers of unions.
6. A need for union recognition to make collective bargaining effective, and the representative union to have the sole right to take up matters with the management.
7. The use of voluntary arbitration in the cases of unresolved disputes rather than compulsory adjudication.

Fairly successful results were achieved through such a planning process initiated after Independence, which created a need for further consolidation of the process for economic growth and development through rigorous implementation of the policies for better results. The consolidation process was done in IRS by laying greater emphasis on bipartism as well as tripartism, for increasing cordial relations between labour and management. During the Second Plan period, two more initiatives were also started: Joint Management Councils (JMC) and worker's training. JMC were introduced in 23 units with a purpose to jointly discuss issues related to the production and productivity of an organization.

In the 15th session of the Indian Labour Conference held in 1957, a groundwork for the Code of Discipline for the industry was evolved. The objective was to voluntarily bind the employer and workers to settle all disputes and grievances by mutual negotiations, conciliation and voluntary arbitration.

The government shifted its emphasis from legislation to voluntary agreements, tried to generate awareness of their obligations and also created in them an attitude of willingness to accept their responsibilities. It was in this context that the question of discipline in the industry was discussed at length by the Indian Labour Conference held in July 1957. The following general principles were laid down in the conference:

- There should be no lockout or strike without a notice.
- No unilateral action should be taken in connection with any industrial matter.
- There should be no recourse to go-slow tactics.
- No deliberate damage should be caused to plant or property.
- Acts of violence, intimidation, coercion or instigation should not be resorted to.
- The existing machinery for the settlement of disputes should be utilized.

- Awards and agreements should be speedily implemented.
- Any action that disturbs cordial IR should be avoided.

A tripartite sub-committee was appointed on whose report and recommendations a Code of Discipline was accepted in March 1958. After due discussion, it came into force on 1 June 1958. The Code of Discipline was accepted on the voluntary basis by nearly all the central organizations of labour and the employers. It was acceptable by both public and private industries. The Code was also accepted by 180 employers and 115 trade unions who were not members of any central employees' organizations.

The Code of Discipline was a set of self-imposed and mutually agreed voluntary principles of discipline and relations between the management and the workers. The Code lays down the norms both for the workers and the management, and provides for the voluntary and mutual settlement of disputes, through mutual negotiations, voluntary arbitrations and conciliations without the interference of an outside agency refraining both the parties from unilateral action. Thus, the Code compels both the parties not to indulge in any strike or lockout without exploring the avenues for voluntary, mutual settlement of any possible misunderstanding or disputes.

The central government amended the ID Act accordingly to include a new provision, and Section 10A provided for reference of disputes to voluntary arbitration. On the social security front, the Employee Provident Fund (EPF) Act was extended to cover industries and commercial establishments having 10,000 workers or more, and the contribution was enhanced from 6.25 to 8.33 per cent. The Employees State Insurance (ESI) Act proposed to extend insurance coverage to the workers' families. This period was a consolidation phase wherein workers' interests were retained and the government's control initiated through the philosophy of bipartism and tripartism.

The government's emphasis in the Third Five-Year Plan was the re-enforcement of the Code of Discipline and the implementation of the works committees and JMC. The government also constituted the Bonus Commission for considering the bonus issue for the workers and also considerations for the relief of the retrenched workers.

There was a big impact on the economy due to the Chinese aggression, which can hardly be overlooked. The war made the need for the Second Industrial Truce Resolution, which was passed on 3 November 1962 at a joint meeting of the employers and workers' representatives at Delhi. The resolution said, 'No effort shall be spared to achieve the maximum production and management workers will strive in collaboration in all possible ways to promote the defense efforts of the country'. The Second Industrial Truce Resolution strengthened the Code of Discipline by laying down that there would be no interruption or slowing down of production; on the other hand, production will be maximized and defence effort promoted in all possible ways. The resolution emphasized:

- The need to maximize production
- That no interruption of work be allowed
- That all disputes should be settled by voluntary arbitration, especially those related to dismissal, discharge and retrenchment of workers
- That unions should discourage absenteeism and negligence on the part of the workers
- Joint emergency production committees to be set up.

A standing committee was also set up in August 1963 to review the implementation of the Truce Resolution.

Box 2.1 Code of Discipline

Managements and unions agree to the following:

1. That no unilateral action should be taken in connection with any industrial matter and that disputes should be settled at an appropriate level.
2. That the existing machinery for the settlement of disputes should be utilized with the utmost expedition.
3. That there should be no strike or lockout without notice.
4. That affirming their faith in democratic principles, they bind themselves to settle all future differences, disputes and grievances by mutual negotiation, conciliation and voluntary arbitration.
5. That neither party will have recourse to (a) coercion, (b) intimidation, (c) victimization or (d) go-slow.
6. That they will promote constructive cooperation between their representatives at all levels and between workers themselves.
7. That they will establish upon mutually agreed basis a grievance procedure, which will ensure a speedy and full investigation leading to settlement.
8. That they will promote constructive cooperation between their representatives at all levels and between workers themselves and abide by the spirit of agreements mutual entered into.
9. That they will abide by various stages in the grievance procedure and take no arbitrary action, which would bypass this procedure.
10. That they will educate the management personnel and workers regarding their obligations to each other.

Managements agree to the following:

1. Not to increase workloads unless agreed upon or settled otherwise.
2. Not to support or encourage any unfair labour practice such as (a) interference with the right of employees to enrol or continue as union members, (b) discrimination, restraint or coercion against any employees because of the recognized activity of trade unions and (c) victimization of any employee and abuse of authority in any form.
3. To take prompt action for the (a) settlement of grievances and (b) implementation of settlements, awards, decisions and orders.
4. To display in conspicuous places in the undertaking the provisions of this code in the local language(s).
5. To distinguish between actions justifying immediate discharge and those where discharge must be preceded by a warning, reprimand, suspension or some other form of disciplinary action, and to arrange that all such disciplinary actions should be subject of an appeal through a normal grievance procedure.
6. To take appropriate disciplinary action against its officers and members in cases where enquiries reveal that they were responsible for precipitating action by workers leading to indiscipline.
7. To recognize the union in accordance with the criteria (Annexure I) evolved at the 16th session of the Indian Labour Conference in May 1958.

Unions agree to the following:

1. Not to engage in any form of physical duress.
2. Not to permit demonstrations, which are not peaceful, and not to permit rowdyism in demonstrations.

3. That their members will not engage or cause other employees to engage in any union activity during working hours, unless as provided for by law, agreement or practice.
4. To discourage unfair labour practices such as (a) negligence of duty, (b) careless operation, (c) damage to property, (d) interference with or disturbance to normal work and (e) insubordination.
5. To take prompt action to implement awards, agreements, settlements and decisions.
6. To display in conspicuous places in the union offices the provisions of this code in the local languages.
7. To express disapproval and to take appropriate action against office bearers and members for indulging in action against the spirit of this code.

Unionization during the Period

With the growth of industries, the unionism in organizations took an aggressive turn. The number of registered unions increased rapidly from 4,623 in 1951–1952 to 11,614 in 1961–1962, and the total number of members of the registered unions became 3,977,000 [35]. C. S. Venkataratnam indicates, 'The total number of membership increased by three times during the said period' [36]. All registered unions made strategic focus to establish themselves in the government-owned industries since the public sector provided a new platform for large-scale unionization.

The principle trade unions, that is, AITUC and INTUC had their respective roles towards the stabilization of IRS in the newly emerging economy. The Communist Party-led AITUC continued to consolidate its dominant position (as they had been doing in the pre-Independence days) with the growth of the public sector in India. Because Congress as a major central political party was very much visible, the party-controlled INTUC had an early acceptability and gained the support of the majority of employees in organizations especially in the public sector undertakings (PSUs). The strategic approach of the two unions was different. Since INTUC had the support from the centre with Congress in power, the union followed an approach of imposing from above in the organizations. So they could make their way for the union formation as well as stabilize their support from the employees. On the other hand, AITUC arose largely from within the workforce. However, there were strong chains of command in both the trade unions, which cascaded from political (affiliated) parties to the unions.

The drawback of the IRS was the inappropriate development of the tools of collective bargaining (the prime mover of IRS). The legal provisions under the ID Act, 1947 provided no framework or procedures for the employees' representation as bargaining units. The colonial regime followed a laissez-faire pattern of collective bargaining, that is, free play within the available scopes. The patterns of society were different so the businesses could continue with collective bargaining without any legal framework. With the business being controlled more by government policies, the trade unions of followed a structure of collective bargaining, which was very much centralized, that is, bargaining used to take place only at the national level (through wage boards or industry-wise), and in some regions, collective bargaining was encouraged at the unit level. On the other hand, in the private sectors, collective bargaining was held at the enterprise level.

The right to strike in public utility services was very much controlled under the provisions of the ID Act, 1947. Since the primary focus of the government was to promote 'responsible unionism' for maintaining industrial peace, the procedure for calling a legal strike in PSUs was made lengthy.

In determination of wage rates, both at the state (minimum wages) and industry levels (wage negotiations), the determinants were more impacted by the political and social institutional considerations [37, 38]. The principles which governed the wage determination systems were through 'tripartism' and 'political bargaining'.

Towards the end of this phase, there were splits in the CTUs because of the emergence of ideological differences between their apex bodies and the groups at the organization levels. Such differences led to split in INTUC to form HMS, the socialist ideology-driven Congress fraction. Similar ideological differences were seen in the Communist Party of India (CPI)-backed AITUC, which was split to create the CPI wing (Marxist) and CITU.

The management style in the PSUs was more of a paternalistic style, that is, focused towards the welfare of the employees with limited links to the business objectives. Such an approach to IRS was termed as a system of 'state pluralism' [39]. In other words, the government encouraged the system to listen to the 'union voices' for the 'collective' interests of the workers, which was felt would lead to rapid industrialization.

2.2.1.2. The Period from 1967 to 1979

This period includes the Annual Plans (1967–1969), the Fourth Five-Year Plan (1969–1974) and the Fifth Five-Year Plan (1974–1979).

A wider government role was visible with the announcement of the formation of the first National Commission on Labour in 1966. The National Commission on Labour was set up on 24 December 1966, under the chairmanship of Justice P. B. Gajendragadkar. The Commission submitted its report in August 1969. The committee's recommendations focused on certain specific areas such as recruitment agencies and their practices, employment and service administration, training and workers' education, working conditions of the workers, labour welfare as a core need, housing and social security, wages including wage policies and bonus, workers/employers' organizations and their roles, and IR machinery for settling industrial disputes.

This period experienced a sharp rise in the number of strikes and labour unrests. The reason for the same can be attributed to the structural changes in the economy and declining employment elasticity leading to the tightening of the labour market. This situation reshaped the trade unions' objectives and thus the activities. The practice of collective bargaining took a different shape since the investors were focused on the return on capital, whereas the trade unions, both to maintain their stand amongst the employees and as political parties at the Centre, resorted to aggressive means for settling the disputes. Collective bargaining was more backed by aggressive labour agitations. This resulted in a phenomenal increase in the number of strikes and lockouts, the number of workers involved and the number of man-days lost due to such labour unrests [40].

The economy underwent a sharp downturn. The factors of the economy which contributed to the adverse IR during the period are attributed to high inflection, low industrial growth, income inequalities and increasing unemployment percentage. Above all these shocks, the impact of the oil price hike was also was felt in the economy. Inflation rose above 10 per cent during the period 1967–1968 as compared to the period 1966–1967. The food price increased by 20 per cent during the same period [41].

With inflation leading to economic stagnation, the industrial growth registered was about 3.6 per cent [42]. There were unequal terms of trade between agriculture and industry, resulting in growing income inequalities. In addition, the economy suffered two oil price shocks in 1973 and 1978. The average annual growth rate in employment fell from 2.2 per cent during 1967–1969 to 1.8 per cent during 1974–1979 [43]. Industrial stagnation, structural changes in the economy and the emerging uncertainties in the economy were the causes of reshaping the trade union movements and their pattern of agitation. In the mid-1970s, the negotiation strategy shifted from 'demanding for rights to demanding for interests'. There were various factors for such shifts, they are as follows:

1. There was an uneven development of firms within an industry; some units were more profitable than others. While bargaining trade unions insisted on the 'capacity to pay' of the firm.
2. The information on a firm's performance was made available to the trade unions, as a right.
3. The leadership of the trade unions was no longer decided by the centrally affiliated party of the trade union. The decision on the leadership was now taken by the leaders driving the union at the units.

The government took the initiative in the early 1970s to re-frame some of the labour policies, procedures and programmes, which were based on the recommendations of the Royal Commission on Labour, 1966. The list includes wage policy and minimum wages, employment services, vocational training, labour statistics, research and workers' education and so on. The National Labour Institute was set up in 1972 on the basis of the recommendations of the Commission. The stagnated economy did not encourage the wages to increase during this period. The wages either declined or remained unchanged. The real wages however declined.

The rising labour unrest and economic downturn were addressed by the government's initiatives in the Fourth Five-Year Plan. The government stressed more importance on the machineries for the settlement of industrial disputes. The development of the processes of collective bargaining, conciliation machineries, voluntary arbitration and adjudication machineries was insisted in this plan period. The enforcement of labour legislations was another area of focus.

The period also witnessed a series of amendments in the existing labour acts since the government implemented the recommendations of the Labour Commission through amending certain labour laws which include the Workmen's Compensation Act, 1923 (recommendations were for the removal of wage ceiling for coverage), the ID Act, 1947 (introduction of the unfair labour practices), the ESI Act, 1948 (for enhancement in the wage limit for exemption from the payment of employees' contribution), the Factories Act, 1948 (for making penalties more stringent for the violation of safety requirements and the provision of welfare facilities) and the Employees Provident Funds and Miscellaneous Provisions Act, 1952 (enhancement in the rate of contribution and making default of dues a cognizable offence). On the basis of the recommendations of the Labour Commissioner, the government enacted certain new laws which include the Contract Labour (Regulation and Abolition) Act, 1970; Limestone and Dolomite Mines Labour Welfare Fund Act, 1972; Iron Ore, Manganese Ore and Chrome Ore Mines Labour Welfare Fund Act, 1976; Equal Remuneration Act, 1976 and Child Labour (Prohibition and Regulation) Act, 1986.

The early 1970s witnessed considerable industrial strife and loss of a large number of man days. During this period, the Indian Labour Commission, which was active till 1971, did not meet from 1972 to 1976. Towards the end of the Fourth Plan, the Railway strike of 1974 was a big IR issue.

The 1974 rail workers' strike was a unique event for several reasons. It occurred at a time when labour militancy was at its highest. The number of man-days lost owing to all industrial disputes in India touched 40 million in 1974, which was more than double the number recorded in any single year in the preceding decade. The strike commenced on 8 May 1974 and lasted for three weeks. About 1,700,000 workers of the railways participated in the strike. The strike was called off on 27 May 1974. The president of the All India Railwaymen's Federation (AIRF) George Fernandes led the strike. During this strike, 50,000 railway workers were arrested, over 10,300 railwaymen were dismissed from services, 5,600 temporary employees were terminated from their services and 4 employees lost their lives.

The railway bureaucracy, working under the government's approval and direction, preferred to deal with 'tamed' leaders of the railways' working class. In doing this, the Government, as an employer, perceived 'the unions as devices with which it could "discipline" the workers' with. But the 1974 strike was symbolic of the fact that the workers' refusal to accept the 'patron–client' character which claimed to work for the government.

In February 1974, the National Coordinating Committee for Railwaymen's Struggle (NCRRS) was formed to bring all the railway unions, the CTUs and the political parties in the opposition together to prepare for the strike which was to start on 8 May 1974. The workers' initiative was matched by the government's determination to put down the strike with a heavy hand. This intention of the government is evident from their actions; for example, on 2 May 1974, as the negotiations were proceeding, the government arrested George Fernandes at the Lucknow railway station; simultaneously, across the country thousands of railway workers were arrested. The provisions of the Defence of India Act and the Maintenance of Internal Security Act (MISA) were used against the workers.

With the countrywide arrest of the top leadership of the unions, the success of the strike now depended greatly on the zonal and local union leaders, and, of course, the rank and file workers. Workers from other industries and services were quick to express solidarity with the striking rail workers. The action of the government provoked the workers to go on an immediate strike in some zones, instead of waiting for 8 May 1974.

The brutal methods adopted by the government against the striking workers and their families have been well documented in various pieces of literature. Railway colonies were practically under siege. For instance, in Mughalsarai (now known as Pt. Deen Dayal Upadhyaya Junction), Uttar Pradesh, which has one of the biggest railway yards, women were assaulted; even children were not spared. The Border Security Force (BSF), the Central Reserve Police Force (CRPF) and the Provincial Armed Constables were deployed in the labour township. There were also instances of workers forced by terror to work. Instances of train drivers who were shackled in their cabins were reported at the height of the strike [43, 44].

The strike was deemed to be a failure, but the strike achieved later what it sought to achieve then. For these reasons, the strike marks a milestone in the labour history. For the first time, bonus was granted to railway employees in 1979 after the Janata government came to power.

C.2.3. Case for Discussion   The Railway Strike

AIRF declared, 'the strike by nearly 1,700,000 Indian railwaymen could have been averted had there been sincere, good faith in collective bargaining on the part of the public authorities'. A charter of railwaymen's demands was submitted to the management and the management accordingly started the negotiation on the matter on 5 February 1974. A number of meetings took place and finally, AIRF had meetings with the minister and deputy minister of railways.

The AIRF announced that a strike notice would be served on 23 April 1974, and they would go on strike from 8 May 1974 in case their discussion with the management was not going to provide any amicable solutions. The discussions continued until 30 April 1974, but no settlements were reached. The railway minister agreed on 30 April that he would resume the discussion on all the demands made and proposed that the next meeting be held on 1 May 1974. The union representatives suggested the minister to provide a written reply to each of their demands so that the document could serve as the basis for further negotiations. They also requested to hold the next meeting on 2 May 1974, to which the minister agreed.

However, on 2 May, Mr George Fernandes, the president of the AIRF, was arrested along with many other trade union office bearers who were leading the negotiation. This brought an abrupt halt to the negotiation. This incidence led to spontaneous work stoppages in some areas/departments as a reaction to the government's step of 2 May 1974. On 8 May 1974, the entire railway system was brought to a halt and the strike was declared.

What followed was the management's action of suspending and dismissing thousands of strikers, eviction with their families from railway quarters, army personnel asking strikers' wives at bayonet point to disclose the whereabouts of their husbands or face eviction, arrest of over 25,000 workers and finally, Territorial Army personnel were compelled to run trains, with no previous experience or training. The Home Ministry issued a circular directing state governments to arrest protestors in consultation with the railway general managers and the divisional superintendents.

The union (AIRF) pointed out that its demands had been pending for over a year without any meaningful negotiations or any genuine efforts being made by the management to resolve the issues. It alleged that the arrests and repressive measures had begun long before the strike started. Instead of referring the dispute to the conciliation machinery under the ID Act, in the event of such breakdown of the negotiations which was a normal course laid down under the Act, the administration had followed a method of exhorting union members by threats, intimidation, persuasion or rewards to relinquish their union membership or causing the dismissal or otherwise prejudicing workers by reason of their union membership.

AIRF also indicated that more than 60,000 workers were arrested and detained without trial, more than 10 million workers were served with dismissal orders and approximately 30,000 were thrown out of their houses or served with eviction notices with immediate effect. There had been ruthless propaganda against railwaymen through the state-owned radio and TV network. The armed forces and police went into action, and the government made use of draconian powers under the measures of the 'maintenance of internal security and the defence of India'. The workers were forced to work at bayonet point, and the authorities unleashed a reign of terror in the railway colony.

The management's/government's point was that the Indian Railways was run as a government undertaking and was deemed to be an essential public utility service. It was the lifeline of the country's transport system. Besides carrying passengers, it assisted in the transportation of coal to power stations, essential raw materials to steel plants and food grains to areas where they were in short supply. They employ nearly 1,400,000 workers and their total wage bill in 1972–1973 amounted to 4,800 million rupees. So being an organization providing employment to the highest number of employees and involved in serving the nation, it was not justified for the AIRF to initiate a strike.

The government's contention was:

A permanent tripartite machinery for the settlement of railway disputes had been functioning since 1952, which was set up in agreement with AIRF. In 1966 the Government introduced a scheme for consultation with its employees' organisations through joint councils at the national, regional and office levels were involved on addressing their issues. The scheme provides for the settlement of all disputes through joint consultation or compulsory arbitration machinery. Compulsory arbitration was provided for all issues relating to the pay and allowances, weekly hours of work and leave of a grade or class of employees. The scheme further provides, 'any matters determined by the Government in accordance with the recommendations of a commission shall not be subject to arbitration for a period of five years'.

The government's contention was also that railwaymen were government servants and that the same pay scales and service conditions were applicable to them as to employees in other government departments. They were also bound by the same rules as concerns, inter alia, strikes, and their pay scales and service conditions were determined by high-level pay commissions appointed by the government from time to time. A third pay commission was set up in 1970 to review the pay scales and service conditions of all government servants. Both the railwaymen's federations—one being the AIRF—took the opportunity to present their views before this commission. The commission submitted its report in March 1973. The government evaluated the recommendations of the commission and discussed with the two federations of railwaymen. The matter was also discussed with the Ministry of Finance. After extensive discussions with the employees' representatives, the government finally announced its decisions on the pay commission's recommendations in October 1973. Despite the agreement was reached under the joint consultation machinery, the AIRF submitted a six-point memorandum demanding for further changes in the pay scales and in the dearness allowance (DA) formula on 8 November 1973. The government felt that it was a clear transgression of the spirit of the agreement in question.

Mr George Fernandes threatened to call a strike if the demands were not accepted by 10 April 1974, even though strikes in an essential service like the railways were prohibited because of the conditions witnessed in the past year. The government added that acceptance of the AIRF's demands would have entailed an additional expenditure of 4,500 million rupees, which was beyond their capacity in the then context of the country's economy. However, with a view of avoiding any disruption of the smooth working of the railways and to find ways and means of arriving at a settlement, the railway minister and his deputy started negotiations with the AIRF and the other recognized federations.

The AIRF refused to make any concession and served strike notices on 22 and 23 April 1974 for a general strike on 8 May 1974. The main objective of this initiative was to secure a negotiated settlement. As a result of the negotiations, most of the issues raised had been resolved. The number of benefits derived from the negotiated settlement over these demands were evaluated at about 800 million rupees a year (in addition to the 1,100 million rupees accruing out of the implementation of the pay commission's recommendations). Two of the demands could not be accepted, that is, the revision of pay scales because they had already been considerably improved upon, and the computation of DA and bonuses because the matter was under consideration of the Bonus Review Committee.

Notwithstanding the government's readiness to resolve the difference through negotiations, the AIRF proceeded with all-out preparations for a strike designed to cripple the national economy. Mr George Fernandes toured the whole country openly inciting his followers to adopt the means of violence and sabotage. A number of instances of intimidation, assaults on officers and supervisors, and adoption of the general atmosphere of violence were reported. By 30 April 1974, the negotiations had reached a decisive stage and a measure of agreement was in sight; it was accordingly agreed that what had already been achieved should be put in writing so that the agreed minutes could be discussed and accepted on 1 May. Mr Fernandes stated that he would not be able to come for the meeting so the meeting was postponed until the next day.

The government added that other railwaymen's federations had openly declared that they would not join the strike. In fact, out of 1,400,000 employees, only about 550,000—that is less than half—took part in the strike. It was on this account, according to the government, that the AIRF resorted to violence, even when the negotiations were on. The government had to act in the interest of the nation and of the majority of the staff who wanted to hold their posts. It was on this account that preventive arrests of Mr Fernandes and his close associates were made. The strike commenced on 8 May 1974. According to the government, the AIRF resorted the acts of organized violence, intimidation and attacks on loyal workers. There were reported cases of sabotage leading to the wanton destruction of railway property and premises. The number of strikers soon dwindled to 250,000, and the strike was called off unconditionally after three weeks.

The government further pointed out that the Railway Ministry had planned to get the dispute arbitrated by their own machinery, namely the Permanent Negotiating Machinery (PNM), which comprised representatives of both the recognized federations including the AIRF and the management. This machinery was fully competent to deal with any disputes arising in the railways. But the AIRF contended that after the negotiations failed, the dispute should have been referred to the conciliation machinery under the ID Act.

The federation's demands included the revision of wage scales, changes in the DA formula and the payment of bonuses. The contention of the government was that such issues could not have been dealt with through the conciliation machinery. These were issues with wider financial implications and were within the authority of the pay commission, and the bonus issues were under the considerations of the Bonus Review Committee.

In order to enforce discipline and restore order, the government admitted to having been obliged to have recourse to preventive detention, but only in respect of those who had indulged in violent activities. Some such workers were subsequently dismissed or removed from service under the disciplinary rules applicable to railwaymen. The affected workers were free to make individual appeals; in fact, such appeals had been received and were under consideration. It is a gross exaggeration, according to the government, to say that army personnel were deployed to terrorize the wives of strikers. As a safeguard against sabotage and to protect the lives, property and families of workers who had stayed at their posts, it was necessary to provide pickets at strategic points and in the railway colonies, as well as arranging for the patrolling of the railway tracks.

The government pointed out that the Territorial Army personnel involved were railwaymen with long years of service who were recruited to meet national emergencies, move essential traffic and to prevent the country from sliding into a state of economic paralysis. They ran thousands of trains during the strike without violating any safety rules. Out of 1,400,000 railway employees, continued the government, 19,883 were arrested during the strike; all except seven were later released. The number of regular employees removed from service was 16,749; on the basis of individual appeals, 10,561 of them were reinstated.

According to the government, all those who actively participated in the strike—which was declared illegal under the Defence of India Rules, 1971—had to forgo their pay for the period of absence due to strike. This break in service, however, did not imply any reduction in pay or loss of seniority, but only the forfeiture of earned leave for the period of the strike. The government indicated that by resorting to a strike and reopening issues which had been settled by joint discussions, the AIRF infringed the existing agreement between the government and the associations. The association was also responsible for violating the law of the land, which prohibited strikes in the railways, run as an essential service.

Case Questions

1. Was the AIRF right in calling a strike across the country in an organization like the railways, which is a PSU?
2. Please list down your points on 'the strike was justified' and the 'strike was not justified'.
3. Please examine the legality of the strike in the light of the provisions of the ID Act and the agreement the railway administration had with the striking federations.
4. List down your comments on the initiatives of the government to deal with the strike.
5. Analyse the impact of the strike in a situation when the economy was not performing at the expected levels.

(The instructor may please refer to the teaching manual for the pedagogy.)

The railway strike of 1974 precipitated the Emergency of 1975. The government had branded this strike as a political strike and considered it as a justification for the declaration of Emergency of 1975.

With the declaration of Emergency in June 1975, a National Apex Body (NAB) was set up in place of the tripartite Indian Labour Commission, which was in consonance with the government's 20-point programme. NAB and some state apex bodies (SABs) were forums for the bipartite settlement of the disputes. NAB consisted of 23 members (12 representing workers and 11 representing employers). It met six times during 1976 for reviewing IR and labour matters, with the government acting as an arbitrator. However, these bodies did not had a long tenure. During the Janata government, they were abolished and the Indian Labour Commission was revived in May 1977. The period of Emergency 1975–1977 experienced considerable tightening of discipline in the industries in India.

IC.2.1. INDUSTRIAL CONTEXT FOR DISCUSSION

Emergency

Indira Gandhi moved away from socialism during the Emergency. The focus was for a more consistent shift towards prioritizing economic growth by embracing the private sectors with the existing industrial sectors. Improving production was the top priority. The incorporated policy changes during the time establishes this shift. *The Times of India* editorialized within a year: 'A change of considerable significance is taking place in India...the emphasis has shifted from distributive justice to growth' (22 February 1981). A close advisor noted that, after returning to power in 1980, Indira Gandhi 'was clearly determined to get back to the firm foundations of economic reform'.

The new model of economic development adopted by Indira Gandhi had three critical components:

- Prioritization of economic growth as a state goal
- Supporting big business to achieve the goal
- Taming labour as a necessary aspect of this strategy.

The emphasis was on 'national situation' ahead of labour's interests. Strikes, 'gheraos', 'go-slow' and 'work-to-rule' movements were increasingly characterized by Indira Gandhi as 'anti-social demonstrations of irresponsibility by a few' [45]. Special legislation was passed to discourage strikes.

The 'growth first' model of development led to the priorities shifting to favour the growth of big business and discourage labour problems and agitations. The State's role was restructured with more focus for the economy towards growth promotion. The preference for business against labour in a situation where labour could never be fully tamed and where the State itself remained relatively 'soft' for gaining the support of the people created numerous problems and inefficiencies in the bureaucracy and public management. It also created significant political problems since the policy could not win the support of the majority, where the majority were poor or near poor [46].

The structural changes in the economy also generated counter actions from the employer's side. For the first time since Independence, in the year 1976, the number of man-days lost due to lockouts exceeded the number of days lost due to strikes [40].

In the post-Emergency period, with the change in the political leadership, there followed a period of reconciliation. The Janata government set up a number of committees to review IR practices. For instance, there was a tripartite committee on workers' participation and a draft

Industrial Relations Bill, 1978. The outcome in result during this phase precipitated that the onus of economic development again shifted to the government. The Janata government adopted the policy of leading industrialization through government interventions.

At the labour front, divisions were created within the union movement. Employers were prepared to negotiate wages and working conditions at the workplace rather than adopting the imposed norms [47]. This led scope for the leftist group to be visible with their ideologies to reach out to the employees. There was large-scale multiplication of unions in India in this period. In 1950–1951, there were 2,002 registered unions, whereas by 1979, there were 10,021 unions [48].

2.2.1.3. The Period from 1980 to 1990

This period corresponds to the Sixth Five-Year Plan (1980–1985) and the Seventh Five-Year Plan (1985–1990). The average annual growth rate during this decade was around 5.7 per cent and the employment growth rate was only around 1.8 per cent [43]. 'The most striking fact is that the 1980s has been the best decade in terms of economic growth but the worst decade in terms of employment generation' [49].

The public sector strike in Bangalore during the period 1980–1981 marks the beginning of this period. The PSUs were: Hindustan Aeronautics Limited (HAL), Bharat Electronics Limited (BEL), Bharat Earth Movers Limited (BEML), Hindustan Machine Tools (HMT) and Indian Telephone Industries (ITI). The PSUs produced capital goods and components which were desperately needed by many industries.

IC.2.2. INDUSTRIAL CONTEXT FOR DISCUSSION

Strike by Public Sector Engineering Workers in December 1980

In December 1980, nearly 125,000 public sector engineering workers, representing five organizations, namely BEL, BEML, HAL, HMT and ITI, located in Bangalore, declared strike. The trade unions of these organizations formed a Joint Action Front (JAF). The strikers demanded pay hikes at par with the pat structure and the benefits implemented at Bharat Heavy Electricals Limited (BHEL). The strike lasted for 77 days and ended in a bitter defeat for the unions and the workers. They were forced to return to work by the government without conceding any of their demands. But protests continued in their agitation for further six weeks, which culminated into 26 days long lockout. It was only after this event that a final settlement was signed between managements and the unions, although the government still refused to concede their demand for wage parity with BHEL. The government however agreed to refer the question of wage and benefit parity question for adjudication to the National Industrial Tribunal. The Tribunal passed its order in the year 1989. Subsequently, the matter continued as a dispute before the Supreme Court.

An economy which was dependent on government-run PSUs was heavily affected due to such a strike. To meet the situation of industrial strife, on 26 July 1981, the government issued an ordinance to ban strikes. A new law, called ESMA, was implemented. With the enactment of this law, the government's authority to intervene in IR was widened. This law encroached into the trade union rights to a great extent and, as a result, major trade unions of India observed a Bharat

Bandh on 19 January 1982. Workers in industrial establishments, banks, life insurance companies and general insurance companies abstained from work on that day [50]. ESMA empowers the government to ban strikes, lay-offs and lockouts in what it deems to be 'essential services'. It also empowers the government to punish any person who participates or instigates a strike which is deemed illegal under ESMA. The values of production loss due to strikes and lockouts in 1980 was ₹12.53 crore, in 1979 was ₹125.63 crore and in 1978 it was ₹108.16 crore.

C.2.4. Case for Discussion   Bangalore: Paying a Heavy Price

The fall-out of the four-month strike in the five premier PSUs in Bangalore is only now being felt throughout the nation. The effects have been particularly severe because nearly all the mammoth concerns where work stopped—HAL, BEL, BBEML, HMT and ITI—produce capital goods and components desperately needed by many industries.

One of the worst affected by the strike which ended in March has been the TV industry which is mostly in the small sector. BEL makes 40 million picture tubes, the most essential component of a TV set.

Orders placed with BEL last year are yet to be processed and delivered. This means production slow-downs and partial lay-offs in TV manufacturing units, resulting in more unemployment. Even if factories go in for imports, being bulky items picture tubes cannot be air-freighted and getting them by sea involves a delay of six to eight weeks. Some TV manufacturers in fact are importing picture tubes from Taiwan at very high prices, an avoidable drain on scarce foreign exchange.

According to the Indian TV Manufacturers' Association, it had pleaded in January, when the strike was in full swing, with the Electronic Trade and Technology Development Corporation (ETTDC), to go in for imports to fill the anticipated shortfall of 100,000 tubes. Since nothing was done, production of TV sets fell steeply resulting in black marketing and causing great inconvenience to customers.

Replacement of even a small BEL component, either by an imported one or by another of indigenous make, presents problems. First of all, the circuits would have to be changed. Most manufacturers, accustomed as they have been to BEL quality and specifications, would not be able to affect the switch.

Use of another make of component also presents the possibility of a higher rejection rate of the end product. The list of items manufactured by BEL is long. Once a component has outlived its stipulated period, it has to be replaced. Again, difficulties arise when such items go off the market. A shortage of X-ray tubes resulted in many patients being referred from hospital to hospital.

Though production at BEL has resumed, it will take months to clear the backlog of orders. For 1980–81, BEL had a production target of ₹84 crore. It achieved only ₹57 crore, thanks to the strike.

Thwarted Plans: BEML had an ambitious plan of achieving a turnover of ₹175 crore. They have lost ₹69 crore worth of production. Thirty six per cent of BEML production goes to the coal industry, 26 per cent to irrigation and power, 14 per cent to iron and steel and 6 per cent to agriculture.

What are their products? Crawler tractors, dumpers, excavators, track shovels—equipment vital to the coal, irrigation, power and mining industries. Added to this is the little-known fact that BEML accounts for 25 per cent of the production of rail coaches in the country, with substantial export orders. Here again the railways, and ultimately the public, will suffer.

Officials of BEML one of the efficiently run PSUs, pointed out that production during any normal year progressively increases and picks up only towards the middle of the year, reaching its peak during the last quarter.

While production had been satisfactory till December (the strike began on December 26), there had been total stoppage since then. In 1979–1980, BEML reported netted a pretax profit of ₹12 crore.

In 1980–81, due to the loss in peak production during the last quarter, all possibilities of breaking even have been wiped out.

Those who entertain ambitions of having a telephone might as well shelve it for the time being. Even at the best of times, getting a telephone line installed is a herculean task. With ITI suffering a loss of 25 per cent of its targeted production of ₹130 crore, the already long waiting lists for telephones will only get longer in the months to come.

A World Bank loan of £53 million (₹92.7 crore) which became operative on 30 October 1978, terminates on 31 March, 1982. This was to help ITI modernise its equipment. A World Bank team was in Bangalore recently, apparently to monitor the progress of the programme, keeping in view the prolonged strike, ITI, which also had a reputation as a consistent exporter, has already sustained a loss of ₹10 crore in overseas orders, according to C. M. Stephen, union communications minister.

Although HAL primarily functions as the principal overhaul, repair and maintenance depot for the air force and for aircraft of other wings of the armed forces, it too suffered from the strike. While no information can be officially released, HAL being a defence undertaking, it is clear that the Jaguar assembly project suffered a serious setback. A new division was set up for this purpose but even the civil construction work on it has been delayed.

Silver Lining: The only silver lining seems to be on the HMT watch front. Though its Bangalore unit was on strike, the company as a whole has made up and produced 3.51 million watches in 1980–1981. Even with the Bangalore unit on strike, perhaps this figure could have been surpassed. Also, HMT'S two vital foreign projects in Algeria and Nigeria, each worth ₹10 crore, are bound to be affected by the strike, apart from inevitable loss of goodwill.

According to Michael Fernandes, president of the ITI Employees Union and one of the leaders of the JAF, the strike was forced on the workers by the government and the managements who refused to negotiate for nearly nine months on the demand for revising wages on the basis of a clause incorporated in the tripartite settlements signed in 1978.

The clause relates to parity with BHEL in respect of a minimum wage. The demand of the striking workers was merely for maintaining this parity which the government flatly turned down.

As the strike progressed, amidst all the early euphoria and whipped-up enthusiasm, the JAF quietly began to play down its demand for parity. Indeed, on three different occasions, when some of its leaders met the prime minister at Bangalore airport, the JAF suggested that it had a 'watered down' version of its demands.

Short of spelling out their eagerness to call off the strike, they did everything possible to persuade Mrs Indira Gandhi to agree to a negotiated settlement.

When this obviously did not happen, the JAF knuckled under amidst all its brinkmanship and bravado. The INTUC unit of HMT, controlling some 6,500 employees of HMT–1 and HMT–2 units manufacturing sensitive and sophisticated machine tools, which had not joined the strike, raced to the forefront through its sustained psychological campaign against the strike, under the stewardship of F. M. Khan, MP, president of the Karnataka INTUC and treasurer of the All India Congress Committee (I).

Though Khan succeeded, through his poster campaign and rough-house street brawl tactics, in causing confusion and disarray among the JAF leadership, he miserably failed to emerge as the hero of the toiling masses. Karnataka Chief Minister R. Gundu Rao also came a cropper in his attempt to play the honest broker in ending the deadlock.

It can truly be said: while neither the workers, nor their trade union leaders, nor the managements of the Bangalore-based PSUs, emerged victorious, the people of India have lost heavily. And they will continue to pay for the folly of these leaders for months to come.

Source: http://indiatoday.intoday.in/story/four-month-strike-in-five-premier-psus-in-bangalore-felt-throughout-india/1/402038.html

Case Questions

1. Please list down the impact of the strike in HAL, BEL, BEML, HMT and ITI on the following:
   a. On their employees
   b. On the depending companies using their products as raw materials
   c. On the employees of the subsidiary companies and their vendors
   d. On the economy at large
2. Analyse the role of the government as owners of the business and government as an institution responsible for designing the framework of law and policies for maintaining harmonious IR.

(The instructor may refer to the teaching note for the pedagogy.)

The Bombay (now Mumbai) textile strike was a more significant event. It started as a wage and bonus issue in few cotton mills in late 1981, which soon developed into an industry-wide strike. The 1947 Bombay Industrial Relations Act (BIRA) had imposed an industry-wide bargaining structure with an unrepresentative union (affiliated to the INTUC) as the sole bargaining agent of workers of the textile mills in Bombay. This was not accepted in general by the workers. By the time the textile strike ended in late 1983, the government-installed union in the industry declined to levels from which it could never recover [51].

C.2.5. Case for Discussion   The Bombay Textile Mill Strike of 1982

The Bombay textile mill strike of 1982–1983 has few parallels in the trade union movements in India. Such a general strike is rarely seen in the history of organized labour [52]. There had been little violence of any kind in this strike. The strike stands out in history as an event for reckoning, an incidence where the labour force showed that the unity was their strength and that numbers did matter. The strike has been explained as 'there was more of political unionism rather than an economic bargaining on the part of the trade unions' [53].

The Bombay textile mill strike began in January 1982 and the agitation continued for one and a half years. Around two and a half lakh workers of 60 mills from all over Bombay participated in the strike.

The cause of the agitation is attributed to the fact that the wages of the Bombay working class in textile mills were disproportionately low. The textile workers in Bombay were dissatisfied with their wages as well as with their trade union, who was not representing their interests to the mill owner. During the years following the Second World War, wages and other benefits in the cotton textile industry in Bombay became reasonably low as compared with other industries in the city, and perhaps in the whole country. In the year 1947, through an award of the Industrial Court, the concept of 'some minimum wage' across the industry emerged. The minimum wage was placed at ₹30 per month as basic. The variable part of the wages, that is, DA was linked with the cost of living index. With the increase in the cost of living index figures, the DA was proportionately increased. The unions in other industries, in Bombay, through militant action and skilful collective bargaining, succeeded in making substantial gains in their emoluments and other service conditions. But the textile workers, represented by Rashtriya Mill Mazdoor Sangh (RMMS), accepted the recommendations of the wage boards for which the workers had to be contented with measly wage increases and stagnant DA formula for over 25 years. The RMMS did make up a little in the years 1973 and 1978. But on both these occasions, the non-recognized unions, who had been attempting to represent the workers, initiated the agitations for wage increases. In 1973, due to prolonged work stoppage by the workers, the ministers had to intervene. The wage agreement, however, was signed by RMMS on behalf of the workers.

One of the main reasons for the poor working conditions of the labour force was the deteriorating conditions of the textile industry. In the 1980s, there were shifts in the customer demand from cotton-based products to synthetic and mixed textiles. In addition, the power loom outperformed the hand-loom both in productivity and the cost of manufacturing, resulting in the downfall of various mills that were using handlooms [54].

Another main feature of this strike was the emergence of Datta Samant as a trade union leader. RMMS was the sole bargaining agent for the textile mill workers of Bombay. But for years, RMMS constantly overlooked the fundamental needs of the workers [52]. Some wage increases on an ad hoc basis were negotiated in each case, but these were limited to only those workers who were engaged in highly skilled areas involving technological improvement. In course of time, when the whole range of the production processes and equipment in several mills were modernized, the basic wage structure of the industry remained unchanged. The textile workers felt quite neglected and as such were aggrieved in the context of the functioning of their representing trade union. Indeed, that is the reason why they turned to Datta Samant for leadership.

Datta Samant, with no experience of the textile industry, but with a reputation of being dynamic and having an understanding of militant trade unionism, had staged a number of extraordinarily long strikes in many factories in and outside Bombay. He was approached by the workers for taking up their leadership. His quality of leadership was different. A number of strikes called by Samant dragged on for extremely long periods, often six months or more. Not all of them succeeded. Several strikes called upon by him resulted in bloodshed. All these attributed to his militancy and his extraordinary ability to mobilize workers and hold their loyalty through long struggles.

However, at the same time, he indicated a lack of essential bargaining skills and sensitivity to understand the problems of IR. An ability to lead workers in strikes is not the only important test of a trade unionist, but his/her real test is to solve the disputes and to secure acceptable solutions of problems without resorting to extremely long strikes or bloodsheds.

The strike of 1982–1983 was a reaction to the inactive approach of RMMS, the legally recognized union in the industry. The state government favoured the recognition of RMMS. But the first challenge to this recognition came in 1950, over the issue of bonus for the workers in the industry. A nine-week industry-wide strike was staged under the leadership of the Mill Mazdoor Sabha. This was very much against the recognition of RMMS. Subsequently, on several occasions, the recognition was challenged by workers through the formation of rival organizations. On each occasion, RMMS was bailed out by the state government. BIRA also supported this approach of the state government. Unlike in the past, the state government initially had not intervened to settle the current dispute in spite of the facts that the strike continued for a longer period, a large number of workers were involved and the loss of production to the industry. Nor the mill owners requested the state government for any such intervention. The reason in all can likely be attributed to the fact that the industry was in recession.

For several reasons, there was much non-acceptance by the mill owners to discuss the issues concerning the workers with Datta Samant. First, legally and technically, Samant's union was not the recognized union. Second, in a situation when RMMS was the recognized union, there were technical problems. A wage settlement which was in force (signed for one year only) was not permitting to open a fresh negotiation, before the expiry of the settlement period. Finally, his personality, aggressive style and unending interventions to work had already made him a legend.

The nature of the leadership would always be seen by the workers as a positive aspect for achieving their organizational goals. Datta Samant was an icon, whose leadership was trusted by people and was felt to generate effective results. On the contrary, towards the whole issue, Datta Samant as a leader of the strike had quite a different view, initially. In his own words, 'I was never keen to enter into any confrontation concerning the textile employers, rather the workers pressed me hard enough to call the strike' [55]. Datta Samant's image was that of 'a hot headed and sometimes a militant trade union goon' [56]. Samant was always ready to walk the extra mile and organize workers from their slum houses. Datta Samant's upfront nature, his fearlessness and ability to face any situation were some of the big reasons why he was chosen as the leader of the strike.

One of the positive aspects of Samant was the fact that he was not getting attracted towards any political party even when both the Congress and the communist parties were bent on getting him in the party. The militancy and the notoriety of Dr Datta Samant were favoured by the working class, who saw him as someone who could win them anything they demanded. His fame had outrun any union leader of his time.

Another strong reason to opt for Datta Samant was the failure of RMMS to crack a deal for the mill workers with the mill owners. The RMMS was the Congress-supported union in the textile industry which had exclusive bargaining rights under the Bombay BIRA 1946 (BIRA). With BIRA norms in place, the Mill Owners Association was not ready to accept any other trade union to be the bargaining agent on behalf of the workers. But even though at a macro level Samant's ways were not all that acceptable, these issues made him the ultimate choice for the workers to represent their case before the industrialists [56].

To Samant, a win in this struggle would mean not only almost total dominance over the labour scene in Bombay, but also the flowering of his political ambitions, for one could not see any other labour organization blocking his path once he consolidated his control over the textile workers. Defeat, on the other hand, would bring his entire labour empire into jeopardy. To the government and the ruling party, a triumphant Samant was an even more intractable challenge, administratively as well as politically, quite apart from the loss of face and of representative status for its portage, the RMMS. For all three, the monetary stakes must now be of secondary importance. But for the presence of Samant on the scene, some compromise on the monetary issue would almost certainly have been found, as so often in the past, and that without RMMS being displaced from its favoured position.

Thus, the power struggle came to dominate, although to begin with the workers were concerned primarily with the wage issue and brought in Samant to lead them to gain that goal. It turned out that in doing so they had unwittingly made themselves cannon fodder in this battle for high stakes and would be the ultimate sufferers, whatever the outcome of the fight. A victory would have no doubt brought sizeable monetary benefits to them, although not of the order they had been led to hope. Besides for that uncertain gain, they had already paid a very heavy price in form of current wages. They may also deem themselves winners in the power struggle inside their mills. But a state of continuous tension and unrest in the mills was unlikely to be of any benefit to workers in the long run. Any political gains Samant made out of the present struggle would be his own and of hardly any benefit to the generality of workers. The mill owners would undoubtedly recoup their strike losses by screwing further concessions from government, manipulating cotton prices and finally raising the prices to pass on to the consumer any additional costs that an eventual settlement may involve. The whole established trade union movement would find itself at a disadvantage vis-à-vis labour adventurists, thereby making workers in other industries suffer the consequences of this strike too.

On the other hand, defeat for the strikers, needless to say, would be a serious disaster not only for them but for labour as a whole. Either way, textile workers seemed to stand to gain not much and to lose a great deal.

For the textile workers, the strike involved more than a demand for wage increases. It reflected the total disillusionment with the institutional framework of the BIRA and with the RMMS as the legally determined sole representative union in the industry. BIRA is unusual in that unlike other IR laws in India, it has provisions for determining the sole representative union in the industry. It requires that the claimant union has a membership of 25 per cent of the industry's workforce for the preceding six months.

When the strike began in the third week of January 1982, the mill owners could have been happy since the industry was going through a recession. Indeed, it allowed the mills to get rid of the piled up stocks. However, the mill owners were not expecting a long strike. The continuance of the strike for few weeks resulted in the downswing of the raw material cost. When the demand for the cotton textiles picked up and with the prices of inputs having fallen, the Bombay mill owners had no option to start the production since the workers were on strike.

Samant had no legal stand under BIRA but had the total support of the workers. The government had taken a very legalistic stand by refusing to invite Datta Samant for the negotiation with the Mill Owners Association. The government's point was that Samant had not applied for legal recognition of his union. The successful Bandh of 19 April 1982 proved his strength. Datta Samant thereafter had the majority support of the textile workers, and ultimately the government and the mill owners accepted his union as the negotiating union.

Mill owners believed that the workers were grossly misled by Datta Samant. Datta Samant asked for wage hikes which would have incurred costs of nearly ₹115 crore per annum on mill owners. He also demanded 239 per cent hike in DA. The strike resulted in massive lay-offs and job losses of nearly 75,000 people. The strike caused the policy makers to come up with laws which benefitted the mill owners. Many cases were filed against Samant's Maharashtra Girni Kamgar Union [52]. Neither the government nor the industrialists did anything to help the workers. The workers were all through at a loss—losing salary and losing jobs. Workers who were part of the strike for one and half years knew that they had not gained anything at the end.

Even though subsequent legal changes were made to the status of the unions, the strength of the workers who were organized brought the grand textile industry of Bombay to its knees.

Case Questions

1. Justify the statement that the 'strike had (there was) more of political unionism rather than an economic bargaining on the part of the trade unions'. Do you agree with this statement? If yes, why?
2. What were the causes for which the workers of the Bombay textile mills went for a strike?
3. What were the reasons for the emergence of Datta Samant as a leader of the workers of the textile mills of Bombay?
4. Why the qualities of militancy of Datta Samant were widely accepted by the workers of the textile mills of Bombay? Please explain the context for such an acceptance with logic.
5. What were the ultimate impacts of such a long strike on different actors of IR?
6. What was the role of the government from time to time?

(The instructor is requested to refer the instructional manual for the pedagogy of the case.)

In 1982, after a major strike of 18 months, the mills were permanently closed and triggered the end of the struggling industry. Later, Phoenix Mill, Dawn Mill at Lower Parel, Kamala Mills, Zenzi Mill and other mills became the sources of survival for lakhs of mill workers in Mumbai. Now, all of them have been sold out and converted to commercial complexes, malls and high-rise buildings.

IC.2.3. INDUSTRIAL CONTEXT FOR DISCUSSION

The Chronological Order of Rise and Fall of Textile Mills in Mumbai

1854: Cowasji Nanabhai Davar set up the first mill, called the Bombay Spinning Mill. It produced cotton textiles for Britain.

1860–1915: There was a significant rise in the number of mills from 13 in 1870 to 70 in 1875 and later 83 mills in 1915. This encouraged hand workers from Konkan to settle in Lalbaug and Parel.

1920s–1960s: Shripad Amrit Dange, the founder of CPI, had led the mill workers union since 1920s and had called for strikes in 1928 and 1929. Left had control over the union till 1960s. Later, Shiv Sena took over the union and renamed it as Bharatiya Kamgar Sena. With the decline of Left, coincidently, the textile industry too started declining.

1982: On 1 January, 2.5 lakh workers went on strike against Bombay Mill Owners Association under the leadership of Datta Samant. They demanded bonus and increase in wages. The strike proved to be a disaster with closure of 58 mills and rendering 1.5 lakh workers jobless.

1991: The state government brought in Development Control Rule 58, which states that mill owners can sell their mills' land by fulfilling the following rules:

1. Brihanmumbai Municipal Corporation should be handed over one-third land.
2. Maharashtra Housing and Area Development Authority to get one-third land, out of which half land should be given to housing projects for mill workers.
3. One-third land is to be developed by mill owners.

2001: The Development Control Rule was amended and the state government said that it applied only to 'open land' and not to all the land of the mills. The open land came to be just over 100 acres out of the total 600 acres of the textile mill land.

2005: In March 2005, the National Textiles Corporation (NTC) had 25 mills in the city worth nearly ₹5,000 crore. They sold their mills in the following ways:

1. Sold Jupiter Mills to Indiabulls for ₹276 crore.
2. In June, the Mumbai Textile Mills was sold for ₹702 crore.
3. In July, Kohinoor Mill number 3 was sold to Manohar Joshi and Raj Thackeray for ₹421 crore.

2006: The Supreme Court said that the sale of the mills was legal and that changes to the rules for developing mills were valid.

2010: NTC decided to reopen three mills—India United Mills no. 5 at Kalachowkie, Podar Mills at Chinchpokali and Tata Mills at Hindmata on 19 January.

The era of unionism had started when the workers started preferring 'independent' unions, which were not affiliated to any political parties of the Centre. Such trade unions started operating in the major industrial units. The independent trade unions were found to compete with the traditional party-affiliated unions who delivered a higher wage and fringe package than the affiliated unions [57]. This conclusion was based on the study conducted in the Bombay–Thane industrial belt. It was observed that there was a noticeable shift in preference for non-political affiliated trade unions across the country.

In the late 1970s and early 1980s, IR in India were characterized by violence (especially in the Thane–Belapur area and Modinagar). For instance, on 29 June 1981, the president of the HMS Workers' Union was beaten and murdered, and on the same day, another worker was murdered [58]. On 14 July 1981, the managing director of the Bombay Tyres Company was assaulted. In another incident, a worker of Wellman India, a company in the Thane area, was murdered [59]. Besides these instances, newspapers and their reports indicated violence in labour–management relations.

IC.2.4. INDUSTRIAL CONTEXT FOR DISCUSSION

The Policy Focus on Growth First, Pro-Business and Anti-Labour by Rajiv Gandhi

Significant changes in the policymaking provisions for the inclusion of the private Indian firms with the State-controlled business houses were made by the government. Indian business groups were also provided significant concessions on corporate and personal taxes, as well as assurances about future patterns of taxation. To link with the international trade, some import barriers on quotas were removed. By the end of Rajiv Gandhi's regime, some significant changes in the domestic political economy and a few changes that altered India's links with the world were put in place.

Three important political economic observations have been made on the initiatives of Rajiv Gandhi. They are as follows:

1. Rajiv Gandhi dropped the concept of socialism altogether and openly committed his government to a new 'liberal' beginning.
2. The government's commitment was for economic growth. In spite of the fact that the economy had growing budget deficits, the government kept up with the pace of public investments, including infra-structure. The objective was that public spending would help growth. The government consciously lowered taxes on the middle classes so as to boost demand, especially on consumer durables.
3. Finally, the policy pattern was more pro-big Indian businesses. Whenever conflicts arose over external opening, especially on the issues of foreign investment, and on trade, the government accommodated the demands of Indian business groups.

The two annual plans (1990–1992) mark the end of this third phase and the beginning of the contemporary pattern of Indian IR. This period was associated with Rajiv Gandhi's economic liberalization measures. Till the beginning of this period, a controlled pattern of industrial development was adopted across Indian states by the government. The objective of the government was also to remove/not encourage regional disparities. Indian economy was planned to grow under this 'License Raj', which slowed the growth rate. Rajiv Gandhi's reforms of the mid-1980s exempted few selected Indian industries from industrial licensing.

2.3. Impact of Globalization on the Liberalized Economy

India is now considered as an emerging nation with a dynamic economy. The economic progress of the country has been tuned to be moving in the right direction, with expectations to emerge as the fourth largest economy in the world. The country has become attractive to foreign investors in due course of time. The economy of India had undergone significant policy shifts in the early

1990s with the adoption of the economic liberalization policy. Indian economic policies were re-framed to the liberalization, privatization and globalization (LPG model) in the early 1990s. With focus to make the Indian economy one of the fastest developing economies in the globe and to match up with the biggest economies of the world, such policy adoptions were made.

Rajiv Gandhi's government initiated the policy of liberalization in the mid-1980s. The objective of economic liberalization of the time had been to increase production, improve quality and get access to foreign markets. In 1991, the country experienced a balance of payments problem following the Gulf War and the downfall of the Soviet Union. The country had to make a deposit of 47 tons of gold to the Bank of England and 20 tons in the Union Bank of Switzerland. This was essential as a recovery pact with the International Monetary Fund (IMF). Furthermore, the IMF necessitated India to assume a sequence of systematic economic reorganizations. The then prime minister of India, P. V. Narasimha Rao, initiated economic reforms. Radical liberalization or globalization measures were adopted on 24 July 1991, which made the Indian economy progressively market oriented and integrated with the emerging global economy structure. The policy of liberalized economy created economic platforms conducive to business enterprises, investments and innovations. At the labour front, to gear up for the increasing expectations of the economy resulting out of the liberalized economy and the increased level of competition from overseas firms, the prerequisites from the Indian workers went through a sea change. To survive and prosper in the competition, the Indian companies countered challenges to develop the employees so as to compete with overseas firms in terms of skills, efficiency and effectiveness [60]. On the other side, globalization brought in an era of economic, institutional and cultural integration among countries. It encouraged unifications in trade, investment and capital flow, technological advances and pressures for assimilation towards international standards in the Indian industries. There were the dissemination of advanced management practices and newer forms of work organization, and in some situations, sharing of internationally accepted labour standards on quality, cost and rate of production including the product and its life.

IC.2.5. INDUSTRIAL CONTEXT FOR DISCUSSION

New Industrial Policy by P. V. Narasimha Rao

Shri P. V. Narasimha Rao's government to accelerate the pace of economic development in India announced its New Industrial Policy (NIP) on 24 July 1991. The important objectives of this policy were as follows:

1. To correct the distortions that may have crept in and consolidate the strengths built on the gains already made
2. To maintain sustained growth in the productivity and gainful employment
3. To attain international competitiveness.

The basic philosophy of NIP 1991 was to adopt change with the renewed initiative towards national economic reconstruction. The policy changes, which the government introduced, were a sharp departure from the earlier industrial policies. These changes focused broadly to the following five areas:

1. Industrial licensing
2. Public sector policy
3. Monopolies and Restrictive Trade Practices Act, 1969

4. Foreign investment
5. Foreign technology agreements.

Above all what was more important for the economy were the expected changes in the attitude of the State towards the foreign industrial nations and the investors, change from centrally planned and controlled economy to market-led economy, change from excessive government intervention to minimal intervention, change from nationalization to privatization, change from subsidization to gradual withdrawal of subsidy and changes from a protected economy to an open economy.

Dr Manmohan Singh was then the finance minister of the Government of India. He played a key role in implementing these reform policies.

Narasimha Rao Committee's Recommendations

The recommendations of the Narasimha Rao Committee were as follows:

- Bringing in the Security Regulations (Modified) and the SEBI Act of 1992 which rendered the legitimate power to the Securities Exchange Board of India to record and control all the mediators in the capital market.
- Doing away with the Controller of Capital matters in 1992 that determined the rates and number of stocks that companies were supposed to issue in the market.
- Launching of the National Stock Exchange in 1994 in the form of a computerized share buying and selling system which acted as a tool to influence the restructuring of the other stock exchanges in the country. By the year 1996, the National Stock Exchange surfaced as the biggest stock exchange in India.
- In 1992, the equity markets of the country were made available for investment through overseas corporate investors. The companies were allowed to raise funds from overseas markets through issuance of GDRs or Global Depository Receipts.
- Promoting foreign direct investment (FDI) by means of raising the highest cap on the contribution of international capital in business ventures or partnerships to 51 per cent from 40 per cent. In high priority industries, 100 per cent international equity was allowed.
- Cutting down duties from a mean level of 85 per cent to 25 per cent, and withdrawing quantitative regulations. The rupee or the official Indian currency was turned into an exchangeable currency on trading account.
- Reorganization of the methods for sanction of FDI in 35 sectors. The boundaries for international investment and involvement were demarcated.

In the 1980s, the position of the trade unions in Indian industries showed a declining trend with respect to the support of their members. The following were the reasons for such a decline:

- The failure of a number of strikes, as a result of which workers started losing faith and confidence in militant trade unionism [61, 62]
- A sharp decline in union membership and growing alienation between trade unions and members
- Changing characteristics of the new workforce
- The waning influence of national federations over enterprise unions [62]
- Multiplicity of unions
- The trend in the number of lockouts, duration of strikes and the number of industrial disputes reduced.

With liberalization, the industrialization policy shifted from ISI to export-oriented industries (EOIs). The other policy initiatives by the government were as follows:

- The concept of licensing of industries was eliminated.
- The rules on monopoly restrictions were relaxed.
- The ceilings on foreign investment were removed.
- The public sector was opened to privatization.
- Scope for free entry into and exit of the firms from all industries except for a few strategic ones.
- The trade policy was revamped to promote exports and free trade.
- The Indian currency was made fully free floating and convertible.
- Restrictions on the import of several goods were removed.
- Fiscal policy was amended to reduce the fiscal deficit.
- Several price controls were removed and financial markets were liberalized.
- Banking regulations have been reformed.
- Stock markets have been freed from government controls [64].

The economy grew at an impressive 6.7 per cent in the first five years after the reforms, but it slowed down to 5.4 per cent in the next five years. India remained among the fastest growing developing countries in the second sub-period because other developing countries also slowed down after the East Asian crisis, but the annual growth of 5.4 per cent was much below the target of 7.5 per cent which the government had set for the period. Inevitably, this led to some questioning about the effectiveness of the reforms.

The IR policy in India was influenced by the close ties between political parties and the labour movement in India. Some of the concepts of the government which structured the policies were as follows:

1. Labour legislation was extremely pro-labour and believed in a protection philosophy.
2. The formation of a trade union was kept relatively simple to have right representation of the labour force. (Any seven persons being able to form a union who comply the provisions of The Trade Union Act of 1926.)
3. Leadership of the trade union could be taken over by someone not an employee of the organization (industrial action therefore was often driven by political considerations, which were not connected with enterprise problems).
4. The practice of collective bargaining occurred at the industry level where the employees were organized. Collective bargaining in unorganized sectors was decentralized at the enterprise level.
5. The rights to fire, lay-off, retrench employees, close down the businesses, and calling strikes and lockouts in public utility services were sufficiently restricted under the ID Act of 1947.
6. The non-compliance of providing the statutory benefits to the employees warranted very heavy penalties on the employers.

The three actors of IR (management, union and the government) have their respective roles in contributing to IR as it exists today. The liberalization of the economy created pressure on the Indian HR functions, and with time demanded for a more rationalized and structured approach to employee relations in Indian organizations. Both employers, who now faced the challenge of international business competition, and the employees, who faced the situation to deliver in the internationally competitive market, accepted the challenges in a positive spirit. The World Bank had also strongly recommended for changes in the IR legislation that would allow organizations to lay off and retrench workers without the lengthy process under the statutory provisions [63].

One significant outcome of structural adjustment and liberalization had been workforce reduction. Given their inability to retrench, employers introduced other ways to shed the HR fat through voluntary retirement schemes (VRS) and negotiated settlements (in individual cases). There is no precise figure on manpower reduction, but the figure would be close to 5 million jobs by 1993. This includes job losses by way of VRS, plant closures and the privatization of inefficient public sector organizations.

Two cases worth mentioning are the case of VRS for public sector banks (PSBs) in 2001 and the privatization of Bharat Aluminium Corporation (BALCO). In April 2001, a VRS was introduced in Indian banks.

C.2.6. Case for Discussion — The Success of Voluntary Retirement Scheme in Public Sector Banks in the Year 2001

VRS for banking officers had been a unique initiative and a bold attempt to accomplish the reduction of excess manpower in the nationalized banks. The old-timers who were not accustomed to the computerized culture of managing their responsibilities were either unable to cope with the changed banking processes or were uncomfortable with the new processes. The process changes were inevitable for the increasing competition in the banking sector due to liberalization and demanded cost efficient approaches to the banking system. The PSBs were left with the only alternative, reducing the manpower and adopting banking processes which supported the adoption of technology. Sending home over a lakh of serving bank officers and employees, who formed part of these banks for years, was a big challenge for the government. Probably any other process other than VRS would have created a high degree of dissatisfaction for the affected employees and would have spread an industrial unrest in the PSBs.

It was implemented at the first go in 26 out of the 27 PSBs. The benefits structure of the scheme was uniform across all the banks, whereas the structure of administration of the scheme was linked more to the cultural adaptability of the respective banks. The scheme was well accepted by the employees of PSBs but certain bank employees initially had perceived it differently. For example, State Bank of India (SBI) promoted the VRS as a 'golden handshake', but its employee unions perceived it to be a retrenchment scheme. They were of the opinion that the scheme will not be effective in the emerging context. The unions of various banks had also argued that the VRS might force the closure of rural branches due to acute manpower shortage.

According to Indian Banks' Association (IBA), the total staff strength in PSB at the end of March 2000 was 863,188 out of whom 126,714 or 14.7 per cent applied for VRS. As per the scheme, about 80 per cent of the applications were accepted. The total number of staff relieved under VRS until 31 December 2001 was 101,300. This constituted 11.7 per cent of the total staff strength of the employees as of March 2000.

The bank officers and employees of all the PSBs were represented by organized trade unions with high bargaining powers. In normal situations reducing the workforce on such a high magnitude would be an impossible proposal. But banks and their employees opted for the choice of downsizing with dignity by widely accepting the VRS termed as the 'Golden Handshake'.

For the growth of the banking system all across the country, all the PSBs went in for a massive recruitment drive at various levels, during the years 1960–1980. The objective had been expansion and development of banking across India to provide support to the industry's demanding vertical growths. The emerging reforms in the banking systems, which happened towards the end of the century, because of technological advancements and the growth of communication and information technology (IT) drove the banks. The new banking philosophy was more focused on performance and customer satisfaction rather than number of people efficiently working in the organization.

It was belatedly realized that productivity is linked to customer satisfaction, which has a significant bearing on the bank's overall performance. It was also realized that it was the one factor which would enable the banks to develop a unique competitive advantage. The profit per employee is an appropriate measure of the success of the banks. During the year 1999–2000, the profit per employee was (an average of all the PSBs) 0.65, whereas for the private banks, it was 1.46 and for the foreign banks it was 5.61. The lower ratio in the PSBs was attributed to over-staffing. The foreign banks, which were already in the liberalized market, operated on global standards with high-tech tools and applications of computerized functions replacing manual operations, with ATMs operating on a 24/7 (full-day and full-week) basis dispersing rush at cash counters and credit cards or plastic money replacing endless counting and recounting of cash (currency notes). Whereas the Indian banks in their traditional banking practice were much behind the performance levels of the international banks.

The PSBs in the post-liberalization period were classified under the following three categories:

- Healthy banks (those that are currently showing profits with zero accumulated loss of the past)
- Banks currently showing profits, but have accumulated losses of the previous years carried in their balance sheets
- Banks which are at loss, that is, showing losses in the past and in the present.

The setback of profitability of the banks could only be rectified by addressing the following two major problems of PSBs:

- Reduction and rationalization of the unproductive labour
- Accumulation of non-productive assets (gross estimated at around ₹100,000 crore of failed credit rendered sticky and difficult of recovery)

The burden of surplus manpower was addressed by the government by accepting the one-time solution of VRS.

There was the strain of the expense on the VRS since it would be affected by the drain on profitability in the short run. This would strain the capital adequacy ratio (CAR).

But the scheme was implemented in consultation with the IBA. There were some package differences from bank to bank but it has been broadly structured around the 'model' prescribed by the IBA. There is no difference in the eligibility criteria of officers or the quantum of compensation. Individual banks had the discretion in defining the category of employees who were to be kept outside the preview of VRS. The model proposed that banks offered to pay 50 per cent of the settlement in cash and the balance in bonds with a lock-in period of three years. However, SBI, the largest Indian bank, offered to settle fully in cash.

The incidence of the success of the VRS scheme, at the macro level, sets a precedent of successful downsizing in PSUs. This is the first time in a public sector industry that a VRS package leading to downsizing of the employees was successful, and became an example for other PSUs to follow.

Case Questions

1. Do you find any difference in the process of managing the business after liberalization of the economy and prior to the liberalization of the economy?
2. What were the considerations of the government in the role of organizers and managers of the business of PSBs for adopting the scheme of VRS?
3. What were the reasons for the bank employees to accept VRS in such large numbers without any disputes?
4. Explain the changing roles of the trade unions in the context?

(Please refer to the instruction manual for the pedagogy of the case.)

Another relevant example is BALCO, which was sold to a private company (Sterlite Industries) in 2000. However, both union and state government fought against the deal for more than six months, resulting in a plant lockout for months and bringing employee relations to an all-time low. Finally, in 2001 the deal went through and things have now normalized with the new establishment. Similar disinvestment processes were followed after the BALCO case. The government sold its stake of the loss-making bread maker, Modern Foods and also the stakes of computer software and maintenance firm CMC as well as Hindustan Teleprinters. The new trend indicated that the government appeared to be more willing to sell strategic stakes to partners who have the competency to manage the business in the competitive market situation.

C.2.7. Case for Discussion   **BALCO: The Disinvestment Strategy**

BALCO is an organization which is into manufacturing of aluminium from aluminium ore. The company was incorporated in 1965 and was closely associated with the growth of the Indian aluminium industry. The company had its captive mines. The organization was involved end to end from mining of the ore to production of aluminium to be used for domestic, industrial, defence and astronomical equipment. BALCO manufactured and supplied special aluminium alloys to the nation's intermediate range ballistic missile Agni and surface-to-surface missile Prithvi. The Government of India prior to the year 2001 held 100 per cent stake in BALCO. In the year 2001 it announced to disinvest 51 per cent of its stake to a long-term strategic partner.

The reason for such a decision of the Government of India was linked to the performance of the organization and the expected near future investment for modernization of the plants. In fact, BALCO was a profit-making company and had a huge reserve capital of ₹500 crore. It was the only public sector enterprise that had paid its 50 per cent equity, that is ₹244 crore to the exchequer. But the fact of the revenue source was that in the late 1990s, only 50 per cent of BALCO's profits had been on account of the company's operating margins while the other half was due to the interest earned on its fixed deposits. But BALCO was under threat as the plant was running on outdated technology and was in profits only because aluminium prices in the international market were ruling high. The Government of India was interested in disinvesting the company while the earning was positive in order to get a good deal. The cash reserve of ₹437 crore was not sufficient for modernization of the plants. The estimated expenses for modernization was estimated at ₹4,000 crore. So the only alternative with the government was to infuse a strategic partner for prospective investments.

Sterlite, the acquiring company was one of India's fastest growing company. The company's turnover in the year 1999 was ₹2,070 crore, and it earned a net profit of ₹105 crore. After this acquisition, the company becomes a formidable player in metals—aluminium, copper and zinc. The group was also into the business of fibre optic cables. The government's decision to sell 51 per cent of its stake in BALCO to Sterlite Industries was considered to a right decision in many ways.

In late 2000 to win the confidence of the agitating employees, the Government of India for the first time announced to offer stock options to the employees. There was assurance from the government both to the employees and the trade unions that the company would not retrench any employee at least within one year of the takeover by the private company. But the more serious consideration for the Sterlite Industries was that all issues involving the 7,000 employees were subjected to the market performance of the company, performance of the employees and overall returns to achieve long-run sustainability.

The 7,000 employees were represented by seven major trade unions, under the banner of the BALCO Bachao Sangharsh Samiti. The association had been protesting against the disinvestment plan of the government. The union affiliated to the BMS, the trade union wing of the BJP, also joined the common agitation platform. The management of Sterlite invited the leaders of the seven unions to Delhi for discussion. The union leaders were not interested to talk to the management of Sterlite.

Although the government and the management of Sterlite Industries had assured that there will be no retrenchment for at least one year, but there was a widespread fear in the employees that the new management will shed workers in significant numbers. If not retrenchment, the expected approach for downsizing the employees would be VRS since VRS schemes had already become a technique of reducing the manpower in PSUs. The union representing the employees initiated protests against the disinvestment plan of the government. In February 2001, the union filed petitions before the Department of Company Affairs (DCA) and the Monopolies and Restrictive Trade Practices Commission (MRTPC) on the issue of the disinvestment process. The union in its petition to DCA indicated several factors and also indicated, 'The process (disinvestment) is likely to be completed without valuation of assets of Balco on fair market value, as recommended by the disinvestment commission'.

On 3 March 2001, the employees through their union launched an indefinite strike. The agitation by the employees brought the operations of the plant to a standstill. The management apprehended not only productivity loss, but also that the employees would resort to damaging the plant facilities. The strike was called for an indefinite period, but the workers were aware of the fact that the smelter will run the risk of being damaged in the event of a complete stoppage of work.

On 9 March 2001, a senior BALCO officer declared that the smelter of the plant had started cooling. To restart operations, it would need about ₹50 crore and three to six months' time. The management appealed to the workers to re-join for saving the smelter. The management also threatened a lockout unless the employees returned to work. The company was yet to declare lockout when the core committee of the unions on the fifth day of the strike issued passes to more than 70 workers to enter the plant in order to keep the smelter alive. They offered *shram daan* (free and voluntary labour) to protect the plant. But the management of Sterlite, declared a lockout on 10 March 2001 alleging that the plant was under risk of being damaged by the workers.

All major trade unions of the region, expressed their support for the 'ongoing struggle of the BALCO workers'. The Supreme Court by an order issued directives both to the management and the union, suggesting a dialogue between the workers and management to resolve the ongoing crisis.

Supporting the agitation of the workers, the opposition in the parliament as well as the chief minister of Chhattisgarh launched attacks on BJP government of 'selling out' BALCO. In spite of such protests they were not able stop the process of disinvestment of the company.

The BALCO management filed an affidavit before the Supreme Court that no workers would be retrenched. In the first week of May 2001, the Supreme Court asked the workers to resume work on assurance of advance payment of salary by the BALCO management. The workers were assured an advance payment of two months' salary by the BALCO management and were requested to return to work. This was rejected by the union. On 4 May 2001, a marathon meeting of the unions was held to discuss on the issue of withdrawal of the strike, in view of the Supreme Court's directives.

On 9 May 2001, a 25-point agreement was signed between the union leaders and the management of Sterlite Industries. With this agreement, the long-drawn-out battle between the union and the management seemed to have come to its logical conclusion. BALCO employees went back to work ending a 67-day strike. Within 48 hours (10 May 2001) of the agreement and the withdrawal of the strike, the management of Sterlite laid off 2,000 contract workers on the grounds that their contracts had expired. The management then reinterpreted the pay agreement, declaring that the two months' pay was an advance on workers' future wages, not back pay for the duration of the strike.

Source: Wickremasinghe N. Collapse of Balco strike opens way for further privatization in India, World Socialist Web Site. 8 June 2001. Available from https://www.wsws.org/en/articles/2001/06/ind-j08.html
Narasimhan CML. The Balco privatisation, The Hindu. 23 February 2001. Available from http://www.thehindu.com/2001/02/23/stories/06230009.htm

Case Questions

1. Why it was essential for the government to disinvest in BALCO?
2. BALCO was disinvested at a stage while the company was still making profit. Do you agree to this statement?
3. Do you think the trade unions represented by BALCO Bachao Sangharsh Samiti had sufficient reasoning valid enough to justify their stands against the government?
4. Do you accept that the trade union was constructive to the business interests of the organization and to its members? If not, what initiatives you would recommend in the context as a leader of the trade union?

(The instructor is requested to refer the instruction manual for the pedagogy of the case.)

Similar developments in different industries changed the focus of the government to consider to accept protecting the management against unions in the liberalized Indian economy. Employers' approach to IR had been more focused at their business objectives. The fact that the number of lockouts have increased dramatically, whereas the frequency of strike have declined establishes the shifting focus of the employers towards the business. Closing the operation rather than running the same at a loss has become the call for the employers.

Employers have adopted the approaches of employee empowerment and for that the employers have gone to the extent of giving additional responsibility by way of promoting the workers to supervisory category. This technique has barred the workers from the unionized category of employees and thereby removing them from the scope of ID Act, 1947.

Employers have adopted schemes like participative management through which the workers have been accepted as stakeholders of business. Joint consultation for productivity improvements and suggestion schemes for improvement in working conditions at workplace have facilitated the employers to involve the employees as contributors to the business.

There are also instances that the government has supported such movement of the employers of the private sectors. For example, in the state of Maharashtra, for the first time, the government has attempted to neutralize labour unrest by declaring several private sector firms 'essential and public utilities', thereby outlawing strikes in these firms.

The trend in IR is highly influenced by the country's IR history, industrial culture and other contextual factors of the economy. Liberalization has changed a growing concern for flexibility and competitiveness in the international market. The impacts of liberalization on different segments of the structure of IR had been different as discussed further.

1. **Impact on trade unions**

   Trade unions in India initially resisted the implementation of economic policy of liberalization. The unions voiced their argument against the new economic policy on various platforms through different means, and tried to establish their logic against liberalization. The new approaches adopted to meet the business needs both by the management and the government changed the approaches of the trade unions in due course of time. A contextual reconcile and adoption of the new approaches to business marked a phenomenal change in the trade union movement in the country. Understanding the need, realizing the essence of the need, adopting the process of the changed needs and expecting results by contributing to the business needs frame the rules of the games of the IR in India today.

2. **Impact on human resource development**

   Liberalization has a positive impact on HRD. HRD strategies for industries of liberalized India have been identified to be performance planning, employee development, encouraging innovation and creativity, motivation building and retraining, developing the aptitude towards different jobs and encouraging job rotation. These initiatives have proved to be success stories in Indian industries.

3. **Impact on wages and benefits**

   Liberalization resulted in higher salaries and benefits for highly skilled, talented and committed employees, and low salaries and benefits for those whose skills and talents are in less demand. The present system of performance management system considers to link individual performance and delivery to determine the individual salary, wages and benefits.

4. **Impact on collective bargaining**

   The process of collective bargaining, which was instrumental in settling disputes between the trade unions and the management, and had taken a shape of hostility during the 1970s and the 1980s reshaped to mutual acceptance, accommodation, realization of the issues in question and devising solutions amicably to meet the ends of the management as well as the employees. The dominance of trade union or the management was replaced by emergence of cooperation and coordination for amicable settlement of the disputes and for a harmonious IR.

5. **Impact on management style**

   The management style of the HR underwent a sea change. Concepts such as participative management, suggestion schemes, quality circles, employee empowerment, innovative technique of motivation and employee engagement were found by the management to be more effective than the traditional technique of 'master and servant relationships'. The adoption of employees as 'stakeholders of business', trusteeship in business and open door policy, which encouraged involvement and engagement of the employees, proved to be better means for achieving organizational results.

6. **Managing diversified cultures**

   The increasing globalization of workforce contributed to the need for managing different cultures and subcultures effectively. The ethnic mix of workforce because of the entry of multinationals and foreign companies with people from their parent countries to India posed challenges to the Indian managers and their ability to adapt, diversified international cultures.

C.2.8. Case for Discussion   Are The Trade Unions Institutionalizing Violence in the Agro-Industries of Bengal

Incidences such as strikes and protests leading to unrest have been common IR phenomena in India, but of late there have been unrests leading to violence and killing of executives in organizations. Incidences since 2008 have registered a trend of violence in organizations, for example in MSIL, Regal Ceramics, Powmex Steel, Allied Nippon, Pricol, Graziano Transmissions India and others. Such incidences have influenced to forming the IR culture of not only the industry in which such incidences have occurred but have also impacted the IR culture of the region, state and the country. All these organizations are in the manufacturing sector. But what about the agro-industries?

The impact of incidence can well be visualized by taking the instance of the trade unions' reaction at Hosur. Some 1,750 km away from the site of Manesar Maruti plant, at a remote place called Hosur, near the Tamil Nadu–Karnataka border, provocative posters expressed their reaction to the incidence of 18 July 2012 at Maruti Suzuki Ltd. They candidly expressed 'We congratulate the workers who burnt down the big boss attitude of the management', through the poster deployed in Tamil language, within a week of the incidence of 18 July 2012, in which Awanish Kumar Dev, the general manager HR was brutally killed. It was a call from the trade union 'New Democratic Labour Front (NDLF)', a splinter group with small pockets of support to celebrate the occasion. Their posters were stuck on factory gates of industrial units in Hosur, Krishnagiri, Dharmapuri and Salem in western Tamil Nadu, and wholeheartedly endorsed the mob violence in Manesar.

The HR head of an auto component manufacturer of this area expressed, 'NDLF is a registered trade union, have demonstrated militant tendencies and forced the management of several industrial units in the Hosur belt by using the threat of violence'. The representatives of NDLF had their own views 'we do not believe in democracy. We believe in fighting it out, fighting for workers' rights. We cannot achieve anything through democracy' [64].

Whereas the incidence of 18 July 2012 at Maruti, was explained as a 'criminal and militancy' action by the trade union, by a senior executive[29] of Maruti. Maruti Suzuki is certainly not the only example. Incidents of violence in Regal Ceramics, Powmex Steel, Allied Nippon, Pricol, Graziano Transmissions India, the jute mill in Bengal, the tea gardens of Bengal, a tractor manufacturing unit in Pune and a textile mill in Kolhapur are few instances which illustrate, 'violent approaches by trade unions are not confined to any particular region, or industry; rather it is prevalent in all types of industries and across the country'.

In a landmark judgement, Justice Siri Jagan of the Kerala High Court while pronouncing an order on a petition filed by Kerala Fibertech in June 2009 said, 'Trade unions are militant in nature and are interested in their own development rather than that of the industry'. The judge went to the extent of ordering the removal of flag posts by the trade unions on the premises of the company in the Kerala Industrial Park with immediate effect. The state police department was ordered to provide adequate protection if necessary for the same. The judge also said that the trade unions do not have any rights to infringe into the KINFRA Park and to play politics [65].

Whereas in the same year (2009), Mr M. K. Pandhe, the General Secretary of CITU, in a statement candidly expressed, 'Since managements are denying workers the right to strike, all trade unions are going to come together. If you think such strikes are militancy, more such action will be seen'. He also explained that militancy means extremism. But in the context of unions, it means struggle, not extremism. With unions becoming more active, the struggle would be visibly seen. Mr Pandhe, commenting on the incidence of Pricol, Coimbatore in which Roy George, the vice-president (human

[29] Mr S. Y. Siddiqui, the chief mentor, Maruti Suzuki India Ltd.

resources), suffered a head injury in the course a talk with a group of workers on 21 September 2009 and succumbed to death the next afternoon, said,

> What happened over there is not a sign of militancy. The reason why workers resorted to killing the official was that the latter refused to talk to them...... It was a spontaneous response. Workers demanded that they be reinstated. The officer refused to talk. So they reacted. It is not that unions are more militant now. [66]

A light on the management's approach will justify that in an era of perfect competition, the management's action are more focused at cost compression. It is very often felt that workers' costs is one such cost which has scope to be compressed and can be brought down. Such efforts to compress labour cost very often results in more aggressive and rigid approaches of the management. To such approaches of the management, the trade unions have their own reactions. Expressing on the reaction of the trade unions, Mr Manish Sabharwal, the chairman, TeamLease Services, expresses that the trade unions view all entrepreneurs and managers as 'myopic vampires'. Even if the literary meaning of such expressions is ignored, the fact continues to hold, 'the concept of class struggle still prevails in industries' [66]. But the facts of the present business and the market dynamics are that the shareholders do not pay salaries or create jobs but the customers do.

The expectations of the present younger workforce are more inspired by their objectives to work as a permanent employee, performance-linked salary differentiation and portfolio careers instead of just a salary package, which ensures a socially just living wage. The changing expectations of such a class of workers title them as 'the neo-working class'.

India has seen militant trade unionism in the 1970s and 1980s. Any discussion on trade union militancy draws the attention to some of the agitations, for example, the railway strike led by George Fernandes of 1974, the Mumbai textile workers' strike led by Datta Samant in 1981 and the public sector strike in Bangalore 1980–1981. The employees of the jute and tea industries in the state of Bengal are increasingly aware of their rights and liabilities and have not lagged behind. In these industries, trade unions led by the left wing ideological and believers of Stalinist and Maoist organizations showed high degree of extremism. These trade unions include All India Federation of Trade Unions (affiliated to the CPI[ML] Janashakti), All India Central Council of Trade Unions, AICCTU (affiliated to the CPI[ML]), All India United Trade Union Center run by the Socialist Unity Center, AITUC (affiliated to the CPI), CITU (affiliated to CPI[M]) and United Trade Union Congress (UTUC) (run by the Revolutionary Socialist Party).

In Mumbai (called Bombay) in the early 1970s Dr Dutta Samant rose to become one of the most prominent INTUC leaders, and grew increasingly militant in his political convictions and activism. He succeeded in organizing strikes claiming substantial wage hikes for the working class in this region. Companys' statistics on business performance and business information were not the factors which were considered by him for settlement of wages, rather the logic of the wage settlements rested more on workers' expectations. In the 1980s, the incidents of violence were more common in the Mumbai, Pune and Nasik industrial belts. Dr Datta Samant was labelled as the initiator of violence in this industrial belt. It is often observed that the 1982 strike gave the textile workers of Mumbai a new identity. The trade unions still feel proud of what had happened at that time.

But violence today is much more widespread and can be seen all over India. The trade unionism as a labour movement is more a matter of interests of the working class in general, rather than interests of the political groups sponsoring affiliated trade unions. The trade union federations declared a general strike on 28 February 2012. The members of all major trade unions participated in the one-day industrial strike, making it the largest strike in India since the nation's independence in 1947 [67]. The movement was against the 'neo-liberal economic and labour policies' of the government. All major trade unions participated including the support of more than 5,000 independent unions. The demands that the unions made were the establishment of a national minimum wage, the ending of temporary employment (contract labour), controlling inflection, guaranteed pensions and ending privatization of publicly owned companies. All these issue raised as demands were more policy issues of the government, which implies that the trade unions are raising their voice to the government for its changed focus towards IR issues.

Acts of violence by unionized workers of the agro-industries of the state of Bengal have not been speared. There had been more extreme incidence of violence in these industries in the past. The following are few instances.

1. Tea industry and tea in Bengal

India is one of the largest tea producers in the world. Also, the population of tea consumers in India ranks among the top 5 per capita tea consumers nations. The Indian tea industry is more than 170 years old. The industry occupies an important place and plays a very useful part in contributing to the GDP of the national economy. The industry also occupies a special status in the national economy since it is highly labour intensive.

Tea plantations are mainly located in rural hills and backward areas of north-eastern and southern states. The major tea growing areas in India are concentrated in Assam, West Bengal, Tamil Nadu and Kerala. The other areas where tea is grown are the states of Karnataka Tripura, Himachal Pradesh, Uttarakhand, Arunachal Pradesh, Manipur, Sikkim, Nagaland, Meghalaya and Mizoram. India has emerged as world leader in all aspects of tea production, consumption and export mainly because it accounts for 31 per cent of global production.

For last more than 150 years the Indian tea industry has retained its leadership over other countries. The industry offers a wide range of varieties of tea which includes the original orthodox to CTC, green tea, the aromatic and flavoured Darjeeling tea as well as the strong Assam and Nilgiri Tea. The quality of Indian tea is the best in the international market. Exports increased by 33.8 mn kg or 17 per cent. In value terms, the increase was ₹669.5 crore or 17.5 per cent [68]. The figures on production and export of tea are provided.

Financial Year	Production (in mn kg)	Increase/Decrease (in per cent)	Export (in mn kg)	Increase/Decrease (in per cent)
2011–12	1,095	13.32	214	0.26
2012–13	1,135	3.60	216	0.88
2013–14	1,209	6.50	226	4.40
2014–15	1,197	−0.96	199	−11.82
2015–16	1,233	3.00	233	17.00

Source: Tea Board of India.

West Bengal is a major tea producing state and contributes about one fourth of the total production of tea in India. Darjeeling, Terai and Dooars are the traditional tea growing areas in the state. There are 309 tea estates in the state in the organized sector, covering 103,431 hectares under tea cultivation. Besides that 8,078 small growers are growing tea in an area of 11,094 hectares. The industry is passing through a crisis due to lack of investment, thereby the maintenance of the health of the tea gardens has gone down. Further the rising cost of inputs, lower yield rate, fall in prices and so on are bottlenecks to the industry in Bengal. The garden owners have neglected the gardens over the years. The capital has not been ploughed back for investment for the growth of the industry.

The tea workers get wages through tripartite collective bargaining and the benefits as per the plantation legislation. But the execution of the agreed wages through negotiation and the statutory benefits had been a matter of question. This phenomenon often resulted in various social issues in the gardens. Reportedly there had been about 100 starvation deaths since January 2014 to December 2014, in the tea gardens in the Dooars, North Bengal [69].

The following incidences of the tea estates of Bengal speak for themselves on the prevailing IR in the tea estates.

On 23 November 2014, Rajesh Jhunjhunwala, the owner of Sonali Tea Estate in Bagrakote, Dooars, was lynched by workers. In the evening, during negotiations for payment of arrears the owner was dragged out by a group of workers in the middle of the discussions and stabbed to death. It was reported that workers had not been paid wages for the last six months, and were agitating since early morning (that day) and gheraoed the management for their arrears. In the afternoon, Jhunjhunwala, who lived in Malbazar, arrived and started negotiating with the workers. There were some heated exchanges after which somebody dragged him to a spot in front of the office, where he was murdered.

Sonali Tea is a small garden of about 426 acres, 40 km from Malbazar on the way to Siliguri. It has a long history of trouble and was shut for some time. According to records, the garden produced nearly 1.63 lakh kg tea leaves in 2010. It had no factory for processing the tea leaves, so it was only involved in the sale of leaves to the larger tea estates. The Sonali Tea Estate had 375 permanent workers and about 150 temporary workers. The tea-worker's union of Sonali Tea Garden was affiliated to Trinamool Congress since 2009. The management had not deposited the workers' due provident fund amount, or supplied regular rations or firewood to the workers, which were a part of the benefits entitled to them as per the Plantation Act. Not much details were available, since the proprietor, Jhunjhunwala, was not a member of any association of tea planters [70].

The tea garden workers were awaiting the payment of their wages at the revised rate, which was due since April 2014, and the management had not paid salaries since then. Talks between the tea unions and the estate owners were deadlocked over the quantum of hike since the proprietor was not accepting the revised rates.

The Terai Indian Planters' Association (TIPA) reports that Sonali Tea Estate had a long history of defaulting wages payment and also the statutory dues to workers. This tea estate had also not implemented the revised wages as were adopted in the industry-wide wage settlement. The mounting dispute between the workers and the management caused such an incidence [71].

A senior manager of the tea estate expressed that, 'We find it difficult to work in the tea estates now, particularly after the recent incidents'. Another officer working in a garden in Naxalbari said,

In tea estates, even a minor issue can snowball into a major one and lead to a law-and-order problem. After the incidence of 23rd November, 2014, we are nervous because the workers have a reason to be discontented. None of the workers in the Terai, Dooars and Darjeeling hills have received wages at a revised rate, which despite being due since April 1, 2014.

The trade unions indicated that they had never supported violence and all those who were responsible for Jhunjhunwala's murder should be punished. A joint forum of trade unions, which is a conglomeration of 23 tea unions, except that of the union sponsored by Trinamool Congress (the party which is in power in Bengal), had decided to fight for the revision of the minimum wage [72].

The low wages had always been a distinctive feature of the plantation industry in India. The wage rates of tea plantation had been lower in comparison to the wage rate of workers in other industries. A tripartite wage agreement signed on 20 February 2015, fixed a raise of ₹37.50 per day (in phases over three years) to tea plantation workers in Terai and Dooars and ₹42.50 to workers in Darjeeling. The daily wage before the agreement was ₹95. The agreement was between the state, planter's associations and workers' unions. 'Workers will therefore be paid a miserly amount of ₹112.50 (per day) in the first year, ₹122.50 in the second year and finally ₹132.50 in the third year. That by no logic such an increase be justified', expressed Progressive Plantation Workers Union (PPWU), which had refused to sign the agreement [73]. In contrast to this rate of minimum wages, the existing minimum wage as declared by the state government for the agricultural sector was ₹206 per day.

This is not the first such incidence happening in the tea estates. Similar incidences had happen in the past.

For example, on 26 December 2012, an Indian tea plantation owner Mridul Kumar Bhattacharya and his wife Rita at Konapathar tea estate in Tinsukia district of Assam were burnt alive after their bungalow was attacked by more than 1,000 workers, following a labour dispute [74].

In 2006, the owner of Govindapur tea estate in Golaghat district, Rupak Gogoi, was lynched and his body burnt by the workers of his tea estate [74].

The growing aspirations of a community of workers deployed in the tea estates causes what the trade union explains as socio-economic struggle, which occasionally goes out of control leading to such incidences.

2. Jute industry in Bengal

The jute industry is an important industry and occupies a special place in the economic history of India. It is one of the major industries in the eastern region. In Bengal this golden fibre is considered as a prime industry. The product meets all the standards for safe packaging, which are natural, renewable, biodegradable as well as eco-friendly. Jute mills, in the 19th century, were the foundational premise of the industrialization in Bengal. Jute mills stretched over an area of 20 miles along the banks of Hooghly, both north and south of Kolkata. The expanding international trade after the year 1850 had been the reason for the growth of these mills in Bengal. The industry linked the agro-based economy of the country with foreign trade.

The jute sector in Bengal in the year 2015 was having around 59 jute mills and was providing employment to over 250,000 workers. In addition to same, the raw material for jute was cultivated by 350,000 farmers in the villages of Bengal. In the 1850s there were only six mills, by 1912, there were 61 factories in this region employing nearly 200,000 workers and by 1945, the industry in Bengal had 85 factories and employing over 350,000 workers.

The decline in the demand for jute packaging material began with the growing popularity of plastic in the mid-1960s. The industry had problems thereafter and by the early 1970s the industry was already deteriorating by losing its price advantage to plastic products. The industry also lost its stake in the international business since after Partition, the new factories with advance technology came up in Dhaka to compete with the Indian manufactures [75].

A tripartite wage agreement was signed in the industry by the government of West Bengal in April 2015. There were serious troubles in various mills on the issue of the implementation of the increased wages. The workers complained against the management that they were not paid their salary in the month of April 2015. On the morning of 1 May 2015, a notice of suspension of work was issued in Nafarchand and Kankinada Jute Mills in the Barrackpore industrial belt. On the same night, similar suspension of work notice was issued in Victoria Jute Mill, Telinipara, in the Hooghly industrial belt. On 2 May 2015, labour trouble erupted in Wellington Jute Mill of Rishra and India Jute Mill in Serampore, Bengal.

The payment to the workers is linked with the performance of the mills. The mills were not getting orders. So their capability to pay the wages at an increased rate had been a matter of question. On 9 December 2015, the cabinet minister declared that at least 90 per cent of food grain output and 20 per cent of sugar production has to be packaged in jute bags. This was definitely a relief to the jute industries.

The jute mills in Bengal had always been a spot of violence. Labour unrest, violence and intimidation were part of the enforcing process of the demands of the workers. There were five general strikes in the industry in Bengal, during the period 1929 to 1971. The trend of conflict between the management and the trade union in jute industries was an old symptom and was identified with the industry itself. The industry had all through been branded as a labour problem sector in Bengal. Few instances are discussed further.

S. K. Maheshwari, the 69-year-old CEO of Northbrook Jute Mill at Bhadreshwar in Hooghly, was attacked on 14 June 2014 by mill workers. The incident happened following the declaration of wage cut due to production cuts. Such production reductions were due to lack of orders, along with a huge pile up of finished products in the mill. Maheshwari was trying to put a point suggesting to cut down on working days from five to three days because of the incurring losses to the organization. The incident happened after a rumour spread stating a possible shutdown of the mill. S. K. Maheshwari had held a meeting with the workers' union in the mill about reducing the number of working days, which meant lower pay for the workers. After S. K. Maheshwari refused to agree to the demand of the workers for increasing the weekly working hours, he was beaten up by the agitated workers of the factory. General Manager Kiranjit Singh said, 'There was sudden brick throwing, we were in the meeting, and didn't see who they were, Maheswari was badly hurt, I also got hurt badly along with our security men'. The general manager and the chief security officer of the mill were also injured and were shifted to hospital [76].

The workers in such an industry are paid according to the hours they worked. They were demanding for increasing the weekly working hours to 40 hours from the existing 25 hours. A worker of the mill, Toton Ali, said:

> In the meeting held in the morning, the management said that from 1st July, there will be work for 3 days and for 3 days the factory will remain closed. Workers got agitated and started throwing bricks, iron rods and sticks wherein I also got hurt. [77, 78]

Such killing of a jute mill executive is not the first such incidence in the jute industries of Bengal. The following are few other registered incidences of similar type of violence in jute industries in Bengal.

On 18 May 2014 in Indian Jute mill three managers were attacked by workers and pelted with bricks and machine spare parts. The death of one of the officers could be averted, narrowly. On 15 July 2011, another LO was murdered in Chandennagore [79]. On 15 May 2008, the personnel manager of Loomtex Jute Mill was lynched to death in Titagurh. The chief personnel officer of Dalhousie Jute Mill was killed on 16 May 2002 as a result of a labour dispute in the organization. The same year, the LO of Hastings Jute Mills was also killed in the month of October. On 29 June 2001, two executives of Barangar Jute Mill were lynched to death by the workers, due to differences in the management and trade union differences and conflicts.

Case Questions

1. Identify the reasons why the IR culture of the the two agro industries of Bengal has continued to be as it was?
2. What do you think should be role of the management in the cases?
3. What do you think should be the role of the trade union in the cases?
4. What do you think should be the role of the government in the cases?
5. What has structurally gone wrong for development of an appropriate harmonious IRS in the context?

(The instructor may refer the teaching notes for the pedagogy of the case.)

Chapter Summary

1. Since 1947 (Independence), the Government of India has played a crucial role in the industrialization of the country. The government's focus for industrialization was achieved through the five-year plans as well as through the industrial policies implemented from time to time.
2. The Indian economy had been predominantly an agricultural economy till 1947. The First Five-Year Plan (1951–1956) laid emphasis on agriculture for economic growth. In the Second Five-Year Plan (1956–1961), the focus shifted towards heavy industries for industrialization of the nation and thereafter the trend continued.
3. Through the Industrial Policy Resolution of 1948, the government adopted a 'mixed economy' approach for economic development.
4. The focus of the government in the Second Five-Year Plan was 'to initiate to secure peace through mutual negotiation, conciliations and voluntary arbitrations'.

5. The government's emphasis in the Third Five-Year Plan was re-enforcement of the Code of Discipline and implementation of the works committees and JMC.
6. Fairly successful results were achieved through planning process initiated after Independence, which created a need for further consolidation of the process for economic growth and development through rigorous implementation of the policies for better results.
7. A wider government role was visible with the announcement of the formation of the first National Commission on Labour in 1966.
8. Post 1967, India experienced a sharp rise in the number of strikes and labour unrests. The reason for the same has been attributed to the structural changes in the economy and declining employment elasticity leading to the tightening of labour market. This situation reshaped the trade unions' objectives and so the activities. Collective bargaining was more backed by aggressive labour agitations. The negotiation strategy shifted from 'demanding for rights to demanding for interests'.
9. The rising labour unrest and economic downturn were addressed by the government's initiatives in the Fourth Five-Year Plan. The government stressed more importance on the machineries for settlement of industrial disputes. The period also witnessed a series of amendments in the existing labour acts, since the government implemented the recommendations of the Labour Commission through amending certain labour laws.
10. The early 1970s witnessed considerable industrial strife and loss of a large number of man-days.
11. The 1980s have been the best decade in terms of economic growth but the worst decade in terms of employment generation. But in the early 1980s, IR in India were characterized by violence.
12. With liberalization in post 1991, industrialization policy shifted from ISI to EOI. The trade unions in India initially resisted the implementation of economic policy of liberalization. But liberalization had a positive impact on HRD.
13. The process of collective bargaining, which was instrumental in settling disputes between the trade unions and the management, that had taken a shape of hostility during the 1970s and the 1980s reshaped itself to mutual acceptance, accommodation, realization of the issues in question and devising solutions amicably to meet the ends of the management as well as the employees due to the impact of globalization.

Questions

1. The Indian IRS was highly influenced by the government policies adopted from time to time and the trend of industrialization. Justify.
2. What were the impacts of industrial liberalization of 1991 on IR?
3. Globalization impacted IRS in India. Discuss.

Project Work for the Students

1. Identify two instances of positive impacts of globalization on IRS from organizations around you and elaborate on the same.
2. Justify how far the statement 'Trade Unions are institutionalizing violence in North India' is correct. Students may collect instances of violence by the trade union in North India for the last 10 years for conclusion on the subject.

References

1. Mathur A. The experience of consultation during structural adjustment in India (1990–1992). Int Labour Rev. 1991; 132(3): 331–345.
2. Sodhi JS. New economic policies and their impact on industrial relations. Indian J Ind Relat. 1993; 29(1) July: 31–54.
3. Venkataratnam C. Impact of new economic policies on the role of trade unions. Indian J Ind Relat. 1993; 29(1) July: 56–77.
4. Reddy YRK. Determination of collective bargaining agency: search for a procedure. Indian J Ind Relat. 1978; 14(1) July: 73–86.
5. Ramaswamy EA. Indian management dilemma: economic versus political unions. Asian Surv. 1983; 23(8) August: 976–990.
6. Kumar A. Trouble in another Gurgaon unit, The Hindu. 2 August 2012. Available from http://www.thehindu.com/todays-paper/tp-national/tp-newdelhi/trouble-in-another-gurgaon-unit/article3714934.ece1
7. Times News Network. Medical company closes facility, workers protest, The Times of India. 29 July 2012. Available from http://articles.timesofindia.indiatimes.com/2012-07-29/gurgaon/32923172 1 workers-protest-labour-union-labour-problem
8. Dhoot V. Another Maruti waiting to happen; Eastern Medikit employees halt work, The Economic Times. 6 August 2012. Available from http://m.economictimes.com/news/news-by-industry/healthcare/biotech/healthcare/another-maruti-waiting-to-happen-eastern-medikit-employees-halt-work/articleshow/15368976.cms
9. Joseph J. Private medical firm workers threaten hunger strike, The Times of India. 2 August 2012. Available from http://timesofindia.indiatimes.com/city/gurgaon/Private-medical-firm-workers-threaten-hunger-strike/articleshow/15320165.cms
10. http://www.medikit.com
11. Bloomberg. Company overview of Eastern Medikit Ltd. Available from http://investing.businessweek.com/research/stocks/private/snapshot.asp?privcapId=31228520
12. Sikarwar, D. (2012). Uttarakhand, Himachal Pradesh manufacturing units to get tax breaks even if company is sold: CBEC. The Economic Times. Retrieved from http://articles.economictimes.indiatimes.com/2012-02-20/news/31079508_1_excise-duty-exemption-hill-states-manufacturing-units
13. Times News Network. Medikit workers lodge police complaint against company, The Times of India. 5 August 2012. Available from http://articles.timesofindia.indiatimes.com/2012-08-05/gurgaon/33048692 1 labour-laws-labour-department-factory-management
14. Eastern Medikit Ltd Workers Threaten Hunger Strike Aug 12, week. Available from http://investing.businessweek.com/research/stocks/private/snapshot.asp?privcapId=312285201
15. Anand D. Workers of closed firm stage protest, Hindustan Times. 19 September 2012. Available from https://www.hindustantimes.com/india/workers-of-closed-firm-stage-protest/story-G6B09K2Dry4NUhuVDFRGeM.html
16. Vaid R. Gurgaon news: Eastern Medikit employees protest against the company's wrongdoings, Faridabad Metro. 18 September 2012. Available from http://faridabadmetro.com/2012/09/18/gurgaon-news-eastern-medikit-employees-protest-against-the-companys-wrongdoings/]
17. Protest against illegal lockout CGPI. 16–30 September 2012. Protest against illegal lockout http://d8.cgpi.org/index.php/mel/struggle-rights/2642-protest-against-illegal-l
18. The Hindu BusinessLine. Unions flay suspension of work in Eastern Medikit, Gurgaon, The Hindu BusinessLine. 24 August 2012. Available from https://www.thehindubusinessline.com/companies/unions-flay-suspension-of-work-in-eastern-medikit-gurgaon/article23080941.ece
19. PTI. Haryana labour dept proceeds against Gurgaon based company. 1 August 2012. Available from http://ibnlive.in.com/generalnewsfeed/news/haryana-labour-dept-proceeds-against-gurgaon-based-company/1033577.html

20. Times News Network. End lockout, govt to Medikit, The Times of India. 12 August 2012. Available from http://articles.timesofindia.indiatimes.com/2012-08-12/gurgaon/33167037 1 labour-department-labour-court -factory-owner

21. Sahoo DP. Industrial relations in NCR in retrospect. FIIB Bus Rev. 2013; 2(3) July–September: 30–39.

22. http://www.thehindu.com/business/companies/maruti-declares-lockout-at-manesar-plant/article3666172.ece, http://articles.economictimes.indiatimes.com/2012-07-20/news/32764423_1_maruti-suzuki-s-manesar-manesar-plant-awanish-kumar

23. http://wap.business-standard.com/article/bs/stir-at-gurgaon-supplier-of-marks--spencer-110090300097_1.html

24. Headlines Today. RICO workers pelt stones on factory; situation tense, India Today. 20 October 2009. Available from https://www.thehindu.com/business/companies/maruti-declares-lockout-at-manesar-plant/article3666172.ece

25. https://www.business-standard.com/article/companies/stir-at-gurgaon-supplier-of-marks-spencer-110090300097_1.html

26. GurgaonWorkersNews. Police attack on Honda workers in Gurgaon, India, Youtube. 18 November 2007. Available from https://www.youtube.com/watch?v=lOMWz7GH33c

27. https://www.business-standard.com/article/companies/rs-65-cr-loss-for-sunbeam-auto-due-to-52-day-stir-109113000193_1.html

28. Kuruvilla S. Venkataratnam CS. Economic development and industrial relations in South and Southeast Asia: past trends and future developments. Ind Relat J. 1996; 27(1): 9–23.

29. Kerr C, Dunlop JT, Harbison F, Myers CA. Industrialism and industrial man. New York, NY: Oxford University Press; 1964. Available from https://economictimes.indiatimes.com/700-injured-in-clash-between-honda-workers-and-police/articleshow/1182154.cms

30. Sharma B. Aspects of industrial relations in ASEAN. Singapore: Institute for Asian Studies; 1985.

31. Frenkel S. 1993. Organized labor in the Asia-Pacific region: a comparative study of trade unions in nine countries. Ithaca, NY: ILR Press; 1993.

32. Bjorkman M, Lauridsen L, Marcussen H. Types of industrialization and capital-labour relations in the third world. In: Southall R, editor. Trade Unions and the New Industrialization of the Third World. London: Zed; 1988.

33. PTI. India's per capita income rises 7.4% to ₹93,293, The Economic Times. 31 May 2016. Available from http://economictimes.indiatimes.com/articleshow/52524152.cms?utm_source=contentofinterest&utm_medium=text&utm_campaign=cppst]

34. The Industrial Policy Resolution of 1956

35. http://www.indiastat.com/table/labourandworkforce/380987/numberandmembershipoftradeunions 19602010/452312/352302/data.aspx]

36. Venkataratnam CS. Industrial relations in India. Paper presented at a seminar on Labour Market and Industrial Relations in South Asia, New Delhi, 18–20 September 1996.

37. Jackson DAS. Wage policy and industrial relations in India. Econ J. 1972; 82 March: 183–194.

38. Fonseca AJ. Wage determination and organized labour in India. Bombay: Oxford University Press; 1964.

39. Chatterjee R. Unions, politics, and the state: a study of Indian labour politics. New Delhi, South Asian Publishers; 1980.

40. Sengupta AK. Trends in industrial conflict in India (1961–87) and government policy, Working Paper Series No. 174/92. Calcutta: Indian Institute of Management Calcutta; 1992.

41. Joshi V, Little IMD. India: macroeconomics and political economy, 1964–1991. Washington, DC: The World Bank; 1994.

42. Nayyar D. Industrial development in India: growth or stagnation? In Bagchi AK, Banerjee N. editors. Change and Choice in Indian Industry. Calcutta: K. P. Bagchi; 1981. pp. 91–118.

43. Papola TS. Employment growth and social protection of labour in India. Indian J Ind Relat. 1994; 30 October: 117–143.

44. Sridhar V. Chronicles of a strike, Frontline. Volume 18, Issue 19. 15–28 September 2001. Available from http://www.frontline.in/static/html/fl1819/18190750.htm

45. Indian Railway Employee. The Indian railway strike of 1974: a study of power and organised labour. Indian Railway Employee. Available from http://www.indianrailwayemployee.com/content/indian-railways-strike-1974-study-power-and-organised-labour]
46. The Times of India, 10 July 1980.
47. Rudolph LI, Rudolph SH. In pursuit of lakshmi. Bombay: Orient Longmans; 1987. Available from https://www.princeton.edu/~kohli/docs/PEGI_PartI.pdf
48. Bhattacherjee D. Organised labour and economic liberalisation India: past, present and future. Discussion Paper DP/105/1999, International Institute for Labour Studies. Geneva: ILO; 1999.
49. Ghose, AK. Economic restructuring, employment and safety nets: a note. In Social Dimensions of Structural Adjustment in India. New Delhi: ILO-ARTEP; 1992. pp. 94–102.
50. Subramanian D. Bangalore Public Sector Strike, 1980–81: A Critical Appraisal: I: The Settlements of 1973 and 1978, Economic and Political Weekly, Vol. 32, No. 15 (Apr. 12–18, 1997), pp. 767–769 and 771–778.
51. Bhattacherjee D. Unions, state and capital in western India: structural determinants of the 1982 Bombay textile strike. In Southall R editor. Labour and Unions in Africa and Asia: Contemporary Issues. London: Macmillan; 1988. pp. 211–237.
52. Nair J. A substantial empirical study: Bombay textile strike 1982–83 by Hubert W.M. Van Wersch. Soc Sci. 1993: 21(1/2) 91–94.
53. Bhattacherjee D. Evolution of unionism and labour market structure: case of Bombay textile mills, 1947–1985. Econ Pol Wkly. 1989: 24(21) M67–M76.
54. Goswami O. Sickness and growth of India's textile industry: analysis and policy options. Econ Pol Wkly. 1990: 25(45) 2496–2506.
55. Tulpule B. Bombay textile workers' strike: a different view. Econ Pol Wkly. 1982: 17(17/18) 719–721.
56. Bakshi R. The long haul: the Bombay textile workers strike of 1982–83. Mumbai: BUILD Documentation Center; 1986.
57. Bhattacherjee D. Union-type effects on bargaining outcomes in Indian manufacturing. Br J Ind Relat. 1987; 27 July: 247–266.
58. Monappa A. et al. Industrial Relations and Labour Laws,2e. New Delhi: Tata McGraw Hill Education. 2012 page 4.
59. Business India, September 28, October 11, 1981, pp. 40–51.
60. Venkataratnam CS. Economic liberalization and the transformation of industrial relations policies in India. In Verma A, Kochan TA, Lansbury RD, editors. Employment Relations in the Growing Asian Economies. London: Routledge; 1995. 248–314.
61. Das H. Trade union activism–avoidable or inevitable? Indian J Ind Relat. 1999; 35(2), pp. 224–236.
62. Ramaswamy E. Organised labour and economic reform. In Oldenburg P, editor. Indian Briefing: Staying the Course. Armonk, NY: M.E. Sharpe; 1995. 97–128.
63. Sodhi JS. Emerging trends in industrial relations and human resource management in Indian industry. Indian J Ind Relat. 1994; 30(1): 19–37.
64. Chandramouli R. Militant unionism raises its head in Tamil Nadu, the Times of India. 29 July 2012. Available from http://timesofindia.indiatimes.com/city/chennai/Militant-unionism-raises-its-head-in-Tamil-Nadu/articleshow/15245233.cms
65. Lakshman A. Trade unions militant in nature, says Kerala HC, Rediff.com, 25 June 2009. Available from http://www.rediff.com/news/report/kerala-hc-slams-trade-unionism/20090625.htm
66. Have trade unions become more militant?, Business Standard. 7 October 2009. Available from https://www.business-standard.com/article/opinion/-have-trade-unions-become-more-militant-109100700039_1.html
67. The Times Network. Trade, bank unions call mega strike on Feb 28, The Times of India. 27 February 2012. Available from http://timesofindia.indiatimes.com/india/Trade-bank-unions-call-mega-strike-on-Feb-28/articleshow/12048343.cms
68. India records highest-ever tea production in 2015–16, Business Standard. 17 June 2016. Available from http://www.business-standard.com/article/markets/india-records-highest-ever-tea-production-in-2015-16-116061700687_1.html

69. Gupta J, Bhattacharya PP. Hunger stalks tea belt, The Times of India. 7 July 2014.
70. Bhattacharya PP. Workers lynch tea garden owner in West Bengal, The Times of India. 23 November 2014. Available from http://timesofindia.indiatimes.com/india/Workers-lynch-tea-garden-owner-in-West-Bengal/articleshow/45244729.cms
71. The Hindu Business Line. Tea estate owner lynched to death, The Hindu Business Line. 22 November 2014. Available from http://www.thehindubusinessline.com/news/states/tea-estate-owner-lynched-to-death-in-w-bengal/article6625295.ece
72. The Telegraph. Fear grips tea garden management—police remand for workers held for planter's murder, The Telegraph. 24 November 2014. Available from http://www.telegraphindia.com/1141124/jsp/siliguri/story_19079200.jsp#.WCm281V97IU
73. The Hindu. Revised wages inadequate, say tea workers, The Hindu. 6 March 2015. Available from http://www.thehindu.com/news/cities/kolkata/revised-wages-inadequate-say-tea-workers/article6966900.ece
74. Sharma M. Labour unrest a simmering problem in Assam's tea gardens, The Times of India. 6 January 2013. Available from http://articles.timesofindia.indiatimes.com/2013-01-06/guwahati/36173149_1_tea-gardens-tea-estate-bidyananda-barkakoty
75. Biswas P. Why Bengal's jute industry is hanging by a thread, The Indian Express, 29 June 2014. Available from http://indianexpress.com/article/lifestyle/why-bengals-jute-industry-is-hanging-by-a-thread/
76. Bagchi S. Bengal jute mill CEO allegedly killed by workers, The Hindu. 15 June 2014. Available from http://www.thehindu.com/news/national/other-states/bengal-jute-mill-ceo-allegedly-killed-by-workers/article6116727.ece
77. ANI. Jute mill CEO killed by workers in Hooghly District over wage dispute, Yahoo News. 16 June 2014. Available from https://in.news.yahoo.com/jute-mill-ceo-killed-workers-hooghly-district-over-040157716.html]
78. Basu M, Datta R. Questions hang over West Bengal's jute mill CEO's murder, Livemint. 17 June 2014. Available from http://www.livemint.com/Companies/RH88utqHbJBzWfPSPNaXbN/Questions-hang-over-Bengal-jute-mill-violence.html
79. Hindustan Times. Bengal jute mill CEO killing: militancy at the gates, Hindustan Times, 17 June 2014. Available from http://www.hindustantimes.com/comment/bengal-jute-mill-ceo-killing-militancy-at-the-gates/article1-1230550.aspx#sthash.BCu8TIFF.dpuf

PART
2

Emerging Shifts in Industrial Relations in Organizations

CHAPTER 3   Industrial Relations: The New Prospective

PART

2

Emerging Shifts in Industrial Relations in Organizations

3

Industrial Relations: The New Prospective

After reading this chapter, you will be able to:

☐ Understand the emerging trend in IR
☐ Understand the impact of the economic, social and political aspects on IRS
☐ Understand IR in a knowledge economy
☐ Understand proactive diagnosis of IR
☐ Understand the difference between IR and employee relations

C.3.1. Case for Discussion   Strike at Chakan Plant (Pune) of Bajaj Auto Ltd

The 50-day-long workers' strike at Chakan Plant (Pune) of Bajaj Auto ended on 13 August 2013, with the workers' union unconditionally calling it off and deciding to go to work from 14 August 2013. Around 80 per cent workers reported for work next day. Workers' union called for strike again on 25 June 2013.

The IR stalemate created by workers union on certain unrealistic demands were far from both economic reality and the trends of framing a charter of demand. The management's tough stand brought results due to 'their conviction in the cause of the stand'.

The question is whether 'strike can beget a win-win situation in labour management relations in organizations'.

The labour union leaders felt that they will not get anything even after 50 days long strike; rather they will lose 50 days' wages and in addition to the same 22 workers were subjected to disciplinary proceedings for misconduct committed by them in course of the strike. It was not loss of salary alone but also a loss of self-respect and pride for workers.

The management on the other hand lost sale of around 20,000 units in June 2013 alone.

This was the first strike at the Chakan Plant of Bajaj Auto in its 16 years of operations. Management and labour union executed an agreement in March 2010 for nine years, which was to last till 2019 with a clause that provided wage revision in three years. This wage revision was due in March 2013. However, the labour union arbitrarily terminated the agreement and submitted a charter of demand to the management.

The workers through their labour union filed a charter of demand for an annual hike of ₹10,000 with an additional correction of ₹5,000 apart from benefits of variable dearness allowance (VDA). The union had then submitted a separate list of 37 demands which also sought clarity on the company's promotion policy, eligibility for a housing loan of ₹5 lakh, education loan of ₹2 lakh and marriage loan of ₹50,000. The union also separately demanded a work study at the site to measure how much production is possible in 480 minutes. Over and above, the union made an audacious demand for allotting 500 shares of the company to each worker at ₹1 only.

The reason for raising such a demand in the charter as was explained by a senior labour union leader of the trade union was that if the company could give 450 per cent dividend to its shareholders, why it cannot pay the same amount of rewards to its own workers? The same labour union leader expressed, 'it is always the investors who benefit from our hard work, so we decided that we also want to be the investors.'

Such a demand appearing in the charter of demand of the trade union in the Indian context would have been unimaginable in the past scenario as well as in the traditional concept of IR in India, but is a reality now.

Probably due to a leading perception among the workers that automation and improvement in productivity has resulted in a significant growth in the profitability of the company and the benefits of the same are not being shared equitably by the management with the labour union.

The eligibility of employee stock option plan (ESOP) was a question which has never been offered to any 'blue collar employees' in Indian manufacturing industry till date. ESOP had never been a part of union negotiations in the Indian industry. It had only been with few IT organizations. Whereas automobile companies such as Tata Motors and Mahindra & Mahindra allotted shares only to the top management in the R&D division and not to the workers [1].

Case Questions

1. In manufacturing culture, can the loyalty of the employees be generated by giving shares to them?
2. Did the management of Bajaj Auto do a right job by rejecting this demand firmly from day one?
3. What would have happened to the trend of labour union demands in manufacturing sectors, had the management of Bajaj Auto accepted such a demand of the labour union? Justify your answer.

3.1. The Emerging Trend

In the new reality, traditional IRSs, with their focus on collective action by the actors and conflicts of interest between management and labour, are becoming more and more obsolete. There is less and less need for a traditional system of IR in industrial societies. There is an emerging new type of employer–employee relationship. The employers in the present situations are more willing to provide a right pay and have an equally contributing return from the employees. In addition to obligation to pay wages for the job done, the approach of the employers in dealing with the employees have undergone a sea change. This has resulted in an emerging trend and willingness not to prefer a collectively organized action by the labour class/labour unions and the same is more visible in emerging new sectors such as service and IT sectors as compared to the old manufacturing sectors.

C.3.2. Case for Discussion   Instances of Employers Not Encouraging a Collective Action

Instances of employers not encouraging a collective action of the trade unions resulting in conflicts of interest between the management and the labour unions are visible in the following recent cases of labour disputes:

1. **Case of MSIL:** In June 2011, workers in MSIL, Manesar Plant, applied to the registrar of trade union at Chandigarh for registration of a new union named Maruti Suzuki Employees' Union (MSEU). The management being aware about the workers' initiative for a new union forced and threatened the workers to sign documents declaring that they will not join the new union. To protest against the management's action, 3,000 workers started a sit-in from 4 June 2011 at the Manesar Plant, demanding recognition of newly formed MSEU. To pressurize the workers, on 6 June, the management dismissed 11 workers including the MSEU office-bearers for allegedly inciting the workers to go on a strike [2].

2. **The unionization of the contract employees in Viva Global:** In the month of April 2010, the workers of Viva Global, a garment company in Gurgaon, Haryana, demanded for a wage increase commensurate with the increase in minimum wages as was implemented by the Government of Haryana since January 2010. The workers also demanded ID cards, PF and ESI membership cards, and salary slips. There was no registered trade union in the organization so the workers contacted MEM, a non-government organization (NGO) platform for workers in Gurgaon, and sought its help in the struggle. Eventually after 10–15 days, their most of the demands were fulfilled. But soon after this, the management started firing out workers and outsourcing the work to other fabricators. The workers initiated for the registration of a trade union and the same was successfully registered in May 2010. The permanent workers along with the contract workers negotiated with the management but the management continued firing workers one by one. Eventually by 21 August, all the contract workers were fired.

3. **Formation of trade union in Rico Auto Ltd:** Rico Auto Ltd is an Indian multinational having 2,500 permanent workers and about 2,000 contract workers. There was no trade union in the company prior to 2009. Only in 2009, the workers started their efforts to form a trade union. On 4 August 2009, they successfully organized the workers without the knowledge of the management and filed an application for registration of the union at the registrar office of trade unions at Chandigarh. In the first week of September 2009, the registrar office of trade unions sent their application to the Department of Labour office at Gurgaon for verification. Thereafter, the management also got the information about the application and started terrorizing the workers. In spite of all such roadblocks, by 9 September, Rico Auto Employees Union was formed. This was followed by labour problems causing both strike and lockout in the plant and death of an employee in a conflict between the security personnel and the workers.

4. **Problem caused due to the managements' action of not permitting to conduct the trade union's election in Sunbeam:** The management of Sunbeam initially formed a works committee to pre-empt the formation of a workers' union. But after the workers initiated for the formation of a union, the management itself formed a union by sponsoring a group of workers in the company and thus 'Sunbeam Auto Shramik Union' was formed. The management controlled this trade union and the office-bearers were representatives selected by the management. There was no formal union election. As a result, the discontent grew among the workers and gradually a parallel leadership emerged which started raising demands for formal elections of union officers, which was due in May 2009. On 1 June 2009, the management formally recognized the new office-bearers elected by the workers.

5. **Pricol labour problem for recognition of trade union:** In Pricol, the management was not ready to recognize the trade union (Kovai Mavatta Pricol Employees' Trade Union, affiliated to AICCTU). The members of the union were victimized and on 21 September 2009, about 40 workers were terminated. A violent physical confrontation erupted resulting in vice-president (HR) of Pricol being attacked and killed by the workers.

6. **The problem of Madras Rubber Factory (MRF) workers' formation of trade union:** MRF workers faced victimization after forming a union and asking the management to recognize their union

for collective bargaining. The management was not ready to recognize their union. Owing to this, Madras Rubber Factory United Workers Union (MRFUWU) filed complaints with the International Labour Organization (ILO) in the years 2006 and 2007. On 9 May 2009, workers of the MRF factories in Arakkonam, Tamil Nadu, and in Puducherry went on a strike demanding salary and wage increases and recognition of MRFUWU as the legitimate representative of MRF workers. The MRF management responded by locking out all staff from the factories on 17 May 2009.

7. **Trade union formation in Nestle India:** In March 2009, the management of Nestle India factory located in Pantnagar, Uttarakhand, started victimizing the workers after they formed a trade union—Nestle Mazdoor Sangh (Nestle Workers Union [NWU]). Fifty-five workers formed the NWU and submitted an application for its official registration. Nestle threatened 25 of those workers and forced them to sign a statement, saying they had joined the union under pressure. The management also attempted to force four workers to 'voluntarily' resign as part of an effort to prevent the setting up of the union. Three of them refused to resign and were therefore dismissed. The Nestle workers protested against these actions of the management and went on a strike on 27 April 2009.

8. **Formation of trade union in Graziano Trasmissioni India Pvt. Ltd (Noida):** The workers faced unimaginable repression and victimization when they started their efforts to register a trade union in Graziano Trasmissioni India Pvt. Ltd (Noida), a subsidiary of multinational firm Oerlikon, in the year 2008. The management in their action started terminating the agitating workers. On 22 September 2008, the workers launched a protest which escalated violent actions on both sides. In the course of the action, the CEO of the company was hit. He died later in the hospital.

9. **Labour problem for trade union formation in Hyundai Motor India Limited (HMIL):** The workers of HMIL, located at Chennai, formed a trade union in 2007. The workforce of Hyundai Motor was around 1,650 permanent workers, 2,000 casual workers, 1,500 apprentices, 1,000 trade apprentices and 1,200 technical trainees in the year 2007. More than 1,300 workers of the company formed a trade union—Hyundai Motor India Employees' Union (HMIEU) in 2007. However, the management was not prepared to recognize the union and a long phase of victimization of union leaders, union members, and supporters in the form of dismissals, suspensions and transfers followed. On 23 July 2007, the management of HMIL signed a wage settlement with the workers' committee set up by management rather than the trade union formed by the workers. It was followed by labour agitations.

Case Questions

1. What had been the general reasons for 'employers not encouraging collective actions'?
2. What do you think would be the impact of discouraging collective actions by the employers on the trade unions?
3. How such restrictions on collective actions would impact IR?

3.2. The Changing Trend

India is one of the most competitive economies. The Global Competitiveness Report 2015–2016, published by World Economic Forum, indicates that after five years of decline, India has moved up to fifty-fifth place gaining 16 positions on a global index of world's most competitive economies. Such changing trends in the Indian industries are the result of the emerging changes in the industries as well as the changes in the nature and operation of the business, including production planning. In the IR front, there had been a progressive reduction in the number of industrial disputes, number of man-days lost on account of strikes and lockouts and the number of strikes and lockouts in India. These are the trends of positive harmonious IR which are more evident during the last decades. The number of strikes and lockouts drastically came down during the period 2012–2014. The figure which was 318 in 2012 came down to 84 by the year 2016.

On the other hand, there had been an increasing trend of lockouts. In the event of a strike by the labour union, the employers had been aggressively locking out the workers and had been using the same as the antithesis of strike. The objective of using lockout had been for two specific reasons, that is,

1. To create a financial and psychological pressure on the labour union and the workers by locking them out.
2. To protect the life and the property of the organization.

Table 3.1 indicates that while the strikes are in the reducing trend, the number of lockouts still continues to be higher than the number of strikes resorted to by the trade unions. The frequency of the strikes and the lockouts and the number of labour problems in India prior to 2013 had a different trend. The reasons for the changing trends may be attributed to various changed initiatives introduced at different levels since the liberalization of the economy. The following are the data on the number of strikes and lockouts since 1992, that is, the period since the post-economic liberalization.

There has been shifts in the focus of organizing the business by the employers as well as in the expectations, preferences and approaches of the employees in relation to their work context and environment in the Indian industries. These aspects have resulted in shifts in the outlook towards the traditional IRS, which focuses more on collectivism of the actors and conflicts of interest between management and labour. There are various factors causing this shift from the traditional IRS. The IR environment majorly contributes to such shifts.

M. Salamon discusses the impact of the environment on IR and the actors of IR [3]. The IR environment consists of three major components, and each of these components constitutes of various sub-components. The components are:

1. Economic component
2. Social component
3. Political component

The economic component includes technology, employment and the market, the social component of the IR environment includes education, class, wealth, whereas the political component includes elements such as the legal, political and governmental systems of the society. All these sub-components and components interact in the space and time to influence the climate and/or context of IR at a particular point in time.

An atmosphere of coexisting competition, collaboration and cooperation among the actors in the economic, social and political frameworks of IR environment emerges to the context. Such coexisting competition, collaboration and cooperation precipitate from the IR environment in which the actors of IR function. Figure 3.1 explains the impact of the social, political and economic frameworks of environment on IRS.

Table 3.1	The Number of Strikes and Lockouts since 1992

		Strikes			Lockouts	
Years	Number	Workers Involved (In '000)	Man-days Lost (In '000)	Number	Workers Involved (In '000)	Man-days Lost (In '000)
1991	1,278	872	12,428	532	469	13,999
1992	1,011	767	15,132	703	484	16,126
1993	914	672	5,614	479	281	14,686
1994	808	626	6,651	393	220	14,332
1995	732	683	5,720	334	307	10,570
1996	763	609	7,818	403	331	12,467
1997	793	637	6,295	512	344	10,738
1998	665	801	9,349	432	488	12,713
1999	540	1,099	10,625	387	211	16,161
2000	426	1,044	11,959	345	374	16,304
2001	372	489	5,563	302	199	18,204
2002	295	900	9,665	284	199	16,921
2003	255	1,011	3,206	297	305	27,050
2004	236	1,903	4,829	241	169	19,037
2005	227	2,723	10,801	229	191	18,364
2006	243	1,712	5,318	187	98	15,006
2007	210	606	15,056	179	118	12,111
2008	240	1,514	6,955	181	66	10,479
2009	167	1,793	8,075	178	74	9,547
2010	199	990	13,150	172	85	9,980
2011	179	645	4,697	191	90	9,761
2012	133	1,221	2,843	185	86	10,094
2013	103	1,774	4,045	155	64	8,600
2014	137	1,051	2,883	25	3	911
2015[a]	112	741	2,663	29	10	1,351
2016[a]	104	654	1,873	26	14	2,746

Note: [a]Provisional.
Source: https://www.indiastat.com/table/labour-and-workforce-data/380987/labour-disputes/78/1264/data.aspx

While the major components, that is, economic, social and political, impact the actors, the IR trend of the past strongly impacts the setting of the future pattern of IR. The future expectations of the business and economy as well as the social and political expectations of the industry's context impact by way of influencing the actors, thereby reorganizing the IRS.

Figure 3.1 Factors Impacting the Actors

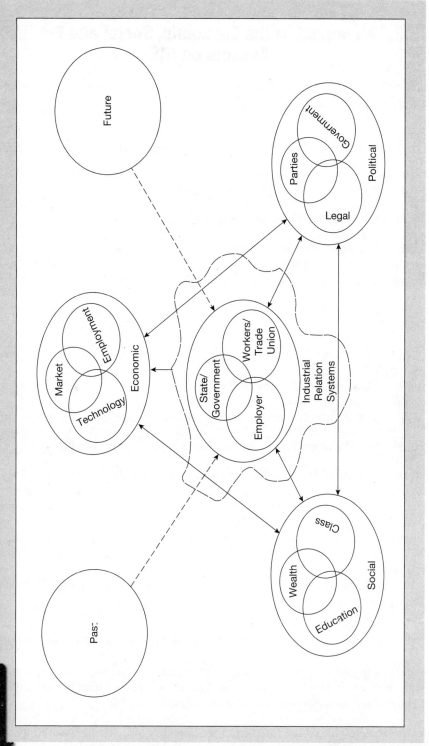

3.3. The Impact of the Economic, Social and Political Aspects on IRS

The impact of the economic, social and political aspects on IRS in the Indian context is studied under the following phenomena.

3.3.1. Globalization and Liberalization of the Market

The globalization has significantly changed the labour market and impacted the IRS. The most important economic effects of globalization in the Indian context include the following:

1. Increasing integration of global economic activities
2. Rising competitiveness
3. Relocation of economic activities
4. Structural changes in the economy
5. Rapid technological advancements and innovation

The increasing changes in the economy have impacted the labour market and the working class in the following manner:

1. Flexibilization of labour markets
2. Increasing labour migration
3. Rising non-standard forms of employment
4. Changing work content and working conditions
5. Increasing skill mismatch leading to multi-skilling and urge for life-long learning

The 'actors' of the IRS have responded to the changing context in various ways such as:

1. Both the agencies of labour and capital, that is, the trade unions and the management looked to the state (government) for specific solutions for favouring their respective interests. Thereby, of late, there had been continuous pressure on the government to provide both infrastructures and opportunities for growth.
2. The government introduced a wide range of labour reforms for enabling the growth of industry without hurting the fundamental interests of working class, that is, securing their employment and providing a better standard of living.
3. The workers in the unorganized sectors also gained importance as the indirect contributors to the industrial development.

3.3.2. Decline of Labour Power in the Era of Globalization

The trade union's negotiating power is a derived function of the support of the working class clubbed with their unity. There had been a decline of such power with the globalization of the economy. The reasons for the declining of the labour power are [4]:

1. The government shifted the focus from welfare state which only ensured 'protection and justice to labour' to productivity enhancement and thereby generating economic efficiency for growth.

2. Employers' increasing consideration of pay for individual performance based on individual and work group productivity and efficiency instead of going by the negotiated norms set by the collective force of the labour unions. The case of Chakan Plant (Pune) of Bajaj Auto Ltd is an example. Such shifts result in individualization of IR and obsolesce of cooperative IRS.
3. Emergence of larger number of service organizations including IT and information technology enabled service (ITES) organizations, where it is comparatively difficult to organize the workforce for cooperative initiatives to create pressure on the management.
4. Emergence of gold-collared employees (describe either young, low-wage workers who invest in conspicuous luxury, or highly skilled knowledge workers, traditionally classified as white collar, but who have recently become essential enough to business operations as to warrant a new classification and knowledge workers) who are less interested in unionization but more interested in self-skill development and personal growth.
5. Employers' greater tendency to employ contract and casual labour rather than engaging permanent workforce leading to decline in organized workforce.
6. There had been an increasing tendency of employers to employ labour law experts to professionally address the issues of the trade unions and the individual workers.

3.3.3. The Changing Power Balance Due to Increased Mobility of Capital

The growing mobility of capital has greatly enhanced the bargaining power of the employers/ management, thereby weakening the scope for labour unions on their efforts to generate any collective pressure on the management. With the globalization of the economy, companies have gained the ability to move operations to countries having low human cost and better working conditions, whereas labour on the other hand, has only limited access to such mobility and is more geographically bounded thereby increasing the overall bargaining power of employers and decreasing the bargaining power of employees. There are also instances where managements have shifted their works from one state to another state for getting the benefits of low cost labour, better subsidies in terms of tax reliefs and low fixed as well as variable costs, for example, land, capital, labour and power.

3.3.4. Neo-liberal Judicial Trends

With the liberalization of the economy in the post 1990s, some significant judgments were delivered by the court of law relating to contract labour, privatization of business units, right to strike and the bandhs (strikes). The focus of the judgments was more on promoting industrial growth and thereby economic growth. The trend of judgment was no more of protecting and generating welfare state for the working population; it rather focused on broader economic interests.

Few of the judgments of the Supreme Court of India went to the extent of:

1. Affirming the policy of independence of the government in the cases of privatization, which promoted the private players to peruse their commercial objectives.
2. Making critical remarks in general against the right to strike and prohibited the right to strike of public employees.
3. Imposing restraints on public protests like bandhs.

4. Endorsing or asking the government to impose the ESMA, reversing the order on automatic absorption of contract labour and arguing that automatic absorption was not provided in the relevant law [5].

Such path-breaking judgments, which were distinctly different, impacted IR as well as the labour management relationships.

3.3.5. Changing Managerial Strategies on Labour Hiring

The government with no changes in the formal system continued to provide sufficient signals and opportunities to the employers in the interest of economic growth to implement various changes [6]. The employers grabbed these opportunities and adopted various forms of labour flexibility, control over work processes, which weakened the collective labour power.

The restrictive practices through stringent regulations and more clarity on the legal norms pronounced by the judiciary on issues such as illogical work stoppages by the labour unions, illegal closures by employers, prolonged lockouts (often closures in disguise), reduction in regular workers (via VRS, labour reallocation, transfers, multi-tasking, freeze on employment, idleness pay and so on) encouraged the employers both in the public and the private sectors to adopt increased use of contract labour, outsourcing of support functions, subcontracting, job freezes and so on. These initiatives reduced the impact of the collective workforce, thereby trade unionism [7].

Such deliberate managerial strategies of employing non-regular workers increased considerably in the last decade. The objectives of such initiatives were not only to achieve labour flexibility and reduction in labour cost but also to gain control over production process and weaken collective labour institutions.

3.3.6. The Changing Trends in Collective Bargaining

Collective bargaining had been one of the important methods of rulemaking in IRS in many industries, but in India, collective bargaining as an effective tool of IRS has only been adopted in very few industries (only 3% of the industries) [8].

Collective bargaining experienced major challenges like:

1. In industries such as cotton, silk, plantations and sugar in regions such as Coimbatore, Mumbai, Bihar and Uttar Pradesh, where industry-wide bargaining has become a historical practice, this has led to the emergence of the enterprise-level bargaining.
2. There was a preference to focus more on linking pay with performance resulting in a new trend in the characteristic of collective bargaining both in the public and private sectors. It shifted the trade unions' united strength more towards linking with the organization's performance and achieving business objectives [9].
3. The managements' approach, as a practice, to consider collective bargaining as an opportunity to reduce labour costs, increase production or productivity, flexibility in work organization (multi-functioning, changes in worker grades and so on), increase in work time, reduction in regular staff strength via VRS, importance of quality and so on in recent years owing to heightened competition in the market changes the nature of collective bargaining [10].

The trade unions learnt to consider themselves as partners of the organization, resulting in introduction of new work measurement systems, flexible working conditions, rise in productivity and so on. There had been several instances where the trade unions have understood the financial constraints of the companies and have offered their cooperation in various ways.

3.3.7. Failure of Political Unionism Model

There has been increasing failure of the 'political unionism model' in India, which focused on perusing labour reform measures based on the political ideological orientation of a political party. The political interests which ruled over labour organizational interests generated splits in the unions on ideological beliefs thereby weakened the labour movement and union power. Further, there also emerged conflicts between the ruling political parties and their labour wings. These factors had important implications on the trade union actions and initiatives.

3.3.8. Launching Nation-wide Agitations on Common Fronts for Reform Programmes

The national trade unions adopted nation-wide agitations on issues based on common fronts and demanded to implement reform programmes through government policies [11, 12]. Since 1992, these trade unions have conducted various strikes and agitations at the national level. Many of these agitations had been conducted under one common banner. On such issues of agitations, the Left-based trade unions came together, each maintained its organizational and ideological identity. However, there has not been absolute unity among the INTUC, BMS and HMS [12].

IC.3.1. INDUSTRIAL CONTEXT FOR DISCUSSION

The Nation-wide Strike of 2016

On 2 September 2016, an estimated number of 1,800 lakh Indian public sector workers went on a 24-hour nation-wide general strike. Ten CTUs participated in the strike bringing many government-run organizations and transportation services to a standstill. The strikers protested in demand for social security including universal health care and an increased minimum wage. It was considered as a strike having the involvement of the largest supporters of strikers in human history in India. This strike cost the economy up to 1,800 lakh rupees (£2 billion), according to an industry group.

The government made a concession by raising the unskilled workers' daily minimum wages by ₹104, which the trade unions considered as 'anti-worker and anti-people' policy of the government. Not only banks, power stations and public transport but also schools and colleges were closed as a precautionary measure in Bangalore, and 4,200 buses sat idle in Haryana. Mumbai and Delhi avoided major disruptions but surgeries were delayed at a major hospital in the capital, while nurses demonstrated outside. Protesters also blocked railway tracks and roads in Assam, Uttar Pradesh and Odisha.

The trade unions had 12 demands in the charter, including a demand for ₹692 in the daily minimum wages, universal social security and a ban on foreign investment in the country's railway, insurance and defence industries. Only one major trade union pulled out of this national strike, that is, the BMS.

3.3.9. A More Inclusive Labour Union Movement

The national trade unions in the early years of liberalization had neglected the unionization of the workers in the informal sectors. There had been two reasons for the same.

1. The ease of organizing formal sector workers (in terms of economies of scale in organizing, high pay offs and so on).
2. The high costs of organizing workers in the informal sector and the perception of the mainstream unions was that over time informal sector will be absorbed into the formal sector.

The mainstream unions revived their organizational outlook towards the workers in the informal sectors as a result the membership count increased so also the support to the trade union movements. Such trade unions had the registration in the informal sectors and one such example is 'SEWA', the most notable among them, which was registered as a trade union. The National Alliance of Street Vendors of India (NASVI), initiated by SEWA, is another organization. The Government of India initiated for the formulation of 'National Policy for Street Vendors' due to the pressure exerted by such organizations [11].

3.3.10. Changing Trend of Labour–Management Conflicts

There had been a significant change in the emerging nature of the management and the working class conflicts. The two emerging nature of conflicts had been on issues like the registration and the recognition of trade unions as the negotiating agency on behalf of the workers. The employer's preference for working in a situation of trade union-less organizations had been the cause for such conflicts. Few instances of such nature of disputes as discussed in the preceding part of the chapter are:

- The organizational efforts of formation and registration of a trade union of workers in Honda Motorcycle and Scooter Ltd in Haryana in 2005 and the struggles that followed, thereafter.
- HMIL in 2008 refused to recognize the labour union, namely the HMIEU. The management victimized the union leaders and sought to reach a collective agreement with the workers' council which provoked workers' protests and agitations.
- MRF preferred a 'company union' to a union formed by the majority of the workers in its plant at Arakkonam in Tamil Nadu, and conflict in the form of strikes, lockout and litigation started for this initiative.
- The Italian Graziano Trasmissioni India Private Limited in Greater Noida, in October 2009, on union negotiation led to killing of a senior officer of the organization followed by serious labour problems.
- The problem between the labour union and the management leading to the killing of a senior HR officer, and further conflicts between the union and the management, in Pricol Limited in Coimbatore in Tamil Nadu.
- The labour problem in 2012 in Maruti, resulting in killing of a senior manager and labour disputes led to very high production losses because of the resistance created by the management to consider to recognize a newly formed trade union in their Manesar plant.

3.3.11. Changing Demographics of Workforce in India

The average age of the workers working in the manufacturing, service and IT sectors in India is low as compared to other developing nations across the globe. The average age of the workers in the newly set up plants in the country had been in the range of 26–30. The employees in this workforce, referred as the Gen-Y employees, possess a different approach to works. Such a group of employees ischaracterized by high aspirations, self-reliant and independent. Gen-Ys are more technology savvy and are eager to take up responsibility, so are more productive at their work. They also have the ability to effectively communicate and articulate their ideas and thoughts.

3.3.12. Role of Social Media in Changing Worker–Management Relationship

Social media have impacted the personal lifestyle, work life, mindset, mode of communication and expectation of the present working class, thereby creating interests for work-life balance. With the advent and proliferation of social media, which is accessible through the smartphones, raising awareness among workers through Facebook, Twitter and other social media communication sites has taken a quantum jump. The technology used across the globe is becoming identical and similar, so are the thought process and the expectations. The Gen-Y group of employees being able to communicate with their counterparts in foreign countries are impacted by the developments worldwide.

3.3.13. Changing Political Environments in the Indian Context and Single Party as a Majority Power

A single political party as the majority party in power at the Centre and their changing focus on industrialization, with the approaches and initiatives, for example, 'Make in India', 'Digital India', 'Skill India', 'Smart Cities' has isolated the controls of the political institutions of the labour unions. A trend for formation of labour unions having no affiliation from any political bodies has developed. Such changes can be linked to a number of factors:

- Employers and employers' associations used the changing political environment and support to put pressure on trade unions and the organized labour bodies for weakening the collective bargaining powers of the trade unions.
- Economic internationalization due to globalization has created scope for competitive positioning of the product and business creating areas like production, trade and investment free from the intervention of the trade barriers.

3.4. The Changing IRS in India

IRS in India, since the economic liberalization announced in 1991, was more determined by the institutions decided by the government (state) and the objective was non-suppression of the workers' rights. The procedures for settling the industrial disputes were compulsory adjudication, conciliation and lengthy arbitration. The conditions of employment were defined for ensuring against exploitation, through various labour legislations and case laws of various courts. The laws and the provisions of the standing orders were executed. The objective of the government during the regulation era was to maintain industrial peace. There appears to exist a 'social pact' between trade unions, employers and the state whereby trade unions promised industrial peace for organizational growth and job security, and in return, both employers and trade unions accepted state regulation [13].

So the general and acceptable perception was that during the regulation era the working class could count on the judiciary as one of their allies. Whereas with time the focus changed. As is evident in the case of Bajaj Auto in the year 2013, the labour union leaders surrendered by withdrawing from the 50 days long strike, unconditionally. The reason for such shift in IR was primarily the changing Indian industrial context.

3.4.1. Redefining IR in the Emergent Indian Context

The economy being challenged by the globalized market, technology and the knowledge era, and the world of intangibles (media, software and services) replacing the world of the tangibles (atoms, objects, steel and oil) have profoundly impacted the HRM practices and IRC. In addition to such exogenous challenges, the changing macroeconomic conditions of the Indian economy, the new initiatives of the government to facilitate the growth of industries and the economy, with its inbuilt ambitious economic growth plan, looking beyond its own economic horizon and with the strength of the available manpower skilled enough for contributing to higher quality and quantity, at a competitive cost the world of Indian works have changed. The contemporary 'information age', the knowledge era and the innovations in capital formation have become the only recognized sources of economic prosperity. In the Indian context, the four forms of capital (as indicated in the following) have a critical interdependency and contribute to each other thereby facilitating growth.

1. Human capital (labour and intelligence, culture and organization)
2. Financial capital (cash, investments, monetary instruments)
3. Manufactured capital (infrastructure, machines, tools and factories)
4. Natural capital (resources, living systems and ecosystems)

The changing paradigm challenges the actors of IR in the emerging Indian context thereby the goal of IR in the changing emerging situation is 'managing the disputes/differences between the management and the trade union thereby creating enablers which facilitate productivity'. The state (the government) being one of the actors of IR has the basis to proceed with the predisposed notion that industrial peace would facilitate higher industrial productivity. But in the emerging changes as discussed, there is a greater need for IRS, which addresses the redefined situations in the emerging knowledge economy.

3.5. A Theory of IR for a Knowledge Economy

The plethora of changes that the knowledge era brings have caused changes in the IRS. There emerges the need for an IR model that seeks to explore and explain the current opportunities and adopts itself as a practice. It also logically explains the casual relationships to the problems. The present model recommends IRS which is a more dynamic approach to the concept of IR [14]. The model is fundamentally designed under the foundations of:

1. The model recognizes the interaction between the actors of IR, that is, the management, the workers and the government. Such interactions are assumed to be happening at the local, national as well as at the international levels. The interactions also include the networked relationship in which there is constant interphase between the parties for addressing each other's business interests. The model recognizes a two-way complex interaction between employers, government and unions in a broader political, social and economic environment.
2. The actors have their individual as well as their combined interests. Such interests are also impacted by the economic, social and political environments (including the market and technology) as well as the legal environments in the local, national and global context. The systems and the sub-systems of these broad environmental (local and international) systems include various groups and sub-groups, for example, community groups, user groups, NGOs, shareholders, ethical groups, families and women, religion, the level of academic excellence and the art and crafts which impact the three actors.

   The principal actors, as stated above, include the management, the labour union representing the body of labour and the state (government) interphased with the industrial, political, cultural economic and legal environments of the business. The interphase is presented in Figure 3.2.
3. The model recognizes the role as well as the impact of the international bodies. The example of such external bodies may include international NGOs, MNCs, offshore outsourcing business, globally networked community groups (e.g., ILO, affiliated labour unions, United Nations Organisation [UNO], IMF, the World Bank and other agencies) which influences, or

Figure 3.2   **The Principal Actors' Interphase with Contextual Factors**

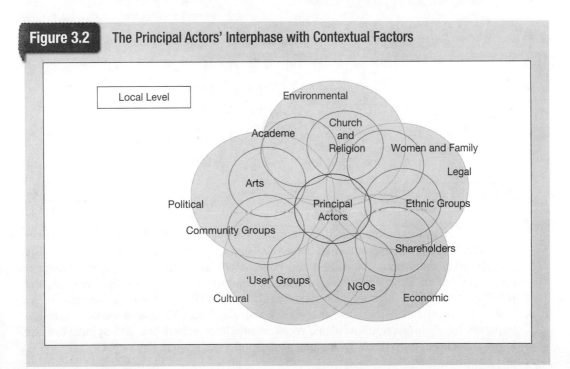

Figure 3.3   The International Factors Impacting the IRS

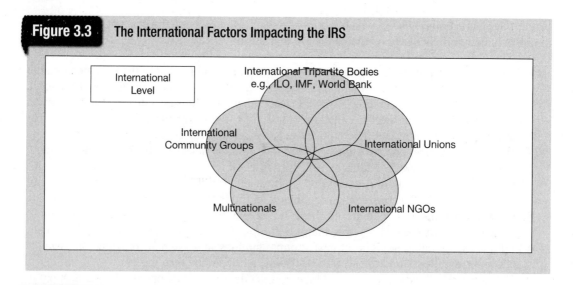

Figure 3.4   The Interphase of the Local/National Context with the International Context

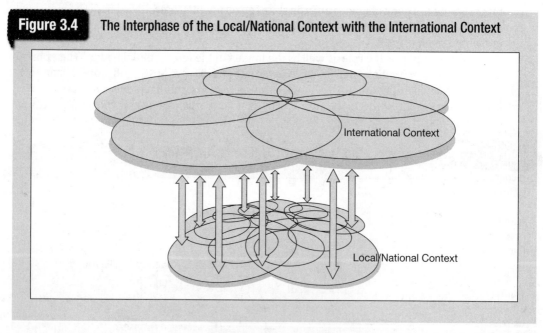

are influenced by international bodies, thereby impacting the IR. The international tie-ups of the labour unions with their affiliated bodies also impact the IRS. The actors of IR, that is, the management, the labour union and the government are influenced by the initiatives, recommendations and norms set by such international organizations thereby influencing the IRS. Figure 3.3 shows the interphase of various international bodies with the actors.

4. The actors being in the local/national context interface with the international bodies are impacted by the prescriptions, ideas, recommendations, experience and opinions of the internal bodies to form the IRS. The interphase model is shown in Figure 3.4.

The interphases at the local, national and international levels of the actors establish that the knowledge era necessitates a fundamental reconsideration of a broad spectrum of assumptions and theories upon which social, political, environmental and economic decisions have been made. Business is being encouraged to view organizations as living systems in which complex networks and systems contribute to a dynamic value rather than as static structure. The business organizations are being encouraged in practice to develop trust, motivation and emotional intelligence of their employees by recognizing and developing the psychological contract in the employment relationship.

5. Finally, the model recognizes the need to develop new networks and partnerships between the traditional industrial parties and community groups on any issue of mutual interests. It assumes to develop 'communities of interest' within structurally separated groups, which in practice becomes 'communities of practice' across these structurally separated groups. It results in the all likely chance of the future partnerships between the industrial parties (particularly unions and employer associations) to become more long term, enabling non-union groups to have some sort of ownership of the unionized activities. A new role of the trade unions and partnership between the employer and employees is the ultimate outcome.

The theory is proposed in consideration of the need for flexible structures to accommodate between the actors of IR instead of a rigid, structured relationship as is presupposed under the traditional IR concept. It provides a proactive solution in a predictive platform to comprehend and initiate actions for the likely things to happen.

C.3.3. Case for Discussion — Case of ICLR, Visiting and Investigating after 18 July 2012 on MSWU Complaint

The workers at MSIL, Manesar unit, decided to form an independent trade union, believing that the existing trade union of Gurgaon unit was a pocket union of the management and was not representing their interests. The newly formed trade union, after a long period of struggle, could get their union recognized by the Labour Department of Haryana. Thus, the union named Maruti Suzuki Workers Union (MSWU) was registered, but MSIL refused to negotiate with the new trade union in good faith.

After two months of MSIL's refusal to involve MSWU, on 18 July 2012, the management negotiated with MSWU, and in course of the negotiation process, a supervisor misbehaved with a worker, causing break out of violence at the MSIL-Manesar facility. It is reported that MSIL management brought thugs known as 'bouncers' into the workplace, dressed as workers, to instigate violence. The violence caused the death of one management official and many other officers and workers were injured.

The police arrested 147 MSIL-Manesar workers. MSIL dismissed 546 permanent workers and 1,800 contract workers.

The trade union claimed before the International Commission for Labor Rights (ICLR) that there were violations of workers' rights.

ICLR, a 501(c)(3) non-profit organization under the USA law, is based in New York. ICLR coordinates the pro bono work of a global network of lawyers, who are committed to advancing workers' rights through legal research, advocacy and cross-border collaboration, using cutting-edge knowledge and technology of international and domestic legal mechanisms.

ICLR believes in the principle that all working people have certain core rights, which this body is committed to defend. The objectives of ICLR are as follows:

- To create scope for the workers to form and join unions, and ensure the workers to bargain collectively for better conditions at work.

- To ensure that the workers earn enough to support themselves and their families so that children do not have to work.
- To ensure the workers to work freely, without force or coercion.
- To make the world of work and the workplace free from discrimination.

Highlights on MSIL

Year	Development
1981	Maruti Udyog Limited (MUL) was created as a public sector enterprise.
1983	MUL entered into a license and joint-venture agreement with Suzuki Motor Co. Japan, which acquired 26 per cent equity and brought in technology and management systems. MUL began production in 1984 at the mother plant of the company at Gurgaon, Haryana.
1987	Suzuki raised its equity stake in MUL to 40 per cent.
1992	Suzuki was allowed through a shareholder agreement to raise its equity to 50 per cent, following which MUL ceased to be a public sector enterprise.
2002	MUL was privatized with the government selling the controlling interest to Suzuki. The first tranche of the government equity was sold through a public offer.
2003	Maruti was listed on the stock exchange.
2006	Second plant at Manesar was set up.
2007	MUL changed its name to Maruti Suzuki India Limited (MSIL). Under the stewardship of MSIL, the company acquired a corporate structure with Suzuki Motor Co. in Japan. Suzuki's majority shareholding was 54.3 per cent.

ICLR convened an international delegation to investigate alleged violations of workers' and trade union rights at the Manesar plant of MSIL. The workers had alleged that dozens of workers had been dismissed and detained without trial, merely for exercising their right to form and join a trade union of their choice. These rights, for example, freedom of association and collective bargaining, are protected as a fundamental right.

The delegation, which included labour lawyers and labour rights experts from the United States, Japan, France, South Africa and India, met widely with workers and their families, civil society organizations including trade unions, public authorities and industry associations. The officers of MSIL refused a meeting in spite of multiple requests.

The delegation visited India from 25 to 31 May 2013.

In their efforts to research on the problem, they had:

- Meetings with members of the committee of MSWU.
- Meetings with other terminated workers of the MSIL Manesar plant including members of the provisional committee of MSWU as well as their families.
- Discussions with local, national and regional trade union representatives. The group met the national leadership of the AITUC, CITU and HMS, and the South Asia Regional Director of the global union federation. It also met plant-level union leaders from the Gurgaon-Manesar-Dharuhera industrial areas.
- Consultations with MSWU's legal counsel, Raghubir Singh Hooda and Rajendra Pathak.
- Interviewed the high-level administrative officials of Haryana, including the Director General of Police in Chandigarh, the Commissioner of Police in Gurgaon and the Joint Labour Commissioner in Chandigarh.
- Meeting with the Haryana Human Rights Commission.

- Meetings with representatives of the Confederation of Indian Industries (CII) and the Associated Chambers of Commerce and Industry of India (ASSOCHAM).
- Reviewed key documents related to the dispute between MSIL and the workers at its Manesar plant, including tripartite and bipartite agreements, court records and police reports.

The delegation established that:

1. The management of MSIL was engaged in significant violations of law with respect to the right to freedom of association, the right to collective bargaining and the right to equal pay for equal work, protected under ILO Conventions 87, 98 and 111.
2. The labour department has been ineffective in ensuring the rule of law.
3. The police has transgressed its powers in ways that amount to gross and inappropriate interference in industrial disputes, and yet failed to act to protect industrial peace when it should have.

To ensure that justice is not further or forever denied, the delegation recommended:

1. Immediate release of 147 MSIL workers.
2. Haryana state police to stop arbitrary arrests of workers. The police must also end the harassment of workers and their families.
3. The constitution of an independent and impartial judicial enquiry to investigate the full scope of events that led up to the industrial violence on 18 July 2012, as well as subsequent events, including but not limited to the custodial torture of workers.
4. The full reinstatement of all workers who were at MSIL-Manesar as of 17 July 2012, whether permanent or precarious workers.
5. Enforcement of tripartite machinery—bringing together the state labour administration, employers' representatives and workers' representatives.
6. To ensure that MSIL enters into constructive good faith negotiations with the union of the workers' choice.
7. Haryana Human Rights Commission to investigate the abuses outlined above.

Case Questions

1. ICLR is an independent body. Please indicate the reasons for ICLR visiting and investigating the incidence of 18 July 2012 at MSWU.
2. How bodies like ICLR would be impacting the actors of IR and IRS?

(For teaching aids, refer the instructor's manual.)

The need for a working concept of IR was felt as the contextual factors impacting IRS underwent a sea change. While emphasizing the need and importance of a working concept of IR, Hyman, in 1975 stated, 'The whole point of an explicit theoretical perspective is to provide a framework within which the complex detail of the real world can be organized and thus understood...'. A working concept calls for an all-inclusive and holistic approach to the subject and thereby needs to be redefined.

Ghosh and Ray proposed a working concept of IR by defining IR as

The sum total of employment relations, addressing the overall socio-political, legal, economic, psychological, technological and corporate dimensions in the industrial set-up involving the mutual participation of employer and employees in an environment regulated by the state, the cumulative output of which determines the collective human factor involved in industrial production [15].

3.6. Working Concept of IR

A working concept of IR essentially includes:

1. The relationships between employer and the employees, arising out of terms of employment.
2. The exogenous factors influencing such relationships, for example, the structures, rules and laws, technology and so on are also influenced by the social, economic, political and technological features emerging from the context of the business and the organization.
3. The spirit of cooperation and adjustment by way of accommodating with each other (management and the labour union). The interest is mutual within the determined/established rules for coexistence.

The above definition considers a 'systems approach' to the concept of IR which implies that there exists a set of inputs, and in a given process results in the output. The inputs to the process are considered and termed as the 'core dimensions' and include 'sociopolitical, legal and socioeconomic dimensions' (Figure 3.5).

3.6.1. Set of Inputs

Sociopolitical: The sociopolitical dimension as pointed by Budhwar would include the impact of social relations, political contacts, caste, religion, economic power and so on. Such factors in the Indian context and organizations contribute substantially to impact IRS. The broad contributing factors to this dimension are as follows:
- Level of collective bargaining
- Employer initiated decentralization
- Union membership and affiliation

As the sociopolitical objectives are linked with the overall economic activities of the nation, very often policy aspects of doing business get impacted or changed. Such changes involve the actors of IR. Issues like national confederations of employers facing the common threat of globalization are normally followed by policy changes by the government for the protection of the domestic industries. There had been other approaches to address the threats of globalization, for example, conscious and joint strategic changes in business models by the federation of employers for confronting the common challenge of globalization or introduction of new institutional norms either by the government with the acceptance of the federation of employers and the trade unions. These changes in the models of doing business impact the approaches to collective bargaining by the trade unions in consensus with the government and the employers, strategies of managing trade unions by the management and In turn the approaches of the trade unions to such policy including reframing their internal policies to manage the members.

Legal: The legal aspects help to understand the legal rights and obligations of the trade unions and the management in the spheres of management and organizational context for business. The phenomenon like historical disagreements among trade unions, management and the government that have prevented the adoption of a standard mechanism for

Figure 3.5   Systems Approach to IR

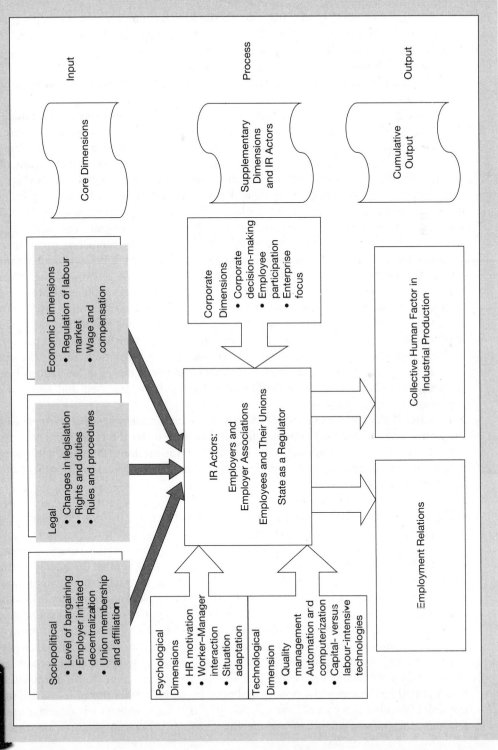

considering the recognition of trade union in the Indian context is explained through these factors. The broad contributing factors to this dimension are as follows:

- Changes in legislations by the government for business reasons
- Rights and duties of the actors and their stakeholders
- Rules and procedure framed by the actors to control business and relationship within the legal framework

The labour laws in India have a history of about 125 years. The labour laws emanate from the constitutional provisions of India. The 44 central labour laws and about 100 state laws, which constitute to the voluminous labour laws in India, are initiatives for 'establishment of social justice' in the country. The labour legislation in India had been instrumental in shaping the IR since the objectives of labour laws include protection of workers from exploitation, facilitate harmonious IR and providing machineries for settling industrial disputes and promoting welfare of workers. The labour legislations are sensitive to the working class without ignoring the nation's objective of economic development. Such sensitive nature of the labour laws is evident from the existing number of labour laws and the frequencies of their amendments. A politico-legal approach helps to understand the historical disagreements among the actors of IR, that is, trade unions, management and government. For example, there has been a continuing difference on the issue of recognition of trade unions in India. The government has prevented the adoption of a standard mechanism for the recognition of trade unions in India. This has resulted in high degree of freedom to the management to frame practising norms which more suitable to their context. There has been increasing trends to change the legislations to suit the specific context and objectives, resulting in changes in the rights and duties of the actors of IR. The state governments having the rule-making authority have designed and adopted rules appropriate to their contexts.

Economic: The socio-economic dimension helps in understanding social partnerships and the formal and informal agreements may be voluntary or by the course of law arrived at between the government, employer groups and the trade unions (industry/national level), explaining and addressing the economic and social needs. The broad contributing factors to this dimension are as follows:

- Regulation of labour market
- Wages and compensation regulations as well as the standard practices, including the benefits

The socio-economic dimension helps in understanding the 'social partnership' emerging from the industrial agreements between the parties (actors), that is, the management, the workers represented either at the individual level or through trade unions and the government. The actors, having their own objectives, frame the socio-economic dimension. It includes aspects such as payment of wages (wage structures) and other issues related to wages (including the long-term wage settlement, arrived out of negotiated outcomes), the tax structure, the constituents of overall social welfare which are tailored for the employees at large (rules framed by the government), attaching special importance to certain sectors for ensuring economic development (decided by the government from time to time and incorporated in the industrial policy) and production objectives linked to market and its dynamics (decided as a part of business policy by the management). For example, the need for the policymakers in Indian organizations to pay serious attention while designing policies on internal labour market were highlighted in the works of Budhwar in 2003. Such factors, as highlighted by him, include social relations, political contacts, caste, religion and economic power, which are unique to the Indian context [16].

The set of inputs may change (may have both inclusion and exclusion) depending on the context, priorities of the actors, logic of the business and its implication for society at large.

3.6.2. The Process

The process of achieving organizational effectiveness is facilitated by the 'supplement dimensions' that include the corporate dimensions (explaining the management and its control system focused on achieving the physical aspects of the enterprise), the psychological dimensions (explaining the human aspects of the enterprise) and the technological dimensions (explaining the man and the machine interface facilitating for achieving the physical aspects of the enterprise, that is, quality product at minimum cost). These dimensions are the internal processes and the systems that facilitate the actors in achieving their respective objectives as well as the corporate objectives. The three sub-components as specified above are interrelated and they either complement or supplement each other. The sub-components of the supplement dimensions include the following:

Corporate Dimensions

- Corporate decision-making
- Employee participation
- Enterprise focus

Psychological Dimensions

- HR motivation (policy and practices)
- Workers–Managers interaction
- Adaption to situation (attitude, individual and the group)

Technological Dimensions

- Quality product at optimum cost
- Capital- versus labour-intensive technology
- Automation and computerization

The corporate dimensions facilitate setting of corporate objectives, and align the strategies for achieving the same with the help of corporate policy, management style and involvement of people, who are the prime contributors to business and corporate vision.

The psychological dimensions, which initiate from the HR policies practised in the organization (principally flow from the management) internally involve the people by forming internal equitation among themselves and the supervisory class (which constitute the culture of the organization). Within the ambits of conflicts and cooperation and the principles of legal obligations, the actors adapt to the context in mutual interest.

The technological dimensions include technology and its upgradation, as well as changes which are adopted for the business objectives. The adoption of new technology normally focuses on better quality of product at lower costs as well as increasing individual productivity. Management strategies, for example, shifting from labour-intensive to capital-intensive technology, moving towards automation and computerization are certain initiatives. Such changes highly impact the work life of the workers. With the change in technology, which is unavoidable in the dynamic market, the expected skill for performing the jobs changes. Workers having attitude to resist to changes, very often react to such changes by expressing militancy behaviours by striking, remaining absent from duties and at times, resigning in extreme situations. Such behaviours have impacted the socio-economic agendas of the workers. Examples of changes which have normally been resisted by the workers include automation of the works, since it threatens their job security, or situations of changes which do not categorically explain why they need to change. The cumulative output is expected to achieve appropriate employee relations and collectivism of human factors in the industrial production.

The government over years have assumed the role of a controller of this relationship and facilitator of this cooperation and determines the policies and rules in terms of social norms and justice.

C.3.4. Case for Discussion   Restructuring the Hiring Process of Temporary Workers

After the management's nightmare incidence of 18 July 2012, a clash between workers and managers at Maruti, Manesar plant, resulting in killing of a senior manager and injuries to several officials, including some of the Japanese staff, the management initiated for winning the trust of their people.

The management alleged that the contract and permanent workers of the unit had planned the violence. So they went for dismissing 1,700 contract and 546 permanent workers. The Haryana police arrested 147 workers and charged them with murder and rioting.

During the years 2011–2012, permanent and contract workers together went on strike thrice, and ultimately the management responded to the same with lockouts. The agitation caused losses of over ₹2,500 crore and a fall in the company's share price by 6 per cent. Finally, the management initiated a series of changes in their management practices including restructuring the hiring process of the temporary workers.

The hiring process of the temporary workers was significantly restructured. The new process replaced the practice of hiring temporary workers through labour contractors and a system of direct hiring was introduced. This new category of employees was called 'company temps'. Such workers would work for seven months and then be laid off for five months. After the lay-off period was over, workers could be recalled for another seven months, in case the need for similar competency of employees arose. The salary of these 'company temps' was decided at ₹14,000 per month, which was about half the salary of the permanent workers.

To safeguard against hiring only local labour, which used to happen while hiring workers on contract through contractors, the HR managers were deputed to several states—Punjab, Madhya Pradesh, Odisha—to hire 'company temps' on the basis of tests conducted at Industrial Training Institutes in these places. Such a process of direct hiring of 'company temps' was expected to promote loyalty, offer labour flexibility in months of shifting demand and give the company greater control in determining who gets hired.

The 'company temps', being directly controlled by the management, were expected to be more loyal and were expected to form the future talent pipeline for expanding the regular workforce.

People Connect

The company has already hired more than 2,000 'company temps' in the MSIL's assembly lines at Manesar plant. An audit done through a third-party survey rated the new system with the emerging culture at 90 per cent.

The People Connect Model of MSIL

Maruti's Toolkit to Improve Worker Relations

Workforce Breakup

5,898: Permanent workers

4,088: Contract workers (being phased out)

2,088: Company temps (new category, offering better terms and security than contract system)

993: Apprentices

Workers As People

360 degree knowledge: Familiarise workers with entire manufacturing process. 834 workers covered. Also change roles and offer skill development programmes

Family visits: Families can visit plants, see work stations, interact with general manager

Communication meetings: Workers start day with supervisor meeting, where a safety oath is taken and work-related issues discussed. In a monthly meeting, company shares sales figures, market conditions and strategy

Better ergonomics: Review processes to reduce worker fatigue and injury. For instance, a worker had to bend 360 times in a shift to clamp a particular harness; eliminated by bringing up the contraption to arm level

Workers As Partners

Suggestion Schemes
Two suggestions per month expected from each operator. About 353,000 suggestions, from 75% of workforce, received in 2012-13. Example: a worker noticed the motor of the shuttle conveyor for body transfer continued to run even after doing its function. Excessive usage reduced to 10 seconds, from 100 seconds; annual saving: ₹17 lakh

Recognise Talent
Workers with ideas for big improvements are taken off the line to coordinate with kaizen (continuous improvement of processes) team to implement changes

Cost-reduction Measures
Drive by group patriarch Osamu Suzuki to reduce weight of components. Suggestions from 200 workers led to 700 improvements. Savings in 2012-13: ₹125 cr

Source: Karunakaran N. How Maruti is trying to win back workers' trust, Economic Times. 1 April 2014. Available from http://economictimes.indiatimes.com/articleshow/33034519.cms?utm_source=contentofinterest&utm medium=text&utm_campaign=cppst

Case Questions

1. Explain how difference in the approach for hiring as well as dealing with people would impact the IR context of the organization.
2. 'Labour by nature is an agitated group. Indicate how the management's initiatives would reduce labour unrest and thereby develop harmonious IR.

3.7. Employee Relations

The terms 'employment relations' and 'employee relations' are being increasingly used in recent years to replace the term 'industrial relations'. Kaufman and others have argued that IR need to become 'employment relations' in order to conceptualize the new trends in IR [17, 18].

Using terms like 'employee relations' rather than 'IR' redefines the boundaries of the subject to include all employment relationships, rather than only involving unionized manual workers of the factories [19].

With the emergence of HRM, emergent technological changes, massive restructuring within organizations and restrictive legislation applicable to the labour and decrease in union membership, there has been a steady decline in the importance of IR. These factors have considerably reduced the power of the labour unions and thereby their roles, resulting in a visible 'end of institutional IR'. With the complexities emerging from the globalized market and the emergent globalized work culture, which are the results of the collaborative business ventures between universal brands, a balanced concept of employee relations is being talked about worldwide. Globalization has enabled free flow of resources, know-how, technology and people competency.

3.7.1. Employee Relations and IR

IR, in general, is the study of relations between the employees and employers. There are various factors at the workplace that shape up the relations between workers, employers and the government. The field of IR came into existence with the advent of the industrial revolution as an important tool to understand the complex relations between employers and employees. From the perspective of the workers, IR means better wages, safety at workplace, job security and training at workplace, on the other hand, IR for an employer would imply all about productivity, conflict resolution and employment laws. So IR is inevitably associated with trade unions, collective bargaining and industrial action.

The term employee relations lays stress on the processes of interpersonal relationships among individuals as well as the behaviour of individuals as members of groups. The focus of employee relations is on the behaviour of individuals, where moral and social elements predominate. The term industrial relations is comprehensive covering human relations and the relations between the employers and workers in an organization as well as matters regulated by law or by specific collective agreement arrived at between trade unions and the management. IR comprehensive covering human relations is generally understood to refer to the relationship between employers and employees collectively.

Business managers recognize that their employees are the most important part of a business and through effective management a business can gain the competitive advantage. The skills, knowledge and creativeness of employees being the main potential drivers that drive the business over its competitors and drive the profitability, there is a shifting focus for such business drivers. Employee relations focuses on the process of finding the people the business needs, developing their skills, knowledge, talents, careers and motivating and maintaining their commitment to the business. The purpose of employee relations is to deal with the people, the business employees and the issues arising from their employment. Acquiring, developing, maintaining and motivating staff are all aspects that are covered by the concept.

'Employee relations' is a concept that is being preferred over IR because of the realization that there is much more at the workplace than IR could look to cover. In general, employee relations can be considered to be a study of relations between employees as well as employer and employees by resolving conflicts and help in improving productivity of the organization by increasing motivation and morale of the employees. The concept believes in providing information to employees regarding the organization so that they have a better understanding of the objectives and policies of the management.

3.7.2. More Frequently Used Terminology

The terminology of 'employee relations' is being used more frequently worldwide. The reasons for the same are normally attributed to the following:

- Falling union memberships around the world have made people realize that relations between employers and employees are more important than the focus given to these relations by IR.
- It is human beings called employees that form the backbone of all operations in an organization and the study of relations between employers and employees are more important than the laws and institutions that govern relations at the workplace. Employment relations is distinctly different from IR because the concept is an attempt to fulfil the criteria of equity, efficiency and voice of the employees. A good employment relationship strikes a balance between these three.

Efficiency and the effective use of resources, being clear implications of economic prosperity, are the focused business objectives of all organizations. For achieving these objectives, the people behind the wheels, that is, the human element at work are entitled to equitable, fair treatment together with opportunities to voice their opinions which need to be listened by their employers. In other words, the principles of equity which ensure equality in terms of economic benefits and rewards, with scopes for a meaningful contribution (voice) at the decisions-making levels (at the individual and collective levels) are being encouraged as management practices. Organizations are facilitating the voices

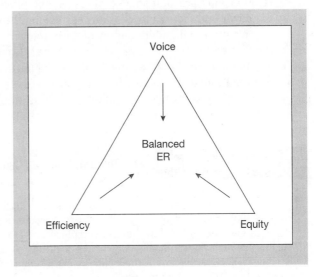

to be heard through focus group discussions, employee surveys, grievance procedures, trade union representation in management and so on. Striking a balance between efficiency, equity and voice of the employees by the employer generates trusting behaviour in the employees, and thereby creates a committed group of employees.

The employees' occupational commitments contribute to the employment relations. Every employee's occupational commitments construct relationships and behaviours at works, which are distinctly different from the conflicting and collectivism approaches conditioned in the stereotyped IRS. 'Except limited choices, occupational commitments are found to be significantly positive' [20]. Bakker and Schaufeli justify that commitment is a crucial motivation for individuals and is a positive organizational behaviour [21].

The considered opinion on 'occupational commitment is that a psychological link exists between an individual and his occupation. In other words, it is the emotional and cognitive attachments to that occupation [22]. (Although there are relatively less works on the linkage between occupational commitment and IR in the Indian context, the theoretical foundations do not rule out the possibility of the links.)

3.7.3. The Difference between IR and Employee Relations

Some experts argue that there are identifiable differences between 'employment relations' and 'IR', whereas others argue that the concepts can be used interchangeably in all respects. The differences between IR and employment relations are as follows:

- IR focuses on employees as a collective body, whereas employment relations put a strong emphasis on employees as individuals.
- Employment relations are based on greater cooperation between management and employee, who being motivated adds value to the organization. Such employment relationships are outcome of management practices which generate trust between the employer and the employees, fairness among the employees, knowledge of works and the organization, and understanding of the employer about employees' aspirations and thereby draw attention to 'employee voice' gathered through a variety of channels (e.g., employee and union representatives involvement and participation).
- IR have come to dominate the workplace because of the need to deal with conflicts, mainly between workers and management, whereas employment relations deals with developing a working environment where conflict is less likely to occur.

C.3.5. Case for Discussion — The Shift from the Culture of IR to Employee Relations in Liberty Shoes Ltd

On 25 June 2006, around 9:30 AM, Mr Shammi Bansal, the Executive Director of Liberty Shoes Ltd, received a phone call from office of the District Magistrate, Karnal, Harayana. The voice on the other side told the executive director that the employees of Liberty Shoes Ltd have barricaded the Delhi–Chandigarh highway (both the sides of the highway) at Gharaunda (where Liberty Shoes Ltd has another manufacturing units). The incidence of picketing on the highway and blocking the free movement of the traffic was initiated around 7:00 AM. The number of employees of Liberty Shoes Ltd picketing on the highway was around 600 (employees from the units of Liberty Puram and Gharaunda[1]). The

[1] Liberty Puram unit is located on the Delhi–Chandigarh Highway, at 13 Mile Stone, G. T. Road, P. O. Bastara, Kutail, Distt. Karnal 132114. Gharaunda is also on the Delhi–Chandigarh highway located about 5 km away from Liberty Puram towards Delhi.

employees were demanding for immediate redressal of their demands through the intervention of the district administrative authorities and the labour department authorities.

At 9:30 AM on 25 June 2006, Mr Shammi Bansal, the Executive Director was in a meeting with his senior officers at the Liberty Puram unit of Liberty Shoes Ltd, and was busy in discussing on a never-before incident which happened on 24 June 2006 at Liberty Puram unit. Three members of the Board of Directors were also present in the meeting.

The Incidence of 24 June 2006

On 24 June 2006, four senior officers were manhandled by the workers at Liberty Puram unit of Liberty Shoes Ltd. The incident happened during the normal working hours in the factory. A mob of about 200 workers encircled the Deputy General Manager, Mr Narender Kumar Joshi in the shop floor and started enquiring on matters related to their pay hikes. Soon the news about the gherao of the deputy general manager (works) spread in the plant. The general manager (HR) with the general manager (works) and general manager (welfare) arrived at the spot to be a part of the discussion. The peaceful shop-floor standing discussion, in which all the four senior officers tried their best to convince the workers, turned to a platform for the trade union leaders to use slogans and provocative languages against the management. The four senior officers had no alternative but to continue to listen to the provocative anti-management slogans among the workers.

Since the initial discussion was quite peaceful, the four senior officers were not expecting the meeting to continue for a longer time, and second such acts of slogans and provocative languages were a never-before incidence so nothing untoward happening was not anticipated by them. The four officers tried to convince the trade union leaders to shift the meeting to the meeting room and peacefully discuss their issues. Since the trade union leaders were not convinced with the proposal, the four senior officers continued to remain silent on the issues. The impatient workers led by the trade union leaders suddenly became violent on the instigation and provocative languages of the trade union leaders. By the time the deployed security staff came to the spot and attempted to gently disperse the gathering mob, the union leaders became extremely violent and instigated the workers to manhandle the senior officers.

The Deputy General Manager, Mr Narender Kumar Joshi, was badly beaten and he was left unconscious in the shop floor. Mr S. C. Parida, General Manager (HR) was also beaten badly and pushed over a stitching machine, which resulted in sustaining serious injuries of broken ribs. Mr Lokesh Tyagi and Kulbhushan Sharma, General Manager (works) and Welfare Officer respectively, were manhandled and beaten badly causing serious multiple injuries on their body. The security people posted on duty rescued the officers and rushed them for medical aids. All the officials were rushed to the Civil Hospital, Karnal. Two of the officers, namely Mr Narender Kumar Joshi and Mr S. C. Parida were referred to Delhi for treatment since their conditions were critical. On reporting at the hospital in Delhi, the medical experts admitted them in the ICU. The medical treatment for the general manager (HR) and deputy general manager (works) continued for six weeks at Delhi.

Such incident of manhandling the senior officers had never happened before in Liberty Shoes Ltd. There had been stray incidence of manhandling of officers at the junior level earlier, but the senior officers were never manhandled. The incident was followed by a series of strikes by the trade union in all the three units of Liberty Shoes Ltd. The active union members forced all the workers to move out of the plants and suspend all the operations.

The Genesis of the Incidence

A trade union representing all the units of Liberty Shoes Ltd (at the material time the organization had units at Karnal, Liberty Puram and Gharaunda) was registered named 'Liberty Shoes Workers Union' in the year 2005. In September 2005, the trade union instigated the workers in all the units of Liberty

Shoes Ltd to go on a strike. Although no demand notice was submitted by the trade union, strike was resorted to on 3 September 2005 at the Gharaunda unit of Liberty Shoes Ltd. The trade union also blocked the Delhi–Chandigarh national highway. The busy Delhi–Chandigarh highway was blocked from 7:00 AM by the workers. The picketing on the road was lifted around 11:00 AM with the intervention of the state government authorities who assured to the agitating workers that they will expedite for early settlement of all the pending issues between the trade union and the management of Liberty Shoes Ltd.

The trade union resorted to a strike at Gharaunda unit of Liberty Shoes Ltd without any prior information to the management. No demand notice was pending for settlement on the date of striking. The trade union submitted a memorandum to the management on 5 September 2005. On 7 September 2005, a tripartite settlement was executed. The District Magistrate, Karnal and the DLC, Panipat were representing the government in the tripartite agreement. The agreement of 7 September 2005 addressed issues related to wages revision, permission for late attendance for five minutes a day for three times in a calendar month. The trade union undertook to maintain discipline in the plants and support a work culture favourable for achieving the targeted rate of productivity per worker. The terms of the settlement had no reference to the period of validity of the agreement.[2]

The tripartite agreement of 7 September 2005 was supposed to settle all differences between the management and the trade union. But the trade union resorted to another strike on 25 September 2005 while the tripartite agreement of 7 September 2005 was in vogue. The strike of 25 September 2005 was in violation of the agreement dated 7 September 2005. The terms of the agreement legally did not allow the trade union to go on such a strike, while during the active enforcement of the settlement dated 7 September 2005.[3] The act of indiscipline by the trade union was in violation of the assurances agreed by them in the settlement dated 7 September 2005. Finally, there were no pending issues of disputes between the trade union and the management.

The trade union raised a further list of demands through a demand notice issued to the management. Since the problems between the management and the trade union were escalating, conciliation meetings were called by the labour department authorities. The meetings were held on 28, 29 and 30 September 2005, in which the DLC, Panipat and the District Magistrate, Karnal, also participated.

On 1 October 2005, the trade union took an extreme step of confining Mr Shammi Bansal, the Executive Director of the company with other senior executives. The confinement of the executive director continued from 10:00 AM to 11:00 PM of 1 October 2005.

Such mounting pressure of the trade union resulted in signing a settlement before the ALC, Chandigarh, on 3 October 2005 under Section 12(3) of the Industrial Disputes Act, 1947 (ID Act). The agreement of 3 October 2005 addressed all financial demands of the trade union, assuring the management to provide further wages and benefit increases and in return the trade union agreed to give better production and to maintain discipline in the units. This settlement was for three years. With this, all salary-related demands were fully and finally settled.

The trade union resorted to another strike on 24 October 2005, which continued until 8 November 2005. The workers of all the three units were either provoked or forcefully restricted from joining duties by the trade union. Meanwhile, the management had moved a request before the Civil Court praying injunction, which was granted by the local Civil Court. But the injunction order of the court was violated by the trade union.

On 25 November 2005, Mr Pritam Sharma, Assistant Manager was beaten in his office by the trade union members. An FIR was lodged by the management in the local police station under sections 147/149/323 and 506 of the Indian Penal Code.

[2] Where no period is prescribed, the period of operation of the settlement is six months as per Section 19 of the Industrial Disputes Act, 1947.

[3] The Industrial Disputes Act, 1947, do not permit for strikes during the pendency of the settlement.

During this period, while Mr Shammi Bansal, the Executive Director, was on round inside the plant, two employees misbehaved with him, which resulted in initiating disciplinary action against these employees in accordance with the standing orders of the company.

The company had a system of different lunch timings for groups of employees engaged in the shop floors. The trade union took a decision to call all the workers for lunch at one time as fixed by them. This was a gross violation of the management's orders. The management in order to restore discipline in the plant initiated disciplinary action against such employees who had violated the management's order. This resulted in suspension of such employees pending domestic enquiry to the charges levelled against them.

The non-cooperation of the workers and failures in delivering in accordance with the production schedule resulted in failures to deliver the finished goods by the dealers. The management could realize that the situation will affect their market stake in no time.

The suspended employees moved before the conciliation officer requesting for an amicable settlement. On the intervention of the labour department and the district administration, a tripartite settlement was arrived on 16 January 2006 between the trade union and the management. The suspended employees were reinstated and undertakings were signed by them in the form of an agreement, which stated that discipline in the shop floor will be maintained and the workers will also honour the terms of the agreements dated 7 September 2005 and 24 November 2005 both in its letter and spirit.

In February 2006, the trade union raised a fresh demand notice, while the agreements of 7 September 2005, 24 November 2005 and the undertaking dated 16 January 2006 were in vogue. This was followed by a series of labour agitation. The trade union forced the workers to boycott the work by going on mass sick leave. In certain sections, the workers who reported for work resorted to 'go slow' as a protest.

Production was seriously affected by such attitude of the trade union. By the end of February 2006, the production figures registered a monthly loss of 40 per cent. Such uncontrolled situation continued until 17 June 2006, when the trade union raised another demand notice, demanding for higher bonus, wages increases, promotions to various categories of employees as per their interests, increase in DA and so on. To enforce their new demand notice, the trade union resorted to dharna.[4] The dharna started from 19 June 2006 and continued until 22 June 2006 resulting in complete suspension of work from 19 June 2006 to 22 June 2006.

The incident of 24 June 2006 was a never-before incident in Liberty Shoes Ltd. Four senior officers were manhandled mercilessly in the shop floor by the workers. Their lives were saved as they were timely rescued from the hands of the agitating trade union members and provided timely medical facility.

The production in the shop floors was totally stopped. The trade union continued to disallow the willing workers to resume on their duties. The company had about 4,000 employees working in its three units (Liberty Puram, Gharaunda and Karnal). On 25 June 2006, employees of the two units, that is, Liberty Puram and Gharaunda totally boycotted the work. Only 15–20 employees turned out at the Karnal plant, which had about 500 employees.

Hundreds of protesting workers of Liberty Footwear blocked National Highway No. 1 near Gharaunda in the morning of 26 June 2006. Police resorted to lathi charge after the workers pelted stones at them and refused to lift the blockade that continued for more than four hours, leading to nearly 10-kilometre-long queues of stranded vehicles on either side of the industrial town of Gharaunda. The clash between the workers and the police resulted in causing injury to six policemen.

[4] Dharna is an agitation of the workers when they leave the workplace and assemble at some conspicuous places, normally in front of the main entrance, and demonstrate for execution of their demands.

The incidence of blocking the highway on 26 June 2006 forced both the district administrative authorities and the labour department to have a series meeting with the agitating trade union and the management. The government finally by its order, dated 13 December 2006, prohibited strike. A memorandum of understanding was signed off on 22 December 2006 between the trade union, management and the government agency represented by the labour department and the district administration. The labour department helped in reaching a 'sahmati'[5] containing 'nine points' clarifying the conditions under which the striking workmen will be eligible to resume on their duties. The period allowed to the workmen for reporting on their duties was from 23 December 2006 to 31 December 2006 with a clear communication that 'after 31 December 2006 no stake could be given by workmen'.

The long agitation for about two years by the trade union, their action of resorting to acts of indiscipline both inside and outside the plant resulted in huge production losses, thereby losing the market stake in the competitive market situation. The management took a series of actions, within the legal framework available to them against the acts of indiscipline, manhandling, remaining away from the job without authority by the trade union and its members. This resulted in filing of 306 labour cases against the indisciplined workers, which were referred to the Labour Court, Panipat, for adjudication.

The years 2007–2009 witnessed the management's efforts to follow up the 306 cases before the Labour Court, and the criminal case for manhandling the officers inside the plant. The production during this period continued to be low. The marketing team was making efforts to regain the company's market stake but the production team was not able to gear up to the market demands.

In the annual board meeting in 2010, Mr Shammi Bansal, the Executive Director expressed his concern on the losing market stake and downswing in the business volume of the company. The total annual sales turnover which had registered slightly more than 500 crores INR in 2004 had been reduced to hardly 300 crores INR in 2010.[6]

The Organization

Liberty Shoes Ltd has been fashioning footwear since 1954. Presently, it figures among the top five manufacturers of leather footwear of the world producing more than 50,000 pairs of leather footwear a day using a capacity of more than three lakhs square feet of leather per month. Its annual sales turnover exceeding ₹1,000 crores as of date.

At present, Liberty's manufacturing base includes six facilities spread across different states in India. These production facilities are:

- Gharaunda, in the state of Haryana (approximately 95 km from Delhi)
- Liberty Puram, in the state of Haryana (approximately 102 km from Delhi)
- Karnal, in the state of Haryana (approximately 124 km from Delhi)
- Dehradun in the state of Uttarakhand (approximately 235 km from Delhi)
- Paonta Sahib in the state of Uttarakhand (approximately 267 km from Delhi)
- Roorkee in the state of Uttarakhand (approximately 172 km from Delhi)

Product Quality

The company is committed to quality and is an ISO 9001:2000 certification company. The products are quality tested under the able guidance of quality analysts. Further, for assuring production of proper quality products the following systems and tools were implemented:

---

[5] A Hindi word which means mutual agreement.
[6] Data source, balance sheet of the company.

- Kaizen was implemented in the year 2000 and practised throughout the organization.
- The concept of 5S was introduced in the year 2001.
- The company received ISO 9001:2000 certification.
- The company established waste management system.
- The company follows the ISES-200 norms to ensure social, health and environmental safety. These standards are closely monitored by Indo-German Export Promotion Council of India.
- The company also has an energy management system.

The Management's Initiative

The situation of labour unrest continued until 2007, resulting in serious losses in production and customers, thereby market stakes. In a situation when the labour department failed to control the situation as well as the legal process failed to create an environment of harmonious IR, the management started feeling the need for generating a wave of 'it's my job attitude' within the employees. The general workplace culture at the units of Liberty Shoes Ltd was not encouraging employees to proactively respond to the production needs. The courage to take the initiative was either totally lacking or existed at a low level. The work culture encouraged by the trade unions during more than two years alienated the workers. The feeling of alienation was natural, since a handful of employees were totally spoiling the work culture and were making the other employees behave as per their decision, the conscious and the duty-bound employees on returning to work felt guilty of all that had happened.[7] In one of the opinion surveys of 231 employees selected from and among the senior workers of the units of Liberty Puram, Gharaunda and Karnal, they expressed a serse of alienation and loss of confidence.

Mr Shammi Bansal, the Executive Director, after the financial closure of the financial year(s), 2007–2008, started meeting the senior workers of all the three major units (Liberty Puram, Gharaunda and Karnal). The units at Dehradun, Paonta Sahib and Roorkee were reasonably new units and had only the assembly lines. Structured communication meets were organized, and the executive director shared the company's performance figures for the year(s) 2007–2008. He expressed his concern on loss of market stake. He also welcomed suggestions from the workers on 'what they feel would be an appropriate way out from the situation'? No responses were received from any corner. The executive director declared in these communication meets that he would be available on specified dates and the workers were free to meet him without seeking any appointment. The dates were announced not only in the communication meets but also on notice boards. It was also announced that for any reason in case the executive director cannot visit any unit at the scheduled time, the same will also be notified to the workers.

The initial response to such an announcement was rather zero. The executive director with the HR head went around the shop floors on his visit to the units and the same became a regular feature. He discussed the production issues as well as the personal issues of the workers. The issues were addressed on the spot by giving appropriate solutions and the concerned functional heads were also involved. The actionable points were noted for records.

A time came when in case the executive director with the HR head was not visible at the appointed time and date, the workers became impatient and enquired from their respective supervisors about the executive director's programme for the day. In one of the opinion surveys, during the period, the supervisors expressed that a culture emerged where the workers became more keen in showcasing their performances and skills to the executive director, who had been constantly appreciating such aspects.

---

[7] The workers working in all the three units, Karnal, Liberty Puram and Gharaunda, hailed from the local villages. Liberty Shoes being a major and the oldest organization in this belt, to work in this organization is considered a matter of pride.

The dates of unit visit of the executive director:

S No.	Days	Units	Timings
1.	Monday, Wednesday	Liberty Puram	2:30–4:30 PM
2.	Thursday, Saturday	Gharaunda	2:30–4:30 PM
3.	Tuesday, Friday	Karnal	2:30–4:30 PM

With focus more on improving performance (both at the individual and group levels), the need was felt to change the culture the desire for which was coming from the experienced workers of the organization. The next step was to empower the employees of the organization in a planned way. This was the result of the continuous efforts of the executive to be close to the people. The management expected the employees to act proactively regardless of whether they are in a formal position of authority to deliver. Converting the disengaged employees into engaged employees and controlling criticism or dismissal of the employees' ideas and suggestions were the immediate needs in the organization. An employee empowerment process was planned out which is depicted in Figure 3.6 with emphasis on implementation of a 'communication process' across the organization, with focus on 'employee empowerment', 'employee development' and 'performance feedback to the employees'. This in totality constituted the 'employee empowerment model' at Liberty Shoes Ltd.

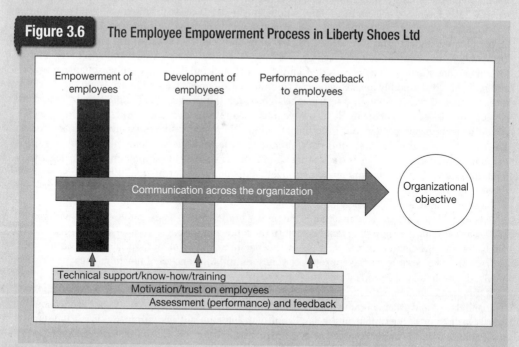

Figure 3.6   The Employee Empowerment Process in Liberty Shoes Ltd

An implementation plan of the model of employee empowerment was designed in consultation and involvement of the departmental heads. The departmental heads were made responsible for implementing the plan for results in their respective areas and departments.

The Plan

The four-stage implementation plan for employees' empowerment implemented in the organization is shown in Figure 3.7.

Figure 3.7 The Four-stage Implementation Plan

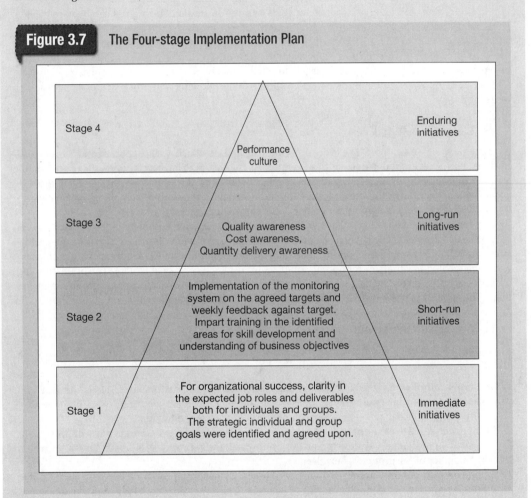

Stage 4	Performance culture	Enduring initiatives
Stage 3	Quality awareness, Cost awareness, Quantity delivery awareness	Long-run initiatives
Stage 2	Implementation of the monitoring system on the agreed targets and weekly feedback against target. Impart training in the identified areas for skill development and understanding of business objectives	Short-run initiatives
Stage 1	For organizational success, clarity in the expected job roles and deliverables both for individuals and groups. The strategic individual and group goals were identified and agreed upon.	Immediate initiatives

Stage 1: The Immediate Initiatives

The focus was on involving people for achieving higher performance, more involvement, engaging the workforce, providing them the benefits of higher delivery and ultimately empowering the employees. So the initiative started with drawing clarity on 'the delivery levels of the individual departments' and synchronizing the same with the organizational business plan. The organizational annual business plan was cascaded to the units, based on the unit's technical ability and human resource availability. The heads of the departments were trained to execute the business plan with a humanistic approach and to be close to the employees in the shop floor. (A training programme titled 'shop floor production heads' was designed to train the heads of the departments. The programme focused on 'how to do better than what had been happening'.)

Each shop-floor head and the employees at the supervisory level were made to understand their expected weekly production targets. (Organizational business goals cascaded to unit business goals, unit business goals cascaded to department goals, the annual unit business goals cascaded to weekly goals, which turned to weekly group goals). The weekly production targets were expressed in measurable parameters in terms of Quantity to be produced, Cost at which to be produced and Quality levels to be achieved. This led to a clear clarity on the expected deliverables at the individual and group levels. Setting the quantifiable targets for such departments was more a top-driven approach and was aligned with the business objective rather than following any other strategic methods of target setting.

Stage 2: Short-run Initiatives

A training session on the topic 'The Process Monitoring and Feedback' was conducted and this enabled the members of different department heads with the supervisors to have a clarity on the process to be adopted to bring efficiency and way to give regular feedback to the employees for involving them in achieving the business goals. The departmental heads acquired the skills of compiling respective performance data to have clarity on their respective performance against the target.

The departmental heads had meetings with the central reviewing authority on every Saturday on regular basis. The weekly performance data of each department were discussed to bridge the performance gaps (gap between actual performance and the target performance). A system of brainstorming was implemented as a practice for finding solutions for bridging performance gaps. The brainstorming process facilitated involvement, thereby putting the onus and pride of achieving the group targets on them. The actionable areas were noted and planned for further implementation.

Stage 3: Long-run Initiatives

The solutions to the problem areas, which were identified, were mostly in any of the following areas:

1. **Implementation of Kaizens** for performance improvement or cost compressions. The idea and Kiazen proposals came from the shop-floor employees. Employees were rewarded based on the quality of the proposal and actual cost compression or wastage reduction.
2. **Some process improvement** implemented for performance efficiency, productivity improvement and cost compression. A systematic process improvement approach was implemented, in which every member of the group was involved.
3. **Employee skill enhancement** for improving individual performance.
4. **Wastage reduction in some form**, that is, wastage of different forms in areas of raw material utilization, machine utilization and downtime reduction, energy utilization, human resource utilization, inventory size of raw material, finished goods inventory were addressed through involvement of employees in the shop floor.

Stage 4: Enduring initiatives

The enduring initiatives which were taken for result were:

- Communication through a properly designed 'communication plan'
- The motivating and the trusting process for empowering the employees

The above processes are detailed as follows.

Communication

The process of communication was designed and adopted across all the units. The objective of communicating across the organization at all levels was to achieve the following:

1. To establish and maintain a system of communicating with all HR employed directly or indirectly and involved in the process of delivery of final output (product).
2. To develop conscientious intrapersonal relationships all through the organization, both vertical and horizontal, thereby having an unhindered channel of information flow.

The structured communication model explained '*What*' (what to be communicated), '*Who*' (who is going to communicate), '*at what interval*' (at what interval/frequency such communications to be made), '*Whom*' (whom to communicate) and '*When*' (meeting schedule).

S No.	Area of Communication ('What')	Communicator ('Who')	Frequency ('at What Interval')	Communication to Be Made to ('Whom')	Meeting Schedule ('When')
1.	Department's performance during the week	Departmental heads and their immediate subordinates	Once in a week	Unit head and works manager	Every Saturday
2.	Gaps in achieving the target, areas to improve, plans for skill improvement, review kaizen proposals and approve for implementation	Unit head and works manager	Once in a week	Departmental heads and their immediate subordinates	Every Saturday
3.	Monthly targets of the units and feedback on the previous month's achievements of the unit	To all departmental heads	Once in a month, in the second half of the last Saturday of the previous month	Executive director with works manager	Every month
4.	Production meeting in the departments	Departmental heads	Daily morning meeting	To all employees associated at the hall level in the production	Daily (standing meeting in the shop floor)

In other words, the employee empowerment, supplemented by the process of employee development and employee performance feedback, was complemented by a communication process across the organization.

The Motivating and Trusting Process for Empowering the Employees

The motivational process in Liberty Shoes Ltd included the following steps/initiatives by the management:

- Information sharing that includes providing information such as vision, mission, goals, financials, performance objectives, quality and productivity to employees throughout the enterprise.

- Autonomy through boundaries that refers to organizational structures, policies, procedures and practices that promote autonomous behaviour among employees.
- Team accountability that identifies the team as the decision-making unit with required authority.

The three-dimensional empowerment model recognizes the power of employee self-efficacy or generating the competence with an attitude to deliver to the organizational goals. A graphic presentation of the three-dimensional empowerment model is depicted in Figure 3.8.

Figure 3.8 The Three-dimensional Approach of Employee Empowerment in Liberty Shoes Ltd

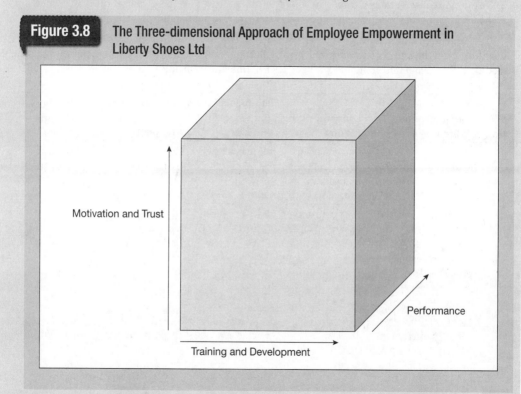

In the model, the X-axis represents the 'training and development' initiative for the employees, the Y-axis represents the initiative of the management to motivate the employees and development of a trusting behaviour and the Z-axis represents the performance monitoring and providing feedback on regular basis.

The model attempts to establish the conceptual link between 'trained/skilled employees under a condition that appropriate motivation and trust on them will contribute positively to the organizational objective'. In other words, there existed a direct relationship between performance and skill as well as performance and motivation/trust.

The employees may have the ability to perform due to the possessed skill level, but may not have a willingness to deliver. This gap between ability and willingness was bridged by the management's process of motivating and trusting the employees.[8]

---

[8] Since the objective of this case study is just to discuss the cases study of Liberty Puram, Liberty Shoes Ltd, the theoretical aspects of performance, motivation/trust and skill have not been discussed in detail.

The Process Results

The shop-floor groups through their team leaders/incharges aligned themselves attitude wise and accepted the change initiatives, valued the initiatives flowing from the top leaders, which resulted in accepting the feedback, as a result, the follow-up change initiatives were more effective through total involvement of people. The company ultimately registered a growth during the financial year(s) 2011–2012.

The Performance Results

Table 3.2 depicts the cost per pair of shoes incurred, productivity per man-day and quality rejection rate during the financial year(s) 2011–2012, 2012–2013 and 2013–2014. The results show a reasonable improvement.

Table 3.2 Performance Data

Financial Year	2011–2012	2012–2013	2013–2014
Labour cost per pair	39	36	36
Productivity per man-day	7	9	10
QC rejections rate	2.25%	1.50%	0.1% (Target year 2014–2015: 0.50%)

Source: Company's records.

Table 3.3 details the percentage of improvement in areas of 'growth in sales revenue increase', 'growth in revenue per person', 'average CTC increase per person', 'manpower strength increase', 'HR cost increase' and 'HR cost percentage of turnover decrease' during the year(s) 2013–2014 as compared to 2012–2013.

Table 3.3 Percentage of Improvement

Key Performance Areas	%age Increase in 2013–2014 over 2012–2013
Growth–sales revenue—increase	37
Growth revenue per person—increased	18
Avg. CTC per person—increase	11
Manpower strength—increase	11
HR cost—increase	23
HR cost percentage of total trunover—decrease	–1.5

Source: Company's records.

Chapter Summary

1. There is less and less need for a traditional system of IR in industrial societies. There is an emerging new type of employer–employee relationship. The employers in the present situation are more willing to provide a right pay and have an equally contributing returns from the employees. In addition to obligation to pay wages for the job done, the approach of the employers in dealing with the employees has undergone a sea change.

2. In the IR front, there has been a progressive reduction in the number of industrial disputes, number of man-days lost on account of strikes and lockouts, and the number of strikes and lockouts in India. These are the trends of positive harmonious IR which are more evident during the last decades.

3. There had been an increasing trend of lockouts. In the event of a strike by the labour union, the employers had been aggressively locking out the organizations and had been using the same as the antithesis of strike.

4. There has been a shift in the focus of organizing the business by the employers, and also there has been shifts in the expectations, preferences and approach of the employees from their work context and environment in the Indian industries. These aspects have resulted in shifts in the outlook towards the traditional IRS, which focuses more on collectivism of the actors and conflicts of interest between management and labour.

5. There had been various impacts of the economic, social and political aspects on IRS in the Indian context.

6. The globalization has significantly changed the labour market and impacted IRS.

7. There has been a decline in the bargaining power of the trade unions with the globalization of the economy. Also, the growing mobility of capital has greatly enhanced the bargaining power of the employers/management and thereby weakening the scope for labour unions to generate any collective pressure on the management.

8. In the post 1990s, with the liberalization of the economy, some significant judgments were delivered by the court of law, which include judgments on contract labour, privatization of business units, right to strike and the bandhs (strikes). The judgments promoted industrial growth more, and thereby economic growth.

9. On the other hand, there has been increasing failure of the 'political unionism model' in India, which focused to pursue labour reform measures based on the political ideological orientation of the political parties.

10. There was a more inclusive labour union movement that emerged with time, which implied that the mainstream trade unions revived their organizational outlook towards the workers in the informal sectors.

11. A new definition of IR emerged in the Indian context with the contemporary 'information age', the knowledge era and the innovations for capital formation.

Questions

1. Elaborate on the emerging new type of employer–employee relationship in the Indian context. Indicate the characteristics of the changing trend.

2. The changing trend of industrial disputes indicates that the number of strikes are reducing, whereas the trend of lockouts is increasing. Indicate the reasons for the same.

3. The post-liberalization period experienced changing patterns in the legal judgments. There had been changes in the role of the government, an actor of IR. What were the reasons for the same?
4. What were the reasons for the mainstream trade unions to consider the inclusion of the trade unions of the informal sectors?

Project Work for the Students

1. Students may be asked to study the changing trend of IR in an organization of repute in the post 1990s.

References

1. (a) DNA. Bajaj auto strike petition to be heard on Wednesday. Pune: DNA; Wednesday, 17 July 2013. Available from http://www.dnaindia.com/pune/1861931/report-bajaj-auto-strike-petition-to-be-heard-on-wednesday (b) Gopalan M. Rajiv Bajaj rules out shares for striking workers at Chakan, The Hindu BusinessLine. 2 July 2013. Available from http://www.thehindubusinessline.com/companies/rajiv-bajaj-rules-out-shares-for-striking-workers-at-chakan/article4873956.ece (c) DNA. Second talk to end Bajaj Auto stir falls flat. Pune: DNA; Saturday, 13 July 2013. Available from http://www.dnaindia.com/pune/1860416/report-second-talk-to-end-bajaj-auto-stir-falls-flatd (d) Dahiwal A. Bajaj workers go on 'stop work' agitation. Pune: DNA; Wednesday, 26 June 2013. Available from http://www.dnaindia.com/pune/1853106/report-bajaj-workers-go-on-stop-work-agitation
2. http://www.industriall-union.org/archive/imf/maruti-suzuki-workers-struggle-for-trade-union-rights.
3. Salamon M. Industrial theory and practice. 2nd ed. New York, NY: Prentice-Hall; 2000.
4. Saini DS. Dynamics of new industrial relations and postulates of industrial justice. Indian J. Labour Econ. 2003: 46(4), 651–656.
5. Venkata Ratnam CS. Industrial relations. New Delhi: Oxford University Press; 2006.
6. Bardhan P. The political economy of reforms in India. In Mohan R, editor. Facets of the Indian Economy. New Delhi: Oxford University Press; 2002.
7. Shyam Sundar KR. Trade unions in India: from politics of fragmentation to politics of expansion and integration? In Benson J, Zhu Y, editors. Trade Unions in Asia. London: Routledge; 2008. pp. 157–176.
8. Venkata Ratnam CS. Negotiated change: collective bargaining, liberalization and restructuring in India. New Delhi: Response Books; 2003.
9. Shyam Sundar KR. Labour reforms and decent work in India: a study of labour inspection in India. New Delhi: Bookwell; 2010.
10. Krishna Murthy R. Negotiating wage settlements experiences of innovative managements. Mumbai: Indian Industrial Relations Institute; 2006.
11. Shyam Sundar KR. Labour institutions and labour reforms in contemporary India: trade unions and industrial conflict. Vol. I. Hyderabad: Icfai University Press; 2009.
12. Shyam Sundar KR. Labour reforms and decent work in India: a study of labour inspection in India. New Delhi: Bookwell; 2010.
13. Shyam Sundar KR. Current Status and Evolution of Industrial Relations in Maharashtra. ILO-Asia-Pacific Working Paper Series. Subregional Office for South Asia. New Delhi; 2009.
14. Jones S. Towards a theory of industrial relations for a knowledge economy. Industrielle Beziehungen. 2004; 11. Jg., Heft 1+2.
15. Ghosh A, Ray P. A contemporary model for industrial relations: relook from global perspective. Manage. Labour Stud. 2012; 37(1). doi:10.1177/0258042X1103700103.
16. Budhwar PS. Employment relations in India. Employ. Relat. 2003; 25(2): 132–148. doi:10.1108/01425450310456442.

17. Kaufman B, editor. Theoretical perspectives on work and the employment relationship. IL: IIRA; 2004.
18. Kaufman B. The study of labour, employment, and work life: central features and core principle. Arbetsmarknad & Arbetsliv. 2007; 13(3–4): 11–28.
19. Blyton P, Turnbull P. The dynamics of employee relations. Oxford: Palgrave; 2004.
20. Ling Yuan, Yue Yu, Jian Li, Lutao Ning. Occupational commitment, industrial relations and turnover intention. Empirical evidence from China. Chin. Manage. Stud. 2014; 8(1): 66–84. doi:10.1108/CMS-08-2011-0065.
21. Bakker AB, Schaufeli WB. Positive organizational behavior: engaged employees in flourishing organizations. J. Organ. Behav. 2008; 29: 147–154.
22. Lee K, Carswell JJ, Allen NJ. A meta-analytic review of occupational commitment: relations with person- and work-related variables. J. Appl. Psychol. 2000; 85: 799.

PART

3

Growth and Development of Trade Unions in India, Their Structure and Positions

PART

3

Growth and Development of Trade Unions in India, Their Structure and Positions

CHAPTER 11, Definitions, Theory and the Growth of Trade Unions in India

CHAPTER 12, Trade Union Structure and Management

4

Trade Unions: Theory and the Growth of Trade Unions in India

LEARNING OBJECTIVES

After reading this chapter, you will be able to understand:

☐ The concept of trade union and the need for such unions in organizations
☐ The theoretical foundation of the trade union movement in India
☐ The link between the movement for Independence and the growth of trade union in India
☐ The link between the government policies for economic development, management's approach to industrialization and trade unionism in India
☐ The factors leading to the growth of trade union in India

C.4.1. Case for Discussion   Spentex Industries Ltd

Spentex Industries Ltd, a textile mill in Butibori, Nagpur, employed around 700–800 permanent workers, and a similar number of workers were employed on contract. There were five contractors engaged in the plant. One of the contractors, the ICEM Contract and Agency project coordinator, indicated that it had been supplying the same set of workers at the plant for four years. Similar opinions were also expressed by other contractors.

A survey on the job profile of the contract workers established that the contract workers were engaged as machinists, packers, drivers and helpers, and they had been working at the plant for more than 10 years on contract. Some of them expressed that they were initially hired by the company directly for a period of three month as trainees, and thereafter their employment was transferred to a contractor. The wage difference between the permanent and the contract workers was about ₹60–70 (i.e., up to €1) per day. The contract workers were not getting the same benefits as the permanent workers. The permanent workers were getting uniforms whereas the contract workers were not. Personal protective equipment (PPE) such as safety gloves, safety shoes or helmets were not provided to the contract workers; they were only provided with safety masks and earplugs after two years of working. One of the employees expressed that, 'If there was any problem, they get fired and the entry into the plant was immediately restricted'. He also said that if they wanted to join a trade union, they would be immediately dismissed.

One worker who had been working at the plant for 12 years through a contractor, informed the management of availing leave for attending a family function. When he returned, he was instructed to sit outside the gate and not allowed to work for two days. Such approaches by the management were not uncommon. An application for leave by a contract worker was treated differently. They were not given any receipt of the application and no communication was made on the approval of leave [1].

Case Questions

1. What do you think will be the reaction of the contract worker in such a context?
2. 'The management approach to discriminate between the contract workers and the permanent workers is likely to lead to the formation of a separate trade union of the contract employees'. Do you agree?
3. List down the expected roles of a trade union representing such a contract worker.

4.1. The Concept of Trade Union

Trade unions represent an association of employees for the purpose of securing improvements in pay, benefits, working conditions and so on through collective bargaining. The Trade Unions Act, 1926 defines a trade union

As any combination, whether temporary or permanent, formed primarily for the purpose of regulating the relationship between workmen and employers or between workmen and workmen or for imposing restrictive conditions on the conduct of any trade or business and includes any federations of two or more Trade Unions.[1]

The Trade Unions Act which is a central legislation, but administered by the state governments, is applicable to all industries in India including the IT industry. The Trade Union (Amendment) Act, 2001 although restrains the multiplicity of trade unions, there are no provisions of barring the IT industry or any other industry from forming of trade unions.

Webb and Webb considered that 'A trade union is continuous association of wage earners for the purpose of maintaining or improving the conditions of their working lives' [2]. Whereas Flippo provided a wider definition, 'A labour union or trade union is an organization of workers formed to promote, protect, and improve, through collective action, the social, economic, and political interests of its members' [3]. The above three definitions can be summed up as:

1. Trade unions are organizations formed by employees or workers
2. Such organizations are formed on a continuous basis as permanent bodies and not casual ones
3. The organization's objective is to protect and promote all kinds of interests of the workers, for example, economic, political and social
4. Trade unions include federations of trade unions
5. Trade unions achieve their objectives through collective action and group effort

[1] http://www.industriall-union.org/sites/default/files/uploads/documents/a4_india_report_new2.pdf

C.4.2. Case for Discussion   A Trade Union Was Born

The Tata Iron and Steel Company (now Tata Steel Ltd) was set up on 27 February 1908 on the direction and initiative of Jamsetji Tata, and the active involvement of his eldest son Dorabji Tata and cousin Shapoorji Shaktalwaia. Workers from different parts of the country, particularly Chhattisgarh, Shahabad and Saran district of Bihar came to work in the plant at Tatanagar. Around 10,000 workers were employed by the company by 1918. The number went up to approximately 23,000 by 1934.

During the First World War, the company made good profits. In spite of high earnings, the wages of the workers remained the same. The wages of the workers were low. The prices of essential commodities had increased during the time of war, which continued over the years which resulted in financial hardships of the workers.

Being illiterate the workers hardly had the guts to raise their voice against the management. But with time they learnt about the effectiveness of workers' association in other organizations and the role of ILO to support the interests of the workers. By then the concept of worker's association was present in the European countries.

In January 1920, some active workers took the lead for organizing themselves against the management. They prepared a charter of demands that included their request to increase their wages, provide paid leaves and benefit of compensation in the event of fatal injury, request for housing accommodation and the framing of service rules for uniform treatment. Thakkar Bapa, superintendent of the Grain Store, placed the charter of demands before the management of Tata.

But since the management did not respond to the charter of demand for over three months, the workers decided to go on agitation. Canvassing and picketing at the gates of the factory began. Some of the senior employees planned to launch a protest against the management's action of not revising the salary and the workers decided to go on strike from February 1920. In the absence of any formal organization among them, the strike was led mainly by foremen, apprentices and a few dedicated workers.

These incidents drew the attention of the national leaders of the Congress Party. Eminent Congress leaders started taking interest in the issue. The workers of Tata factory, as their next step, approached Byomkesh Chakravarty for helping them. They also informed Mahatma Gandhi, Motilal Nehru, Pandit Madan Mohan Malviya and C. R. Das. Byomkesh Chakravarty sent his close friend Surendra Nath Haldar, a renowned barrister at the Calcutta High Court, to help the workers.

On 25 February 1921, a general meeting was called. More than 10,000 workers participated in the meeting. The then deputy commissioner of the district who favoured the worker's agitation, J. E. Scott, addressed the meeting as the chief guest. In view of the massive response from the workers, the middle and lower level management team of the organization started paying attention to the workers' agitation.

The management invited and requested the agitating workers to participate in a negotiation. But the leaders of the striking workers insisted that they would only negotiate with T. W. Tutwiler, the General Manager of the plant. They also started raising funds to ensure the success of their agitation. The management, in turn, managed to deploy a large number of police to protect the company's property and maintain law and order. Despite this suppression, increasing number of workers started participating in the agitation.

On 27 February 1921, Surendra Nath Haldar addressed a large meeting of the workers before he proceeded to meet J. E. Scott. The same day Tutwiler reached Jamshedpur. A tripartite meeting was subsequently convened, but nothing came out of it.

On 28 February 1921, the administration deployed additional armed forces near the factory premises and in vulnerable areas of the town. Another tripartite meeting was held on the same day in which the management spoke about the concessions it was ready to offer. However, Haldar insisted for a written statement, which the management refused. Thus, the negotiations failed again. In view of the gravity of the situation, Haldar sent a telegram to Mahatma Gandhi requesting his intervention. Gandhiji sent Lala Lajpat Rai and Shaukat Ali to Jamshedpur.

Meanwhile, Scott requested Haldar to prepare a fresh charter of demands. On 1 March 1921, the new charter was presented to Tutwiller to forward to the Board of Directors at Bombay.

On 3 March 1921 the management, local administration and police officials held secret meetings to discuss the volatile situation in the city. On 5 March 1921, a tripartite meeting was again organized in which Byomkesh Chakravarty played the role of the anchor. The same afternoon, a general meeting of the workers was called to convey to them that the management was not accepting any of their demands. A proposal came up in the meeting for formation of a trade union. The Jamshedpur Labour Association was thus formed in 1937; the trade union was named Tata Workers' Union.

Case Questions

1. Do you think it was the right step to form a trade union in Tata Steel?
2. How was it going to help the peace-loving uneducated workers?
3. What advantage did the agitating workers gain by calling the national leaders? Was it essential?

4.1.1. The Organization of Trade Union

May Day celebrated on 1 May refers to the struggle of 1886 in Chicago, when the labour class demanded to have 'eight hours of work, eight hours of rest and eight hours of recreation' in their daily lives. The logic for such a demand was that 'there should be a limit to the exploitation of workers'. This was a movement to stop workers working from dawn to dusk. In India, May Day was first celebrated in 1923 in Chennai. The problem of workers organizing themselves every time to protest against any act of injustice was streamlined with the enactment of the Trade Unions Act of 1926, which provided workers the right to register a trade union and become its member, and the right of a trade union to be a legal entity. The right to form association/unions and the right to collective bargaining (collectively raising/bargaining) constitutes as a right under the Constitution of India. The ILO in its conventions 87 and 98, respectively, ensures these rights to the workers. India is a founding member of the ILO, and has a permanent place in the ILO governing body.

4.1.2. Formation of a Trade Union

The importance of the formation of a trade union are the following:

1. Trade unions represent the workers to support their demands and facilitate settlement.
2. Trade unions ensure a safe working condition by highlighting the adverse working condition to the management, thereby protecting the workers by ensuring better safety measures at workplace.
3. Trade unions ensure job security to their members.
4. Trade unions protect the interests of the workers, thereby safeguarding their members' economic, social and political interests.
5. Trade unions protect workers against exploitations of all kinds, for example physical and mental torture, and exploitation by superiors at the workplace.
6. Workers' individual rights and liberties are better protected by trade unions.
7. Trade unions protect women employees against sexual harassment.
8. Trade unions negotiate with management for higher incentives for increased productivity.

9. Trade unions ensure a better bargaining power, thereby negotiating with employers for better terms and conditions of employment collectively.

10. Trade unions provide legal support to workers when they face legal implications.

11. Trade unions in advanced countries often provide educational support and training for skill upgradation.

C.4.3. Case for Discussion   The Kagad Kach Patra Kashtakari Panchayat: A Trade Union of Waste Pickers

Suman Mariba More, a waste picker from the city of Pune who was in her forties said:

An entrepreneur offered a doorstep garbage collection service with a motorized vehicle and two workers for a fee in an area where we had been serving the residents by 'picking up the wastes'. This had a direct negative impact on our livelihoods since our earnings from waste picking stopped. We all protested against this. We appealed to the entrepreneur and then to the residents for allowing us to resume work. We had been doing this job for generations. Since we received no positive response from the residents and the entrepreneur, all the waste pickers decided to go for 'bin chipko andolan' (i.e., held on to the waste bins) so that they could not be used either by the residents or the entrepreneur. The residents on being threatened by the waste pickers, without getting into any complications, discontinued the services of the entrepreneur.

Such emerging threats to the livelihood of the waste pickers made them realize that in future there could be others who would try to step into the business of waste picking and put an end to their earnings. The threat created an urgent need for the waste pickers in different parts of Pune to associate to form a union. Dr Baba Adhav, the president of the Hamal Panchayat (trade union of coolies/head loaders) and a labour leader of the unorganized sectors of workers, came forward to help this section of people. The transformation of these waste pickers in an organized manner started in May 1993 when Dr Baba Adhav organized a convention of waste pickers in Pune. This convention was attended by more than 800 waste pickers from across Pune. The convention ended with a thought of forming of a trade union. With time the Kagad Kach Patra Kashtakari Panchayat (KKPKP), a union of scrap collectors, was formed to enable these waste pickers to protest for their rights as legitimate workers. Another reason for the formation of the union was that the waste pickers felt that other entrepreneurs with more capital intensive and innovative tools may step into the business and become claimants to the 'wealth in waste'.

Organizing the waste pickers preceded the concept of formation of a trade union. The organized activities provided an opportunity to the waste pickers for establishing close and enduring reciprocal relationships within themselves. Mr Narayan, the General Secretary of the KKPKP, expressed, 'individuals and small groups had no power or voice to counter the threats of other claimants to "wealth in waste" and there was an immediate need to establish an identity for waste pickers as workers' [4].

The benefit of unionizing and working in an organized way was soon felt by the waste pickers. There was a serious need for changing these workers' working conditions. Organized efforts and assistance from NGOs changed their working conditions. With time the association gathered an inherent authority to negotiate for better wages from the residents, and the segregated wastes when sold to the scrap dealers brought them better incomes.

They were finally identified as a class of workers and they started feeling dignity in their labour, and the KKPKP proved to be a perfect platform. It not only represented the collective identity and interests of scrap collectors, but also gave them a platform to voice their grievances and concerns. Unlike conventional unions, it also focused on social development activities, such as credit provision, education of children and abolition of child labour.

Suman Mariba More recalls how she toiled from dawn to dusk, walking miles with her sack to collect scrap and sort it with the help of her children. All that changed after 1993 when she joined the trade union, now she works for four hours and earns more money since she collects waste from door to door. The quality and condition of waste she gets is much better. So she was working for fewer hours in better working conditions and earning more than what she was earning earlier.

'Door-to-door collection had social benefits as well. Simple pleasures like a cup of tea, a friendly chat during lunch breaks, in addition to getting soap to wash hands and feet are just some of the unsaid benefits', expressed Suman Mariba More.

But the best of benefits were from the association. Over the years, KKPKP evolved to a union of 9,000 plus members. About 80 per cent of the members were women. Their identity cards were endorsed by the Pune Municipal Corporation (PMC), which entitled them to benefits such as interest-free loans and educational support for children and coverage under two different insurance programmes (started for them by the state government). For their life insurance coverage, members paid a yearly fee of ₹50 only, while the state government paid a matching sum and in addition the Central Government contributed ₹100. There was also a medical coverage of ₹5,000, the premium for which is paid by the PMC.

For Suman Mariba More, a higher income and health insurance meant that she could afford proper medical care instead of indulging in self-medication. Now not only her sons are educated but her daughter-in-law is a computer engineer and is from a Brahmin family. Even her daughter was married off only after she turned 18 years, and that too with no dowry. Suman Mariba More no more segregates waste at home but goes to the shed provided by the municipal corporation for segregating them.

A state government report indicates that the KKPKP's initiatives and the efforts proved to be extremely valuable for the city in terms of keeping the city clean [4, 5, 6].

Case Questions

1. Had you been a resident of the area, how would you have reacted to the concept of 'bin chipko andolan' of the waste pickers?
2. 'The formation of the trade union led to performing the job of waste picking in an organized manner, which added value to various groups of individuals, for example, the members of the trade union, the customers of the waste pickers and the society'. Do you agree? If yes, please list the benefits to these three beneficiaries.
   (The class may be divided into three groups. Each of these groups may be assigned the task of answering the benefits to one of these beneficiaries. The groups may brainstorm to arrive at a common answer.)
3. Do you think the formation of trade union was essential? Why?

4.1.3. The Formation of a Trade Union and Its Roles and Responsibilities

The first four CTUs in India, that is, AITUC (affiliated to CPI), INTUC (affiliated to Indian National Congress), HMS (affiliated to Socialists) and CITU affiliated to CPI(M), established in the years 1920, 1947, 1948 and 1971, respectively, had the following objectives.

The main role of the trade unions is to put forward ideas to the management and get them converted into well-structured implementable plans through negotiations. The process assumes that the result of the same will be good for the organization [7]. However, broadly, the objectives of trade unions in India are as follows:

1. **Maintenance of full employment:** This implies the struggle of maintaining enough jobs with good pay for full employment. Though in a liberalized economy achieving this objective is beyond the control of the trade unions.
2. **Rationalization of personnel policies for job security:** This is a protection initiative of the trade unions against an illegal action. Economic security is ensured by ensuring job security. While economic security addresses employees' living standards fairly, job security protects employees against the management action of laying off, retirement, disciplinary action, illegal transfer and promotions. Job security has a nexus with the economic security.
3. **Voice in decisions affecting workers:** A voice to all such decisions affecting the workers negatively is raised through the union. The trade unions may successfully pressurize for higher wages or may achieve a satisfactory rationalization of personnel policies, but raising a voice against certain decisions, for example change in the scale and schedule of production, introduction of labour-saving devices and the closure or relocation of plant remain outside the effective influence of the trade unions.
4. **Recognition and participation:** Another objective that unions seek to achieve is winning recognition for the fact that they are equal partners with management in the activity of production. This equality is considered more valuable than the equality on the bargaining table.
5. **Gaining legislative enactments:** Strategically, the unions always target to provide legal sanctions to their demands. In such efforts, the outcomes of negotiations are framed within the available legal framework or in extreme situations they pressurize the government for an enactment.
6. **Miscellaneous services:** The trade unions also engage in providing educational, medical, recreational and other developmental activities with the objective of providing welfare to their members and the families in case sufficient funds are available with them.

C.4.4. Case for Discussion   Role of Trade Unions: The Strike Call of Central Trade Unions

Trade unions represented by 10 CTUs in India went for a nation-wide strike on 2 September 2016. It was a joint decision to organize this all-India general strike by CTUs of the country along with independent national federations of employees of different industries and services including the Confederation of Central Government Employees. The strike was against what they termed as anti-people, anti-workers policies and the authoritarian attitude of the present Central Government. The government's 42 per cent hike in minimum wage, that is, an increase of ₹350 per day was considered as completely inadequate by the trade unions. Millions of workers belonging to the 10 CTUs participated in this general strike demanding higher wages and protested against the revised wages announced by the government. The government's decision to close down/disinvest in some of the loss-making firms run by the Central Government was termed as a 'unilateral' action by the trade unions.

The trade unions alleged that the government had not taken any meaningful step to curb the price rise of essential commodities and to generate employment. In the charter of demand, the trade unions had also pointed out that the government had been mysteriously silent on the question of retrieving the black money stashed abroad and recovering lakhs of crores of rupees of bad debts of PSBs. A whole range of social security measures were under severe attack including the pension of post-2004 entrants in the Central Government services. The goverment launched an atrocious attack, drastically cutting the interest on small savings deposits. Totally ignoring the united opposition of the working class, the goverment had been moving fast to demolish existing labour laws, thereby empowering the employers with unfettered rights to 'hire and fire' and stripping the workers and trade union of all their rights and protection provided by the law. Along with the peasantry, agricultural labourers were also under severe attack. Attack on public sector had been pushed to unprecedented height with goverment announcing mega strategic sale and also allowing unlimited FDI in strategic sectors such as railways, defence and financial sector as complementary to the move of privatization and public–private partner-ship. The anti-worker and authoritarian attitude of the government was nakedly reflected in its refusal to implement the consensus recommendations of 43rd, 44th and 45th Indian Labour Conference for formulations of minimum wages, equal wage and benefits of regular workers to contract workers.

The Central Government through the finance minister announced the revised minimum wage of the unskilled non-agricultural workers in 'C' category of employments for the areas under the central sphere to be ₹9,100 per month (for 26 days). This increase was much below the demands of the trade unions, which was ₹18,000 per month. A 12-point charter of demand was raised by the unions before the Central Government. The issues in the charter of demands related to the workers of both organized and unorganized sectors. The trade unions were quite considerate of the hardship undergone by this category of employees, as per the statement of the unions.

The government made it categorically clear that they were not in a position of fixing a universal minimum wage in the existing legal provisions since the minimum wages are determined as per the Minimum Wage Act, and the authority to determine such minimum wages is with the respective state governments. But it was assured that the government was initiating steps for making it possible to have a universal minimum wage in the country.

The government targetted to shut down 77 state-run loss-making companies, because a loss of more than ₹400 crore was made by these companies in the in the fiscal year (2014–2015). The government aimed to raise ₹56,000 crore through privatization of these organizations.

The neo-liberal economic policies pursued by the government landed the entire national economy in distress and decline, affecting working people the most, opined the trade unions. The trade unions also raised a nine-point charter of demand concerning the 'Central Government employees'. The areas these demands included are appended here.

Part A: The general demands for the workers

1. Urgent measures for containing price rise through universalization of public distribution system and banning speculative trade in commodity market.
2. Containing unemployment through concrete measures for employment generation.
3. Strict enforcement of all basic labour laws without any exception or exemption and stringent puni-tive measures for violation of labour laws.
4. Universal social security cover for all workers.
5. Minimum wage of not less than ₹18000 per month with provisions of indexation (for unskilled worker).
6. Assured enhanced pension not less than ₹3000 per month for the entire working population (including unorganized sector workers).
7. Stoppage of disinvestment in Central/state PSUs.
8. Stoppage of contractorisation in permanent/perennial work and payment of same wage and ben-efits for contract workers as that of regular workers for the same and similar work.
9. Removal of all ceilings on payment and eligibility of bonus, provident fund and increase in quan-tum of gratuity.

10. Compulsory registration of trade unions within a period of 45 days from the date of submitting application and immediate ratification of ILO conventions C–87 and C–98.
11. No FDI in Railways, Defence and other strategic sectors.
12. No unilateral amendment to labour laws.

Part B: Demand of the Central Government employees

1. Avoid delay in implementing the assurances given by Group of Ministers to NJCA on 30th June 2016, especially increase in minimum pay a fitment formula. Implement the assurance in a time bound manner.
2. Settle issues raised by the NJCA, regarding modifications of the 7th CPC recommendations, submitted to Cabinet Secretary on 10th December 2015.
3. Scrap PFRDA Act and New Pension System (NPS) and grant Pension/Family Pension to all Central Government employees under CCS (Pension) Rules 1972.
4. No privatization, outsourcing, contractorisation of Government functions.
5. Treat Gramin Dak Sevaks as Civil Servants and extend all benefits on pay, pension and allowances of departmental employees.
6. Regularize casual, contract, contingent and daily rated workers and grant equal pay and other benefits.
7. Fill up all vacant posts by special recruitment. Lift ban on creation of new posts.
8. Remove ceiling on compassionate appointments.
9. Extend benefit of Bonus Act amendment 2015 on enhancement of payment ceiling to the Adhoc bonus/PLB of Central Govt. employees with effect from the financial years 2014–2015. Ensure payment of revised bonus before Pooja holidays.
10. Revive JCM functioning at all levels [8, 9].

Case Questions

1. What are your comments on the areas of demand raised by the CTUs?
2. Are the trade unions going beyond their roles and responsibilities? Justify your answer.
3. Categorize the initiatives of the CTUs under different roles of trade unions.

4.2. Theories on Trade Unionism

The theories have been formulated from time to time considering the contextual framework of the society and the level of industrialization. The theories are broadly categorized as follows.

4.2.1. Webbs' Theory

The profounders of the theory were Sidney Webb and Beatrice Webb. They were dominant leaders of the Labour Party in Great Britain during the 1920s and 1930s. Trade unionism as a concept for them was, 'A trade union is continuous association of wage earners for the purpose of maintaining or improving the conditions of their working lives'.

Sidney Webb and Beatrice Webb had extensively and intensively studied various facets of trade unionism. Their books titled *The History of Trade Unionism* and *Industrial Democracy* are often regarded as 'bibles of trade unionism'. The book *Industrial Democracy* was published in 1897, three years after the Webbs published *The History of Trade Unionism*, which was an account of the roots and development of the British trade union movement. This work of the Webbs highly influenced trade unionists like Lenin who translated the book from English into Russian language. These books contain significant ideas pertaining to assumptions, purposes, objectives and methods of trade unionism, which hold true even in the present industrial context.

Webbs' Theory of Industrial Democracy is an extension of democracy from the political sphere to that of industry in order to overcome the dangers of managerial dictatorship. The objective of the concept was to improve the economic status of the working class. The process assumes the infusion of industrial democracy through the method of mutual insurance between the managers and the working class. It assumes the adoption of collective bargaining as a tool for achieving this objective with the help of legal enactments. The Webbs believed in public ownership of the means of production. Their theory underlines that a trade union is a continuous association of wage earners. They associate for the purpose of maintaining and improving the conditions of their work life. The concept originated from the fact that capitalists who possessed the means of production, purchased labour owned by the labourers. The workers/labourers did not own the means of production, but possessed the power to sell their labour to the owners of the means of production however they want. So trade unionism as a concept was as old as capitalism. Trade unionism existed both under capitalism (when there is private ownership of the means of production) as well as under socialism (when there is social ownership of the means of production).

The underlying ideas of the theory are as follows:

1. Reconstruction of the society by eliminating capitalist profit makers who live merely by owning the means of production
2. Democratic administration of the industry
3. The organized labour follows the methods of mutual insurance at the workplace, collective bargaining and legal enactments
4. The trade unions seek to maintain a progressively rising 'national minimum' wages for the entire wage-earning class for better conditions of living

4.2.2. The Marxian Theory

The Marxian theory is found on Karl Marx's concept of 'class straggle' in the economy. In the opening statement of the *Communist Manifesto,* Marx indicates 'the history of all hitherto existing society is the history of class struggles'. Marx explains that the emergence and growth of trade unionism is a result of the rise of two opposed classes in the society—the capitalists, termed by him as the *bourgeoisie*, and the labourers, termed by him as the *proletariat.* His theory of trade unionism is based on 'the existence of inherent conflict between these two classes in the society'. Marx's concepts on the growth and role of trade unions are evident in most of his writings, that is, *The Poverty of Philosophy* (1847) and *The Communist Manifesto* (1848), the inaugural address of the First International Workingmen's Association (1864) and his correspondence with Friedrich Engels and others.

In the post-Industrial Revolution period, labour was paid only subsistence wages. Marx considered this phenomenon as exploitation. He observed in 1865 that wage levels can only be 'settled by the continuous struggle between capital and labour; the capitalist constantly trying to reduce wages to their physical minimum, and to extend the working day to its physical maximum, while the working man constantly presses in the opposite direction' [10]. The struggle between the capitalists and labour was initially at the level of the individual worker and the capitalist, but with time and industrialization, the combined voice against exploitation of the workers resulted in the formation of trade unions. Thus in Marx's view, the birth of trade unions had been the result of struggle between the two classes, that is, the bourgeoisie and the proletariat. Marx says that 'the only social power of the workmen is their number'.

Marx uses the concept of profit in terms of 'surplus value'. Marx did not himself invent the term 'surplus value'. He had developed the concept of surplus value, which means value added (sales revenue minus the cost of materials used up). Marx distinguished between labour-time worked and labour power. A worker who is sufficiently productive can produce an output value greater than the costs of hiring him. In other words, wage does not reflect the full value of what the worker produces. Effectively it is not labour which the worker sells, but his capacity to work. Marx considers that surplus value is the fruit of the exploitation of workers' labour. The capitalists who possess the means of production, sell the same for capital. In the process of capital formation a certain quantity of value is augmented through the exploitation of labour.

The next stage is the formation of permanent associations in the form of trade unions to necessitate the struggle against the capitalist and their exploitations.

4.2.3. Perlman's Job Consciousness Theory

The theory of Selig Perlman on trade union movement is also called 'job consciousness theory'. The theory was primarily based on his examination of labour movements in the United States, Great Britain, Germany and Russia.

Perlman rejected the idea of class consciousness as an explanation for the origin of the trade union movement. He substituted the concept of class consciousness by what he called 'job consciousness'. The underlying assumption of his theory was that a large group succeeds in pursuing their collective aims when individuals in the group are compelled to work together for the common aim rather than follow what rationality tells them is their best interest; it is *the logic of collective action* which leads to the formation of a trade union. According to him, 'working people in reality felt an urge towards collective control of their employment opportunities, but hardly towards similar control of industry.' Trade union is the outcome of the pessimistic outlook of the workers, who becoming conscious of the scarcity of job opportunities start looking for alternatives. In order to protect his limited job opportunity, he starts uniting with fellow employees facing similar situations. Perlman established that the impact of 'job scarcity' on the workers had been true not only for workers in the medieval guild system of European countries, but also for modern industrial labour. 'Just as to the guildsman opportunity was visibly limited to the local market, so is to the industrial wage-earner it is limited to the number of jobs available, which is always fewer than the number of job seekers'. The scarcity of jobs makes conscious workers to form trade unions by coming together.

4.2.4. Robert F. Hoxie's Socio-Psychological Approach

Robert F. Hoxie advocated the socio-psychological approach to study trade unionism in his book *Trade Unionism in the United States* (1920). According to him, the 'social and the psychological' environment of the workers are the cause of the growth of trade unionism. He contends that workers in similar economic and social situations, and who are not very divergent in temperament and educational and training levels will tend to develop similar interpretation of the social situation and adopt similar/common solutions to their problems of living. Such psychological behaviours may emerge in them gradually or spontaneously, or it may be a sudden outcome of some crisis or context.

Hoxie brushes aside or reduces the concepts of economic and technical reasons and the context of the competitive markets to a secondary position while explaining the reasoning behind trade unionism. He gives importance to non-industrial factors such as the social environment and the subjective differences of temperament in the workers. Hoxie considers that the economic reasoning may indicate an orderly succession of unionism from one stage of industry to another, but the psychological or the functional (as he calls it) analysis in the context will provide the multifaceted reasoning to unionism.

The logic underlying the concept of Hoxie lies in the fact that group psychology differs widely for different groups, which has linkage with the political, religious, traditional, educational and circumstantial factors in which the individual frames his own attitudes.

The functional classification which he tentatively proposes is that there are four main types of trade unionism: Business unionism, uplift unionism, revolutionary unionism and predatory unionism. The two varieties of revolutionary unionism are the socialistic and quasi-anarchistic. Two varieties of the predatory are the 'hold-up' and the 'guerilla' unionism. Hoxie's followers added a fifth type—dependent unionism—to the list.

1. **Business unionism:** Such unionism, clearly recognized as a functional type, is essentially trade conscious as opposed to class conscious. It accepts the capitalistic organization of wage systems and seeks the best obtainable terms of employment for its members. It is conservative in outlook and generally tries to limit its membership to the craft, trade or industry. Its method is collective bargaining supplemented by mutual insurance and occasional resort to strikes.
2. **Uplift unionism:** This is also called as friendly unionism. Such unionism aims mainly at elevating the moral, intellectual and social life of workers. Such a type prefers to rely on political action, mutual insurance activities and cooperative enterprises. It accepts the existing wages system and social orders. Its mission is the diffusion of leisure-class culture.
3. **Revolutionary unionism:** Revolutionary unionism is extremely radical both in outlook and action. It acknowledges or declares openly to overthrow the existing socio-economic order by and for the working class. Hoxie has further subdivided this unionism into (a) socialistic unionism and (b) quasi-anarchistic unionism. It is distinctly class conscious rather than trade conscious.
4. **Predatory unionism:** This is characterized by 'ruthless pursuit of the thing in hand by whatever means seen most appropriate at the time, regardless of ethical and legal codes or effect'. It practices secret rather than open violence. It is lawless and is far more anarchistic. It does not professes any far-reaching philosophy nor does it aim at anything beyond the immediate economic advantage of its own membership. Two varieties of the predatory are the 'hold-up' and the 'guerrilla' unionism.
5. **Dependent unionism:** This unionism is defined in terms of (a) company unionism and (b) union label unionism. Company unionism is dominated by the employer and is dependent on him. Union label unionism depends upon the union label being imprinted on the products made by the union members so that consumers, particularly workers, may opt for union label products in preference to those not labelled so.

4.2.5. Tannenbaum's Technological Theory

Frank Tannenbaum developed a technological theory of trade unionism in 1951 in *A Philosophy of Labor*. He considers a cause and effect relationship between 'labour movement' and 'machine'. 'Labour movement is the result and machine is the major cause'. This implies that any process/mode of production through machines, irrespective of whether it is in factories or mines or any industry, will give birth to trade unions. It is mechanization which breaks the society, which provides the social norms—'security, justice, freedom and faith'—to the workers. When workers are led to look after themselves individually and with the advent of machines resulting in 'social atomization', the workers needed to congregate under one roof as trade unions to restore their lost position.

Tannenbaum states,

> What the workers had in common was their employer, the industry they worked in, the hours they laboured, the bench or the machine they worked at, the wage rate they received, the foreman who ruled over them, the materials they worked, the whistle that called them from beds in the morning or brought to halt to their labours. [11]

Thus they dependeded on one another's cooperation for restoring 'security, justice, freedom and faith'. The need for a sense of identity, which was inevitable, led to the formation of the trade union. Lastly the common unity based on craft, job, shop or industry led to the establishment of 'self-conscious' groups.

Tannenbaum holds that 'the trade union movement is an unconscious rebellion against atomization of industrial society. It suggests that the men, skilled and unskilled who do the labour of the world want to return to ... older way of life'. Tannenbaum further considers that trade unionism is 'conservative and counter-revolutionary'. He also considers that the aim of trade unionism is participation in all the affairs of the management.

4.2.6. Mahatma Gandhi's Approach

Mahatma Gandhi was not only a leader of the freedom struggle in India but also a trade unionist. His views had direct and indirect relevance to many other facets of the social life of the people and the nation. Gandhiji, after his return from South Africa, was actively associated with the labour movements in Ahmedabad, especially with the women's labour movement of the Textile Labour Association (TLA) founded by Anasuya Sarabhai. Gandhiji's approach was based on his ideals of truth and non-violence. His ideology was greatly influenced by the writings of Leo Tolstoy and John Ruskin. His firmly believed in the dignity of labour. He clarified his own stand on matters relating to the importance of labour, role of trade unions, relationship between labour and capital, and the settlement of industrial disputes. He recognized the importance of labour in society and workers' contribution in production and, therefore, considered them as the sources of all wealth.

The Gandhian ideology was based on the ideologies of the socialist and communist contemporaries, which were aligned by him to the Indian tradition. He sought to evolve 'a truer socialism and a truer communism that the world was yet dreamed of' [12]. His concept on IR was based on some of his fundamental principles which constituted the core of his philosophy. The principles were as follows:

1. Truth and non-violence
2. *Aparigraha* (non-possession)

Mahatma Gandhi's philosophy was based on the concept of sarvodaya, that is, the principles of truth, non-violence and trusteeship in which class harmony prevailed. Gandhiji's main ideas relating to labour issues, trade unionism and IR are contained in many of his writings, for example, *Young India* and *Harijan*. R. J. Soman's *Peaceful Industrial Relations: Their Science and Technique* (1957) and Mahadeva Desai's *The Righteous Struggle* (1951) are important sources of information on the views of Gandhiji.

Gandhiji's vision was to create a new social order, which he called sarvodaya. His vision was for transforming the existing capitalistic society to a new order, evolved in his theory of trusteeship, in which the welfare of all would be looked after. He developed the theory of trusteeship as an alternative to private ownership.

The tool of voluntary arbitration was considered as the means for settling conflicts in IR. In the event of differences between workers and employers, Gandhiji considered voluntary conciliation between the parties to be the first tool for settling the dispute. In case conciliation fails, the next step is to refer the matter to an impartial third party for arbitration. The award of the arbitration is binding on the parties. In case the employer does not abide by the award of the arbitration, the workers have the option of resorting to non-violence or non-cooperation with the employer, which otherwise implies the resort to strike. But Gandhiji, as a practice, imposed certain conditions before workers called a strike. The conditions were as follows:

1. The reason for the strike needs to be just.
2. There should be complete unanimity amongst the workers who are on a strike.
3. Workers should not resort to while being on strike.
4. There should not be any sort of intimidation or coercion of workers who are not supporting the strike.
5. No financial help from third parties for strike.
6. A sense of solidarity to be maintained amongst workers till the strike lasts.
7. Workers should not resort to a strike without involving the trade union to which they belong.

The concept of 'satyagraha' for Gandhiji was characterized by adherence to truth by means of one's behaviour which is not violent but includes self-suffering. Thus, the concept of satyagraha when applied to labour agitation in any form meant merely a compromise in the context of conflict. So strike as a form of agitation was viewed differently than an ordinary strike. The stoppage of work at Ahmedabad, which Gandhiji was leading, was not merely a strike, but satyagraha, that is, striving for truth and compromise.

Gandhiji held that trade unions should aim to raise the moral and intellectual standards of labour and thus by sheer merit make labour the master of the means of production instead of being slaves. According to him, trade unions should cover all aspects of workers' lives both inside the factory and at home. Gandhiji was not in favour of strike in public utility services. He held that there was a conflict of interest between capital and labour and suggested a trusteeship approach to the relation between them. In his view, capital was the trustee for the good of the workers. He viewed that capital and labour should supplement and help each other. There should be a great unity and harmony between capital and labour; capital should not only look after the material welfare of labourers but also their moral welfare.

When workers are considered equal to the shareholders, they have the right to information regarding mills. If material information is withheld from workers, their confidence cannot be won. Gandhiji summed up his trusteeship theory in the following words:

My theory of trusteeship is no makeshift, certainly no camouflage. I am confident that it will survive all other theories. It has the sanction of philosophy and religion behind it. That possessors of wealth have not acted up to the theory does not prove its falsity; it proves the weakness of the wealthy. No other theory is compatible with non-violence.[2]

To solidify the trusteeship theory, Mahatma Gandhi suggested three steps: (a) persuasion, (b) state legislation and (c) dispossession and nationalization. He advised individual workers to practise self-control, self-discipline and self-imposed simplicity.

C.4.5. Case for Discussion   The Dispute at Graziano[3]

On 22 September 2008, Lalit Kishore Chaudhary, the managing director of Graziano Limited, Greater Noida, was lynched by factory workers. Chaudhary, an IIT Kanpur graduate, who built the factory from its inception, worked as a plant manager. He was appointed as the managing director in 2005. He had a good control over the people, plant and technology.

The workers who had lynched Lalit Kishore Chaudhary had come for L. K. Gupta, general manager, HR, who hid under the table of his cabin. The workers armed with stones and iron rods shattered windows and tore the blinds of the general manager's room from outside. The mob went looking for the managing director, who was on the first floor of the guest house and was talking to a group of Italian executives from Graziano's parent company. The Italians went hid in different rooms while the managing director jumped out of the balcony into the porch, where the workers caught up with him and beat him to death.

Mr Gupta returned to work when the plant was partially re-opened a week after this incidence. There was fear in all the factories in the vicinity of Graziano at Surajpur in Greater Noida, as was expressed by Mr Atul Ghildyal, the president of Association of Greater Noida Industries (AGNI). Mr Ghildyal was also the HR head at New Holland Tractors located right next to Graziano.

The then 10-year-old Surajpur facility of Graziano is now owned by Oerlikon Graziano, Italy. The plant located in Greater Noida is spread on 15 acres of land (60,000 sq. m) having a 32,860 sq. m covered area with a fully capitalized power plant (6,875 KVA PLC controlled generators). It is specialized in the production of gears, shafts, synchronizer assemblies, crown wheel and pinion for AG tractors, construction equipment, commercial vehicles and other off-highway applications. The facility is equipped with advanced technologies for crown wheel and pinions (Gleason face milling and face hobbing), and electron beam welding (EBW) technology, and it has the state-of-the-art heat-treatment capabilities and a fully robotic continuous type gas carburising furnace (CGCF).

Business was as per the expectations during the first nine years of its inception. From a modest turnover of ₹15 crore in 2000, it made an impressive growth of ₹270 crore in 2007. In the year 2007, it expanded its Greater Noida plant from 13,000 to 23,000 sq. m and added axles and synchronizer assemblies to its production. The plant is a certified ISO 9001:2008, ISO/TS 16949:2009, ISO 14001:2004 and OHSAS 18001:2007 facility.

There was no registered trade union in the company till 2008. It was only in the third quarter of 2007 that the workers felt the need for registering their trade union under the Trade Unions Act, 1926. In the year 2007, out of the 1,200 workers employed in the factory, only 500 were regular workers and the rest were on contract. M/S Graziano in 2008 paid its regular workers ₹3,200 per month for working 12 hours a day and contract workers were paid ₹2,200 per month. Most workers were not locals but migrants from other states. The workers attempted to register a trade union; three such attempts were made, but the registrar rejected their application s every time.

[2] M. K. Gandhi, *India of My Dreams: Ideas of Gandhi for a Vibrant and Prosperous Modern India*. New Delhi: Diamond Pocket Books; 2017.

[3] The case is presented only for academic objective. The author does not claim the authenticity of the data in the case. This case is purely from the prespective of the trade unions. The source of the data has been declared.

The Agitation

According to a trade union leader, the labour problems first started towards the end of 2007 when the factory's permanent workers asked the management for issuing them appointment letters which would have enabled them to register a trade union. Because three workers initiated the process of registration of a trade union, the management terminated their services.

The sequence of events that had taken place since 4 December 2007 is as under:

According to the company officials, signs of unrest were first seen in December 2007 when workers came up with a charter of demand. The key focus of this charter of demand was the revision of salaries. On 4 December 2007, 100 workers who were involved in the agitation were locked out by the management. The management agreed to negotiate with the workers on the restoration of normalcy in the plant. On 7 December 2007, AITUC, the trade union front of the CPI, to which the workers were initially affiliated, made a settlement with the management to restore normalcy in the plant. But the workers rejected this agreement. Thereafter, AITUC abandoned the workers.

Subsequently, the protest of the workers started over the demand for an increase in wages. The protesters had also demanded not to make deductions of wages on the grounds of improper punching of their attendance cards. They claimed that there were technical faults in the punching system, which caused such problems.

A tripartite wage settlement was reached on 24 January 2008 in the presence of DLC, Noida, and five representing members of the workers. The management agreed for a wage revision. The terms of the agreement were an increase of ₹1,200 for the first year (2008), ₹1,000 for the second year and ₹800 for the third year. The company signed the agreement with all the workers and with the external union AITUC, and the agreement was registered with the labour department. The agreement was valid for three years.

In the month of February 2008, immediately after this settlement, the management hired 400 workers on contract through three local contractors. Reportedly, the contractors, with the force of those 400 workers, started bullying other workers. Indiscipline grew post-March when the workers switched allegiance from AITUC to CITU.

The agitation which started in May 2008 was neither for the registration of the union nor for a claim for higher wages. In the month of May 2008, the management decided not to offer employment to five trainees at the end of their probationary period. Some workers went on strike to put pressure on the management for reverting their decision about those five trainees. But the management terminated the services of those five workers on the pretext that they manipulated the 'setting/programmes' of the automated machines without any instructions to them. The workers in their demands claimed the reinstatement of the five trainees, but the management besides terminating those five workers also terminated the production manager on the charge of supporting those workers.

In the same month, on one occasion, the cooling system of the works was switched off, which resulted in an increase of temperature on the shop floor. The workers protested to such unfair labour practices and made complaints, but complaints had no results. The workers also demanded for 8-hour shifts, as per law, instead of 12-hour shifts. Though all such demands were justified, they were not accepted by the management. Thereafter, the workers called a strike and despite labour officials' interventions, the strike continued and 27 workers were suspended.

On 30–31 May 2008, a disturbance started on the instigation of a local muscleman of the management, undercover as a contractor. The muscleman lodged a false complaint with the police on the basis of which 30 workers were implicated in a case and were taken to custody by the police. These employees were released by the police on a personal bond of ₹100,000 each.

With effect from June 2008, the 400 contract workers hired by the management were made to stay inside the plant. Apart from them, a large number of armed 'security guards' were employed by the contractors. The total required manpower was not so high to recruit the contract workers. So it was evident that the management was planning to throw out the permanent workers and replace them with those contract workers.

On 19 June 2008, the management terminated other 35 permanent workers. With this, the total number of permanent workers terminated gone up to 97. CITU agreed to the proposal of the management to restore the normal work culture in the plant by stopping all agitations inside and outside the plant. The workers, in general, disagreed to the conditions. CITU, thereafter, withdrew their support. In the meantime, the workers had the affiliation from HMS, the trade union front of Rashtriya Lok Dal.

The approach of the management was indifferent. An officer of the labour department in the course of an interview indicated the indifferent approach of the management that every time though the management assured to reinstate the terminated employees, they did not honour its promise.

On 1 July 2008, a meeting between the employers and HMS took place in the office of the DLC, in which the workers agreed to normalize the work culture by 4 July 2008. But on 2 July 2008, the management took a different stand. They terminated the remaining 192 workmen. This led to the workers resorting to protests and agitations. They first organized dharna in front of the office of the DLC for seven days. Thereafter for three days in fount of the office of the district magistrate and finally in fount of the office of the Italian Embassy in New Delhi.

On 11 July 2008, a settlement was arrived at in the presence of the DLC and the sub-divisional magistrate in which the workers agreed to maintain a normal work environment and the management agreed to reinstate the workers. On 13 July 2008, as a pursuant to the settlement, the workers presented themselves at the factory, but it was of no avail. On 16 July 2008, out of the 27 suspended workers, only 12 workers were reinstated. Notices were issued to 55 workers communicating that the remaining 15 workers would be reinstated soon, but this was never complied. The management obtained an order from the court restricting the agitation of any kind within 300 m of the factory premises by any employee.

All these incidents were followed by a series of meetings at the tripartite level held on 4 and 16 September 2008. In the meetings, it was agreed that the workers would tender an apology to the management. The DLC, Noida directed the workers to tender an apology on or before 22 September 2008.

On 18 September 2008, the workers on reporting in the factory within a day to tender an apology were informed that they would be called on 22 September 2008, and on the same day, the DLC refused to accept the apology in his office when the workers reported at his office. They were informed that only two workers at a time would go inside the 'time office' to tender the apology. They were told to specifically admit in their apology that they had indulged themselves in sabotage and violence. Some workers out of duress signed the document, but some refused.

Reportedly, in the course of this incidence, the time officer slapped one of the workmen for refusing to write the apology in the desired format. A scuffle started, and reportedly the workman was beaten up by the security personnel. On hearing about the commotion, the workmen present outside entered the time office; the management was unable to prevent the workers from entering the plant. It was also reported that the management ordered the security people and the goons present inside the plant to attack the workers. The security men opened fire on the workmen. About 34 workers were injured in the scuffle. The police implicated 63 workers for conspiring and participating in the killing of the CEO, whereas 74 others were implicated for rioting and other activities.

On 2 October 2008, the workers staged a sit-in protest at Jantar Mantar, New Delhi, against their victimization, and on 16 October 2008, another protest in support of the workers was held at the same place by the trade unions of NCR.

After the incident, the state government took the following steps:

1. Set up two new police circles for the Noida urban area, including one industrial police circle; appointmented a special circle officer, industries, to provide security to industrialists, and a special force was raised for that; launched a special helpline to solve the problems of employers within

two hours; and a decision was taken to issue arm licenses to the private security agencies working in the special economic zones.
2. Issued two government orders directing that the powers of the Labour Commissioner of Uttar Pradesh for the industrial areas of Noida and Greater Noida to be vested in the CEOs of the Noida and Greater Noida regions. The post of the DLC was relinquished. The authority of the DLC was now to assign the assistant labour commissioners (ALCs) of the areas who would discharge their duties directly under the two CEOs of Noida and Greater Noida of the respective regions.
3. Established a quick reaction team and an 'IR committee' comprising the CEOs of Noida and Greater Noida authorities and senior district police officers to look into the problems of industrialists, including labour disputes.

Annexure 1.

A petition by the Graziano Workers' Solidarity Forum (reiterated without any changes):

To
The Minister of Labour,
Government of India,
Shram Shakti Bhawan, New Delhi
Subject: Repression upon the workers of Graziano Trasmissioni in Noida.

Hon'ble Sir,

We, the various labour and social organizations, NGOs and individual social activists in and around Delhi, having come together under the banner of 'Graziano Workers' Solidarity Forum', with all humility represent to you as under:

We want to attract your attention towards the repression being launched against the workers of Graziano Trasmissioni at Noida, by the local administration and police in connection with the death of the CEO of the said company. This is apparently being done by the authorities in collusion with the Employers, not only of Graziano but of the entire Noida. It seems that the employers there want to settle accounts with the workers, and for this purpose are misusing the machine of the state.

We draw your humble attention to the fact that it is the same authorities who did not pay any heed to the very genuine and legitimate grievances of the workers for more than a year. The prayer of the workers for registration of their Trade Union, which is their statutory right, was kept pending for long. Neither did the employers recognize the Union nor did the department of labour permit it to be registered.

While the State authorities connived in depriving the workers of their minimum and modest rights, the employers went on exploiting the workers without challenge. Graziano Trasmissioni could thus earn super profits. The capital of 20 crore [200 million Rs.] invested by this company in 2004 grew over to 240 crore [2,400 million Rs.] in 2008. This could happen only through super-exploitation of the labour of poor workers. All peaceful protests of workers had fallen on deaf ears of the authorities. The employers, however, did everything in their control to crush the protests of workers, from suspension, lockout to outright terminations.

The unfortunate incident of 22nd September, cannot be made a tool to crush the workers further. The false charge being mischievously attributed by the police to the workers, of alleged conspiracy to harm the CEO, is beyond comprehension. There is no history of workers in Graziano of resorting to violence, much less a conspiracy. Moreover, the workers could not have expected any gain through such act. It is also underlined that even the wife of the CEO Smt. Ratna, who is a well-educated lady, has herself claimed that the killing of the CEO is the result of conspiracy by the rival business groups, from whom the CEO, Mr. L. K. Chaudhary himself had been expressing apprehension, immediately before his elimination.

We would also like to point out here, that according to our knowledge the dispute between the workers and management had already been settled amicably and thus there was hardly any occasion for the workers to enter into a tussle. Yet another side of the matter is that it has appeared more than once in the media that some rival business factions may be behind the elimination of the CEO. Be that as it may, the charge against the workers of conspiracy to kill the CEO is not only misplaced but also mischievous.

We apprehend, on the contrary, a conspiracy on the part of the employers in Noida, hand in hand with the police, to drown the peaceful and legitimate struggle of the workers in violence and blood and thereby vitiate the industrial atmosphere in Noida for the time to come. It is not the repression upon the workers, but a process of conciliation among the parties, which may help to restore the congenial atmosphere in Noida.

The Government cannot permit itself to be used as a tool at the behest of those who have the might of millions in their hands and cannot be turned into a vehicle of vested interests against the toiling workers. It goes without mention that Noida and its vicinity, Delhi included, is saturated with these toilers. The apparent bias of the state authorities against the workers, with an indifference towards their sufferings in the past and present, would result in perpetuating an environment of unwarranted hostility in the entire region.

We, therefore, humbly present the following demands before Your kind self:

1. Arrested workers to be released immediately and the false charges imposed upon them to be withdrawn.
2. Suspended and dismissed workers to be reinstated in their jobs.
3. Adequate compensation to be given to the victimized workers [13, 14].

Case Questions

(Instruction to the faculty: (a) divide the class into six groups, (b) each group to be assigned to analyse the questions relating to one of the theories on trade unions in the context of the above case, (c) the groups may brainstorm on the questions and come to a common answer and (d) the groups may be made to present the answers for class discussion).

Group 1. Questions on Webbs' Theory

1. What are the various factors that led to the formation/unionization of the workers of Graziano?
2. Please justify with the help of instances from the case whether the workers were democratic in their approach.
3. Do you think that the workers in any way could have initiated for a better method of settling their issues? Explain how.

Group 2. Questions on Marxian Theory

1. Please list down the instances of class straggle in the instant case.
2. Do you agree that 'the struggle between the trade union and the management led to the unionization of the workers'? Justify your answer in the light of the above case.
3. Do you think that the situations of the case study can be explained with the help of 'Marxian theory'? Explain.

Group 3. Questions on Perlman's Job Consciousness Theory

1. Identify the instances of collective action by the workers of Graziano.
2. Please indicate whether any of the collective actions were associated with any pessimistic outlook of the workers.
3. 'The threat of job security led to unionization in the instant case'. Explain how far the statement is true.

Group 4. Questions on Robert F. Hoxie's Socio-psychological Approach Theory

1. List down the factors of Graziano's environment impacting the psychology of the workers.
2. Please indicate the chance of such impacts on unionization in the case of the workers of Graziano.
3. To which category of unions (as per Robert F. Hoxie's) the present case can be justified? How?

Group 5. Questions on Tannenbaum's Technological Theory

1. Please list down 'how the factors such as security (job and working environment), freedom and justice to the employees, and faith of the workers are impacted in the instance case'.
2. Explain whether such instances have any connection with unionization in Graziano. How?

Group 6. Questions on Mahatma Gandhi's Approach

1. Can the actions of the trade union of Graziano be explained with the help of Gandhiji's concept on trade unionism?
2. How could the trade union manage the situation more effectively without violence? What changes would you recommend?

4.3. History of the Trade Union Movement in India

The history of trade unions' development in India is linked with the movements for reforming the society, the movements for making India independent and achieving the economic objectives of the industrialization of the country. The national leaders and social reformers took active roles in organizing workers and protecting them against inhuman working conditions and exploitations in factories. To protest against the acts of exploitation by employers, committees were formed from time to time to lead labour agitations and strikes. But such associations did not have the features of a trade union. Associations were more like ad hoc committees emerging to the specific requirements of workers, and they were not taking the responsibilities of a trade union. Industrialization in India started in the mid-19th century. The British tea companies started tea plantation in Assam in the year 1839, the Bengal Coal Company started in 1843, the first cotton mill in Bombay was established in 1854 and the first jute mill in Calcutta (now Kolkata) was started in 1855. The British established a network of railways in 1854 to transport raw materials and manufactured goods. Railways became another major employer of labour by 1860.

The major employment centres in India during the time were jute mills, cotton mills and tea plantations. By 1870, more than 5,00,000 Indian workers were working in these industries. But a 16-hour work day, low wages and no compensation for accidents marked the employers' labour-engaging culture.

The factory system encouraged the employment of women and children, long and excessive hours of work, undermining morality, lack of education, poor housing and an excessively high death rate owing to unhealthy and unsecured working conditions. The labour movement in India started in 1875, although some opine that the movement started in 1960. The study of the phases of development of trade unions in India, considering their activities and movements, are broadly categorized under six periods, and they are as follows: (a) pre-1918, (b) 1918–1924, (c) 1925–1934, (d) 1935–1838, (e) 1939–1946 and (f) 1947 and since.

4.3.1. Pre-1918 Period

In India, the first strike was organized in April–May 1862. At that time, the railway workers of Howrah Railway Station went on strike over their demand for an eight-hour shift duty. The working class, who were living below the poverty line, called for a strike to have a permanent solution to their miseries and protest against their exploitation, despite personal inconveniences in going for the strike. These workers in 1862 neither had the support of political power nor economic power to resist against the management's action of making them work for 10 hours a day.

There was a growing consciousness among the factory workers to demand for better working conditions in the factories. In the year 1875, for the first time, the Indian factory workers united for securing better working conditions in the factories. In the same year, the first factory commission was appointed because Mr Sarobji Shapuri protested against the poor working conditions of workers in the factories and started agitations in Bombay to draw the attention of the government. He brought the lamentable conditions of women and child labour in industries in India were brought to the knowledge of the Secretary of State for India, who realized that the working conditions of the workers were inhuman. Such factors resulted to the enactment of the Factory Act of 1881. But the Act was inadequate and it failed to address the issues of child labour and working conditions of women workers.

The next factory commission was appointed in 1884 to address these issues. In the same year, Mr Narayan Meghaji Lokhande (considered as the 'father' of the trade union movement in India) organized a conference of factory workers at Bombay. A memorandum was signed by 5,300 workers demanding to the managements and the government a complete day of rest on Sunday, half-an-hour recess as lunch break, working hours from 6.30 AM to sunset, payment of wages not later than 15th of the next month and compensation for injuries. Because some of these points were not addressed either by the factory owners or by the government, the agitation on demand for a rest day on Sunday and compensation in the case of an accident continued in 1889 by the workers of spinning and weaving mills of Bombay. Another representation was made to the government in 1890, which was signed by 17,000 workers. In 1884, the Bombay Mill Hands Association (BMHA), the first labour association, was founded by Mr Lokhande, at Bombay. Mr Lokhande was appointed as its president.

Mr Lokhande started a labour journal named *Deenbandhu*, which with time became the voice of workers. Mr Bangs Lee, a great philanthropist, was associated with the BMHA to project the sufferings of the workers of Bombay. Under the leadership of Mr Lokhande, the workers placed their demands before the Factory Labour Commission in the year 1890. It was high time for the Commission to give due consideration to the demands of the labour.

The post-1890 period saw the formation of several labour associations, and the list includes the following:

1. The Amalgamated Society of Railway Servants in India and Burma was formed in April 1897 and registered under the Indian Companies Act.
2. The Printers Union, Calcutta, was formed in 1905.
3. The Bombay Postal Union was formed in 1907.

4. The Kamgar Hityardhak Sabha and Social Service League were formed in 1910.
5. TLA was founded in 1917.
6. The Madras Labour Union at Madras was formed in 1918.

This period also witnessed several strikes in various parts of India. The notable of these strikes were as follows:

1. In 1894, two strikes in Bombay.
2. In February 1895, the strike of mill operators of Ahmedabad.
3. In 1896, when the Ahmedabad Mill Owners Association decided to substitute the system of payment of wages from weekly to fortnightly over 8,000 weavers went on strike.
4. In 1896, the strike in the jute industries in Calcutta.
5. In 1897, after the epidemic of plague, the mill workers in Bombay went on strike for the payment of daily wages instead of the monthly payment of wages.
6. In 1903, the employees of the press and machine section under the Madras government went on strike against the non-payment of overtime. This strike prolonged for six months.
7. In 1905, the workers of the Government of India Press, Calcutta, launched a strike over the question of the (a) non-payment for Sunday and gazetted holidays, (b) imposition of irregular fines, (c) low rate of overtime pay and (d) the refusal of authorities to grant leaves on a medical certificate. The strike continued for over a month.
8. In December 1907, the workers of the Eastern Railways Workshop at Samastipur, Bihar, went on strike on the issue of increment of wages. They went back to work after six days when they were granted allowance owing to the famine at that time in the region.
9. In the same year, the Bombay Postal Union and Indian Telegraph Association called a strike.
10. In 1908, workers of textile operators in Bombay went on strike in sympathy with Shri Bal Gangadhar Tilak who was imprisoned for sedition.
11. In 1910, the workers in Bombay went on strike demanding the reduction in working hours. As a result of this agitation, the Government of India set up a commission to enquire into the desirability of reducing the working hours. On the basis of the recommendations, the working hours were reduced to 12 hours a day.

Similar strikes continued in Bengal and Bombay demanding an increase in wages and improving the working benefits.

Immediately after the war time of 1918, an important landmark event in the history of the Indian trade union movement took place, that is, the establishment of TLA in Ahmedabad under the guideance of Mahatma Gandhi. The Association declared a strike demanding higher wages, war bonus and so on.

TLA was considered at that point of time as India's biggest organized labour union which was associated with Gandhian philosophy and principles of trade unionism. But the labour movement during the period did not have any qualities of agitation as in modern trade unionism. The efforts of the social reformers and the leaders of the agitation were aimed at organizing workers and making them aware of their rights. The important characteristics of the early trade union movement were as follows:

1. The leadership was from outside, philanthropists or social reformers and not anyone from the workers' side.

2. There was no organized body of trade unions in the modern sense. Even BMHA did not have the features of a trade union. It was never registered; hence, it neither had a legal stand nor was it recognized by the management. It was not having any membership of workers, no funds and no rules. The leaders like Lokhande who served both as the president of the union and the member of the factory commission worked more as a volunteer and not as a leader of the agitating group.

3. Associations mainly relied on petitions and memoranda for projecting their demands. No other means of placing their demands were followed. Such demands were focused only in the areas of hours of work, health, wages for overtime, leave and holidays.

4. No strike was organized as a means of getting grievances redressed; only the early movements were against conditions of child labour and women workers employed in various factories.

5. The association of workers worked with the cooperation of the management and the government officials, and some of them considered it as their duty.

6. Strikes were considered as against the legal system of the time.

7. Unions adopted a constitutional approach to redress grievances as they were led by philanthropists and intellectuals. However, workers were reactive to inhuman conditions prevailing in the organized industry.

IC.4.1. INDUSTRIAL CONTEXT FOR DISCUSSION

Narayan Meghaji Lokhande: The Father of the Trade Union Movement in India

Narayan Meghaji Lokhande, the father of the trade union movement in India, founded the first trade union in India—BMHA—in 1884 and was its president. He worked for some time as a store keeper in a Bombay textile mill and gathered knowledge on the working conditions in the Indian factories and various problems faced by workers. He edited the first labour weekly *Deenbandhu* (the friend of the oppressed) from 1880 to the end of his life in 1897. When the Government of India appointed the factory commission in 1890, Lokhande was appointed as an associate member of the commission for the Bombay presidency. He mobilized men and women from the working class to present evidence before the commission on the hardships they undergo in the factories. He was both a social reformer and a trade union leader. He worked for the social upliftment of the people against the social vice caste untouchability.

Lokhande was born to a poor family of the phulmali caste in Thane near Bombay in 1848. The phulmalis grew flowers, fruits and vegetables for the urban market and so lived mostly on the periphery of the towns. Being closer to the towns, they were the first amongst the non-brahmin castes to receive Western education.

After completing his schooling, Lokhande joined as a store keeper in a textile mill in Bombay. He was impressed by Jyotirao Govindrao Phule's teachings and became an active member of the Satyashodhak Samaj. Phule (11 April 1827–28 November 1890) was an Indian activist, thinker, social reformer and writer from Maharashtra. He formed Satyashodhak Samaj (society of the seekers of truth) and was the first president and treasurer to focus on the rights of depressed classes).

Lokhande with Bhalekar, a co-worker of Phule, started publishing *Deenbandhu* in Pune in 1877. He published it at great personal loss and ultimately had to discontinue it after two years owing to the shortage of funds. In 1880, the journal was brought to Bombay. Lokhande gave up his job to work to edit the journal. With the help of his Telugu friends, who were builders and contractors, Lokhande published *Deenbandhu* without interruption till his death caused by the epidemic plague in 1897.

The appointment of the commission gave factory workers an opportunity to put their grievances before the government. Lokhande and his associates formed the BMHA and on behalf of the association organized a meeting of mill workers in Parel on 23 September 1884. This was the first meeting of industrial workers in Bombay's history. In a resolution adopted at the meeting, the following demands were made:

1. One complete day of rest every Sunday for all mill hands
2. Half an hour rest at noon on every working day
3. Hours of work from 6:30 AM to sunset
4. Payment of wages be made no later than 15th of the next month
5. A workman sustaining serious injuries in the course of work at the mill, disabling him for some time, should receive full wages until he recovers, and in the case of being maimed for life, suitable provisions be made for his/her livelihood.

As the president of the association, Lokhande forwarded the petition to the government. The Government of India appointed another factory commission in September 1890. The scope of this commission was to study the conditions of labour in Indian factories and make recommendations. Sorabji Bengalee was one of the members of the commission. A new factory Act based on their recommendations was passed in 1891. Because of the initiatives of Mr Lokhande, the Act had provisions such as improving the working conditions of workers, limits on engaging children below nine years, and restricting children's working hours to 9 hours and that of women to 11 hours.

The first Hindu–Muslim riot occurred in Bombay on 2 August 1893, and after the riots, workers felt insecure to come to duty. Lokhande and other activists of the Satyashodhak Samaj went to the labour areas and restored confidence in them to come to duty. Lokhande also took a lead role in helping the riot-affected people by distributing donations collected by him through *Deenbandhu*.

Lokhande was not only a trade union leader but also a social reformer working for social justice and communal harmony [15–17].

4.3.2. The Period from 1918 to 1924

The period from 1918 to 1924 is termed as the era of formation of trade unionism in India that was focused on protecting workers' interests. This period witnessed the formation of a large number of organized trade unions. But initial trade unions had to face a lot of problems such as 'internal dissension' and persistent opposition from employers. They also suffered merciless persecution and suppression from the British Government. Trade unions were even considered as criminal conspirators. In England, the Combinations Acts of 1799 and 1800 were enacted which prohibited the workmen from uniting and declared any unions to be illegal. Trade unions were considered as criminal conspirators for creating restraints on trade. Taking such a clue from the British law, the Madras Labour Union in the case of the Buckingham and Carnatic Mills in the year 1921 was termed as a criminal organization by the Madras High Court. But despite these stigmas, trade unions continued to grow in India.

The association of Mahatma Gandhi with Ahmedabad TLA in 1917 was the most significant incident. The first systematic attempt in the similar direction was made by B. P. Wadia who established the Madras Labour Union in 1918. Wadia was a leader of the Indian National Congress and a close associate of Dr Annie Besant. The birth of the Madras Labour Union was the result of the difficulties, hardships and problems which the workers faced in the Buckingham and Carnatic Mills. The trade unions of that period had twofold objectives, that is, to protect the general interest of the workers and to provide militant force to the national freedom movement.

The important active trade unions of this period were as follows:

1. TLA
2. Madras Labour Union
3. Indian Seamen's Union
4. Calcutta Clerks' Union
5. All India Postal and RMS Association
6. AITUC, formed in 1920.

This period experienced a more number of strikes in industries than other periods. The strikes were in reaction to the misery of the working class in factories and their deteriorating economic conditions.

The factors responsible for the growth of trade unions during this period were as follows:

1. **The economic conditions of workers:** Low economic conditions clubbed with rising prices of essential commodities were some of the prime causes of the growth of trade unions in this period. The prices of essential commodities, namely salt, cotton, cloth and kerosene increased, whereas the existing salaries were not meeting the ends of the working class.
2. **The influence of the political movement for Independence:** The Independence movement had started which charged employees with the spirit of agitation. Workers were also influenced by political leaders, who took the lead for helping the growth of trade unions.
3. **Workers' revolution in Russia:** The Russian labour movement was an example for the workers in India to think along similar lines in the Indian context.
4. **The impact of war:** The economic effects of the First World War prompted the industrial workers to unite to demand for better wages and working conditions.
5. **The impact of the ILO:** The setting up of the ILO in 1919, of which India was a founding member, and the government's decision to appoint Shri N. M. Joshi as the representative, without consulting trade unions, was a major point of discontent. As a reaction, AITUC was formed in 1920.

4.3.3. The Period from 1925 to 1934

This period is termed as the period of left-wing unionism. In the year 1924, trade unions were involved in violent and long-drawn strikes. Such actions of the trade unions led to the arrests and imprisonment of the active union members. AITUC was the only CTU which emerged as the sole representative of the Indian working class. By the year 1927, about 57 unions had joined AITUC bringing its membership to 150,555, across India. The factors which were responsible for the rapid growth of trade unions were as follows:

1. The growth of the anti-imperialist national movement in India
2. The brutal violence of the British Government in the Jallianwala Bagh massacre, imposition of the Rowlatt Act, and indiscriminate arrests and imprisonment of national leaders and freedom fighters
3. Exploitation of workers and high profits earned by capitalists at a time when real wages were falling.

In the meantime, the Trade Unions Act, 1926 was enacted by the government, which had become the contextual requirement of the time for managing the emerging number of trade unions in the country.

In the historic Buckingham and Carnatic Mills case, 1921, the Madras High Court issued an injunction order against the strike of the Madras Labour Union prohibiting them from going on strikes. The trade union leaders were also liable to prosecution and imprisonment for bona fide trade union activities. A sequence of events after this incident helped in the process of the enactment of the Trade Unions Act, 1926 and safeguard of the freedom of such associations, such as follows:

1. After the establishment of the ILO in 1919, the need for some legislation was felt for the protection of trade union activities in India.
2. Trade unions were organized and in 1920, AITUC was founded. Mr N. N. Joshi, the general secretary of AITUC, in March 1921 moved a resolution in the Central Legislative Assembly recommending the Government of India to introduce a legislation for the registration of trade unions.
3. The interest of trade unions and the national movement in favour of the protection of the rights of the workers in different organizations across the country coincided.

Employers opposed to the adoption of such enactments. However, ultimately, the Trade Unions Act was passed in the year 1926.

The Act continues to be an important legislation and instrument for the formation of new trade unions, controlling the existing trade unions, and continuance and functioning of the trade unions in India. The Act provides legal sanctity to the infant trade unions and a social status and organizational cohesiveness to such associations. Legally, trade unions are no longer conspiratorial associations against the management.

The enactment of the Trade Unions Act, 1926 was a very important landmark in the history of the trade union movement in India.

The year 1928 witnessed the formation of All India Workers' and Peasants' Party, which was a union of workers and farmers. With this, the leadership in AITUC shifted to the Left. The philosophy of the Left led to an increasing number of strikes during this period. In the same year, the total man-days lost were of 316 lakh. The communists were supported by the trade unions of the cotton mills of Bombay and the workers union of the G.I.P. Railways. These trade unions had 54,000 and 45,000 members, respectively, during that time. The support to Left was visible in the activities of the trade unions in Bombay, Ahmedabad, Delhi and Calcutta. The British Government in order to control the impact of the leftists, initiated measures of control. The Meerut Conspiracy case filed by the government in the year 1929 was one such example. The case continued for 4.5 years. The verdict of the case ordered for the arrest of 31 leading left-wing trade unionists across the country. This was a big blow to the leftist's movement.

The leftist's ideology was that 'the working class should resort to militant action and combine economic struggle with political struggle in order to capture political power'. On the other hand, the moderate section of AITUC found such ideologies to be far from their conceptual approach to unionization. Under the leadership of Mr N. M. Joshi and Mr V. V. Giri, supported by 21 affiliated unions having a membership of 94,000, a separate organization by the name of the National Trade Unions Federation (NTUF) was formed. The objective of this federation was to follow a constructive approach for furthering the interests of the working class. This approach of NTUF was widely accepted by trade unions across the country, and by the year 1930, the federation had an affiliation of 104 trade unions with a total membership of 2.42 lakh.

In the year 1931, there was another split in AITUC, in the Calcutta session, owing to the fundamental differences between the communists and the left-wing unionists. The communists led by B. T. Ranadive and S. V. Deshpande formed the Red Trade Union Congress (RTUC).

Thus, at the beginning of the 1930s, three CTUs were formed:

1. AITUC led by royalists and militant nationalists
2. AITUF led by congress nationalists and moderates
3. RTUC consisting of orthodox communists.

There were also other independent organizations, for example, AIRF and TLA of Ahmedabad.

4.3.4. The Period from 1935 to 1938

This period was termed as the Trade Unions' Unity Period. The trade union movement during this period tended towards unifying the larger body of associations.

After the splits in AITUC, some efforts were made to unite the fragmented units. The initiative taken by AIRF, which was a neutral body, had some fruitful results. This federation in its conference in the year 1932 at Bombay formed the Trade Union Unity Committee. In the year 1933, the National Federation of Labour (NFL) was formed, and it further facilitated the unity of CTU. AITUF and the railway unions amalgamated themselves with the NFL under the name of NTUF. However, AITUC and RTUC remained out of this reunion.

The following developments happened subsequently:

1. In 1935, the All India RTUC merged itself with AITUC.
2. In 1938, the All India National Trade Union Federation and AITUC arrived at an agreement leading to NTUF getting affiliated to AITUC.

The factors which led to the revival trade unions to unite were as follows:

1. The political setup and the movement by the Congress Party, which formed its government in several provinces in 1937, strengthened the trade union movement and improved the conditions of labour.
2. The awakening of the working class and becoming conscious of the rights led to demand for better terms and conditions of service.
3. The management's approach to trade unions also changed.

The year 1939 saw the most important state enactment, namely the Bombay Industrial Disputes Act, 1938. The significant features of the Act were as follows:

1. Compulsory recognition of unions by the employer
2. Giving the right to workers to get their case represented either through a representative union, elected representatives of workers or through the government LO
3. Certification of standing orders which would define with sufficient precision the conditions of employment
4. The setting up of an industrial court, with both original as well as appellate jurisdiction
5. Prohibition of strikes and lockouts only under certain conditions. But the scope of the Act was limited to certain industries in the province.

4.3.5. The Period from 1939 to 1946

The Second World War broke in September 1939. By the time, some differences in the different political fractions of AITUC were developed. The group led by the members of the Radical Democratic Party, under the leadership of J. Mehra, V. K. Karnik and M. N. Roy, were of the opinion that AITUC should support the British Government. On the other hand, the group supported by Shri S. C. Bose and others were against such views. So there was another split in AITUC in the year 1941. The radicals left AITUC, with nearly 200 unions with a membership of 300,000, and formed a new central labour federation known as the Indian Federation of Labour (IFL). In 1942, this federation had its recognition from the government. IFL mobilized the Indian labour for participation in such industrial programmes, which were geared to meet the needs of the war and made efforts to secure for the workers minimum wages and benefits which were needed in the wartime conditions. This effort of IFL was supported by the Government of India by funding ₹13,000 per month. The number of trade unions affiliated to IFL by the year 1944 was 222 with a membership of 407,773 workers.

Certain factors were favourable to the trade union movement during this period which helped the growth of trade unions, that is (a) the government and employers launched a number of labour welfare activities with intention to increase the production of war materials and other essential goods, (b) many employers recognized trade unions, (c) there were bans on strikes and lockouts under the 'Defence of India Rules 81A' and (d) a tripartite labour conference was held in the year 1942 to provide a common platform for discussions and mutual settlement of disputes between the employer and workers.

The Defence of India Rules, 1942 remained in force during this time. The Rule 81A of the Act empowered the government with some of the specific powers relating to the management of factories. Such provisions were as follows:

1. To instruct employers to observe such terms and conditions of employment in their establishments as may be specified
2. To refer any dispute to conciliation and adjudication
3. To enforce the decisions of the adjudicators
4. To make general and special orders to prohibit strikes and lockouts in connection with any trade dispute unless reasonable notice has been given.

The provisions empowered the government to use coercive methods for the settlement of 'trade disputes'.

In the post Second World War period, the membership of the registered trade unions increased to 1,087 by 1945. There were also increasing number of labour disputes. The reasons attributed to the disputes were as follows:

1. There was a rise in the prices of essential commodities.
2. There was a split in AITUC owing to the nationalist movement.
3. The post-Second World War period witnessed retrenchment and, therefore, the problem of unemployment. The period also witnessed a large number of strikes.

In 1946, the Industrial Employment (Standing Orders) Act, 1946 was passed with a view to bring uniformity in the condition of employment of workmen in industrial establishments, and thereby minimizing industrial conflicts. In 1946, BIRA was also enacted. The Act had elaborate provisions for the recognition of trade unions and defined their rights.

4.3.6. The Period after 1947

The proliferation of trade unions in the post-Independence period in India had been identical to the pattern of proliferation of political parties.

INTUC was formed in May 1947 by the members of the Congress Party; by then, AITUC was controlled by the communists. The Congress socialists who were with AITUC subsequently formed HMS in 1948. Subsequently, HMS was split up with a group of socialist and formed a separate association, namely, BMS—which is now an affiliate of the Bharatiya Janata Party (BJP). Years after, the Communist Party split into various fractions forming the UTUC and the CITU. Later again, a group disassociated itself from the UTUC and formed another UTUC-Lenin Sarani. Of late, with the emergence of regional parties since 1960, most of the regional parties have shown their inclination to a trade union wing, thereby adding to the proliferation of trade unions in the country. Thus, it is clear that the origin and growth of the trade union movement in India are riddled with fragmented politicization.

The trade union movement and the emergent IR in the country went hand in hand with the economic policy on the industrialization of the government. With the growth of industry, there were changes in the social and personal expectations of the labour class. Such changes were also impacted by the structural changes in the environment, impacting the three actors, that is, the management, the workers represented by the trade unions and the government. The Ministry of Labour and Employment, India, in its Orders No. L–52025/20/2003–IR (Imp–I), dated 11 January 2008, New Delhi, declared the names of 13 trade unions under the Central Trade Union Organizations (CTUOs). They are as follows:

1. AITUC: All India Trade Union Congress (CPI) is the oldest trade union federation in India. It was founded on 31 October 1920 in Bombay by Lala Lajpat Rai, Joseph Baptista, N. M. Joshi and a few others. Since then, it has been associated with CPI. According to the provisional statistics from the Ministry of Labour, AITUC had a membership of 2,677,979 in 2002.
2. INTUC: Indian National Trade Union Congress (Indian National Congress) is the trade union wing of the Indian National Congress. It was founded on 3 May 1947 and is affiliated with the International Trade Union Confederation. According to the provisional statistics from the Ministry of Labour, INTUC had a membership of 3,892,011 in 2002. INTUC is widely accepted as a trade union that works with the management and is not a typical confrontational organization.
3. HMS: Hind Mazdoor Sabha (Unaffiliated) was founded in Howrah on 29 December 1948, by socialists, Forward Bloc followers and independent unionists. It is claimed to have 380 affiliated unions with a combined membership of 618,802.
4. UTUC: United Trade Union Congress (Revolutionary Socialist Party) is politically tied to the Revolutionary Socialist Party. UTUC was founded at an All India Labour Conference in Calcutta on 1 May 1949. According to the statistics from the Ministry of Labour, UTUC had a membership of 383,946 in 2002.
5. BMS: Bharatiya Mazdoor Sangh was founded by Dattopantji Thengdi on 23 July 1955. It is the labour wing of RSS (Rashtriya Swayamsevak Sangh, a wing of BJP). It can also be noted that BMS is not affiliated to the International Trade Union Confederation. According to the provisional statistics from the Ministry of Labour, BMS had a membership of 6,215,797 in 2002.
6. AIUTUC: All India United Trade Union Centre formerly known as United Trade Union Centre (Lenin Sarani) or UTUC-LS, is the labour wing of the Socialist Unity Centre of India

(Communist). All India UTUC was founded at a conference held in Calcutta on 26–27 April 1958, following a split in UTUC. Presently, its activities are spread over 19 states. The organization claims to have 600 affiliated unions, comprising an individual membership of over two million. According to the provisional statistics from the Ministry of Labour, UTUC-LS had a membership of 1,368,535 in 2002.

7. NFITU: National Front of Indian Trade Unions, Dhanbad and National Front of Indian Trade Unions, Kolkata: The union was founded on 14 August 1963, at Dhanbad, and subsequently at Kolkata. It achieved the status of CTUO in the year 2008 by the Ministry of Labour and Employment, Government of India. NFITU has its presence in around 35 industries across 15 states in India. It comprises 138 affiliate unions and has more than 60 lakh membership of workers in organized and unorganized sectors.

9. CITU: Centre of Indian Trade Unions is affiliated to CPI(M). It was established in the year 1970. It has a strong presence in the states of Tripura, Bengal and Kerala. However, this trade union has an average presence in Tamil Nadu and Andhra Pradesh. CITU had a membership of 3,222,532 in 2002.

10. LPF: Labour Progressive Federation (Dravida Munnetra Kazhagam) was founded on 1 May 1970. It is a trade union federation in the South Indian state of Tamil Nadu. The LPF is politically attached to Dravida Munnetra Kazhagam. According to the statistics from the Ministry of Labour, LPF had a membership of 611,506 in 2002.

11. SEWA: Self Employed Women's Association is the trade union of independently employed female workers. SEWA was founded in 1972 by the Gandhian and civil rights leader Ela Bhatt as a branch of TLA (a labour union founded by Gandhi in 1918). SEWA has over two million participating women as members, it is the largest organization of informal workers in the world and largest non-profit organization in India.

12. AICCTU: All India Central Council of Trade Unions is politically attached to Communist Party of India (Marxist–Leninist; CPI[ML]) Liberation. Founded in 1989 in its Chennai conference, it is spread over 32 of 50 scheduled industries (including miscellaneous) in 11 states and achieved the status of a recognized CTUO in 2008. According to provisional statistics from the Ministry of Labour, AICCTU had a membership of 639,962 in 2002.

13. TUCC: The Trade Union Coordination Centre is the trade union wing of All India Forward Bloc, a party founded by Netaji Subhas Chandra Bose. According to the statistics from the Ministry of Labour, TUCC had a membership of more than 16 crore in 2011.

A changing trend in trade unionism was visible in the first decade of the 21st century. The phases of growth of trade unionism in the period of post-Independence can be broadly categorized under five phases. The analysis of the five phases is appended in the context of 'the background', 'the relation among the three actors' and 'the trade union movements'.

4.3.6.1. The First Phase of Unionism (1951–1966)

The background: The first phase of unionism is generally termed as national capitalism [18]. This includes the growth of trade unionism during the first three Five-Year plans (1951–1956, 1956–1961 and 1961–1966). This was a period of government-led industrialization policies. The government encouraged a policy of import substitution during this period. In this period, large, employment-intensive public sector enterprises emerged. The average employment during this period grew rapidly, that is, from 0.4 per cent in 1951 to 2 per cent per annum by 1966. The membership of the registered trade unions increased threefold during this period. The number of registered trade unions also increased from 4,623 in 1951–1952 to 11,614 in 1961–1962.

The relationship among the actors: The management and labour relationship was more of a paternalistic nature, where the government was aware of workers' needs. On the other hand, because the government was more inclined towards early industrialization, it expected that the trade unions will work to contribute to this objective. The relationship between the ruling government and its affiliated trade union federation during the first phase was well controlled by the provisions of the ID Act of 1947, which had initially the answers to all related issues of labour. The structure of collective bargaining was more centrally controlled by CTUs, except in some industries like textiles. *Tripartism and political bargaining* predominantly controlled the sphere of wage negotiations.

The trade union movements: During this period, the communist-led CTU, AITUC, had established well-organized movements in the textile and engineering industries of Bombay, Calcutta and Kanpur. The Congress Party felt the need for the formation of a trade union of its own, grounded on its ideology, resulting in the formation of INTUC. AITUC established itself with the support of the rank and file workers, whereas the INTUC was imposed as a labour movement from the outside with the support of the Congress Party. By the end of the first phase, further splits occurred in the labour movement, that is, the socialists formed HMS, thereby breaking away from the Congress. The Indo-Chinese issues divided the CPI, and CPI(M) emerged which formed its own trade union CITU.

The institutional structures of IR like collective bargaining continued at an underdeveloped stage. However, the government attempted for developing the participatory involvement of workers through Works Committees (under the ID Act, 1947) and later through JMCs in the year 1958.

C.4.6. Case for Discussion   The National Freedom Fighters in the Trade Union Movement

The need to voice the genuine demands of the working class in India, and at the same time, national interests of economy appeared in the agenda of national leaders in the post-Independence period. As Sardar Vallabhbhai Patel in his presidential address in a labour conference held on 3–4 May 1947 indicates:

The workers in India are only a section of the people and not a class apart. The culture and their tradition form part of the common heritage of the people of India. In organizing them and seeking the redressal of their grievances, ways and means have to be evolved in consonance with our condition. No more grafting or transplantation of a foreign ideology or method however suited to the condition elsewhere, is likely to yield healthy results here. What is required is an indigenous movement having its roots in the Indian and soil. Such a movement has for long been in existence and has attained a remarkable centre. A new organization, that would give the correct lead to the working class and strives to established social justice, peace and security with a constitution and working. Which would be essentially democratic giving every one of its constituent units ample scope for free expression of views and action has become imperative.

Thus, INTUC was born in the year 1947.

The conference was attended by the national leaders such as Pandit Jawaharlal Nehru, Jagjivan Ram, Aruna Asaf Ali, Ram Manohar Lohia, G. Ramanujam, V. V. David, B. G. Kher, O. P. Ramasami Reddiar, Ravishankar Shukla, Harekrishna Mahtab, S. K. Patil, Kamaladevi Chattopadhyaya, Ashok Mehta, R. R. Diwakar and Bhim Sen Sachar. The prominent labour leaders of the time who were attending the conference were G. L. Nanda, Khandubhai Desai, Suresh Chandra Banerjee, Abid Ali Jaffarbhoy, Michael

John, Deven Sen, Harihar Nath Shastri, S. R. Vasavda, S. P. Sen, R. K. Khedgikar, G. L. Mapara and G. D. Ambekar.

The national freedom fighters, political thinkers, social reformers and leading labour leaders attended this conference to constitute a new form of CTU. The focus was the creation of a CTU which could voice the genuine demands of the working class of the country, without defeating the national interests. About 200 trade unions attended this conference, which was a call of these national freedom fighters and social reformers. The combined membership of these unions was roughly over 565,000.

The conference was inaugurated by Acharya J. B. Kripalani, the then president of the Indian National Congress who in his address said:

> The proposed organization should not hesitate to employee the weapon of strike, if it were essential to promote the true interest of labour. But that weapon is to be employed only after due consideration and with aim was to achieve any legitimate economic and social objective. But it would however, not only be misuse of this weapon but doing actual harm to labour's own interests if it were to be employes for the attainment of sectional political ends. If labour were to submit its organized strength to such exploitation. It would become a mere tool in the hands of unscrupulous party politicians.

The national leaders and social reformers were considered by him as 'trusted leaders' to lead the trade union.

Shri Ghulzari Lal Nanda, the secretary of the Hindustan Mazdoor Sewak Sangh, who explained the circumstances that led to the formation of such a trade union, stated:

> There is no common ground between those inspired by communist philosophy and those who have fail in democracy, the proposed organization can provide a broad platform and ensure the largest measure of unity as the latter in pursuit of the aim of the labour movement.

According to the resolution of the conference which was moved by Dr Suresh Chandra Banrjee:

> Whereas the course of the labour movement in the country is taking under the leadership of those who are opposed to peaceful change and democratic methods has proved to be extremely detrimental to the growth of strong and healthy trade unionism and is doing incalculable harm to the true interest of the masses of the country and whereas it has become a scared and imperative obligation of those who are for the well-being of the working class to take concerted action to safeguard and promote its interest, it is resolved that to give effect to this purpose, an organization called the Indian National Trade Union Congress be formed.

Thus, INTUC was born on 3 May 1947 as a historic necessity, just before India attained independence [19].

Case Questions

1. What are the reasons for the involvement of the freedom fighters in the trade union movement?
2. 'The freedom fighters were equally concerned for an economic reform as well as a social reform in the country.' Do you agree with this statement? Give your justification to what you agree.

4.3.6.2. The Second Phase of Unionism (mid-1960s to 1979)

The background: The period includes the Annual Plans for 1967–1969, the Fourth and the Fifth Five-Year Plans (1969–1974 and 1974–1979, resp.). There had been structural changes in the economy during this period, which had effects on trade union activities. There was a rise in the cost of living owing to inflation which had increased above 10 per cent during the years 1966–1967 and 1967–1968. The food price inflation was also even higher, that is, around 20 per cent. There was a general industrial stagnation in the economy. In the context of such an uncontrolled economy, where the bulk of the industrial organizations were under the control of the government, the efficacy of the paternalistic management style and philosophy, which was followed by the government, was questioned. Further, the government's decision to impose Emergency in the year 1975, which continued till 1977, was nothing but a failed attempt by the government to impose its policy decisions on the trade unions and workers. This led to a dissension between the government and the trade unions.

An analysis of industrial disputes revealed that most of the disputes involved two or more CTU federations, concluding more of inter-union rivalry. There was a deep sense of uncertainties within the organized workers. Instances like the railway strike of 1974 were the obvious steps taken by the trade unions. The suspension of the right to strike in 1975 (during Emergency), reduction of the statutory bonus from 8.33 to 4 per cent, transfer of increments in the cost-of-living allowance to a compulsory savings scheme, freezing of wages, formation of the NAB of 12 trade unions and 11 employers' representatives for settling disputes were something uncalled for by the trade unions. With the Janata government (1977–1980) coming to power, there were qualitative changes in the political climate as well as in the thought process of IRS.

The relationship among the actors: By 1977, the major CTUOs were INTUC, AITUC, HMS and CITU. The labour–management relationship had turned to an informal decentralized bargaining mode, no more looking at a centralized negotiation structure through the involvement of CTUs. A visible shift was there in the trade union structure, that is, going for smaller groups rather than centrally controlled larger groups proved to be more effective.

The trade union movements: The second phase of unionism saw significant changes in industrial labour markets, labour relations, in general, and collective bargaining practices, in particular. By the 1970s, unions shifted their goals from focusing on their rights to those of interests. This led to decentralized collective bargaining as per the interests, resulting in an increase in the number of strikes and lockouts, number of workers involved and the number of workdays lost [20]. Local trade unions followed new approaches of agitations, for example, gheraos, dharna and go-slow. These forms were more visible in West Bengal. These shifts and fractures within the organized labour in the country had serious implications for union strategies, especially in maintaining solidarity across the entire organized labour movement.

C.4.7. Case for Discussion   The Formation of Tea Plantation Labour Unions in Bengal

After Independence in 1947, the Indian economy changed as per the policy of the government. During this period, a pro-labour approach was adopted by the government. Trade unions were allowed to organize the tea plantation workers in Assam, the state with the largest number of tea plantation workers, and a major union—the Assam Chah Mazdoor Sangh—was formed. This union was affiliated to INTUC and with time became a recognized trade union.

Trade unions from other industries had influenced tea plantation workers to form trade unions. The Bengal Dooars Railway Workers Union (BDRWU) played a major role in the formation of trade unions in the tea gardens of Bengal. First, the workers of Haihaipathar (now called Rapali) near Mal came under the influence of BDRWU. The workers of other tea gardens who had also formed trade unions under the influence of BDRWU were Denguajhar, Bagrakote and Lakhipara. The trade union leaders Mr Ratanlal Brahman and Deb Prasad Ghosh were in the lead roles of influencing these workers. Ultimately, the trade union movement received a proper direction in July 1946 when the Zilla Cha Bagan Mazdoor Union was formed with the workers of nearly 13 gardens. This trade union happened to be the first CTU of the tea garden workers, which was later affiliated to AITUC [21].

The union had a high expectation in the post-Independence period. Their expectations were of better facilities and wages, which were assumed to be announced by the national government. But that did not happen. This resulted in labour unrest in the form of labour agitations, strikes and lockouts in different tea estates. The two newly formed CTUs, that is, HMS and UTUC also influenced these. (At the centre, there emerged other CTUs, such as HMS in 1948 and UTUC in 1949, in addition to the INTUC which had been existing since 1947.)

In the early 1950s, a union affiliated to the local party known as Gorkha League was formed under the leadership of Deo Prakash Rai. The new union was named 'Darjeeling District Chai Kaman Shramik Sangh'. In the early 1960s, under the leadership of Dr Maitree Bose, another union known as National Union of Plantation Workers was formed which was affiliated to INTUC, and the Darjeeling District Chia Kaman Mazdoor Union, formed thereafter, was affiliated to CITU. Much after, in 1989, another trade union known as the 'Himalayan Plantation Wokers' Union' emerged for plantation workers.

With the multiplicity of unions in the region, each worker was a member of one or another union, or some of them had been members of more than one union.

In spite of the multiplicity of the trade unions in the region, plantation workers had been able to form a common front to take up their issues at an industry level. In 1962, all major trade unions of plantation workers came together to form the Co-ordination Committee of Tea Plantation Workers (CCTPW). This committee had joint affiliation with CITU, INTUC, AITUC, UTUC and Hind Mazdur Kissan Panchayat (HMKP). Smaller unions not having an affiliation with CTUs also formed their own joint forum known as the Committee for Defence of Plantation Worker's Rights (CDPWR).

The employers' associations of tea planter in the region were the Indian Tea Association (ITA), the Indian Tea Planters Association, Terai Indian Tea Planters Association and Darjeeling Planters. All the planters had not initially implemented the provisions of Plantation Labour Act (PLA) in totality. There was a general tendency to avoid the payment of benefits, for example, weekly offs once a week, housing, health care and education. Regarding wages, DA and VDA, as per the declaration of the government, arrears due after every wage agreement, PF and gratuity were hardly paid. No welfare amenities were provided to workers.

The industry experienced very few strikes, although there were frequent agitations in individual tea estates against the management. The major strikes at the industry level were in the years 1969 for 21 days (demanding regularization of temporary workers) and 1999 for 10 days. The strike of 1969 led to the absorbtion of about 10,000 temporary workers in the industry.

The present major trade unions in Bengal are as follows:

- All West Bengal Tea Garden Labourers Union, affiialiated to CPI (ML)
- Cha Bagan Mazdoor Union, affiliated to CITU (CPI[M])
- Darjeeling District Chia Kaman Majdoor Union, affiliated to CITU (CPI[M])
- Darjeeling District Chia Kaman Majdoor Union, affiliated to AITUC (CPI)
- Darjeeling Terai Dooars Cheeya Kaman Mazdoor Union (Communist Party of Revolutionary Marxists)
- Dooars Cha Bagan Workers' Union, affiliated to UTUC (Revolutionary Socialist Party)
- Himalayan Plantation Workers' Union (Gorkha National Liberation Front)
- National Union of Plantation Workers, affiliated to INTUC (Indian National Congress)
- Terai Sangrami Cha Sramik Union, affiliated to the AICCTU (CPI [ML] Liberation)
- West Bengal Cha Mazdoor Sabha, affiliated to HMS

Thus, the history of the trade union movement in Bengal tea gardens gives an account of the tremendous amount of struggle of workers who fought against all odds to establish trade unions in tea gardens. BDRWU also made an enormous contribution which made the task much easier for plantation workers. The full-fledged support of BDRWU was instrumental in the formation of trade unions in the tea gardens of Bengal.

Case Questions

1. List down the circumstances which led to the formation of trade unions in the tea estates of West Bengal.
2. What was the condition of the workers of the then tea estates? Elaborate.

4.3.6.3. The Third Phase of Unionism (1980s to 1992)

The background: The period includes the Sixth and Seventh Five-Year Plans (1980–1985 and 1985–1990, resp.) and two Annual Plans (1990–1992). The average GDP during this period was 5.7 per cent, but the growth in employment was around 1.8 per cent [22]. The economy experienced:

1. Drought in 1979
2. Industrial recession in 1980–1981
3. Rising inflation and increasing oil bills
4. Balance of payments crisis followed by a massive IMF loan
5. Rajiv Gandhi's economic liberalization and government's policy of export promotion and encouraged domestic competition
6. The 1990 Gulf War, followed by economic recession and political turmoil. Macroeconomic changes during this phase affected the political economy of trade unionism and labour markets, as well as the structure of IR.

On the union front, this phase started with a massive public sector strike in Bangalore during 1980–1981 and the Mumbai textile strike of 1982, which ended in late 1983.

The relationship among the actors: The relationship among the actors had not been congenial during this period. The militants bargaining strategies of the local unions initially received a high degree of hostility from the management. The proliferation of 'independent' unions operating in the major industrial centres and competing with the traditional party-affiliated trade unions developed more inter-trade union rivalry.

The trade union movement: 'Independent' unions were formed in Western India from within the rank and file. These unions were formed primarily because of workers' dissatisfaction with the bargaining styles of the traditional trade unions with the management at the enterprise level. There emerged more trade unions who were 'selfish' to their own interests [23]. There was a fall in the membership of the registered trade unions. By 1989, the Labour Ministry listed the following CTUOs in their registry: INTUC, AITUC, CITU, HMS, BMS (affiliated to BJP), the Hind Mazdoor Kamgar Party, UTUC, UTUC-LS, National Labour Organisation and a number of small independent unions.

The trade union movement during the period was more aligned to the self-interests of the employees of different regions of the country. In West Bengal, a highly politicized IR regime prevailed with the dominant trade union federation (the CITU) working under the close watch of the dominant political party, the CPI(M). This created considerable inflexibilities for the management and prohibited the growth of independent trade unionism. On the other hand, Bangalore, a city where there was growth of both private and public sector enterprises, especially in the IT industry, witnessed the rise of plant or organization-based unions (as in Mumbai). The inter-city/zone differences, resulting from the existing difference in political, social, cultural and past history of unionism, contributed to the labour relation system. The trade unions in the more profitable sectors (often 'independent' unions), through bargaining with their management, managed better wages and incentive structure than other trade unions.

4.3.6.4. The Fourth Phase of Unionism (1992–2002)

The background: This phase includes the year 1992 and thereafter, that is, the Eighth and Ninth Five-Year Plans (1992–1997 and 1997–2002, resp.). There was political instability at the Centre since 1992 (several coalition governments failed to complete their full term). The political instability resulted in differences within CTUs and political parties. In June 1991, the ruling minority government decided to adopt the World Bank–IMF stabilization and structural adjustment programme. The rupee was also devalued twice during this time. Quotas on the import of intermediate and capital goods were reduced. The economy became more open than earlier because of the adaptation of the liberalization policy. During this phase, people largely through the print and visual media became aware of the fact that trade unions only represent a 'sectional interest group' [24]. This resulted in declining connections with trade unions, particularly with CTUs.

On 10 January 1999, the government announced the formation of the Second National Labour Commission. The terms of reference for this commission included the rationalization of existing labour laws for the organized sector and recommend an umbrella legislation to ensure minimum protection for unorganized workers. The commission had a term of two years and was constituted of representatives from the government, trade unions and industry. Trade unions felt that workers had little protection from the management and that any changes in the labour laws would mean only adding to management's power. In terms of the labour market and IR, it was felt that the economic liberalization would undoubtedly lead to more employment flexibility, greater decentralization in bargaining structures (especially in public enterprises) and less government intervention.

The relationship among the actors: With the liberalized economy and market competition, there was a thrust for every organization to be ahead in market competition. So the organizational objectives changed to not only make a visible profit but also to be better off than others in the open competitive market. Labour being a critical factor in achieving such an objective, the outlook towards the labour class changed. The management, instead of considering labour to be a class of *wage earners,* started considering the concept of *partnering* with them in the business interest.

To overcome the differences between the management and trade unions, and amicably settle differences for the business interests, there was the need for consultation. The government partially diffused possible differences through its consultative approach, but trade unions had 'serious doubts on the adequacy of consultation at (the) industrial or enterprise level' [25]. Trade unions had a suspicious outlook on such attempts.

The trade union movements: This phase witnessed the growth of BMS, affiliated to BJP. In the state of Maharashtra, the trade union movement became quite volatile because the local Shiv Sena Party and its affiliated union, the Bharatiya Mazdoor Sena, made deep inroads into the industries through the support of the people. But the CTU fell short of workers' expectations. This resulted in creating ways for more independent and decentralized trade unions, replacing the central unions [26–27].

4.3.6.5. The Post-2002 Period

The trade union movement had undergone a number of changes since early 2000. Earlier, left-affiliated trade unions were more active in calling strikes against the government's actions. But for the first time in 2009, all CTUs came on a common platform to decide the course of action on their charter of demands jointly. Since then, five strikes have taken place—one each in 2010, 2012, 2013, 2015 and 2016. Figure 4.1 portrays the evolution of trade unions and their active movements during the period 2005–2014. The numbers of disputes have been presented in the decreasing trend since 2013.

Figure 4.1   The Evolution of Trade Unionism

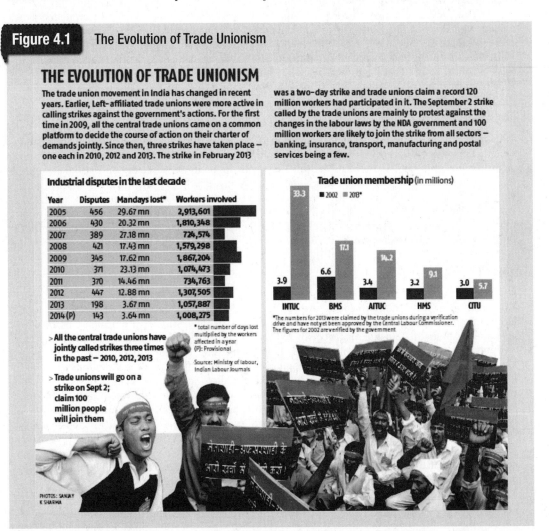

THE EVOLUTION OF TRADE UNIONISM

The trade union movement in India has changed in recent years. Earlier, Left-affiliated trade unions were more active in calling strikes against the government's actions. For the first time in 2009, all the central trade unions came on a common platform to decide the course of action on their charter of demands jointly. Since then, three strikes have taken place – one each in 2010, 2012 and 2013. The strike in February 2013 was a two-day strike and trade unions claim a record 120 million workers had participated in it. The September 2 strike called by the trade unions are mainly to protest against the changes in the labour laws by the NDA government and 100 million workers are likely to join the strike from all sectors – banking, insurance, transport, manufacturing and postal services being a few.

Industrial disputes in the last decade

Year	Disputes	Mandays lost*	Workers involved
2005	456	29.67 mn	2,913,601
2006	430	20.32 mn	1,810,348
2007	389	27.18 mn	724,574
2008	421	17.43 mn	1,579,298
2009	345	17.62 mn	1,867,204
2010	371	23.13 mn	1,074,473
2011	370	14.46 mn	734,763
2012	447	12.88 mn	1,307,505
2013	198	3.67 mn	1,057,887
2014 (P)	143	3.64 mn	1,008,275

* total number of days lost multiplied by the workers affected in a year
(P): Provisional

Source: Ministry of labour, Indian Labour Journals

> All the central trade unions have jointly called strikes three times in the past – 2010, 2012, 2013

> Trade unions will go on a strike on Sept 2; claim 100 million people will join them

Trade union membership (in millions)

■ 2002 ■ 2013*

	INTUC	BMS	AITUC	HMS	CITU
2002	3.9	6.6	3.4	3.2	3.0
2013*	33.3	17.1	14.2	9.1	5.7

*The numbers for 2013 were claimed by the trade unions during a verification drive and have not yet been approved by the Central Labour Commissioner. The figures for 2002 are verified by the government.

PHOTOS: SANJAY K SHARMA

Source: Jha S. The evolution of trade unionism, The Business Standard. 31 August 2015.

C.4.8. Case for Discussion — Changing Role of Siemens Workers Union

Siemens had set up a small workshop under Mahalakshmi Bridge, Central Mumbai, in 1956 to manufacture switchboards. The company has grown over the last 60 years into one of India's largest multinational conglomerates. The business world of Siemens included designing, producing, and sales and servicing a wide range of electrical equipment. Siemens in India is now active in four sectors: energy, industry, health care and infrastructure. The company in India during the past decade had an unprecedented growth through several acquisitions and joint ventures, introduction of new services in electrical and electronic fields, and new manufacturing facilities.

Siemens' Initial Manufacturing Phase in India

The company was founded in India in 1922, though Siemens set foot in India way back in 1867 when the company was contracted to build an 11,000 km telegraph system in India between London and Calcutta. In the year 1956, Siemens started manufacturing switchboards in India. The initial products were switchboards; but in the year 1959, manufacturing and assembling of medical equipment like low-voltage X-ray machines were added to the product range of Siemens at Worli, Bombay. The company enhanced its production of switchgears in 1960 and began production in Worli, and, in the same year, manufacturing of switchboards was extended to Calcutta Works.

The Union in the 1960s

In the year 1960, employees in Siemens organized to form their first trade union 'the Engineering and General Employees Union (EGEU)'. This union was led by R. J. Mehta, as the president, and J. H. Pinto, as the general secretary, along with Narayan Shetye, as the honorary secretary. In December 1961, EGEU regularized the working and service conditions of the workers by signing the first settlement with the management. The settlement only had the terms for the blue-collar workers; the white-collar workers were not included. The Siemens Employees Union (SEU) representing the clerical, administration and supervisory staff was formed in 1962. SEU signed a settlement on the service conditions of the white-collar employees in the year 1962.

The First Workers' Strike

By the year 1964, the workers were dissatisfied with EGEU and formed an internal union Siemens Workers Union (SWU) under the leadership of Mr A. D. Shastry. In the same year, SWU launched its first industrial action in the form of a strike demanding better wages and bonus for its members. The strike continued for 45 days, but the management refused to negotiate with Mr Shastry labelling him an 'extremist'. The leadership of SWU moved to Mr B. S. Dhume as the president of the union. SWU signed a wage settlement in December 1967, which improved the working and service conditions considerably. The wages were increased by nearly 25 per cent and working hours were reduced by 8 per cent. SWU is now the recognized trade union of Siemens India under Section 12 of the Maharashtra Recognition of Trade Unions and Prevention of Unfair Labour Practices Act, 1971 and affiliated since year 2006 with IG Metall—a union of metal workers in Germany which includes Siemens and International Metal Workers Federation. Now, SWU raises all issues internationally hoping to build pressure on Siemens to accept trade union rights of all employees of Siemens. With the joining of the engineering, clerical and administration staff from across the country as members of SEU, the union decided to change its name to All India Siemens Employees Union (AISEU).

Since 1965 the company in its growth track has been establishing works at Aurangabad, Bangalore, Kolkata, Goa, Gurugram, Hyderabad, Kalwa, Kharagpur, Nashik, Puducherry, Vadodara and Winergy. TSWU was present in all the units. For the reason SWU enjoyed maximum membership, the management consideres to settle all major issues of employees and workers after discussion with SWU, and thereafter the same is communicated to other trade unions.

During the period of the late 1960s and early 1970s, a large number of industrial training institutes' trainees were recruited, and they all joined SWU as members. Their issue of regularization on completion of the training period was raised by SWU, and the trainees were regularized.

Festival Bonus Based on Ability to Pay

The company had a practice of disbursing bonus before Diwali in Bombay and before Durga Puja in Calcutta. In the year 1972, SWU signed an agreement with the management for the first time to pay the festival bonus based on company's ability to pay, thereby doubling the bonus amount as compared with the previous years.

SWU in the Turbulence Period

By the early 1970s, the economy stagnated, which led to a drop in employment rates. Workers across the country started losing faith in the unions including CTUs. This was followed by the National Emergency of 1975, when all the trade union rights were curtailed and the trade union activities were banned. The right to strike was withdrawn and collective bargaining was restricted. Wages were frozen in organizations. SWU supported this step of the government. The management, taking advantage of the situation, connived with SWU to sign a settlement which resulted in only a 6 per cent wage increase for workers over the next five years. With the lifting of the National Emergency in 1977, and Janta Party (JP) coming to power at the centre, SWU faced intense trade union rivalry. The workers tried to break away from SWU to form small units or local-level unions. This resulted in the formation of a new militant union named the Association of Engineering Workers (AEW), led by Dr Datta Samant. In spite of the overwhelming support of workers for this new union, the company refused to recognize AEW which demanded that the question of recognition of union should be settled by seeking the mandate of the workers through a secret ballot. However, the company refused to settle the controversy. This resulted in hostility between two sets of workers/supporters of both the unions. In February 1978, violence erupted between the two factions and the company declared a lockout. Following this, AEW declared a strike.

SWU took the lead to break the strike, and after a month, with the support of the management, SWU convinced the workers to return to work by giving an undertaking that they would never take part in any industrial unrest. The workers refused to that and the stalemate continued. After 10 months of deadlock, with the intervention of the chief minister of the state, the strike was called off. The management dismissed more than 100 workers for indulging in violence during the strike. But AEW continued to enjoy the support of majority of the workers and pursued its efforts for attaining recognition. In the early 1980s, AEW again launched an agitation for reinstating workers who were dismissed but were acquitted by the courts.

Youth Win through Secret Ballot in 1987

Though AEW withered away, a large number of workers refused to accept SWU as their representative body, causing serious differences among the leaders of SWU in 1985. Sensing an opportunity to take control of the leadership of SWU, some members demanded elections of the union through secret ballot. In 1987, for the first time, SWU held elections through secret ballot in the factory premises. This brought about significant change in the leadership of the union. External leaders were replaced by workers working on the shop floor as central office bearers.

Economic Liberalization

The wind of economic liberalization, which started to sweep over India in 1991, brought policy shifts from being import centric to export oriented, and open market competition led to the adoption of new strategic focus for industries. Multinational companies were the biggest gainers of liberalization, and there was phenomenal growth in these companies. Many restrictions were removed for these companies, giving them a distinct advantage over Indian counterparts. Organizations expected more flexibility in employment, which in practice meant the recruitment of employees on contract. This caused more pressure on trade unions. VRS was introduced across industries to replace older, permanent workers with new contract labour at a lower labour cost. This affected the bargaining power of trade unions. The management started hiring of employees on contract in the new units which were commenced in 1992 at Waluj, in Aurangabad District of Maharashtra; in 1993 at Salt Lake, Calcutta and in 1995 at a factory in Verna, Goa. SWU with the new leadership of young, technically educated and fully conversant leaders, with the technicalities and working of manufacturing activity of the company, convinced workers to duly consider the needs of the management. SWU, under the new leadership, brought transparency and accountability in its working culture. Though the government policy of liberalization had an immediate impact on unions in hundreds of companies across India, it had not affected IR between the Siemens management and SWU.

In 1987, the manufacturing activity of industrial electronic equipment was expanded to the new Nashik factory in Ambad. Workers were transferred to this new unit. A settlement for relocated workers was signed between the union and the management, which gave each transferred worker a huge subsidy on housing loans, thereby facilitating them to own houses. This settlement also opened avenues for career development, and many workers were promoted to the white-collar category. This initiative of the union was widely accepted by the workers of other units of Siemens, for example, Kalwe Works and Aurangabad. The workers of these units joined SWU.

Despite the organization supporting relatively stable and collaborative IR in the early 1990s and thereafter, the management found a novel way to prohibit the formation of unions. They designated all workers recruited at the permanent status for the Salt Lake factory at Calcutta and Verna, Goa as 'executives'. The service conditions kept this category of employees away from the scope of the ID Act and other labour laws. This initiative was a threat to the union.

In the financial year 1997, the company for the first time registered losses to the tune of ₹149.6 crore which resulted a negative profit of ₹60.3 crore. The losses were carried forward in the subsequent years. To over come the financial losses, the company planned restructuring and structural changes by reducing the workforce through launching VRS, forcing many workers to opt for the golden handshake and adopted outsourcing of manufacturing jobs. The target was to reduce its workforce by 50 per cent, with more focus on reducing the workmen category. The jobs of housekeeping and office maintenance and manufacturing activities of the components were outsourced, and the company only held the jobs of vendor development and controls, assembly line functions and quality assurances.

Owing to job losses, the unions became weak and easily succumbed to these changes. The structural changes came in the form of outsourcing of manufacturing activities. Inside the offices, the unions were forced to accept contract workers in service areas of housekeeping and office maintenance. SWU considering the business objectives supported this action of the management.

Thereafter, the company went into the aggressive mode of closing down some of the units and adding new units. In 1998, it closed down the Worli unit, which was manufacturing medical products, and shifted operations to Verna, Goa. There was no union in the Verna factory because all the workers were 'executives'. In 2000, the company closed the Joka factory, Calcutta. The emerging new work culture and process of production, which the SWU supported, helped the company in business expansion. Since

1995, Osram India Pvt. Ltd became a group company of Siemens and manufactured lighting equipment and systems at its manufacturing facility at Sonepat, Haryana. In the year 1998, the company set up a factory for manufacturing high-voltage circuit breakers alongside the switchgear unit in Aurangabad. In 2005, the automotive component production of Siemens VDO was integrated with Siemens Ltd. The Siemens VDO had manufacturing facilities in Bangalore in Karnataka, Pune in Maharashtra and Gurgaon in Haryana. In 2005, Siemens acquired Demag Delaval Industrial Turbomachinery (DDIT). In 2006, the company commissioned a new unit for the manufacturing of Traction Motors specially required for Indian Railways in Kalwe Works alongside the motors unit. In 2007, a new transformer factory was commissioned which was manufacturing high-voltage transformers in Kalwe Works. In 2007, the company acquired a factory at Hyderabad, which was manufacturing isolators for vacuum circuit breakers. In 2007, Flender Ltd, a company, manufacturing gear boxes for the sugar and cement industry, was incorporated in the Siemens Group of Companies. It had its manufacturing facility at Kharagpur, West Bengal. In 2007, the company acquired small manufacturing facilities in Puducherry and Tamil Nadu. Fire alarms for buildings and establishments are manufactured in Puducherry, whereas in Tamil Nadu special gearboxes for windmill generators are manufactured.

The company has now 20 manufacturing units, but only half of them have organized unions. In the rest of the units, the company has designated all workers as 'executive' and barred them from forming or joining any union [28].

Case Questions

1. Do you think there was a change in the approach of the trade unions in the early 2000? Justify your answer with the help of instances from the case study.
2. 'A strong bondage of cooperation between the trade unions and the management is essential for organizational growth.' Do you agree? Justify your answer from the case study.
3. List down the differences in the approach of the earlier trade unions and the recent trade unions as is evident in the present case study. Give the reasons for the same.

Chapter Summary

1. Trade unions represent association of employees for the purpose of securing improvements in pay, benefits, working conditions and so on through collective bargaining. The Trade Unions Act which is a central legislation, but administered by the state governments, is applicable to all industries in India including the IT industry.

2. India is a founding member of the ILO, and has a permanent place in the ILO governing body. The right to form association/unions and the right to collective bargaining (collectively raising/bargain) constitutes a right under the Constitution of India. The ILO in its conventions 87 and 98, respectively, ensures these rights at the works.

3. AITUC, INTUC, HMS and CITU—the first four trade unions—were established in the years 1921, 1947, 1948, 1971 respectively. The main role of the trade unions was to put forward ideas to the management and get those converted into well-structured, implementable plans through negotiations. However, the theories of trade union, formulated from time to time, considered the contextual framework of the society and the level of industrialization.

4. The development of trade unionism in India is linked with the movements for reforming the society, and the movements for making India independent as well as achieving the economic objective of the industrialization of the country. The national leaders and the social reformers

took active roles in organizing the workers and protecting them against inhuman working conditions and exploitations in the factories.

5. For the first time, in the year 1875, the Indian factory workers united for securing better working conditions in the factories, that is, against long working hours, and bad and inhuman working conditions. Protests and several strikes were organized in various parts of India during this period which continued from 1884 to 1910. After the war time of 1918, the TLA was established under the guideance of Mahatma Gandhi. The leadership of trade unions during this period was from outside, by the philanthropists or social reformers and not by workers. There was no organized body of trade unions in the modern sense.

6. The period 1918–1924 experienced the formation of trade unionism in India which focused on protecting the worker's interests.

7. During the period 1925–1934, AITUC was the only CTU, which emerged as the sole representative of the Indian working class and this period was termed as the period of left-wing unionism. In the year 1924, the trade unions were involved in violent and long-drawn strikes. Such actions of the trade unions led to arrest and imprisonment of the active union members. By the year 1927, about 57 unions had joined AITUC bringing its membership to 150,555 across India. This was the period of growth of anti-imperialist national movement in India.

8. Under the leadership of Mr N. M. Joshi and Mr V. V. Giri, supported by 21 affiliated unions having a membership of 94,000, a separate organization by the name of the NTUF was formed. By the year 1930, NTUF became a widely accepted trade union with an affiliation of 104 trade unions and a total membership of 2.42 lakh.

9. In the year 1931, there was another split in the AITUC, in the Calcutta session, due to the fundamental differences between the communists and the left-wing unionists. The communists led by B. T. Ranadive and S. V. Deshpande formed the RTUC.

10. The trade union movement during 1935–1938 tended towards associating with the larger body of associations. In 1935, the All India RTUC merged itself with the AITUC. In 1938, the All India NTUF and the AITUC arrived at an agreement leading to NTUF getting affiliated to AITUC.

11. There was another split in AITUC in the year 1941. The Radicals left the AITUC with nearly 200 unions with a membership of 300,000, and formed a new central labour federation known as the IFL.

12. INTUC was formed in May 1947 by the members of the Congress Party. The Congress socialists who were with AITUC subsequently formed the HMS in 1948. Subsequently, the HMS was split to form a separate association, named, Bhartiya Mazdoor Sabha. Years after, the communist party split into various factions forming the UTUC and the CITU.

13. The growth of trade unionism during the first three Five-Year Plans (1951–1956, 1956–1961, 1961–1966) was considered as national capitalism. But in the Fourth and the Fifth Five-Year Plans (1969–1974, 1974–1979) there were deep sense of uncertainties within the organized workers in India. During the Sixth and Seventh Five-Year Plans (1980–1985, 1985–1990), and two Annual Plans (1990–1992), the relationship between the management and the trade unions was not congenial. In the year 1992, and thereafter, that is, the Eighth and Ninth Five-Year Plans (1992–1997, 1997–2002), there was political instability at the centre resulting in differences within the centralized trade unions and the political parties. The trade union movement underwent changes since early 2000, and for the first time in 2009, all the CTUs came on a common platform to decide the course of action on their charter of demands, jointly.

Questions

1. The trade union movement in India is linked to various contextual aspects. Please identify the contexts against various time periods.
2. Indicate the roles of political parties in the trade union movement in India.
3. How far was the government successful in achieving the objectives of industrialization and economic development through the trade unions in the post-Independence period?

Project Work for the Students

1. Political leaders had an agenda of linking their political ideologies with the trade union movement in India. Identify from time to time how different political leaders had initiated to develop the political objectives along with trade unionism.

References

1. IndustriALL Global Union. Precarious work in India. Available from http://www.industriall-union.org/sites/default/files/uploads/documents/a4_india_report_new2.pdf
2. Webb S, Webb B. The History of Trade Unionism. 2nd edn, London: Longmans; 1920.
3. Edwin B Flippo. Principles of Personnel Management, McGraw Hill Kogakusha, New Delhi; 1976.
4. Pai S. Together scrap dealers have changed their lives, standing united, The Weekender Leader. 10 May 2013. Available from http://www.theweekendleader.com/Culture/1601/pickers-pick.html
5. Pai S. A union that accords dignity and safety in numbers to women waste pickers, The Better India. 30 October 2013. Available from http://www.thebetterindia.com/8527/a-union-that-accords-dignity-and-safety-in-numbers-to-women-waste-pickers/
6. Deia. Press Release: Waste pickers frame common struggles and demands, Global Alliance of Waste Pickers. 26 April 2012. Available from http://globalrec.org/2012/04/27/press-release-in-pune-waste-pickers-frame-common-struggles-and-demands/
7. Subramanyam S. Trade unions in IT industry, Business Line. 11 October 2005. Avialable from https://www.thehindubusinessline.com/todays-paper/tp-opinion/Trade-unions-in-IT-industry/article20291030.ece
8. PTI. Trade unions stick to Sept 2 strike, reject govts wage hike, India Today. 30 August 2016. Available from http://indiatoday.intoday.in/story/trade-unions-stick-to-sept–2-strike-reject-govts-wage-hike/1/752482.html
9. Rajasinghmurugesan. 2nd September 2016—all India general strike—make it a grand success, Govtempdiary. 1 September 2016. Available from http://www.govtempdiary.com/2016/09/2nd-september–2016-all-india-general-strike-make-it-a-grand-success–2/20801
10. Marx Karl. Value, price and profit. In: Karl Marx and Frederick Engels, Collected Works, Vol. 20. New York: International Publishers; 1985. p. 146.
11. Tannenbaum Frank. A Philosophy of Labor. New York: Alfred A. Knopf; 1951.
12. Gandhi MK. Socialism of my conception. In Ananad T Hingorani, editor. Collection of Gandhi's Writings. Bombay: Bharatiya Vidya Bhavan; 1957. p. 265.
13. Graziano Workers' Solidarity Forum. India: The dispute at Graziano – a chronology of events, In Defence of Marxism. 22 October 2008. Available from http://www.marxist.com/india-dispute-at-graziano-chronology.htm
14. http://pakusastry.blogspot.in/2014/01/trade-union-repression-in-india.html

15. Kadam M. Narayan Meghaji Lokhande: Bharatiya kamagar chalvaliche jamah. Mumbai and Pune: Akshar Prakashan and Mahatma Phule Samata Pratisthan; 1995.
16. Morris DM. Emergence of an Industrial Labour Force in India. 1965.
17. Pandit N. Narayan Meghaji Lokhande, the father of trade union movement in India. Econ Pol Wkly. 1997; 32(7) 15–21 February: 327–329.
18. Sabyasachi B. Coolies, Capital, and colonialism: Studies in Indian labour history. Int. Rev. Soc. Hist. 2006; 51(14): 7–19.
19. indianlabour.org, History of Indian National Trade Union Congress. Available at: http://indianlabour.org/index.php/labour-centers/nlc/intuc/ (accessed on 21 Oct 2019).
20. Sengupta, AK. New generation of organised workforce in India: Implications for management and trade unions. In: Sodhi JS, Ahluwalia SPS, editors. Industrial Relations in India: The Coming Decades. New Delhi: Sri Ram Centre for Industrial Relations and Human Resources; 1992.
21. Bhowmik S. Labour and social issues in plantation in South Asia. New Delhi; People's Publishing House; 1981. pp. 140–145.
22. Papola TS. Structural adjustment, labour market flexibility and employment. Indian J. Lab. Econ. 1994; 37(1, January–March).
23. Bhattacherjee D. Economic liberalisation, democracy and industrial relations: India in a comparative perspective. Ind. J. Lab. Econ. 1996; 39(4): 1011–1021.
24. Bhaduri, Nayyar. The intelligent person's guide to liberalization, 139. Penguin publishing; 1996.
25. Mathur. The experience of consultation during structural adjustment in India (1990–1992). International Labour Review 1993; 132(3): 331–345.
26. Davala S. Employment and unionization in Indian industry. New Delhi: FES; 1992.
27. Muralidhar S. Slipping through the holes in the safety net, The Economic Times. 26 December 1993, Calcutta: 7.
28. http://www.siemensworkersunion.com/2012-02-15-19-28-11/2012-02-15-19-29-04

5

Trade Union Structure and Management

LEARNING OBJECTIVES

After reading this chapter, you will be able to:

☐ Understand the reasons as to why employees join trade unions
☐ Understand the changing trend of trade union membership
☐ Understand the changing trend of the trade union movement and the factors impacting the same
☐ Understand the importance of the recognition of trade unions
☐ Understand the provisions of the Trade Unions Act, 1926
☐ Understand the paradigm shift in trade unions and the new trend

C.5.1. Case for Discussion   The HMSI Workers' Agitation of 2005

The Honda Motorcycles and Scooters India Ltd (HMSI), which was established on 20 October 1999, is a wholly-owned subsidiary of Honda Motor Company Limited (HMCL), Japan. The company followed HR policies which it claimed to be transparent and were aligned with the philosophy of its parent company. The policies were structured on the following two fundamental management beliefs:

1. Respect for individual differences.
2. The three joys: the joy of buying, the joy of selling and the joy of manufacturing.

However, the workers felt an unfair treatment for the first time in November 2004 when they were offered by the management a Diwali gift of ₹600. They had an expectation of more than what was paid. This expectation generated feelings that the management arbitrarily decided the figure and forced the workers to accept the same. Reportedly, at this period, a Japanese vice-president (production) kicked a worker (though he considered it to be a friendly behaviour due to the closeness of the individual with him) who was slightly late in joining work after the tea interval.

The discipline enforced on the workers was no doubt very strict. The workers were taken to task for their indiscipline behaviour at works, which they did not like. Whereas Japanese top management was strict, the Indian managers were practising favouritism.

On the other hand, the workers had grievances that there was a high wage difference between the payments made to the workers of HMSI and those of Hero Honda for the similar work. (Hero Honda being the competitor of HMSI, such salary comparison was obvious.)

All these factors led to the workers of HMSI to plan for the registration of a union. The workers also submitted a charter of demand to the management in December 2004. The management in their efforts tried to stop the formation of the trade union. Reportedly, the registrar of trade unions denied union registration to the workers on the ground that the registration would vitiate the peaceful atmosphere in the Gurgaon industrial region. Eventually, the political figures like Mr Gurudas Gupta, an MP, who belonged to CPI, supported the movement of the workers and the trade union was registered in May 2005.

The matter of dissatisfaction of the workers also caused some instances of minor violence initiated by them at the workplace. But the worst happened on 25 July 2005 at the office of the deputy commissioner (who was the chief of the civil administration) of the Gurgaon (now Gurugram) district, where the workers had gone to protest against the alleged high-handedness of the HMSI management. A violent conflict took place between the HMSI workers and the local police, that is, a collusion with the state administration. This resulted in severe injuries to some 70 workers.

The Indian TV channels and TV news made a live telecast of atrocities by policemen on the workers. Owing to the pressure of workers' representatives on the government, the state chief minister was directed by the Congress (the then ruling party) President, Mrs Sonia Gandhi, to facilitate a settlement between the HMSI management and its workers. On 30 July 2005, an agreement was signed between the workers and the management with the intervention of the chief minister, according to which the workers who were on strike would resume duty from 1 August 2005, suspended workers would be taken back on duty and the workers would not raise any new demand causing financial implications during the next one year.

The management was concerned about not only the losses but also about the magnitude of alienation among the workers and the untoward event that took place between the workers and the police. In the post-25 July scenario, the management allowed several concessions to workers on many fronts. The union office-bearers were allowed to do full-time union work. Despite the losses, the workers could secure an impressive amount of money from the management as bonus for the year 2004–2005.

Post 25 July 2005, the management started imparting the managers with management development programmes (MDPs) in areas such as interpersonal skills, team building, negotiation and conflict management. It decided to appoint a senior manager IR. Union office-bearers were given training by the HR department on building cooperative IR.

The fact is that the company wanted to pursue a non-union model. It thought that such policies of paying slightly higher wages than the average in the automobile industry in the Gurugram region, providing uniform for all employees and offering attractive welfare facilities would secure their commitment to the company. The Japanese top management left HR issues to be handled by the senior Indian managers who were basically production specialists and were not experts in handling IR issues. But the management was caught unaware of the fact that the accumulated grievances led the workers to become hostile and form a union with the help of the AITUC.

As a result, the company suffered a loss of ₹13 lakh and saw the emergence of a strong trade union. The major shortfall was that the HR practices that the company was following were quite different from the projected HR policies and practices. The managers were conducting themselves like autocrats and misused their authority vested in them. Steps such as unreasonable restrictions on employees, refusal to grant leaves even on genuine grounds and threatening the workers of termination from services were not accepted by the knowledge workers. The employees were not treated with dignity.

Finally, the large-scale use of contract and casual labour were taking place who supported the workers' struggle. With the call for a strike, there was a complete shutdown of the plant.

Case Questions

1. After going through the above case, what do you think were the major reasons for the formation of the trade union?
2. Indicate the solutions for addressing such IR issues proactively.
3. Such IR issues being common in various industrial belts indicate the contextual factors which contributed to such problems. Please discuss.

5.1. Impact of Industrialization on Trade Unions

In Chapter 4, it was discussed that the trade union movement in India started as early as in the 18th century. It started with the industrialization of the nation. The earliest industries were tea in 1839, coal in 1843, cotton and jute in 1854 and the railways in 1854. The early major employment centres in India were jute mills, cotton mills and tea plantations. But subsequently, railways were added to the list with the British Government taking initiatives for the same. By 1870, more than 5 lakh Indian workers were working in these industries for 16 hours a day, getting low wages and no compensation for accidents, which was frequent because of the bad working environment. The earliest known trade unions which came into existence as a reaction to the above work culture were the following:

1. BMHA was formed in 1890.
2. The Amalgamated Society of Railway Servants of India and Burma was formed in 1897.
3. The Printers Union was formed in Calcutta (now Kolkata) in 1905, and the Bombay Postal Union was formed in 1907.
4. The Kamgar Hitwardhak Sabha of Bombay was formed in 1910.

Trade union movements in India are linked with reforming the Indian society as well as initiating the movement for making India independent. Subsequently, the objective of achieving the economic objective of industrialization of the country was added. So the national leaders and the social reformers took active roles in organizing workers, and protect them against inhuman working conditions and exploitation at the hands of the factory owners.

5.2. Why Employees Join Trade Unions

The question 'why employees join trade unions?' continues to be clubbed with dilemmas and attitudinal aspects of individual employees. With time, the distrust of employees on trade unions because of the fear of their corrupt practices can hardly be overruled. Such attitudes emerged because of the following:

1. They thought that their wages and working conditions were proper and their needs were substantially satisfied, which made them believe that they could manage things on their own without any support of the group.

2. The white-collar, technical and professional workers identified themselves with the management and accordingly expected promotion to supervisory and management positions in due course of time. Such individuals maintained a distinct professional association and viewed unions as below their status and dignity.
3. There were workers who distrusted trade unions because they considered them as opposed to individual freedom and their individual initiatives.
4. Corrupt images were often attached to trade unions. That is why workers did not join trade unions because they considered them as the root cause of corruption.

But the general motives of workers in joining trade unions were normally grievance representation, security, improvement in their economic conditions and protection in times of trouble. The elaborate reasons for the same are as follows.

1. **Greater bargaining power**: Individual employees to enhance their bargaining power, which they possess very little individually as compared to that of their employer, prefer to join the trade unions. The threat of strike is a powerful negotiating tool that often causes the employer to accept the demands of the employees. For ensuring better conditions of employment through such negotiations, employees join trade unions.
2. **Sense of security**: Employees may join trade unions because of their belief that it is an effective way to secure adequate protection from various types of hazards and a means of income security. Other motives may include security in the cases of accidents, injuries and illness in the event of unemployment or even the threat for the same and so on. A trade union secures retirement benefits for workers and compels the management to invest in welfare services for the benefits of workers.
3. **Sense of belongingness**: Many employees join a trade union because their co-workers are the members of the union. At times, an employee joins a trade union under group pressure; if he does not do so, he often faces tough times at works. On the other hand, those who are the members of a union feel that they gain respect in the eyes of their fellow workers. It also gives an opportunity to discuss their problems with the trade union leaders.
4. **Sense of participation**: Employees can participate in the management of matters that may impact their interests only if they join a trade union. They can influence the decisions that are taken as a result of collective bargaining between the trade union and the management.
5. **Betterment of relationship**: Employees feel that unions can fulfil the important need of adequate machinery for the proper maintenance of employer–employee relations. Trade unions help in the betterment of IR among the management and workers by solving problems peacefully.
6. **Better legal support:** Trade unions provide legal support to workers at the time of their needs. The court cases, legal advices and settling legal complications faced by a worker are normally helped out by trade unions.
7. **Support the demands and facilitate their settlement**: Trade unions negotiate with the management for better terms and conditions of employment by ensuring better bargaining power in collective bargaining. They represent workers to support their demands and facilitate for settlement, while ensuring a safe working condition and job security to them.

5.3. Trade Unions in the Eyes of the Management

The management considers that 'trade unions restrict the management's discretion'. On the other hand, the trade union as an association only admits that 'they attempt to regulate the discretion of the management at points where the management's action affects the welfare of their members'. The contradiction arises from the fact that it is the management who is responsible for the success and failure of the enterprise and not the trade union, so it wants to retain its authority to make all important decisions even if that impacts the welfare of the people. The management also often argues that the trade unions hamper the optimum utilization of manpower and thus influence the productivity adversely. To sum up, the main reasons for managers resisting or restricting the development and growth of trade unions are as follows:

1. Managers consider unions as outsiders; as such they have no right to intervene in the affairs of the enterprise and works. Whereas managers seek to maximize the profits of the enterprise, trade unions seek to increase the bargaining powers of their members.
2. Managers consider trade unions as troublemakers. They think that the unions cause a gulf between them and the workers even where there is no ground for it. Trade unions often encourage employees' grievances to secure their positions among the workers.
3. Managers believe that unions undermine employee loyalty to the enterprise because unionized workers tend to have dual loyalty, that is, to trade unions as well as to the enterprise.
4. Trade unions are resisted because of their poor historical image in the public. This is evidenced in publicized reports of 'irresponsible union strikes, union leaders' offences and allied malpractices'.
5. Managers oppose unions because of their perceived major values of the labour movement. Frequently, the trade unions stress seniority and group consciousness which are in conflict with managerial values relating to merit and individualism.

5.4. Are Trade Unions Losing Their Grounds?

Trade union participation is defined as the behavioural involvement of trade union members in the operation of their local labour organization. It refers to the involvement of members in collective action and other union-related activities, which are closely related to effective working of the union. It is considered that in India, the united action through trade unionism by the working class had been a strong instrument to earn higher standards of living [1]. Since 1991, there have been deliberations regarding the utility of trade unions in Indian IR. There had been decreasing interests of the workforce to join the trade unions and simultaneously decrease in the number of trade unions. The following data provide the decreasing trend of the number of trade unions in India.

Year	Registered Trade Unions	Membership of Trade Unions ('000)
1991	53,535	6,100
1992	55,680	5,746
1993	55,784	3,134

Year	Registered Trade Unions	Membership of Trade Unions ('000)
1994	56,872	4,094
1995	57,988	6,538
1996	58,988	5,601
1997	60,660	7,409
1998	61,992	7,249
1999	64,817	6,408
2000	66,056	5,420
2001	66,624	5,873
2002	68,544	6,973
2003	74,649	6,277
2004	74,403	3,397
2005	78,465	8,719
2006	88,440	8,960
2007	95,783	7,877
2008	84,642	9,574
2009	22,284	6,480
2010	18,602	5,097
2011	10,264	7,421
2012	16,098	9,128
2013	11,556	3,231
2014	12,486	7,886

Source: Data for the years 1991–2014 has been compiled from Indiastat. Available at https://www.indiastat.com/table/labour-and-workforce-data/380987/trade-nions/282/40515/data.aspx

There had been various inherent difficulties and obstacles in the growth of trade unions in India. The reasons for the decreasing trend of the workforce joining the trade unions and the decrease in the number of trade unions are given in the following sections.

5.5. Impact of Labour Legislations and Enactments

The history of the trade union movement indicates that it was only through agitations or protests of some nature that the need for various enactments was made felt to the government authority. In the year 1875, for the first time in India, factory workers united together for securing better working conditions in the factories. The growing consciousness of a common cause brought the working class closer despite several hindrances. The Secretary of State for India was kept informed of the evils of the modern factory system and the first Factory Commission was appointed in Bombay in the year 1875 and the first Factories Act was passed in 1881.

A trade union agitation took place in the Buckingham and Carnatic Mills during October–December 1920, when workers striked in protest against working conditions [2]. To this agitation, on 9 December 1920, the government responded by ordering the police to shoot down workers who were on strike to bring the strike to a forceful end.

The need for a 'Trade Union Act' was felt during the case of Buckingham Mill, 1921, in which the Madras High Court granted an interim injunction against the strike committee of the Madras Labour Union, forbidding them to induce workers not to return to work. In the instant case, the trade union leaders were liable for prosecution and imprisonment for union activities. So it was felt that some legislation for the protection of trade union was necessary. In March 1921, Mr N. M. Joshi, the then general secretary of the AITUC, successfully moved a resolution in the Central Legislative Assembly recommending that the government should introduce legislation for the registration and protection of trade unions. The Indian Trade Unions Bill, 1925, was introduced in the Central Legislative Assembly to provide for the registration of trade unions and in certain respects to define the law relating to registered trade unions in the provinces of India. It was in 1926 that the Indian Trade Unions Act was passed. The Act came into force on 1 June 1927 as the Indian Trade Unions Act, 1926 (16 of 1926). It was by Section 3 of the Indian Trade Unions (Amendment) Act, 1964 (38 of 1964) that the word 'Indian' has been omitted and now it is known as the Trade Unions Act, 1926 (16 of 1926).

I.C.5.1. INDUSTRIAL CONTEXT FOR DISCUSSION

The Buckingham and Carnatic Mills

On 20 May 1921, the workers in the Spinning Department of the Buckingham and Carnatic Mills refused to work until the management agreed to discuss their demands for wage rise. The protest reached a serious turn since an official strike was declared on 20 June 1921 [3]. The workers who were on strike were led by Congressman V. Kalyanasundaram Mudaliar. A meeting was convened in Madras on 10 July 1921 by the Indian National Congress. In this meeting, C. Rajagopalachari moved for a resolution sympathizing with the workers of the Buckingham and Carnatic Mills and supporting their cause.

The strike lasted for a total of six months. The management tried to suppress the agitation. On 29 August 1921, the police opened fire, killing six workers. All other party leaders joined hands with the Indian National Congress and supported the strike. The management tactfully broke up the unity of the workers by allegedly enlisting the support of Dalits and Indian Christians who had not joined the strike.

The strike eventually evolved into a confrontation between caste Hindu and Muslim workers who were determined to continue the strike and the Dalits and Indian Christians who were not interested to proceed with the strike. A communal riot broke out on 28 June 1921 when the caste Hindu mob attacked the Dalit village of Puliyanthope and burnt a hundred houses.

The strike eventually came to an end in October through the mediation of C. Natesa Mudaliar [4].

5.6. Politics and Trade Unions

The trade unions, founded on the strength of the supporters, normally have a weak structure. So very often they find themselves in very difficult situations in their decision-making process and need to be bailed out. Such bailouts can be provided either by the management or the external political parties or the government. Since they do not trust either the management or the government, they are only left with the political parties. Since labour movement was closely associated with the Indian freedom movement, the leaders of the Independence movement had also been the leaders of the labour movement. The pioneering work of establishing trade unions has also been done by them. So till Independence, trade unions were almost completely dominated by the political movement. As a result, some outside leaders have emerged as national leaders for the trade unions. This had also been a strong reason for the influence of the national political leaders on the trade unions.

On the other hand, for the political leaders, the trade unions provide the grassroots base for the prospective political leadership. A period of trade union leadership in their career tends to pay-off in the political field and there are instances where several trade union leaders have occupied high political positions in the country by the strength of their trade unions career [5].

But the trade unions are very often marked by political rivalry and disunity. Very often the trade unions are also supported by the ruling party in power for the political party desires to accomplish its immediate short-term objectives of getting support of the trade union members. But it has the dark side too. The opposition party's trade unions' members, due to their inability to bag the support of the ruling party, miss the opportunities and may turn militant in character to attain their unions' goal.

On the basis of the dependency aspect of the trade unions on the political parties, the trade unions can be classified as follows.

1. **Fully dependent:** The trade unions that are completely dominated by the political parties. Such unions accept the leadership of their parent political party in matters of policy and functions as the labour wings of the party.
2. **Semi-dependent:** The trade unions which are functionally within the 'sphere of influence' of the political parties. Unions of this type are semi-independent but they lean heavily on parties for guidance in all important matters.
3. **Independent:** Independent unions maintain close relationship with political parties but such relationship is characterized by mutual understanding and non-interference.

Following is a list of national-level CTUOs as recognized by the Ministry of Labour, Government of India. The list is for the reference year 2002 whose verification was completed in 2008 (in alphabetical order). All these trade unions are affiliated to some political party or are independent.

1. **All India Central Council of Trade Unions (AICCTU):** It is politically attached to CPI(ML) Liberation. Founded in 1989 in its Chennai conference.
2. **All India Trade Union Congress (AITUC):** The AITUC is the oldest trade union federation in India. It is not politically affiliated to any political party including the CPI.
3. **Bharatiya Mazdoor Sangh (BMS):** BMS is the labour wing of RSS.
4. **Centre of Indian Trade Unions (CITU):** CITU is politically affiliated to the CPI(M).
5. **Hind Mazdoor Kisan Panchayat (HMKP):** HMKP is the India Workers Peasants Council.
6. **Hind Mazdoor Sabha (HMS):** HMS is affiliated with the International Confederation of Free Trade Unions.
7. **Indian Federation of Free Trade Unions (IFFTU):** IFFTU is the trade union wing of CPI(ML) Janashakti
8. **Indian National Trade Union Congress (INTUC):** INTUC is the trade union wing of the Indian National Congress.
9. **Labour Progressive Federation (LPF):** LPF is affiliated to Dravida Munnetra Kazhagam.

10. **National Front of Indian Trade Unions (NFITU):** NFITU is not affiliated to any political body.
11. **Self Employed Women's Association (SEWA):** SEWA is not affiliated to any political body.
12. **Trade Unions Co-ordination Centre (TUCC):** is not affiliated to any political body.
13. **United Trade Union Congress (UTUC):** UTUC is affiliated to the Revolutionary Socialist Party.

The dependence of trade unions on outside leadership, who were interested in achieving their political objectives and exploited the strength of the trade unions to meet their political objectives, vitiated the objectives of trade unions and retreated the growth.

5.7. Militancy Approach of Trade Unions

Militancy expresses a sense of combativeness and aggression. The attribute of militancy has been attached to trade unions in India since the first trade union came into being. Trade unions in India had been formed to counter against the exploitation of the working class. So there was some degree of aggression in the basic reason and intention of the foundation of the trade union. The history of trade unions also establishes the fact that they were registered in various companies to counter the oppressions of the managing class.

Industrial unrest had been explosive since the post-Emergency period. Incidences like strikes of late had shown signs of diminishing trend. But sporadic labour militancy had continued to the present times in spite of the fact that militant trade union policies are opposed by the modern management policies. Employees are becoming apathetic towards trade unions because they consider them to be 'weak and ineffective'. The trade unions on the other hand are not able to mobilize their members for various forms of trade union actions including demonstrating the militant forms.

Instances of labour militancy had been rampant; to cite few recent ones, incidences at the MSIL Manesar factory in 2012, Rico Auto Industries Ltd in 2009, Pricol Ltd in September 2009, Honda Motor Co. in September 2009, Graziano Trasmissioni India Pvt. Ltd in September 2008 and Hyundai Motor Co. in December 2009. Some of the older cases of militancy include the following.

On 8 January 1979, N. P. Godrej, vice-chairman of Godrej & Boyce Pvt Ltd, was stabbed by an unidentified knife-wielding assailant.

On 30 November 1977, the personnel manager of Britannia Biscuits, S. D. Deolalkar, was stabbed in the back and seriously injured. In Kerala, the small southern state provides its workers the highest wages and best working conditions in the country. The workers are under an umbrella of protective legislation which regards labour exploitation as a dirty word. An instance from Kerala is given below.

Headload workers earn, on average, ₹2,500 and some make ₹5,000 a month. They get what they ask, otherwise they will not let goods be lifted. In 2014, cashew worth over ₹5 crore could not be shipped from Cochin Port because the CPI(M)'s trade union wing, CITU, wanted its own men to be used for loading. In the Cochin Port, 51 workers handle a container for loading and unloading, while the same job is done by only 18 in Madras. So while it costs around ₹2,300 to unload a container at Cochin, the cost in Madras is just ₹225.

There had been instances where the non-workers have resorted to militancy approaches. For example, on 28 December 1978, 500,000 workmen employees of the 14 public sector and major private sector banks declared strike. On the next day, 100,000 bank officer employees in the

30,000 branches of the nationalized and private sector banks across India joined the workmen who were on strike and cheques worth ₹1,000 crore remained unclear in the vaults of the banks. This brought the financial transaction within the economy to a virtual halt, indicating the white-collar organizational solidarity and power [6].

There was also a strike by power engineers in Uttar Pradesh, a stir by port trust officers and merchant navy officers. This period also saw strikes by doctors in the state-managed hospitals, and in the labour courts in Bombay, a strike by the Labour Law Practitioners Association in protest against the appointment of a judge to the Labour Tribunal [7].

Militancy of labour converted the collective bargaining to what may be termed as 'terrorists' bargaining'.

For example, Dr Datta Samant and his unions converted collective bargaining virtually into terrorists' bargaining by the adoption of strong arm-twisting tactics. The nine and a half months old strike in 60 textile mills in Bombay was sustained by Dr Samant. The prolonged strike resulted in a colossal loss of production of more than ₹1,000 crore, while workers have lost wages of about ₹200 crore and the government was deprived of revenue to the tune of ₹200 crore. Many other ancillary industries, trades and occupations depending on the textile industry and employees therein also greatly suffered because of this strike [8].

I.C.5.2. INDUSTRIAL CONTEXT FOR DISCUSSION

Murder of N. P. Godrej

Seconds later as the 62-year-old managing director of Godrej & Boyce, N. P. Godrej, opened the door in response to the doorbell he was found lying bleeding on the floor, who was stabbed twice in the lower abdomen by a stranger wielding a Rampuri knife. It was just after 8.10 PM on 8 January that the assailant stabbed N. P. Godrej.

The assault has thrown business and industrial circles into a state of panic and highlighted the grim reality of deteriorating labour–management relations. Frantic telegrams were sent to the Central Government by, among others, the Indian Merchants' Chamber, the Bombay Merchants' Chamber, the Maharashtra Chamber of Commerce, the All India Manufacturers' Association and the Association of All India Engineering Industries. The messages claimed that the assault was incited by a militant labour union leader, and was more a reflection of inter-union rivalry than of management–worker conflict.

The crime branch of the Bombay police arrested the militant trade union leader, Dr Datta Samant, and three others, all members of the INTUC, in connection with the assault. They were remanded to police custody for a week. The case against Samant was that the assault was a desperate gambit provoked by the realization that he had all but lost his undisputed hold over the workers at Godrej & Boyce, one of the largest engineering units in the Western region.

5.8. Terrorists' Bargaining

The labour movement in India during the 1970s experienced a typical collective bargaining process. The process is termed as terrorists' bargaining. The initiators of this process were leaders such as Dr Datta Samant and George Fernandes.

The approach of such leaders was hostile on the negotiating table, which was not based on any logic and reasoning. They whimsically desired and demanded to the management and on the negotiation table expected the agreement to be executed as per their expected terms. Dr Datta Samant and his unions were typical outstanding examples who had convened collective bargaining virtually into terrorists' bargaining by adopting arm-twisting tactics and methods. The consequences of this brand of trade unionism which unfortunately has been permitted to grow and flourish was realized in the nine and half months old strike in 60 textile mills in Bombay, launched and sustained by Dr Samant. Misguiding the workers and making them tall promises, thereby prolonging the strike, resulted in a colossal loss of production of ₹1,000 crore, while workers lost wages of about ₹200 crore and the government was deprived of revenue to the tune of ₹200 crore (the then figures).

5.9. Outside Leadership of Trade Unions

The outside leaders do not belong to the ranks of the workers to whom they led, as they are not employees of the organization. Such leaders are normally politicians or social workers who had taken up trade unionism as a full-time vocation. The interest and influence of such outsiders very often cut across the interests of the workers. On the other hand, in many cases, the insiders are more influenced by the outsiders, so the former generally work under the guidance of the latter without any questions. In one sense, the insiders are the leaders of the workers but the followers of the outsiders.

The Trade Unions Act, 1926, (Section 22) provides for the proportion of office-bearers to be connected with the industry to which the trade union belongs. The subclauses provide the following:

'(1) Not less than one-half of the total number of the office-bearers of every registered Trade Union in an unorganized sector shall be persons actually engaged or employed in an industry with which the Trade Union is connected. Provided that the appropriate Government may, by special or general order, declare that the provisions of this section shall not apply to any Trade Union or class of Trade Unions specified in the order'.
('Unorganized sector' means any sector which the appropriate Government may, by notification in the Official Gazette, specify.)

'(2) Save as otherwise provided in sub-section (1), all office-bearers of a registered Trade Union, except not more than one-third of the total number of the office-bearers or five, whichever is less, shall be persons actually engaged or employed in the establishment or industry with which the Trade Union is connected.'
(For the purpose of this sub-section, an employee who has retired or has been retrenched shall not be construed as outsider for the purpose of holding an office in a Trade Union.)

'(3) No member of the Council of Ministers or a person holding an office of profit (not being an engagement or employment in an establishment or industry with which the Trade Union is connected), in the Union or a State, shall be a member of the executive or other office-bearer of a registered Trade Union'.

Over the years, trade unions in India have dominated by the influence of political leaders. In the process, often the interests of workers and their aspirations have been totally neglected. On the other hand, the nature of leadership majorly influences the union–management relations because of the presence of outsiders in the executive body of the trade union.

On the other hand, the unions and ILO feel that it is a fundamental right of any union to form its own structure and elect its own members. The ILO Convention No. 87 states that it is up to the trade union to decide the structure, composition and method of selection or election of its office-bearers. The government will play the role of a facilitator. The logic of ILO is supported by the fact that the outside leader has the knowledge of industrial practices in comparable organizations, and therefore has more experience while bargaining on the table.

The objective of government for including outside leaders in trade unions was to provide professional advice to the employed union leaders in an established manner with regard to labour laws and IR practices.

The government had proposed the move in the Code on Industrial Relations Bill, 2015, as an attempt to keep a check on 'politicization of trade unions'. The CTUs viewed this as an attack on the trade union movement. The provisions on restricting outsiders from becoming office-bearers in trade unions were dropped.

Finally, the outside leadership has been playing a pivotal role in the Indian trade union movement due to the inability of insiders to lead their movement. The factors for the same had been low education standards, poor command over English language, which is still the principal language of labour legislation and negotiations, low level of knowledge about labour legislation, unsound financial position, fear of victimization by the employer and lack of leadership qualities.

However, this practice proved to be counterproductive as most of these outside political leaders championed the interests of their political parties and other political causes rather than the causes that concerned the workers. There was a huge gulf in what the union leaders thought the workers need and the real pain points and demands of the workers. The workers were even exploited by these outside leaders.

5.9.1. The Evil Effects of Outside Leadership

The evil effects of outside leadership as pointed out by National Commission on Labour are as follows:

1. Outside leadership undermined the purposes of trade unions and weakened their authority. Aspects such as personal benefits and prejudices sometimes weighed more than unions.
2. Outside leadership has been responsible for the slow growth of trade unions.
3. This has resulted in not developing internal leadership fully.
4. Most of the leaders cannot understand the workers' problems as they do not live the life of a worker.

5.10. Small Size and Multiplicity of Trade Unions

The unions are getting smaller in size. Their finances are generally in bad shape. Trade union leadership faces several dilemmas. The unions often cannot make a constructive approach because of intensive inter-union rivalries and multiplicity of unions. Then, there is the heterogeneity of membership with workers from different areas, classes, castes and regions. The main reason for the development of such industry-centric trade unions had been the concentration of certain industries in particular areas. For example, textiles in Bombay, Ahmedabad, Indore and Kanpur; plantation in Assam, West Bengal, Tamil Nadu and Kerala; jute mills in Bengal; engineering in Calcutta and Bombay; chemical and pharmaceutical industries in Bombay and Vadodara.

The Indian trade unions are of various sizes. The membership number ranges from few thousands to countable few. The projected figure of average membership per union in India is less than 800 as compared with the United Kingdom (17,600) and the United States (9,500) [9]. The small size of the unions is due to the following factors:

1. The provision of the Trade Unions Act provides for any seven workers to form a union and get registered. This has resulted in large number of small unions.
2. The structure of a trade union organization depends on the size of the factory or the unit to which the employees belong. So the size of the factory or the unit impacts the size of the trade union. The membership has been impacted by the small size of units and a portion of the employees' preference to join trade unions.
3. Multiplicity of trade unions in the same factory or the unit had been another reason for the low membership. There are instances where in a single factory or unit, each agitated group has preferred to go for the formation of their own trade unions.
4. Multiple political parties supporting different groups of employees in the same factory or unit.
5. Employees getting organized on the basis of different craftsmanship, followed by the formation of craft-wise trade unions.
6. Employees splitting in terms of the nature of employment, for example, permanent, casual/contract, bad, apprenticeships and trainees, often go for the formation of their own trade unions, leading to impact the membership size of the trade unions.
7. Location of the units of the same organization. Employees of different units of the same organization located in different places form separate trade unions also result in the small size of membership of the unions. Rapid industrialization has increased the pace of capital formation in India, but skill development has not matched the process of capital formation. The agrarian labour force which was converted into industrial labour force in the early stage of industrialization had no scope for imparting systematic training for skill development. So the early foundation stage of the trade union formation suffered a lot and there had been no alternative for the same.
8. Most of the trade unions were linked to the political parties. Since Independence, India has experienced formation and reformation of political parties by splitting and sub-splitting based on ideological differences. The large number of political parties has caused the formation of a number of trade unions linked to different ideologies.
9. Rivalry among the leaders and the central organizations of trade unions has resulted in the multiplicity of unions, thereby reducing the average membership.

5.11. Financial Weakness

The trade unions suffer from financial weakness as the average yearly income of the unions has shown to be low and inadequate even for the individual trade union body [10]. The average income has been low not because of the low earnings of the workers but because of the following:

1. Workers are indifferent towards contributing their hard-earned money to the trade unions and do not want to do the same. The National Commission on Labour observed that the trade unions generally do not claim anything higher nor do the workers feel like contributing

more because the services rendered by the unions do not deserve a high face value. The members instead of making regular payment to the union make ad hoc payment if a dispute arises which is the indication of lack of commitment to the trade unions.

2. Under a condition of multiplicity of trade unions, the trade unions would be interested in increasing their membership. For that they usually keep their union contribution rates unduly low and do not collect the subscription regularly. For the improvement of the financial conditions of the trade unions, the National Commission on Labour recommended increase in the rate of minimum subscription.

The National Commission on Labour recommended various measures for improving the financial conditions of the trade unions. It recommended the mode of collection to be the 'checkoff system', under which an employer undertakes, on the basis of a collective agreement, to deduct towards the trade union dues from the worker's pay and transfer the same to the trade union. But no deductions can be made on this account under the Payment of Wages Act.

A recommendation for the solution to improve the financial condition of the trade unions was to remove trade union rivalry by strictly adhering to the principle of 'one union in one industry' [10]. The possibility for the same continues to be a question mark.

5.12. The Changing Economic Scenario

Till 1991, the labour department was considered to be the labour welfare department. But 1991 onwards, with the background of the international developments and introduction of neoliberal policies in India, workers came under attack where many existing benefits were either stopped or the government made serious efforts to amend them. The government started talking about 'reforms' and 'rightsizing' of workers. With the government initiating towards such new looks, the organizations being business oriented proceeded in an organized way to lead what may be termed a 'business for business'.

The right to form an association and the right to collective bargaining are part of the Indian Constitution. The conventions of the ILO also acknowledge the right to organize (No. 87) and the right to collective bargaining (No. 98).

Since 1991, in the wake of LPG accompanied by the need for growing emphasis on flexibility and downsizing for reorganization of work, the trade unions have been under severe stress and pressure [11]. The new economic environment, not only in India but also worldwide had not been favourable to trade unions and labour movements. The trade unions are either no longer capable of protecting the interests of their members or have no role in this 'new world' of constant flux and change [12]. The changing economic scenario has threatened the interests of Indian workers as well as the trade unions, resulting in a diminishing trend in membership [13].

Employers, on the other hand, have tended to become both economically and excessively powerful, thereby enjoying the privilege to hire and fire. There had been instances of the reduction of manpower in the name of efficiency. Schemes such as 'VRS and the exit policy' were adopted to retrench the organized workers.

Studies indicate that there had been several instances of political, administrative, legal and police support to the investors; in other words, 'protection being given to prospective investors' (e.g., Honda Motors case). Gone are the days of providing blanket support to the working class, and thereby to the trade unions by the government, which has been replaced by a protectionist approach towards industries for the sake of industrialization [14]. In short, it is the economic liberalization which has brought about more harm to trade unions through job losses in the organized sector.

5.13. Effect of Mechanizations

The management adopted easy means to retrench workers by replacing them with machines. It also caused decreasing incentives for trade union activities. Increased unemployment levels in different sectors reduced the chances of workers to unite for a movement. Through mechanization, re-engineering and technological upgradation, there had been loss of employment. Numerous manual jobs became outdated even if technology placed demand for high-quality jobs. The capital-intensive organizations became leaner where the trade unions did not fit into the structure since the technology demanded quality jobs [14]. The new technology having labour saving capacity caused redundancy and unemployment and consequently shrieked the trade union's power. Further, it created a new set of neo-workers, whose interests were different from traditional workers. The freedom to innovate enabled the firms to rapidly introduce new technology and products to satisfy the swiftly changing consumer choices and demands. The firms adopted modern sophisticated technology, management and production practices, involving the use of specially trained and educated workforce in the production and marketing of goods and services. All this resulted in the manifold increase in international trade flows during the emerging new economic environment [15].

The changed approach of the management caused the trade unions to face enormous difficulty in managing these young, enthusiastic and skilled workforce. The situation weakened the bargaining strength of trade unions [14]. This also resulted in the union membership showing declining trends [16].

5.14. Impact of Casualization of Labour

With the increasing privatization of the public sector industries, there had been mass scale casualization of the labour force since 1991. About 50–60 per cent of the workers, including those working in Maharatna and Navratna public sector companies, are working on contract. So the informal nature of the job has spread to even the organized sector, both in private and public. The mounting size of the informal employment is the key challenge to the present trade unions [17]. Technically, contract workers cannot raise an industrial dispute with the principle employer. As per the Indian law, their labour rights are mostly exercisable against the contractor, their employers only. However, these categories of workers had lent a supportive hand to the workers' struggle. Researchers have established that the casual and temporary workers in the informal sectors are generally less enthusiastic about trade union's activity. This has further aggravated the reduction of the importance of the trade unions [14].

5.15. The New Type of Negotiated Settlement

With time there emerged new types of negotiated settlements, which reflect a greater degree of employee cooperation, a different type of IR mode in which the employers tried to shift to the 'no-union model' or 'weak union model'. Such models are becoming popular, especially in multinational companies, as they believe that trade unions adversely obstruct managerial autonomy. The new way of managing collective labour power is through the implementation of the modern philosophy of HRM and various HR tools for involving, engaging, thereby controlling the workforce. The HRM strategy seeks to change behaviour and attitudes through HR interventions to promote competitive advantage for the employers and the organization. The empowerment model of human resources is also considered as the commitment model.

5.16. The Emergence of Service Organizations and Globalization

The emergence of service organizations, including IT and ITES, has led to an increase in knowledge employees, with better pay packages and emergence of gold-collared jobs, who are less interested in unionization. Globalization has substantially influenced the nature of IR policies being followed by employers and reduced the power of trade union. Strategic shifts in the management's approach to manage IR are noticeable at covert as well as overt levels [18].

5.17. Adoption of New HRM Strategy

The adoption of a new HRM strategy by most organizations in their efforts to gain competitive advantage through people has declined the collective labour power. The strategic HR interventions are broadly divided into the following two categories:

1. 'Instrumentalist' (hard) that implies enhanced managerial control on people. The hard HR interventions are generally resisted by employees as it considers the employees as any other resources. Hard interventions also involve a greater degree of measurement of cost-effectiveness of workers' efforts, which is normally not appreciated.
2. 'Empowerment' of HR interventions, on the other hand, involves trusting employees, ensuring transparency and fairness in the organizational working, and involving employees in decision-making as individuals. But HR interventions in actuality are generally an amalgam of hard and soft measures.

I.C.5.3. INDUSTRIAL CONTEXTS FOR DISCUSSION

The Changing Paradigm of Trade Union Leadership

There is no denial that in the spear of trade union leadership, a paradigm shift is emerging, which is more tending towards a situation of reasonability in considering the problems and the emerging issues. The management of the organizations have also grown tough to accept anything and everything. Further, the lockout is now a powerful weapon and often results in devastating effect on the working class. The business environment is becoming more firm these days as businesses are becoming more competitive and are posing a variety of challenges which were not experienced earlier. The trade union leaders have started understanding these changing contexts. So it is often considered that the militant days are getting over. There are emerging new approaches of the trade union leaders; few examples might include the activities of Madhukar Satpotdar, head of Shiv Sena's Maharashtra

Kamgar Sena, Chand Bibi, Damodar Thankappan of Bombay-based Kamani Tubes, with other emerging similar leaders.

The new leaders have not quite taken over from the George Fernandes and the Datta Samants, but they are waiting in different wings to take the organization and the employees to new heights. A few are not attached to any political parties. They are not only educated but many of them began their careers on the shop floors to understand the reality of work life. So they are intimately familiar with the nitty-gritty of company affairs and are better equipped for the negotiating table. They are not for repeating what happened with the Bombay textile industries with the continuation of a long gestation strike. What is true to the context was that the Bombay textile industry strike was that the mills were no longer viable—an aspect Samant seems to have ignored and that would not have survived the market competition. So the new class of leaders at the enterprise level of the management are emerging to give new future direction to IR in industries.

Madhukar Satpotdar, the head of Shiv Sena's Maharashtra Kamgar Sena, considers that he is interested in workers getting a good deal, but the same should not be at the expense of overburdening the organization. Aspects such as workers maintaining discipline and achieving higher productivity are taking their priority. Such an attitude is probably the result of their shop floor experience. Satpotdar represents over 200 companies, including Air India, Mahindra Ugine and Century Enka, leaders and over 50,000 members. But he has hardly supported strike except once at Bombay's Bhatia Hospital, which was more on reasonable grounds. (Satpotdar was the personnel manager at H&R Johnson, the Bombay-based ceramic tile unit. It was when Shiv Sena supreme, Bal Thackeray, requested him to launch a union, he agreed for it.) Today, the health of the units whose unions they head is a major concern.

Damodar Thankappan, who is 50 years old and took over as the working president of the employees union of the Bombay-based Kamani Tubes, is a remarkable example of a grassroots trade union leader. He came to Bombay in 1957 and, for five years, worked as a full-time unionist. In 1963, he joined Kamani Tubes and not long after began to work with the trade union. He was general secretary for a decade and since 1976 worked as the president. When the owners refused to run the company, he took the lead of taking over 'Lamani Tubes' by forming a workers' cooperative. He is presently a part of the management and also a faculty of the Indian Institute of Management, Calcutta. He addresses in various seminars and conferences. His turn-around experience as a leader of 'Kamani Tubes' is quoted as a true sign of trade union leadership. Now the workers' cooperative owns 50 per cent of the company's equity.

Chand Bibi is another example of trade union leader who has risen from the ranks and is an Arts graduate from Meerut University. She started her career as a clerk in R. J. Mehta's Engineering Mazdoor Sabha and later joined Mumbai Mazdoor Sabha. Just a decade later, she became its general secretary. She has negotiated many successful settlements for her union (which has 1.5 lakh workers in 475 companies, including Tata Consultancy Services, Cable Corporation of India and the foods company Herbertsons). She has proven to be a tough negotiator but also considerate of the competitive context of the business. She has stood for higher productivity with higher benefit to the working class.

5.18. The Objects of Trade Unions

Some of the aims and objectives of trade unions are as follows:

1. To secure for the worker fairer wages in the light of the cost of living and the prevailing standard of living in India.
2. To improve the workers' working conditions by securing shorter working hours, better leave facilities, adequate social security benefits, appropriate educational facilities and other welfare benefits.

3. To assure the workers a share in the increased profitability of an industrial unit by providing them the payment of adequate bonus.
4. To protect the workers' interest and more specifically to avoid their exploitation.
5. To ensure the workers' security of employment by resisting retrenchment and victimization likely to harm them.
6. To protect the larger interest of society by aiding in the improvement of trade and industry.

5.19. The Advantages of Trade Unions

There is no denial that there are certain benefits offered by trade unions to the working class which can be summarized as follows:

1. Trade unions help in getting the best professional assistance, be it legal or any other including personal.
2. They have proved to induce a spirit of self-reliance and self-respect among the workers, thereby helping to build up national character.
3. As unions act as an organized body, workers can negotiate with the employer on the basis of their status and self-respect. Pressure can be created by employees on the employer to maintain a healthy working condition including safety, hours of work and other service conditions. Any grievances case can be presented through the union, thereby preventing unnecessary strife and disruption to work.
4. Trade unions help maintain the wages at a uniform level in terms of the actual economic value.

Although strike had been a strong weapon in the hands of the trade union for projecting their demands, it is in its decreasing trend of utilization by the trade union leaders. On the other hand, some extremists have observed that workers' dissatisfaction is not finding an outlet in the form of non-violent agitation or strikes, as both government and factories discourage formation of trade unions and, by extension, collective bargaining and bipartite and tripartite negotiations. The statutory methods of settling disputes have gone a long way to address workers' dissatisfactions. The Trade Unions Act, 1926, provides another regulatory norm on the trade unions.

5.20. Recognition of a Trade Union

The registration and recognition of union by an employer are independent issues. The recognition of a trade union is generally a matter of agreement between the employer and the trade union which ensures that appropriate modes of collective bargaining take place and that the agreements, which are collectively reached, are mutually observed. Trade union recognition also works as much in the interests of the employer as it does in the interests of employees.

Recommendations by the National Labour Commission, 1969, strongly recommended that the trade union registration be made compulsory.

Recognition of trade union is the backbone of collective bargaining, but managements in several states have refused to recognize a trade union mainly on the following five grounds:

1. Most of the office-bearers of the union were outsiders.
2. Sometimes, those disapproved by management were particularly politicians and ex-employees.
3. The union consisted of only small number of employees.

4. There were many rival unions in existence.
5. The trade union was not registered under the Trade Unions Act, 1926.

The right to grant recognition to trade unions within the meaning of the Constitution of India, Article 19(1)(c) is a fundamental right or not is answered in negative because the right to form association does not carry with it the concomitant right that the association must be recognized by the employers. Hence, withdrawal of recognition does not infringe the fundamental rights guaranteed under the Constitution of India, Article 19(1)(c).

The Labour Code on Industrial Relations Bill, 2015, is silent on recognition of the trade union. But few state governments have enacted special statute or rules and provided a mechanism for recognition. Broadly speaking, these enactments are as follows:

- Maharashtra Recognition of Trade Unions and Prevention of Unfair Labour Practices Act, 1971.
- West Bengal has made an amendment by way of Chapter III A to the Trade Unions Act under the heading 'Recognition of Trade Unions as Bargaining Agents'.
- Kerala Recognition of Trade Unions Act, 2010.
- Orissa Verification of Membership and Recognition of Trade Union Rules, 1994.

It is a normal IR practice that in a multi-union situation the management has to decide with which trade union it is supposed to negotiate. The general norm is that the negotiating trade union should be the true representative of the workmen.

The Trade Unions Act provides for registration of the union but is silent on the recognition of the trade union. In this connection, reference may be made to the case between Puducherry Shasun Chemicals and Drugs Niruvana Thozhilalargal Muneerta Sangam versus Labour Officer, (2010 LLR 498 [Mad HC]). The Hon'ble Madras High Court, inter alia, ruled that the Trade Unions Act 'except for providing registration of the union do not oblige any employer to recognize any particular trade union and no procedure has been prescribed for grant of any recognition'. Further, the High Court also ruled that 'the grant of recognition of the union cannot be brought under Section 2(k) of the Industrial Disputes Act and thereby cannot be the subject matter of the industrial dispute'.

There had been a general practice in few organizations and establishments to follow the criteria for the recognition of trade unions as specified in the code of discipline recommended in the 16th Labour Conference in the year 1958. Although this code of discipline has no statutory force, courts have recognized its importance in securing industrial peace.

In the case of Hind Mazdoor Kisan Panchayatt Vasavadatta Cement Workers Union versus The Commissioner of Labour & Registrar of Trade Union in Karnataka (2001 LIC 3260 [Karn]), it was held that the code of discipline has no statutory force. The court was of the opinion that though the code has no statutory force, this needs to be followed both by the employer and employees to secure industrial peace. The court observed[1]

The code of discipline was accepted by all employers' and workers' organizations at the 16th Session of the Indian Labour Conference held at Nainital in May 1958. No doubt, the code of discipline has no statutory force but, this code of discipline has to be observed, in order to have industrial peace.

In establishment/s where code of discipline is not followed and in the absence of any prescribed law or rule for recognition, it is left to the discretion of the management to recognize the sole

[1] https://www.businessmanager.in/recognition-of-a-trade-union-by-the-employer.php

bargaining agent of the workmen; this is a management's prerogative. But there are instances where such actions have been challenged by the rival trade unions if the decision of the management appears to be unfair or arbitrary.

The Kerala High Court in Travancore Cochin Chemicals Thozhilali Union versus Travancore Cochin Chemicals Ltd (1982 (1) LLJ 425) has opined two important aspects. They are as follows:

1. Recognition is a matter of volition on the part of the employer.
2. A trade union has neither common law right nor statutory right which enables and entitles it to compel an employer to give recognition to it as the bargaining agent of its members.

This view of the Kerala High Court had the concurrence from the Apex Court in its judgment in Delhi Police Non-Gazetted Karmachari Sangh versus Union of India (1987 (1) LLJ 121). It was held in the instance case that there is no fundamental right for a trade union to be recognized.

In Board of Trustees, Port of Calcutta versus Haldia-Calcutta Port and Dock Shramik Union ((1994) IILLJ 575 Cal), the division bench of the Calcutta High Court was of the opinion that neither a registered trade union could automatically get a right for recognition from the authorities nor there was any statutory rights whereby any union could not compel the management to recognize it. Further, the court observed that a trade union had to establish a reasonable standard whereby it could be said that they represented a substantial section of the workforce.

In the case of IATA union Hyderabad versus Chairman and MD Indian Airlines (1995 (1) LLJ 578 1994 (2) LLN 493), the court was of the opinion that with regard to the limited recognition, though it may be said that it was not the fundamental right or a statutory right, the fair play required that such recognition should be conceded wherein the trade union sought a general recognition to negotiate as a majority union on behalf of all workmen.

5.21. The Trade Unions Act, 1926

The Trade Unions Act, 1926, provides provisions to protect workers against exploitation and safeguard their rights. The Act under various chapters specify various legal provisions as enumerated below:

1. Chapter I deals with the objective of the Act. The Trade Unions Act, 1926, was enacted during the British rule in India. It came into force with effect from 1 June 1927 and extends to the whole of India except the state of Jammu and Kashmir. It deals with the registration of trade unions and the law connected with such registered trade unions. The Act, after the preamble, defines certain concepts which have been used in the Act.
2. Chapter II deals with the registration of trade unions, which is an important area. The registration process of the trade unions as laid down under the Act is as follows:
    a. Appropriate government shall appoint a person as registrar of trade unions for each state (Section 3(1)). The appropriate may also appoint additional and deputy registrars as per necessity.
    b. Application for registration is required to be made and signed by at least seven members. The Act provides that any seven or more members of concerned trade union can apply for registration of that trade union by subscribing their names to the rules of that trade union and also by complying with the provisions of this Act. Provided that no trade union of workmen shall be registered unless at least 10 per cent or 100 of the workmen, whichever

is less, engaged or employed in the establishment or industry with which it is connected, are the members of such a trade union on the date of making of application for registration: provided further no trade union of workmen shall be registered unless it has on the date of making application not less than seven persons as its members, who are workmen engaged or employed in the establishment or industry with which it is connected.

c. Such applications are required to be tabled before the registrar and should also be accompanied with a copy of rules of trade union and also a statement showing names, occupations and so on of the applicants. It should also have the name of the trade union and its head office's address. Such rules of the trade union are to be provided for name of union, its objects and purposes, maintenance of list of members thereof, admission of member thereof and so on for getting registered under this Act (Section 5). Rules should contain provisions as prescribed in Section 6.

d. The Registrar, on being satisfied that the trade union has complied with all the requirements of the Act in regard to registration, shall register the trade union and enter particulars related to the trade union in the register maintained by him (Section 8). While registering such trade union, the registrar is required to enter its name in the register and issue the certificate of registration. Trade union will have a registered office (Section 12).

e. Section 10 provides for situations in which such registrations can be cancelled, including if any application as to same was received from the trade union or if the registration is found to have been obtained by fraud or mistake. There are also other situations in which such cancellations can be made. An appealing provision is given in case persons feel aggrieved by the decision of refusal to grant or cancellation of the registration of trade union. An appeal can be preferred before the Civil Court not below the rank of additional or assistant judge of a principal Civil Court. Further, Section 13 of the Act requires incorporation of such trade unions which are registered under this Act.
Section 13 provides the features of registered trade union, which are as follows:
- Registered trade union will have perpetual succession (will not stop after the death of the members of the trade union).
- Every registered trade union will have common seal.
- Every registered trade union can acquire and hold both movable and immovable properties.
- Every registered trade union can sue others.
- Every registered trade union can be sued by others.

3. Chapter III deals with the rights and liabilities of such registered trade unions. Section 15 specifies certain objects in respect of which the general funds of such registered unions should be spent, including salaries, allowances, administrative expenses, prosecuting or defending the legal actions and so on, and the list is inclusive. Section 16 requires the registered union to constitute a separate fund for the political purposes which are to be spent on the given objects. Under Section 19, the office-bearers are entitled to inspect the account books of the registered trade unions. Besides all these rights there are also several rights provided under subsequent provisions of this Act.

4. Chapter IV of the Act makes provisions to regulations, and Section 29 empowers the concerned government to make such regulations for the purpose of this Act and on the matters enlisted thereunder. Such regulations are to be published by the appropriate government.

5. Finally, Chapter V of the Act makes penal provision under the Act and also prescribes the procedure in relation thereto. Sections 31 and 32 describe certain offences, including providing false information, committing default in giving notices, documents and so on which

are required under this Act to be given by registered trade union. The punishment is provided in the form of fine. Section 33 provides for taking cognizance of such offence by the court which should not be below the rank of presidency magistrate or a first class magistrate.

6. Rights and liabilities of a registered trade union: A registered trade union has the right to maintain a general fund and a separate fund for political purposes. But the unions are bound to utilize the funds only for the purposes specified in the Act.

7. Objectives for using general fund (Section 15): The following are the purposes for which the general funds of the union may be spent:
   a. Payment of salaries, allowances and so on to the office-bearers of the union.
   b. Payment of expenses for the administration of the union including other expenses spent on defending any legal proceedings by or against the union.
   c. Settlement of trade disputes.
   d. Special allowances to the members (including dependants) of the trade union on account of death, sickness, accidents and so on.
   e. Compensation to members for loss arising out of trade disputes.
   f. Provide educational, social and religious benefits to the members.
   g. Issue of assurance policies on the lives of members and also against sickness, accidents, unemployment, insurance and so on.
   h. For the publication of periodicals for the members' benefit.
   i. Any other object that may be notified by the appropriate government in the official gazette.
   If funds are spent for any purposes other than the above, such expenditure is treated as unlawful and the trade union can be restrained by the court for applying its funds in any other purposes.

8. Constitution of a separate fund for political purposes (Section 16): Apart from the primary objects, a trade union may have certain other political objects. As per Section16, a registered union may constitute a separate fund in addition to the general fund and the payment of such a fund shall be utilized for serving civic and political interest of its members. The fund can be utilized for the following purposes:
   a. Holding of any meeting or distribution of any literature or document in support of any candidate for election as a member of legislative body constituted under the Constitution or of any local authority.
   b. For maintenance of any person who is a member of any legislative body constituted under the Constitution.
   c. For convening of political meeting of any kind or distribution of the political literature or documents of any kind.
   d. The registration of electors for selection of a candidate for the legislative body.
   The funds collected for political purposes shall not be clubbed with the general fund. No workman is compelled to contribute in this fund and the non-payment in this fund cannot be made a condition for admission to the trade union.

9. Amalgamation of trade unions: Section 24 provides that any two or more registered trade unions may become amalgamated together as one trade union with or without dissolution or division of the funds of such trade unions or either of them, provided that the votes of at least one-half of the members of each or every such trade union entitled to vote are recorded, and that at least 60 per cent of the votes recorded are in favour of the proposal.

In the case of an amalgamation of a trade union with another trade union, a written notice of an amalgamation signed by the secretary and seven members of the trade union is required to be sent to the registrar of the trade union. The trade union's name should not match with the other trade union's name. If the registrar is satisfied with all requirements provided by the members of both the trade unions, the registrar will change the name of the union, and the same will be entered in the register. Also, if the registrar is satisfied with all requirements provided by the members of trade unions, he or she will validate amalgamation and the same will be entered in the register.

10. Section 25 provides that in case of change in the name of the trade union, written notice of the change of name signed by the secretary and seven members of the trade union is required to be sent to the registrar of the trade union.

11. Dissolution of the trade union: Section 27 provides for the dissolution of the trade union. The procedure is as follows:

   a. Notice of dissolution signed by the secretary and seven members of the trade union should be sent to the registrar of the trade union within 14 days from the date of the dissolution of the trade union.

   b. If registrar is satisfied with the provisions and rules followed by the members of the trade union for dissolution, he will confirm the dissolution.

   c. Funds shall be divided by the registrar among its members, if there are no rules mentioned by the trade union for distribution of the funds.

C.5.2. Case for Discussion   Settlement in PepsiCo's Naroda Plant

On 30 December 2008, every worker, after their names were announced, came to the vice-president (HR) and received three different cheques and congratulated each other. Some of them even hugged him. Naroda Plant was taken over by PepsiCo from Gujarat Bottling Plant on 7 November 1995. The plant had two lines of production, that is, carbonated soft drink incorporated in 1995 and juice incorporated in 2001. The management introduced total productivity maintenance (TPM) methods in the year 2007. The plant had an excellent track record of social responsibility but the performance of the plant on production volume and productivity showed a downward trend during 2005–2008.

Naroda Plant employed 138 persons including 85 workers (associates), 22 executives and about 31 in other categories. On average, 67 workers were needed for operating two lines. The need for contractual workers ranged between 25 and 175 depending on the volume of the production. The plant normally used to run in three shifts. The overall operations of the plant were taken care of by the plant manager and the responsibilities of people management remained with the plant personnel manager. Out of 85 workers, 84 completed 20 years of service. Half of the workers were SSC and above in terms of educational qualification; 9 out of them were graduates and 11 of them were having technical qualifications to their credit.

The sales team with 130 distributors and 60,000 outlets in Gujarat strived for getting more and more market stakes. But Cola was experiencing a downfall for the following reasons:

1. Glass bottle consumption was going down, polyethylene terephthalate (PET) bottles and cans sales were growing up. The Naroda Plant was only manufacturing in glass bottles.
2. The taste of consumers was changing towards health drinks.
3. The Cola market was price-sensitive; consumer preference was going down.

In spite of the best efforts being made by the sales team, there was not much of any improvement in sales. So business being not viable, the alternative was VRS.

The trade union, after due consideration of the context, considered to give the following options to the management:

1. The workers of Naroda Plant agreed to postpone the issues of wage revision for a period of two years.
2. The age of retirement of workmen was accepted to be reduced from 60 years to 58 years.
3. Workmen were also ready to work other than in production activities like marketing.
4. The trade union agreed to reduce the strength by 20 per cent by way of introducing VRS in consultation with union.
5. The VRS amount which was demanded to be ₹20 lakh was finally reduced to ₹10.5 lakh. The VRS commenced from 26 December 2008 and closed on 29 December 2008. The VRS package and legal dues included the following:
   a. Salary for the month of December 2008
   b. Loyalty bonus
   c. VRS amount
   d. Bonus
   e. Gratuity
   f. Leave encashment

The agreement was signed off and everything got settled peacefully in just three weeks time.

Case Questions

1. Explain the approach of the trade union.
2. Was the trade union right in giving the offers to the management as stated in the case? Justify.
3. Do you think there were other alternatives which the trade union could have adopted? Give reasons.

Chapter Summary

1. The trade union movements in India are linked with reforming the Indian society as well as initiating the movement for making India independent. Subsequently, the objective of achieving the economic objective of industrialization of the country was added.
2. The general motives of workers for joining trade unions were normally grievance representation, security, improvement in their economic conditions and protection in times of trouble.
3. The management considers that 'trade unions restrict the management's discretion'. The management also often argues that trade unions, as outsiders, have no right to intervene in the affairs of the enterprise, and they also hamper the optimum utilization of manpower, thereby influencing the productivity adversely.
4. There had been decreasing interest of the workforce to join trade unions and consequently, the number of trade unions decreased.
5. There had been a changing paradigm of trade union leadership. Instances of the same are provided in the chapter.
6. There are certain benefits of trade unions to employees; for example, they help in getting the best professional assistance, they act as an organized body and negotiate with the employer, and they help in maintaining the wages at a uniform scale of increase.
7. The Trade Unions Act, 1926, provides for the rules for the trade union formation, registration, liabilities and obligations, and for its management and control.

Questions

1. What are the impacts of industrialization on the trade unions in India?
2. What are the reasons for employees joining the trade union?
3. How does the management consider the trade unions?
4. Do you think that militancy is a general feature of the trade unions? Discuss.
5. Explain the concept of 'terrorists' bargaining'. Give examples.
6. What are the impacts of mounting size of informal workers?
7. Explain the features of the changing paradigm of trade union leadership.

Project Work for the Students

1. Identify one instance of changing role of trade union leadership from an industrial context and elaborate.
2. What are the major challenges you see ahead for the trade unions in the organizations? Elaborate with examples from the organizations you have come across.

References

1. Michael, VP. Industrial relations in India and workers' involvement in management. Bombay: Himalaya Publishing House; 1987.
2. Basu RS. Nandanar's children: The Paraiyans' tryst with destiny, Tamil Nadu 1850–1956. New Delhi: SAGE Publications; 2011. pp. 241–257.
3. Reddy KV. Working class and freedom struggle: Madras presidency, 1918–1922. New Delhi: Mittal Publications; 2005. pp. 58–59.
4. The Hindu. 22 December 2008. Available at https://www.thehindu.com/archive/print/2008/12/22/.
5. Thakur CP. Indian J. Ind. Relat. July 1976; 12(1): 6.
6. Editorial. Forty years ago, December 28, 1978: Bank strike begins, Indian Express. 28 December 2018. Available at https://indianexpress.com/article/opinion/editorials/forty-years-ago-december-28-1978-bank-strike-begins-5512539/
7. Business India. 8–21 January 1977.
8. Dubey S, Singh CU. Datta Samant: A lion who prowls the embattled frontier between labour and capital, India Today. 19 October 2013, Issue Date: 28 February 1982. Available at https://www.indiatoday.in/magazine/cover-story/story/19820228-datta-samant-a-lion-who-prowls-the-embattled-frontier-between-labour-and-capital-771550-2013-10-19
9. Cornfield D, McCammon H. Labor revitalization: Global perspectives and new initiatives. London, UK: JAI Press; 2003.
10. Ghosh G. Indian Trade Union Movement. US: The Peoples History Publication; 2005.
11. Reddy DN. Changing world economic order and world of worker. Indian J. Labour Eco. 2003; 46(2).
12. Yates MD. The new economy and labour movement, Monthly Review. 2001; 52(11): 28–42.
13. Sodhi JS. Emerging trends in industrial relations and human resource management in Indian industry. Indian J. Ind. Relat. 1994; 30(1): 19–37. Available at http://www.jstor.org/stable/27767337.
14. Ghosh B. Economic reforms and trade unionism in India—a macro view. Indian J. Ind. Relat. 2008; 43(3): 355–384. Available at http://www.jstor.org/stable/27768140.
15. Anker R. Gender and jobs. Geneva: ILO; 1990.
16. Mamkoottam K. Labour and change-essays on globalization. New Delhi: SAGE Publications; 2003.
17. Bagchi AK. New technology and the workers' response. New Delhi: SAGE Publications; 1995.
18. Saini D. Dynamics of new industrial relations and postulates of industrial justice. Indian J. Labour Econ. 2003; 46(4).

PART

4

Administrative Aspects of Industrial Relations

6

Collective Bargaining

LEARNING OBJECTIVES

After reading this chapter, you will be able to:

- ❑ Understand the concept, nature and scope of collective bargaining based on labour relations literature
- ❑ Understand the importance of collective bargaining
- ❑ Understand the structure of collective bargaining in India
- ❑ Describe the process (or procedure) of collective bargaining embracing varied strategies and tactics widely used in contract negotiation and administration
- ❑ How collective bargaining is conducted in real-work settings

C.6.1. Case for Discussion   The Wage Problem with the Workers of Tea Estates in Darjeeling

Sojan, the HR manager of a tea estate of Darjeeling, West Bengal, is eagerly looking forward for the settlement of the issue of minimum wages, which has been pending for three years. As the system prevails since 1977, the daily wage of tea workers is negotiated once in three years. But the industry has not been able to finalize the new wage rates for last three years, after the expiry of the last term on 31 March 2014.

Around seven lakh tea workers in Bengal participated in the labour agitation over implementation of minimum wages in 2014 in the tea-growing areas of Darjeeling. But such agitations had not yielded any fruitful results, since the authority under the Minimum Wages Act, the labour department, had not pronounced any solutions. This agitation spurred to a level, which caused disruption in the production process in the tea gardens and the factories in the tea-growing region of Darjeeling.

The labour department was unable to provide any specific solutions to the issue, so also the management, who were the members of the employer's association. The matter with passage of time had moved to the level of the State Labour Minister, the ultimate government authority for the decision. Commercially, and from the business perspective, it could prove to be a tough task for planters to withstand any kind of unrest in gardens at a time when plantations were approaching towards the first flush—season's first and best quality yield that comes after winter.

Almost all major trade unions, for example, INTUC and CITU, jointly asked for implementation of the Minimum Wages Act, instead of following a system of periodic negotiation for a wage settlement. After initial reluctance, following nine rounds of meetings, Bengal Government finally formed a special committee in 2015 comprising representatives from planters, workers and government to propose a new wage structure and other modalities as per Minimum Wages Act. But the committee being too slow in providing a suitable solution, there was no solution to this long pending issue. So, there were no options left for the workers other than agitating across the industry in demand for a suitable solution.

The planter association was also pressed from both the sides, that is, the restless tea garden workers at one hand, and on the other hand they did not want the government to settle the issue in haste, without considering all aspects of minimum wages settlement. As any hasty or populist settlement by the government would put the planters under tremendous financial pressure. On the other side, delay in settlement may ignite aggressive workers' movement grossly hampering the business.

Sojan, the HR manager of a major tea estate, believes that his organization's performance rests on the well-being of the HR. So under such a situation, where there were no solutions to the problem, Sojan approached his management for adoption of an independent wage policy of their own. But being a member of the planter association, the management was unable to find a way out to move out of the decision of the tea planter's association.

The big planters also voiced their concern and said, 'we are ready to accept any wage structure under any system. But that should be acceptable and rational. Any hasty and populist settlement, accepted by the government, will come as an unjustified financial overload for us. On the other side, delay in settlement may ignite aggressive workers' movement. That will badly damage the industry'.

Case Questions

1. Are the workers of the tea estate right in their approach of adopting an industry-wise agitation only because the issue of settlement of their wage structure is taking a longer time?
2. The workers started the agitation at a time which was very critical for the tea industry and tea business. Any agitation continuing for a longer period at such critical phase of the business is likely to affect the planters' business, the industry's market performance both at the national and international levels. What are the possible solutions to this problem?
3. Of all the solutions recommended, which solution do you feel is the best fit to the context and why?

6.1. Introduction and Concept

Collective bargaining implies that a group of employees negotiate as a unit with their employer over pay, benefits and working conditions and other conditions of service related to the job they perform. The belief and the logic which back collective bargaining are that as a group, employees have more strength which is termed as 'bargaining power' rather than negotiating with their employer individually. Because of the reason of 'collaborating for a common cause', collective bargaining is inherently a democratic process. Collective bargaining is a dynamic process at work and adopted in all developed and developing economies as a tool for facilitating negotiation between management and workers represented through labour unions. Collective bargaining is universally acknowledged as the ideal method for regulating and settling differences between the labour and the management. As such, the process of collectively bargaining has been considered to be a 'fundamental human right'.

IR being inherently a bipartite relationship, the parties to this relationship, that is, the labour union representing workers and management representing the employer, for settling the differences arising out of the condition of employment collectively negotiate for amicable settlements. Due to the diverse interests, differences in expectations and difference in the guiding value systems of the two parties, that is, the labour and the management, their relationship is often fragile and complex. The possibility of developing incongruent goals, leading to misunderstanding and conflict is inevitable in the organizational context. Both the parties, that is, the labour union and the management for resolving their differences or conflicts offer for mutual discussions and negotiate without the intervention of any third party. Such a process of resolving the differences between the labour union and management without involving any third party is termed as collective bargaining.

The 'collective bargaining process' is not an outdated practice or belief for maintaining 'harmonious IR', rather it is still a contemporary acceptable practice. On 26 February 2011, the Human Rights Watch Press, which is a non-profit, non-government human rights organization having international representation, recommended to honour 'public employee bargaining rights' in the United States. They elaborated the reasons as to why collective bargaining needs to be recognized as an 'international human right'. The reason was 'that the bargaining right facilitates for compromises resulting from a process in which workers have an autonomous voice and reflects principles of dignity, equality and democracy which are consistent with human rights principles'.

The principles of dignity, equality and democracy which are constituents of collective bargaining recognize the right to join and be involved in the trade union activities. The *collective relationship* between trade union and employer, which emerges out of the terms of employment, is strengthened through the approaches of collective bargaining, which ultimately results in harmonious IR. All these aspects qualify the process of collective bargaining to be 'a means to an end'.

The concept of collective bargaining can be further defined as follows.

1. **A tool for settling differences:** The phrase 'collective bargaining' was first coined by Sidney and Beatrice Webb and was accepted worldwide as a tool for settling differences between the employer and the workers, represented by the trade unions. Webbs considered 'collective bargaining' as an economic institution, with trade unions representing the labour as a factor of production. The present conceptual understanding is contrary to the belief that 'the management having the purchasing power procures HR, which is a factor of production, thereby enjoys the unlimited power to exploit the HR'.

   Harbinson [1] defines collective bargaining as 'a process of accommodation between two institutions (management and labour, represented by trade unions) having both common and conflicting interests'. The major dimensions of collective bargaining are enhancement of dignity, worth of labour and freedom of individual workers. It relates to group bargaining about wages and salaries and working conditions. The parties may be trade unions or their federations on the one hand and an employer or his representative or an employers' association or federation, on the other. The concept and the approach of collective bargaining has been considered as a process, a technique and a means for reaching the end of maintaining 'harmonious IR' in the industries by ensuring against labour exploitation. It embraces formal labour agreements impacting the day-to-day relationships between the management and the trade unions.

2. **Collective bargaining—a process of settling disputes:** Collective bargaining is a process of negotiating between management and workers represented by their representatives for determining mutually agreed terms and conditions of work which protect the interest of both the workers and management. According to Dale Yoder, 'collective bargaining is essentially a process in which employees act as a group in seeking to shape conditions and relationships in their employment' [2]. Michael J. Jucius also defined collective bargaining as 'a process by which employers, on the one hand, and representatives of employees, on the other, attempt to arrive at agreements covering the conditions under which employees

will contribute and be compensated for their services' [3]. Also, Edwin B. Flippo considered that 'collective bargaining is a process in which the representatives of a labour organization and the representatives of business organization meet and attempt to negotiate a contract or agreement, which specifies the nature of employee–employer–union relationship'.

3. **Solution to settle the terms of employment and condition of services:** In the year 1990, the Supreme Court of India provided a more practical sense of the concept in the case of 'Karnal Leather Karmachari Sangathan versus Liberty Footwear Co.'[1] The Supreme Court defined collective bargaining as 'a technique by which disputes as to the "Conditions of Employment" are resolved amicably, by agreement rather than coercion. The dispute is settled peacefully and voluntarily, although reluctantly, between the labour and management'. In other words, collective bargaining provides the solutions by mutually discussing, negotiating and concluding to the negotiated terms between an employer and employee, and finally culminating in a written agreement or contract. It is a process of accommodation between two conflicting interests where power stands against power. In 1960, in the manual published by the ILO, collective bargaining has been defined as 'negotiations about working condition and terms of employment between an employer or one or more employers' organizations, on the one hand, and one or more representative workers' organizations, on the other, with a view for reaching an agreement'.[2]

4. **A process in which parties have willingness to compromise:** According to Leap and Crino [4], collective bargaining is an indication of good faith bargaining and willingness to compromise during negotiations. The key to its success is the role of the negotiators who is to maintain a flexible attitude and willingness to listen to proposals submitted by the other side and to make counter offer on those proposals. As such it is a dynamic activity in the employer and employee relationships as with the expiry of the agreement period, a similar agreement maybe with a different sets of demands and the nature and duration of agreement may change with the changing expectations, circumstances and position of the parties.

It is worth indicating the court's order in the case of 'Bharat Iron Works versus Bhagubhai Balubhai Patel', [5] it was held that

> Collective bargaining, being the order of the day in the democratic, social welfare State, legitimate trade union activities, which must shun all kinds of physical threats, coercion or violence, must march with a spirit of tolerance, understanding and grace in dealings on the part of the employer. Such activities can flow in healthy channel only on mutual cooperation between the employer and the employees and cannot be considered as irksome by the management in the best interests of its business. Dialogue with representatives of a union help striking a delicate balance in adjustments and settlement of various contentious claims and issues.

Similar observations are embedded in the thoughts of Louis E. Howard,[4] who considered collective bargaining as

> To get together (right of meeting), to enter a common organization (right of association), to determine that whatever conditions of work are allotted shall be the same for all workers and to make a bargain with employers to that effect (rights of combinations and bargaining) and eventually in case the employers should refuse to enter on such a bargain or fail to honour it

[1] AIR 1990 SC 247.
[2] ILO. Geneva: ILO;1960.

when entered upon, to confront them with a united refusal to go to work or to continue at work (right of strike).

5. **Collective bargaining is the beginning of a long-term relationship:** The process of collective bargaining does not end with arriving at an agreement. It is a continuous process because the agreement is only the beginning of a long-term relationship. Since all the bargaining processes terminate to an implementable negotiated agreement, the process is not a temporary or one-time solution. It generates a long-lasting harmonious IR. In the case of 'Ram Prasad Viswakarma versus Industrial Tribunal' [6], the court observed,

> It is well known how before the days of 'collective bargaining', labour was at a great disadvantage in obtaining reasonable terms for contracts of service from its employer. As trade unions developed in the country and collective bargaining became the rule, the employers found it necessary and convenient to deal with the representatives of workmen, instead of individual workmen, not only for the making or modification of contracts but in the matter of taking disciplinary action against one or more workmen and as regards of other disputes.

The following are the recommendations of the ILO on 'collective bargaining for the settlement of industrial disputes':

- The Collective Agreements Recommendation, 1951 (No. 91), dealing with collective bargaining machinery, the definition of collective agreements, their effects, their interpretation and the supervision of their application.
- The Voluntary Conciliation and Arbitration Recommendation, 1951 (No. 92), which aimed at promoting the establishment of conciliation and arbitration machinery with equal representation on both sides; it stresses the voluntary nature of such machinery and specifies that none of its provisions may be interpreted as limiting the right to strike.
- The Collective Bargaining Convention (No. 154) and Recommendation (No. 163), both adopted in 1981 and aimed at promoting free and voluntary collective bargaining.

Source: ILO's 84th session, 1994.

6. **The ultimate impact is beyond the visible outcome:** The above definitions explain the term collective bargaining as a means of improving conditions of employment. But invisible dimension of the concept serves more than just a means of fair harmonious IR. Perlman [7] aptly indicates,

> Collective bargaining is not just a means of raising wages and improving conditions of employment. Nor is it merely democratic government in industry. It is above all a technique, collective bargaining as a technique of the rise of a new class is quite different...from the desire to displace or 'abolish' the 'old ruling class'...to gain equal rights as a class...to acquire an excessive jurisdiction in that sphere where the most immediate interests, both material and spiritual, are determined, and a shared jurisdiction with the older class or classes in all other spheres.

This sense of the concept is widely accepted, particularly in the developed countries. It implies that collective bargaining, a term thus used to describe:

a. The procedure, whereby employers must attempt to reach agreement about wage rates and basic conditions of labour with trade unions, instead of with individual workers.

b. It is an essential element of economic democracy, a 'two-party' procedure for arriving at a commonly agreed solution.

c. It is the process of discussion and negotiation between an employer and a union culminating in a written agreement or contract and the adjustment of problems arising under the agreement.

d. Collective bargaining implies 'good-faith bargaining' which essentially implies that both parties make every reasonable effort to arrive at an agreement.

e. It does not mean either party is compelled to agree to a proposal or requires either party to make any specific concessions.

6.2. Objective of Collective Bargaining

The objectives and focus of collective bargaining are listed as follows:

1. To recognize trade unions as having similar authority at the workplace as the employer.
2. To agree upon an acceptable contract—acceptable to management and the trade union representatives.
3. Collective bargaining is an industrial peace treaty and at the same time a source of terms and conditions of employment for the stability of jobs.
4. To protect the legitimate expectations of both management and labour.
5. The right to profit-sharing for improving workers' standards of living and claiming enhanced share in the profits of the enterprise.
6. The workers' democratic participation in decisions influencing their working conditions.
7. Development of orderly practices for sharing decisions of the day-to-day working of the enterprise, and settlement of disputes which may form the broad general objectives of the workers, including defending and promoting the workers' interests.
8. To generate pressures for enhancement of the dignity, worth and freedom of individual workers.
9. To attain industrial peace.

6.3. Some of the Important Features of Collective Bargaining

1. **It is a collective two-way bipartite process:** Through this process the workers and management jointly arrive at an amicable solution through negotiations.
2. **It is a complex process:** The process of collective bargaining has been considered to be a complex process since it involves a number of procedures, techniques and tools including preparation for negotiations and so on.
3. **It is flexible, voluntary and continuous:** Since it is a group action, it has sufficient flexibility. In such a process, no party can afford to be inflexible and rigid. The unique feature of collective bargaining is that usually the parties concerned start negotiations with entirely divergent views but finally reach a middle point acceptable to both.

   It is voluntary as both workers and management come to the negotiating table voluntarily in order to have a meaningful dialogue on various troubling issues. They try to probe each other's views thoroughly before arriving at an acceptable solution.

It is continuous collective bargaining since it does not commence with negotiations and end with an agreement. The agreement is only a beginning of collective bargaining. It is a continuous process which includes implementation of the agreement and also further negotiations.

4. **It is backed by collective strength, demonstrated across the table:** Both parties bargain from a position of equal strength. It is more of industrial democracy at work.

5. **It is dynamic:** Collective bargaining is a dynamic process because the mental make-up of parties keeps changing. So the concept itself changes, grows and expands over time.

6.4. Types of Collective Bargaining

The types of collective bargaining can be broadly categorized as follows.

1. **Conjunctive:** Conjunctive bargaining is also termed as distributive bargaining. In the process of conjunctive bargaining, the parties try to maximize their respective gains. They try to settle economic issues such as wages, benefits and bonus through a zero-sum game (where my gain is your loss and your gain is my loss). The trade unions negotiate to maximize their interests, which may be wages and other benefits. Whereas the management makes similar efforts to pay as little as possible, while getting things done through workers.

2. **Cooperative:** Cooperative bargaining is also termed as integrative bargaining. In situations when companies are hit by recession or a situation is created where the management cannot offer the kind of wages and benefits demanded by workers, but at the same time the management cannot survive without the latter's support, the trade union has to continue to get their wages to survive. Both parties realize the importance of surviving in such difficult times and thereby willing to negotiate the terms of employment in a flexible way. Labour may accept a cut in wages in return for job security and claim higher wages when things improve. Management may agree to modernize and bring in new technology and invest in marketing efforts in a phased manner. There are instances in India, companies such as TELCO and Ashok Leyland, where both the management and the trade union resorted to cooperative bargaining with a view to survive during the recessionary trends.

Settlement under Conciliation to Collective Bargaining Agreement

There had been instances of arriving at collective bargaining agreement through settlements under conciliations.

Examples

In 1981, collective bargaining agreements were signed between the managements of HMT, BEL, HAL, BEML and ITI and their workers represented by the trade unions of these enterprises which had formed themselves into what was called the 'Joint Action Front (JAF)'.

Though such agreements are arrived at after negotiations between the workers represented by a trade union and employers, this was done in the presence of the government conciliation officer, making them appear like the conciliated or settled agreements. These agreements were not the product of mutual negotiations and collective bargaining between the parties. The reason for the practice of arriving at the agreements in the presence, and under the counter signature of the conciliation officer, was that the possibility of the non-signatory union members disowning responsibility for the agreement [8].

3. **Productivity:** Productivity bargaining is the method in which workers' wages and benefits are linked to productivity. At the start of the negotiation process, a standard productivity index is finalized through discussion between the parties. Workers perform at a rate to achieve the preset figures of the index. In the event of exceptionally high levels of productivity where the workers beat the index they get higher benefits as per the productivity norms. The management gains control over workplace relations and is able to tighten the norms still further in future negotiations.

C.6.2. Case for Discussion — Productivity Agreements in TISCO

(The historic agreement between TISCO and Tata Workers' Union, 1956, and subsequently modified in 1989, contains important clauses related to productivity.)

The agreement provides that the trade union, its officers and other representatives agree to give their full support and cooperation in the matter of securing improvement in labour productivity. The parties agreed on the need to establish a standard workforce in each of the existing departments and agreed that such standard workforce will be fixed by the company after consultation with the trade union, for securing improvement in labour productivity. The company assured the union that:

1. There will be no retrenchment of existing employees.
2. Those employees who may be required to do jobs other than those in which they are at present employed, will, wherever necessary, be trained for other jobs.
3. The present average earnings of employees transferred or under training will be guaranteed to them.

The agreement also provided the details regarding the adjustment of workforce in the event of redundancy in particular departments or sections.

The agreement of 1956 was modified by the memorandum of settlement between the company and the union in 1989. The settlement contained enlarged and detailed provisions related to productivity, technological improvement and modernization. The relevant clauses of the settlement are reproduced below.

The Company and the Union recognized the importance and need for technological development, modernizing the facilities, better utilization of labour force, good working conditions and cordial management–employee relations for growth and efficient operation of the company's business. So there was a need for the effective and timely implementation of schemes of modernization, and capacity expansion which the company to undertake by making capital expenditure.

The parties also committed themselves to continue to work together in attaining higher levels of production and productivity and profitability. Joint efforts would be made continuously in the following areas:

1. Efficient handling of raw materials and reducing wastes
2. Improvement in yields and reducing operational costs

3. Reducing energy consumption
4. Improving quality in all operations
5. Improvement in house-keeping
6. Necessary improvement in working conditions, health and safety of workers
7. Continuously adopt better working practices
8. Reducing unauthorized absenteeism
9. Improve effective utilization of all resources including HR.

The union recognizes the right of the company:

a. To fix the number of men required for the normal operation of a section or department, in consultation of the trade union.
b. To eliminate, change or consolidate jobs, in consultation of the trade union.

Modifications in 1989 agreement:

The memorandum of settlement between TELCO and TELCO Workers' Union (1 April 1989–31 March 1992) contained some important clauses related to productivity. The contents of the settlement are reproduced follows:

1. The union and the management agreed that TELCO can remain viable only through improved standards of productivity throughout the Jamshedpur Works and by optimum utilization of plant, equipment and HR. Both parties recognized that it will be essential to utilize state of the art or the latest technology available in manufacturing methods in order to remain competitive and both will work jointly to ensure that the company remains modern and maintains the highest standards of productivity.
2. The union recognized adherence to production quotas or any restrictive practices which inhibit production and productivity.
3. The union recognized that the productivity principle is based on the concept of 'return ability' with respect to input and agreed to work jointly with the management to ensure an improvement in productivity at the rate of 10 per cent in terms of output per man per year. The union will work with the management to remove all restrictive practices which come in the way of increasing productivity of plant and equipment.
4. All technical, clerical and other indirect employees working in areas such as maintenance, inspection, shop cleaning, sanitation and hospitals will also achieve the targeted levels of productivity in their respective areas. They will also make commensurate efforts to help the direct men enhance productivity.
5. The union accepts that an individual's unwillingness or inability to attain targeted performance levels retards the improvement in overall performance. The union, therefore, agrees to cooperate with the management in counselling and training such individuals whereby they can achieve targeted performance levels.
6. The union appreciates the fact that with change in market conditions changes in methods of production, retraining and deployment of workers are also essential. The union agrees to cooperate with the management in such deployment plans so as to ensure optimum utilization of HR in the Jamshedpur Works and flexibility in production to meet changing market conditions.
7. The union also agrees to support the management in its efforts to identify and eliminate wasteful practices and to improve quality through replacement of outdated methods, equipment, tooling and systems with more effective and efficient alternatives.
8. The union and the management recognize that participation of employees in 'small group activities' will go a long way in promoting goals of productivity, quality of product and quality of work life. The parties, therefore, agree to encourage employees in their role in achieving their goals through participation in small group activities.

9. The management and the union believe that quality is produced and not inspected. Hence, joint efforts will be made for self-certification of products by concerned employees, backed by an effective feedback system so as to ensure products and services of the highest quality.

The union and the management agree that special attention needs to be paid and results achieved in the following areas through joint efforts of both parties:

1. Full capacity utilization of each plant/equipment/facility.
2. Improvement/effective utilization of resources, including HR.
3. Optimum energy consumption.
4. Improvement in quality of all operations and products.
5. Efficient handling of raw materials and reduction of wastages.
6. Improvement in yields and reduction in operation costs.
7. Improvement in housekeeping.
8. Improvement in environment.
9. Continuous adaptation of better working practices.
10. Reduction in unauthorized absenteeism.
11. Improvement in customers' services and delivery.

The union and management agree to discuss each of these issues in detail department/division wise to arrive at specific targets and to jointly implement plans to achieve the same.

(The provisions of the first agreement were retained in subsequent agreements between the company and the trade union, and have continued to provide the base for productivity measures in the company even till today.)

Case Questions

1. Indicate the productivity aspects in both the agreements.
2. Indicate the reasons for the management to maintain continuity in the features of agreement of 1956 and 1989 and thereafter.
3. What is the importance of productivity agreement for an organization?

4. **Composite:** In the composite bargaining method, labour bargains for wages and goes a step further demanding equity in matters relating to work norms, employment levels, manning standards, environmental hazards, sub-contracting and so on. It is normally alleged by the workers that productivity bargaining agreements tend to increase their workload. The introduction of high technology and tight productivity norms has made the life of a worker somewhat uneasy. As an answer to such problems, labour has come to favourable composite bargaining. Under this process the trade unions negotiate on manning standards, while they ensure the workload of workers does not increase. Similarly, by negotiating sub-contracting clauses, the trade unions prevent management from exploiting the contract labour at low rates. Workers are no longer interested in monetary aspects to the exclusion of work-related matters. There is no doubt that wages, bonus and other monetary aspects continue to occupy the central focus in bargaining sessions, but there is a definite shift towards composite bargaining. Without proactive bargaining, workers may not be able to withstand the forces of liberalization, automation, farming out business to outsiders and survive in the long run. Through composite bargaining, trade unions are able to prevent the dilution of their powers and ensure justice to workers by putting certain limits on the freedom of the employers.

The process of composite bargaining does not suffer from periodic wage hikes and day-to-day tussles over productivity norms and other related issues. There is no danger of workers going on a strike or threat of strike every now and then.

C.6.3. Case for Discussion — Hindustan Foods Ltd, Goa: An Agreement of Voluntary Unemployment

Hindustan Foods Ltd, a factory at Usgao, Goa, manufactured processed food products such as Bonny Mix, Farex Rice, Farex Fruits and Rozanna. These products were manufactured under propriety trademarks of Glaxo India Ltd. The entire marketing was done by Glaxo India Ltd. From 1 January 1993, M/s. Glaxo India Ltd withdrew its participation in business with Hindustan Foods Ltd resulting in the business coming to a standstill. Hindustan Foods Ltd had not developed any of its own products, so the company had no alternative but to suspend its plant operations at Usgao, for an indefinite period, until alternative arrangements are made. The company therefore proposed to close down its operations. The same was communicated to the trade union and the workers.

There were 60 workmen in the permanent role. They were unionized under the 'All Goa General Employees' Union', Vasco da Gama. In response to the company's proposal of closing down the plant operations, the trade union requested for a discussion with the management for an amicable solution. Accordingly, this issue was discussed on 14 January 1993, 20 January 1993 and finally, on 21 January 1993. After prolonged discussions, the parties arrived at the following memorandum of understanding:

Terms of memorandum of understanding are as follows:

1. It was agreed by the workmen that all 58 of them will accept the voluntary unemployment, with effect from 1 February 1993, until the company restarts its operations. It was agreed by the company that during this voluntary unemployment, the workmen will be paid compensation at the rate of 50 per cent of their wages drawn as on 31 December 1992. The wages for this purpose would mean basic wage + fixed DA + VDA + house rent allowance.
2. It was agreed that the existing terms of the settlement will remain suspended in animation until the operations restart. All other details regarding the manner of collecting compensation every month, the requirement of the company for some of the workmen to work as and when required for maintenance purpose and manner of recording of attendance during the voluntary unemployment period are to be further discussed and be settled.

Terms of the Settlement

1. It was agreed by the company that all 58 workmen who were on the permanent rolls of the company will be called upon to report to the factory at Usgao, Ponda, Goa, on 14 December 1993, and resume their duties at 8:30 AM. Further, it was agreed that those workmen who will fail to report to factory and resume their duties within five days time, that is, on or before 21 December 1993 will be treated to have been not interested in the employment with the company and have resigned and relieved from the services of the company on the close of working hours of 21 December 1993.
2. It was agreed between the parties that initially in the process of restarting the factory operations, the company plans to start manufacturing of its products in a small way. The company therefore, to begin with, requires the services of only 38 workmen from the total number of workmen, who are on the permanent rolls of the company. The requirement of 38 workmen category-wise will be as per Annexure 'A' attached to this settlement. It was agreed and understood that at any given time, the strength of 38 workmen as per Annexure 'A' will be maintained. These 38 workmen will

be employed periodically on a rotation basis. The workmen whose services will not be required will be treated as laid off during their unemployment period. However, all such workmen will have to present themselves at the commencement of the working hours at the factory main gate and record their attendance and report to the factory manager, who shall communicate within half an hour as to whether their services will be required or otherwise. The workmen who are not provided with work will be treated as laid off and will be entitled for compensation as provided under Section 25(c) of ID Act, 1947. This arrangement shall continue to be operative until the company starts its production to its full capacity.

3. It was agreed by the company that all the workmen whose services will be retained for work according to the requirement of the company will be entitled to same terms and service conditions which were applicable to them as on the date prior to their accepting voluntary unemployment, effective from 1 February 1993. The union and workmen agreed that they shall extend their full cooperation in the process of restarting factory operations. The workmen specifically agreed that they shall carry out their work responsibility as entrusted to them by their superiors so as to overcome the difficult times in reorganizing and restarting the factory operations.

4. Annexure I: Category of workmen whose services would be required at the time of restarting the factory.

S. No.	Category	Total Number on Roll as on 10 December 1993	Required after Restarting	Number of Workmen at the Time of Restarting
1.	Electricians	3	2	1
2.	Mechanics	3	2	1
3.	AC operators	2	1	1
4.	Instrument mechanic	1	1	–
5.	Operators	2	1	1
6.	Prod. operators	9	5	4
7.	Helpers	34	22	12
8.	Clerks	3	3	–
9.	Chemists	1	1	–
		58	38	20

It was agreed by both the parties to enter into a valid settlement incorporating these and any other understandings that will be reached in accordance with the provisions of ID Act.

Case Questions

1. Indicate and explain the unique features of collective bargaining as appear in the case.
2. The workmen's approach to adopt to the context and amicably settle the issues indicates certain basic objectives to the approach of collective bargaining. Indicate which objective is under discussion here.
3. Indicate the type of collective bargaining happened in the above case and justify.

6.5. ILO and Collective Bargaining

The 'Right to Organise and Collective Bargaining' has been dealt under Convention C98 of 1949. The relevant extracts of this convention are reproduced here from the text of the ILO Document on C98. This convention contains 16 articles out of which only four are the operational articles, which are reproduced here.

(The two main instruments of the ILO that protect the freedom of association and the collective bargaining theory are the Freedom of Association and Protection of the Right to Organize Convention, 1948 [Convention No. 87] and the Right to Organise and Collective Bargaining Convention, 1949 [Convention No. 98]. On account of the importance of the principles contained in the two Conventions, they have been categorized as 'fundamental conventions' requiring universal observance.)

TThe General Conference of the International Labour Organization, having been convened at Geneva by the Governing Body of the International Labour Office, and having met in its thirty-second Session on 8 June 1949, and having decided upon the adoption of certain proposals concerning the application of the principles of the right to organise and to bargain collectively, which is the fourth item on the agenda of the session, and having determined that these proposals shall take the form of an international Convention, adopts this first day of July of the year one thousand nine hundred and forty-nine the following convention, which may be cited as the Right to Organize and Collective Bargaining Convention, 1949:

Article 1

1. Workers shall enjoy adequate protection against acts of anti-union discrimination in respect of their employment.
2. Such protection shall apply more particularly in respect of acts calculated to:
   a. make the employment of a worker subject to the condition that he shall not join a union or shall relinquish trade union membership;
   b. cause the dismissal of or otherwise prejudice a worker by reason of union membership or because of participation in union activities outside working hours or, with the consent of the employer, within working hours.

Article 2

1. Workers' and employers' organization shall enjoy adequate protection against any acts of interference by each other or each other's agents or members in their establishment, functioning or administration.
2. In particular, acts which are designed to promote the establishment of workers' establishments under the domination of employers or employers' establishments, or to support workers' establishments by financial or other means, with the object of placing such establishments under the control of employers or employers' establishments, shall be deemed to constitute acts of interference within the meaning of this Article.

Article 3

Machinery appropriate to national conditions shall be established, where necessary, for the purpose of ensuring respect for the right to organize as defined in the preceding Articles.

Article 4

Measures appropriate to national conditions shall be taken, where necessary, to encourage and promote the full development and utilization of machinery for voluntary negotiation between employers or—iployers' establishments and workers' establishments, with a view to the regulation of terms and conditions of employment by means of collective agreements. Right to Organize and Collective Bargaining Convention (No. 98) is also one of the four conventions of the ILO that the Government of India is yet to ratify. However, the right to organize a trade union has been enshrined in the Trade Unions Act, 1926. Following this, the concept of collective bargaining has taken deep roots in the Indian labour scene, particularly in the organized sector.

6.6. The Legal Framework of Collective Bargaining under Indian Laws

Freedom of association including the right to form and join unions for the protection of one's rights and interests has been recognized as one of the fundamental human rights. The Indian laws which contribute to the formation of the legal framework of collective bargaining include:

Article 19(1)(c) of the Indian Constitution, which guarantees freedom of association and union, and formation of trade unions as a fundamental right. The Constitution of India in the parts on fundamental rights justify the legality of collective bargaining. In this context, Article 19(1)(c) guarantees the right to form association and unions. Directives principles of the state policy also justify the provisions for improving the conditions of the labour in general and Article 43-A in particular provides that state shall ensure the participation of workers in the management.

The Trade Unions Act, 1926, deals with the formation, registration and purpose, and constitution of a trade union; the Trade Unions Act provides for the registration of trade union and determines the rights, liabilities and immunities of the union. The object of this piece of legislation was to regulate the relations between the employer and employee or among themselves and it is well established that collective bargaining is one of the means of regulating such a relation. In the case of 'D. N. Banerjee versus P. R. Mukherjee', [9] the court has recognized the concept of collective bargaining.

In the case of 'Tamil Nadu Electricity Workers Federation versus Madras State Electricity Board', [10] the Madras High Court observed that the whole theory of organized labour and its statutory recognition in industrial legislation is based upon the unequal bargaining power that prevails as between the capital employer and an individual workman, or disunited workman.

So there are various court rulings wherein collective bargaining has been recognized by the Apex Courts.

The ID Act, 1947, deals with the process of settlement of industrial disputes and all associated aspects of disputes concerning the management and the labour, and has various provisions having nexus with collective bargaining. Aspects, for example, *a settlement* and *the binding/applicability of a settlement* on the parties, which constitute to form the backbone of collective bargaining are dealt under the following sections:

Section 2(p), 4 and 18(3) of the ID Act, 1947, provides that collective agreements to settle industrial disputes can be reached with or without the involvement of the conciliation machinery.

Section 18(3) of the ID Act provides that a settlement/agreement being a written agreement, between the employer and the workmen is arrived at in the course of conciliation proceedings, and is binding, not only on the actual parties to the industrial dispute but also on the heirs, successors or assignees of the employer on one hand and all the workmen in the establishment, present or future.

Section 36(1) of the ID Act deals with *representation of workmen*. Any collective agreement would be binding on the workmen who negotiated and individually signed the settlement. It would not, however, bind a workman who did not sign the settlement or authorize any other workman to sign on his behalf. A settlement with one trade union is not binding on members of another or other unions unless arrived at during conciliation proceedings.

6.7. Steps in Collective Bargaining

There are three distinct steps in the process of collective bargaining:

1. The creation of the trade agreement
2. The interpretation of the agreement
3. The enforcement of the agreement

Each of these steps have sub-steps which are elaborated as follows.

1. The creation of the trade agreement
   The sub-steps of 'creation of the trade agreement' are as follows:
   a. Selection of negotiators
   b. In negotiating the contract, a union and management present their demands to each other
   c. Identification of the problem
   d. Collection of data
   e. Creating the climate of negotiations
   f. The trade union and the management discuss and negotiate for settling the differences
   g. The conditions are agreed under which the workers' interests are to be addressed
   h. The application and the duration of the contract are determined with mutual consent
2. The interpretation of the agreement
   a. The administrative process is the day-to-day application of the provisions of the contract that are worked out including its application to the context or to the work situation.
   b. At the time of writing the contract, it is impossible to foresee all the special problems which will arise in applying its provisions and sometimes, it is a matter of differing interpretations of specific clause in the contract, even at times, it is a question of whether the dispute is even covered by the contract. On case-to-case basis, the issues are settled. Without affecting the spirit of the contract, the management and the trade union jointly accept amicable settlement of the differences.
3. Enforcement of the agreement
   Timely enforcement of the contract is very essential for the success of collective bargaining. If a contract is enforced in such way that it reduces or nullifies the benefits expected by the

parties, it will defeat basic purpose of collective bargaining. It may give rise to fresh industrial disputes.

6.8. Collective Bargaining Levels

Collective bargaining takes place at five different levels in India. They are, national level, industry level, corporate level, plant level and craft level.

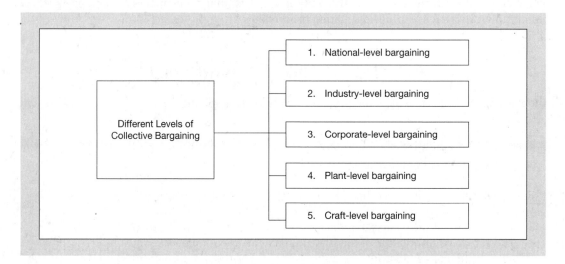

6.8.1. National Level

The agreements at the national level are generally bipartite agreements and are finalized at conferences of labour and management. This is a centralized bargaining unit. National-level bargaining is common in public sector where wages, compensation and various other employees benefit schemes are decided at national level.

IC.6.1. INDUSTRIAL CONTEXT FOR DISCUSSION

Instances of Formation of the Joint Negotiating Committee in Steel Industries

The National Joint Committee for the Steel Industry (NJCS), formerly the Joint Wage Negotiating Committee for the Steel Industry, was set up in October 1969. This committee arrived at a memorandum of agreement on revision of wages and benefits in the steel industry on 2 October 1970. This covered the workers of the then Hindustan Steel Ltd, TISCO, Indian Iron and Steel Company (IISCO) and the then MISL and VISL. Initially, the committee was formed under the aegis of the Labour Ministry and the then Deputy Chief Labour Commissioner (I) was the secretary of the committee; it was decided by the Minister of Steel and Mines that the committee would work independently.

The NJCS membership comprises 21 union leaders—three each from four national centers of trade unions: INTUC, AITUC, CITU and HMS, one each from recognized unions of the steel plants such as Bhilai, Durgapur, Rourkela, Bokaro, TISCO, IISCO, Alloy Steels, Salem and VISL and 12 management staff managing directors of the steel plants of Bhilai, Rourkela, Durgapur, Bokaro and IISCO, Bumpur; executive directors of Alloy Steels Plant, Salem Steel Plant and VISL; vice-president (HRM), TISCO; vice chairman and director (finance) of Steel Authority of India Ltd (SAIL). The director (personnel) of SAIL is the convener-member of the committee.

Since its inception, the NJCS had many unique features.

- The committee never had any Chairman, but a convener was appointed by the committee itself.
- The decisions were taken by consensus.
- No strike occurred so far on account of wage negotiations—before, during or after negotiations since 1969.
- The decision of the committee was binding on both the parties.
- The expenditures of the committee were borne by the member steel plants and workers' representatives in an agreed proportion.
- It was a permanent bipartite committee whose scope extends beyond wage negotiations to implementation aspects and other matters of concern to the industry and its employees.

Salient features of 2001 agreement: The agreement of 2001 was signed on 23 July 2001. This agreement covered all plants as mentioned above. However, taking into account the financial position of IISCO and in view of the fact that the revival package of IISCO was not by then finalized, it was mutually agreed that IISCO employees who were on the rolls of IISCO as on 31 December 2000 will be paid monthly adjustable advance at 12 per cent rate of their basic pay plus FDA as on 31 December 1996. This monthly adjustable advance would be paid with effect from 1 January 2001. This advance would not be counted for any other purposes and would be adjusted against future wage revision benefits. The extension of other provisions of this agreement and payment and adjustment of ad hoc adjustable advance for the period 1 January 1997 to 31 December 2000 will be considered separately at the time of revival package which management agrees to submit at an early date. Other benefits enjoyed by IISCO employees before signing this agreement would continue.

This agreement covered the issues as were agreed earlier, and in addition the following issues were agreed:

1. Due to the adverse financial position the Arear Payments from 1-1-1997 to 31-12-2000 have been deferred along with city compensation allowance.
2. SAIL employees' superannuation benefit fund and performance benefit schemes will continue.
3. Achievement of payment under life cover scheme to ₹62,000 will continue.
4. Participation in national health programmes will continue.

6.8.2. Industry Level

Industry-level collective bargaining is the agreement arrived at in course of negotiation between the managements and the trade unions representing at the industry level or at a specific geographical level. When collective bargaining takes place at the industry level, the employers' organizations of one industry jointly bargain with unions in that industry. These unions are organized as industry federations on industry basis.

For example, wage negotiation of the sugar mills of Bihar. It is a form of centralized collective bargaining where negotiations arrived at are applicable to a particular industry or sector. Here, all unions of an industry enter into an agreement with the employers in general. If there are multiple unions, the bargaining can take place between an employer and multiple unions.

Many a time, industry-level bargaining agreements are being supplemented by plant-level agreements. The two-tier bargaining or a combination of industry-level and plant-level bargaining has become a common practice in the jute industry where industry-level bargaining has been supplemented by plant-level agreements. This has also been the case with IBA.

In India, collective bargaining of this type is very popular in textile industry, sugar industry, tea gardens (state wise) and so on, where agreements are reached between labour unions and the various management bodies.

6.8.3. Corporate Level

Collective bargaining at corporate level takes place when the management of a corporate with multi-plant enterprise negotiates one agreement with various unions for all its plants. The collective bargaining is usually conducted by corporate management with its representatives from different plants.

The advantage of corporate-level bargaining is that it gives uniformity in its various establishments and avoids disputes which arise out of disparity. This type of collective bargaining is common in most PSUs which have several establishments in various regions of the country, for example, BHEL, HMT, ONGC.

6.8.4. Unit/Plant Level

Collective bargaining at plant level is very common with most of the private sector enterprises in India. A unit/plant-level collective bargaining agreement is reached at the single unit/plant level for which it has been agreed, between the parties and its scope and extent of application are limited only to that particular unit of the undertaking. The issues are relevant to that plant or factory only. The other advantage of plant-level bargaining is that negotiations take place independently. The agreement generally provides for certain common norms of conduct with a view to regulate labour–management relations and to eliminate confusions and misunderstanding. It contains provisions for a quick and easy solution of those issues which require immediate and direct negotiation between the management and the trade union, and lays down a framework for their future course of action whenever similar controversial issues arise.

In IT industry, there is educated workforce. There are no trade unions in this type of industry. So whenever negotiation takes place, it happens at individual level.

IC.6.2. INDUSTRIAL CONTEXT FOR DISCUSSION

The Agreement of Informal Workers in Jivraj Bidi Works

SEWA is a CTU of women workers in India's informal economy. SEWA was founded in Ahmedabad in Gujarat by Ms Elaben Bhatt in 1972. SEWA's main goal was to organize informal economy women workers for full employment and self-reliance whereby they would obtain work, income and food security at the household level. The organization is guided and managed in accordance with Gandhian philosophy.

Jivraj Bidi Works (JBW) is a relatively large bidi manufacturing and marketing organization located in Gomtipur area of Ahmedabad, Gujarat.

In 1983, bidi workers of JBW filed a suit for a provident fund at the office of the provident fund commissioner. One hundred and seventy-four bidi workers were trying to prove that there was an employer–employee relationship. The workers did not have any evidence to prove their claim. The JBW owner took back the logbooks they had issued to workers. But one woman was not at home and therefore still had her logbook, which became significant evidence in the case. The case proceedings took place in the office of the provident fund commissioner. The workers could not prove an employer–employee relationship.

SEWA assisted the workers in filing an appeal in the Gujarat High Court in 1989. During this period, a change was made in the Provident Fund Act and the case was transferred to Appellate Tribunal in Delhi. Here the employer–employee relationship was established and the Provident Fund Commissioner issued an order to calculate and determine the amount due to the workers. One thousand and two hundred workers received provident fund money which was due from the office of the provident fund commissioner.

In 1998, JBW filed an appeal in Gujarat High Court. The High Court set aside the appeal and ordered provident fund calculations as per the Delhi Appellate Tribunal.

The concerned workers filed an appeal on 18 March 18 2007. SEWA and JBW jointly came to an agreement, after which JBW deposited 479,960 rupees in the provident fund office. The Bidi Trade Committee of SEWA calculated the earning wages amount to be 1,020,040 rupees on the basis of the duration of work and number of bidis made by the concerned 174 bidi workers. The owner of JBW joined in the calculation process and accepted the amount determined by the committee. It took 23 years to prove the provident fund claim of the workers. At last, on 6 November 2007, the 174 bidi workers received their provident fund payments of 15 lakh rupees [11].

(This incident shows the power of collective bargaining, determination and patience on the part of bidi workers as well as the power of the role played by SEWA.)

6.8.5. Craft Level

When an enterprise has many craft unions, collective bargaining at craft level is possible. The representatives of the management and the representatives of the craft union bargain for effective solutions. Collective bargaining at this level was very common in the early years of industrialization in many countries. In India, it is not so common except for airlines industry such as Air India and Indian Airlines where they have pilots association, engineers association, cabin crew association and ground staff union. They have different agreements for different category of employees.

6.9. Hurdles to Collective Bargaining in India

Since Independence, collective bargaining as a concept for the settlement of differences between the management and the trade unions had continued to grow at a steady pace. But the growth of collective bargaining was not free from hurdles causing roadblocks in its growth. Few of the roadblocks causing the hurdles in the growth areas are as follows.

1. **Recognition of trade unions:** It is essential that the trade unions get recognized by the management for the purpose of collective bargaining. There is no compulsion for the

employers to recognize trade unions nor there are any statutory bindings. The management is only under moral obligation to follow the code of discipline. Such a provision does not have much significance in the absence of statutory obligation to recognize representative unions for the purpose of bargaining. But it is only the recognition of trade unions compulsorily, and clear-cut definitions of the roles of recognized and minority unions, which will provide a sound basis for the growth of collective bargaining.

The first NCL recommended that it would be desirable to make recognition compulsory under a central law. Such a recommendation was stipulated only for undertakings employing 100 or more workers and/or where the capital invested is above a certain stipulated size. It was also stipulated that a trade union seeking recognition as a bargaining agent from an individual employer should have a membership of at least 30 per cent of workers of the establishment. The minimum membership expected was recommended to be at least 25 per cent if recognition is sought for an industry-level representation in a local area.

The second NCL in 2002 recommended compulsory recognition of representative trade unions and also worked on a comprehensive draft legislation covering various aspects of IR.

2. **Non-existence of an effective procedure for the determination of a representative trade union:** Even under situations where the employers are willing to recognize the representative unions, the determination of the representative body of unions had been a difficult task.

   A procedural aspect adopted by the government is the verification of membership which has been widely used. There is no law on the subject. The problem of finding a representative trade union has become more acute on account of fierce rivalries among the trade unions and the existence of large number of trade unions.

3. **Outside leadership:** Outside leadership is a well-developed procedure for the trade unions in India, and a large number of trade unions are dominated by outside leaders who are also active workers of political parties. Due to the existence of multiple political parties, the representatives of such political parties develop rivalry among the trade unions which is reflected in the trade unions activities. The result is that when a representative union having allegiance to one political party is recognized, the other unions affiliated to other political parties try to dislodge it and claim for their recognition too. Such a situation becomes worse when a representative trade union recognized as a bargaining agent is in opposition to the political party in power. The outside leaders having no interest in the affairs of the trade union hardly look at the negative effect of such rivalry.

4. **Adjudication machineries being dominant, affect collective bargaining:** The ID Act, 1947, has laid down a network of adjudication machineries. The state acts have established the labour courts, tribunals and national tribunals. Such machineries had been operating for more than half a century. Such courts being under this law, the government as part of its procedure is empowered to refer industrial disputes to these authorities, whether the parties like it or not. The adjudication awards are binding on the parties. The trade union and the management cannot resort to strike or lockout since the same are prohibited during the pendency of disputes before these authorities and the period of operation of the awards. Disputes in large numbers are referred for adjudication every year and, during the pendency, it is not possible for the parties to enter into negotiations.

5. **Restrictions on strikes and lockouts:** In collective bargaining, resorting to strike by the trade union and lockout by the management are considered to be the last resort. Collective bargaining without this right has little significance. In India, considerable restrictions

have been imposed on the exercise of these rights under the ID Act, 1947. In addition, state IR laws like 'ESMA' are also imposed. The Supreme Court on 3 August 2003, observed that 'the trade unions, which have a guaranteed right for collective bargaining, have no right to go on strike', and that 'government employees have no fundamental, legal or moral right to go on strike'.

6. **Comprehensive coverage of labour laws:** A number of protective, social security and welfare laws have been in operation in the country. These laws cover a wide range of subjects of direct interests of industrial workers such as hours of work, physical working conditions, wages, social security benefits, protection of service, personal matters, welfare amenities and holidays. Many of these are subject matters of collective bargaining in many developed countries. Had the coverage of labour laws been narrow, the trade unions would have relied more on collective bargaining methods.

7. **Inadequate development of the trade unions:** In a country where only a small percentage of workers in the organized sectors have joined the trade union, expecting effective collective bargaining is not supported by either the strength of workers or their bargaining power. Second, the average size of Indian trade unions is very small and finally the financial condition of the Indian trade unions is also poor. The organizations of workers at the industry or regional level are confined only to few industries only. These features do not encourage the growth of collective bargaining in the country.

8. **Other factors:** Other factors have also affected the growth of collective bargaining in India which include the following.
   a. Inadequacy of education among workers.
   b. Unwillingness on the part of many employers to part with their freedom and to sit along with their workers on the bargaining table.
   c. Poverty of the workers and inadequate capacity of the industry to pay.

6.10. Conditions for Collective Bargaining

1. **Existence of a stable, democratic and acceptable trade union:** The union participating in the collective bargaining process must have the quality of stable, democratic and acceptable trade union to workers in general. The trade unions which are weak, fragmented, small and suffering from instability of their membership as well as rivalries with other trade unions hardly project a stable form of trade union for collective bargaining.

   The management-formed trade unions also very often do not get the support of the workers. Collective bargaining cannot become fully effective, if management continues to regard the trade union as an alien or an outside force.

2. **Voluntary recognition to trade unions:** One of the principles for establishing and promoting collective bargaining is to give voluntary recognition to trade unions as one of the negotiating parties. It may also have the positive benefit of improving IR, production and productivity.

3. **Willingness of both the parties to give and take:** There should be willingness of both the parties to give and take. There should be also genuine interest on the part of both to reach to an agreement. Exaggerated demands put forth by the trade unions or management and not accepting genuine demands will create roadblocks to effective negotiation. Both the parties must realize that collective bargaining is, by its very nature, a part of the compromise process.

4. **Avoidance of unfair practices:** The whole atmosphere of collective bargaining gets vitiated, and the relations between the management and the trade union become bitter and strained if one or both the parties engage in unfair practices. Both the union and the management, therefore, must restrain from committing unfair practices. Having a healthy regard for mutual rights and responsibilities generates trust and openness which is essential for collective bargaining.

5. **Existence of an understanding:** To make the collective bargaining process more successful, it is essential on the part of the representative of employers and the trade unions to hold meetings at regular intervals to consider matters of common interest. Such an ongoing process would enable them to understand one another's problems better and make it easier to find solutions to questions.

6. **Awareness of the economic conditions:** The trade union must have the knowledge of the economic condition of the plant or the industry as the case may be. The management must have a developed awareness of the nature of the trade union as a political institution operating in the environment and their interests.

7. **Maturity of leadership:** The effectiveness of collective bargaining cannot be attained without maturity of leadership on both sides of the bargaining table. The negotiators should have qualities such as experience, skill, intelligence, resourcefulness, honesty and technical know-how.

6.11. Theories of Collective Bargaining

6.11.1. The Market Theory

The marketing concept considers collective bargaining as a negotiated contract for the sale of labour. According to this theory, employees sell their individual labour only on terms which are collectively determined on the basis of negotiated contract. Such contracts are arrived at through the process of collective bargaining. It is the open market which determines the exchange relationship and justifies the voice of the organized workers in the matter of sale of their labour.

So collective bargaining is a means for employees to sell their manpower through the agency of the trade union, which bargains for an optimum wage in the market context. The need for such bargaining is due to the uncertainty of trade cycles, the spirit of mass production causing cost compression and competition for jobs. The trade union's collective action provides strength to the individual workers. It enables the workers to resist the pressure of the management creating circumstances of disadvantageous situation.

6.11.2. The Governmental Theory

The governmental concept considers collective bargaining as a constitutional system in industry. The agreement enables for the formation of an industrial government at the enterprise or industry level. The concept establishes a statutory relationship of a contractual nature. The trade union being the representative of the workers uses authority on behalf of the workers and enters into an agreement with the management within the statutory bindings. The principle function of the constitution is to establish the organs of the government, specify them, provide executing, interpreting rules and enforce the same.

An agreement arrived at in this process is determined on case-to-case basis depending on the merits and circumstances of the case. The agreement lays down the machinery for executing and interpreting the governing laws for the context and the particular case. Thus, the agreement is viewed as having a constitutional force. In case the management fails to conform to the agreed norms of the agreement, the judicial machinery takes care of the context. This creates a joint industrial governance where the unions share sovereignty with management over the workers and defend their group affairs and joint autonomy through the exercise of external interference.

6.11.3. The Managerial Theory

The managerial theory is also called IR concept which considers collective bargaining as a system of IR. It is a functional relationship. Discussions take place in good faith and agreements are arrived at jointly on matters in which both the management and the trade union have interests.

Thus, the agreements are arrived at between the trade union and the management with each other's cooperation. When the terms of agreement fail to provide the expected direction to the parties, it is the joint objective, which determines and controls the context. Hence, this theory recognizes the principle of mutuality, joint concern and the extension to workers of the corporate responsibilities.

The earliest form of negotiations were matters of contracting for the terms of sale of labour. Developments of the latter period led to the emergence of the Government theory. The IR approach can be traced to the ID Act of 1947 in India, which established a legal basis for union participation in the management.

C.6.4. Case for Discussion   Agreement of 1977 in Eastern Press Ltd (EPL)

About the company and the trade union.

EPL was established in western India in 1960, in collaboration with one Indian and one foreign company. The company had 567 employees on its payroll in 1960. At the material time, it was one of the best presses in Asia and was equipped with all modern machineries.

In September 1977, a labour union under the name 'Eastern Press Employees Union' was formed and registered. It had affiliation with the CITU and claimed the support of 100 per cent of the employees. All office-bearers of the trade union were then employees of the company. Only the chairman was an ex-employee of the company who was earlier terminated from the services on the charges of man-handling a foreman.

The Charter of Demands

On 20 December 1977, the union, on behalf of the workers, served 14-point charter of demands to the management.

The demands included:

1. Recognition of trade union
2. A total of 25 per cent share in profit and 12 per cent production bonuses
3. Allowance for children's education
4. Washing allowance
5. Conveyance allowance
6. Night allowance

7. Increase in DA rates
8. An interim relief of ₹125
9. Revision of pay scales
10. A total of 20 per cent house rent allowance
11. Reduction in canteen rates
12. Regularization of casuals
13. Revision of overtime rates and
14. Improvement in several administrative practices related to security department, office time, accounts and establishment

To explore the possibility of implementation of these demands, negotiations were held between the parties on several dates in January and February 1978 before the conciliation officer and also bilaterally. As a result of these negotiations, the parties reached an amicable conciliation settlement during the last week of February 1978.

The Negotiation

Nine rounds of discussion took place between the management and the trade union. The management finally withdrew totally to agree to any of the demands of the trade union. Two rounds of negotiations were held in the presence of the conciliation officer on 22 and 25 February 1978.

The Agreement

During these negotiations, the trade union realized that production bonus would be more beneficial to the employees. Therefore, they dropped the annual profit-sharing bonus and expected production-linked bonus.

The Production Bonus Agreement

1. A minimum net saleable production targets was mutually agreed to by the parties and for that the trade union studied the production figures of the preceding five years. The raise in the base figures for the future years was nearly 10 per cent keeping in view the increase in the cost of raw materials, wages and other expenses. As regards the method of calculation for additional percentage, it had been agreed that on every additional net saleable production slab of ₹5 lakhs over and above the minimum target for each year as shown in column 2 of the following table one per cent of the total wages/salaries earned/paid to the employees during the year would be paid to the eligible employees over and above the minimum 8.33 per cent as shown in column 3. In case the additional net production was less than five lakhs, the bonus would be paid on pro rata basis. However, casuals and persons on trial would not be eligible for the payment of bonus.

Period (Accounting Year)	Minimum Net Saleable Production Targets (in ₹)	Percentage of Production-Linked Bonus on the Minimum Net Production
(1)	(2)	(3)
1 March 1978 to 28 February 1979	2.10 crores	8.33
1 March 1979 to 29 February 1980	2.30 crores	8.33
1 March 1980 to 28 February 1981	2.50 crores	8.33

2. The agreement also embodied the method of calculating ratio of machinery/equipment to the net production. The net production figures indicated in column 2 of the above table were based on the

present-day book value of the installed machinery/equipment and installation in the factory. In case there was any addition or deletion, the machinery/equipment and installation, the net production figures, as in column 2 were to be automatically increased or decreased in the ratio of ₹1 lakh:₹2 lakh per annum.

3. It was further agreed by the union that the cost of machinery and so on as provided by the management will be in accordance with its book value duly audited, which would not be disputed by the trade union. The date of start of a machinery would be the date of starting the production.

4. It was also agreed that the rebates and discounts allowed to the customers would not be included under net saleable production, and the net saleable production figure as certified by the audit team of the company for the particular year would be acceptable to the trade union.

5. It was further agreed that the payment of bonus would be made in lump sum on or around 20 July of the following year.

6. The demand for interim relief was unconditionally withdrawn by the trade union.

The Other Points of the Settlement

1. During the tenure of the settlement, the workmen/union would not raise directly or through union any demand involving financial liability or implications on the company of any nature whatsoever.

2. In the event of breach of any of the clauses of the settlement on the part of workmen/union, the management reserved the right to withdraw all or any part of the benefit of the settlement. The management had agreed to provide a substantial increase in the benefits to its employees as a gesture of goodwill and for maintaining industrial peace and harmony not only for the period of the settlement but for future as well.

3. The workmen also agreed that they would not resort to any direct actions like strike, go-slow, tool-down or sit-down strike and any concerted action detrimental to the interest of the company during the tenure of the settlement without giving due notice to the management as provided in the existing certified standing orders of the company.

4. It was also agreed by the workmen that on being aggrieved by an order from the management, the concerned workman would himself file a written appeal to the managing director of the company within 30 days of the occurrence of the cause of action and that the managing director would dispose of the same within 15 days from the date of receipt of the said appeal. In case the workman did not feel satisfied with the order given by the managing director, he might take up the matter further to the appropriate authorities.

5. It was agreed that the settlement would be binding on both the parties up to 28 February 1981 [12].

Case Questions

1. Which theory of collective bargaining is most appropriately applicable to the context? Justify.
2. What are the features of an agreement?
3. What are the steps of a negotiated settlement?

6.12. Scheme for Joint Consultative Machinery and Permanent Negotiating Machinery of the Railways

On 30 October 1975, as part of the 20-point economic programme, an IR promotion strategy was adopted for the organizations in India. The important objectives of this scheme were reduction of industrial conflict and improvement of productivity. Railways adopted three schemes which include schemes on collective bargaining, workers' participation in management (WPM) and reference for arbitration. For collective bargaining, the PNM was formed, whereas for worker's participation in management, the Joint Consultative Machinery (JCM) was formed. The Railways also adopted the Compulsory Arbitration which is discussed below.

With the object of promoting harmonious IR and securing the greatest measure of cooperation between the government in its capacity as an employer and the general body of its employees in matters of common concern, the government established the machinery for collective bargaining, Joint Consultation and Compulsory Arbitration. This scheme is also known as 'Joint Consultative Machinery'. It came into effect from October 1996. At the same period, the scheme was implemented by the government in Posts and Telegraphs, and Defence.

The scheme of JCM visualizes two-tier structure, namely departmental councils and national council. National council deals with matters affecting all central government employees, whereas departmental council deals with matters affecting the staff in a particular ministry. The scope of council includes all the matters relating to the conditions of service and work, welfare of employees and improvement of efficiency and standards of work. The scheme also provides limited compulsory arbitration on three subjects, namely pay and allowances, weekly hours of work and leave of a class or grade of an employee. In departmental council, both federation representatives attend the meeting and in national council representatives of Railways, Posts and Telegraph, Defence and few others attend. In case of disagreement, the matter is referred to compulsory arbitration.

The Railway's labour and administration have set up PNM and JCM not only for the purpose of collective bargaining but also to secure cooperation, consultation, discussion and negotiation between the staff and administration. As per ID Act, 1947, if collective bargaining fails, the dispute is referred to adjudication; there is another stage in between, namely conciliation. Under PNM there is no scope for conciliation. If negotiation fails, PNM envisages reference of the matter to the 'ad hoc tribunal'. The PNM also provides that all disciplinary matters and subjects such as promotion and transfer of the staff would be excluded from the scope of discussions at all the levels. This was an anomalous situation. The most important defect of the PNM is that when negotiations fail, there is no other remedy to secure justice.

6.13. The Changing Trend of Collective Bargaining in India

There has been a growing recognition for a new collective bargaining paradigm. The traditional relationship between labour and management has been an adversarial one breeding hostility and distrust between labour and management and has proven to be a hindrance to organizational success. The changed paradigm distinctly distinguishes itself empowering the working class to contribute in all spears of management function.

The new paradigm embraces an equal partnership between labour and management, which is very often found in the private sectors. With the emerging competition in the global marketplace, it is being felt by the managements that trade unions must have a role in firms' strategic decisions. This paradigm involves union participation in decisions regarding the direction of the business, including access to financial and business decisions. With these responsibilities, the trade unions and managements would share the success of the organization.

It is admitted that at the workplace of the future, the actors' relationship, that is, the workers represented by the trade union and the management is seen to be of cooperation, openness, and trust working towards a common goal to improve economic performance. Information sharing and communication hold the key to such paradigm shift between labour and management. Two-way communication and continuous dialogue promote a climate of transparency, mutual understanding and trust, which are critical aspects in present-day collective bargaining. Bargaining in good faith can take place when there is:

- Interdependence of the parties concerned in solving problems through a shared understanding.
- A preference among the parties to focus on their interests without taking positions.
- An attitude that seeks to invent creative options for mutual gain rather than encourage win-lose zero-sum game.

A large number of organizations have achieved good results through cooperative collective bargaining. Few outcomes are discussed as follows.

1. **Prior consultation and communication:** Prior consultation and communication facilitate mutual understanding. Under the condition when the rationale behind the proposed decisions is clear, even harsh decisions may find acceptance. For instance:

   In BOC India Ltd, when input costs were rising and output prices were beginning to fall, to overcome the challenges of competition in a liberalized market environment, the company decided for tripling the output and reducing the workforce to a third for a period of seven years. This was possible due to diligent handling of employees, among other reasons.

IC.6.3. INDUSTRIAL CONTEXT FOR DISCUSSION

Communications by the Management

When the company's business environment changed from a dominant monopoly to a competitive scenario due to the liberalization of the policies of the government, the management presented an action plan for the company's survival and growth to the trade union. After laying its cards on the table, the management asked for suggestions from the trade union and informally obtained the union's consent to go ahead.

In 1991, when one of the welding units employing 1,600 employees was to be sold to a Swiss firm, ESAB, as part of BOC's divestment of non-core businesses, the management team communicated this to all trade unions and workers ahead of divestment. The managing directors of both BOC India Ltd and ESAB made it a point to be present at all the communication meetings and answer the questions related to the transfer of ownership. The management was prompt in incorporating any positive suggestions that emanated from these interactions.

The sale agreement covered specific clauses in respect of its employees' terms and conditions of service. The ESAB management agreed to take over the business as an ongoing one on better conditions of service for the employees of BOC India Ltd [13].

---

2. **Continuous interaction:** When information sharing takes place prospectively, trust too is established prospectively, not retrospectively. This was the position of the union in Kamani Tubes in Mumbai, a sick unit eventually taken over by the union through employee stock ownership, which they could manage effectively [14].

Cooperation between labour and management can take root only when the matter in focus is a concern for both parties. The cordial and cooperative relationship establishes the understanding. This is achieved through continuous dialogue rather than just collective bargaining. Bargaining in good faith is possible only if both parties perceive the need, opportunity and responsibility to implement whatever is agreed upon.

3. **Mutual concern for each other's benefits:** Workers and their unions, in turn, reciprocate by keeping the company interests above their own because they believe that unless the company is secured, their own job and income will not be secured. In the traditional trade union and the management relationship, in India, this attitude is usually lacking from both the sides. Hence, the initiative to develop cordial and cooperative relationship is on the management and their considerate initiatives which guide the trade union for subsequent cordial and cooperative relationship and behaviour.

4. **Overcome economic crisis:** In the event of economic crisis, before an organization is declared sick and referred to the Board for Industrial and Financial Reconstruction (BIFR), the management initiates any of the following practices or a combination of two or more practices:

    a. Wage cut/freeze until at least the company achieves break-even sales volume and/or wipes out losses
    b. DA freeze
    c. Freeze/deferment of certain employee benefits
    d. Freeze/deferment of leave travel concession
    e. Reduction in jobs (in rare cases, this is avoided with just a trade-off with wages)
    f. An assurance not to resort to industrial action

    But any of the above six clauses may not be easy to implement without assurance and involvement of the workers' organizations/representatives. These assurances are given/extracted as a precondition for considering the revival of sick companies on the brink of liquidation. They are supposed to remain in force for a certain number of years, until the company overcomes its financial problems and achieves break-even.

    In 1993, the government stopped budgetary support to the public sectors to meet the costs of wages and employee benefits, and asked such enterprises to meet the costs from their internal resources. Unions cooperated with the managements to reduce the redundant staff in a phased manner to help make the units economically viable. The agreement in Hindustan Insecticides Ltd, New Delhi (24 August 1995), is an example of the same. Similar approaches were there in public sector agreements during 1993–1994—Fertilizers and Chemicals Travancore Ltd (FACT) and Indian Rare Earths Ltd.

5. **Make adjustment to change:** Making the trade union to accommodate for adjustments for change is another dimension where trade unions have accepted and realized the context. An example is the case of IISCO.

    In IISCO, Burnpur, which is part of SAIL, the restructuring agreement in 1989 provided dismantling the entire plant and machinery and modernizing it with help from a Japanese steel giant. The agreement incorporated various action plans for retraining, redeployment and, for the first time, a VRS even for contract labour. The workers to the context showed a high degree of understanding effecting radical business changes. The workers agreed for a temporary suspension of employment and later a relay lockout to give their employer time to secure business and provide them gainful employment.

IC.6.4. INDUSTRIAL CONTEXT FOR DISCUSSION

IISCO Scrapping the Old Plant and Modernization of IISCO, Burnpur

The agreement in IISCO, Burnpur, was signed two years before the economic policy was announced in 1991. In 1989, it was decided to modernize the plant. The existing plant was to be reduced to scrap and a new plant to be built with the help of Japanese steel giant.

IISCO was established in the private sector and taken over by the government. After the takeover, it became one of the production units of the public sector steel giant, SAIL. Shortly after the 12 July 1989 agreement, there was a change in government at the centre and the modernization decision was stalled over some allegations. Subsequently, there were several rounds of discussions about the future of the company, including its privatization, but the workers supported the modernization of the plant by SAIL. Although certain factors including politics and unviable economics stopped the implementation of the agreement of 1989, nothing could devalue the intrinsic merits of the agreement.

The management's agreement with the trade union was distinctly different from the trend of agreements happening in the belt. The agreement provided for:

1. Modernizing the IISCO Burnpur plant by scrapping the existing plant.
2. Building a new 21.5 lakh tons plant over a period of four to five years.
3. Detailed provisions related to the schedule for phasing out the units, plant for operating units and installation on new plants for operating the units.
4. Guidelines and terms and conditions for deployment of workforce.
5. A separate VRS not only for regular workers but also, for the first time in India, for contract workers.
6. Principles for the review of arrangements made in the agreement.
7. The need to evolve a code of conduct for the management and unions.

This agreement is an example of the extent to which the trade union cooperated with the management for their long-term benefits [15].

6. **Improve productivity:** Trade unions through their efforts can and have contributed to productivity. A cooperative approach of the management through collective bargaining has greatly facilitated for this.

In the pre-liberalization period, trade unions in India did resist modernization and technological changes which were for improving productivity, since they felt the threat of losing jobs. With the introduction of India's structural adjustment policies in 1991, marking a shift towards a market-oriented economy, trade unions accepted retraining and redeployment to ensure lifelong employability of their members and thus improving productivity.

IC.6.5. INDUSTRIAL CONTEXT FOR DISCUSSION

Tata Motors Signs Landmark Wage Agreement with Pune Plant Workers

A landmark agreement was signed with Pune plant workers and Tata Motors, India's largest automobile company by revenues. The new measurement of performance was well received by workmen. This move of the management has brought 15,000–20,000 blue-collar factory workers to a wage structure that is performance linked.

The company concluded a long-term wage settlement agreement with its Pune Workers Union that covers 6,400 workers, after 19 months of negotiations. Tata Motors then worked towards getting workers from Sanand, Lucknow and Jamshedpur factories to sign a similar agreement.

About 10 per cent of the Pune plant workers' salary was variable pay and was linked to the performance. The wage settlement for Pune plant workers had been signed for a period of three years, that is, 1 September 2015 to 31 August 2018. The agreement was effective with immediate effect. The total wage package was bifurcated as: a fixed rise of ₹8,600 (in the ratio of 72%, 15% and 13% for a period of three years) and ₹8,700 non-actual, that is, a total of ₹17,300.

Source: https://economictimes.indiatimes.com/jobs/tata-motors-signs-landmark-wage-agreement-with-pune-plant-workers/articleshow/57902091.cms

Tata Motors has manufacturing plants in Sanand, Jamshedpur and Lucknow, and a similar wage agreement was offered to the workers of these plants.

In addition to the increment amount, the company had also agreed to pay a gratuity amount to the families of deceased workmen and give a wrist watch to the spouse of an employee on the completion of 25 years of service. Additionally, various other facilities were agreed upon, including increased in block closure days by six days [16].

Source: Economic Times. Tata Motors signs landmark wage agreement with Pune plant workers. Economic Times. 30 March 2017.

7. **Overcome legal rigidities:** Labour laws in India are generally considered to restrict employers' flexibility. The employers do not even have the right to override any provision of the legal provisions. Various enactments provide the legal framework for managing the organizations. For example:

Section 9A: Notice of Change. 'No employer, who proposes to effect any change in the conditions of service applicable to any workman in respect of any matter specified in the Fourth Schedule, shall effect such change' without 21 days notice to effected employees. But in a collective bargaining agreement in the case of Ingersoll-Rand (India) Ltd, Bangalore, arrived on 31 March 1994, the trade union accepted that in 'recruitment, placement, promotion, deployment, flexibility of operation, internal transfers, job rotation, farming out of work', the decision of the management shall be final and binding. This was accepted to meet the exigencies of production. It was also agreed that the association/employees will cooperate in allotting employees from one division/department to another provided that this does not result in retrenchment.

Also in the case of ITC Ltd (Tribeni Tissues Division, Kolkata), arrived at in November 1993, it was agreed by the trade union in course of a collective bargaining agreement that:

a. Regardless of the causes, there will be continuous effort by all to achieve higher levels of productivity to offset the rising cost of operations including the additional cost that results from the settlement.

b. There is a need to continuously improve the systems and procedures (backup system), operational planning and control, job safety, working conditions and productivity, and reduce wastage and eliminate wasteful and unproductive practices. Towards this end, the management will come out with action plans, from time to time, and the unions/workers will support these and cooperate in their implementation. Also, unions/workers will cooperate with the management in eliminating all wasteful and unproductive practices.

There are numerous other agreements, where similar agreements have been arrived at for business interest by normalizing the legal rigidities.

8. **Downsizing/workforce reductions:** In enterprise-level restructuring, workforce reductions are effected via a variety of measures, which include:

a. Ban on recruitment, particularly, in unskilled and semi-skilled jobs, both in the public and private sectors

b. Not filling positions of employees who are superannuated or have resigned

c. Adjusting the existing workforce with or without retraining, through redeployment in new jobs or new facilities

d. Voluntary separation schemes

There had been instances where the trade union through agreements has accepted the above provisions realizing the organizational objectives. For example:

In the VRS agreement dated 24 June 1994, in Indian Metals & Ferro Alloys Ltd, Therubali, Odisha, provides that: 'Anybody applying for retirement benefit under VRS shall not be granted the benefit automatically and the decision of the management in this respect shall be final'. This agreement gives the management the choice or discretion to accept or not to accept a VRS application.

The trade union surrendering the right to terminate the services of an employee at the discretion of the management was an acceptable phenomenon in the above case.

9. **Foster workers' participation:** Cooperation ensures participation, which implies essentially sharing information, exchanging ideas and experiences, taking decisions jointly, and owning up and sharing responsibility for results. This requires transparency in motives, mutual trust, ability and willingness to participate. Further, worker participation through involvement encourages empowerment. For instance:

Indian Aluminium agreed with the trade union to set up, among others, a bipartite job classification and job evaluation committee to take care of the need to dynamically adjust jobs to changes in job contexts.

Chapter Summary

Collective bargaining implies that a group of employees negotiate as a unit with their employer over pay, benefits, working conditions and other conditions of service related to the job they perform.

1. The 'collective bargaining process' is not an outdated practice or belief for maintaining 'harmonious IR' rather it is still a contemporary acceptable practice.

2. Collective bargaining is:
   - A tool for settling differences
   - A process of settling disputes
   - A solution to settle the terms of employment and condition of services
   - A process in which parties have willingness to compromise
   - The beginning of a long-term relationship
3. The ultimate impact of collective bargaining is beyond the visible outcome.
4. The four types of collective bargaining are: conjunctive, cooperative, productivity and composite.
5. Article 19(l)(c) of the Indian Constitution, the Trade Unions Act, 1926, and the ID Act, 1947, provide the legal framework of collective bargaining.
6. The three distinct steps in the process of collective bargaining are:
   - Creation of the trade agreement
   - Interpretation of the agreement
   - Enforcement of the agreement
7. Collective bargaining takes place at five different levels in India. They are: national, industry, corporate, plant and craft.
8. Hurdles to collective bargaining in India are:
   Recognition of trade unions
   - Non-existence of an effective procedure for the determination of a representative trade union
   - Outside leadership of trade unions
   - Adjudication machineries being dominant affects collective bargaining
   - Restrictions on strikes and lockouts
   - A detailed and comprehensive coverage of labour laws
   - Inadequate development of the trade unions

Questions

1. Explain the concept of collective bargaining.
2. What are the objectives of collective bargaining?
3. Explain the types of collective bargaining.
4. Explain how the ILO conventions impact collective bargaining in India.
5. What are the different legal provisions contributing to the framework of collective bargaining?
6. Explain the various steps in collective bargaining.
7. What are the different levels in collective bargaining? Explain.
8. What are the hurdles in collective bargaining?
9. Explain the changing trend of collective bargaining in India.

Project Work for the Students

1. Identify two cases of collective bargaining happening in any organizations and discuss its unique features.

References

1. Harbinson FN. Goals and strategy of collective bargaining. New York, NY: Harper & Brothers; 1951.
2. Yoder D. Personnel management and industrial relations. New York, NY: Prentice Hall; 1972.
3. Jucius MJ. Personnel management. R. D. Irwin; 1975.
4. Leap TL, Crino MD. Personnel/human resource management. New York, NY: Macmillan Publishing Company; 1990. p. 637.
5. LAWS(SC)-1975-10-32, Supreme Court of India, Decided on October 10, 1975.
6. Ram Prasad Vishwakarma v The Chairman, Industrial case decided on 12 December 1960, published in 1961 AIR P 857.
7. Perlman, Selig. The principle of collective bargaining. *Ann Am Acad Pol Soc Sci* 1 March 1936; 184: 1: 154–160.
8. Aziz, Abdul. Collective bargaining in Karnataka: A review. *Indian J Labour Econ* January 1982; 25: 4: C74.
9. D. N. Banerji v P. R. Mukherjee And Others judgment on 5 December 1952, reported in 1953 AIR 58.
10. Tamilnad Electricity Workers v Madras State Electricity Board ordered on 1 March, reported in (1962) II LLJ 136 Mad.
11. WIEGO. Collective bargaining by workers of the Indian unorganized sector: Struggle, process, achievements, and learning, http://www.wiego.org/sites/default/files/resources/files/Collective-Bargaining-%20India.pdf (2012, accessed 28 August 2019).
12. Dwivedi, R. S. Collective bargaining in Eastern Press Ltd. *Indian Manag* April 1979: 16–19.
13. Das, Subash. *Managing people at work: Employment relations in globalizing India*, Chapter 5. New Delhi: SAGE Publishers, 2011.
14. Bhowmik, Sharit K. Workers take over Kamani tubes. *Econ Pol Wkly*, 21 January 1989; 24: 3: 124–126, https://www.jstor.org/stable/4394270 (accessed 28 August 2019).
15. *The Economic Times*. Burnpur: One of the country's earliest steel towns, is springing back to life, //economictimes.indiatimes.com/articleshow/45154206.cms?from=mdr&utm_source=contentofinterest&utm_medium=text&utm_campaign=cppst (2014, accessed 28 August 2019) http://egyankosh.ac.in/bitstream/123456789/16763/1/Case%20Study-5.pdf (accessed 28 August 2019).
16. *The Economic Times*. Tata Motors signs landmark wage agreement with Pune plant workers, //economictimes.indiatimes.com/articleshow/57902091.cms?utm_source=contentofinterest&utm_medium=text&utm_campaign=cppst (30 March 2017, accessed 28 August 2019).

7

Industrial Disputes and Grievance Redressal Mechanism

LEARNING OBJECTIVES

After reading this chapter, you will be able to:
- ☐ Identify various industrial dispute settling processes and systems
- ☐ Describe the mechanism for the prevention and settlement of industrial disputes
- ☐ Understand the importance of code of discipline
- ☐ Understand procedures of settling disputes as provided under the ID Act, 1947
- ☐ Understand the procedure for grievance handling

C.7.1. Case for Discussion   Volvo Strike for 60 Days in 2011

The workers of a reputed bus-manufacturing firm Volvo stopped work for around 60 days starting from 2 August 2011. Every regular employee of Volvo had protested outside the factory premises against what they termed as 'the oppressive management practices' by the company.

The organization is located about 30 km from Bengaluru. The strike of the workers proceeded even though the management made all efforts to push production using the less experienced trainees, probationers and the contract workers hired from staffing agencies. This resulted in quality issues and the quantity of production was also impacted. The clients expressed their concern as the supply was affected. Since Volvo buses were sold between ₹70 lakh and ₹1.2 crore, the clients were obvious to raise their concerns and the company was under the threat of losing business.

The oppressive management practices were termed as exploitation of the workers by the workers represented by a trade union which was registered by then. The trade union was interested in getting its voice heard.

The genesis of the conflict lies in the low wages at the factory, right from the time the Volvo buses division was set up in 2001. In 2008, when the share of Azad Builders, who had a 30 per cent minority stake in Volvo India, was bought out by the management of Volvo, the Swedish giant, the workers were paid monthly wage of ₹5,500. Since then the workers were demanding for higher wages and the management in 2009 (July) consented to give a salary hike of ₹650. But the workers continued to demand for further hikes to which the management expressed the requirement for negotiating with the representatives of the trade union. This requirement led to the creation of the VBWU, which was registered in October 2009. The VBWU presented its official charter of demands to the management in January 2010.

On 23 April 2010, the management negotiated with the elected heads of the trade union. The negotiations went on for a long time and came to a conclusion only at 5:30 PM on that day. Since the negotiations were to result in the long anticipated wage increases, there was a lot of curiosity among a section of the workers who waited near the meeting room to know what had happened.

The office bus departure time for dropping employees at home was 05:40 PM. Mr Raghuram, who was the manager in the administration, asked the buses to leave at 05:35 PM, that is, five minutes before their usual time. Some other workers who were peacefully sitting in the bus disembarked to protest this decision and the bus left early. These buses were the workers' sole mode of transport after work since the nearest town from the work was 10 km away. On finding that the buses had already left, all the workers went to the management and asked for recalling the buses, but the management refused. It was during this argument that there was a surge in the crowd which resulted in some people being pushed—both among the workers and the management. The Volvo management complained that Mr Schwartz, a foreigner, was manhandled in the crowed. The workers surrounded the management asking for transportation and this went on till the early hours of the next day which was a Saturday, a holiday. The management decided to suspend the representatives of the trade union and two others on the same day.

Since there was no progress either in the wage hike or reinstatement of the suspended employees, in August 2010, the workers went on a strike demanding the wage hike and the reinstatement of their union representatives.

The strike led to tripartite negotiations and successfully ended with the long awaited wage settlement (valid for three years) with salaries increasing in the range of ₹3,500–5,000 for the employees. However, the workers, to their dismay, found themselves being increasingly harassed at the shop floor. Few examples of harassment were as follows: the probation periods were increased to one year, the managers started accusing employees of product sabotage and dragging them to the police, the trainees were not regularized and there was an increase in the number of contract workers' utilization (who were paid around half the salary of a regular employee). Apart from this, the management started to resort to other petty actions such as denying workers any kind of leaves (even for personal problems), reducing the quality of transportation (without changing the employee contribution under the transportation head), harassment on duration of the breaks and so on.

Despite the fact that the findings of the domestic enquiry indicated that there were lapses by the management on 23 April, the management did not reinstate the suspended trade union representatives. The management of Volvo internally kept the union members under suspension for over a year.

The workers, when started facing increased harassment at the workplace, saw no other option but to go on strike again on 2 August 2011. Their demands were primarily to reinstate the elected representatives of the union and stop harassment of probationers/trainees and regular employees. But subsequently, the trade union representatives were dismissed by the management.

Source: https://www.newsclick.in/node/2616

Case Questions

1. Indicate the attitudinal aspects of the management and the trade union that caused conflicts.
2. Indicate the behavioural aspects of the management and the trade union that caused conflicts.
3. Do you agree that industrial disputes are first manifested in the form of some conflict? Discuss in the light of the above case.

7.1. Concept of Conflict

Liberalization, globalization and privatization were expected to weaken the bargaining power of workers, thereby reducing the number and frequency of industrial conflicts. But the reform measures were in some cases opposed by the trade unions, and in some cases, they led to aggressive labour market practices by employers [1]. As a result, there were work stoppages and even violence in which both the organized and unorganized workers participated.

Industrial conflicts are unavoidable because they are natural in any organization as long as people expect to better themselves in their jobs with better resources, power, recognition and security, and, on the other hand, the management expects higher productivity from workers and higher returns from the market. Such contexts create perceived incompatibilities that result in some form of opposition, which is termed as 'conflict'. Industrial conflicts involve the total range of behaviours and attitudes that are in opposition to owners/managers, on the one hand, and working people, on the other. It is a state of disagreement over issues. It involves emotional antagonism which may arise owing to anger, mistrust or personality clashes.

Conflict is a social phenomenon, that is, in personal, group or organizational interactions. It comprises several dimensions, beyond just overt behaviours. Theorists suggest three interrelated dimensions of conflict, which are as follows:

1. Conflicting situation
2. Conflicting attitude
3. Conflicting behaviour.

The above three dimensions emphasize that it is essential to consider the situation in which parties (individuals, groups or organizations) come to possess incompatible goals. Because organizations are living systems, consisting of interacting units that perform a task in a mutually dependent manner within a structure of scarce resources, the parties in an organization may have conflicts about the distribution of resources. They may have fundamental conflicts about the very structure of their organization, including the basic nature of their interaction. Once the parties are in a situation of goal incompatibility, their conflict develops in a dynamic fashion.

It is true that conflict may be uncomfortable to both the parties. It may even be a source of problems to them. But it is absolutely a necessity if change is to occur, and if organizations are to survive, as well as to adapt growth. Researchers have observed that organizational change and innovation do not just happen; they require a stimulant and that stimulant is conflict. As the goals of different stakeholders are often incompatible, conflicts are an inevitable part of the organizational life.

Industrial conflicts occur when employees express their dissatisfaction with the management over the current state of the management–employee relationship. Employees can express such dissatisfaction in formal or informal ways. Industrial conflicts can occur at various levels, which are as follows:

- between two employees
- between two groups of employees
- between members of a group
- between employees and employers as a group
- between an individual employee and an employer
- between employees in a group or individually with agencies like the government.

The impact of such conflicts is different on work groups and individuals' behaviours. An example of the industrial conflict is HMSI-2005.

In June 2005, employees at the HMSI factory in Gurgaon started protesting against differentiation in wage rates. This led to the loss of job of four workers for strike, slowdown, protests and, finally, a situation where the company's president was gheraoed.

At this point, the protesting employees clashed with the police near the company's MG Road showroom. Nearly 100 people were injured. The production at the company's plant went down from 2,000 to 400 units per day. The company suffered a revenue loss of ₹130 crore.

According to Karl Marx, a conflict is inevitable between the owners of capital and workers who sell their labour. He had said that the owners of capital could prosper only by ensuring that there was surplus in the capitalist's favour. So conflict is endemic as an inevitable part of the wage system as visualized by Marx. Disputes arising from power struggles at the workplace may be a frequent part of the process. A conflict of interest between various groups is essentially the progeny of an organization in a capitalist economy. As it is a kind of negotiation situation where wants of both parties are unlimited and resources are limited, it leads to conflicts. The parties (such as employers, employees and the state) to IR have divergent interests and objectives, thereby creating contexts for potential forms of conflicts. For some scholars, industrial conflict is an inherent part of the nature of the organizational life because work relations are an inevitable source of dispute. Because what is good for one may not be the same for the other, it results in conflicts.

Industrial peace and harmony are the objectives of every business organization. If differences are not prevented or resolved in time, they are likely to result in industrial actions in the form of production and other losses. So another potent source of industrial conflict is the distribution of revenue. Conflicts relating to this source may be concerned with either absolute or relative shares of the revenue pool. It is possible for employees in a profitable and growing firm or an industry to make huge gains, whereas in the pay packages, this share is reflected as a diminishing share of revenue. The perception of the value of one's economic benefit, relative to others, is likely to be a greater stimulus to conflict.

Industrial conflict theorists conceive that organizations are an inevitable battleground of differences. The differences are traceable not only to the characteristics of individuals but also to the structural and inter-group attributes of the organizations. It is construed that the conflict of one type or another is likely to exist in most organizational settings, which is often expressed in a wide variety of ways. Typical lists of the forms of conflict include absenteeism, labour turnover, accidents, pilferage, sabotage, withdrawal of cooperation, work to rule, go-slow, overtime ban, restriction of efforts as well as strikes, lockouts and other collective actions. Industrial conflict is not necessarily dysfunctional or bad in IR. It can be a necessary and even a desirable feature in certain specific industrial contexts.

7.2. Dispute

A dispute is considered as a disagreement over a particular issue between two people or groups. A dispute has been considered as a short-term occurrence. The difference is resolved with time. In other words, the short-term disagreements that are relatively easy to resolve are disputes. So the concept supposes the existence of a scope for negotiation.

The main objective of the IR legislations in India was to protect the economy and assure a favourable labour market. A series of legislations were enacted for achieving this objective, which include the Merchant Shipping Act, 1859; the Workmen's Breach of Contract Act, 1860; Workmen's Dispute Act, 1860; Indian Factories Act, 1881; Trade Unions Act, 1926; Trade Disputes Act, 1929; Trade Disputes (Extending) Act, 1934; and Trade Disputes Amendment Act, 1938. After the failure of these Acts for providing a harmonious IR, the ID Act, 1947, was enacted with provisions for the investigation and settlement of industrial disputes, in the industries.

It is admitted that in the industrial context, difference is a reality between the actors of IR, and the same is realized by them. An elaborate framework, including statutory and non-statutory approaches, for the prevention and settlement of the industrial disputes has been discussed in the chapter.

7.3. Industrial Disputes

Industrial disputes may be said to be disagreements or controversies between the management and labour with respect to wages, working conditions, union recognition or other employment matters. Such a dispute may include controversies between rival unions. ILO recommended various industrial dispute settling instruments. The main instrument of ILO dealing with industrial dispute prevention and settlement is the Voluntary Conciliation and Arbitration Recommendation, 1951 (No. 92). It recommends that voluntary conciliation should be made available to assist in the prevention and settlement of industrial disputes between employers and employees. It also recommends that parties should refrain from strikes or lockouts while conciliation or arbitration procedures are in progress, without limiting the right to strike. Dispute resolution has been further addressed under the Collective Bargaining Convention, 1981 (No. 154), which provides the bodies and procedures for the settlement of labour disputes. One objective of dispute resolution is, in fact, to promote the mutual resolution differences between employees and employers, and, consequently, to promote collective bargaining and the practice of bipartite negotiation.

Section 2k in the ID Act, 1947, provides industrial dispute as 'any dispute or difference between employers and employers or between employers and workmen, or between workmen and workmen, which is connected with the employment or non-employment or the terms of employment or with the conditions of labour, of any person'.

The following conditions qualify for an industrial dispute:

1. There must be a dispute or difference and that must be between:
    a. employers and employees
    b. employees and employees
    c. employers and employers.
2. Such disputes must be connected with:
    a. employment or
    b. non-employment or
    c. terms of employment or
    d. the conditions of labour of any person.

The other conditions that qualify any dispute as an industrial dispute are as follows:

1. There should be a factum of dispute not merely a difference of opinion.
2. It has to be espoused by the union in writing at the commencement of the dispute. Subsequent espousal will render the reference invalid.

3. It affects the interests of not merely an individual workman but several workmen as a class who are working in an industrial establishment.
4. The dispute may be in relation to any workman or workmen or any other person in whom they are interested as a body.

In the case of Chandrakant Tukaram Nikam and others v. Municipal Corporation of Ahmedabad and another [2], the Supreme Court held that neither the Civil Court nor the Code of Civil Procedure has jurisdiction to decide the cases of dismissal or removal from service. The appropriate forum for such relief was with the court constituted under the ID Act, 1947.

7.3.1. An Individual Dispute Can Be an Industrial Dispute

In the case of J. H. Jadhav v. Forbes Gobak Ltd [3], it was held that a dispute relating to a single workman may be an industrial dispute if it is espoused either by the union or by a number of workmen, irrespective of the reason that the union espousing the cause of workman was not the majority of the union.

Before the insertion of Section 2A of the Act, an individual dispute was not considered to be an industrial dispute. The scope for raising a dispute by an individual was a process of sponsoring the dispute through a trade union or a number of workmen. It was considered that a dispute raised by a dismissed employee would not be treated as an industrial dispute, unless it is supported by a trade union or by a body or section of workmen. For an individual dispute to be declared as an industrial dispute, the following conditions were to be satisfied:

1. A body of workmen (trade union) or a considerable number of workmen are found to have made common cause with the individual workman.
2. The dispute (individual dispute) was taken up or sponsored by the workmen as a body (trade union) or by a considerable section of them before the date of reference.

The present conditions of law provide that for an individual dispute to be considered within the definition of the industrial dispute, it must be sponsored by the trade union of the workmen, or if there is no trade union, it must be sponsored by the majority of the workmen or must comply with the requirements of Section 2A of the ID Act, 1947.

Section 2A provides that[1]

Where any employer discharges, dismisses, retrenches or otherwise terminated the services of any individual workman, any dispute or difference between that workman and his employer connected with, or arising out of such discharge, dismissal, retrenchment or termination shall be deemed to be an industrial dispute, notwithstanding that no other workman nor any union of workmen, is a party to the dispute.

So the conditions for raising an industrial dispute by a workman are as follows:

1. A workman may make an application directly to the Labour Court or Industrial Tribunal for the adjudication of such dispute after the expiry of three months when an application was made before the conciliation officer for conciliating the matter. This has been done to prevent inordinate delay.

[1] https://indiacode.nic.in/bitstream/123456789/2169/3/A1947-14.pdf. Page 11. Accessed on 08-09-2019.

2. The said application, however, should be made within three years of the date of dismissal, discharge, retrenchment or termination of service.
3. The court shall proceed to hear the matter as if it was referred under Section 10 of the ID Act, 1947.

However, Section 2A does not consider all individual disputes to be industrial disputes. It is only when a dispute is connected with a discharged, dismissed, retrenched or terminated workman that it will qualify to be treated as an industrial dispute. If the dispute or difference is connected with some other matter, for example, payment of bonus/gratuity, then it would have to satisfy the test laid down in judicial decisions.

Where an individual dispute is espoused by the union, the question of the employee being a member of the union when the cause arose is immaterial. Those taking up the cause of the aggrieved workman must be in the same employment, that is, there must be a community of interest when the act complained against happened and not when the dispute was referred to. An example of this is, a May 2009 incident, when the workers at Mahindra's Satpur, Nashik Plant, protested over the suspension of the union leader Madhavrao Dhatrak on disciplinary grounds.

7.4. Meaning: 'Any Person'

The dispute can either be raised for a workman or for any person about whose employment or non-employment or terms of employment or conditions of labour the workmen have substantial interest. The concept 'any person' in the definition has not been equated with workmen, and it has rather a wider connotation. Even the judicial interpretation has limitations on the concept of 'any person'. The term 'any person' must have a direct relation with the workmen whose employment or non-employment or terms of employment or conditions of labour workmen have direct and substantial interest. In other words, it is implied that 'any person' must be an employee of the industry which the workmen are employees.

The term industrial dispute connotes the existence of a real and substantial difference, which is having some elements which might endanger the industrial peace of the undertaking or the community. When the parties are at variance and the dispute or difference is connected with the employment or non-employment or terms of employment or with the condition of labour, there exists an industrial dispute. The issues could include wage demands, union rivalry, political interference and unfair labour practices as described in the 5th Schedule of the ID Act, the multiplicity of labour laws, industrial sickles and so on.

Bad IRs are caused by a strained relationships between the employer and employees, resulting in industrial disputes. Following are the examples of situations that may cause such stained relationships and thereby bad IRs:

1. Employers' approach to extract maximum work with minimum remuneration
2. Employee's approach, for example, to avoid work and get more benefits in pay and wages
3. Not mutually acceptable wage system and structure
4. Poor working environment, including unsafe and unhygienic conditions
5. Poor human relations and lack of dexterity on the part of management personnel

6. Employers' or trade unions' lack of control over situations leading to the erosion of discipline
7. Reactions to the introduction of new technology or automation or mechanization, including computerization without proper consultations with the trade union
8. Employers' actions leading to nepotism, unequal workloads, disproportionate wage and so on
9. Adoption of unfair labour practices either by employers or employees including trade unions
10. Trade union rivalries
11. Strikes by trade unions
12. Lockouts by employers
13. Lay-offs and retrenchments of employees
14. Ignoring or overriding existing agreements and arriving at new settlements
15. Militancy of the trade unions.

7.5. Causes of Industrial Disputes

Broadly, the causes of industrial disputes can be classified, along with a brief description of each, as follows.

1. **Economic causes:** Economic causes include questions pertaining to wages, salary and remunerations that include the following:
   a. Demand for higher bonus
   b. Demand for an increase in wages on account of the increase in All-India Consumer Price Index for Industrial Workers
   c. Demand for better social security benefits
   d. Demand for paid holidays
   e. Demand for a rise in DA
   f. Demand retrenchment benefits of workmen by the employer owing to rationalization and automation
   g. Demand for leave pay
   h. Demand for certain allowances such as
      i. House-rent allowance
      ii. Medical allowance
      iii. Night shift allowance
      iv. Conveyance allowance.
2. **Managerial causes:** Some of the management systems lead to discontent and are inherent in the industrial system; they are as follows:
   a. Workers do not get any opportunity for self-expression.
   b. Their social needs are not fulfilled, that is, the position of workers within informal groups formed in industrial undertakings and problems of conflict within the groups may not be taken into account.
   c. Lack of communication, on the one hand, between the workers and management may turn petty differences into industrial unrest.
   d. Indiscipline, on the other hand, in industrial units may assume serious dimensions.

e. Mental inertia on the part of the management and labour.

f. Management's general attitude of hatred towards their workers.

g. Lack of competence of the supervisor and other managers in terms of human relations.

h. Management's desire to pay a comparatively lesser amount of bonus or DA against the desire of workmen.

i. Efforts to introduce modernization without any prior notice or an appropriate environment.

j. Excessive workload and inadequate welfare facilities.

k. Defective policy of lay-offs.

l. Denial of the workers' right to recognize the union.

m. Unfair practices like victimization or termination of services without assigning any reasons.

n. Lack of definite wage policy and stabilization of prices.

o. Lack of a proper policy of union recognition.

p. Denial of worker's right to organize.

3. **Personal causes:** Sometimes industrial disputes may arise because of personal causes and the list includes the following:

   a. Dismissal
   b. Retrenchment
   c. Lay-offs
   d. Transfer
   e. Promotion

4. **Job-related methods and processes:** Sometimes industrial disputes may arise owing to job-related methods and processes and the list includes the following:

   a. Terms and conditions of employment
   b. Reduction of working hours
   c. Better working conditions
   d. The managements, to curb indiscipline and violence, resort to disciplinary action
   e. Violation of a registered agreement or settlement or award
   f. Demarcation or role clarity about a job or function
   g. Absence of grievance redress machinery or procedure
   h. Grievance machinery provided by the government for the resolution of industrial conflicts may be inadequate and slow
   i. Workers' resistance to rationalization
   j. Automation and the introduction of new machinery
   k. Change of place owing to transfer
   l. Forced unemployment resulting from the implementation of rationalization schemes and the installation of new machines because of which fewer persons would be employed

5. **Political causes:** The present trade union practice in India has allowed various political parties to control the trade unions. People having political affiliations and leading a trade union may have vested interests, which may be political in nature. There had been instances in the past where some important political strikes were organized by industrial workers in India. Such strikes had been for the following causes:

   a. Against the sentence of imprisonment
   b. Trial of political leaders
   c. Reorganization action of state governments
   d. National language and so on

7.6. The Consequences of Industrial Disputes

Consequences of industrial disputes are many, a brief description of which is as follows:

1. **Impact on the economic, social and political life of a country:** The national dividend expressed in terms of GDP suffers when the whole or any part of an industry is rendered idle because of a strike or lockout.
2. **Loss of output:** Loss of output in an industry when affected by an industrial dispute also restricts the activities of other industries.
3. **Decline in the demand for goods and services:** Strikes reduce the demand for the goods which are produced by other industries.
4. **Loss to the workers:** Loss of wages and effect on their well-being become a lasting injury to the workers. This situation economically affects the workers.
5. **Mental worries to self and the family members of the workers:** Workers and their family members also suffer from mental worries resulting from the loss of wages.
6. **Problem to consumers:** Non-timely availability of goods and commodities owing to non-supply to the market caused by strikes and lockouts creates problem to consumers.
7. **Loss to the management/employer:** When workers stop working, the plant and machinery remain idle. Fixed expenses are to be borne by the employer even under the stoppage of production. Thus, the employer suffers from loss.
8. **Bad effect on labour relations:** Strikes and lockouts bring bad effects on IR. They make the workmen and the employer suffer from mental pressure.
9. **Obstruction to the economic growth:** Strikes and lockouts obstruct economic growth.

C.7.2. Case for Discussion　Agitation against the Implementation of the Provident Fund Act

An agitation, appropriately termed as 'spontaneous', 'leaderless' and 'massive flash strike', launched by the women employees of the garment factories in Bengaluru on 18 and 19 April 2016, was against the central government's decision to implement the amended provisions of the Provident Fund Act with effect from 1 May 2016. The agitation/struggle was spontaneous and was not backed by any large labour unions. Neither the blistering hot summer days of the month of April nor the fear of facing the police of the city of Bengaluru could stop the thousands of women workers of the five garment factories in Bengaluru. They blocked the arterial Hosur Road for over seven hours; on the Bangalore–Mysore Highway, thousands more squatted on the road, causing a gridlock. It took the country by surprise as lakhs of women workers, working in atrocious working conditions, came out on the road and protested against the government's proposal, which constrained the withdrawal of the provident fund. The protestors were so militant that the government decided to call back their decision of implementing the amended proposal of the Provident Fund Act. The agitation was only for two days, which forced the government to withdraw the proposed scheme.

There were no defined leaders of these agitators who would have enabled the police to negotiate. The police too were hesitant to use force against women.

The Changed Scheme

On 10 February 2016, the labour minister issued an amendment restricting the withdrawal of the provident fund. The EPF comprises a contribution of 12 per cent of an employee's basic salary plus DA made by the employer and employee every month. The existing practice was that in case a worker who was unemployed for two months could withdraw the entire provident fund savings. But the Labour Ministry revised withdrawal norms of this fund vide a notification in the month of February 2017. The new rules laid down that the employees could only withdraw their own contribution, and that the employer's contribution could only be withdrawn on attaining the retirement age of 58 years. Of the 12 per cent of a worker's salary contributed by the employers to the provident fund, only 3.67 per cent goes to the provident fund, the remaining 8.33 per cent becomes part of a pension fund. The new order was applied to this 3.67 per cent of workers' savings.

The agitation remained fairly peaceful. The central government announced a rollback and the women returned to their jobs. The agitation ended as suddenly as it had started.

Case Questions

1. Will the above case be fit enough to be considered as an industrial dispute? Justify.
2. Had the Central Government not withdrawn their decision, what were the alternatives left to such workers who were not unionized?
3. Will such stoppage of work come under the purview of a strike?

7.7. Types of Disputes

ILO refers to two main types of disputes relating to terms of employment published in the first Indian edition in 1980 under the 'conciliation of industrial disputes'. They are as follows.

1. **Interest disputes:** These are also called 'conflicts of interests' or 'economic disputes' or 'collective labour disputes'. They arise out of deadlocks in the negotiations of a collective agreement. Such disputes originate from trade union demands or proposals, and maybe for improvement of wages, fringe benefits, job security or other terms or conditions of employment. These demands or proposals are normally made with a view to conclude a collective demand.

2. **Grievances or right disputes:** These disputes are also known as 'conflicts of rights' or 'legal disputes'. They arise from day-to-day worker's grievances or complaints. Grievances typically arise on questions such as discipline and dismissal, the payment of wages and other fringe benefits, working time, overtime, promotion, transfer, the relationship of work rules to the collective agreement, and the fulfilment or obligations relating to safety and health laid down in the agreement. Under the Indian context, disputes regarding the implementation of labour laws and regulations, standing orders, arbitration awards, collective agreements and settlements, wage board's recommendations and administrative orders of the government fall under this category.

There are two other types or disputes relating to organizational rights. They are as follows:

3. **Disputes over unfair labour practices:** These types of disputes are also termed as 'victimization for trade union activities'. The attempts by the management of an undertaking to discriminate against workers for being trade union members, or for participating in trade

union activity are the examples of this dispute. Other unfair labour practices of this category include the following:

a. Management's interference, restraint or coercion of employees from exercising their right to organize, join or assist a union

b. Refusal of the management to bargain collectively in good faith with the reorganized union

c. Management recruiting new employees during a strike which is not an illegal strike

d. Failure to implement an award, settlement or agreement and indulgence in acts of force or violence.

4. **Recognition disputes:** This type of dispute arises when the management of an undertaking or an employers' organization refuses to recognize a trade union for purposes of collective bargaining. The reasons of the same may be various. Some of them are as follows:

a. Management's refusal may be on the ground that the union requesting recognition is not sufficiently representative.

b. There are several unions in the undertaking to make claims of recognition. (In such a case, the resolution of the issue may depend on the existence or non-existence of rules for determining the representative character of trade unions for the purpose of collective bargaining.)

7.8. Forms of Industrial Unrest

Although the term 'industrial dispute' in general implies disagreement between workers and employers, ultimately it is expressed in the forms of certain industrial action taken either by the trade union or the management. These actions include (a) strikes and (b) lockouts.

7.8.1. Strike

Section 2(q) of the ID Act, 1957, defines a strike as 'cessation of work by a body of persons employed in any industry, acting in combination or a concerted refusal under a common understanding, of any number of persons who are or have been so employed to continue to work or to accept employment'.

Following are the essential elements of a strike:

1. Plurality of workers
2. Stoppage of work or refusal to work
3. In combination or concerted action.

Strike implies the following:

1. Strike is a temporary stoppage of work by a group of employees in order to express a grievance or enforce a demand. The employees return to work only under certain conditions acceptable to them.
2. The second essential feature of a strike is that it is a group concept. There is a mass action in a particular direction and an implied willingness for the same.

7.8.2. Forms of Strikes

Strikes may be classified in the following categories.

1. **Primary strikes:** Such strikes are generally against the employer with whom the disputes exist. Some of the forms of primary strikes are stay-away strike, stay-in strike, sit-down, pen-down or tools-down strikes, go-slow and work to rule, token or protest strike, lightning or cat-call strike and picketing or boycott.
2. **Secondary strikes:** These strikes are pressure that is intentionally applied not against the employer with whom the workers have contract of employment but against some third party who has good trade relations with the employer for which the primary employer gets involved in incurring losses.

Other classification of strikes is by the nature of initiation.

1. **Authorized strikes:** Trade unions resort to such strikes only with a consent or permission.
2. **Unauthorized strikes:** This is commonly known as the wildcat strike and is called without the approval of the union. It is called by a section of workmen on the spur of the moment without any formal preparation or any formal notice to the employer, or obtaining any consent. It is an outburst caused by any sudden provocative action on the part of the management or supervisors.

Considering the scope of strikes, they may be classified as follows:

1. **General strikes:** General strikes, as the terminology connotes, have a wide coverage. But the degree of generality or the nature of coverage varies considerably from strike to strike. Bandhs at the national levels are the typical examples. The objectives behind organizing such bandhs are primarily political in nature. Such general strikes may cover a wide range of industries and all or a large part of the country. Some general strikes may be confined to a city or an industrial town.

   An example is the general strike on 2 September 2016, in which an estimated 15 [4] to 18 crore workers participated [5]. Indian public sector workers went on a 24-hour nation-wide general strike against the Prime Minister Narendra Modi's plans for increasing privatization and other economic policies [6]. A total of 10 trade unions participated [7]. Many government-run locations and transportation services were closed. Strikers also protested in favour of social security, universal health care and an increased minimum wage. The strike mainly took place in states where opposition parties were the most influential such as Karnataka and Kerala. It was called the largest strike in human history [8].

2. **Particular strikes:** These are limited in scope and are usually confined to a single plant or a few plants and to a single trade or occupation in a particular town or city. Ordinarily, such strikes are called by the plant-level unions. Majority of strikes come under this group.

   An example is the Maruti strike on 26 November 2011 which began at 2 PM and work was stopped at its Manesar Plant. The strike began after one of the supervisors was assaulted by some workers in the Manesar Plant. In a disciplinary action, the management had suspended two workers. The strike was led by the same group of workers who went on strike in the month of June 2011 [9].

On the basis of the techniques adopted, strikes may be classified as follows.

1. **Slow-down strike:** The workers intentionally reduce the speed of the work and adopt dilatory tactics to reduce the production or efficiency while pretending to be engaged. Workers resort to go-slow when the union does not want to resort to a full-fledged strike but still wants to take some alternative action which may be less risky but equally effective.

   An example is the Air India strike on 20 August 2015 after a section of commanders went on a 'go-slow' protest against a government notification removing airlines' commanders from the workmen category. This resulted in delay in its flight operations. A total of 13 flights—eight from Mumbai and five from Delhi—were delayed by two hours till the evening owing to this protest.

2. **Token or protest strikes:** Workers remain in their place of work, but they stop work for a brief period, that is, for a few minutes or few hours. The purpose is to exert moral persuasion than to precipitate the issue.

3. **Sit-down strikes:** Workers remain in their place of work but do not work. The difference between a token and a sit-down strike is only that of duration. In a sit-down strike, workers stop working altogether.

4. **Work-to-rule:** Under a work-to-rule situation, employees declare that they will perform their tasks strictly in accordance with the rule prescribed. By this, they succeed in slowing down the pace of work and reducing output without going on a formal strike and without any dereliction of duty.

   It has proven to be an effective instrument of exerting pressure on the management. Mostly in service sectors such as insurance and banking, post and telegraph employees often resort to work-to-rule method for the fulfilment of their demand.

5. **Picketing:** This is an act of posting pickets and marching or patrolling of the workmen in front of the premises of the employer carrying and displaying signs, banners and placards (in connection with the dispute) for the purpose of preventing others from entering the place.

   Some of the union workers are posted at the factory gate for the purpose of persuading others not to enter the premises but to join the strike. This type of picketing is said to be peaceful.

6. **Boycott:** Employees boycott the work with an aim to disrupt the normal functioning of the enterprise. It is an appeal for all voluntary withdrawal from work so it is persuasive in nature.

7. **Gherao:** The practice includes the confinement of authorities (often managerial personnel) by workers in their offices, lasting for hours or even days, and they are prevented from going out until the workers' demands are fulfilled.

On the basis of the generic purposes for which the strikes are undertaken, they can be classified as follows.

1. **Sympathetic strikes:** It is conducted out of sympathy for the cause of another group or workers, whether on strike or not. Thus, the workers resorting to a sympathetic strike have no immediate grievance against their employer. Such a strike strengthens the morale of workers for whom they are expressing their sympathy by going on a strike.

2. **Jurisdictional strikes:** These are conducted with a view to force an employer to recognize or bargain with a particular trade union instead of another. One of the contestants may go on strike to pressurize the employer to accept his/her representational claim.

3. **Political strikes:** Strikes of this sort are intended to put pressure on the government or a public authority to do something or desist from doing something. Such strikes are also intended to express worker's support to a particular cause.

7.8.3. Whether Rights to Strike Is Guaranteed by the Constitution of India

The fundamental rights guaranteed under Articles 19, 14 and 21 of the Constitution are as follows.

1. Article 19(1)(c) of the Constitution of India guarantees the right of citizens of the country to form and join associations and unions as a fundamental right.

   In the case of All India Bank Employees' Association, the Supreme Court of India [10] considered the issue whether the right guaranteed by Article 19(1)(c) would be inclusive of the right to collective bargaining and the right to strike. The Court held that even a very liberal interpretation of Article 19(1)(c) cannot lead to the conclusion that trade unions have a guaranteed right to effective collective bargaining or to strike.
2. Article 19(1)(a) guarantees to all citizens of the country the freedom of speech and expression.
3. Article 19(1)(b) protects the right of citizens to assemble peacefully without arms.
4. In Kameshwar Prasad and others v. the state of Bihar and another [11], the Supreme Court held that the right of workers to participate in peaceful and orderly demonstrations flows from Articles 19(1)(a) and (b).
5. Article 19(1)(d) guarantees the freedom of movement throughout the territory of India. The Supreme Court has held that the right of citizens to take out public processions and hold public meetings flows from Article 19(1)(b) guaranteeing the freedom of assembly be read together with Article 19(1)(d).
6. Article 14 guarantees to all citizen equality before the law and the equal protection of the law.
7. Article 21 provides that 'no person shall be deprived of his life or personal liberty except according to the procedure established by law'.
8. Article 21 and Articles 21(1) and (2) guarantee protection against arbitrary arrest and detention.

7.8.4. Lockouts

Ordinarily, 'lockout' means the action where an employer temporarily closes down or shuts down the undertaking or refuses to provide his or her employees with work with the intention of forcing them either to accept demands made by the employer or to withdraw demands made by the workers.

The ID Act, 1947, defines lockouts as 'the closing of a place of business or employment or the suspension of work, or the refusal by an employer to continue to employ any number of persons employed by him'.

But lockout does not mean the closure or closing down of business. It only means the closing down of the place of business. It means suspension of work, not discontinuance of the carrying of the business. Lockout is an antithesis of strike. Just as the employees have a weapon in their hands to put pressure on the employer by going on strike, so also, the employer has a weapon against the employees to lockout his premises and not to allow the workers to come to work.

7.9. Historical Perspective of Industrial Disputes in India

In India, with the progress of industrialization, there was a growing trend in the number of industrial disputes. Factors such as increasing price level, rising cost of living, growing industrial inefficiency, and indiscipline and sickness of industries have been attributed to be the general causes for the growing industrial disputes in the country. The historical perspective of industrial disputes in India gives an understanding of the IR in the country. The industrial dispute's history of India is discussed in three distinct periods.

7.9.1. Period Prior to Independence

The frequency of strikes and lockouts is normally considered as the indicator of industrial disputes. Any difference between the management and workers of any serious nature, in case not resolved in time, gets manifested as industrial disputes. The Royal Commission on Labour observed that the number of strikes till the First World War were rare. The fact which cannot be denied is that because the workers were illiterate, unorganized, submissive and not conscious of their rights, and there was a dearth of able trade union leaders to lead, the grievances might not have been ventilated in the form of strikes or industrial disputes. The first strike, as reported, was in the year 1882 in a textile factory in Bombay. In 1885, strikes also occurred in Ahmedabad as a protest against the substitution of a fortnightly payment of wages to weekly payment. But the efforts made through this strike had resulted into failures to achieve any results. Data reveals that the period from 1926 to 1930 registered 49 million man-days lost due to strikes mainly in textile mills.

With the breakout of the Second World War in September 1939, prices of the commodities increased, making lives of workers miserable. This, obviously, resulted in demand for an increase in DA for workers all over the country. In consequence, the number of industrial disputes almost doubled from 406 in 1939 to 820 in 1945.

The legislative history of industrial disputes provides some degree of understandings on the importance of the authorities given for the settlement of industrial disputes. The conflicts between European Railway Contractors and their workmen in Bombay causing the death of one of the contractors took place in 1859. The cause of the dispute was delay in the payment of wages. The Employers and Workmen's (Disputes) Act, 1860, was enacted by the government as a remedy for settling such disputes. But the earliest legislation in India was Bengal Regulation VII of 1819. Under this legislation, the breach of contract was treated as a criminal offence and this was also followed by the Merchant Shipping Act (I of 1859) and the Workmen's Breach of Contract Act, 1860.

The Bombay Government enacted The Trade Disputes Act, 1929, which was codified for five years as an experimental measure. The Act was amended in 1932 and was made permanent by the Trade Disputes (Extending) Act, 1934. Since 1937, the scope of trade disputes legislation had considerably been extended both at the centre and in a number of provinces. The Act had provisions for permanent machinery for the speedy and amicable settlement of industrial disputes.

The Trade Disputes Amendment Act of 1938 provided for the appointment of conciliation officers with authority for mediating and promoting the settlement of trade disputes. Table 7.1 shows the available data on industrial disputes during the pre-Independence period.

| Table 7.1 | Industrial Disputes in India during Pre-Independence | | |

Year	No. of Disputes	No. of Workers (in '000) Involved	Man-Days Lost (in Lakhs)
1921	396	600.3	69.8
1926	128	186.8	10.9
1930	148	196.3	22.6
1936	157	169.0	23.6
1940	322	452.5	75.7
1944	658	550.0	34.4
1947	1,811	1,840.7	165.6

Source: Compiled by the author from various issues of the handbook of labour statistics and annual report of Ministry of Labour & Employment.

7.9.2. Post-Independence Period

The post-Independence period experienced a large-scale industrial unrest. The cause for the same was factors like the overwhelming feeling of Independence in the minds of workers owing to the transfer of power to the national government. The fear of termination of service was gone. The rising cost of living affected the working class. Table 7.2 shows the data of industrial disputes since Independence till liberalization.

As evident from Table 7.2, there was a wide fluctuation in the rate of industrial disputes during the post-Independence period. The government implemented the 'Code of Discipline in 1958' and adopted the 'Industrial Truce Resolution in 1962', which led to a decline in industrial disputes in the country. But the economy experienced an eventful decade from 1964 to 1974; there was an

| Table 7.2 | Industrial Disputes in India (1951–1990) | | |

Year	No. of Disputes	No. of Workers (in '000) Involved	Man-Days Lost (in Lakhs)
1951	1,071	691.3	128.1
1961	1,357	511.9	49.2
1971	2,752	138.9	165.5
1976	1,308	11,873.7	127.4
1981	1,589	1,588.4	365.8
1990	1,825	1,308.0	240.9

Source: Compiled by the author from various issues of the handbook of labour statistics and annual report of Ministry of Labour & Employment.

unprecedented rise in the prices because of the Indo-Pak conflict in 1965, and a recession took place owing to the oil price hike in 1973.

During this period, there were an increased number of strikes and industrial disputes. The year 1974 was marked by all India railway strike. This was followed by the government's strong measures to ensure uninterrupted production during the period of Emergency, that is, 1975–1976, which made the period different marked by the declining number of industrial disputes. But with the lifting of Emergency in the early 1977, industrial disputes again experienced a steep increase, that is, 2,589 in 1981. It was in 1982 that the nation witnessed the world's longest strike (for over 18 months) in Bombay textile mills, started on 13 January 1982 and led by Dr Datta Samant (a militant trade union leader). The seeds of liberalization were sown from the mid-1980s by the Rajiv Gandhi government. The Government of India introduced its new economy policy in 1991 to open the Indian economy for world-level players.

7.9.3. Post-liberalization Period

The post-liberalization brought in a shift in balance of power in favour of the management. This was reflected in the declining number of strikes and increasing number of lockouts during this period. Table 7.3 provides the data on the number of strikes and lockouts from 1991 to 2014.

The trade unions and the labour considered to adopt a softening stand. An example of the same is the case of 12 January 1994, when more than 1.5 lakh insurance workers went on strike across the country to protest against the recommendation of the Malhotra Committee on reforms in the insurance sector. However, they were back at their jobs within two hours. On the contrary, in the pre-liberalization time, a nation-wide protest of this nature would have kept employees away from work for several days or even weeks. The percentage of strikes for less than five days had declined from 66 per cent in 1961 to 51 per cent in 1996. Of these 51 per cent strikes in 1996, strikes less than a day accounted for 35 per cent. There was a shift in the preference of the trade unions for striking during this period.

Table 7.3 Strikes and Lockouts in India (1991–2014)

		Strikes			Lockouts	
Years	Number	Workers Involved (in '000)	Man-Days Lost (in '000)	Number	Workers Involved (in '000)	Man-Days Lost (in '000)
1991	1,278	872	12,423	532	469	13,999
1992	1,011	767	15,132	703	484	16,126
1993	914	672	5,614	479	281	14,686
1994	808	626	6,651	393	220	14,332
1995	732	683	5,720	334	307	10,570
1996	763	609	7,818	403	331	12,467

(Table 7.3 Continued)

(Table 7.3 Continued)

		Strikes			Lockouts	
Years	Number	Workers Involved (in '000)	Man-Days Lost (in '000)	Number	Workers Involved (in '000)	Man-Days Lost (in '000)
1997	793	637	6,295	512	344	10,738
1998	665	801	9,349	432	488	12,713
1999	540	1,099	10,625	387	211	16,161
2000	426	1,044	11,959	345	374	16,804
2001	372	489	5,563	302	199	18,204
2002	295	900	9,665	284	199	16,921
2003	255	1,011	3,206	297	805	27,050
2004	236	1,903	4,829	241	169	19,037
2005	227	2,723	10,801	229	191	18,864
2006	243	1,712	5,318	187	98	15,006
2007	210	606	15,056	179	118	12,111
2008	240	1,514	6,955	181	66	10,479
2009	167	1,793	8,075	173	74	9,547
2010	199	990	13,150	172	85	9,980
2011	179	645	4,697	191	90	9,761
2012	133	1,221	2,843	185	86	10,094
2013	103	1,774	4,045	155	64	8,600
2014	137	1,051	2,883	25	3	911
2015*	112	741	2,663	29	10	1,351
2016*	104	654	1,874	26	14	2,746

Source: Compiled by the author from various issues of the handbook of labour statistics and annual report of Ministry of Labour & Employment.
Note: * Provisional

7.10. Dispute Resolution

The dispute resolution framework (Figure 7.1) under the ID Act consists of conciliation, arbitration and adjudication. Apart from this, there are preventive procedures which include recommendations of ILO, code of discipline, joint management committees, provisions of the standing orders, grievance-handling procedure, works committee and collective bargaining. All these machineries help prevent industrial disputes. Joint management committees and provisions of the standing orders are discussed in the subsequent chapters, whereas collective bargaining has been discussed in the previous chapter.

Figure 7.1	Dispute Resolution Framework

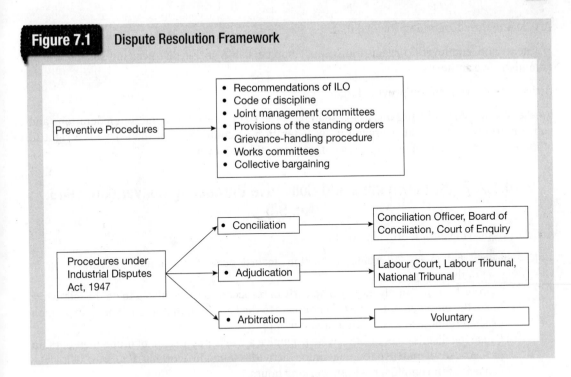

7.10.1. Settlement Machinery of Industrial Disputes

ILO recommended various provisions for settling differences and disputes between workers and the management. The principle recommendations are the following.

7.10.1.1. Freedom of Association and Protection of the Right to Organize Convention, 1948 (No. 87)

Part I. Freedom of Association

Article 2 of the convention provided that:

Workers and employers, without distinction whatsoever, shall have the right to establish and, subject only to the rules of the organization concerned, to join organisations of their own choosing without previous authorization.

Article 3 of the convention provided that:

1. Workers' and employers' organisations shall have the right to draw up their constitutions and rules, to elect their representatives in full freedom, to organise their administration and activities and to formulate their programmes.
2. The public authorities shall refrain from any interference which would restrict this right or impede the lawful exercise thereof.

Article 4 of the convention provided that:

Workers' and employers' organisations shall not be liable to be dissolved or suspended by administrative authority.

Article 5 of the convention provided that:

Workers' and employers' organisations shall have the right to establish and join federations and confederations, and any such organisation, federation or confederation shall have the right to affiliate with international organisations of workers and employers.

7.10.1.2. Right to Organise and Collective Bargaining Convention, 1949 (No. 98)

Article 1 of the convention provided that:

1. Workers shall enjoy adequate protection against acts of anti-union discrimination in respect of their employment.
2. Such protection shall apply more particularly in respect of acts calculated to do the following:
   (a) Make the employment of a worker subject to the condition that he shall not join a union or shall relinquish trade union membership;
   (b) Cause the dismissal of or otherwise prejudice a worker by reason of union membership or because of participation in union activities outside working hours or, with the consent of the employer, within working hours.

Article 2 of the convention provided that:

1. Workers' and employers' organisations shall enjoy adequate protection against any acts of interference by each other or each other's agents or members in their establishment, functioning or administration.
2. In particular, acts which are designed to promote the establishment of workers' organisations under the domination of employers or employers' organisations, or to support workers' organisations by financial or other means, with the object of placing such organisations under the control of employers or employers' organisations, shall be deemed to constitute acts of interference within the meaning of this Article.

Article 3 of the convention provided that:

Machinery appropriate to national conditions shall be established, where necessary, for the purpose of ensuring respect for the right to organise as defined in the preceding Articles.

7.10.1.3. Voluntary Conciliation and Arbitration Recommendation, 1951 (No. 92)

I. Under the heading 'voluntary conciliation', the following provisions have been provided:

1. Voluntary conciliation machinery, appropriate to national conditions, should be made available to assist in the prevention and settlement of industrial disputes between employers and workers.

2. Where voluntary conciliation machinery is constituted on a joint basis, it should include equal representation of employers and workers.
   (1) The procedure should be free of charge and expeditious; such time limits for the proceedings as may be prescribed by national laws or regulations should be fixed in advance and kept to a minimum.
   (2) Provision should be made to enable the procedure to be set in motion, either on the initiative of any of the parties to the dispute or ex officio by the voluntary conciliation authority.
3. If a dispute has been submitted to conciliation procedure with the consent of all the parties concerned, the latter should be encouraged to abstain from strikes and lockouts while conciliation is in progress.
4. All agreements which the parties may reach during conciliation procedure or as a result thereof should be drawn up in writing and be regarded as equivalent to agreements concluded in the usual manner.

II. Under the 'voluntary adjudication', the following provisions have been provided:

5. If a dispute has been submitted to arbitration for final settlement with the consent of all parties concerned, the latter should be encouraged to abstain from strikes and lockouts while the arbitration is in progress and to accept the arbitration award.

7.10.1.4. Examination of Grievances Recommendation, 1967 (No. 130)

ILO recommends the procedure within the undertaking. Such provisions have been dealt under the following clauses:

10. (1) As a general rule an attempt should initially be made to settle grievances directly between the worker affected, whether assisted or not, and his immediate supervisor.
    (2) Where such attempt at settlement has failed or where the grievance is of such a nature that a direct discussion between the worker affected and his immediate supervisor would be inappropriate, the worker should be entitled to have his case considered at one or more higher steps, depending on the nature of the grievance, and on the structure and size of the undertaking.
11. Grievance procedures should be so formulated and applied that there is a real possibility of achieving at each step provided for by the procedure a settlement of the case freely accepted by the worker and the employer.
12. Grievance procedures should be as uncomplicated and as rapid as possible, and appropriate time limits may be prescribed if necessary for this purpose; formality in the application of these procedures should be kept to a minimum.
13. (1) The worker concerned should have the right to participate directly in the grievance procedure and to be assisted or represented during the examinations of his grievance by a representative of a workers' organization, by a representative of the workers in the undertaking, or by any other person of his own choosing, in conformity with national law or practice.
    (2) The employer should have the right to be assisted or represented by an employers' organization.

(3) Any person employed in the same undertaking who assists or represents the worker during the examination of his grievance should, on condition that he acts in conformity with the grievance procedure, enjoy the same protection as that enjoyed by the worker under Paragraph 2, Clause (a), of this recommendation.

14. The worker concerned, or his representative if the latter is employed in the same undertaking, should be allowed sufficient time to participate in the procedure for the examination of the grievance and should not suffer any loss of remuneration because of his absence from work as a result of such participation, account being taken of any rules and practices, including safeguards against abuses, which might be provided for by legislation, collective agreements or other appropriate means.

15. If the parties consider it necessary, minutes of the proceedings may be drawn up in mutual agreement and be available to the parties.

16. (1) Appropriate measures should be taken to ensure that grievance procedures, as well as the rules and practices governing their operation and the conditions for having recourse to them, are brought to the knowledge of the workers.

   (2) Any worker who has submitted a grievance should be kept informed of the steps being taken under the procedure and of the action taken on his grievance.

ILO recommends for the 'adjustment of unsettled grievances' in the following manner:

17. Where all efforts to settle the grievance within the undertaking have failed, there should be a possibility, account being taken of the nature of the grievance, for final settlement of such grievance through one or more of the following procedures:

   (1) procedures provided for by collective agreement, such as joint examination of the case by the employers' and workers' organizations concerned or voluntary arbitration by a person or persons designated with the agreement of the employer and worker concerned or their respective organizations;

   (2) conciliation or arbitration by the competent public authorities;

   (3) recourse to a Labour Court or other judicial authority;

   (4) any other procedure which may be appropriate under national conditions.

18. (1) The worker should be allowed the time off necessary to take part in the procedures referred to in Paragraph 17 of this Recommendation.

   (2) Recourse by the worker to any of the procedures provided for in Paragraph 17 should not involve for him any loss of remuneration when his grievance is proved justified in the course of these procedures. Every effort should be made, where possible, for the operation of these procedures outside the working hours of the workers concerned.

7.10.1.5. Collective Bargaining Convention, 1981 (No. 154)

Under Article 2 of this convention, ILO provided that:

For the purpose of this Convention the term *collective bargaining* extends to all negotiations which take place between an employer, a group of employers or one or more employers' organizations, on the one hand, and one or more workers' organizations, on the other, for:

(a) determining working conditions and terms of employment; and/or
(b) regulating relations between employers and workers; and/or

(c) regulating relations between employers or their organisations and a workers' organisation or workers' organisations.

Under Article 5 of Part Promotion of Collective Bargaining of this Convention, ILO provides the following terms:

1. Measures adapted to national conditions shall be taken to promote collective bargaining.
2. The aims of the measures referred to in Paragraph 1 of this Article shall be the following:
   (a) collective bargaining should be made possible for all employers and all groups of workers in the branches of activity covered by this Convention;
   (b) collective bargaining should be progressively extended to all matters covered by subparagraphs (a), (b) and (c) of Article 2 of this Convention;
   (c) the establishment of rules of procedure agreed between employers' and workers' organizations should be encouraged;
   (d) collective bargaining should not be hampered by the absence of rules governing the procedure to be used or by the inadequacy or inappropriateness of such rules;
   (e) bodies and procedures for the settlement of labour disputes should be so conceived as to contribute to the promotion of collective bargaining.

7.10.1.6. Termination of Employment Convention, 1982 (No. 158) Entry into Force: 23 November 1985

Article 4 of the convention provides:

The employment of a worker shall not be terminated unless there is a valid reason for such termination connected with the capacity or conduct of the worker or based on the operational requirements of the undertaking, establishment or service.

Article 5 of the convention provides:

The following, inter alia, shall not constitute valid reasons for termination:
(a) union membership or participation in union activities outside working hours or, with the consent of the employer, within working hours;
(b) seeking office as, or acting or having acted in the capacity of, a workers' representative;
(c) the filing of a complaint or the participation in proceedings against an employer involving alleged violation of laws or regulations or recourse to competent administrative authorities;
(d) race, colour, sex, marital status, family responsibilities, pregnancy, religion, political opinion, national extraction or social origin;
(e) absence from work during maternity leave.

Article 6 of the convention provides:

1. Temporary absence from work because of illness or injury shall not constitute a valid reason for termination.
2. The definition of what constitutes temporary absence from work, the extent to which medical certification shall be required and possible limitations to the application of Paragraph 1 of this Article shall be determined in accordance with the methods of implementation referred to in Article 1 of this Convention.

7.11. Code of Discipline

The problem of industrial discipline was debated by the Indian Labour Conference held in 1957. A subcommittee was appointed to draft a model 'code of discipline' acceptable to all. A code of discipline drafted by the subcommittee was duly ratified by the central organizations of workers and employers at the 16th session of the Indian Labour Conference held on March 1958 and it became operative from 1 June 1958.

7.11.1. Principles of the Code of Discipline

1. There should be no strike or lockout without proper notice.
2. No unilateral action should be taken in connection with any industrial matter.
3. There should be no resource to go-slow tactics.
4. No deliberate damage should be caused to a plant or property.
5. Acts of violence, intimidation, coercion or instigation should not be resorted to.
6. The existing machinery for the settlement of disputes should be utilized.
7. Awards and agreements should be speedily implemented.
8. Any action which disturbs cordial IR should be avoided.

7.11.2. Objectives of the Code of Discipline

The code has been aimed at establishing cordial relations between managements and workers on a voluntary basis to promote harmony and to put an end to industrial unrest. The objectives, as stated in the code, are as follows:

1. To ensure that employers and employees recognize each other's rights and obligations
2. To promote constructive cooperation between the parties considered at all levels
3. To secure settlement of disputes and grievances by negotiation, conciliation and voluntary arbitration
4. To eliminate all forms of coercion, intimidation and violence in IR
5. To avoid work stoppages
6. To facilitate the free growth of trade unions
7. To maintain discipline in industry.

7.11.3. Features of the Code of Discipline

The code of discipline is applicable to both public and private sector units. Its important features are as follows:

1. It prohibits strikes and lockouts without prior notice and also intimidation, victimization and the adoption of 'go-slow' tactics by workers.
2. No one-sided (unilateral) action can be taken by either party in any IR matter.
3. All disputes are to be settled through the existing machinery provided for this purpose by the government.

4. The employers will not increase the workload without prior agreement with the workers.
5. A common grievance procedure for the settlement of grievances of the workers after full investigation has been provided for.
6. The employers will provide all facilities for the growth of trade unions.
7. Prompt action will be taken against those officers whose conduct provokes indiscipline among the workers.
8. The workers will not indulge in any trade union activity during the working hours. They will not engage in any demonstration or activity which is not peaceful.
9. The workers will implement their part of the awards and settlements promptly and will take action against those office-bearers of the union who have violated the code.
10. The unions will discourage the negligence of duty, careless operation, damage to property, insubordination and disturbance in normal productive activities. They will discourage unfair labour practices and will not engage in rowdy demonstrations.

7.12. Settling Industrial Disputes under the ID Act, 1947

The systems of establishing industrial peace and to settle industrial disputes as specified under the ID Act, 1947, are discussed in the following sections.

7.12.1. The Works Committee

In the case of any industrial establishment in which 100 or more workmen are employed or have been employed on any day in the preceding 12 months, the appropriate government may by general or special order requires the employer to constitute in the prescribed manner a works committee consisting of representatives of employer and workmen engaged in the establishment. It shall be the duty of the works committee to promote measures for securing and preserving amity and good relations between the employer and workmen and, to that end, to comment upon the matters of their common interest or concern and endeavour to compose any material difference of opinion in respect of such matters. The committees will attempt to remove the causes of friction between employers and workers in the day-to-day working of the factory.

The other machineries as provided under the ID Act, 1947, for the settlement of the industrial disputes are as follows.

7.12.2. Dispute Resolution in the Indian Context

In the Indian context, because disputes are resolved under the ID Act and the procedure of settling industrial disputes is equally applicable to all categories of organizations, the emergence of non-unions firms would have no effect on the dispute resolution framework of conciliation, adjudication and arbitration. Section 2A of the ID Act provides that where any employer discharges, dismisses, retrenches or otherwise terminates the services of an individual workman, any dispute or difference between that workman and his employer connected with, or arising out of, such discharge, dismissal, retrenchment or termination shall be deemed to be an industrial dispute not withstanding that no other workman nor any union of workmen is a party to dispute.

Section 10 of the ID Act provides that when an industrial dispute occurs or is apprehended, the appropriate government may refer it to the following:

1. A conciliation officer
2. Board of Conciliation for promoting a settlement
3. A Court of Enquiry
4. A Labour Court for Adjudication
5. An Industrial Tribunal for Adjudication.

A flowchart of the process which is followed for the settlement of industrial disputes is provided in Figure 7.2.

With the emergence of non-union forms of worker's associations, the procedures of the settlement of disputes through collective bargaining is becoming redundant. The dispute resolution process, as specified under the ID Act, 1947, mainly involves the following:

- Mediation and conciliation
- Adjudication (the litigation process)
- Arbitration.

Figure 7.2 Process for the Settlement of Industrial Disputes

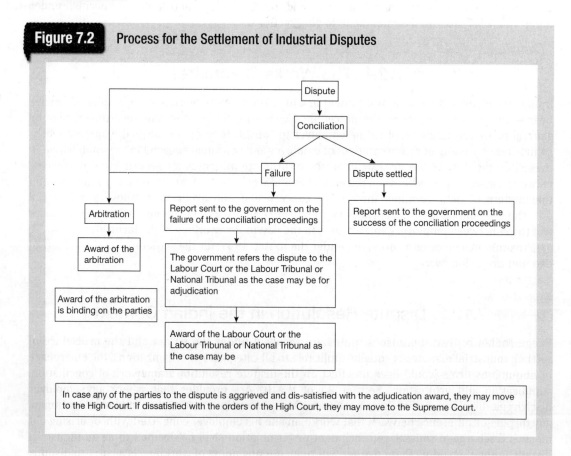

7.12.2.1. Mediation and Conciliation

Conciliation or mediation assumes the third-party intervention in promoting the voluntary settlement of disputes. It is a mediation process for settling industrial disputes. ILO defines conciliation as the practice by which the services of a neutral third party are used in a dispute as a means of helping the disputing parties to reduce the extent of their differences and to arrive at an amicable settlement or agreed solution. The ID Act, 1947, has made provisions for conciliation as an important tool for dispute settlement process though conciliation has not been defined under any of the Indian Labour Laws. Neither do the conciliators work in the judicial capacity nor do they enjoy any 'powers' to impose an agreement or settlement between the parties. The effort of the conciliation process is to narrow down the differences through discussions and suggestions. The conciliation machinery, as provided under the ID Act, 1947, comprises conciliation officers and the Board of Conciliation and the Court of Enquiry. So, the conciliation machinery comprises the following:

- Conciliation by an officer (Sn.4 & 2(d))
- A board (an ad hoc board consisting of a chairman and equal number of workmen and the employer's representatives (Sn.5&2(e))
- Court of Enquiry

Conciliation Officers

The ID Act, 1947, provides for the appointment of conciliation officers, permanently or for a limited period, for a specific area or for a specific industry. Section 4 of the ID Act, 1947, confers power upon the government to appoint conciliation officers by notification in the official gazette, for a specified area or for one or more specified industries for the purpose of mediating in and promoting the settlement of industrial disputes. The conciliation officer enjoys the powers of a Civil Court; he can call and witness parties on oath. The conciliation officer examines all the facts relevant to the disputed matter and then helps both parties with discussion on the areas of dispute with the aim of progressively narrowing down the dispute. It is also open for either party to submit a request in writing to the conciliation officer, requesting to start the conciliation process.

The conciliation officer is required to submit his report within 14 days of the commencement of the conciliation proceedings, but the time for the submission of the report may be extended further on the written request of the parties to the dispute. The conciliation officer is empowered to enquire into the dispute and suggest possible solutions to bring the parties to a mutually accepted solution. If the conciliation efforts are not successful, the officer may submit a failure report with his recommendations to the appropriate government. The appropriate government may make a decision to refer the dispute to the Labour Court/Tribunal or National Tribunal for adjudication (ID Act [Act XIV of 1947] sub Sections 12(4), (5)). A failure of conciliation at the regional level will automatically involve the conciliation officer at the state level to conciliate to settle the dispute. Such conciliations are normally conciliated at the level of the ALC, or the Labour Commissioner of the state. Therefore, as disputes move up the hierarchy of conciliation officers, the chances of settlement of the dispute increase. A failure of conciliation proceedings at the state level might draw the state labour minister in the role of conciliating officer depending on the seriousness of the case. Normally, disputes get settled at this level due to the power and authority exercised by the office of the minister. A failure at the state level implies that the appropriate government will refer the dispute for adjudication (ID Act [Act XIV of 1947] sub Sections 7(1), 10,...). If a settlement is arrived at during conciliation proceedings, the conciliation officer will send a copy of the report and the memorandum of the settlement to the government.

All disputes do not go to the levels of the labour commissioner or labour minister after the conciliation fails at the regional level. Only such disputes that involve a large number of workers or have resulted in a strike tend to go to these levels. The law empowers appropriate governments to make a reference to the Labour Court/Tribunal or the National Tribunal for the adjudication on failure of the conciliation.

Disadvantages of Conciliation

There are many disadvantages of conciliation, which are as follows:

1. The process takes a long time. In certain cases, the time taken for conciliation exceeds a month. It is being observed that if a dispute goes through all the stages of the conciliation procedure, it could take about six months for the dispute to be resolved. This time gap might increase tensions at the workplace.
2. Conciliation officers generally do not receive any organized training to conciliate. They are sent to occasional training programmes on concepts.
3. There is the issue of commitment. Being part of a large bureaucracy with guaranteed job security and promotions based on length of service, it provides little incentive for a conciliation officer to take a great interest in his job.
4. Conciliation officers are rarely viewed as a totally impartial third party. Frequently, union presidents, who are invariably politicians, possess enormous power over conciliation officers by threatening transfers and interfering with career advancement. Consequently, they tend to stay on the good side of these politicians and this affects their neutrality in dispute settlement process.

The major advantage of conciliation is that the appropriate government has the authority to prohibit any strike during the pendency of conciliation proceedings (ID Act [Act XIV of 1947] sec22, 23,...). The strike that continues during the pendency of conciliation proceedings becomes an illegal strike. In an illegal strike, workers' entitlement of wages becomes nil.

Board of Conciliation

Where a settlement is not reached, the appropriate government, after considering the report of the conciliation officer, may refer the dispute to a Board of Conciliation or Labour Court or Industrial Tribunal or National Tribunal as the case may be. The ID Act, 1947, empowers the government to appoint a Board of Conciliation for promoting the settlement of disputes where the conciliation fails.

Section 5 of the ID Act, 1947, provides for the creation of Board of Conciliation which is simply an extension of conciliation officers' work. Unlike a conciliation officer, the board may not be a permanent body and can be set up as the occasion arises. It comprises two or four members representing parties to the dispute in equal numbers and a chairman who has to be an independent person. The board has the status of a Civil Court and can issue summons and administer oaths. Where the appropriate government is of the opinion that any industrial dispute exists or is apprehended, it may at any time, by order in writing, refer the dispute to a Board of Conciliation by an order in writing, to promote settlement of industrial disputes. Such references are also possible where the parties to an industrial dispute make an application in the prescribed manner whether jointly or separately, for a reference of the dispute to a Board of Conciliation.

Where the dispute is referred to the board, the appropriate government may prohibit the continuance of any strike or lockout in connection with such dispute which may be in existence on the date of reference.

The Duties and Powers of the Board of Conciliation

When a dispute has been referred to the Board of Conciliation, it may take suitable steps to induce the parties to come to a fair and amicable settlement. If settlement is arrived at, the board is required to send a report and a memorandum of the settlement signed by the parties to the appropriate government. If no such settlement is arrived at, the board is required to submit a conciliation failure report to the appropriate government. The board is required to submit report within two months of the date of the reference of the dispute or within shorter period as determined by the appropriate government.

Court of Enquiry

The appropriate government is empowered to constitute a Court of Enquiry as occasion arises, for the purpose of enquiry into any matter appearing to connect with or relevant to an industrial dispute. Generally, Court of Enquiry is constituted when no settlement is arrived at as a result of the efforts made by the Conciliation Board.

7.12.2.2. Adjudication in the Labour Courts/Tribunal

Labour Court

Labour Court is one of the adjudication authorities under the ID Act, 1947. It was introduced by amending the ID Act in 1956. Setting up of a Labour Court is at the discretion of the government. The function of Labour Court is to adjudicate on matters referred to it by the appropriate government. The listed matters in the schedule II, appended to the Act include the following:

- The legality of an order passed by an employer under the standing orders
- Discharge or dismissal of workmen including reinstatement of or grant of relief to workmen wrongfully dismissed
- Withdrawal of customary concession or privilege
- Illegality or otherwise of a strike or a lockout
- All matters other than those provided in the third schedule appended to the Act

The appropriate government may refer the dispute to a Labour Court/Tribunal or National Tribunal for adjudication. The Labour Court is empowered to adjudicate upon matters specified in second schedule and an Industrial Tribunal on those specified in second or third schedule. Thus any matter which is important for the industry as a whole and is listed in second or third schedule maybe referred for adjudication to a tribunal. However, where a dispute relates to a matter specified in the third schedule, and is not likely to affect more than 100 workmen, the appropriate government may refer it to the Labour Court.

The Labour Court is vested with the powers of a Civil Court. The Labour Court after examining all relevant documents and conducting detailed hearing, issues its decision. By the legislative amendment in 1971, the Labour Courts were given additional powers to give appropriate relief to any worker wrongfully discharged (including the authority to set aside the order of discharge dismissal) and to impose a lesser punishment if deemed appropriate. A proceeding can also be initiated by the Labour Court on receipt of a petition filed in the Labour Court by either party under copy to the appropriate government.

Decisions of the Labour Court may be appealed by either party in the High Court. If that decision is considered unsatisfactory, the matter may be appealed before the Supreme Court.

Tribunals or Industrial Tribunals

The appropriate government may constitute one or more Industrial Tribunals for the adjudication of industrial disputes relating to any matter as specified either in second schedule or in the third schedule appended to the ID Act, 1947, which includes the following:

1. Wages, including the period and mode of payment
2. Contribution paid or payable by the employer to any provident or pension fund or for the benefit of the workmen under any law for the time being in force
3. Compensatory and other allowances
4. Hours of work and intervals
5. Leave with wages and holidays
6. Starting alteration or discontinuance
7. Classification by grades
8. Withdrawal of any customary concession or change usage
9. Introduction of new rules of discipline or alteration of existing rules, except in so far as they are provided in standing orders
10. Rationalization, standardization or improvement of plant or techniques which is likely to lead to the retrenchment of workmen
11. Any increase or decrease in the number of persons employed or to be employed in any occupation or department or shift not occasioned by circumstances over which the employer has no control

National Tribunals

A National Tribunal can be set up by the Central Government. Disputes involving issues of national importance for industrial establishments situated in more than one state are normally referred to such National Tribunals. The state governments are debarred from referring the matter for adjudication to National Tribunal.

7.12.2.3. Arbitration

Under Section 10(a) of the ID Act, the parties may agree to refer the dispute for arbitration at any time before the dispute is referred for adjudication. The statute requires the parties to sign an arbitration agreement specifying the terms of the reference and the names of the arbitrator or arbitrators. An arbitrator has the power to bind unions and workers who are not parties to the arbitration agreement if he is satisfied that the union represents the majority of the workers in the unit (ID Act (Act XIV of 1947) Section 18).

The Act does not provide any structured arbitration procedure. However, the procedure which is followed is that the arbitrator provides opportunity to the parties to file their written submission. Further, evidence is normally called for from the parties by calling either party for hearing. The arbitrator studies the case and arguments put forward by both parties after which he gives his award. The award is then published in the official government gazette thus obtaining legal validity.

Once the arbitration agreement is signed, the government has the power to terminate and prohibit any strikes and lockouts or the continuation of any strikes and lockouts in connection with the dispute.

Advantages

Following are the advantages of arbitration:

- If the arbitration is voluntary, acceptability of the settlement by both parties are higher.
- It gives an opportunity of flexibility when the arbitration is established by agreement.
- The process is more expeditious than other methods of settlement.

Disadvantages

Following are the disadvantages of arbitration:

- It deprives workers of their right to strike.
- There is likely a chance of the judgement to be biased.
- There may be delays which can affect the morale of the parties.

Types of Arbitration

Arbitration can be compulsory or voluntary.

Compulsory arbitration: When the parties are required to accept arbitration without any willingness on their part, it is called compulsory arbitration. In case any of the parties feels aggrieved to an industrial dispute by an act of the other, it may apply to the appropriate government to refer the dispute to adjudication machinery. Under compulsory arbitration, the parties are forced to arbitration by the order of the State. It leaves no scope for strikes and lockouts.

Voluntary arbitration: Voluntary arbitration refers to, getting the disputes settled through an independent person, chosen by the parties to the dispute, mutually and voluntarily. It is a choice made by the contending parties for arbitration, before referring it for adjudication. The ID Act, 1947, was amended in 1956 to include a provision relating to voluntary arbitration (Section 10A). On the failure of conciliation proceedings, the parties may refer the dispute to a voluntary arbitrator. Voluntary arbitration became popular as a method of settling differences between workers and the management with the advocacy of Mahatma Gandhi, who had applied it in the textile industry of Ahmedabad.

An arbitrator is not vested with any judicial powers. It is a quasi-judicial process, where the arbitrator sits in judgement on the proceedings. He/she after coming to a decision makes the decision known to the parties and submits his/her award to the government. The government then may publish it within 30 days of its submission.

Voluntary arbitration has been considered as the next best alternative to conciliation, which is built on a democratic process and is a substitute to collective bargaining. It not only provides a voluntary method of settling industrial disputes but is also a quicker way of settling them.

Following are the main ingredients of voluntary arbitration:

1. The industrial dispute must exist or be apprehended.
2. The agreement must be in writing.
3. The reference to voluntary arbitration must be made before a dispute has been referred to under Section 10 to a Labour Court/Tribunal or National Tribunal.
4. The name of arbitrator/arbitrators must be specified.
5. The arbitrator or arbitrators shall investigate the dispute and submit to the appropriate government the arbitration award signed by the arbitrator or all the arbitrators, as the case may be.

National Arbitration Promotion Board

The National Arbitration Promotion Board (NAPB) was set up by the Government of India in 1967. The objective was to strengthen the system of voluntary arbitration in our country. The board consists of representatives from the employer and worker organizations, PSUs and central/state government officials.

The model principles of NAPB broadly laid down the circumstances under which individual as well as collective disputes can be referred to voluntary arbitration.

The functions of the board are as follows:

1. To examine the factors inhibiting arbitration.
2. To evolve principles, norms and procedures for the guidance of the arbitrator and the parties.
3. To advise parties, in important cases, to accept arbitration for resolving disputes so that litigation in courts may be avoided.
4. To look into the cause or causes of delay and expedite arbitration proceedings, wherever necessary.
5. To specify, from time to time, the types of disputes that would normally be settled by arbitration in tripartite decisions.
6. To maintain a panel of suitable arbitrators.

7.13. Grievance Redressal Machinery

The ID (Amendment Act), 2010, had substituted a new chapter for Chapter IIB.

1. Every industrial establishment employing 20 or more workmen shall have one or more Grievance Redressal Committee (GRC) for the resolution of disputes arising out of individual grievances.
2. The GRC shall consist of equal number of members from the employer and the workmen.
3. The chairperson of the GRC shall be selected from the employer and from among the workmen alternatively on rotation basis every year.
4. The total number of members of the GRC shall not exceed more than six. Provided that there shall be, as far as practicable, one woman member if the GRC has two members and in case

the number of members are more than two, the number of women members may be increased proportionately.

5. Notwithstanding anything contained in this section, the setting up of GRC shall not affect the right of the workman to arise industrial dispute on the same matter under the provisions of this Act.

6. The GRC may complete its proceedings within 30 days on receipt of a written application by or on behalf of the aggrieved party.

7. The workman who is aggrieved of the decision of the GRC may prefer an appeal to the employer against the decision; and the employer shall, within one month from the date of receipt of such appeal, dispose of the same and send a copy of his decision to the workman concerned.

8. Nothing contained in this section shall apply to the workmen for whom there is an established GRC in the establishment concerned.

Any discontent or dissatisfaction which an employee faces or even imagines, when not addressed properly in a company, is reflected as a grievance. Grievance brings out important information about creeping problems to the management in advance. It may be real or imaginary, valid or otherwise, genuine or false. The grievance of employees ought to be addressed since it may result in unhappiness, frustration, discontent, poor morale and very importantly, it adversely affects production. A grievance is a sense of resentment of an individual or a group of workers working in an organization. It is an expression of discontent made by the worker or the group of workers because there is a certain standard which is explicitly or implicitly expected by the workers. Discontent or dissatisfaction cannot be said to be a grievance. Normally such discontent initially finds an expression in the form of a complaint. When a complaint of this nature remains unattended and the employee concerned feels a sense of lack of justice and fairness to him, the dissatisfaction assumes the status of grievance.

In the 15th Session of the Indian Labour Conference held in 1957 it was emphasized to have a grievance procedure that will be acceptable both to the union and the management. A model grievance procedure was drawn up in the 16th session of Indian Labour Conference held in 1958. In the 'code of discipline' it was laid down that the management and workers will establish a mutually agreed grievance procedure that will ensure speedy investigation to the grievances, leading to its settlement. The procedure was a time-bound application of the procedure.

The Model provided that:

1. The aggrieved worker will indicate verbally his complaint to the supervisor or the officer designated for the purpose.

2. The supervisor has to reply within 48 hours of the receipt of the complaint. If the reply is satisfactory, the process ends there.

3. If it is not satisfactory, the worker may move the grievance to the departmental head within 72 hours.

4. If the worker is satisfied, the matter ends or else the worker may move to the Grievance Committee for redressing the grievances within 72 hours.

5. The Grievance Committee needs to be a joint committee having at least two to three representatives from the workers and the management. The committee has to give a suitable solution within seven days.

6. If the worker is dissatisfied with the decision, he/she may appeal to the chief executive, expressing his/her grievances. The chief executive has to reply to the worker within next three days.

| Table 7.4 | Causes and the Nature of Dissatisfaction in the Form of Grievance |

Causes of Grievance	Nature of Dissatisfaction
Economic	Pay fixation, computation, over time bonus and incentives
Work environment	Poor working condition, defective system/equipment and materials
Supervision	Perceived notion of favouritism, bias, superior's lack of managerial and technical skills, and bullying
Work group	Incompatibility with peers and feeling of neglect
Work organization	Rigid unfair rules and lack of recognition

Grievances may occur for a number of reasons, which are as follows:

- The primary reason for a large number of individual grievances can be attributed to discontent with regard to wage fixation and wage revision, leading employees to feel that they are underpaid in comparison to their peer.
- Grievances among individuals due to inferior working conditions and restrictive practices towards production efficiency.
- Grievances may also arise due to the inability of a worker to adjust in the work environment and efficiently work with his co-workers.
- Grievances among workers on issues relating to violations in respect of promotions, transfers, fines and granting leaves. In short, employees grievances may be grouped into economic, working environment, supervision, work group and work organization.

Table 7.4 provides the various causes of a grievance resulting in different nature of dissatisfaction in the employees of an organization.

The morale of the employees is affected badly when grievance arises, thereby the employees' work is affected adversely. Even for top performers, when they have grievance, their performance is affected badly. Some of the effects of grievance are as follows:

- Loss of interest in work
- Lack of morale and commitment
- Poor quality of production
- Increase in wastage and costs
- Increase in employee turnover
- Indiscipline

7.13.1. Objectives of a Grievance-handling Procedure

Tricia Jackson [12] lays down the objectives of a grievance-handling procedure as follows:

1. To enable the employee to air his/her grievance.
2. To clarify the nature of the grievance.

3. To investigate the reasons for dissatisfaction.
4. To obtain, where possible, a speedy resolution to the problem.
5. To take appropriate actions and ensure that promises are kept.
6. To inform the employee of his or her right to take the grievance to the next stage of the procedure, in the event of an unsuccessful resolution.

7.13.2. Benefits of a Grievance-handling Procedure

According to Tricia Jackson [12], the benefits that will accrue to both the employer and employees are as follows:

1. It encourages employees to raise concerns without the fear of reprisal.
2. It provides a fair and speedy means of dealing with complaints.
3. It prevents minor disagreements developing into more serious disputes.
4. It saves employers' time and money as solutions are found for workplace problems.
5. It helps build an organizational climate based on openness and trust.

7.13.3. Steps in a Grievance-handling Procedure

In a grievance-handling mechanism, the dispute/difference must be handled by some members of the management. The responsibility of redressal of grievance lies largely with the management. It is essential that grievances should be settled promptly at the first stage itself. The following are the steps for grievance handling.

1. **Acknowledge the dissatisfaction:** Acknowledging the grievance is an important step and needs a through attention of the managerial/supervisory. The managers handling the grievance should necessarily focus their attention on grievances and not turn away from it. Condescending attitude on the part of supervisors and managers would aggravate the problem.
2. **Define the problem:** It is essential to understand and define the problem correctly instead of trying to deal with a vague feeling of discontent. At times wrong complaints are lodged, so proper investigation for finding out the facts is an essential step. Effective listening might turn out to be one way to address this issue and one can make sure that a true complaint is voiced.
3. **Get the facts:** It is essential to get the facts through proper method of enquiry, separated from fiction. Though grievances result in hurt feelings, the effort should be to get the facts behind the feelings. There is a need for a proper record of each grievance.
4. **Analyse and decide:** Decisions on each of the grievances will have a precedent effect. However, no time should be lost in dealing with grievances. Grievance settlements provide opportunities for managements to improve the employer and the employee relationship, and thereby come closer to the employees. Horse-trading in grievance redressal process due to pressures of the trade union may temporarily bring trade union leaders closer to the management, but it will alienate the workforce away from the management.
5. **Follow up:** Decisions taken by the management needs to be followed up and be promptly communicated to the employee concerned. If a decision is favourable to the concerned employee, the immediate boss should have the privilege of communicating the decision.

7.13.4. Principles for Handling Grievances

There are seven principles for handling grievances, which are as follows.

1. **Fair demonstration of the grievance procedure:** The situation assumes that the attitude of the supervisor is very important. The condition should facilitate for acceptance of the employee's right to be heard and appeal. In an organization having an active trade union, the supervisors can encourage the employee to be represented by a trade union official, if he so desires.

2. **The procedure of a grievance handling should be definite and clear:** No grievance procedure can work satisfactorily unless there are definite provisions, consistently adhered to determining what, when and by whom various initiatives to be done. There needs to be a clear clarity on:
    a. to whom grievances are to be filed
    b. in what form, written or oral

3. **The grievance procedure should be simple:** The procedure needs to be simple enough so that it can be easily understood even by the employees who have had little formal education.

4. **The procedure needs to be prompt and speedy:** Prompt action is an essential feature of the grievance procedure. Promptness is essential not only from the complaint's point of view, but also from the management's point of view. Since delay causes frustration and negative reactions, it is essential that grievances needs be dealt with speedily. Any unnecessary delay may constitute to another grievance. It is considered that settlement of grievances in the shortest possible time and at the earliest is the ideal one.

5. **The supervisor to develop an attitude towards his employees that generates confidence:** In the grievance procedure it is essential that the supervisor gain the confidence of the employee in order to generate a trusting behaviour. To gain confidence, the supervisor must show the right attitude towards the aggrieved employees. He should display a sincere interest in the problems of the employees and a willingness to be of help. Although the supervisor is mainly the representative of management to the employees, he is also a representative of employees to the management.

6. **Supervisors to be aware of their responsibilities and be ready to carry them out:** The supervisor must have confidence in carrying out his responsibilities. An executive who has no self-confidence soon finds that his employees are aware of this and tend to be wary of him. Most of the employees never go to such supervisors with their grievances.

7. **The total effects of the decision to the grievance to be considered:** The effect of the decision on the grievance to be considered in its totality, which implies consideration of both short-run effects and its long-run implications. Any decision reached at the present moment has an immediate effect and also likely to have an influence upon the future relationship between the employees and the management. Every grievance has to be considered with due importance, and its long-term effect. For in handling grievances, it takes a long time to gain the confidence of employees but it can be lost overnight by a foolish decision or inapt handling of a single grievance.

Last, encouraging decisions to disputes by negotiation between labour and management have been considered as a better work culture. It solves the problem through the process of bargaining and negotiation.

Grievances take a wide variety of forms in its result. In case it is handled well, it will help in avoiding issues from escalating and will increase the faith of the employees in their employer. In case it is handled badly, the result may be anything from disillusionment to full-blown litigation. Five mistakes are normally committed by the employers while handling grievances, which are as follows.

1. **Being too formal and too fast:** The action taken by the management after receiving a grievance is crucial. There might be a general tendency of processing every grievance through formal channel, but sometimes this escalates the matter since a more informal resolution could prove to be a better approach.

   To launch issues like a grievance on unfair criticism of a worker's work from his manager immediately into a formal process can be counterproductive—particularly as manager and employee will probably need to continue working together. Instead a more informal route can be much more effective. There may have been a simple misunderstanding, or it may be a communication issue which can be resolved through an informal conversation.

   It is important to understand what the employee wants. Wherever possible employers need to discuss the expectations of the employee as a part of the grievance-handling procedure.

   There may be occasions where the allegations are serious enough and demanding a formal action.

2. **Judgements considering a part of the fact:** Not having all the facts is a dangerous position and jumping into conclusions/decisions may prove to be more serious. The grievances in general give a clear understanding of facts for enabling the employer to decide what action needs to be taken. This expects proper investigation, a key to any grievance process, thereby collecting facts in totality. A reasonable investigation will not only help to establish the facts, but will help to shield the employer from allegations of unfairness.

3. **Skipping the steps for scarcity of resources:** A formal grievance procedure should involve an investigator, decision-maker and appeal manager. Small employers with only one or two managers may struggle to have enough appropriate people to fill each of these roles. Some smaller employers use external consultants to manage the investigation process and reserve the decision-making to a senior manager. This may not be appropriate in all cases.

4. **Not following all the steps of the procedure:** Employers spend a considerable time ranging from many weeks (and sometimes months) to investigate and conclude a grievance. Thereafter, when a communication that 'I have decided not to uphold your grievance' reaches the employee, it creates a series of reactions. The emotion which is often attached by an employee to his grievance is bound to lead to problems with the passing of time. Often it results in an appeal, but frequently in disillusionment with the process.

   It may seem crucial to explain to an employee (particularly where grievances are being rejected) how a decision has been reached. Even an employee who disagrees with the decision can at least feel that there is logic to it and that their views have been considered. Moreover, if that decision was ever to be challenged, the employee may do so through an appeal. Documenting the action to be taken is also important.

5. **Moving too slow:** The subject of a grievance is often something an employee will face daily, so each passing day without resolution will take its toll. Leaving an employee for weeks and months without information or resolution is asking for trouble. It is the greatest source of frustration for employees and one of the biggest risks for employer. Handling a grievance properly can take time, but all employers are under a duty to conclude grievances promptly.

I.C.7.1. INDUSTRIAL CONTEXT FOR DISCUSSION

Grievance Redressal OXFAM (India)

1. **Policy statement**

   The Grievance redressal procedure at Oxfam India aims to reinforce the organization's commitment towards providing fair and equitable work opportunities to all employees. The objective of the grievance resolution process is to provide employees with an easily accessible mechanism for settlement of their individual grievances. This policy applies to all the staff of Oxfam India and those of partner organizations who are in a relationship with Oxfam India.

   a. For the purpose of the policy, grievances means individual grievance and include all matters but exclude the following:

      i. Annual performance appraisal

      ii. Grievance pertaining to, or arising out of, disciplinary action or appeal against such actions

      iii. Grievance arising out of termination/dismissal

2. **Grievance statement and policy**

   a. A grievance can be defined as any sort of dissatisfaction which needs to be addressed in order to enable staff to function efficiently and effectively within the organization. A grievance is a sign of an employee's discontentment with his job or his relationship with his colleagues. Broadly, a grievance can be stated to be any discontent or dissatisfaction with any aspect of the organization.

   b. Oxfam India's grievance policy is designed to provide an effective procedure for the resolution of problems. Oxfam India's policy ingrains a disciplinary procedure that will afford consistent and equitable treatment to all employees.

   c. The purpose of the disciplinary procedure is to ensure that unacceptable conduct is addressed promptly and appropriately.

   d. The disciplinary procedure applies to all Oxfam India employees.

   e. The procedure takes account of the Oxfam India code of conduct and will be reviewed periodically in line with developments in good practice.

3. **Criteria**

   a. Except for gross misconduct, no employee will be dismissed for a first breach of discipline. The level of any formal action will be dependent on the seriousness of the offence, having regard to the need for fairness and natural justice.

   b. The procedure is internal to Oxfam India and does not allow for any external representation.

   c. No disciplinary action will be taken against an employee until the case has been fully investigated.

4. **Grievance redressal procedure**

   The following process should be followed for expressing and seeking redressal to a grievance:

   a. Employees may communicate their grievance in writing to their line managers while at the same time, addressing a copy to the HR manager. In case the grievance involves the line manager, then the employee can contact the line manager's manager, while simultaneously copying the HR manager.

   b. The concerned manager must immediately acknowledge the receipt of the grievance in writing, informing the employee of the receipt of grievance and inviting the employee for a formal meeting. Managers may consult with the HR manager and revert to the employee with a course of action/solution within seven working days from the date of receipt of grievance.

   c. In case an employee is not satisfied with the solution, the employee may choose to represent the grievance to director operations (or the CEO, if the grievance concerns the director operations).

d. The senior leadership team (SLT) member will convey their decision to the aggrieved employee through the HR manager within five days of receipt of the complaint. If, however, the SLT is of the view, that the matter should be referred to the grievance resolution committee, they may do so.

e. The grievance resolution committee consists of three members from the India leadership team, and the HR manager and should try to have at least two women representatives. The grievance resolution committee (as mentioned below) will provide an opportunity to the aggrieved employee to present their concern.

f. The grievance resolution committee will give their recommendation to the SLT within four working days. The SLT will take a decision based on this recommendation and communicate their decision through the HR manager to the aggrieved employee within 15 working days from the commencement of enquiry.

g. Grievances will be treated with utmost confidentiality and sensitivity.

h. HR shall maintain a record of all grievances referred to the grievance resolution committee, number of grievances settled/pending and report to the senior management team on a quarterly basis.

Chapter Summary

1. Industrial conflict occurs when employees express their dissatisfaction with the management over the current state of the management–employee relationship. Employees can express such dissatisfaction in formal or informal ways. Industrial conflicts can occur at various levels which are as follows:
   a. between two employees
   b. between two groups of employees
   c. between members of a group
   d. between employees and employers as a group
   e. between an individual employee and an employer
   f. between employees in a group or individually with agencies like the government.

2. Industrial disputes may be said to be disagreement or controversy between the management and labour with respect to wages, working conditions, union recognition or other employment matters. Section 2k in the ID Act, 1947, defines industrial dispute as 'any dispute or difference between employers and employers or between employers and workmen, or between workmen and workmen, which is connected with the employment or non-employment or the terms of employment or with the conditions of labour, of any person'.

3. The statutory machineries for the settlement of industrial disputes in India include works committee, conciliation officer, Board of Conciliation, Labour Court/Tribunal and National Tribunal, and GRC.

4. The ID Act, 1947, requires an employer to constitute a works committee consisting of equal representatives of employers and workmen engaged in industrial establishments where 100 or more workmen are employed.

5. The methods of settling industrial disputes without state intervention comprise (a) collective bargaining (discussed earlier) and (b) voluntary arbitration.

6. The methods of settling industrial disputes with state intervention include (a) conciliation or mediation by the conciliation officer, Board of Conciliation, (b) adjudication at the level of Labour Court/Tribunal and National Tribunal and (c) compulsory arbitration.

7. Conciliation or mediation is a form of settling industrial disputes through the mediation of a third party, who is a government representative. Such endeavours are to help the parties to arrive at a mutually acceptable settlement.

8. Adjudication or compulsory arbitration involves a legal requirement that empowers the government or a prescribed authority to refer an industrial dispute to an adjudication authority usually known as the tribunal or Labour Court, whose award is generally binding on the parties.

9. Voluntary arbitration is the procedure voluntarily chosen by the parties to an industrial dispute whereby the dispute is settled by an impartial arbitrator or an umpire of mutual selection. The acceptance of the award of the arbitrator may be voluntary or binding, depending on the choice of the parties.

10. A code of discipline in the industry is a voluntary measure from the partners to ensure industrial peace. The code of discipline in the industry, which applies both to the public and the private sectors, has been accepted voluntarily by all the central organizations of employers and workers, and has been in operation since the middle of 1958. The code lays down specific obligations for the management and the workers with the object of promoting cooperation between their representatives at all levels, facilitating the free growth of trade unions and eliminating all forms of coercion and violence in IR.

11. The ID (Amendment Act), 2010, had substituted a new chapter for Chapter IIB.
    a. Every industrial establishment employing 20 or more workmen shall have one or more GRC for the resolution of disputes arising out of individual grievances.
    b. GRC shall consist of the equal number of members from the employer and the workmen.
    c. The chairperson of GRC shall be selected from the employer and from among the workmen, alternatively on a rotational basis every year.
    d. The total number of members of GRC shall not exceed 6. Provided that there shall be, as far as practicable, one woman member if GRC has two members and in case the number of members is more than 2, the number of women members may be increased proportionately.
    e. Notwithstanding anything contained in this section, the setting up of GRC shall not affect the right of the workman to arise industrial dispute on the same matter under the provisions of this Act.
    f. GRC may complete its proceedings within 30 days on receipt of a written application by or on behalf of the aggrieved party.
    g. The workman who is aggrieved of the decision of GRC may prefer an appeal to the employer against the decision, and the employer shall, within one month from the date of receipt of such an appeal, dispose of the same and send a copy of his or her decision to the workman concerned.
    h. Nothing contained in this section shall apply to the workmen for whom there is an established GRC in the establishment concerned.

Questions

1. Differentiate between a conflict and an industrial dispute. What are the conditions for a dispute to be termed as an industrial dispute?
2. Explain the various statutory and non-statutory machineries for the settlement of industrial disputes.
3. What are the types and forms of industrial disputes? Explain.
4. What is the grievance redressal mechanism? How is it useful in the industrial context?

References

1. Sunder KRS. Who said all is quiet on the industrial front? Industrial conflicts in India in the post reform period, Econ. Pol. Wkly. 17 January 2015.
2. (2002) I L.L.J. 842 (SC).
3. (2005) I L.L.B. 1089 (SC).
4. Banerji A. Tens of millions in India strike for higher wages, The China Post. 3 September 2016.
5. Workers strike back: 180 million Indian workers strike for higher minimum wage, Sputnik. 2 September 2016. Available from https://sputniknews.com/asia/201609021044893835-india-workers-strike/
6. Karuna M. Strike call evokes mixed response in India, Gulf News India. 2 September 2016.
7. Shehab K. Humanity's biggest ever strike is underway, The Independent. 3 September 2016.
8. The Hindu. General strike: Trade unions claim success, normal life unaffected, The Hindu. 3 September 2016.
9. https://www.ndtv.com/business/another-strike-hits-marutis-manesar-plant–147602
10. All India Bank Employees' Association versus The National Industrial Tribunal (Bank Disputes), Bombay and others AIR 1962 SC 171.
11. Kameshwar Prasad and another versus State of Bihar and others AIR 1963 SC 1166, 1168.
12. Jackson T. Handling grievances. London: Institute of Personnel and Development; 2000.

The Indian Labour Market

C.8.1. Case for Discussion Thyrocare Technologies

There is a continuous increase in the eligibility of the working population to join the labour market. Every month, millions become eligible in terms of their age, qualification and skills to join the workforce. This is true for every sector of the Indian industry. But the growth in jobs has not kept pace with the rising number of job seekers in different skills. It is a matter of concern for an economy which is supposedly one of the brighter spots in a slow global market.

For instance, 33-year-old R. S. Dubey, father of two, who hailed from Chhapra in Bihar, recently lost his job for resisting a decision of the management to change him from a permanent to a temporary employee in the company.

Aspects such as the reasons for losing jobs and getting rejected in an interview for a job are more controlled by the market rather than organization's HR philosophy.

An explanation for the 'whys' behind the symptom of unemployment in a growing economy may very often be attributed to examples such as those discussed below.

In a pathology lab named Thyrocare Technologies, about 200 young trained technicians, who are experts in their own skills, start their job at 8 AM every day in its automated clinical chemistry laboratory at Turbhe in Navi Mumbai. They work till 8 PM and perform the skilled activity of operating a range of state-of-the-art diagnostic equipment. Such equipment processes up to 200,000 investigations a night for thyroid, kidney and liver diseases, testing nearly 45,000 samples flown in from 1,300 collection centres in India. This would have taken several days of investigation by at least 1,000 technicians a decade ago, but is now being done by a workforce of one fifth size, in less than a day.

Some sectors have also lost their market stakes. The reasons for the same have been changing global customer demands. For example, employment in export units in India saw a sharp decline due to shrunken global demands. In the automobile sector, 23,000 jobs were lost—the reason for the same had been somewhat identical. The overall figures indicate that there were only 5,000 job additions in the first half of fiscal year (FY) 2016 compared to 271,000 in the corresponding period of FY 2015.

The market also forced large manufacturers to trim their operations, resulting in reduced employee strength. Few examples are as follows:

1. In November 2014, the mobile handset giant, Nokia, rendered 8,000 employees jobless, and shut down its handset-making factory in Chennai after being locked in a tax dispute with the Indian Government.
2. The new owner of the Nokia handset brand, Microsoft, considered the business of manufacturing smartphones in China and Vietnam to be more cheaper than that of Chennai, India; so never thought of reinstating the 8,000 job less employees.
3. Lafarge, the cement major, also is planning an exit after selling its 11 mt business in India. The global cement industry is beset by overcapacity and falling demands.
4. A three-year-old Mumbai-based food ordering software start-up, TinyOwl is still in dire state, even after it fired more than hundred employees.
5. A food-tech company, Zomato, laid off 300 employees, that is, almost 10 per cent of its workforce in the year 2015 as business went down.
6. The real estate and infrastructure sectors had been down sizing for the last few years because of the market situation where the organizations are struggling to arrange for resources.
7. Some MNCs in the financial sectors had also exited India market, after they found that the competition is tougher. For example, JP Morgan Asset Management of the United States exited its India-based mutual funds business, selling it out to Edelweiss Asset Management. On March 2016, Edelweiss Asset Management had announced the acquisition of JP Morgan's mutual fund business in India. There are also similar other examples.
8. The $3,500 crore Essar Group for meeting its steep debt is reported to be in talks to sell off a part of its refinery business as well as a portion of its ports business.

The traditional labour-intensive industries are becoming increasingly mechanized by upgrading their operation processes, resulting in shrinkage of job and new opportunities.

The 27th Quarterly Employment Survey of eight employment-intensive industries, that is, textiles, leather, metals, automobiles, gems and jewellery, transport, IT/BPO and handloom/power loom by the Labour Ministry indicates that there were 91,000 net new jobs created in the first half of FY 2015–2016, whereas the second quarter was better with 134,000 new jobs.

The previous records on job creation had been much better than 2016. In the year 2010, the total number of jobs created were 0.11 crore.

The question is why an economy supposedly growing at a rate of over 7 per cent is not creating enough jobs. Have the organizations become less labour-absorbent? What are the reasons for the economy becoming less labour labour-absorbent?

(The instructor is requested to go through the instruction manual before leading the case for discussion in the class.)

Case Questions

1. Identify the causes for the job shrinkage in the Indian industries.
2. Identify expected impacts for such changing dynamics in the labour market in the Indian context.

8.1. The Labour Market

It is only an assumed condition that economic growth ultimately translates into a better labour market by creating further scope for employment generation, thereby increasing per capita income and creating economic surplus for further investment. There are talent gaps in all developed and developing economies. In the globalized market conditions, all emerging world economies look for closing the existing talent gap as well as creating scope for development, thereby generating employment.

Industrial growth leads to economic growth of a nation. There is a direct relationship between aspects such as industrial growth, economic growth and the labour market. Conceptually, higher the industrial growth, higher would be the labour utilization, thereby creating a demand for the employable labour. The employable labour from the labour market contributes to the workforce of the organizations. So it is important to understand the labour market for understanding the employable labour.

In the present chapter, the Indian labour market will be studied in the context of its economic growth and the initiatives of the government for achieving industrialization, thereby creating opportunities for more employment in the context of available manpower, population growth and the labour market institutions. The Indian economy is emerging as a giant in the global economy. The appropriately coined phrases such as 'amazing India' and 'shining India' define the Indian economy today. Economists predict that at its present trend of economic growth, the Indian economy would overtake the US economy in about two and a half decades [1, 2].

The model in Figure 8.1 depicts the relationship between economic growth, government's initiatives for improving the economic growth through policy measures and statutory compliance, the pressure of the population growth on the labour market, the need for employable labour by various employable sectors and employers, and the impact of the globalized market. The model explains that in the context of the global competitive market, there is a continuous pressure from the increasing population of the nation on the labour market. The government is making efforts for industrialization, and thereby economic growth within the legal frameworks to increase job creation. The employable sectors of the Indian labour market include the IT and ITES sectors, the service sector, the manufacturing sector and the agriculture sector. So understanding the labour market is the understanding of the employable resources in the context of the job market.

To start with, let us look at the need for closing the talent gap in the emerging world economies.

8.2. The Global Need for 'Closing the Talent Gap in the Emerging World Economies'

In the year 2016, the IMF projected that the emerging economies will grow at a faster pace, while advanced economies will see lower economic growth. Figure 8.2 indicates the economic performance of the emerging economies as compared to the developed economies.

The rates of growth in emerging markets (EM) picked up during the years 2003–2007. The financial crisis of 2007–2008 affected the developed economies adversely. The trend of difference in the economic growth rate between EM and advanced economies continued to be substantial thereafter.

It is projected that the economic growth of the developing nations will outpace that of the developed nations. Figure 8.3 is the projected rate of economic development in the G7, BRIC and N11 nations by 2020.

Figure 8.1   Various Factors Impacting the Labour Market

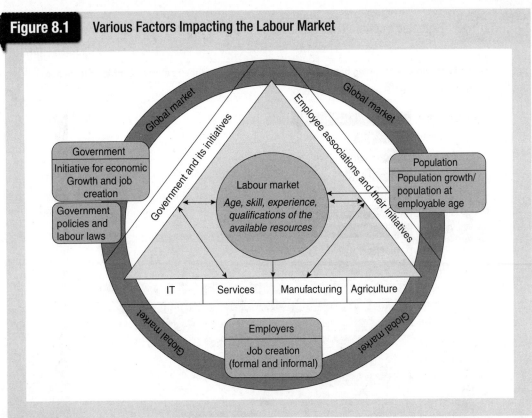

Figure 8.2   The Growth of the Global Emerging Market

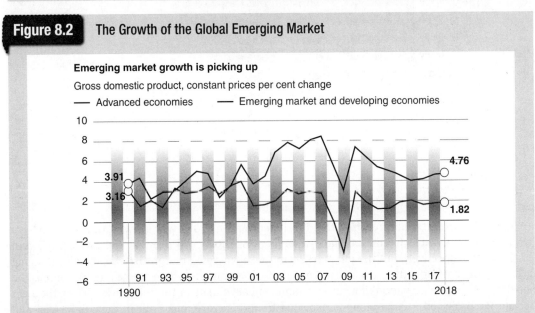

Source: The IMF, World Economic Outlook Database, October 2016.

Figure 8.3   Expected Economic Growth of the Emerging Nations

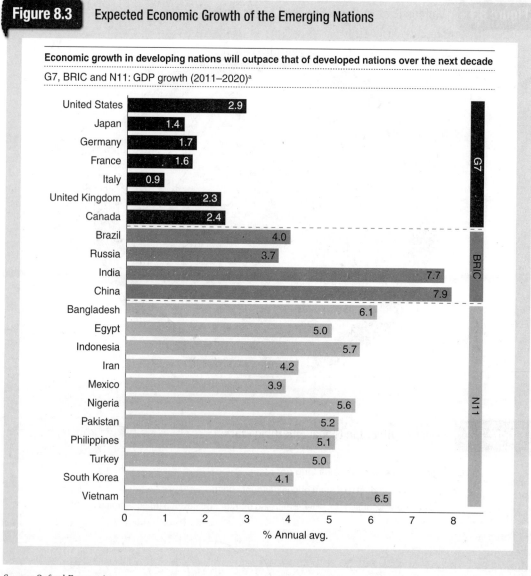

Economic growth in developing nations will outpace that of developed nations over the next decade

G7, BRIC and N11: GDP growth (2011–2020)[a]

Source: Oxford Economics.
Note: [a]Local currency constant prices.

Figure 8.3 projects that by 2020 the developed nations (G7) will grow within the range of 0.9–2.9 per cent, while China and India (members of BRIC) will grow at the rates of 7.9 and 7.7 per cent, respectively. But the job markets in these emerging nations had been a discouraging factor by not enabling further transformation of the economic growth to create jobs. So there is the need for the emerging nations for an enormous enhancement in the job market. Over the next decade (as projected), China alone is expected to add 8 crore jobs both in their industrial and service sectors. India, being the second largest emerging economy after China, is likely to add 6.5 crore jobs during the said period in the industry and service sectors.

Figure 8.4   The Share of Investment in the Emerging Economies

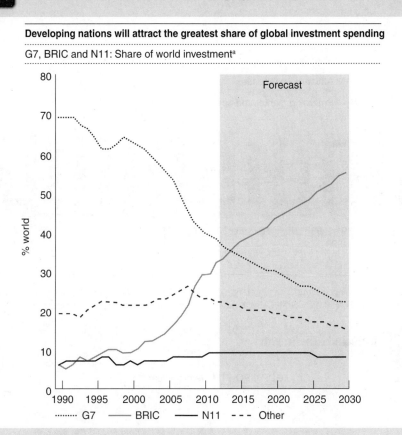

Developing nations will attract the greatest share of global investment spending

G7, BRIC and N11: Share of world investment[a]

Source: Haver Analytics, Oxford Economics.
Note: [a]Nominal US$ investment.

The positive aspects of the developing nations are that will attract greater share of investment spending. Figure 8.4 shows the forecasted trend of investment spending in the G7, BRIC and N11 countries. The projection indicates that by 2030, 58 per cent of the global investment spending will be in the BRIC nations, whereas N11 nations will continue to maintain their investment spending at 8 per cent and the investment spending of the G7 countries will come down to 24 per cent.

Figure 8.5 indicates that while investments as a percentage of GDP have come down in the advanced economies, the same have considerably gone up in the EM as well as the developing economies. The rate of investment as a proportion of GDP in the year 2016 was higher in the EM and developing economies as compared to developed economies. The available scope in the EM for infrastructure development for growth was considered as the prime cause for the same.

EM with their better performance tend to tap the global capital flows. In the year 2016, the IMF estimated that the GDP growth of EM will at least grow for the next five years, whereas the developed economies will continue to stagnate (Figure 8.6).

Figure 8.5 Investment in EM

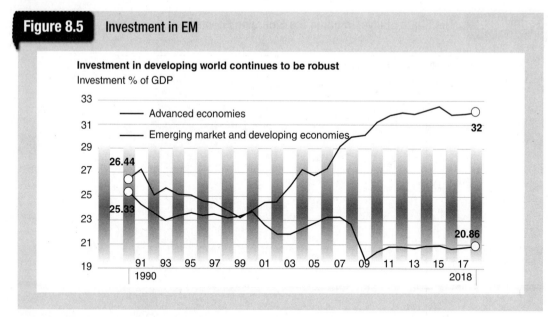

Investment in developing world continues to be robust
Investment % of GDP

Source: Chakravarty M. Advanced economies vs emerging markets, Livemint. 26 October 2016. Available from http://www.livemint.com/Opinion/ck1EMSGaPQvksrMeC45QsI/Advanced-economies-vs-emerging-markets.html

Figure 8.6 Expected GDP Growth

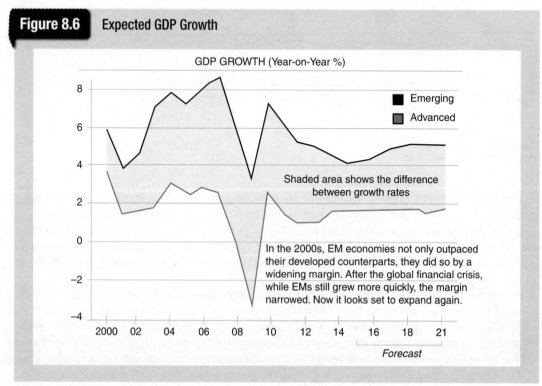

GDP GROWTH (Year-on-Year %)

Source: World Economic Outlook 2016.

So, to sum up, as per the IMF report:

1. The economic growth rate in the EM would be higher than in the advanced countries.
2. The figures project that by 2020, the developed nations (G7) will grow within the range of 0.9 per cent to 2.9 per cent, while the developing countries (BRIC) will grow at the rate of 7.9 per cent and 7.7 per cent as in the case of China and India, respectively. So, there is the need in the emerging nations for an enormous enhancement in the job market.
3. The investments as a percentage of GDP have come down in the advanced economies, the same have considerably gone up in the EM as well as the developing economies.
4. EM with their better performance trends will better tap the global capital flows.

8.3. The Indian Labour Market

The key economic and labour market indicators are as follows:

1. The growth in GDP
2. The investment as percentage of GDP
3. Employment
4. Unemployment
5. Labour force participation rate (LFPR; male and female)
6. Population growth

The following data provides some important information on the above areas (key economic and labour market indicators).

Macro Indicators	2012–2013	2013–2014	2014–2015	2015–2016
Real GDP (% change year to year)	5.6	6.6	7.2	7.6
Investment (% of GDP)	36.3	34.2	34.1	32.4
Labour Market Indicators	**2004–2005**	**2009–2010**	**2011–2012**	**2013–2014**
Employment (in crore)	45.79	45.90	47.29	–
Unemployment (in crore)	1.13	0.98	1.08	–
LFPR (in %)	63.7	57.1	55.9	55.6
Male LFPR (in %)	84.0	80.6	79.8	75.7
Female LFPR (in %)	42.7	32.6	31.2	31.1
Unemployment rate (%)	2.3	2.0	2.1	3.4
Male unemployment rate (%)	2.1	1.9	2.1	2.9
Female unemployment rate (%)	2.6	2.3	2.3	4.9
Share of employment in manufacturing (%)	11.6	11.0	12.5	10.7
Share of employment (male) in manufacturing (%)	12.0	11.1	12.2	10.7

Share of employment (female) in manufacturing (%)	11.0	10.8	13.2	10.6
Share of regular wage and salaried wage workers (%)	14.4	15.7	17.9	15.7
Share of regular wage and salaried wage workers (male) (%)	17.3	17.8	19.9	16.5
Share of regular wage and salaried wage workers (female) (%)	8.4	10.2	12.8	12.1

The above indicators, which provide a snapshot of all aspects of the trend of the labour market, conclude the following:

1. The GDP of the economy shows a rising trend.
2. Even with increasing economic activities and positive economic trends, there has been a downswing in the employment.
3. LFPR has reasonably decreased in spite of higher economic activities.
4. The employment in the manufacturing area also shows a decreasing trend.
5. The percentage of workers depending on the salaries for living is at a decreasing trend.

Various works of literature on the Indian labour market attempt to establish that the economy is characterized by an increase in GDP. It is also characterized by surplus labour force and unemployment, existence of a high degree of unskilled labour force, inappropriate work culture with militant trade unionism, and finally there is a need for labour reforms. Some of the critical characteristics are discussed as follows.

1. Faster growth in GDP

Various economic surveys conducted during the years 2015–2016 by organizations such as the Central Statistics Organisation (CSO) and IMF indicated that the 'Indian economy will continue to grow at more than 7 per cent in 2016–2017'. The IMF in World Economic Outlook (October 2016) indicated that the GDP growth rate of India in 2016 was 7.6 per cent, and India was the fourth fastest growing nation of the world. The average growth rate from 1980 to 2016 stood at 6.32 per cent, reaching an all-time high of 10.26 per cent in 2010 and a record low of 1.06 per cent in 1991.

The reason for this has been attributed to the combined impact of strong government economic reforms and RBI's initiative to control inflation. Similar observation appears in one of the reports of Goldman Sachs released in September 2015. They observed that, on average, India could grow potentially at 8 per cent during the fiscal years 2016–2020 powered by greater access to banking, technology adoption, urbanization and other structural reforms.

The global consumer confidence index created by Nielsen[1] indicates that India's consumer confidence score for the quarter April–June 2016 declined to 128 as compared to 134 during the

---

[1] Nielsen takes the pulse of consumer sentiment towards the global economic climate by questioning consumers about their job prospects, personal finances and spending and saving intentions.

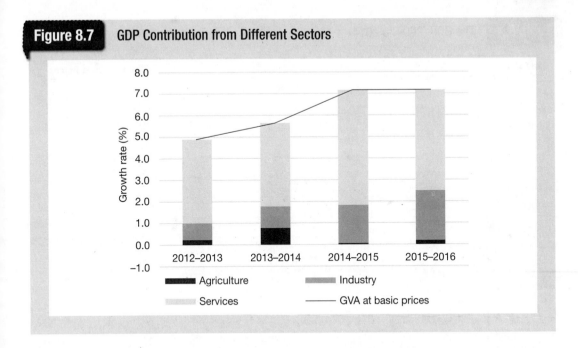

| Figure 8.7 | GDP Contribution from Different Sectors |

quarter of January–March 2016. During the quarter October–December 2015, the Indian economy was ranked at the highest, globally, in terms of consumer confidence. The economy maintained this position during the first three quarters of 2015.

The 12th Five-Year Plan (2012–2017) envisaged a 9 per cent annual average economic growth rate, which was later fixed at 8 per cent by the National Development Council (NDC) in December 2012. But there had been slower economic growth rates of 4.5 per cent in the first year of the 12th Plan (2012–2013) and 4.9 per cent in the second year (2013–2014). The economic growth during the FY 2014–2015 had been 6.9 per cent. During the FY 2015–2016, the economy had a growth of 7.3 per cent. Due to the lower economic growth during the first two years, the average economic growth rate target for the entire 12th Five-Year Plan might have been revised downwards for the lower performance during the years 2012–2014.

The growth rate in per capita income had also increased from 5.8 per cent in 2014–2015 to 6.2 per cent in 2015–2016. The real gross value added (GVA) revealed that the higher economic growth rates followed by increase in per capita income had been followed by strong industrial growth. In FY 2015–2016, growth in agriculture and related activities was estimated at just 1.2 per cent, while growth in the industrial and service sectors reached 7.4 and 8.9 per cent, respectively. Figure 8.7 shows the GDP contribution of different sectors to GVA (at basic prices).

The GDP from the year 2000 to 2014 is provided in Table 8.1.

Similar trends in GDP were also visible during the years 2015 and 2016. The GDP during the years 2015 and 2016 had been at the rate of 6.5 and 7.4, respectively. The study of the Ministry of Finance, Government of India, indicates that:

The year 2015–2016 witnessed a major economic slowdown. However, the Indian economy emerged as the fastest growing economy with a high growth rate of over 7 per cent in the subsequent years.

Table 8.1 The GDP (2000 to 2014)

Year	GDP, Constant Prices
2000	3.975
2001	4.944
2002	3.907
2003	7.944
2004	7.849
2005	9.285
2006	9.264
2007	9.801
2008	3.891
2009	8.48
2010	10.26
2011	6.638
2012	5.081
2013	6.899
2014	7.168

Source: India GDP—real growth rate (http://www.indexmundi.com/india/gdp_real_growth_rate.html).

The manufacturing sector was a major contributor in sustaining this high growth rate. As per the data released in January 2016 on revised estimates of the national income, the growth of the industrial sector broadly comprising mining, manufacturing, electricity and construction was 5.9 per cent during 2014–2015, as against a growth of 5.0 per cent during 2013–2014. As per the estimates of the national income 2015–2016, the growth of the industrial sector was estimated to be 7.3 per cent with the manufacturing sector growing at 9.5 per cent. [3]

The Indian economy experienced a rapid growth in GDP in the last three decades. The trend of growth was first manifested in the 1980s and picked up pace in the 1990s when domestic and external sector economic reforms were first introduced. In the period preceding that of high growth, the economy had grown at around 3 per cent per annum and with a population growth rate of about 2.5 per cent, resulting in only a very small increase in per capita income in the three decades. During the three decades of high growth, the average rate of GDP growth had been close to 6 per cent and during the two decades since the early 1990s and thereafter, it had been above 6.5 per cent. With the economy experiencing a population growth rate below 2 per cent per annum, it has resulted in a substantial rise in per capita income. In the years 2009–2010 and 2010–2011, which followed the slowdown due to the global financial crisis in 2008–2009, the Indian economy responded strongly and achieved a growth rate of 8.6 per cent and 9.3 per cent, respectively. But in the years 2011–2012 and 2012–2013, the growth rates slowed to 6.2 per cent and 5.0 per cent, respectively, because of factors such as high fiscal deficits and slowing down of saving and investment rates, including foreign investment. But during the years 2001–2002 and 2011–2012, the growth rate was 7.8 per cent per annum with per capita income growing at around 6.3 per cent per annum [4].

GDP growth has been close to 7 per cent since the 1990s. This with a population growth rate below 2 per cent has resulted in a substantial rise in per capita income. It is widely believed that the high growth of the Indian economy had been largely due to the process of economic reforms in which the entrepreneur class has played a crucial role, propelled by rising labour productivity.

2. Economy's resilience to external and internal shocks

The growth story of the Indian economy has features of its resilience to internal and external shocks. The economy had been able to withstand both internal and external shocks to a large extent. The internal shocks include the effect of calamities such as droughts and floods, which had been happening at regular intervals in the country. There was a time when such calamities used to impact the GDP and often resulted in inflationary trends. But over the years, the impact of such calamities is neutralized, having no impact on the economy.

The external shocks include the global financial crisis of 2008 which had an adverse impact on the Indian economy as well. But the economy was able to absorb the shock significantly. With several fiscal measures and stimulus packages, no significant adverse effect was witnessed.

The next financial crisis—the eurozone crisis—impacted the Indian economy more severely since the same was in combination with the several domestic constraints (both economic and non-economic). The second slowdown had come on the heels of the previous crisis of 2008 so much so that the issues went uncontrolled.

3. Most of the workers in India have very low education and skill levels

It was estimated that less than 30 per cent of the workforce in the year 2011–2012 had educational qualifications up to secondary school level and above. The National Sample Survey Organization's (NSSO) 68th round survey, as of 2011–2012, indicates that less than one-tenth of the workers had received vocational training, either formal or informal. Although NSSO surveys grossly underestimate several types of skills of workers acquired informally (e.g., those working in cottage and handicraft household enterprises), there is no doubt that levels of skill are very low in the country.

4. Agriculture still accounts for about half of the total workforce

ILO estimates that 43 per cent of the total workforce in 2017 are agricultural workers. Whereas share of agriculture and allied sector to GDP had been at 18.20 per cent in 2013–2014.

5. The level of poverty is very high

A large proportion of the workers are poor and as such poverty is typical of a labour-surplus economy where most people are engaged in low-income activities and cannot afford to be 'unemployed'. With about half of the workers being self-employed, they share whatever work is available, leading to widespread underemployment and poverty.

6. The Indian labour market is dualistic

The Indian labour market is characterized as dualistic, where a large traditional economy coexists with a high level of growth, surplus productivity and modern economy.

7. A large majority of the workers are casual and irregular workers or petty self-employed producers and own-account workers

The following table provides the employment data from 1983 to 2011–2012. The regular wage employment percentage in 2011–2012 was 18, whereas the casual and self-employed percentage was 82.

Share (%) in Total Employment	1983	1993–1994	1999–2000	2004–2005	2009–2010	2011–2012
Regular wage employment	13.5	13.2	14.0	14.3	15.6	17.9
Formal[a]	–	–	5.4	5.6	6.4	6.8
Informal	–	–	8.6	8.6	9.2	11.0
Casual wage employment	29.0	32.0	33.2	28.9	33.5	29.9
Self-employment	57.5	54.7	52.8	56.9	51.0	52.2
Casual and self-employment	86.5	86.7	86.0	85.8	84.5	82.1
Organized sector	–	–	9.3	11.1	14.0	16.4
Unorganized sector		–	90.7	88.9	86.0	83.6

Source: Computed from unit level data of various NSSO rounds.
Note: [a]Formal employment includes the regular workers with social security in the organized sector.

8. There had been an increase in GDP, but growth in employment had been significantly low

The GDP grew at 4.7 per cent per annum during 1972–1983, employment growth was 2.4 per cent; GDP increased to 5 per cent, but employment growth declined to 2.0 per cent during 1983/1993–1994; during 1993–1994/2004–2005, GDP accelerated to 6.3 per cent, but employment growth further declined to 1.8 per cent; and during the period 2004–2005/2011–2012, when GDP growth was as high as 8.5 per cent, employment growth was insignificant, that is, at the rate of 0.5 per cent.

9. The unorganized sector contributed majorly to employment growth

The following table depicts the data of sector-wise growth in employment. As is evident from the data, most of the employment growth had been contributed by the unorganized sectors. This is characterized by low incomes and poor conditions of work.

Sectors	1972–1973/ 1983	Employment 1983/ 1993–1994	Growth 1993–1994/ 2004–2005	2004–2005/ 2011–2012
Primary	1.70	1.35	0.67	–1.98
Secondary (including mining and quarrying)	4.43	2.82	3.97	4.46
Tertiary	4.21	3.77	3.41	2.09
Non-agricultural	4.30	3.36	3.64	3.15
Total	2.44	2.02	1.84	0.45

Source: Estimated on various rounds of NSS data on employment and unemployment.

10. India's labour market is characterized by the low female participation rate

The overall LFPR stands at around 40 per cent, which for women is 23 per cent. While the male LFPR had been stable at 55–56 per cent during three decades from 1983 to 2011–2012, the female LFPR has shown a decline from around 30 per cent in 1983 to 23 per cent in 2011–2012 as evident in the following table.

Labour Force Participation Rate and Workforce Participation Rate (UPSS) by Gender (All Ages): 1983 to 2011–2012

Year	LFPR			WFPR		
	M	F	P	M	F	P
1983	55.1	30.0	42.9	53.9	29.6	42.0
1993–1994	55.6	29.0	42.8	54.5	28.6	42.0
2004–2005	55.9	29.4	43.0	54.7	28.7	42.0
2011–2012	55.6	22.5	39.5	54.4	21.9	38.6

Source: Computed from unit level data of various NSSO rounds.
Note: M—Male; F—Female; P—Persons; UPSS—Usual Principal and Subsidiary Status; LFPR—Labour Force Participation Rate and WFPR—Workforce Participation Rate.

It is a fact that a large percentage of women in India, particularly in rural India, are involved in various part-time economic activities along with their domestic care duties, which are often not measured by national surveys; this results in under-reporting of economic participation of women.

8.4. Industrial Growth in India and the Labour Market

The economy's present situation comes with a long history of policy regulations and high promises by the government, whereas in reality, the pace and level of India's industrial development has been well below expectations. It is a fact that the maximum recorded value of the share of manufacturing value added in GDP has never exceeded 19 per cent in India. In sharp contrast, that figure is above 34 per cent in Brazil, 40 per cent in China, 31 per cent in Korea and 31 per cent in Malaysia. The general observation had been that the Indian industrialists have been successful in capital-intensive areas such as automobiles, petrochemicals and pharmaceuticals, but there has been little growth in the more labour-intensive industries like the electronics manufacturing industry. The trend of industrial growth (five-year plan-wise) is shown in Table 8.2.

Plan periods from the Eighth Five-Year Plan to Eleventh Five-Year Plan had shown a steady industrial growth within 6.3–8.2 per cent. An analysis of the economic growth during the last three five-year plans depicts a very bright picture regarding the economy. The economy had 8.2 per cent plus growth during the 10th Five-Year Plan (2002–2007). Against a projected growth target of 9 per cent per year during the 11th Five-Year Plan (2007–2012), the Indian economy recorded an average annual economic growth rate of 7.5 per cent. The shortfall in achieving the targeted economic growth in the 11th Five-Year Plan was attributed to both internal and external factors, for example, global slowdown, fluctuations in international prices, strong inflationary pressures and negative growth in agriculture due to a drought-like situation [5]. The period from 2011 to 2012 saw a severe slowdown in the industrial growth and production. Figure 8.8 shows the growth rate of industrial production from 2005 to 2016.

Table 8.2 The Trend of Industrial Growth

Sl No	Plan Period	Growth Rate Plan-wise (in %)
1	Third Plan	8.2
2	1966–1967 (Annual Plan)	0.6
3	1967–1968 (Annual Plan)	1.2
4	Fourth Plan	4.4
5	Fifth Plan	5.9
6	Sixth Plan	5.9
7	Seventh Plan	8.5
8	1990–1991 (Annual Plan)	8.3
9	1991–1992 (Annual Plan)	0.6
10	Eighth Plan	7.3
11	Ninth Plan	6.3
12	Tenth Plan	8.2
13	Eleventh Plan	7.5

Source: Ministry of Commerce, Government of India.

Figure 8.8 The Growth Rate of Industrial Production

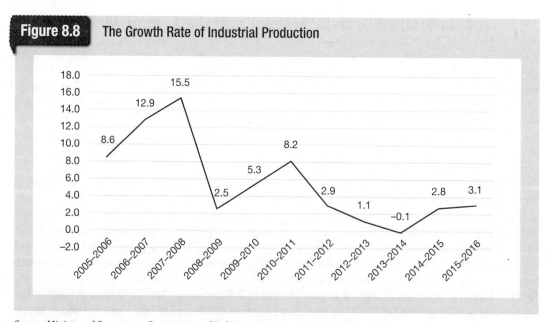

Source: Ministry of Commerce, Government of India.

As Figure 8.8 shows, the industrial production fell from 8.2 per cent in 2010–2011 to 2.9 per cent in 2011–2012. The industrial production further fell to 1.1 per cent in 2012–2013, negative 0.1 per cent in 2013–2014 and 2.8 per cent in 2014–2015.

8.5. The Changes in the Indian Labour Market in the Context of Economic Growth during the Last Three Decades

The labour market was challenged to change in the context of such economic growth. The significant changes since the economic reforms, which started in the 1990s, have radically transformed the labour market and employment conditions in the country. As is evident, there are both negative and positive aspects to these changes. Some major areas of change are as follows.

- **There has been increasing informalization of the workforce:** The economy which was supposed to transfer the workers from agriculture to non-agriculture had been slow. Post 2015, some degree of acceleration is visible which is mostly in generating employment in the informal sectors. The percentage share of contract workers in organized manufacturing sector has increased from 13 per cent in 1995 to 34 per cent in 2011, whereas the growth of regular and protected jobs has been low.
- **The increasing informalization of employment has gradually eroded the strength of trade unions:** There had been a sharp decline in the percentage of man-days lost due to strikes. Whereas there had been a considerable increase in the incidence of lockouts and closures. The scope for collective bargaining for settling industrial disputes had been constantly shrinking. It is only in the recent years that some rise in industrial unrest in certain sectors and several new manufacturing units is visible challenging the industrial peace, which is detrimental to the growth of the manufacturing sectors.
- **The decline in the participation of females in employment during 2012 as compared to 2005**: Women participation in employment (taking all age groups into account) stood at 29 per cent in 2004–2005, which decreased to 22 per cent in 2011–2012. This substantial decline has much to do with lack of appropriate opportunities for females. The employment of women remains at 20 per cent to 40 per cent, less than that of men.
- **The labour market disparities and inequalities have increased:** Disparity has emerged between the regular and casual workers as well as organized and unorganized sector workers. In 2011–2012, the average daily earnings of a casual worker stood at ₹138 in rural areas and ₹173 in urban areas and that of a regular worker at ₹298 in rural areas and ₹445 in urban areas.
- **The gap between per worker earnings in agriculture and non-agriculture has widened:** The gap between per worker earnings in agriculture and non-agriculture has considerably widened and stands at a ratio of 1:6.
- **The share of wages in total value added in manufacturing has been declining consistently**: With increase in the labour productivity, the real wages have increased on an average of over 3 per cent per year. But there had been a constant decline in the share of wages to total value added in the manufacturing sectors. The figures had been around 0.45 per cent in the 1980s, which have fallen to around 0.25 in 2009–2010.
- **Increased diversification of employment away from agriculture**: There had been diversification of employment from agriculture. A large share of this shift has gone to services and construction, and only marginally to manufacturing. Labour productivity in the manufacturing sector had been increasing. During the period 1993–1994 to 2011–2012, the productivity level of per worker has increased three times. The wage share in the organized manufacturing sector, after declining steadily until 2007–2008, has started to recover to some extent over the past few years.

- **The rise in wages has led to decline in absolute poverty:** The decline in poverty has been across all social groups. The largest decline has been observed among the SCs, STs and OBCs as well as among upper Muslims. The government's reservation policy has increased the employment of such social groups in the public sectors between 1999–2000 and 2011–2012. The most noticeable trend is the significant increase in the proportion of OBCs employed in both private and public sectors, and a significant decline in the proportion of upper-caste Hindus as well as 'others' in both categories.
- **Recent years have also witnessed a rise in the unionization of informal sector workers:** The schemes like the Mahatma Gandhi National Rural Employment Guarantee Act (MGNREGA) have contributed to worker awareness and improved their bargaining power.
- **The new emerging threat in the labour market:** The traditional IT sector is experiencing a big change which is likely to impact job profiles and opportunities. The adoption of newer techniques, for example, automation, self-service portals, cost sharing, are all dampeners on job creation in the ITES segment. The customers are seeking more productivity and value-added services, leading to innovative approaches to cost compression and adoption of automations. There is an increasing demand for higher level of skill resulting in lesser job opportunities.
- **The disruptive technologies:** The disruptive technologies such as using social media, mobility, analytics and cloud are offering new avenues of growth across verticals for IT companies. Artificial intelligence (AI) is another upcoming area. The areas of job creation which are likely to be in demand in the coming years include big data scientists, retail planners, product managers and digital marketers. There are instances of advancement of technology leading to replacement of labour-intensive approaches.
- **There has been shift of ITES jobs to tier-2, tier-3 cities and rural areas:** This shift is to make the businesses simple and cost-effective. The euphoria over call centre jobs is vanishing.

8.6. Surplus Labour Force and Unemployment

Labour market in India is suffering from surplus labour force combined with unemployment. A huge number of labourers are rendered surplus due to lack of adequate demand in different sectors which include primary, secondary and tertiary sectors. Due to high population growth rate, a huge number of labourers are continuously being added with the existing labour force leading to a huge surplus in the labour market. So to understand the impact of these factors on the labour market, one needs to study the (a) impact of population growth and (b) existing labour surplus economy and unemployment in the following discussions.

1. Population growth

India stands at the second position in the world in terms of the size of population. It is next to China. India's population constitutes nearly 17.74 per cent of the total world population, whereas her geographical area is only 2.4 per cent of the world area. The median age in India is 27 years. India's national income which is barely 2 per cent of the total global income is a clear indicator of the fact that there is a disproportionate income to the size of the world population. The population of India was 1,362,215,659 as of 21 January 2019 based on the UNO estimates. The statistics of population of India are as follows.

Population of India (2019 and Historical)

Year	Population	Yearly Change (in %)	Yearly Change	Migrants (Net)	Median Age	Fertility Rate	Density (P/Km²)	Urban Population (in %)	Urban Population	Country's Share of World Population (in %)	World Population	India Global Rank
2019	1,368,737,513	1.08	14,685,659	−490,000	27.0	2.41	460	33.6	460,249,853	17.74	7,714,576,923	2
2018	1,354,051,854	1.11	14,871,727	−490,000	27.0	2.41	455	33.2	449,945,237	17.74	7,632,819,325	2
2017	1,339,180,127	1.13	15,008,773	−490,000	27.0	2.41	450	32.8	439,801,466	17.74	7,550,262,101	2
2016	1,324,171,354	1.15	15,117,374	−490,000	27.0	2.41	445	32.5	429,802,441	17.73	7,466,964,280	2
2015	1,309,053,980	1.24	15,614,658	−515,643	26.7	2.44	440	32.1	419,938,867	17.73	7,383,008,820	2
2010	1,230,980,691	1.47	17,372,403	−582,766	25.1	2.80	414	30.3	372,901,884	17.69	6,958,169,159	2
2005	1,144,118,674	1.67	18,213,552	−390,182	23.8	3.14	385	28.8	329,516,783	17.49	6,542,159,383	2
2000	1,053,050,912	1.86	18,513,623	−143,380	22.7	3.48	354	27.4	288,365,219	17.14	6,145,006,989	2
1995	960,482,795	2.00	18,069,863	−110,587	21.8	3.83	323	26.5	254,314,016	16.70	5,751,474,416	2
1990	870,133,480	2.17	17,693,362	9,029	21.1	4.27	293	25.5	221,979,229	16.32	5,330,943,460	2
1985	781,666,671	2.33	16,976,631	116,619	20.6	4.68	263	24.4	190,338,784	16.04	4,873,781,796	2
1980	696,783,517	2.32	15,096,359	231,436	20.2	4.97	234	23.2	161,445,950	15.63	4,458,411,534	2
1975	621,301,720	2.34	13,544,641	428,664	19.8	5.41	209	21.4	132,732,329	15.23	4,079,087,198	2
1970	553,578,513	2.15	11,175,230	−69,036	19.4	5.72	186	19.8	109,709,315	14.96	3,700,577,650	2
1965	497,702,365	2.06	9,644,351	−21,142	20.8	5.90	167	18.8	93,540,800	14.90	3,339,592,688	2
1960	449,480,608	1.89	8,042,311	−30,805	20.3	5.90	151	17.9	80,586,315	14.82	3,033,212,527	2
1955	409,269,055	1.69	6,588,771	−21,142	20.8	5.90	138	17.6	71,906,548	14.76	2,772,242,535	2

2. Population and rise in job seekers

The Indian economy has been distinctly identified to be having a different structure of population growth. A stand-alone analysis provides the following picture on the growth of population:

1. During the years 1960–2000, the country's population more than doubled—from 44.8 crore to 140 crore.
2. During the years 2001–2011, the population of India grew by 181 million.
3. The population increased to 1.27 billion by 2013. By 2013, Indian population constituted 17.5 per cent of the world's population.
4. It is predicted that the Indian population 'is likely to grow substantially in the coming few decades' and is likely to touch 170–180 crore. The state of stabilization will come only after 2050–2070.
5. According to the WHO, the life expectancy of the Indian population has nearly doubled since the 1950s, from 38.7 for men and 37.1 for women to 64.4 for men and 67.6 for women today.
6. The death rate of the Indian population has been declining since Independence. Infant mortality stands at around 44 per 1,000 live births in 2013, which was 200–225 out of 1,000 in the year 1947. This figure is still continuing to fall.
7. Population ages 15–64 (% of total) in India was 66 as of 2016. It is the highest value over the past 56 years, whereas its lowest value was 55.22 in the year 1966.

8.7. Employment Growth in the Indian Economy

The approaches and policies adopted for employment generation in the Indian economy had varied with changing perceptions and conditions. The development agenda of the Indian economy, since the very beginning of development planning post-Independence, adopted the strategy of industrialization-based growth to generate adequate employment to absorb the moderately growing labour force [6]. In the initial years of development planning, unemployment was not expected to emerge as a major problem. It was assumed that reasonable growth rate and labour-intensive sectors would prevent any increase in unemployment and this expectation continued from one five-year plan to another during the 1950s and 1960s. Economy grew at a rate of around 3.5 per cent as against the planned rate of 5 per cent per annum. Yet employment grew at a rate of 2 per cent per annum. However, since labour force growth was at 2.5 per cent as against the assumed growth of less than 2 per cent per annum, there was an increase in unemployment.

In the mid-1970s, it was clear that the achievements relating to growth and employment had fallen far short of expectations and the employment growth was too little to absorb the growth in the labour force of 2.5 per cent, resulting in the growth of unemployment.

The Fifth Five-Year Plan (1974–1979) sought to address the employment issue by reorienting the pattern of growth in favour of employment-intensive sectors. A strong opinion emerged that growth alone cannot solve the problems of poverty and unemployment, and therefore, a number of special employment and poverty alleviation programmes were launched. The programmes were mostly of the following two kinds:

- Providing financial and other assistance for productive self-employment.
- Offering supplementary wage employment to the underemployed.

The fact is that over the years, these programmes have been continued in one form or the other since they have been modified or integrated.

NIP of 1991 with market-led growth had envisaged to generate substantial employment by restructuring production in favour of labour-intensive activities. NIP, initiated in 1991, had duel objectives. They are as follows.

1. **Achieving stabilization in the short run:** The stabilization policies were seen on two fronts: the fiscal policy and balance of payments.
2. **Structural adjustment in the long run:** The structural adjustment policies aimed at bringing about a series of changes in the existing industrial and trade policies that would lead to a shift from public sector-led investment and growth to market-led private domestic and foreign investments, with an emphasis on efficiency and competitiveness as the drivers of growth.

It was argued that liberalization of trade, finance and an increased role for market-driven growth would not only generate a higher rate of output for growth but would also lead to restructuring of production in favour of labour-intensive activities and, therefore, contribute to an increase in employment. Evidence, however, indicates that this expectation has not been realized despite the achievement of relatively high growth.

The fact was that NIP hardly accorded any priority to employment generation. There had been changes in the macroeconomic plan which was more of outward-oriented liberalization in 1991, and this resulted in a kind of rise in joblessness in the 1900s. The macroeconomic reforms and policies led to actions that went against the goals of generating employment creation as part of the development strategy. Such governmental strategy included:

1. The government was under compulsion to reduce public expenditure in order to contain the fiscal deficit during this period.
2. This resulted in the reduction in budgetary provisions for employment programmes in the 1990s.
3. The government policies aimed at the reduction of subsidization in interest rates, and the non-performing assets (NPAs) of banks also had an adverse impact on the availability and cost of credit for employment-intensive sectors such as small and rural industries.

> However, such instances of conflict between the objective of employment creation and macroeconomic policies have been few and prevailed for shorter periods, and public expenditure and conducive policy initiatives to promote employment have largely been restored. [6]

4. FDI increased from 0.3 per cent in 1991 to over 3 per cent in 2010 of the GDP. Most of it, however, has been concentrated in the sectors pertaining to chemicals, engineering, transport equipment and fuel, and very little in the labour-intensive sectors such as textiles and clothing. Though some of the employment-intensive sectors that attracted a significant inflow of foreign investment during the period 1991–2003 are food processing and services. In general, there had been a bias for investing in labour-saving industrial processes so as to get the benefits of increased labour productivity, thereby resulting in growth in GDP.

During the 1990s, the export sector was also seen as an important source of employment. Trade policy had thus become, for the first time, an important instrument not only for achieving faster growth but also for facilitating for more jobs. Trade and the inflow of investment were expected to boost employment in the following two major ways:

1. By accelerating the growth rate.
2. By offering a comparative advantage based on exports and investment in labour-intensive industries.

But the employment growth which was averaged to around 2 per cent during the 1980s was lowered during the 1990s. The employment in the manufacturing sector had grown reasonably fast, averaging around 2.5 per cent per annum. The notable point was that there was no significant difference between the employment growth in EOI and import-competing industries in the manufacturing sectors. During the 1980s, the employment performance of export-oriented manufacturing industries was significantly better; the employment in these industries grew at the rate of 3.36 per cent per annum, as against the corresponding 2.67 per cent in import-competing manufacturing industries during the period 1990–1997 [7]. The following table compiles the unemployment data from 1972 to 2000.

Unemployment Rates (% of Labour Force)				
Year	UPS	UPSS	CWS	CDS
1972–1973	3.80	1.61	432	8.35
1977–1978	4.23	2.47	4.48	8.18
1983–1984	2.77	1.90	431	8.28
1987–1988	3.77	2.62	4.80	609
1993–1994	2.56	1.90	3.63	603
1999–2000	2.81	2.23	4.41	7.32

Notes:
UPS: Usual principal status. A person is considered unemployed according to this concept, if available, but without work for major part of the year.
UPSS: Usual principal and subsidiary status includes, besides UPS, those available but unable to find work on a subsidiary basis during a year.
CWS: Current weekly status. A person is unemployed, if available, but unable to find work even for one hour during the reference week.
CDS: Current daily status measures unemployment in terms of person days of unemployment of all persons in the labour force during the reference week.

Looking at different rates of unemployment, it is clear that underemployment is a problem of much larger magnitude than unemployment. In the year 1999–2000, the UPS unemployment rate was estimated to be 2.81 per cent as compared to the CDS rate of 7.32 per cent. Thus, the employment challenge in the Indian economy consists not only of creating jobs for the unemployed but also providing additional work to the underemployed.

An analysis on efforts to enhance employment generation from the Seventh to Twelfth Five-Year Plan indicates that:

1. During the Seventh Five-Year Plan (1985–1990), the focus was to generate productive employment as the centre of development strategy [8].

2. The focus on employment continued during the Eighth Plan (1992–1997), which adopted a strategy for achieving a high rate of growth along with emphasis on employment generation by promoting the growth of employment-intensive sectors.
3. The Ninth Five-Year Plan (1997–2002) reiterated the employment-oriented strategy by emphasizing that growth could be made more employment-friendly by 'concentrating on sectors, sub-sectors and technologies that are more labour intensive, in regions characterized by a higher incidence of unemployment and under-employment' [9].
4. The Tenth Five-Year Plan period (2002–2007) witnessed the creation of about 4.7 crore employment opportunities, which was quite close to the target of 5 crore (Planning Commission, 2008: 92). But before strategizing for the Tenth Five-Year Plan, it was well realized that the growth in employment was slow in the 1990s, despite a relatively higher growth in GDP, which led to renewed urgency among the planners to focus on employment by the end of the 1990s. The Planning Commission constituted the following two committees in quick succession:
   - Task Force on Employment Opportunities in 1999
   - Special Group on Targeting 10 Million Employment Opportunities per year in 2001
   The focus of these committees was to examine the trends and potential for employment generation and suggest a strategy for creating employment opportunities in order to attain the goal of employment for all within a specified period of time. Their assessments and recommendations [10] were used in the formulation of the Tenth Plan (2002–2007).

   During the Tenth Five-Year Plan, it was realized that mere job creation was not sufficient to address the issue of persisting poverty among more than one-fourth of the workers. A group commonly termed as the 'working poor', which was mainly the outcome of low levels of productivity and poor-skill endowments, among them needed to be addressed. The strategy, therefore, had to be re-designed for approaching the issue of employment generation on two fronts:
   - Accelerating the growth of employment in the formal segment.
   - Improving the quality of jobs (in terms of productivity, earnings and protection of workers) in the unorganized segment.
   So a number of special programmes pertaining to different sectors were introduced, particularly in the agriculture sector and related activities, small and medium enterprises, the non-farm rural sector and social sectors such as education and health care. There were also policy changes for the faster development of sectors of high labour intensity such as construction, tourism, information and communication technology and financial services.
5. The achievement of the Eleventh Plan for employment generation has been less than satisfactory. There has been an addition of only 0.276 crore job opportunities during the periods 2004–2005 and 2009–2010. The Eleventh Plan (2007–2012), strategically, called for more 'inclusive' growth and focused on employment as a central element of such growth. The Plan had set a target of generating 5.8 crore employment opportunities with emphasis on the productivity and income aspects of employment. The objective was to address the problems of the working poor and to effect improvements in the employability of the poor through the implementation of a concerted and large-scale programme for training and upgradation of skills, particularly among the poor [11].
6. The Twelfth Plan (2012–2017) reiterated the centrality of employment creation for achieving faster and more inclusive growth. The Plan had set the target of 3.38 crore job creation. It proposed to make the manufacturing sector a growth engine for employment generation [12].

The data of employment growth against GDP is as follows.

Year	1972–1977	1977–1982	1982–1986	1986–1993	1993–1999	1999–2004	2004–2009	2009–2011	2011–2015
Employment growth (in %)	2.6	2.1	1.7	2.4	1	2.8	0.1	1.4	0.6
GDP growth (in %)	4.6	3.9	4	5.6	6.8	5.7	8.7	7.4	6.8

Between 2013 and 2015, total employment actually shrank by 0.7 crore, and since 2015, there has also been an absolute decline in job growth. There will be stagnation in job creation in India as indicated in the 2017 World Employment and Social Outlook report of UNO. UNO's observations are that in India, the economic growth trends would be lagging behind employment needs.

The economy is not creating enough high-paying jobs either, so the problem is not unemployment but underemployment. The average monthly earnings were estimated to be up to ₹10,000 in 2015. In comparison, the minimum salary recommended by the Seventh Central Pay Commission (CPC) was ₹18,000 per month. This suggests that a large majority of Indians are not being paid what may be termed a living wage. During the 1970s and 1980s, when GDP growth was around 3–4 per cent, employment growth was around 2 per cent per annum. Since the 1990s, and particularly in the 2000s, GDP growth has accelerated to 7 per cent but employment growth has slowed to 1 per cent or even less. The ratio of GDP growth to employment growth is less than 1 per cent.

8.8. Informality Persists and the Quality of Employment Remains the Main Challenge

The Indian economy is characterized by a very high degree of informal natured jobs. The majority of workers in India are informally employed.

The organized sector in the Indian labour market in 2017 generated only about 3 crore jobs, but the informal sector created nearly 44 crore jobs. As per the NSSO survey, the organized sector accounted for only about 10 per cent of total employment in 1999–2000 and 12 per cent in 2004–2005. The percentage further increased to 17 in 2011–2012. The NSSO survey also indicates that all those employed in the organized sector were not formal workers; only 7.5 per cent of the total workers were formally employed and enjoyed regular jobs with social security benefits. The organized sector which comprises about 8 crore workers has 58 per cent (i.e., 4.6 crore) workers in the 'informal workers category', with neither a secure tenure of employment nor any protection against the contingent risks during or after employment. In fact, the proportion of informal workers rose over time from 41 per cent of organized sector employment in 1999–2000 to 48 per cent in 2004–2005 and further to 58 per cent in 2011–2012. Thus, of all the workers in the organized and unorganized sectors together 92.5 per cent were in 'informal employment'. Only 7.5 per cent had secure job tenures and social security against contingent risks of work and life. The share of informal workers in the organized sector (i.e., workers without access to social security) increased significantly because of a greater use of workers on contract and other forms of casual labour.

The overall proportion of informal workers in total employment (e.g., unorganized sector workers plus informal workers in the organized sector) has remained around 92 per cent, which is relatively stable. The available data also indicates the following nature of employment in the informal sector:

- A large group, 32.2 per cent, of informal workers are own-account workers.
- The informal employees in the informal sector are 30 per cent.
- The informal workers contributing family workers is 17.9 per cent.

The following table indicates the distribution of workers by the production unit and employment status (2011–2012 in %).

| Employment Status | Informality | Production Unit | | | |
		Formal Sector Enterprises	Informal Sector Enterprises	Households	Total Employment
Own-account workers	Informal		32.3	–	32.3
	Formal	0.5			0.5
Employees	Informal		1.3		1.3
	Formal	0.1			0.1
Contributing family workers	Informal	0.1	17.9		18.0
Employees	Informal	9.6	30.0	0.8	40.4
	Formal	7.0	0.4	0.01	7.4
Members of producer's cooperatives	Informal		–		–
	Formal				–

Source: Calculated from NSSO's Employment-Unemployment Survey, 2011–2012.
Note: Covers employed persons of all ages. Cells shaded in dark grey refer to jobs which, by definition, do not exist in the type of production unit. Cells shaded in light grey refer to formal jobs. Unshaded cells represent various types of informal workers.

Some examples of informality in job market have been discussed further.

R. C. Bhargav, the Chairman of MSIL expressed that Maruti Suzuki, India's largest carmaker, had not been making any substantial additions to its workforce. However, when it rolled out 1.5 million cars a year, it created anywhere between 800,000 and a million jobs in the unorganized sectors. These jobs were in the area of driver training, repairs, spare parts shops, insurance, dealerships and so on. That applied to a whole lot of other industries as well, where informal jobs were created in the thousands in the downstream sector.

Many of them are created by Flipkart, Myntra and Snapdeal and similar organizations in India, and these jobs are not captured in the data generated by the government.

To conclude, three decades of rapid growth have not significantly transformed the labour market and employment conditions in the country. The growth process has not been inclusive, and a significant proportion of the population has not benefited. A disconnect appears to exist between growth and employment, and so between the economic growth and the labour market. Generating employment in the context of both economic and population growth has all along been a priority of the Indian Government because employment generation has an effect on both economic growth and poverty reduction. But there had been incidences of jobless growth in the economy.

The Labour Ministry's 27th Quarterly Employment Survey report identified eight employment-intensive industries, that is, textiles, leather, metals, automobiles, gems and jewellery, transport, IT/BPO and handloom/power loom. The said report further reported that by FY 2015–2016, these sectors had lost 43,000 jobs in the first quarter. The second quarter was better with 134,000 new jobs. The same sectors had a record of creating 0.11 crore jobs in 2010. But in the following five years, however, 0.15 million jobs were lost. The FY 2014–2015 saw a growth of 500,000 new jobs and the year 2013–2014 saw 300,000 new jobs.

Some disconcerting features of employment growth that have emerged in recent years are as follows:

- The employment growth has declined.
- Sectors with higher employment potential have registered relatively slower growth.
- Agriculture continues to be the largest employer because the non-agricultural sectors have not generated enough employment to cause a shift of workforce.
- Most of the employment growth had been contributed by the unorganized sector, which is characterized by low incomes and poor conditions of work.
- Although employment growth in the organized sector has picked up, it has largely been led by an increase in employment of casual and contract labour.
- There has been a steady growth of workers in the organized sector in the recent decade; while there has been some increase in regular formal wage employment, the bulk of this increase has been in the informal component.

8.9. The Pace of Employment Creation

The pace of employment creation in the Indian economy as discussed above, with the quality of the jobs that are created is a matter of concern. The highlights are as follows:

1. **The growth of regular jobs is slow:** While the number of jobs in the organized sector is now rising, only 18 per cent of employment can be described as regular wage employment, and about 7 per cent is formal; two-thirds of the growth in regular jobs since 2004–2005 has been informal.
2. **Most wage work is casual, contract work is on the rise:** There is a great deal of informal self-employment which is subject to a variety of market and other insecurities, and only a small fraction of workers have adequate social security coverage.
3. **Indian labour markets are poorly regulated:** There are a large number of laws regulating employment conditions, especially in the organized sector, but these laws are largely not followed. This is due to many reasons: (a) they are poorly designed and often inapplicable, (b) enforcement mechanisms are weak, (c) incidence of corruption is high and (d) occasionally they undermine the short-term interests of both workers and employers. Trade unions are fragmented.

4. **Most employment is of low quality with low productivity:** Safety standards are widely ignored and health risks are given low priority. This is to some extent a consequence of informality and under-regulation, and also reflects lack of training and awareness, and the priority of workers for meeting their urgent income needs regardless of the consequences. Child labour is declining but not yet eliminated.

5. **There is a highly unbalanced regional pattern of employment creation:** This has in some areas led to vast and uncontrolled migration in search of work. In rural Bihar, for example, up to half of adult men migrate regularly for work outside the state for shorter or longer periods.

6. **Regional inequality is just one dimension of widening inequality in Indian labour markets in general:** While real wages are rising across the board, they have clearly risen more at the top of the labour market hierarchy.

7. **A variety of discriminations and vulnerabilities persist and underpin the segmentation of labour markets:** Women workers are particularly disadvantaged in terms of their access to the labour market, the quality of work and wages. Home-based work, mainly undertaken by women, is often paid at extraordinarily low rates.

8. **Disadvantaged social groups are mostly concentrated in low-productivity sectors such as agriculture and construction:** The poverty rate among these social groups when compared to the all India level is disproportionately high.

But there is an important positive side to the labour market as well, which is as follows:

1. Employment growth has, by and large, kept pace with labour force growth, and unemployment rates are low, except for some particularly deprived groups and for relatively better-off young people who are seeking formal jobs.

2. While some part of the employment growth may be due to work sharing at low productivity, it is not the only or even the main factor—for real wages have been rising and poverty has been declining steadily.

3. There is a growing middle class, which includes many better-educated and skilled workers, with rising incomes and high levels of consumption.

4. There is extraordinary growth in some advanced sectors, including IT, pharmaceuticals, automobiles and other areas, and while direct employment creation in these sectors may be limited, there are important spillover effects which lead to job creation elsewhere, especially in services. The construction sector is growing particularly fast.

5. There is a popular movement for both rights at work and the right to work, which has given rise to innovative and successful new policies like MGNREGA.

6. Persistent structural inequalities by caste and gender are increasingly being recognized and tackled by popular movements and reservation policies.

7. After a long period of organized sector employment stagnation, recent data suggests that economic growth is finally leading to substantial job creation in the modern industry, where employment was growing at 8 per cent per annum in the mid-2000s and continued to grow through the economic slowdown.

8. At least until 2011–2012, the labour market improved through the period of crisis with a decline in the share of casual wage work, decrease in the wage gap between casual and regular workers and between women and men, and some increase in the share of wages in organized industry.

Downsizing

There had been instances of large manufacturers trimming operations, thereby throwing many jobs out of the labour market.

- Nokia, locked in a tax dispute with Indian authorities, shut down its handset making factory in Chennai in November 2014, rendering 8,000 workers jobless. For Microsoft, the new owner of the Nokia handset brand, making smartphones in China and Vietnam was cheaper.
- In October 2015, Goldman Sachs Asset Management of the United States exited its onshore India-based mutual funds business, selling it out to Reliance Capital Asset Management (RCAM) in India for ₹243 crore.
- Cement major Lafarge in January 2016, planned to sell its 11 metric ton business in India.
- Crompton Greaves divested its consumer business for ₹2,800 crore from March 2016.
- It has been announced by Larsen & Toubro (L&T), the engineering and construction giant, that they will exit all businesses with revenues under ₹1,000 crore, even if it means closing some without finding buyers.
- The $3,500 crore Essar Group is reported to be in talks to sell part of its refinery business as well as a portion of its ports business to reduce its steep debt.

8.10. The Initiatives of the Government to Meet the Challenges in the Labour Market

In the context of such economic growth and globalized market in an emerging economy like India, the projection is of having a skilled labour surplus of 245 million workers by 2030, whereas most of the developed and developing economies are expected to grapple with talent crunch at that time, according to the organizational consulting firm Korn Ferry [13]. The business organizations in India are encountered with various challenges. Such challenges include getting 'employable resources' at the competitive cost, who are competitive in the globalized market context. There have been various government initiatives to initiate economic growth and generate employment. Some of these initiatives which have nexus with the labour market are: 'Make in India', 'Digital India', 'Startup India' and 'Skill India'. All these initiatives have the focused objective of economic growth, employment generation and ensuring a quality life for citizens.

1. Make in India

In the month of September 2014, the Government of India launched Make in India, an ambitious initiative. The mission was to transform India into a global design and manufacturing hub. The initiative planned to increase the contribution of manufacturing sector to India's GDP to 25 per cent from current 15 per cent, as in 2014, and also to generate employment. This initiative is expected to increase the purchasing power of the Indian consumers, resulting in a multiplier effect which would further boost demand and economic development. This is likely to turn out as a bonus above the new investors, initiatives.

Programme Structure of Make in India

The implementation plans of the Make in India initiative can be studied under the following segments:

a. The government identified 25 key industries having high growth potential for promoting investment in these industries through marketing, infrastructure development, reducing compliance requirements and providing monetary concessions. The objective of the government was to increase employment as well as FDIs in these industries. In these identified sectors, the government policy had scope for 100 per cent FDI. The 25 industries are: automobiles, automobile components, aviation, biotechnology, chemicals, construction, defence manufacturing, electrical machinery, electronic systems, food processing, IT and business process management, leather, media and entertainment, mining, oil and gas, pharmaceuticals, ports and shipping, railways, renewable energy, roads and highways, space and astronomy, textiles and garments, thermal power, tourism, and healthcare and wellness.

b. The business process was made easier from setting up through production, distribution and sales. To encourage production, the government policy made provisions to extend the licences, self-certifications and reduced compliance requirements for encouraging FDI. The focus was to improve the system and facilitate the ease of doing business in India. The objective was to facilitate more production, distribution and sales, thereby achieving higher levels of employment and increasing the purchasing power of consumers. In addition, the objective was to achieve higher money circulation and thus economic growth through Make in India. This was deemed to create opportunity by way of the ease of doing business in India.

c. Five industrial corridors were identified across the country which would provide a framework of manufacturing and logistics network. National Industrial Corridor Development Authority (NICDA) was established to converge and integrate the development of all industrial corridors. The five industrial corridors were:
    *   Delhi–Mumbai Industrial Corridor (DMIC)
    *   Bengaluru–Mumbai Economic Corridor (BMEC)
    *   Chennai–Bengaluru Industrial Corridor (CBIC)
    *   Visakhapatnam–Chennai Industrial Corridor (VCIC)
    *   Amritsar–Kolkata Industrial Corridor (AKIC)

d. The government continued to provide necessary support and concessions required over a period of time until its vision to convert India into a manufacturing hub and the top FDI destination became a reality. The various concessions were:
    *   Amending labour laws to provide flexibility in working hours.
    *   Simplifying the process of obtaining industrial licence.
    *   Extending validity of industrial licence to three years from the current two years.
    *   Twenty-four manufacturing cities were identified and are being developed in phases.

2. Digital India

The Digital India programme is a flagship programme of the Government of India with focus to transform India into a digitally empowered society and knowledge economy. The history of e-governance of India indicates that e-governance initiatives in India took a broader dimension in the mid-1990s, with emphasis on citizen-centric services. Later on, many states/union territories started various e-governance projects. Since these e-governance projects were citizen-centric, they could make lesser than the desired impact. The Government of India launched National e-Governance Plan (NeGP) in 2006 under which 31 Mission Mode Projects covering various domains were initiated. Despite the successful implementation of many e-governance projects across the country, e-governance as a whole was not able to make the desired impact and fulfil all its objectives. The Digital India initiative of the government which focuses on three core components, that is, creating digital infrastructure, delivering services digitally and increasing the digital literacy, will go a long way in facilitating the economy's growth process. It was felt that a lot more thrust was required to ensure e-governance in the country to promote inclusive growth. So in order to transform the entire ecosystem of public services through the use of IT, the Government of India launched the 'Digital India Programme' with the vision to transform India into a digitally empowered society and knowledge economy.

The objective of Digital India is to come out with innovative ideas and practical solutions to empower every citizen with access to digital services, knowledge and information. This also includes best practices and policies that help in achieving the vision of Digital India and make it a reality. Digital India is a campaign launched by the Government of India to ensure the government services are made available to citizens electronically by improved online infrastructure and by increasing the Internet connectivity or by making the country digitally empowered in the field of technology. The initiative includes plans to connect rural areas with high-speed Internet networks. Digital India consists of three core components: the development of secure and stable digital infrastructure, delivering government services digitally and universal digital literacy. Bharat Broadband Network Limited (BBNL) which executes the BharatNet project is the custodian of Digital India project. It was planned that BharatNet will connect all the 625,000 villages of India by December 2018. Some of the facilities which were to be provided through this initiative are Bharat net digital locker, e-education, e-health, e-sign, e-shopping and national scholarship portal. As part of Digital India, the Indian Government planned to launch Botnet cleaning centres.

The NeGP aims at bringing all the front-end government services online.

- MyGov.in is a platform to share inputs and ideas on matters of policy and governance through which a citizen can engage in the process of governance, through the 'Discuss', 'Do' and 'Disseminate' approach.
- UMANG (Unified Mobile Application for New-age Governance) is a Government of India all-in-one unified secure multi-channel, multi-platform, multi-lingual and multi-service freeware mobile app for accessing over 1,200 central and state government services in multiple Indian languages over Android, iOS, Windows and USSD (feature phone) devices, including services such as Aadhar, DigiLocker, Bharat Bill Pay, EPFO services, Pradhan Mantri Kaushal Vikas Yojana (PMKVY) services, AICTE, CBSE, tax and fee or utilities bills payments, education, job search, tax, business, health, agriculture, travel, Indian railway tickets bookings, birth certificates, e-District, e-Panchayat, police clearance, passport, other utility services from private companies and more.
- The eSign framework allows citizens to digitally sign a document online using Aadhar authentication.
- The Swachh Bharat Mission mobile app is being used by people and government organizations for achieving the goals of Swachh Bharat Mission.
- The e-Hospital application provides important services such as online registration, payment of fees and appointment, online diagnostic reports and enquiring availability of blood online.

3. Startup India

Startup India is a flagship initiative of the Government of India. The campaign was first announced by the Government of India on 15 August 2015. It was intended to build a strong ecosystem for nurturing innovation and startups in the country that would drive sustainable economic growth and generate large-scale employment opportunities. Through this initiative, the government aims to empower startups to grow through innovation and design. With this plan, the government hopes to accelerate spreading of the startup movement from digital/technology sector to a wide array of sectors including agriculture, manufacturing, social sector, health care and education, and from existing tier-1 cities to tier-2 and tier-3 cities including semi-urban and rural areas.

The Startup Action Plan was divided across the following areas:

- Simplification and handholding
- Funding support and incentives
- Industry–Academia partnership and incubation

An additional area of focus relating to this initiative was to discard restrictive state government policies within this domain, such as Licence Raj, land permissions, foreign investment proposals and environmental clearances.

4. Skill India

Skill India is a campaign launched by the Government of India on 15 July 2015 which aims to train over 40 crore people in different skills by 2022. It includes various initiatives of the government such as 'National Skill Development Mission', 'National Policy on Skill Development and Entrepreneurship, 2015', 'PMKVY' and the 'Skill Loan Scheme'.

The schemes for the skill development launched by the Government of India are as follows:

1. Deen Dayal Upadhyaya Grameen Kaushalya Yojana
2. PMKVY
3. Financial Assistance for Skill Training of Persons with Disabilities
4. National Apprenticeship Promotion Scheme
5. Craftsmen Training Scheme
6. Apprenticeship Training
7. Skill Development for Minorities
8. Green Skill Development Programme

The National Skill Development Corporation India (NSDC) was set up as a one of its kind public–private partnership company with the primary mandate of catalyzing the skills landscape in India. It is based on the following pillars:

1. Create large and good quality vocational institutes.
2. Reduce risk by providing patient capital. Including grants and equality.
3. Enable the creation and sustainability of support systems required for skill development. This includes the industry-led sector skill councils.

PMKVY is the flagship scheme of the Ministry of Skill Development and Entrepreneurship. The objectives are to enable a large number of Indian youth to take up industry-relevant skill training that will help them in securing a better livelihood. Individuals with prior learning experience or skills will also be assessed and certified under Recognition of Prior Learning (RPL). Under this

Scheme, training and assessment fees are completely paid by the government. PMKVY is applicable to any candidate of Indian nationality who is unemployed, school or college dropout, or as identified by the Sector Skill Council (SSC) for their respective job roles.

The objective of the National Policy on Skill Development and Entrepreneurship, 2015, was to meet the challenge of skilling at scale with speed and standard (quality). It aims to provide an umbrella framework to all skilling activities being carried out within the country, and align them to common standards.

Skill Loan scheme was launched by the government on 15 July 2015 with a view to support youth who wish to go through skill training programmes in the country. This scheme has replaced earlier IBA Model Loan Scheme for Vocational Education and Training. Any Indian national who has secured admission in a course run by Industrial Training Institutes, Polytechnics or a school recognized by central or state education boards or in a college affiliated to a recognized university, training partners affiliated NSDC Sector Skill Councils, State Skill Mission, State Skill Corporation can avail loan for the purpose.

The Government of Kerala with the objective of 'skilling the young workforce of Kerala and elevating their skills to global standards for employment in India and abroad' has set up an academy under the name Kerala Academy for Skills Excellence (KASE). The academy is a non-profit organization, and is the nodal agency for facilitating and coordinating various skill development initiatives of the state. The total workforce in Kerala, according to the 2001 Census, is around 1.03 crore out of which 0.78 crore are males and only 0.25 crore are females.

The reported figures of unemployment indicate that the state of Kerala has the highest rate of unemployment among the big states in the country, which stands at 7.4 per cent. It puts Kerala's unemployment rate at three times higher than the national average (2.3%) unemployment rate. Following is some data on unemployment rates in Kerala:

1. The percentage of unemployment among the age group between 15 and 29 in the rural areas is 21.7.
2. The percentage of unemployment among the age group between 15 and 29 in the urban areas is 18.

The situation is worse in the case of Kerala women. The unemployment rate of women is 47.4 per cent, as compared to 9.7 per cent of men. The number of those employed in the organized sector fell from 12.26 lakh in 2000 to 11.4 lakh in 2005 and then to 10.88 lakh in 2013. There was a reduction of 11.3 per cent over 13 years.

The state employment data also projects that employment in agriculture fell from 7.5 per cent in 2004–2005 to 5.9 per cent in 2014–2015. Whereas there had been marked improvement in the service sector which increased from 44.7 per cent in 2004–2005 to 50.43 per cent in 2014–2015.

The manufacturing sector in the state accounted for only 20.4 per cent of the total employment. Self-employed workers made up 37.7 per cent of the total workforce during the year. In comparison, regular/salaried employees accounted for 22.5 per cent and casual labourers comprised 39.8 per cent of the workforce [14].

The youth workforce participation rate is quite low in Kerala as compared to India as a whole. In India the youth workforce participation rate is 42 per cent, whereas in Kerala it is only 24 per cent. Again among the males it is 53 per cent in India and 38 per cent in Kerala. On the other hand, the female youth workforce participation is about 30 per cent in India and in Kerala it is only 10 per cent. In spite of the fact that there are sufficient state government initiatives for skill development and availability of skilled manpower, the unemployment rate continues to be alarming.

8.10.1. Skill Development and Growth Initiatives

- Government of India has prioritized sustainability as the key aspect of India's development. To achieve this, the government aims to encourage education, skill development, digital connectivity and entrepreneurship in a sustainable manner.
- The government launched the Startup India initiative and unveiled the Startup Action Plan which includes creation of a dedicated startup fund worth ₹10,000 crore (US$ 148 crore) apart from other incentives such as no tax on profits for first three years and relaxed labour laws.
- The Government of India has certified 20 private organizations as incubators under the Startup India Action Plan, which are expected to promote entrepreneurship, provide pre-incubation training and a seed fund for high growth start-ups in the country.
- The Government of India aims to improve its ease of doing business ranking from 130 at present to within the top 100 by 2016 and the top 50 by 2017, based on reforms undertaken in areas such as construction permits, enforcing contracts and starting business, especially by top cities such as Mumbai and Delhi.
- The Ministry of Commerce and Industry plans to establish India as a hub for world-class designing by setting up four National Institute of Design (NIDs) across the country, aimed at providing skills to empower India's human capital.

A part of the report was published in 'HuffPost.in' on 25 September 2018.[2]

Rate of Unemployment in India Highest in 20 Years: Report

NEW DELHI—The biggest new challenge facing India's policymakers and administrators is rapidly rising unemployment, says a report released on Tuesday by the Centre for Sustainable Employment of the Azim Premji University.

'Unemployment levels have been steadily rising, and after several years of staying around 2–3%, the headline rate of unemployment reached 5% in 2015, with youth unemployment being a very high 16%,' the State of Working India 2018 (SWI) report said. 'This rate of unemployment is the highest seen in India in at least the last 20 years,' the report added.

This shortage of jobs is compounded by depressed wages, with 82% of men and 92% of women earning less than ₹10,000 per month.

The report also notes that the growth in GDP hasn't resulted in a commensurate increase in employment.

'A 10% increase in GDP now results in less than 1% increase in employment,' says the study.

'It used to be said that India's problem is not unemployment but underemployment and low wages. But a new feature of the economy is a high rate of open unemployment, which is now over five percent overall.'

The report, co-written by a group of researchers, policymakers, journalists and civil society activists, has primarily relied on data from the National Sample Survey Office and the Employment-Unemployment Survey (EUS) of the Labour Bureau—the last of which was conducted in 2015–2016.

[2] https://www.huffingtonpost.in/2018/09/25/rate-of-unemployment-highest-in-india-in-the-20-years-says-report_a_23541136/

Chapter Summary

1. There is a global need for 'closing the talent gap in the emerging world economies'. During the coming periods, the economic growth rate in the EM would be higher than the advanced countries. Since the developing countries (BRIC) will grow at the rate of 7.9 per cent and 7.7 per cent, as in the case of China and India, respectively, there is the need in the emerging nations for an enormous enhancement in the job market.

2. The investments as a percentage of GDP have come down in the advanced economies, the same have considerably gone up in the EM as well as the developing economies, and EM with their better performance trends will better tap the global capital flows.

3. The Indian labour market is characterized by:
   a. Faster growth in GDP.
   b. There is economic resilience to external and internal shocks.
   c. Most of the workers in India have very low education and skill levels.
   d. The agricultural sector still accounts for about half of the total workforce.
   e. The level of poverty is very high.
   f. The Indian labour market is dualistic, where a large traditional economy coexists with a high level of growth, surplus productivity and modern economy.
   g. A large majority of the workers are casual and irregular workers or petty self-employed producers and own-account workers.
   h. There had been an increase in GDP but growth in employment had been significantly low.
   i. The unorganized sector contributed majorly to employment growth.
   j. India's labour market is characterized by low female participation rate.

4. The changes in the Indian labour market in the context of economic growth during the last three decades are as follows:
   a. There has been increasing informalization of the workforce.
   b. The increasing informalization of employment has gradually eroded the strength of trade unions.
   c. There is a decline in the participation of females in employment.
   d. The labour market disparities and inequalities have increased.
   e. The gap between per worker earnings in agriculture and non-agriculture has widened.
   f. The share of wages in total value added in manufacturing has been declining consistently.
   g. There is increased diversification of employment away from agriculture.
   h. The rise in wages has led to decline in absolute poverty.
   i. Recent years have also witnessed a rise in the unionization of informal-sector workers.
   j. Emerging threats in the labour market. The traditional IT sector is experiencing big change which is likely to impact job profiles and opportunities.
   k. The disruptive technologies such as using social media, mobility, analytics and cloud are offering new avenues of growth across verticals for IT companies.
   l. There had been shift of ITES jobs to tier 2, tier 3 cities and rural areas.

5. India stands at the second position in the world in terms of the size of population. It is next to China. India's population constitutes nearly 17.74 per cent of the total world population, while her geographical area is only 2.4 per cent of the world area. The median age in India is 27 years. India's national income which is barely 2 per cent of the total global income is a clear indicator of the fact that there is a disproportionate income to the size of the world population. The current population of India was 1,362,215,659 as of 21 January 2019.

6. Underemployment in India is a problem of much larger magnitude than unemployment. In the year 1999–2000, UPS unemployment rate was estimated to be 2.81 per cent as compared to CDS rate of 7.32 per cent. Thus, the employment challenge in the Indian economy consists not only of creating jobs for the unemployed, but also providing additional work to the underemployed. The labour market on creation of jobs is characterized by:
   a. The growth of regular jobs is slow.
   b. Most wage work is casual, contract work is on the rise.
   c. Indian labour markets are poorly regulated.
   d. Most employment are of low quality with low productivity.
   e. There is a highly unbalanced regional pattern of employment creation.
   f. Regional inequality is just one dimension of widening inequality in Indian labour markets in general.
   g. A variety of discriminations and vulnerabilities persists and underpins the segmentation of labour markets.
   h. Disadvantaged social groups are mostly concentrated in low productivity sectors such as agriculture and construction.
7. There have been various government initiatives to initiate economic growth and generate employment. Some of these initiatives which have nexus with the labour market are: Make in India, Digital India, Startup India and Skill India. All these initiatives have the focused objective of economic growth, employment generation and ensuring quality life for citizens.

Questions

1. What are the major characteristics of the Indian labour market? How are these characteristics different from the other developing countries?
2. How is the jobless economic growth likely to affect the Indian labour market?
3. Discuss the major initiatives by the Government of India to improve the labour market and generate employment.
4. Discuss the socio-economic effect of jobless economic growth on the Indian industries.

References

1. Panagariya A. India: The emerging giant. New York: Oxford University Press; 2008.
2. Winters LA and Yusuf Shahid (eds.). Dancing with giants: India, China and the global economy. Singapore: World Bank and the Institute of Policy Studies; 2007.
3. Press Information Bureau. 'Several initiatives taken would help transforming infrastructure sector; results achieving & sustaining higher economic growth. 26 February 2016. Available from http://pib.nic.in/newsite/PrintRelease.aspx?relid=136863
4. Economic Survey, 2012–2013. Government of India; 2013.
5. PTI. India recorded 8% annual average economic growth in 11th plan, The Hindu BusinessLine. 20 February 2014. Available from http://www.thehindubusinessline.com/economy/india-recorded-8-annual-average-economic-growth-in-11th-plan/article5709485.ece
6. Papoli TS. Employment challenge and strategies in India; ILO Asia–Pacific Working Paper Series, New Delhi: ILO. 2008.
7. Ghosh AK. Jobs and incomes in the globalized world. Geneva: ILO; 2003.

8. Planning Commission. Annual report. New Delhi: Government of India; 1985, 23.

9. Planning Commission. Annual report. New Delhi: Government of India; 1998, 14.

10. Planning Commission. Annual report. New Delhi: Government of India; 2001, 2002.

11. Planning Commission. Annual report. New Delhi: Government of India; 2008.

12. Planning Commission. Annual report. New Delhi: Government of India; 2012.

13. PTI. India to havetalent surplus of 245 million workers by 2030: Study, The Hindu BusinessLine. 7 May 2018. Available from https://www.thehindubusinessline.com/economy/macro-economy/india-to-havetalent-surplus-of-245-million-workers-by-2030-study/article23802698.ece

14. The Hindu. Kerala tops in unemployment rates, The Hindu. 12 February 2016. Available from https://www.thehindu.com/news/national/kerala/kerala-tops-in-unemployment-rates/article8226139.ece

Managing Discipline in Industries and Disciplinary Procedure

After reading this chapter, you will be able to:

☐ Understand the importance of discipline in industry
☐ Understand the concept of domestic enquiry
☐ Understand the procedure of conducting domestic enquiry
☐ Understand rules of natural justice and its importance
☐ Understand the concept of suspension pending enquiry

9.1. Introduction

The average modern management system has provisions to manage the acts of misconducts committed either inside any establishment or outside having nexus to the employment through a well-defined and structured disciplinary procedure. The organizations have adopted in due course the philosophical embodiments of Article 14 and Article 16, which provide that 'the state shall not deny to any person equality before the laws or equal protection of the laws and equal opportunity in matters of public employment, respectively' [1].

In private sector, the holding of a domestic enquiry is laid down under the standing orders framed under the Industrial Employment (Standing Orders) Act, 1946. The procedure for holding enquiries has also been laid down by awards or settlements under the ID Act, 1947. Even where no procedure for enquiry has been laid down by any statute, award or settlement, the employers are required to follow a reasonable procedure for the simple reason that otherwise their action is liable to be set aside by the industrial adjudication. Such principles are commonly known as 'principles of natural justice'. The principles underlying the domestic enquiry are essentially that the employer has to justify that the disciplinary action which he proposes to take against an employee by holding a domestic enquiry is fair and impartial in every respect.

9.2. Domestic Enquiry

'Domestic enquiry' in the context of industrial management means 'management's search for truth or otherwise of facts/circumstances/allegations/charges alleged by it, against its employee' [2]. The role played by the management in a disciplinary proceeding includes:

- To allege a fact/circumstance against its employee and issue a charge sheet against him
- To provide an opportunity to the chargesheeted employee to be heard
- To seek for the truth or facts as alleged
- To initiate appropriate disciplinary action on the basis of management's own findings

The term, 'domestic enquiry' implies an enquiry into the charges of indiscipline and misconduct framed against an employee or a workman. It occupies an important position in industrial law. It is called 'domestic enquiry' because it is considered purely an internal matter between an employer and his employees. Such domestic enquiries are not empty formalities but are conducted with scrupulous regard to the requirements of natural justice. Under the common law, a practice was developed to the effect that the courts insisted upon the employer to hold an impartial fact-finding enquiry before taking any disciplinary action against the delinquent employee.

So as a part of the proceedings, it is customary to have a preliminary enquiry/investigation into the allegations alleged against a workman, and finding out whether there is any prima facie case justifying initiation of formal proceedings. Preliminary enquiry is a fact-finding enquiry, which establishes whether there are evidences to proceed against the delinquent employee.

9.3. Procedure of Preliminary Enquiry

It is desirable to have a preliminary enquiry/investigation into the allegations against a workman for finding out whether there is any prima facie case justifying initiation of formal proceedings. When it is brought to the notice of head of the department or an officer authorized to act on his behalf/a disciplinary authority that a workman under his control/department has committed one or more acts of misconduct, a charge sheet is issued and for that it is essential to ensure that there is material evidence to proceed against the concerned employee for the misconduct committed. There should be sufficient reasons to justify breach of law, discipline or conduct rules. If the evidence initially is sufficient, the disciplinary proceeding can be started forthwith. If, however, the evidence available apparently appears or proves to be insufficient, it becomes essential to probe into the matter in order to ensure further that the case really deserves to be proceeded. This procedure of probing for ensuring that there are sufficient reasons to proceed against the concerned employee is technically termed as 'preliminary enquiry' or 'fact-finding enquiry'.

Preliminary enquiry is done with a view to decide whether there is adequate material for initiating a domestic enquiry against a workman. The preliminary enquiry is objectively for the purpose of framing a charge sheet. It also determines whether a prima facie case for a formal enquiry is made out or not. It is conducted merely for the satisfaction of the employer to conclude that a regular domestic enquiry for the purpose of inflicting punishment can be held against the delinquent employee.

There is no hard and fast procedure laid down for conducting a preliminary enquiry. It is also not necessary that the workman should be present while the preliminary enquiry is being conducted. The statements recorded during the preliminary enquiry have nothing to do with the regular enquiry unless they are produced by the management in the course of the domestic enquiry proceedings as an evidence. Figure 9.1 depicts the steps associated with a preliminary enquiry in a situation in which the delinquent employee participates in the preliminary enquiry.

Such preliminary investigation does not form a part of proper domestic enquiry, and rigid principles of domestic enquiry like natural justice and other related procedural aspects do not apply to it. In case the management is initially satisfied that a prima facie case exists against the wrongdoer, the management may initiate forthwith a domestic enquiry without going into the steps of preliminary enquiry. However, in case of existence of any doubt of any nature related to or incidental to the alleged misconduct, it becomes necessary to proceed through the procedures of preliminary enquiry.

So to prove the validity of the complaint, a preliminary enquiry is conducted in order to decide whether to proceed with the complaint or to drop the same. Sometimes when it is found that the person who has committed the misconduct is unknown, that is, some misconduct has been committed and it is not known who has committed the same, preliminary enquiry may be initiated for finding out either the nature of misconduct or the person who has committed the misconduct. The observations of the enquiring officer also give a bird's-eye view of the material available to proceed against the accused.

The preliminary enquiries are of very informal character and the methods are likely to vary in accordance with the requirements of each case. Further, the procedure changes with the changing facts and circumstances of each case as well as prospective outlook of the management engaged in the management of misconduct. The book *Disciplinary Proceedings against Government Servant* [3] published by Indian Law Institute mentions:

> Preliminary Enquiry may take several forms depending on the judgement of the vigilance officer and the nature of complain. The vigilance officer may ask for explanation from the concerned employees, they may make physical inspection of work, they may seek information from other departmental employees or from persons outside the department (though most serious charges involving outside persons will be referred to other investigating agencies like police agency etc.), they may examine records. In some cases, preliminary enquiry may be closed with the examination of the explanation submitted by the accused officer.

In some cases, in preliminary enquiries or investigations it may be found that there is no serious misconduct but there are irregularities or failure of observations of some rules or procedures. In such cases, instead of holding formal departmental enquiry, the disciplinary authority may opt to close the case by administering the employee a simple warning. The book *Disciplinary Procedure against the Government Servant* [4] indicates,

> [I]n some cases, preliminary investigations may depict doubtful decrees of culpability on the part of the officer accused. In some other preliminary investigations involved may be a substantial character of stray instances of lacking in performance of official duties, failure to observe the proper administrative channel for official connection are example of such relatives minor official lapses. These are the cases whether the officer accused of irregularities cannot be exonerated from the allegation. In such situation the disciplinary authority would rather like to take up the complain to a further stage of formal disciplinary proceedings.

The records of the preliminary enquiry are not a part of the formal enquiry as such and cannot be utilized as an instrument either to take a disciplinary action in the form of punishment or termination of employment in the form of dismissal. It has been observed that under circumstances when the findings of the preliminary enquiry officer became instrumental and a primary tool against the charge sheeted employee for establishment of the charges alleged against him, such instruments become legally void.

The report of the preliminary enquiry officer cannot be considered to be either evidence or an instrument for utilization and to meet the opportunities for establishment of any charges against the chargesheeted employee in course of domestic proceedings (held in the cases of Tribhuwan versus State of Bihar [5] and Chowdhury versus Union of India [6]).

In case the enquiry officer wants to use the findings of the preliminary enquiry officer to be an instrument for establishment of the facts against the chargesheeted employee, the same should be utilized with the full knowledge of the delinquent employee; otherwise the said enquiry is liable to be considered as void.

The participation in the preliminary enquiry by the employee or submission of the evidence by the delinquent is not mandatory.

So the purpose of this enquiry is to determine whether there is a prima facie case for institution of departmental proceedings (held in the case of Champak Lai versus Union of India [7]). Such proceedings are not to be confused with the regular departmental proceedings which may be instituted later. The holding of such an enquiry does not mean that the disciplinary authority has made up its mind with regard to the guilt of the delinquent (held in the case of Badri Das versus Industrial Tribunal [8]). There is neither element of punitive proceedings in such an enquiry nor it is governed by Article 311 (2) of the Constitution (held in the case of Champak Lai versus Union of India [7]). In fact, it is an informal type of enquiry without any definite form or procedure and the preliminary enquiry may be held confidentially, (held in the case of Tribhuwan Nath versus State of Bihar [5]) or even ex parte (held in the case of N. K. Roy versus Commissioner [9]). Non-participation does not disentitle from taking part in the regular enquiry (held in the case of Dadaro Tidke versus State of Maharashtra [10]). In case evidence taken in preliminary enquiry is to be relied upon during regular proceedings, the delinquent should be supplied with copies of such evidence so that he can put up his defence effectively. It is, however, not necessary to disclose the source of information to him (held in the case of Subharao versus P. S. C. [11]). In case the witness is examined during preliminary enquiry, their statements should again be recorded at the time of regular enquiry, (held in the case of Surendra Chandra Das versus Union Territory [12]) and in the presence of the delinquent officer.

9.4. Difference between 'Domestic Enquiry' and 'Preliminary Enquiry'

A preliminary enquiry is not to be confused with a domestic enquiry. A preliminary enquiry is also known as a fact-finding enquiry, and is not a formal enquiry. Preliminary enquiry is done to decide whether there is adequate material for initiating a domestic enquiry against a workman. The preliminary enquiry is only for the purpose of framing a charge sheet and for concluding 'whether a prima facie case for a formal enquiry is made out or not'.

When a complaint is made to an employer alleging certain breaches of employment terms and thereby committing a misconduct by an employee, the employer can conduct such preliminary investigation to find out the truth in the case. This is done with a view to enable the employer to frame specific charges against the workman.

The domestic enquiry initiates with the issue of the charge sheet against the workman. The main differences between the preliminary enquiry and a domestic enquiry are as follows:

1. After the complaint is received against an employee, preliminary enquiry is the first step that is usually taken by the employer. But the first step is by no means essential, whereas domestic enquiry is essential for taking disciplinary action against an employee.

2. It is not obligatory to do a preliminary enquiry. Where a preliminary enquiry is conducted, it is usually the forerunner of a domestic enquiry. It may happen that as a result of preliminary enquiry, charges may be dropped and in that case domestic enquiry is not required to be conducted.
3. The object of the domestic enquiry is to determine whether charges are established or not, whereas the object of the preliminary enquiry is very limited, that is, to find out whether a prima facie case has been made out against an employee or not.
4. The report of the preliminary enquiry often is the basis for framing the charge sheet, whereas the report of the domestic enquiry is the basis for awarding punishment.
5. While the preliminary enquiry is not subject to any rules, domestic enquiry is subject to principles of natural justice.
6. The results of the preliminary enquiry are not conclusive, whereas the results of the domestic enquiry are very much conclusive in as much as they decide the fate of an employee.

9.5. Guidelines for Domestic Enquiry Proceedings

Normally, disciplinary proceedings against an employee are instituted on receipt of a complaint and the complaints are dealt in the manners indicated as follows:

1. If there are no substantial facts against any employee in the complaint, there is no need to take any action other than a reasonable and careful examination of the complaint.
2. If the complaint is doubtful or the employee has committed an ordinary offence for the first time, the employee may be let off with a verbal warning.
3. Written warning may be issued if the misconduct is minor and repetitive in nature, and under such circumstances whether it warrants any further disciplinary action is determined by the disciplinary authority.
4. On the basis of the observations of the enquiry officer in the enquiry report, the employee may be awarded punishment in accordance with the rules of the company, which depends on the degree of misconduct committed.

It is the elementary principle of natural justice that one should not be condoned or punished without being given an opportunity of being heard or substantiate reasonable defence in his favour through a disciplinary proceeding.

9.6. What Is a Charge Sheet?

A charge sheet is a written statement of specific allegations addressed to communicate the delinquent 'what he is supposed or alleged to have done which is not acceptable as per the code of conduct of the organization'. The object being to give the employee the exact idea of the misconduct committed by him so that he may submit his explanation in his defence.

The concept of charge sheet has been derived from the criminal law. In case of the complaint to police where documents under Section 173 of the Criminal Procedure Code are produced, the magistrate can discharge the accused person if, on consideration of the documents, the charge is groundless, otherwise the magistrate is required to frame the charges. Charge sheet under the criminal law is a formal document stating the offence with which the accused is charged.

In disciplinary proceedings, such charge sheets are framed by the disciplinary authority on consideration of a complaint or after holding a preliminary enquiry if material evidence, sufficiently strong enough, is available against the employee. The framing of charge sheet is provided in various Acts, rules, regulations, standing orders and so on, related to public and private sectors.

The delinquent has a right to defend through examination of witnesses, cross-examination of the witness produced by the management and argument. Copies of statement of preliminary enquiry (if utilized in the domestic enquiry) and the statement of witnesses examined are to be supplied to the charge-sheeted employee. All copies of documents relied upon for framing the charge sheet to be supplied to the delinquent. Merely saying that the delinquent would have the opportunity to inspect the documents at any time of enquiry is not enough effective opportunity in the enquiry. In addition to the above, the charge sheet should also mention the particulars of time, place of occurrence and the manner in which the incident alleged to have taken place so as to remove vagueness and make the charge definite by mentioning these essential factors.

One of the fundamental rules of natural justice is that the person affected should have full and true disclosure of the facts sought to be used against him. He must know the nature of the misconduct alleged against him and must be acquainted with it in the first instance, it means that the charge sheet is the sine qua non of the domestic enquiry. The point is that no disciplinary action can be initiated against the employee or a workman unless he is first served with a charge sheet containing all charges and their essential particulars.

The basic requirement of drafting a charge sheet is that it should give the employee a fair idea of the case which he is to face. If a particular act is misconduct when committed on the premises of the establishment, then the place is a part of the charge itself. So while drafting a charge sheet, the attempt should be to ensure that the charges mentioned in the charge sheet are specific as well as complete in all essential constituents.

The principles of natural justice require that the person charged should know precisely the nature of the offence so that he may be able to explain what he has to say about it and prove innocence in the matter. Vague allegations should be avoided while drafting a charge sheet.

9.7. Essential Ingredients of a Charge Sheet

A charge sheet being root of the disciplinary action, when vague, will vitiate the whole proceedings and hence, the imposition of penalty on delinquent is liable to be quashed. So it is essential that the charge sheet is drafted with sufficient precaution. There are few basic ingredients of a charge sheet which are as follows:

1. Details of the identity of the individual against the charges are levelled.
2. Details of the exact specification of the time and place of commitment of the misconduct.
3. Details of the allegation of the charges, specifying the gravity of the charges levelled against the delinquent employee.
4. The relevant provisions of the standing orders, as applicable to the concerned employee, which consider that a misconduct has been committed by the concerned employee.
5. An opportunity to defend by way of replying to the charges levelled against the delinquent employee within a reasonable time as specified under the standing orders of the organization.[1]

[1] Draft charge sheets are provided at the chapter-end.

9.8. Points to Consider while Drafting a Charge Sheet

1. The charge sheet must be specific and must set out all the necessary particulars. It will serve no useful purpose at all to presume that the employee is fully informed of the charges because of any previous proceedings against him.
2. The enquiry itself must be preceded by serving the workman concerned a regular charge sheet devoid of any vagueness. It is imperative to hold a regular enquiry before terminating the services of a workman.
3. Vague accusation, which the workman could not possibly follow, should not be made in the charge sheet.
4. The charge sheet must accurately and precisely state whether the act of commission or omission constituting misconduct is in violation of any standing order or not.
5. The time, date and place, that is, when and where the incidence occurred must be clearly mentioned.
6. When under the standing orders or service rules, an act such as absence without leave, late attendance, negligence or disobedience is misconduct, if it is committed habitually, then in such a case the word habitual forms an essential constituent of the charge and must be expressly mentioned in the charge sheet.
7. Similarly, if the standing orders or service rules provide that damage to property or disobedience or insubordination must be wilful, then the wilfulness is an essential part of the charge and must be stated in the charge sheet.
8. If theft or dishonesty is a misconduct only if it is committed in connection with the employer's business or property, then this must be so stated in the charge sheet in all its details.
9. If the charge is for arrogant conduct towards a superior, then it must be so stated in the charge sheet giving the occasion on which the misconduct was committed and in respect of which particulars of the superior.
10. When an employee is charged for habitually disobeying the instructions, then each set of disobedience on his part must be separately mentioned in details in the charge sheet.
11. When an employee is charged for using objectionable and offending language, then the actual words used must be stated in the charge sheet.
12. When the previous record of the employee is relied upon, then sufficient particulars of the previous bad record should be specified in the charge sheet.
13. While verbiage is to be avoided, use of any abbreviations such as etc. must be equally shunned.
14. The language of a charge sheet, while being precise, must not give the impression that the employer has taken the question of the employee's guilt as a foregone conclusion. It should be simple and be one that is commonly understood or in common usage.
15. When the charge to be levelled is that an employee altered the relevant entries in the record with some ulterior motive then, in such a case, the workman should be informed as to what precisely was the motive being attributed to him because unless this is done, the charge sheet would suffer from the disqualification of vagueness.
16. Make use of the term 'about' in relation to the date and time of a particular incident of misconduct.
17. In the case of a theft, it is most necessary to mention full particulars of the goods or articles stolen.
18. The charge sheet should also not be issued with a bias and closed mind.

19. The charge sheet must be signed by the competent authority.
20. A charge sheet, issued after long delay of the misconduct, will vitiate the enquiry.

9.9. The Steps of Domestic Enquiry

The steps of domestic enquiry are enumerated in Figure 9.1. The steps of the proceedings are as follows.

Step I: Issue of a letter calling explanation to all relevant charges and allegations, which is normally termed as a 'charge sheet'.

Step II: The charge sheet is followed by submission of reply to the same by the chargesheeted employee within the stipulated time period which is normally termed as 'the reply to the charge sheet'. This reply contains the basic defence which the chargesheeted employee pleads in his favour.

Step III: If the explanation is not considered to be satisfactory by the disciplinary authority, an enquiry is conducted and the same is conveyed through a notice of enquiry.

Step IV: In course of the enquiry, the enquiry officer will extend all reasonable opportunities both to the chargesheeted employee and the management to establish their cases. In other words, the management will get an opportunity to state and establish the allegations levelled by them against the chargesheeted employee and the chargesheeted employee will get the opportunity to defend himself in course of the enquiry and establish his innocence on the issue.

Step V: The enquiry officer follows the principles of 'natural justice'—he records all relevant activities including the submissions and after considering all relevant facts deposed by the management and the chargesheeted employee, the enquiry officer gives his findings which is normally termed as the 'enquiry findings'.

Step VI: The disciplinary authority considers the findings of the enquiry officer and determines the extent to which the concerned employee is guilty of the charges levelled against him. The determined quantum of punishment to be imposed on the chargesheeted employee is normally informed in writing.

The procedure of domestic enquiry is based on the principle of natural justice which is fundamental to all judicial procedures and which is enforceable under all courses of law, statutory or otherwise and to all persons and bodies acting in judicial or quasi-judicial capacity.

The main initiation to a disciplinary proceeding is embodied in the master and servant relationship of employer and employee in industry. The employee in the capacity of a disciplinary authority enjoys certain privilege, which is a limited privilege. After holding a preliminary enquiry, the disciplinary authority if satisfied that there are valid grounds for initiation of a disciplinary proceeding, issues a notice conveying the 'articles of charges', that is, a statement of allegations on which such articles of charges are based to the accused employee. The chargesheeted employee is required to submit an explanation in writing within a stipulated time. Such notice, which is titled as 'charge sheet' is kept completely free from spelling out any proposed penalty for the wrongful acts on the part of the delinquent. The logical reason for this is ingrained in the concept of natural justice as per which it is essential that an open mind be kept with regards to the charges against the delinquent, until they are conclusively proved.

Figure 9.1 Procedure of Domestic Enquiry

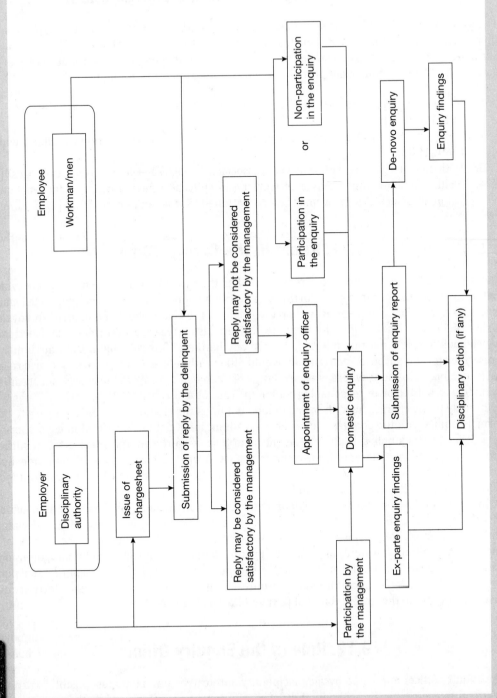

9.10. Some Vagueness in the Charge Sheet

The charges framed should not be vague. It should be definite and written in clear words so that there remains no chance for misconstruction and it is free from ambiguity (held in the case of Surendra Chandra Das [13]). The motives attributed to the delinquent should be stated in clear and precise terms. Certain examples of vague terms are appended as follows:

1. 'He used to accept bribes'—without indicating the specific incidence (Niranjan Prasad's case, 1960 [14]).
2. 'With ulterior motive'—such allegations are open-ended allegations (Saligram's case, 1969 [15]).
3. 'With other allegations, with which he is associated'—vague allegations (Ahir's case, 1957 [16]).
4. 'Failure to show improvement in working in spite of repeated confidential reports'—no instances of lack of improvement was mentioned (Ratnanand's case, 1962 [17]).

9.11. Reply to the Charge Sheet

The delinquent is to be extended a reasonable fair time to submit his defence reply. Any act of calling for a reply to a charge sheet forthwith, without an opportunity for a thought on the charges levelled against the delinquent, is withholding right of the chargesheeted employee from *natural justice* (held in the case of B. D. Kaushal [18]). There also appear certain well-established norms which spell that it is not possible to lay down any hard and fast rule about the time limit to be prescribed for the purpose, which in fact would differ with reference to the circumstances of each case. Instances are there, where even six days were allowed to reply to the charge sheet, the time granted was held to be unreasonable (held in the case of A. S. Raval [19]).

In reply to the charge sheet, in case delinquent admits the charges, it is not necessary to hold a formal enquiry into the charges. However, such admission must be expressed in clear terms and in writing. Matter implied in the statement or in a reply to the charge sheet is not a sufficient ground for dropping the enquiry. Any orders passed on the basis of clear admission by the delinquent will not violate the principles of natural justice (held in the cases of Rabindra Mohan [20], Krishan Lal [21] and J. M. Ajwani [22]).

In reply to a charge sheet, in case a delinquent tenders an unconditional apology and begs to be excused, there does not arise any necessity for a formed enquiry; it is open to the disciplinary authority to straightway close the matter without proceeding further into the details of the enquiry. Any admission or apology made by the delinquent during preliminary or informal enquiry is considered totally irrelevant for the purpose of dropping the enquiry unless the conditions, for example, unconditional and unreserved apology in writing comes forth from the delinquent (held in the case of Ram Lal [23] and Karan Singh [24]).

9.12. Role of the Enquiry Officer

The enquiry officer appointed by the disciplinary authority is ultimately responsible for applying his mind to the matter in question and decide the issue of considering whether the concerned delinquent is guilty of the charges levelled against him. The enquiry officer must be a person who is neither related directly or indirectly and subordinate to the disciplinary authority. He must be impartial and free from bias. He must conduct himself objectively, without any bias and certainly without vindictiveness. Such enquiries must not be conducted by an officer who is associated with the matter in question as there is a likelihood to be biased (held in the case of A. S. Razvi [25]).

The domestic enquiry is based on the well-known principle called natural justice. One of the principles is—'no man should be a judge of his own cause' (the principle of natural justice has been discussed further in this chapter). It may be that though a person who is personally connected with the matter may have the most upright motive and may not allow his judicial discretion be impaired by personal interest, his conducting the enquiry would violate the principles of natural justice. In the case of Nageswara Rao [26], the Supreme Court observed, 'it is of fundamental importance that justice should not only be done but should manifestly and undoubtedly be seen to be done'. So an enquiry officer should bear the following qualities:

1. Should not himself be personally interested in the case
2. Should be a person with an open mind who is not biased against the delinquent
3. Should not have prejudged the issue
4. Cannot act both as a judge and a witness

Often the question is raised that the person holding the post of an enquiry officer should be in rank superior to the person against whom the enquiry is conducted. There are no statutory limitations to such. So, it is not necessary that the person appointed as enquiry officer should hold a position not inferior to that of the appointing authority. Further, so long as the enquiry officer conducts the enquiry in a judicious manner in accordance with the principles of natural justice, he is not disqualified to hold the enquiry even if he had held the preliminary enquiry and had come to a prima facie conclusion (held in the case of D. A. Koregaonkar [27]). The only condition which is required to be fulfilled is that there should be a formal order issued by the disciplinary authority appointing such person as the enquiry officer to enquire into the charges levelled against the delinquent.

There may arise conditions for change of enquiry officer during an ongoing enquiry proceeding. For that, it is essential to have reasonable safeguards, such as de-novo enquiry may be provided to the delinquent which is within the discretion of the disciplinary authority and cannot be claimed as right (held in the case of Amalnath [28]). However, there is no bar to start the enquiry from where it has been left by the predecessor enquiry officer and in any way it will not vitiate the same (held in the case of Harjit Singh [29]).

9.13. Co-worker to Assist the Delinquent Employee

In course of an enquiry proceeding, the delinquent enjoys right to be assisted by a co-worker of his choice. On the issue 'who can be the assistant to the delinquent'—normally the answer to the same is—'a co-worker of his choice'. However, instances often appear where the chargesheeted employee prefers to have the assistance of a professional lawyer which in all normal cases is not allowed in an enquiry proceeding (held in the cases of K. N. Gupta [31], Harjit Singh [32] and Kula Chander [33]). But in case where a person presenting the case on behalf of the disciplinary authority is a professional lawyer, the delinquent can also have the right of availing the services of a legal practitioner at the enquiry proceeding (held in the cases of R. C. Varma versus R. D. Varma [34] and

K. N. Gupta's case [35]). However, under certain cases legal assistance to a delinquent may become necessary in view of the extraordinary nature of the enquiry, for example,

1. Where rightly or wrongly the delinquent was under reasonable apprehension that the enquiry was the result of a preconceived plan and a concerted action on the part of the department held in the case of K. Subha Rao [36]).
2. Where the government's handwriting expert was to be cross-examined by or on behalf of the government servant (held in the case of A. N. Chopra [37]).
3. Where the records of the case were voluminous (as in the instant case 91 number of witnesses were examined and the volume of their deposition was 437 pages; held in the case of Nitya Ranjan [38]).

However, it is a considered opinion that the above circumstances are not exhaustive. The permission to allow to engage a professional lawyer depends on the facts and circumstances of each case. It has been held that if a particular case is complicated enough, the assistance of a lawyer may not be refused on the ground of extending reasonable opportunity to the concerned delinquent which is in accordance with the principles of natural justice. It is often opined that though the normal rule does not permit a delinquent to be represented by a legal practitioner/ expert, domestic enquiries are not only administrative forums, these are also quasi-judiciary or in other words judicial procedures which are often a part of the proceeding. Hence, assistance by an expert may be necessary in cases where judicial aspects dominate the legal technicalities which are involved (held in the case of Nripendra Nath [39]).

However, the normal procedure does not bar any person in the status of a co-worker to represent on behalf of the delinquent. This representation has been considered part of the enquiry proceeding because the delinquent may need from time to time assistance in course of the enquiry which may be clerical, advisory or of some other nature including understanding the language and so on. Further, considering representation through an assistant is also advisable because this ensures that whatever is recorded in course of the proceeding is countersigned by a witness on behalf of the delinquent. This practice safeguards the role of the enquiry officer to be considered as bias.

9.14. Delegating the Power to Hold Enquiry

On the question 'whether the power to hold enquiry can be delegated', the considered view of the Honourable Supreme Court is that since the exercise of the power to appoint or dismiss an officer is the exercise not considered as a judicial power but administrative power, the functionary who has to decide an administrative matter can obtain the material on which he is to act, in such a manner as may be feasible and convenient, provided the affected party has a fair opportunity (held in the case Kapur Singh versus Union of India [40]). In coming to such a conclusion, the Honourable Supreme Court has referred to an English case in which it was observed that a functionary who has to decide an administrative matter can obtain the material on which he is to act in such a manner as may be feasible and convenient. The said decision of the Honourable Supreme Court has been consistently applied in various other cases.

It is normally accepted that the administrative functions can be delegated, whereas the judicial functions can rarely be delegated unless it is enabled to do so expressly or by necessary implication (Shardul Singh versus State of Madhya Pradesh [41]). If executive functions also involve quasi-judicial function, then they can also be delegated as a part of the executive functions (held in the case of Raipur Transport Company Private Limited versus State of Madhya Pradesh [42]) since quasi-judicial implies acts not fully judicial. Certain examples of the extent of delegation are appended:

1. Administrative functions to dismiss and suspend can be delegated (held in the case of Vine versus National Dock Labour Board [43]).
2. A member of the board can be authorized by the board to give personal hearing to the employee.
3. Statutory body of numerous persons can authorize an officer to act on its behalf for conducting the disciplinary enquiry because it is not possible to collect the material facts.

What cannot be delegated is 'to give one's decision'. Under situations when bodies, for example, boards and statutory bodies delegate such administrative powers, the material collected is sent to such bodies, who consider the report and such materials to make up the mind independently for coming to conclusion on the issue (held in the case of A. Krishnaswamy versus Electricity Board [44]).

9.15. Reasonable Opportunity to a Delinquent

Reasonable opportunity to a delinquent for his/her own defence in course of the enquiry ensures for inspection of such records which are material to the facts and circumstances of the case. In the case of 'Jugraj Singh versus Delhi Administration [45]', it was held that there are two classes of documents. The first class are the documents on which the enquiry officer relies, that is, documents which are intended to be used by the prosecution agency to prove the charges against the delinquent and the second class includes documents which, even if are not to be relied upon by the enquiry officer, may be utilized by the delinquent for his defence. The delinquent is entitled for both these classes of documents for his defence. Similar observations appear in the case of Surat Singh versus S. R. Bakshi [46].

A list of records which the delinquent is normally entitled to inspect includes the following:

1. The first information report, if any.
2. Copies of the report forming the basis of the charges.
3. Copies of the statements of witnesses, which are to be utilized in the enquiry made prior to the enquiry.
4. Copies of report of the confidential or preliminary enquiries, if the same are to be utilized in the enquiry.
5. The materials in the form of evidence, oral or documentary, which form the basis for decision-making.
6. Confidential reports on the work and conduct, if the charges against the delinquent relate to his efficiency in the work.
7. Other records considered by the delinquent essential for defence.

The relevance of the record is to be judged from the viewpoint of defence—documents likely to be of any use for defence, which may appear to be relevant initially cannot be denied, but this does lead to conclusions that access to documents cannot be denied. Such denial needs to be exercised in such a way so that the delinquent is neither prevented from reasonable opportunity for defence nor any prejudice is caused to him.

The principles of natural justice firmly establish that no materials should be utilized against the chargesheeted employee, unless they are disclosed to him and he is given an opportunity to explain or rebut the same (held in the case of Jiwaram versus State of Rajasthan [47]).

The enquiry authority unlike court can obtain all the material information from all sources and channels without being moved by rules or procedures. However, any material cannot be used against a delinquent unless it is put to him (held in the case of Bakhtawar Singh versus State of Punjab [48]).

In course of the enquiry, the enquiry officer records all statements and documents utilized in the enquiry, which form a part of the proceedings. However, in course of the proceedings, the delinquent enjoys the liberty to produce any evidence, oral or documentary, for proving his case or for demolishing the case sought to be made out against him by the disciplinary authority.

9.16. Examination-in-Chief and Cross-examination of the Witnesses

Examination-in-chief and cross-examination of the witnesses are the most vital steps of a domestic enquiry. This opportunity is equally enjoyed by the management representative in the enquiry as well as the delinquent. The delinquent in course of the enquiry will not prove the negative of anything unless the same is established positively against him. So, it is the presenting officer appearing on behalf of the management who leads the evidence first which is followed by cross-examination of the witnesses by the delinquent.

The presentation of the defence witnesses by the delinquent follows the production of witnesses on behalf of the management. In case the delinquent is not provided the opportunity to produce witnesses and evidence in defence, this would mean that the enquiry has not been held in accordance with the rules of natural justice (held in the case of Union of India versus T. R. Verma [49]).

The delinquent is to be provided with all material on records placed before the enquiry officer by the management representative, presenting the case on behalf of the management, before he proceeds for cross-examination of any witness. It was held in the case of Phanindra Chandra Shome versus Union of India [50] 'to invite a person to cross examine a witness while keeping back from him earlier statements made by the witness would be like blind folding a man and asking him to find his way out'. The charge sheeted employee may ask for copies of the statement of the witnesses who are to be cross examined by him. In case the same is not supplied the procedure vitiates the principles of Natural Justice (held in the case of Jugraj Singh versus Delhi Administration [51]).

Further, cross-examination need not be confined to the testimony of a witness in his examination-in-chief, its scope is unlimited and may cover the entire field of defence except that the questions must be relevant to the facts of the case or relate to the credibility of the witness or the evidence given by him.

While it is essential to keep the chargesheeted employee posted of all material evidence against him, it is highly improper for an enquiry officer during the conduct of an enquiry to attempt to collect any materials from outside sources and not make that information so collected available to the delinquent and further make use of the same in the enquiry proceedings. There may also be cases where a very clever and astute enquiry officer may collect outside information behind the back of the delinquent and without any apparent reference to the information so collected may influence the conclusions recorded by him against the delinquent concerned. If it is established that the materials have been collected during the enquiry without disclosing the same to the delinquent, it can be stated that the enquiry proceedings are vitiated (held in the case of State of Assam versus M. K. Das [52]).

Reasonable opportunity as has been visualized by various courts of law requires the compliance of the norms of natural justice and sufficient due opportunity for defence to the delinquent and for availing the scope for having all knowledge of the materials utilized against him. Following are some of the instances where it was deemed that reasonable opportunity has not been extended to the delinquent:

1. Enquiry officer acting hurriedly and taking witnesses arbitrarily out of the long list of witnesses submitted by the delinquent for coming to conclusions in the matter of the charges levelled against the delinquent (held in the case of Gajindra Singh versus State of Punjab [53]).
2. Evidences not examined in course of the enquiry but were considered against the delinquent (held in the case of R. Yadav versus Chief Security Officer [54]).
3. Where enquiry officer relied partly on relevant and partly on irrelevant evidences (held in the case of State of Punjab versus Asanand [55]).
4. Where statements of witnesses were recorded in his presence and opportunity to cross-examination was not extended (held in the case of Krishna Lal versus State of Rajasthan [56, 21]).
5. Where the actual enquiry was a confidential and secret enquiry and disciplinary action was taken on the basis of such secret enquiry (held in the case of State of Uttar Pradesh versus C. S. Sharma [57]).
6. Where the delinquent was not permitted to produce defence witnesses (held in the case of S. N. Singh versus State of Manipur [58]).
7. Where the enquiry officer relied on his own evidences for coming to a conclusion in the matter of the charges levelled against the delinquent (held in the case of Sivanandan Sinha versus State of West Bengal [59]).
8. Where the delinquent was not allowed to argue his case (held in the case of State of Uttar Pradesh versus C. S. Sharma [57]).
9. Where the delinquent was not allowed to cross-examine the witness appearing on behalf of other side (held in the case of Lalita Prasad versus I. G. Police [60]).
10. Where the task of hearing the witnesses was sub delegated by the enquiry officer (held in the case of Amulya Sikdar versus L. M. Bakshi [61]).
11. Where the enquiry officer based his conclusion on the evidence taken behind the back of the delinquent (held in the case of Sashi Bhushan versus State of Orissa [62]).
12. Where the punishing authority has made up his mind finally and recorded the detailed order considering the quantum of punishment not less than dismissal from services but further indicating that before imposition of the said punishment a verbal hearing may be given to the delinquent—an instance of fraud on the requirement of the rule (held in the case of Sri Ram versus States of Punjab and Haryana [63]).

13. Where the evidence was led by the prosecution but no charges were made against the delinquent (held in the case of Surjit Kaur versus States of Punjab and Haryana [64]).
14. Where the enquiry was held in a pre-functionary manner and completed in one day. No personal hearing was granted (held in the case of Surjit Kaur versus States of Punjab and Haryana [64]).
15. Where the leading questions were put by the enquiry officer, leading to biasing the witness on behalf of the management (held in the case of Ram Netra versus Superintendent of police [65]).
16. Where the statements of the witnesses were not taken in presence of the accused (held in the case of M. P. Chanda Kutty versus A. O. Medical College [66]).
17. Where adequate time was not granted for inspecting the statements of witnesses (held in the case of State of West Bengal versus S. N. Bose [67]).
18. Where instead of following the regular procedure of recording evidence, enquiry officer reached the conclusion by putting questions to the chargesheeted employee (held in the case of P. Banerjee versus D. C. E. [68]).

There are also various cases where the requirement of reasonable opportunity was considered not to be violated. Such examples are:

1. The chargesheeted employee desired to cross-examine the witnesses only after all the witnesses had been recorded but the request was not granted (held in the case of Jagadish Chandra Bhasin versus State [69]).
2. Where some of the witnesses examined by the enquiry officer were subordinate to the enquiry officer (held in the case of Govind Shankar versus State [70]).
3. Where the assistance of lawyer was refused (held in the case of Lakshmi Narayan versus A. N. Puri [71]).
4. Where the delinquent did not cross-examine the witnesses, though he was given an opportunity to do so (held in the case of Naubat Rai versus Union of India [72]).
5. Where the delinquent expressly stated before the enquiry officer that he did not wish to tender any evidence but later complained to the court of law that he was not given adequate opportunity to defend his case (held in the case of K. Behari Chakravarty versus Union of India [73]).

9.17. The 'Doctrines of Bias'

One of the well-founded norms of the domestic enquiry is that the enquiry officer should not be biased. To act impartially, objectively and without bias is normally demanded in all judicial procedures. Conceptually, 'bias' implies one-sided inclination of mind. 'A biased man does not hold his opinion, as his opinion holds him, therefore, he cannot have an impartial mind' (held in the case of Hareram Samant versus Superintendent of Police, Hooghly [74]).

According to the 'doctrines of bias':

1. No man should be a judge of his own cause.
2. Justice should not only be done but manifestly and undoubtedly seem to be done.

The above doctrines of bias are a technical ramification of instances of good faith in the authority in the matter. Lord Denning observes:

The rule against bias is one thing. The right to be heard is another. These two rules are essential characteristics of what is often called natural justice. They are the twin pillars supporting it. The Romans put them as two maxima—*nemo debet esse judex in propria causa* and *audi alteram partem.*

The existence of bias need not be established. Reasonable ground for believing that there was likelihood of bias on the part of the enquiry officer is efficient to vitiate the enquiry and the findings (held in the case of Zonal Manager, Life Insurance Corporation of India versus Mohanlal Saraf [75]).

'Bias' has been classified in the cases of Ramniwas Sharma versus Union of India [76] and includes:

1. **Bias on the subject matter:** which implies that a mere general interest in the object phrase would not disqualify, unless there is some direct connection with the specific litigation or the prejudice is so strong that court has reached fixed and unalterable contention.
2. **Pecuniary bias:** which implies that even a slight pecuniary interest would disqualify.
3. **Personal bias:** which implies that where a report or determination lacking final effect has a serious judicial effect on the interest of an individual, then he should not take part in the adjudication.

The following instances indicate the situation where bias is caused.

1. **Whether a person lodging complaint against an employee can hold the enquiry?** The answer to this question has been dealt in the case of Mansukhla versus J. D. Nagarwala [77], where it was held that when an officer has made a report which is basis of the charge, then some connection must be established between the report and the conduct of the enquiry officer to establish bias. But under a situation when an officer has made the initial complaint and has recommended several punishments after forming an opinion, then the officer is not a fit person to be appointed as an enquiry officer.
2. **Whether the officer investigating the complaint should hold the enquiry?** The mere fact that an officer holding the enquiry was himself investigating officer would not vitiate the enquiry (held in the case of M. V. Jogarao versus State of Madras [78]). But a person should not be both a prosecutor and a witness (held in the case of Workmen versus Lambadari Tea Estate [79]). For instance, in the case of Hari Singh versus Committee, Batala [80], an officer himself ordered the search of the employee who was alleged to have taken bribe and took interest in that matter. Such an officer should not be appointed as an enquiry officer. Similarly, an officer who admittedly conducted investigation or conducted a preliminary enquiry should neither be appointed as an enquiry officer or act as a disciplinary authority. There are likely chances that such a person would unconsciously be prejudiced by the materials gathered by him, and if he is a witness during the enquiry, there are all possible chances that he may be called upon to appreciate his own evidence. So following the principles that 'justice must not only be done but it must seem to be done'— such a person loses his right to act as an enquiry officer.
3. **Whether an authority recording confession can hold the enquiry?** Such a question has been answered in the case of Lakshminarayan versus State of Rajasthan [81]. In the

instant case, it was hold that it is always advisable for a magistrate who recorded confession or before whom identification have taken place to leave it to some other court, but that would not make him personally interested in the case and would not vitiate the proceedings.

4. **Whether an officer issuing the charge sheet can hold the enquiry?** In a disciplinary proceeding, which is a quasi-judicial proceeding, the employer is entitled to frame the charge sheet, conduct the enquiry and award the punishment. Under this system, an officer only issues the charge sheet when tentatively comes to the conclusion that there are materials to show that the employee is guilty of the particular charge, and therefore further investigation is necessary. The formation of such tentative opinions does not mean that an officer is biased against the employee concerned to such an extent that he is incompetent to hold the enquiry. The principle 'no man shall be a judge of his own case' means that he should not have personal interest in the case (M. L. Joshi versus Director of Estate [82]). Even under a situation where an officer merely serves the charge sheet under the instruction of the general manager, he does not become a prosecutor so as to be disentitled to hold enquiry. There are instances where it was held that a person issuing the show cause notice can hold enquiry because the principle that a prosecutor cannot be a judge is not strictly applicable to departmental enquiries (held in the case of A. R. S. Choudhury versus Union of India [83]). The enquiry officer is biased only when he is prejudged in the matter.

5. **Whether mentioning of penalty in the charge sheet shows bias?** Where there is clear proof in the charge sheet that the issuing officer has made up his mind on the question of guilt of an employee by stating the proposed penalty, it indicates clear proof of bias. The charge sheet or the show cause notice is required to contain only the charges not a finding of guilt or a proposal as to the punishment to be imposed if the guilt is proved (held in the case of Gouri Prasad Ghosh versus State of West Bengal [84]).

6. **Whether passing of an interim suspension order amounts to bias?** Suspension has been defined as temporary deprivation of office. An employee under suspension, pending domestic enquiry or some judicial proceedings against him, is debarred for the time being from further functioning in his office or holding the position of privilege. Suspension does not put an end to the relationship of master and servant. By reason of suspension the person suspended does not lose his office nor does he suffer from degradation. He ceases to exercise the powers and to discharge the duties of the officer for the time being. His rank remains the same and his pay does not suffer any reduction. He cannot draw his full salary during the period of suspension. His power, functions and privileges remain in abeyance. Suspension has always been considered as an implied term of every contract of service. In the case of V. P. Gidroniya versus State of Madhya Pradesh [85], the Supreme Court has observed that there are three kinds of suspension known to law. These are:
   a. Suspension as a mode of punishment
   b. Suspension during the pendency of an enquiry
   c. The act of merely forbidding an employee from discharging his duties

Every master has an implied right to suspend his employee, which is the result of the master and servant relationship. So suspension cannot be construed to mean that a decision to dismiss the workman was taken and the manager or the enquiry officer was biased. There is no bar for an officer passing the suspension order to hold the enquiry for the same and this does not conclude that there was contravention of natural justice or there was a preconceived notion (held in the case of Rameshwar Singh versus Union of India [86]).

Provisions related to the 'Right to Suspend' by the employer was made by the Supreme Court in the case of Balwantary Patel [87]. The observation of the Supreme Court is quoted as follows:

> The General law on the subject of suspension has been laid down by this Court in three cases, viz. The management of Hotel Imperial, New Delhi versus Hotel Workers Union [88], T. Cajee versus U. Jormanik Siem [89], and R. P. Kapur versus Union of India [90]. It is now well settled that the power to suspend in the sense of a right to forbid a servant to work, is not an implied term in an ordinary contract between master & servant and that such power can only be the creature either of a statute governing the contract, or of an express term in the contract itself. Ordinarily, therefore, the absence of such power either as an express term in the contract or in the rules framed under some statute would mean that the master would have no power to suspend a workman and even if he does so in the sense that he forbids the employee to work, he will have to pay wages during the period of suspension. However, where there is power to suspend either in the contract of employment or in the statute or the rules framed there under, the order of suspension has the effect of temporarily suspending the relationship of master and servant with the consequence that the servant is not bound to render service and the master is not bound to pay. This principle of law of master and servant is well established. It is equally well settled that an order of interim suspension can be passed against the employee while an enquiry is pending into his conduct even though there is no such term in the contract of appointment or in the rules, but in such a case the employee would be entitled to his remuneration for the period of suspension if there is no statute or rule under which it could be withheld. In this connection it is important to notice the distinction between suspending the contract of service of an officer and suspending an officer from performing the duties of his office on the basis that the contract is subsisting. The suspension in the latter sense is always an implied term in every contract of service. When an officer is suspended in this sense it means that the Government merely issues a direction to the officer that so long as the contract is subsisting and till the time the officer is legally dismissed he must not do anything in the discharge of the duties trials to which the legal rules of procedure must be applied.

9.18. Evidence in the Domestic Enquiry

The rules related to the appreciation of evidence in a criminal proceeding are different from those of a departmental proceeding, for example:

1. In a criminal trial, the court invariably proceeds on the presumption that accomplice evidence is suspect and shall not be acted upon without any independent corroboration in material particulars. In a departmental enquiry, the officer holding the enquiry is not bound by any such rule.
2. In a criminal enquiry, an incriminating statement made by an accused in certain circumstances or before certain individuals is totally inadmissible in evidence. In a departmental enquiry, the enquiry officer is not bound by any such technical rule.
3. The following has been held by the Supreme Court,

   > [T]here is no warrant for the view expressed by the High Court that in considering whether a public officer is guilty of the misconduct charged against, the rule followed in a criminal trial that an offence is not established beyond reasonable doubt to the satisfaction of the court must be applied. (Held in the case of State of Andhra Pradesh versus Sree Rama Rao [91])

The enquiry held by the Administrative Tribunal is not governed by the technical rules of the Evidence Act. Rule 7(2) of the Disciplinary Proceedings (Administrative Tribunal) Rules, 1951, provides that in conducting the enquiry, the Tribunal shall be guided by the rules of equity and natural justice and shall not be bound by formal rules related to procedure and evidence (held in the case of the State of Orissa versus Murlidhar Jena [92]).

In considering whether an employee is guilty of the misconduct charged against him, the rule followed in criminal trials that an offence is not established unless proved by evidence beyond reasonable doubt to the satisfaction of the court does not apply and even if that rule is not applied, the High Court in a petition under Article 226 of the Constitution is not competent to declare the order of the authority holding a departmental enquiry invalid (held in the case of the State of Andhra Pradesh and other versus S. Sree Rama Rao [91]).

Strictly speaking, neither the provisions of the Evidence Act nor those of the criminal procedure code apply to departmental enquiries, but some of these provisions which are based on rules of natural justice may be held to apply. Thus, if a witness is examined against a delinquent officer, the latter should be given copies of the previous statements of that witness so as to enable him effectively to cross-examine that witness. If such statements had been recorded in regular police investigation under Chapter XIV of the Cr. P. C, the delinquent officer should be given copies of those statements even though there was no regular criminal case, in as much as the spirit of Section 162 of that code should be followed.

Similarly, if there was preliminary enquiry (not of a confidential nature) proceeding the holding of a regular departmental enquiry, the delinquent officer should be given copies of statements made by witnesses during that preliminary enquiry.

The Evidence Act has no application to enquiries conducted by enquiry officer, even though they may be judicial in character. The law requires that such tribunals should observe rules of natural justice in the conduct of the enquiry.

9.19. Rules of Natural Justice

It has been held by the Supreme Court that the principles of natural justice must be observed in all departmental proceedings, whether there be prescribed rules or not. There are two main principles which form the dicta of an enquiry proceeding.

Principle Number 1:

'No man should be a judge of his own cause (nemo debet esse judex in propria causa).'
Under this rule, a person is disqualified to act as a judge:

1. If he is a party to the dispute.
2. If he has any interest whatsoever in the dispute before him.
3. If he is interested in the result of the dispute.
4. If he does not give his own decision on evidence placed before him by the parties.
5. If he does not act according to his own judgement, if he acts at the dictation of others.

Principle Number 2:

'Hear the other side (audi alteram partem).'

This is a duty caused on a judge to hear the evidence of the party to be proceeded against before passing order contrary to his interest. Under this rule, a judge is required to give notice to the party as to why he proposes to proceed in that matter.

1. Fair and reasonable opportunity to the opposite party to deny his guilty and to establish his ignorance
2. To defend himself by cross-examination and by producing witness in his defence
3. To make representation as to why the proposed disciplinary action should not be inflicted on him

In other words, the above rules confirm that the judge acts without bias or prejudice and with a sense of fair play. The principles lay down the procedure required to be followed by authorities entrusted with the task of deciding disputes between the parties.

The principles of natural justice are therefore such principles which are considered as vital to ensure justice and to give all reasonable opportunities to the employee for his own defence. It is necessary to extend full and reasonable scope or otherwise if any authority fails to observe such rule, then the consequence will be that the entire proceedings are liable to be set aside.

To understand the importance of these principles, it would be noteworthy to refer to the observations of Justice Krishna Ayer in the case of Mohinder Singh Gill versus Chief Election Commissioner[2]:

Natural justice is a pervasive facet and secular law where a spiritual touch enlivens legislation, administration and adjudication to make fairness a creed of life. It is of many colours and shades, many forms and shapes and save where valid law excludes it applies when people are effected by acts of authority. It is the home of healthy government, recognized from earliest times and a mystic testament of judge made law. Indeed, from the legendary days of adam and Kautilya's Arthasastra—the rule of law has had this stamp of natural justice which makes it social justice.

It would be prudent to go through some of the salient features of natural justice which are enumerated as follows:

1. The principles of natural justice are such principles which have already received statutory recognition since ancient times. These principles are not static and due to the development of administrative law some subsidiary principles are also being recognized from time to time.
2. Principle of natural justice does not refer to any one principle. There are more than one principle which act as basis to the procedure related to fair determination of the disputes between parties.
3. The principles of natural justice only lay down the procedure and they have nothing to do with the merits of the case.
4. The principles arose out of crystallization of the judicial thinking regarding necessity to evolve minimum norms of fair procedure and they do not owe their origin to either nature or any divine agency.

So the doctrine of natural justice is subservient to positive law, which cannot override the law of a land but can be utilized as a touchstone to find out the validity of any piece of legislation. In this context, reference is normally made to the observation of the Supreme Court in the case of

[2] https://indiankanoon.org/doc/1831036/

A. K. Kraipaka versus Union of India, wherein the Honourable Supreme Court observed that the aim of rule of natural justice is to secure justice or, to put it negatively, to prevent miscarriage of justice. These rules can operate only in areas not covered by any law validly made. In other words, they do not supplant the law but supplement it.

9.20. Constitutional Provisions Attributing to the Principle of Natural Justice

At this juncture, it would be improper not to discuss the constitutional provisions which positively attribute to the above principle. The following constitutional provisions contribute to the growth of industrial justice and are subservient to natural justice.

Articles 14 and 16

Article 14 of the Constitution deals with the fundamental rights and speaks on equality before law for every individual who is a citizen of India. The Article provides that the state shall not deny to any person equality before the law or equal protection of the laws within the territory of India.

Article 16 of the Constitution also provides equality of opportunity in matters of public employment. Previously, it was held that the fundamental rights enshrined in Articles 14 and 16 of the Constitution of India are related to the doctrine of classification and this means that the State will treat equally all persons belonging to a particular category but the State can make reasonable classification and there will be no discrimination where classification is founded on intelligible differential having a rational relation to the objects sought to be achieved. As far as the termination of service of any employee is concerned, constitutionally it is accepted that if the services are terminated in an arbitrary manner by public authorities, then the termination will be violation of Articles 14 and 16.

Article 19

Article 19 of the Constitution provides that all citizens shall have freedom of speech and expression to form associations or unions and to practise any profession or to carry on occupation trade or business. The said Article further provides that the State can impose reasonable restrictions to the exercise of the fundamental rights. So, the Article guarantees the right of freedom of movement and association which contributes positively to the philosophy of industrial justice.

Article 21

Article 21 of the Constitution provides that no person shall be deprived of his life or personal liberty except according to the procedure established by law. So it is obvious that Article 21 of the Constitution deals with the substantive rights as well as procedural rights in so far as the termination or appointment of an individual is concerned.

The industrial justice thus guaranteed by the constitutional provisions ensures the fundamental rights, the rights for association, the rights for doing any trade and business or taking of any occupation which does not affect the social interest and the right to like and personal opportunity. The principle of 'natural justice' asserts a fundamental principle of justice and not specific rule of law and is not susceptible to more than general statement. In the field of procedural rights, the doctrine occupies an important place in laying down fundamental principles for protection of individuals against oppression.

The standing orders of the organizations provide a detailed procedure of management of misconduct. Such a document is an accepted (trade union and management) agreement and is binding on both the management and the trade union/workers.

9.21. Suspension Pending Domestic Enquiry

'Suspension' connotes temporary cessation of the right to work. A person, while holding an office and performing its functions or holding a position or privilege, should be interrupted in doing so and debarred for the time being from further functioning in the office or holding the position or privilege. He is intercepted in the exercise of his functions or his enjoyment of the privilege and put aside, as it were, for a time, excluded during the period from his functions or privileges.

During suspensions, an employee is only prevented from discharging the duties of his office for the time being.

Suspension of employee is prerogative of employer for initiating disciplinary proceedings [93], except when the authority suspending the employee is not competent [94].

There are three kinds of suspension. They are as follows:

1. An employee may be suspended as a mode of punishment.
2. He may be suspended during the pendency of an enquiry against him.
3. Statutory provisions governing his service provide for such suspension.

The employer's right to suspend as a measure of punishment, as well as the right to suspend the contract of service during the pendency of an enquiry are both regulated by the contract of employment or the provisions of the conditions of service.

9.22. Circumstances Justifying Exercise of Right to Suspend

The following circumstances justify the exercise of the right to suspend an employee pending enquiry into the acts of misconduct alleged to have been committed by him:

1. Where the continuance of the employee may endanger industrial peace or security or where the suspension of the employee may be in the interest of the industry itself or its employees in general.
2. Where the continuance of the employee at workplace may prejudice investigation, trial or any enquiry, for example, apprehension of tampering with witnesses or documents.
3. Where continuance at workplace of the employee is likely to be subversive of discipline at the workplace where he is working.
4. Where the continuance at workplace of the workman may be against wider industrial interest, for example, if serious act of misconduct is committed and it is considered

necessary to place the employee under suspension to demonstrate the policy of the management to deal strictly with workers involved in such cases.

5. Where preliminary enquiry into allegations made has revealed a prima facie case justifying criminal or departmental proceedings which are likely to lead to his conviction and/or dismissal or removal from service.

6. Where the employee is suspected to have engaged himself in activities prejudicial to the interest of the security of the company.

Even an employee may be placed under suspension only in respect of the following instances:

1. An offence of conduct involving moral turpitude.
2. Corruption, embezzlement, theft or misappropriation of company's money.
3. Serious negligence and dereliction of duty resulting in considerable loss to the company.
4. Desertion of duty.
5. Refusal or deliberate failure to carry out written orders of supervisory staff.
6. Where it is necessary in the interest of the company itself and the employees in general.
7. Where the continuance of employee may endanger industrial peace and harmony and discipline as well.

The power of suspension should be exercised with circumspection, care and after due application of mind.

9.23. Payment of Subsistence Allowance

(1) Where any workman is suspended by the employer pending enquiry against him, the employer shall pay to such workman subsistence allowance as per Section 10A of Industrial Employment (Standing Orders) Act 1946 at the following rates:

   (a) at the rate of 50 per cent of the wages which the workman was entitled to immediately preceding the date of such suspension, for first 90 days of suspension; and

   (b) at the rate of 75 per cent of such wages, for the remaining period of suspension if the delay in the completion of disciplinary proceedings against such workman is not directly attributable to the conduct of such workman.

(2) If any dispute arises regarding the subsistence allowance payable to a workman under Industrial Employment (Standing Orders) Act 1946, section 10A sub-section (1), the workman, or the employer concerned, may refer the dispute to the Labour Court, constituted under the Industrial Disputes Act, 1947 (14 of 1947), without the local limits of whose jurisdiction the industrial establishment wherein such workman is employed is situated and the Labour Court to which the dispute is so referred shall, after giving the parties an opportunity of being heard, decide the dispute and such decision shall be final and binding on the parties.

(3) Where provision relating to payment of subsistence allowance under any other law are in force, in any State and are more beneficial than the provision as provided under section 10A of Industrial Employment (Standing Orders) Act 1946, the provisions of such other law shall be applicable to the payment of subsistence allowance in that State.

Annexure

General Charge Sheet

To

_____

It is reported against you _____ (name) that on...(date) at...(time), while you were on duty (provided the employee was on duty), you committed the following misconduct as detailed below:

(Mention clearly the act or acts of misconduct as alleged.)

The acts, as alleged above, amount to a misconduct under the clause number _____ of the standing orders of the company which is applicable to you, and is read as under:

(Quote the relevant clauses of the standing orders as appears in the original document.)

The acts, as alleged above, to have been committed by you amount to misconduct which, if proved, would warrant serious disciplinary action. You are required to explain in writing within...(as provided in the standing orders) days of the receipt hereof as to why disciplinary action should not be initiated against you.

Should you fail to submit your explanation as required, it will be presumed that you have no explanation to offer in the matter. The matter will be disposed of without any further reference to you.

The receipt of this letter should be acknowledged.

Authorized Signatory

_____

Charge Sheet for Habitual Absence

To

_____

It is reported against you _____ (name) that you are in the habit of absenting from duty, without obtaining prior permission/approval of leave from your leave sanctioning authority. Your frequent absence from duty has caused dislocation of work, inconvenience to the colleagues and harassment to the management.

The details of your absence from duty without any sanction of leave during the last six months is appended:

(Give the details of the dates of absence date-wise.)

Advisory letters were issued on various dates requesting for the amendment of your habit of remaining absent from duty without authority. The details of the advisory letters specify that you should improve your attendance and are given below:

(Give the details of the advisory letters issued.)

You were also issued a warning letter dated...intimating that in your own interest you should try to be regular in your duty, but despite of that you have not shown any improvement.

The acts, as alleged above, amount to a misconduct under the clause number _____ of the standing orders of the company which is applicable to you, and is read as under:

(Quote the relevant clauses of the standing orders as appear in the original document.)

The acts, as alleged above, to have been committed by you, amount to misconduct which, if proved, would warrant serious disciplinary action. You are required to explain in writing within...(as provided in the standing orders) days of the receipt hereof as to why disciplinary action should not be initiated against you.

Should you fail to submit your explanation as required, it will be presumed that you have no explanation to offer in the matter. The matter will be disposed of without any further reference to you.

The receipt of this letter should be acknowledged.

Authorized Signatory

_____

Charge Sheet for Theft

To

_____

It is reported against you _____ (name) that on...(date) at...(time) when you were leaving the establishment after working during the shift hours _____ to _____, certain articles (goods) belonging to the company as detailed below were recovered from your possession by the watchman, on duty, while you were going out of the factory gate number 2 (exit gate):

(Herein, give details of articles/goods.)

The act of taking out materials without authority is a serious misconduct and amounts to theft of company's property under the standing orders of the company which is applicable to you.

The act, as alleged above, amounts to a misconduct under the clause number _____ of the standing orders of the company which is applicable to you, and is read as under:

(Quote the relevant clauses of the standing orders as appear in the original document.)

The act, as alleged above, to have been committed by you, amounts to misconduct which, if proved, would warrant serious disciplinary action. You are required to explain in writing within...(as provided in the standing orders) days of the receipt hereof as to why disciplinary action should not be initiated against you.

Should you fail to submit your explanation as required, it will be presumed that you have no explanation to offer in the matter. The matter will be disposed of without any further reference to you.

The receipt of this letter should be acknowledged.

Authorized Signatory

_____

Appointment Letter to an Enquiry Officer for Holding Enquiry

To

_____

Since some misconduct was alleged to have been committed by Shri...(name, designation and address), a charge sheet dated...was issued calling for his explanation. Since the explanation, as submitted by the delinquent was found to be unsatisfactory, it has been considered expedient to hold an enquiry into the misconduct alleged as enumerated in the charge sheet.

Accordingly, it has been decided to appoint you as the enquiry officer to conduct enquiry into the charge/charges levelled against the chargesheeted employee daily during office hours and complete your enquiry by...(date) except for unforeseen reasons and submit your report thereafter to the undersigned. The charge sheet, explanation by the delinquent employee and other relevant papers are sent herewith. You are also requested to keep in safe custody the record of all the proceedings of the enquiry. The report of the said enquiry must accompany the order sheet. On the order sheet, you should please take the signature of the worker if any information is given to him personally.

All the persons concerned including witnesses and the management's representative be informed accordingly the next date, time and venue of the enquiry.

Authorized Signatory

Encl.: As above
CC to: 1. The management's representative
          2. Delinquent employee

_____

Letter to the Enquiry Officer for Conducting Enquiry

To
Mr/Ms...

Sir/Madam,

The management has issued a charge sheet to one of its employees calling for his explanation thereto. The explanation by the delinquent employee, on careful consideration, has been found to be as unsatisfactory. The management has decided to hold an enquiry by giving an opportunity to the delinquent employee to defend himself.

The management has decided to appoint you as an enquiry officer and we need your formal approval which may kindly be conveyed at your earliest. Please be assured that the management will extend full cooperation in this context and Mr/Ms...has been appointed as its representative.

Thanking you,
For and on behalf of the management

Authorized Signatory
CC to: Mr/Ms...You are appointed as management's representative to coordinate with the enquiry officer.

Chapter Summary

1. The standing orders of the organizations, certified under the Industrial Employment (Standing Orders) Act, 1946, provide the provisions for maintenance of discipline and taking disciplinary action in the event of an employee commits a misconduct. The standing orders have the list of accepted misconducts (accepted by the employees through their recognized/representative trade union).

2. The detailed procedure of the enquiry proceedings is framed in accordance with the principles of 'natural justice' which are as follows:

Principle Number 1

'No man shall be judged of his cause (*nemo debet esse judex in propria causa*).'
    Under this rule, a person is disqualified to act as a judge:
a. If he is a party to the dispute.
b. If he has any interest whatsoever in the dispute before him.
c. If he is interested in the result of the dispute.
d. If he does not give his own decision on evidence placed before him by the parties.
e. If he does not act according to his own judgement, if he acts at the dictation of others.

Principle Number 2

'Hear the other side (*audi alteram partem*).'
    This is a duty caused on a judge to hear the evidence of the party to be proceeded against before passing order contrary to his interest. Under this rule, a judge is required to give notice to the party as to why he proposes to proceed in that matter.

a. Fair and reasonable opportunity to the opposite party to deny his guilty and to establish his ignorance.
b. To defend himself by cross-examination and by producing witness in his defence.
c. To make representation as to why the proposed disciplinary action should not be inflicted on him.
3. The constitutional provisions that attribute to the principle of natural justice are: Articles 14, 16, 19 and 21.
4. Steps followed in domestic enquiry are as follows:
   a. Step I: Issue of a letter calling explanation to all relevant charges and allegations, which is normally termed as a 'charge sheet';
   b. Step II: The charge sheet is followed by submission of reply to the same by the chargesheeted employee.
   c. Step III: If the explanation is not considered to be satisfactory by the disciplinary authority, an enquiry is conducted and the same is conveyed through a notice of enquiry.
   d. Step IV: In course of the enquiry, the enquiry officer will extend all reasonable opportunities both to the chargesheeted employee and the management to establish their cases.
   e. Step V: The enquiry officer follows the principles of 'natural justice'.
   f. Step VI: The disciplinary authority considers the findings of the enquiry officer and determines the extent to which the concerned employee is guilty of the charges levelled against him.
5. An employ may be suspended pending domestic enquiry until the charges are levelled against him. Such suspensions are not considered as major forms of punishment.

Questions

1. Discuss the difference between preliminary enquiry and domestic enquiry. Why a preliminary enquiry becomes essential?
2. Comment on how the 'principles of natural justice' are critical to disciplinary proceedings?
3. Elaborate the steps of conducting a domestic enquiry?
4. Comment on 'suspension pending domestic enquiry against a delinquent is guaranteed within the contract of employment'.
5. Why a delinquent is suspended pending domestic enquiry to the charges levelled against him?

References

1. The Constitution of India, Article 14 and Article 16.
2. Jagadeesh TK. Demostic enquiry and industrial law. In Domestic Enquiry Principles, Procedures and Practice. Kolkata: Indian Institute of Personnel Management; 1977.
3. Disciplinary Proceeding against Government Servant - New Delhi: Indian Law Institute.
4. Disciplinary Proceeding against Government Servant - New Delhi: Industrial Law Institute.
5. Tribhuwannath v. State of Bihar, AIR 1960, Patna–116.
6. Chowdhury v. Union of India, AIR 1956, Cal–662.
7. Champklal v. Union of India, AIR 1964, SC–1854.
8. Badri Das v. Industrial Tribunal, AIR 1961, Punj–515.
9. N. K. Roy v. Commissioner, AIR 1955, Cal–56.
10. Dadarao Tidke v. State, AIR 1958, Bom–204.

11. Subharao v. P. S. C., AIR 1961, AP–378.
12. Surendra Chandra Das v. Union Territory, AIR 1962, Tri–15.
13. Surath Chandra v. State of West Bengal, AIR 1971, SC–752.
14. Niranjan Prasad v. State, AIR 1960, All–323.
15. State v. Satigram, AIR 1960, All–543.
16. Raghuban Ahir v. State, AIR 1957, Patna–100.
17. Ramanand v. DMF, AIR 1962, Rajasthan–265.
18. Bua Das Kaushal v. State, AIR 1965, Punjab–342.
19. State of Bombay v. Amar Singh Raval, AIR 1963, Gujrat–244.
20. Rabindra Mohan v. Union Territory, AIR 1961, Tripura–1.
21. Krishan Lal v. State (Rajasthan), SLR 1969, 666.
22. J. M. Ajwani v. Union of India (SC), SLR 1967, 471.
23. Ram Lal v. Union of India, AIR 1963, Rajasthan–57.
24. Karan Singh v. Transport Commissioner, AIR 1965, J&K–53.
25. A. S. Razvi v. Divisional Engineer, AIR 1964, Gujarat–139.
26. Nageswara Rao v. Transport Company, AIR 1956, SC–3 08.
27. D. A. Koregaonkar v. State, AIR 1958, Bom–167.
28. DIG Police v. Amalnath, AIR 1966, Madras–203.
29. Harjit Singh v. I. G. Police, AIR 1963, Punjab–90.
30. G. M. v. Jawala Prasad Singh, AIR 70, SC–1095.
31. K. N. Gupta v. Union of India, AIR 1968, Delhi–85.
32. Harjit Singh v. I. G. Police, AIR 1963, Punjab–90.
33. Union of India v. Kula Chander Singh, AIR 1963, Tripura–20.
34. R. C. Verma v. R. D. Verma, AIR 1958, All–532.
35. K. N. Gupta v. Union of India, AIR 1968, Delhi–85.
36. K. S. Rao v. State of AP, AIR 1957, AP–414.
37. A. N. Chopra v. Union of India, 1, DL–1967, P–407 (Punjab).
38. Nitya Ranjan v. State of Orissa, AIR 1962, Orissa–78.
39. Nripendra Nath v. Chief Security, AIR 1961, Cal–1.
40. Kapur Singh v. Union of India, AIR 1956, Punjab–58.
41. Shadul Singh v. State of MP, AIR 1966, MP–193.
42. Raipur Transport G. Pvt. Ltd. v. State of MP, AIR 1961, MP–150.
43. Vine v. National Dock Labour Board (1957), AC–488.
44. A. Krishnaswamy v. T. N. Electricity Board (1981), ISLR (Mad-HC).
45. Jugraj Singh v. Delhi Admn. (Delhi), SLR–1970.
46. Surat Singh v. S. R. Bakshi, AIR 1971, Del–133.
47. Jiwaram v. State of Rajasthan, AIR 1965, Raj–32.
48. Bakhtawar Singh v. State of Punjab, AIR 1971, P&H–220.
49. Union of India V. T. R. Verma, AIR 1952, SC–882.
50. Phanindra Chandra Shome v. Union of India (1961), 3 FLR–1(Cal-HC).
51. Jugraj Singh v. Delhi Admn. (Delhi), 1970 SLR–400.
52. State of Assam v. Malendra Kr. Das, AIR 1970, SC–1255.
53. Gajinder Singh v. State of Punjab, 1972, SLR–432, (P&H-HC).
54. R. Yadav v. Chief Security Officer, 1967, AIR-MP–91.
55. State of Punjab v. Asanand (P&H) 1968, SLR–638.
56. Krishan Lal v. State (Rajasthan) 13 I LLJ–478.
57. Supreme court of India, State of UP v. C. S. Sharma. May, 1967. SCS, May 1967.
58. S. N. Singh v. State of Manipur, 1956, AIR, Manipur–31.
59. Sivanandan Sinha v. State of West Bengal, 1954 AIR, Cal–60.
60. Lalit Prasad v. I. G. Police, 1954 AIR, All–138.

61. Amulya Sikdar v. L.M. Bakshi, AIR 1958. Cal–470.
62. Shashi Bhushan v. State (Orissa), 1969, SLR–63.
63. Sri Ram v. State (P&H), 1967, SLR–686.
64. Surjit Kaur v. State (P&H), 1968, SLR–362.
65. Ram Netra v. Superintendent of Police, AIR 1966, MP–58.
66. Chandra Kutty M. P. v. A. O. Medical College (Kerala), 1968, SLR–453.
67. State v. S. N. Bose, AIR 1964, Cal–184.
68. P. Banerji v. D. C. E., AIR 1960, Assam–51.
69. Jagdish Chander Bhasin v. State, AIR 1957, All–436.
70. Govind Shankar v. State, AIR 1969, Cal–161.
71. Lakshmi Narayan v. A. N. Puri, AIR 1954, Cal–335.
72. Naubat Rai v. Union of India, AIR 1953, Raj–137.
73. K. Behari Chakravarty v. Union of India (SC), 1970, SLR–321.
74. Hareram Samant v. Superintendent of Police, Hooghly (1961), 3 FLR_2 74, (Cal-HC).
75. Zonal Manager, LIC of India v. Mohan Lai Saraf (1978) 2, SLR–868 (J&K-HC).
76. Ramniwas Sharma v. Union of India, 1983 Lab IC–828 (Gau HC).
77. Mansukhlal v. J. D. Nagarwala (1967), I LLJ–455 (Guj-HC).
78. M. V. Jogarao v. State of Madras, AIR–1957, AP–197.
79. Workmen v. Lambadari Tea Estate (1966) 2, LLJ–315 (SC).
80. Hari Singh v. Management of Muncipal Committee, Batala [Punj Gaz. dt. 21 April 1967 p. 353 (IT)].
81. Lakshminarayan v. State, AIR 1956, Raj–34.
82. M. L. Joshi v. Director of Estate, AIR 1967, Del–86.
83. A. R. S. Choudhury v. Union of India (1957) 1, LLJ–494.
84. Gouri Prasad Ghosh v. State of West Bengal (1981) 1, SLR–673 (HP-HC).
85. V. P. Gidroniya v. State of MP, AIR 1967, MP–231.
86. Rameshawar Singh v. Union of India (1963) 1, LLJ–792 (MP-HC).
87. Balwantary Patel v. State of MP, AIR 1968, SC–800.
88. Management of Hotel Imperial, New Delhi v. Hotel Workers' Union (1959) 2, LLJ–544.
89. T. Cajee v. Jormanik Siem (1961) 1, LLJ–652.
90. R. P. Kapur v. Union of India (1966) 2, LLJ–164.
91. State of AP v. Rama Rao, AIR 1963, SC–1723.
92. Supreme Court of India, Appeal (Civil) 129 of 1961, State of Orissa v. Murlidhar Jena. https://indiankanoon.org/doc/186277747/
93. BEST Workers Union v. The BEST Undertaking, 2007.
94. Prem Nath v. State of Uttar Pradesh, 2008 LLR 821.

Workers' Participation in Management

LEARNING OBJECTIVES

After reading this chapter, you will be able to understand:

☐ The nature, forms and the importance of WPM
☐ The advantage of worker–management cooperation in an industry

10.1. Introduction

The complexity of the modern industry had 'dwarfed the importance of the individual worker and tended to tie him for lifetime to his bench'. It was a general trend of employers to neglect human problems arising from mass production techniques, so workers were becoming less and less involved with their jobs, and more and more alienated from the factory life. The remedy was clear—workers must be treated as human beings and managers must realize their individual traits and characteristics, for which a number of labour laws supporting such a view were enacted within a short period after the Independence. Yet the central values of the country's IR system remained competitive. The old attitude of key parties continued to exist; employers and their managers considered trade unions as 'unavoidable nuisance' or 'unavoidable hurdle', whereas trade unions continued to consider their managers as 'exploiters' or 'obscurantist'. Such an industrial climate could not foster the development of basic prerequisites of an ideal IR, that is,

1. The mutual acceptability of the legitimacy of each other's role
2. Mutual perception of interdependence (co-partners in production and distribution) between the key parties.

It is an admitted fact that a harmonious IR in an industry is a means to higher production; second, higher production is a crucial factor for the economic development for a lower-middle income country like India.[1] The essential requirement in the post-Independence period in all Indian industries was to bridge the gap between the management and workers for facilitating a harmonious IR. The scheme of participative management was deemed to be a suitable tool for the purpose.

---

[1] As per the classification of the World Bank.

10.2. The Objectives of Workers' Participation in Management

The objectives of workers' participation in management (WPM) are as follows:

- To achieve industrial peace and harmony
- To build the most dynamic human resources by developing internal motivation in workers
- To boost the morale of employees and satisfy workers' social and esteem needs
- To raise the levels of employee production, productivity and product quality
- To satisfy workers by making them feel that they have their voice in the management
- To give workers a better understanding of their role in the working of industry
- To develop a better mutual understanding so that workers do not resist a change for the betterment of the concern (e.g., the introduction of work-study)
- To minimize the number of grievances and, therefore, industrial disputes
- To make the management of subordinates easy.

10.3. Definition

The concept of workers' participation is widely used but indistinctly defined and understood. The basic philosophy and the ideology are either over-understood or misunderstood. It is often considered as a principle of attaining industrial democracy by ensuring the total involvement of workers in achieving the organizational goals. 'It is the mutual and emotional involvement of a person in a group situation, which encourages him to identify himself with the group goals and share responsibility with them'. In other words, 'the influence of the subordinates on actions taken by the superiors'. 'It is the principle of democratic administration of industry, that is, sharing the decision-making power by rank and file of an industrial organization through their representatives at all the appropriate levels of management in the entire range of managerial action', or it is a distribution of social power in the industry among all the workers. Based on the principle of equity and voluntarism, it gives the workers the right to criticize, to offer constructive suggestions and to become aware of various issues involved in decision-making.

When these definitions are analysed, 'mutual and emotional involvements' or 'influence of the subordinates on the action of the superiors' may be of the following two different forms:

1. Giving ideas and suggestions for improvement anywhere, for example, work methods and working conditions, improvement in the techniques of production and so on
2. Decision-making, that is, participating in a variety of ways in the decision-making process.

ILO had been encouraging its member nations to promote the schemes of WPM. It is a mechanism where workers have a say in the decision-making process of an enterprise formally. It promotes harmony and peace between workers and management by providing them a unique motivational power and a great psychological value. According to ILO,

Workers' participation, may broadly be taken to cover all terms of association of workers and their representatives with the decision-making process, ranging from exchange of information, consultations, decisions and negotiations, to more institutionalized forms such as the presence of workers' member on management or supervisory boards or even management by workers themselves. [1]

According to Keith Davis, 'Participation refers to the mental and emotional involvement of a person in a group situation which encourages him to contribute to group goals and share the responsibility of achievement'.

On the other hand, Walpole defines it as, 'Participation in Management gives the worker a sense of importance, pride and accomplishment; it gives him the freedom of opportunity for self-expression; a feeling of belongingness with the place of work and a sense of workmanship and creativity'.

But participation only becomes meaningful in situations where the participation of each is strictly confined to the field for which he or she is competent and is concerned with. Everybody poking his/her nose into everything is not participation but proliferations. So a group of participating managers defined WPM as the 'involvement of the workers only in such areas of activities of the enterprise where they can make same positive contribution for the betterment of the enterprise'. But this statement does not mean that participation to be limited to a certain isolated area, which is favourable and convenient to the management alone. Such forms of participation should also be conducive to the direct and the indirect well-being of the workers at large. Finally, participation cannot be limited to the formal participation of one or few trade union leaders. A whole-hearted involvement of each concerned worker is true participation. Accordingly, management experts and executives consider participation:

A tool for improving the performance of an enterprise which provides opportunity to workers to take part in the decisions related with their wages, working condition, job and also helps to increase the productivity and efficiency by making harmonious industrial relations. [2]

The concept of WPM is an attempt on the part of an employer to bind his/her employees into a team which works towards the realization of common objectives.

According to Mc Gregor, 'Workers' participation consists basically in creating opportunity under suitable conditions for people to influence decisions which affect them'. It bridges the communication gap between the management and workers and provides greater control and freedom of choice to subordinates. So participation has been described in many ways—as a behavioural mood, as a result of reallocating power within the organization and as an institutional structure.

The various types of involvement with employees varied greatly as several organizations established different practices in India. Information sharing, suggestion schemes, consultation and, only in a few cases, co-determination or participation in its true sense exist in many organizations. Broadly speaking, the range of issues in any enterprise on which decisions need to be taken from time to time can be classified under five major heads: safety and welfare issues, work-related issues (production on the shop floor, quality, machine maintenance), sharing of gains (wages, incentives and allowances) production-related issues (product-mix, plant production targets and technology) and business policy (expansion, contraction and pricing). Even the most reluctant manager would agree that workers should have some say in the first three categories, although there may again be doubts about the second category. The third category obviously influences workers up to some extent through the process of collective bargaining.

Other participative models adopted by various enterprises can be classified into the following three groups:

1. **Superficial participation:** Comprising information sharing and suggestion schemes
2. **Intermediate participation:** Comprising collective bargaining in both traditional and non-traditional areas, and consultation on restricted issues

3. **Real participation:** Comprising consultation on unrestricted issues and co-determination on restricted and unrestricted issues.

Thus, the concept of WPM encompasses the following:

- It provides scope for employees in the decision-making of the organization.
- Participation may be at the shop, departmental or corporate level.
- Participation includes the willingness to share the responsibility by workers as they are committed to execute their decisions.
- Participation is conducted through the mechanism of forums which provide for the association of workers' representatives.
- The basic idea is to develop self-control and self-discipline among workers.

The concept of WPM is aligned with the objectives of IRs in the following manner:

- It safeguards the interest of labour and management by securing the highest level of mutual understanding and goodwill among all sections which participate in the process of production.
- It avoids industrial conflicts and develops harmonious relations.
- It enhances productivity to a higher level.
- It establishes and promotes the growth of an industrial democracy based on labour partnership.
- It eliminates or minimizes the number of strikes, lockouts and gheraos by providing reasonable wages and improved living and working conditions.
- It improves the economic conditions of workers.

10.4. Why Participation?

The promotion of WPM serves the following two main purposes in the organizations:

1. **Economic:** It ensures the increase in production. The process motivates workers to work harder and also makes them more committed to the objectives of the enterprise and more responsive to its needs, as they find greater job satisfaction from their involvements in organizing working methods, setting production targets, having control over their own work and so on.
2. **Social:** It ensures full recognition of the importance of the human elements at work, thereby generating greater interest of workers in the general operation of their undertaking. Workers' participation leads to the 'humanization of the work' in the undertaking and gives them the feeling 'that they are not just a cog in the very big wheel, but also that their personal effort is essential for the achievement of the overall production plan'. For ensuring the development of workers' individuality and recognizing their rights, the concept of workers' participation is an effective tool.

In general terms, the object of workers' participation implies the mental and emotional involvement of a worker in a group situation which encourages him or her to contribute to group goals and share responsibilities with them. Labour participation in the management of business provides some 'status' and a feeling of self-importance to the employees of an organization. Such participation leads to better IRs. Workers are encouraged to give their best to the organization that results in the increase in productivity and generates a sense of belonging to the organization, and leading to industrial growth. But workers' participation had never been an easy game in Indian organizations, as it literally appears. There are various reasons for this as follows:

1. The dual roles played by the trade union or workers' representatives make participation quite difficult.
2. Managements are often reluctant to share responsibility.
3. There are often perceived differences in social status, education and awareness between the two parties, that is, the management and the workers. This obstructs transparency and trust.
4. Trade unions find themselves party to decisions which they do not really influence.
5. It is also clear that real participation cannot be continued for long in the current context. It may prove successful in a particular context and crisis. However, it is very difficult to sustain when conditions improve or change completely.

10.5. The Development of Participation in Management in India

WPM in India was introduced by Mahatma Gandhi in 1920. He emphasized that equal importance should be given to each worker, with the dignity of work and mutual exchange of interest between labour and management. He observed that there should be a perfect relationship of friendship and cooperation among employers and employees. Gandhiji's concept of joint consultation was first adopted by the cotton textile industry in 1937. The Royal Commission on Labour, who supported the works committee, suggested that strong trade unions should be developed and LO should be appointed to set up the works committee to promote industrial harmony, as well as to avoid misunderstanding and settle industrial disputes. The Royal Commission on Labour (1929–1931) said, 'We believe that if these committees (works committees) are given proper encouragement and the past errors are avoided they can play a useful role in the Indian industrial system'. But the importance was given to WPM in India only after Independence. All these recommendations were translated into law only in 1947.

The ID Act, 1947, recommended for setting up of 'works committees' with the purpose of settlement and prevention of industrial disputes. Next, the Industrial Policy Resolution of 1948 advocated WPM, according to which all matters of industrial production should be dealt with labour. In 1958, JMCs were established with the purpose to increase the labour participation in management, and the two-tier participation was also introduced in July 1975, which was known as the shop council at the shop level and the joint council at the plant level. In 1977, the equity participation schemes were suggested by the Ravindra Verma Committee and the Sachar Committee. But such schemes were not accepted by the workers and management, and they remained only on the paper.

On the basis of experience and after the review of old schemes of workers' participation, the Government of India formulated a new scheme for workers' participation in 1983, which was applicable to all central public sector enterprises, and decided that workers would be allowed to participate at the shop and plant levels. A Tripartite Committee was constituted by the Ministry of Labour to review the working of this scheme and also to suggest corrective measures.

A bill on workers' participation was introduced by the government in the Parliament on 30 May 1990 for legalizing the provision of WPM in Indian industries. But the bills could never become an Act owing to the sudden collapse of the government body who had introduced the bill.

For the convenience of our discussion, the entire evolutionary period of workers' participation can be divided into the following five distinct periods:

1. 1910–1930, that is, the period prior to the recommendation of the Royal Commission on Labour
2. 1930–1947, that is, the pre-Independence period
3. 1947–1956, that is, the post-Independence period
4. 1957–1974, that is, the period of JMC
5. 1975 onwards, that is, the period of the new scheme.

10.5.1. 1910–1930

In 1910, a rudimentary form of informal consultation was developed in the organized textile industries through the trade unions which were slowly taking shape in these organizations. Such a development in these industries cannot be ignored altogether because this was the first step in the right direction for the participation of workers, and it was introducing a new dimension to the existing practice of the management.

Then, after the First World War, the idea of forming a consultative committee was taken up by TISCO at Jamshedpur. This form of participation was developed more or less in the British pattern of works council, the objective of which was to maintain industrial peace and boost production. But with the development of rivalry between trade unions in TISCO, the entire scheme was a failure.

In the later part of the 1920s, the ideology of Mahatma Gandhi tried to develop a new relationship based on the mutual decision and consultation between the workers and management in Ahmedabad. Gandhiji's view on WPM was an integral part of his thought on the administration of the economy. Consultation based on goodwill and trust was viewed by him to be the solution of all industrial disputes.

The need for 'works committee' in all organizations for solving industrial unrest was also recommended by the Committee of 1921, appointed by the Government of Bengal. During this period, one of the first industries to set up a Joint Committee in Madras was Buckingham and Carnatic Mills.

On analysing the development till 1930, it can be concluded that the nature of participation was more informal and consultative. Consultation was taken as a means to enhance production and maintain industrial peace. Goals of organizations were given importance, whereas the interest of workers was either given very little importance or neglected.

10.5.2. 1930–1947

The second period starts with the recommendation of the Royal Commission in 1931. The Royal Commission on Labour examined the working of these committees and recommended that the causes of the poor performance of the committees till 1930 were as follows:

1. Existence of trade union rivalry in industries
2. Lack of sincerity and interest on the part of employers
3. Illiteracy and ignorance of the workers

The Commission expressed the importance of the committees in the field of IR and also advocated for the formation of joint machineries similar to the pattern of the informal consultative machinery of Ahmedabad. The Royal Commission on Labour, 1931 observed:

> The organization of the employees as a rule, weak, but we believe that in many centers it would suffice to make a start and the working of the Joint Machinery would go far to strengthen the better elements and to increase the sense of responsibility in trade unions, which so many employees are anxious to develop. The board line of organization, therefore, should include not only Joint committees or councils within the individual establishments, but also a large body representative of both sides of the industry a la the center concerned. (The small body)...would deal with disputes affecting single establishment. The large body would deal with more general questions and might also act as an advisory appellate body in respect of disputes.

The importance of the Great Depression of the 1930s on participation cannot be ignored. With the emergence of the worldwide Depression, the recommendation of the Royal Commission could not make much headway. A further blow to the system came from the Emergency declared during 1939 (Second World War), and the Defence of India Rule which prohibited strikes and lockouts also gave a setback to the movement.

During the post-Second World War period, the trade union movement was identified with the national movement for Independence. The time experienced a graving demand for the nationalization of the basic industries, voiced by the trade unions as well as by the political parties. The People's Plan of 1944 further supported the growing claim for nationalizing the basic industries. When the question of the form of management desirable for these industries was raised, there was a demand for associating labour with management. It was thought that such an association would be a check on the unrestrained power of the management. While the movement for political independence was gradually reaching its success, some of the managements introduced consultative machinery. During that time, the management committee of TISCO reintroduced the scheme.

An analysis of the second phase reveals that the development of participation in management was rather slow and irregular. The form of participation which developed at this stage was more confusing, for the recommendations of the Royal Commission could not successfully give a concrete shape to the form. They advocated something which the economy could not accept owing to unexpected economic hazards such as the Great Depression and the Second World War. In the latter half of this period, socialistic ideas of nationalization tried to dominate the recommendation of the Royal Commission. This was more politically based and the objective was to achieve the national Independence.

10.5.3. 1947–1956

The scheme got a firm legislative foundation with the government's enactment of the ID Act of 1947. The Act recommended for the establishment of the works committees in every industrial establishment where more than 100 workers were ordinarily employed. The committee was intended 'to remove the causes of frictions between the employer and the workmen in the day-to-day working of the establishment and to promote measures for securing amity and good relations between them'. The role of works committee was only consultative and advisory in nature.

In the Tripartite Industrial Conference held in December 1947, both workers and employers accepted the principle of joint consultation. It also gave a positive headway to the scheme by further encouraging the constitution of both works committees and production committees for promoting efficiency and productivity in industries. The issue was later taken up by the state governments, as a result of which by September 1951, the number of committees set up stood at 1,141. Besides this, there were 428 production committees in operation throughout the country. The largest number of works committees was in Madras (486), followed by Bombay (now Mumbai) (245), Punjab (96) and West Bengal (78).

Importance was attached to the works committees in the First Five-Year Plan by the Planning Commission. The Planning Commission observed, 'These committees will be the best vehicle for improving labour relations and promoting the employer and employee collaboration in the interest of higher production and greater well-being of the workers through progress of the industries'. By the end of 1954, there were 2,095 works committees across the country.

The Second Plan recommended for the establishment of councils of management consisting representatives of the management, technicians and workers in each undertaking. Such councils were entitled to recommend steps for better working of the undertaking. Such associations, the Commission felt, would be useful in:

1. Promoting the increased productivity for the general benefit of the enterprise.
2. Giving employers a better understanding of their role in the working of the industry.
3. Satisfying the workers' urge for self-expression, thereby leading to industrial peace, better relations and increased cooperation.

So with Independence, formal participation was introduced in Indian industries through legal enactment. A closer collaboration between the management and labour was sought for maintaining industrial peace and promoting production.

But later, the 'works committee', advocated in the ID Act of 1947, proved to be a failure in Indian industries. Commenting on the failure of the 'works committees', the ILO expert, Professor J. H. Richardson observed:

> The causes of the failures whether in the public or private sector, were the apathy or disapproval of the management, opposition from the trade union or rivalry between them, uncertainties because the subjects which could be discussed and which could not, have not been clearly laid down, and the dissatisfaction of the workers and the representatives.

10.5.4. 1957–1974

In this period, rigorous venture was made to establish the joint council on a strong foundation and simultaneously to introduce the participative management in both public and private sectors. A study group of 1956 which had visited a number of European countries such as Britain, Sweden, France, Belgium, Germany and Yugoslavia produced their report in 1957, which consisted of two parts. The first part gave the information and pattern of the participative management that existed in the countries they visited, and the second part laid down the preconditions that are necessary for the introduction of joint consultation in management in India.

Most of the recommendations of the study group were accepted in the 15th session of the ILO held on 11 and 12 July 1957. The Conference advocated to introduce workers' participation in selected industrial units on a voluntary basis. They were against the compulsory implementation of worker's participation, though they realized that if the voluntary method would fail, the compulsory introduction through legal measures would be the last alternative. The Conference also realized that all the undertakings were not fully matured to accept the scheme. So the Conference had to appoint a Tripartite Subcommittee for laying down the criteria for the selection of undertaking for introducing the scheme.

The Subcommittee laid down the criteria for the selection of undertaking for introducing the scheme of workers' participation. They proposed that undertakings having a fair record of IRs, with at least 500 workers, and well-established strong trade union function, should be accepted for the introduction of the scheme. Later, the Subcommittee itself was reconstituted to 'Committee on Labour-Management Corporation' to advise on all matters connected with the scheme.

A Labour Management Cooperation seminar was held at New Delhi on 31 January 1956 and 1 February 1956, to consider the constitution and function of the JMC, and the administrative problems connected with such a council. The seminar was attended by some 101 representatives of the Central Ministry, state government, All India Employer and Workers Organization, representatives of workers and employers. They reached some conclusions relating to:

1. Size of the council
2. Representation of different departments
3. Office-bearers of the JMC
4. Constitution of sub-committees
5. Schedule for the meeting of the JMCs
6. Minimum qualification
7. Liaison between the JMC and the Ministry of Labour & Employment
8. Guidance for a panel of experts
9. Training programmes in the units
10. Dissemination of information to workers
11. Informal meetings

The report of the conference of the public sector held in 20 January 1959 depicted the willingness on the part of the management to give a trial to the JMC. A restatement of the scheme was also made in the seminar of 1960, and a major rigorous step was taken to extend the scheme to as many units as possible. By 1962, the scheme was introduced in 95 establishments, out of which 35 were public sectors and 60 were private sectors. By 1966, it was introduced in 140 establishments, out of which 34 were public sectors and 97 were private sectors. In 1968, it was introduced in 131 establishments, out of which 46 were public sectors and 85 were private sectors.

The trend shows that by 1968, the private sectors had developed a pessimistic view towards this scheme, whereas the public sectors were gradually trying to accept the same.

Another evolution study was attempted in the report on the working of the JMC published by the Government of India in 1965. The first part of the report indicated certain observations of the general working of the JMC. The report gave a pessimistic picture of the functioning of the JMC. It indicated that the very objectives of participation had neither been realized by the management nor by the workers. As a result, proper communication and the information sharing had not been adequately developed. Although the joint councils were set up with the administrative responsibility with regard to welfare measures, safety measures and so on, in actual practice, no administrative responsibilities were transferred to the workers. In some cases, the worker representatives were interested more in the enlargement of amenities and facilities; as a result, joint councils turned into grievance committees.

The third report on the working of the JMC was made by the Chief Labour Commissioner, New Delhi, in 1966. This report also gave a pessimistic picture of the working of the joint councils. The National Commission on Labour made the following observations about the working of the JMC.

Considering the above, by 1966, it is not wrong to conclude that the scheme of the JMC had failed miserably in India. The question was whether the cause of such failure was the ill modelling of the scheme or defect in the system of acceptance. To be precise, there were some inherent forces in the system, that is, the attitudinal, structural and environmental forces that were hindering the effectiveness of participation.

10.5.5. 1975 Onwards

In 1975, as a part of the 20-point Economic Programme announced by the government, the scheme of workers' participation was implemented on 13 October 1973. It provided for shop council at the shop floor level, consisting of equal number of representatives of management and the workers. The council was to discuss all forms of improvement in production and productivity, and enhance efficiency. Industrial units employing 500 or more workers were required to set up these bodies. There was no compulsion behind the implementation of such a scheme. There was a fair extension of the scheme to a number of public sector enterprises, but not much in private sectors. Some state governments later made an attempt to extend the scheme to the smaller units also.

The second version of the scheme was introduced on 4 January 1977. This scheme was meant only for public sectors' service organizations having an employee strength of 100 or more. These organizations included commercial and service organizations having large-scale public dealings such as hospitals, post and telegraphs, railway stations/booking offices, government provident fund and pensions organization, road transportation, electricity boards, insurance, institutions like FCI, Central Warehousing Corporations, State Warehousing Corporations, Public Distribution System including Fair Price Shops, Super Bazaar, all financial institutions, educational institutions, air and inland water transport, ports and docks, handlooms and handicrafts export corporations, municipal services, milk distribution services, the irrigation system, tourist organizations, public hotels and restaurants, and establishments for public amusements.

The second scheme also had the same flexible characteristics as the first scheme; there was no statutory force behind the enactment of such scheme. Different organizations formed different forms of participative structures or the skeleton of the proposed scheme. As a result of which, a variety of participative styles have emerged in different organizations and it has completely given farewell to the basic purpose for which the scheme was implemented.

10.6. Recommendations of the Verma Committee (1977–1978)

On the recommendations of the tripartite labour conference, the Government of India constituted a Committee on WPM under the chairmanship of Mr Ravindra Verma, the then Minister of Labour and Parliamentary Affairs. The Committee commented that the experience of voluntary schemes of participative management implemented from time to time in the past had not been very effective. So the Committee recommended for the introduction of the scheme through legislative enactments.

The Committee was in favour of the adoption of a three-tier system of participation at the corporate, plant and shop floor levels. The scheme of participation would be introduced in undertakings employing 500 or more workers with an enabling provision to extend it to others employing at least 100 workers. It was also suggested that an organization both at centre and in the states be constituted to monitor the implementation of the scheme of WPM and also to review its working.

10.6.1. Prerequisites for Effective Participation

The prerequisites for the success of any scheme of participative management are as follows:

- There should be a strong, democratic and representative unionism for the success of participative management.
- There should be mutually agreed and clearly formulated objectives for the participation to succeed.
- There should be a feeling of participation at all levels. The working environment must be congenial enough to create a participatory culture.
- There should be effective consultation of the workers by the management to inculcate enthusiasm in them in the formulation of policies that affect them directly.
- A relationship based on mutual trust and respect is essential for effective participation.
- Education and training make a significant contribution to the purposeful working of participative management. Employers, trade unions and the government can play a major and meaningful role in organizing and conducting training programmes, and in developing the necessary skills in the representatives of workers and employees.
- Forums of participation, areas of participation and guidelines for implementation of decisions should be specific, and there should be prompt follow-up action and feedback.

10.7. Schemes of WPM

Since Independence, various schemes have been recommended and implemented by the Government of India to encourage WPM. The history of WPM in India establishes that the participative styles as we see today had not been the outcome of a single short effort, rather based on the industrial experience from time to time. The various schemes implemented for WPM in India are as follows:

- The earliest form of participative management was the 'works committees', implemented through Section 3 of the ID Act, 1947. It empowered the central and state governments, in their respective jurisdictions, to make general or special order, requiring the employer of an industrial establishment employing 100 or more workmen to constitute a works committee. The composition, functions and working of works committees have been discussed in detail subsequently in the chapter.
- In 1947, the Industrial Truce Resolution adopted at the Industries Conference recommended inter alia the formation of unit production committees in industrial establishments for promoting the efficiency of workers and improving production.
- Under the Industrial Policy Resolution of 1948, the Government of India accepted, in principle, the establishment of bipartite production committees consisting of the representatives of employer and workers. Subsequently, a model constitution for the establishment of unit production committees and for enabling the existing works committees to function as production committees was adopted.

- In 1958, an ambitious scheme of JMCs was introduced.
- Subsequently, in 1975, forums of shop councils and joint councils were introduced under the old 20-point programme.
- In 1977, institutions of WPM were established in commercial and service organizations in the public sector.
- In 1976, Article 43A was inserted in the Indian Constitution under the Directive Principles of State Policy. The new Article provides that 'the state shall take steps, by suitable legislation or any other way, to secure the participation of workers in the management of undertakings, establishments or other organizations engaged in any industry'.
- A new scheme of Employees Participation in Management for PSUs was introduced in 1983. This scheme is still in operation in the country.
- Besides, schemes of workers' participation have been in operation in some government services and in establishments of the private sector.
- In 1990, a comprehensive WPM Bill was introduced in the parliament, but it has still not been passed. The schemes are elaborated below.

10.7.1. Works Committee

With the enactment of the ID Act, 1947, the scheme of joint consultation received legislative approval in India. Section 3 of the ID Act, 1947, provides for the provision of the 'works committee' as[1]:

(1) In the case of any industrial establishment in which one hundred or more workmen are employed or have been employed on any day in the preceding twelve months, the appropriate government may by general or special order require the employer to constitute in the prescribed manner a Works Committee consisting of representatives of employers and workmen engaged in the establishment, so however that the number of representatives of workmen on the Committee shall not be less than the number of representatives of the employer. The representatives of the workmen shall be chosen in the prescribed manner from among the workmen engaged in the establishment and in consultation with their trade union, if any, registered under the Indian Trade Unions Act, 1926 (16 of 1926).

(2) It shall be the duty of the Works Committee to promote measures for securing and preserving amity and good relations between the employer and workmen and, to that end, to comment upon matters of their common interest or concern and endeavour to compose any material difference of opinion in respect of such matters.

10.7.1.1. Items to Be Dealt by the 'Works Committee'

1. The conditions of work such as ventilation, temperature and lighting.
2. The amenities such as drinking water, canteens, crèches, medical and health services.
3. The safety and accident prevention, occupational diseases and protective equipment.
4. The adjustment of festivals and national holidays.
5. The administration of welfare and fine funds.
6. The educational and recreational activities such as libraries, reading rooms, sports, games, community welfare and celebrations.
7. The promotion of thrift and savings.
8. The implementation and review of decisions arrived at meetings of works committees.

[1] https://labour.gov.in/sites/default/files/THEINDUSTRIALDISPUTES_ACT1947_0.pdf

Although a large number of committees were set up in accordance with the provisions of Section 3 of the ID Act, 1947, experience has shown that a major hindrance was caused in the way of effective functioning of works committees. There was a lack of clear-cut demarcation between the responsibilities of the committees and the trade unions, causing overlapping of the responsibilities. The trade unions' dominating behaviour and management's silence on such issues resulted in operational failures of the committees.

10.7.2. Participation through JMCs and Committees

The Industrial Policy Resolution of 1956, through their policy statement with regards to WPM, recommended for joint consultation of the workers and the management. The workers and technicians should, wherever possible, be associated progressively in management. It was recommended that the public sector organizations will have to set examples in this respect.

Similar recommendations were also there in the Second Five-Year Plan for the establishment of councils of management consisting of representatives of management, technicians and workers in the larger industrial undertakings.

The Government of India, with a view to get available materials on the subject, sent a tripartite study group to a few industrially advanced countries of Europe, for example, Great Britain, Sweden, France, Belgium, West Germany and Yugoslavia. In the report of the committee, they recommended a non-statutory approach on the participative management style. The draft prepared by this tripartite committee was subsequently modified by two national seminars organized by the Ministry of Labour in 1958 and 1960. From the deliberations of the seminars emerged a draft model agreement relating to the establishment of JMCs.

10.7.2.1. The Objectives of JMC

The following objectives of the JMC were a part of the scheme:

- To promote cordial relations between management and workers.
- To develop understanding and trust between the management and the workers.
- To sustain productivity.
- To secure welfare facilities for workers.
- To train the workers to understand and share the responsibilities of management.

10.7.2.2. Composition and Function of JMC

All organizations/plants were employing at least 500 or more employees to have JMCs. These councils consist of equal number of representatives of the employers and employees, not exceeding 12 at the plant level. Representation of workmen in the JMCs was based on the nominations by recognized trade unions. If it was decided to constitute technical committees or subcommittees, their composition would be decided according to the need of the situation which may also include outside expert on these committees. Whether chairmanship of the JMC should be fixed or rotated should be left to the local agreement.

The JMCs were entrusted with the administrative responsibilities for various matters relating to welfare, safety, vocational training and preparation of schedule of working hours and holidays.

They were to be consulted in matters of change in work operation, general administration and alteration in standing orders, rationalization, closure and so on to encourage smooth work operations and enhanced productivity. Mainly these bodies were consultative and advisory, with decision-making being left to the top management.

JMCs did not receive much support from the trade unions or the management. There had been some issues in the adoption of JMCs and their smooth functioning. Some of these are specified as follows:

- Employers already having an effective system of consultation in their establishments found a JMC, in its existing form, superfluous.
- Many employers and trade unions became averse to having a multiplicity of schemes.
- In undertakings characterized by adverse IR, it was futile to expect the formation and smooth functioning of JMCs.
- Many trade union leaders thought that the JMCs had no scope for focusing on matters such as wages, bonus and allowances, and thus they were not enthusiastic about the success of the scheme.

10.7.2.3. The Amendment of the Constitution of India

In 1975, during the Emergency, the Constitution was amended by the introduction of Article 43A. The objective of this amendment was to raise productivity, promote industrial peace and create a sense of involvement among the workers. The inserted Article 43A formed a part of the Directive Principles of State Policy, which provided that 'the state shall take steps by suitable legislation or in any other way to secure participation of workers in the management of undertakings, establishments or other organizations engaged in the industry'. So the scheme of 1975 was implemented expecting effective participation of workers in the management of industrial establishments.

10.7.3. Shop Councils and Joint Councils of 1975

A scheme of 'workers' participation in industry at the shop floor and plant levels' was implemented on 30 October 1975 during the National Emergency. The scheme applies to the units employing 500 or more workers of manufacturing and mining industries in all the sectors—public, private and cooperative—as well as to those that run departmentally. The scheme provides for the establishment of shop councils at the shop/departmental level and joint councils at the enterprise level.

10.7.3.1. The Composition of Shop Councils

Shop council represents each department or a shop in a unit consisting of an equal number of representatives of both employer and employees. The employer's representatives are to be nominated by the management from among the persons from the unit. The representatives of workers were to be made from among the workers engaged in the department or shop. The total number of members in the council should not exceed 12 members. The number of members of each council is to be determined by the employer in consultation with the recognized or registered trade union or workmen in a manner best suited to the local conditions of the unit. The number of shop councils and the departments to be attached to each council of the undertaking or establishment are to be decided by the employer in consultation with the recognized union or registered trade unions or with workers, as the case may be. The scheme did not prescribe a uniform pattern of the constitution of shop councils, in view of the existence of different practices in different industrial units.

All decisions of a shop council shall be on the basis of consensus and not by the process of voting, provided that either party may refer the unsettled matters to the joint council for consideration. Every decision of a shop council shall be implemented by the parties concerned within a period of one month unless otherwise stated in the decision itself, and compliance report shall be submitted to the council. Such decisions of a shop council which have a bearing on another shop, or the undertaking or establishment as a whole will be referred to the joint council for consideration and decision. A shop council once formed shall function for a period of two years. Any member nominated or elected to the council in the midterm to fill a casual vacancy shall continue to be a member of the council for the unexpired portion of the term of the council. Meetings were held at least once in a month. The chairman of the shop council was nominated by the management, the worker members nominated the vice chairman.

10.7.3.2. Scope and Coverage

The scheme applied to manufacturing and mining industries (whether in public, private or cooperative sector, including department run enterprises) employing 500 or more employees. In 1977, the Government of India extended the scheme to commercial and service organizations of the public sector including hospitals, railways and so on. Some states have extended the application of this scheme even in establishments employing less than 500 workers. For instance, Punjab has extended the scheme in establishments employing 200 or more workers.

10.7.3.3. Functions of Shop Council

The main function of the shop council is to increase production and overall efficiency of the shop or department in the following matters:

1. Assist management in achieving monthly/yearly production targets.
2. Improve production, productivity and efficiency, including elimination of wastage and optimum utilization of machine capacity and manpower.
3. Specifically identify areas of low productivity and take necessary corrective steps at the shop level to eliminate relevant contributing factors.
4. Study absenteeism in the shops/departments and recommend steps to reduce them.
5. Safety measures.
6. Assist in maintaining general discipline in the shop/department.
7. Physical conditions of work such as lighting, ventilation, noise and dust, and reduction of fatigue.
8. Welfare and health measures to be adopted for efficient running of the shop/department.
9. Ensure proper flow of adequate two-way communication between the management and the workers, particularly on matters relating to production figures, production schedules and progress in achieving the targets [3].

10.7.4. Joint Council

10.7.4.1. The Constitution of Joint Council

Under the scheme, every industrial unit employing 500 or more workers is required to constitute a joint council for the whole unit. This scheme of workers' participation, which was introduced by the Government of India, is a voluntary scheme and not a compulsory one. But some states, however, made the scheme compulsory. The main features of the scheme of joint council are as follows:

1. Only such persons who are actually engaged in the unit shall be the members of the joint council.
2. The council shall function for a period of two years.
3. The chief executive of the unit shall be the chairman of the joint council; there shall be a vice-chairman who will be nominated by worker–members of the council.
4. The joint council shall appoint one of the members of the council as its secretary. Necessary facilities for the efficient discharge of functions by the secretary shall be provided within the premises of the undertaking/establishment.
5. The term of the council, once formed, shall be for a period of two years; if, however, a member is nominated in the midterm of the council to fill a casual vacancy, the member nominated in such vacancy shall continue in office for the remaining period of the term of the council.
6. The joint council shall meet at least once in a quarter.
7. Every decision of the joint council shall be on the basis of consensus and not by the process of voting, binding on employers and workmen, and implemented within a month unless otherwise stated.

The constitution is equal number of representatives from the management and the workers not exceeding 12 members in total. One of the members from the management team would function as the chairman, whereas a vice-chairman would be nominated by from and among the workers.

10.7.4.2. Functions of Joint Council

The main function of the joint council is to deal with matters relating to

1. Optimum production, efficiency and fixation of productivity norms of man and machine for the unit as a whole;
2. Have a watch on the functions of a shop council which have a bearing on another shop or the unit as a whole;
3. Deal with matters emanating from shop council which remain unresolved;
4. Matters concerning the unit of the plant as a whole, in respect of matters relating to work planning and achieving production targets; more specially, tasks assigned to a shop council at the shop/department level but relevant to the unit as a whole will be taken up by the joint council;
5. The development of skills of workmen and adequate facilities for training;
6. The preparation of schedule of working hours and holidays;
7. Giving rewards for valuable and creative suggestions received from workers;
8. Optimum use of raw materials and quality of finished products;
9. General health, welfare and safety measures for the unit or the plant.

The government was aware of the fact that various schemes were in vogue in different organizations. So to encourage high degree of flexibility and adoption of this scheme, it was suggested that since there is considerable diversity in the situation prevailing from unit to unit in different industries, even departmental undertakings and public enterprises under the same Ministry of the Government of India have had to adopt different systems depending on the local conditions and their individual needs. Keeping the diversity in view, no uniform pattern was laid down for the constitution of shop councils and joint councils, particularly relating to the representation of workers. The managements in consultation with workers were open to evolve the most suitable pattern of representation so as to ensure that the representation of the workers results in effective, meaningful and broad-based participation of workers.

Two-way communication was given due importance since for any scheme of workers' participation to succeed, the exchange of information between the management and the workmen was essential. With this end in view, it was recommended to devise suitable systems of communication within the undertaking.

10.7.5. Continuation of the Functioning of the Works Committee

The government recommended the continuation of the functioning of the works committee as prescribed under the ID Act as it had been functioning.

I.C.10.1. INDUSTRIAL CONTEXT FOR DISCUSSION

Scheme of WPM in Bharat Petroleum Corporation Ltd (BPCL) Mumbai

The Business of the Organization

BPCL produces a diverse range of products, from petrochemicals and solvents to aircraft fuel and specialty lubricants, and markets them through its wide network of petrol stations, kerosene dealers, LPG distributors and 'Lube Shoppes', besides supplying fuel directly to hundreds of industries, and several international and domestic airlines.

Employee Involvement

The plant has several employee involvement programmes, termed as 'collaborative initiatives'. These can be classified into the following two groups.

1. Structured, which includes the following.
   a. **Works committee, set up under the ID Act, 1947:** It has six workers elected from among the employees. Four of them represent operators, one represents clerical employees and one represents service and maintenance workers. Six managers too are members of the committee.
      Quarterly committee meetings are held and utilized mainly for discussions on welfare activities, working conditions, suggestions for improvement made by any workman and for counselling workmen who have problems with alcoholism or drugs, or are chronic absentees.
   b. Various committees are constituted for ISO standards certification, which was achieved for the plant through union–management cooperation.

   c. **Constitution of quality circles:** Quality circles with concerns for maintaining the appropriate quality and addressing issues related to quality are formed.

   d. **Suggestion schemes:** Both managers' and unions' suggestions are often made and the good ones by the unions were given recognition.

2. Unstructured, which are convened from time to time on specific issues, include the following.

   a. **Communication:** Various plant functions and events are utilized by the management for spreading awareness about performance and creating a competitive environment. The plant management conveys all major issues to the unions, for example, production; additional working hours during January–March each year due to increase in demand; irregularity in working cycles caused by the availability of ships for loading and time taken for tests to achieve best quality.

   b. Discussions among management and union representatives to
      • Increase capacity utilization
      • Redeploy some workers from cleaning and canteen tasks to operations
      • Improve packaging unit for small packages
      • Reduce the costs of various operations

   c. Unions also communicate with the plant management in the areas of improvements they feel are necessary (for instance, they sought two annual health check-ups and also discuss issues such as overtime, problems related to work, ship loading and Saturday working).

10.7.6. The 1983 Scheme of Employees' Participation in Management

A new scheme called Employees' Participation in Management was formulated in 1983. It was a new comprehensive scheme for workers' participation in central PSUs, but excluded departmental undertakings such as the railways and post and telegraphs. It was applied to all central public sector enterprises except those which are specifically exempted. This scheme is also currently in force in many PSUs. It envisages the constitution of bipartite shop floor and plant-level forums and, wherever needed, the establishment of board-level forums also. This scheme was ordinarily a two-tier scheme, like the 1975 scheme, but in situations where the government desired it to be beneficial, it could be extended to the board level with worker directors. Hence, it could be referred to as a three-tier scheme and largely a modified version of the 1975 scheme. The following table provides the salient features of the scheme. To understand the scheme, tabulation has been made under various categories which include safety and welfare, and work-related matters, production related, and business policy-related matters as a part of the scheme.

Category	Shop	Plant	Board
Safety and welfare	Safety; welfare; medical; transport; sports; housing	Township; canteen; control of gambling, drinking, indebtedness; community development	–

Category	Shop	Plant	Board
Work-related	Storage facilities; material economy; operational problems; wastage control; hazards; quality; cleanliness; work systems; group working; housekeeping; productivity; problems of women employment; absenteeism; suggestions	Designing productivity schemes; planning and review; materials shortfall; storage and inventory; quality and technology; machine utilization	–
Production-related	Production facilities; monthly targets; production schedule; cost reduction	Product development; operational performance; shop floor matters remaining unresolved; review of shop councils' functioning; financial statements, costs and sales review; training programmes; pollution	–
Business policy	–	–	All policy matters as well as review of the functioning of shop and joint councils

10.7.6.1. Composition

Both in the shop and plant-level forums, equal number of representatives of workers and the management constitute to the body. The size of the forums did vary between 10 and 20, depending on the size of the workforce in the undertaking. The exact number of the members to the forum was decided by the management in consultation with the trade union leaders of the undertaking. The representation of workers on the forums covered different categories of workers, including skilled and unskilled, technical and non-technical and so on. The representation of women was also considered in situations where they constituted 10 per cent or more of the total workforce.

10.7.6.2. Functions

10.7.6.2.1. Shop-Level Forum

The areas of deliberations of shop-level forums included the following:

- Production-related matters
- Storage-related matters in a shop
- Economizing the use of materials including raw materials and reduction of wastage
- Operational problems
- Wastage control
- Safety hazards and problems
- Quality improvement

- Cleanliness
- Achieving monthly targets
- Production schedules
- Cost reduction programmes
- Formulation and implementation of work system and design
- Group working and welfare measures related to the shop

10.7.6.2.2. Plant-Level Forum

The plant-level forums deliberated on operational, economic, financial, personnel, welfare and environmental aspects.

The operational areas of the plant-level forums included the following:

- Evolution of productivity schemes
- Planning, implementation, fulfilment and review of monthly targets and review
- Supply of materials and shortfalls
- Storage and inventories
- Housekeeping
- Improvement in productivity
- Encouragement to suggestions
- Quality and technological improvement
- Machine utilization, knowledge and development of new products
- Operational performance figures
- Matters not resolved at the shop level or those concerning more than one shop
- Review of the working of the shop-level bodies

In August 1984, to monitor the progress in the implementation of the scheme, a committee was constituted of the representatives of the centre ministries, state government enterprises, central public sector enterprises, central workers' organizations and representatives of private sector manufacturers' organizations. The Annual Report of the Ministry of Labour, 1987–1988, reports that 100 public sector enterprises had adopted the scheme by December 1983 at the shop floor and plant levels, and another 33 public sector enterprises had implemented their own scheme, a variant of proposed scheme as notified by the government. About 64 public sector enterprises have not been able to implement the scheme. Organizations such as SAIL, BHEL, IOL, HMT and Cement Corporation of India had implemented the scheme.

10.8. WPM at the Board Level

After the JMC experience in Indian industries, the government decided to make a fresh attempt in PSUs to implement WPM. It announced in 1971 a scheme for worker directors on PSU boards and accordingly one worker director, being the representative of the recognized union, was made mandatory for each PSU boards. The practice barely survived by the 1990s. For example, in the entire steel industry by the 1990s, the only employee director was in IISCO, West Bengal.

For the banks, statutory amendments in 1973 to the State Bank of India Act, 1959, and the Banking Regulation Act, 1969, provided for the appointment of one workman (non-executive) director and one non-workman (officer/executive) director in each bank. The working of the scheme was delayed by both managements of various banks and unions, for the trade unions protested against officer directors. Their contention was that the officers were in any case represented. The controversy continued for many years till it was settled by the Supreme Court in 1989.

However, the performance and role expectations of the nominees proved major hurdles to the banks. The top management envisaged the role of a worker director as one of coordination and cooperation, whereas the employees felt that the worker's director role should be involving policy formulation, improvement in working conditions and reduction in unjust treatment of employees.

10.9. Participation of Workers in Management Bill, 1990

A Bill titled 'Participation of Workers in Management Bill, 1990 (Bill No. XXVIII of 1990)', was introduced by the then government in the Rajya Sabha on 30 May 1990. Till the introduction of this Bill, all the schemes pertaining to the WPM had been non-statutory for which the earlier schemes had failed to provide meaningful participation to workers in management. The focus was on the following:

1. To provide for specific and meaningful participation of workers in management at the shop floor level
2. To establish WPM at the Board of Management of the industrial establishments

The Bill was referred to the Parliamentary Standing Committee on Labour and Welfare of the Lok Sabha on 12 July 1994 which submitted its report on 18 December 2001. The Bill (Participation of Workers in Management Bill, 1990) as was recommended is presented below graphically.

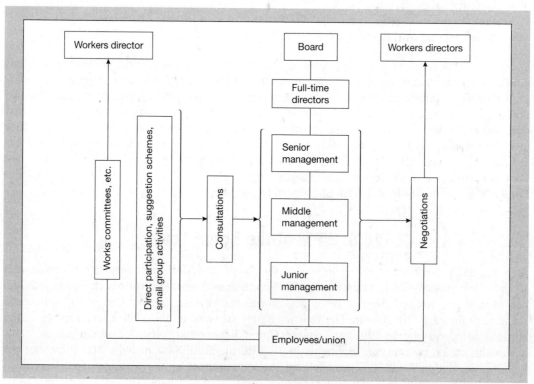

The salient features of the Participation of Workers in Management Bill, 1990, were as follows:

- The Bill was to be applicable to all units covered under the ID Act, 1947, and the Bill recommended for the applicability of the definition of appropriate government prevailing in the ID Act, 1947.
- The central government was supposed to be responsible for enforcing the law in all cases where the central government is the appropriate government under the ID Act, 1947, and also in enterprises where the central government holds 51 per cent or more of the paid up share capital. In the remaining cases, the responsibility for enforcement will be that of the state government.
- The Bill provided for the formulation of one or more schemes to be framed by the central government for giving effect to the provisions of the law which will include, among others, the manner of representation of workmen at all the three levels, that is, the shop floor, unit and board levels.
- The Bill proposed to constitute one or more councils at the shop floor level and a council at the establishment level. These councils shall consist of equal number of persons to represent the employers and the workmen. The appropriate government shall in consultation with the employer and taking into account the total number of workmen, the number of levels of authority and the number of shop floors determine the number of persons who shall represent the employer and the workmen in a council.
- The Bill also envisaged a Board of Management at the Apex level where representatives of the workmen as defined under the ID Act shall constitute 13 per cent and persons representing other workers shall constitute 12 per cent of the total strength of such management. The persons to represent the workmen and other workers in the Board of Management shall be elected by and from among workmen and other workers of the industrial establishment or by secret ballot.
- If any person contravenes any of the provisions of this Act or the scheme made thereunder, he/she shall be punishable with imprisonment which may extend up to two years or with the fine which may extend up to ₹20,000 or with both. It has also been indicated that appropriate government by notification shall appoint such persons as it feels fit to be inspectors for the purpose of this Act.
- The Bill further provides that a Monitoring Committee comprising equal number of members representing the appropriate government, the workers and the employers may be constituted by the appropriate government to review and advise on matters which arise out of the administration of the Act, any scheme or any rules made thereunder.
- The proposed Bill empowers the government to exempt any employer or classes of employees from all or any of the provisions of the Act.

The Bill became a subject of discussion at various forums, and while discussions and comments were in progress, the Bill could not be passed as yet and the Labour Minister, on 1 August 2017, moved for withdrawal of the 'Participation of Workers in Management Bill, 1990', which was approved by the Upper House.

I.C.10.2. INDUSTRIAL CONTEXT FOR DISCUSSION

Workers' Participation in BHEL: The Case of Tiruchi

BHEL decided to introduce the concept of labour participation in management in the early 1970s in its various units. A formal beginning was made with the constitution of a joint committee at the corporate level on 3 April 1973.

Background of Tiruchi Unit

The Tiruchi unit of BHEL manufactures high-pressure boilers for thermal and nuclear power stations of unit's size up to 500 MW and 235 MW, respectively, and also manufactures the related auxiliary equipment. The other products include industrial process steam boilers of different sizes to meet the requirements of fertilizer, petrochemical, steel and paper industries. The boilers are designed for operation on a wide range of fuels, namely coal, fuel oil, gas, asphalt, black liquor and a combination of some of these fuel types.

Beginning from 1980 till the year 1985, the Tiruchi unit witnessed a phenomenal growth in personnel from 13,791 employees in 1980–1981 to 17,541 in 1984–1985. Of the total employees, 1,702 belonged to the executive cadre, and 3,621 and 12,218 fell in the category of supervisors and workers/ministerial staff, respectively. The growth of manpower over the years is evident from Table 10.1.

Table 10.1   Growth of Personnel in the Tiruchi Unit (1980–1985)

Category	1980–1981	1981–1982	1982–1983	1983–1984	1984–1985
Executives	1,290	1,390	1,493	1,614	1,702
Supervisors	2,844	2,841	3,249	3,546	3,621
Others	9,657	10,139	10,824	11,477	12,218
Total	**13,791**	**14,370**	**15,566**	**16,637**	**17,541**

The main responsibilities of the executives were the following:

- To resolve day-to-day grievances of the workers
- To provide feedback to the IR's manager and personnel manager about shop floor processes
- To maintain personal files of the workers to carry out routine administrative work
- To counsel the workers on issues such as absenteeism, code of conduct, behaviour at the workplace, attitude towards superiors, alcoholism, money lending and other undesirable practices
- To act as an important channel of communication between the workers on the shop floor and the management
- To be available to the workers and help them on any matters as and when the need arises.

IRs and Trade Union Structure

In the year 1985, there was a tool-down strike resulting in the loss of 161 man-days. Another strike of eight hours duration took place in support of teachers and fishermen who were on strike, which resulted in the loss of 2,114 man-days. There were nine unions operating at the Tiruchi unit, out of which the following four were recognized by the corporation as participating unions:

1. BHEL Workers' Union (CITU)
2. Boiler Plant Employees' Union (TNTUC)

3. BHEL Employees' Progressive Union (LPF/DMK)
4. Boiler Plant Anna Workers' Union (ATP/AIADMK).

Despite the existence of many unions, the problem was handled by evolving the concept of 'participating union' and by not allowing other unions to take part in negotiations on any issue whatsoever. 'The concept of participating union entitles unions to take part in negotiations with the management on both work-related and interest-related issues as well as represent their representatives onto various committees'.

Workers' Participation in Tiruchi Unit

Works Committee

The first works committee started functioning from 1967 and the third works committee was formed in 1972 in accordance to the rules framed by the Tamil Nadu government under the ID Act, 1947.

The Constitution and Functioning of the Committee

The tenure of the committees would be for a period of six years and one third of the members should retire every two years. The works committee consists of one chairman, one vice-chairman, one secretary and a joint secretary, all appointed by the committee members. In case the elected chairman is from among the management representatives, the vice-chairman must be from among the worker's representatives, and vice versa. Similar is the condition for the position of secretary and joint secretary.

For election purposes, the whole unit is divided into 10 constituencies and one representative from each constituency is included in the committee. The members of the works committee were also nominated to other committees such as the Township Committee, Staff Benefit Committee, Death Relief Fund Committee and Safety Committee. All these committees, combined together, work for the betterment of the employees while channelizing their efforts for achieving the growth and attaining excellence in the unit.

The Major Issues Taken Up by the Works Committee

Following were the major issues taken up by the works committee:

- Conditions of work such as ventilation, lighting, temperature and sanitation, including latrines and urinals
- Amenities such as drinking water, canteens, dining rooms, creches, rest rooms, and medical and health services
- Safety and accident prevention, occupational diseases and protective equipment
- Adjustment of festival and national holidays
- Administration of welfare and fine funds
- Educational and recreational activities such as libraries, reading rooms, cinema shows, sports, games, picnics, community welfare and celebrations
- Promotion of thrift and savings
- Implementation and review of decisions taken in the meetings of the works committee.

Shop Council

Structure

There were 15 shop councils in the Tiruchi unit of which 8 were major and 7 were minor. The shops where production was involved were considered as major and those in non-production areas constituted minor shop councils. Workers' representatives in the shop councils were nominated by the participating unions on the basis of the percentage of votes they used to secure in the election to the joint committee.

Functions

The shop councils dealt with operational problems of all kinds, some of which are as follows:

- Controlling wastage
- Ensuring material economy and proper storage of materials
- Quality improvement
- Absenteeism, reduction and redesigning of work
- Attaining monthly targets for production
- Reviewing cost reduction, inventory reduction, technological development, productivity as well as utilization of capacity of critical machines
- Formulating schemes for job redesign, group working, job enrichment and evolving guidelines for implementation
- Any matter referred to by the plant council for consideration of the shop council.

Plant Council

Structure

The Plant Council was responsible for the overall working of the plant and discussions on matters which had unit-wide repercussions. Workers' representatives were nominated by the participating unions who were elected to the joint committee.

Eight workers' representatives were nominated to the Plant Council. An equal number of management representatives were also nominated to the Council. The tenure of the Council was two years with effect from the date of the first meeting. The Plant Council used to once in two months and all decisions were taken on the basis of consensus. Only those issues which pertained to the entire plant or those which the shop councils could not resolve or which fell beyond the purview of the shop councils were taken up for discussion in the Plant Council meetings. The general manager of the plant used to be the chairman of the Plant Council and one of the members acted as the secretary to the Council.

Functions

The major functions of the Plant Council were as follows:

- To review production targets for the plant as a whole, keeping in tune with the overall target set by the corporation
- To resolve inter-council problems that were referred to the Council
- To provide suitable guidelines for reducing absenteeism
- To periodically review cost-reduction schemes, including wastage reduction, quality improvement, target achievement for production, inventory reduction and so on
- To develop information systems regarding site failures, mechanical defects, rejection rates and overall performance of the plant.

Suggestion Scheme

A suggestion scheme had been in operation in the Tiruchi unit since 1964 with the objective of ensuring a greater involvement of workers on matters of importance regarding employee welfare, as well as effective working of organizations as a whole. Under this scheme, there were 12 Area Committees and 1 Central Suggestion Committee. Employees and workmen at various levels were encouraged to put forward their suggestions. Boxes for receiving suggestions were placed at different locations in the factory premises and good suggestions were awarded cash prizes. Suggestions were being received on various issues pertaining to safety, efficiency, IRs, public relations, cost reduction and so on [4].

10.10. Other Forms of WPM in India

The other forms of participation in management are as follows.

1. **Participation through collective bargaining:** Collective bargaining is the process of negotiation between the management and workers, represented by trade unions for the resolution of disputes/differences related to wages, bonus, and other financial and non-financial benefits, including the working conditions. The ILO considers collective bargaining to be a bipartite process and defined it as all negotiations which take place between an employer, a group of employers or one or more employers' organizations, on the one hand, and one or more workers' organizations, on the other, for:

   (a) determining working conditions and terms of employment; and/or
   (b) regulating relations between employers and workers; and/or
   (c) regulating relations between employers or their organisations and a workers' organisation or workers' organisations. [5]

   Briefly speaking, it is an intuitional procedure of joint determination of the rules to govern the terms and conditions of employment of the workers. The objective of collective bargaining was to regulate a harmonious IR.

   Collective bargaining, on the other hand, is essentially a process which involves confrontation process. In this process, the management and the trade unions across the table discuss and settle issues depending on their relative bargaining strengths.

   There are some general observations that trade unions, in general, sought to promote collective bargaining rather than participation. The general conceptual understanding is that collective decisions between the managements and the trade unions must be arrived at through participative methods rather than coercive methods, but that is normally not the case.

2. **Participation through suggestion schemes:** An employee suggestion scheme (ESS) is one of the oldest acceptable forms of an employee's involvement in the management process of an organization. This tool is widely used by managements to elicit employees' creative ideas. Experts observe that it plays a pivotal role for organizations wishing to become more innovative. It is a formalized mechanism that encourages employees to contribute constructive ideas for improving the organization in which they work.

   The process involves getting suggestions from employees, classifying them and sending them to the experts for evaluation. After this, the suggestion might be adopted, in which case the suggestion may well be rewarded. The experts are either managers or dedicated committees who evaluate the suggestions and implement those which are workable and beneficial to the organization in its production process. Suggestion schemes help in the following:

   o Tapping the untapped potentials and knowledge of the employees that could improve organizational processes and effectiveness.
   o Facilitating the process of motivating employees to think more creatively and to share their creative thoughts as well as convert creative ideas into valuable innovations.
   o Encouraging employees to think innovatively and creatively about their work and work environment, and to produce ideas which benefit the organization. It also creates contexts for the employee to receive recognition.

3. **Financial participation:** This method involves that the performance of the organization is linked to the performance of the employee. The logic behind this is that 'if an employee has

a financial stake in the organization, he/she is likely to be more positively motivated and involved'. Some schemes of financial participation are as follows:

a. Profit-linked pay
b. Profit-sharing and employees stock option schemes
c. Pension fund participation

4. **Quality circles:** A quality circle is a participatory management technique which helps the employees in solving problems related to their own jobs. Such circles are formed of employees working together, who meet at intervals to discuss problems of quality and find out solutions for improvements.

They are a small group of 6–12 employees doing similar work, who voluntarily meet together on a regular basis to identify improvements in their respective work areas. They are led by a supervisor or a senior worker. Employees who participate in quality circles are trained in formal problem-solving methods such as brainstorming, Pareto analysis and cause-and-effect diagrams which they apply for solutions.

Quality circles are generally expected to produce the following two types of effects:

a. The enhancement of quality and productivity.
b. The fostering of a sense of participation in work-related decisions among workers, leading to increased job satisfaction and better IR.

The concept of quality circle is primarily based upon the recognition of value of the worker as a human being, as someone who is willing to put efforts to improve the job.

The objectives of quality circles are as follows:

a. Change in attitude
b. Self-development
c. Development of team spirit
d. Improvement in organizational culture

The process of operation of quality circles is as follows:

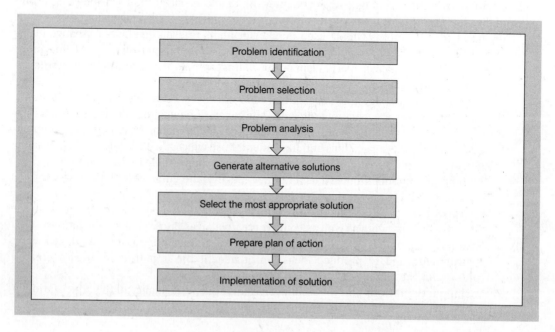

The quality circles proved to be the most risk-free way of involving workers in the organizational decision-making process. So the quality circles provided the management with a number of advantages which the earlier participative schemes did not provide.

Chapter Summary

1. It was a general trend of the employers to neglect the human problems arising from the mass production techniques, so the workers were becoming less and less involved with their jobs and more and more alienated from the factory life. The remedy was clear—workers must be involved so that they contribute their best to the organization and do not feel alienated from their work life.
2. The objectives of WPM had been to maintain industrial peace and harmony, motivate the workers, raise the levels of the employee production, productivity and product quality, and better mutual understanding so that the workers do not resist any change and minimize the number of grievances.
3. WPM encompasses the scope for employees in the decision-making of the organization, willingness to share the responsibility, develop self-control and self-discipline among workers.
4. WPM is aligned with the objectives of IR by safeguarding the interest of labour and management by securing the highest level of mutual understanding and goodwill, avoiding industrial conflict, enhancing productivity, promoting the growth of an industrial democracy based on labour partnership, minimizing the number of strikes, lockouts and gheraos, and improving the economic conditions of workers.
5. WPM serves the economic and social purposes in the organizations.
6. The prerequisites for the success of any scheme of participative management are a strong, democratic and representative trade union, mutually agreed and clearly formulated objective of participation, a feeling of participation at all levels, effective consultation of the workers by the management, a relationship based on mutual trust and respect, proper education and training.
7. Since Independence, various schemes have been recommended and implemented by the Government of India to encourage WPM. The earliest form of participative management was the 'works committees' implemented through Section 3 of the ID Act, 1947. In 1947, the Industrial Truce Resolution adopted at the Industries Conference recommended inter alia the formation of unit production committees in industrial establishments. Under the Industrial Policy Resolution of 1948, the Government of India accepted in principle the establishment of bipartite production committees consisting of the representatives of employer and workers. In 1958, an ambitious scheme of JMCs was introduced. In 1975, forums of shop councils and joint councils were introduced under the old 20-point programme. In 1977, institutions of WPM were established in commercial and service organizations. Employees' participation in management for PSUs was introduced in 1983. In 1990, a comprehensive Workers' Participation in Management Bill was introduced in the parliament, but it has still not been passed.
8. The other forms of participation in management are participation through collective bargaining, participation through suggestion schemes, financial participation and quality circles.

Questions

1. Discuss the importance of WPM in India and how the organizations are benefited out of the same.
2. Discuss the various schemes of WPM introduced from time to time.

3. What are the prerequisites of WPM?
4. A comprehensive Workers' Participation in Management Bill was introduced in the parliament in 1990, but it has still not been passed. From the trend of the government's initiative to make the WPM successful, can you suggest the reasons for not passing the Bill of 1990?
5. Critically justify how far the objectives of WPM have been achieved in India.

References

1. Aswathappa K. Human resource and personnel management—text and cases. 4th ed. New Delhi: Tata McGraw Hill; 2005. 396.
2. Bhagoliwal TN. Economics of industrials. Agra: SBPD Publishing House; 2009. 315.
3. Ministry of Labour Resolution No. S. 6101 l(4)/75-Dk, New Delhi, 30 October 1975.
4. Gautam M. Workers participation in management in India concept1. Available at https://www.academia.edu/8848729/WORKERS_PARTICIPATION_IN_MANAGEMENT_IN_INDIA_concept1
5. ILO. Collective bargaining convention, 1981 (No. 154). Geneva: ILO.

PART

5

Industrial Relations in Emerging Industries and Impacts of International Bodies on Industrial and Employee Relations in India

11

Industrial Relations in IT and ITES Organizations

LEARNING OBJECTIVES

After reading this chapter, you will be able to:

☐ Understand the contribution of IT and ITES organizations to the industrial development of India
☐ Understand the contribution of IT and ITES organizations to employment generation
☐ Understand the problems faced by the employees of IT and ITES organizations
☐ Understand the application of various labour laws in IT and ITES organizations

C.11.1. Case for Discussion   The Trade Union in IT and ITES Organizations

India's first independent trade union for IT employees was formed as a cause of large-scale lay-offs by several Indian software companies. The Forum for IT Employees (F.I.T.E), which evolved from the campaign to protect the Tamils in Sri Lanka, in 2008, after nine years, in 2017, involved itself in the process of getting registered formally as a union for technology employees in India. It was the first independent association of the IT employees. Previous attempts to organize the employees of the IT sector had failed to make much headway. This might be due to the possibility that the middle class has an aversion to political activity.

With insecurity running high among India's IT employees, such changes were obviously evident. Reports attributed companies' preparedness in adapting to newer technologies and dealing with the fallout from US protectionist policies to be the cause for the same. It was forecasted that a large number of employees of top software companies such as Infosys, Wipro and Cognizant were expected to lose their jobs over the next few years. This uncertainty has made employees realize the need for collective action. The companies consider this as trimming the extra fat.

Since most of the members were technology professionals, they decided to form a support group for their co-workers, listening to their grievances and finding ways to tackle them. Presently, the F.I.T.E has over 1,000 online members and around 100 active members. It has opened chapters in eight other cities including Bengaluru, Hyderabad, Mumbai and Delhi.

The group has already fought several cases on behalf of employees who were indiscriminately fired. In one instance, its efforts resulted in Tata Consultancy Services (TCS) reinstating a pregnant woman employee who had been dismissed despite a good performance record.

Another such group working for software professionals in Chennai is the IT wing of the NDLF, a labour union that is active across Tamil Nadu and Puducherry. The wing, which came up at around the same time as the F.I.T.E, was instrumental in getting the state government to clarify in June 2018 that IT employees have the right to form labour unions under the Trade Unions Act, 1926.

Getting the workforce together to protest against unfair company practices has not been easy. Since the industry's growth in the 1990s and subsequent boom in the early 2000s, resistance among workers to unfair practices such as forced resignations, low pay, indiscriminate firing and wage discrimination has been low. The fear of being blacklisted by companies for voicing their problems is always at the back of IT employees' minds and even if the employee applies for a job elsewhere, they are worried that a background check would show them as a troublemaker.

Source: From war protestors to labour activism: India's first IT workers union is being formed in Tamil Nadu https://scroll.in/article/838147/from-war-protestors-to-labour-activism-indias-first-it-workers-union-is-being-formed-in-tamil-nadu

Case Questions

1. IT companies had gone ahead to make large recruitments in anticipation of incoming businesses in the future but had to dismiss a large number of employees to sustain themselves in the adverse market conditions. How far is such practice congenial to the Indian conditions?
2. 'The fear of being blacklisted by companies for voicing their problems is always at the back of IT employees' minds and even if the employee applies for a job elsewhere, they are worried that a background check would show them as a troublemaker.' This unique feature is among the IT employees. Explain why?

11.1. Introduction

India, the second fastest growing economy has grown to become a trillion dollar economy characterized by foreign investment. The economy has positioned the country for a decent growth in its GDP at an average rate of 7–8.5 per cent every year and is considered as one of the best among the emerging economies. It has also projected itself as a leading destination for foreign investment. The key driver of Indian growth is a booming domestic market which is fuelled by increasing consumption. The Indian IT sector has played a significant role in changing the economy to attract global players with its world-class technology solutions and business services. The IT sector has become one of the most significant growth catalysts for the Indian economy by actively contributing both directly and indirectly towards socio-economic parameters such as employment, standard of living and overall economic activity. IT occupies an important sector of the Indian economy. The Indian IT industry comprises software industry and ITES, which also includes BPO industry. Indian IT industry is considered as a pioneer in software development and a favourite destination for ITES worldwide. India is the leading sourcing destination across the world, accounting for approximately 55 per cent market share of the US\$185–190 billion global services sourcing business in 2017–2018. Indian IT and ITES companies have set up over 1,000 global delivery centres in about 80 countries across the world. India has become the digital capabilities hub of the world with around 75 per cent of global digital talent present in the country. The Indian IT sector is poised to become a USD \$225 billion industry by 2020.

11.2. Market Size

The IT sector's contribution to India's GDP increased from 1.2 per cent in 1998 to 7.7 per cent in 2017 as per the NASSCOM report. The market size of India's IT and ITES industry grew to US$167 billion in 2017–2018. Exports from the industry increased to US$126 billion in FY18, while domestic revenues (including hardware) advanced to US$41 billion [1]. In the year 2019, the spending on IT in India is expected to grow over 6.7 per cent and growth to $89.2 billion. The industry is expected to be over by 13 per cent as per the NASSCOM report. Similar reports have been provided by IT research firm Gartner in its forecast. The revenue from digital segment is expected to comprise 38 per cent of the forecasted US$350 billion industry revenue by 2025.

In the global markets, the Indian IT industry has built very valuable brand equity for itself. The Indian IT industry was started by a Bombay-based conglomerate that entered the business by supplying programmers to global IT firms located overseas. The mainframe manufacturer, Burroughs asked its Indian sales agent, TCS to export programmers for installing system software for a US client.

During the 1970s, the industry was state controlled and the approach for the promotion of IT as a business was not favourable for the software industry. Even the import tariffs were as high as 135 per cent on hardware and 100 per cent on software. Financing by banks was not encouraged by the bankers in India. There were no local markets for the industry, and the government policies towards private enterprise were not attractive.

The Government Policy of 1984 (during the period of Rajiv Gandhi) changed towards the IT sector with the implementation of the New Computer Policy-1984, (NCP-1984) which reduced import tariffs on hardware and software to 60 per cent. The software exports were also 'delicensed'. This enabled the banks to finance these companies. There were even permissions for foreign firms to set up wholly owned subsidiaries in India. Some of the well-known IT organizations of today also started their business in India during this time, for example, Wipro in 1966 and Infosys in 1981. But in spite of changes happening for IT business, things were not that easy in India due to government's strict restrictions and regulations. Things brightened up only after 1991 with the government's policies of liberalization.

The working model of IT organization in India with time emerged to the model depicted in Figure 11.1.

Firms in the United States, the United Kingdom and other developed countries outsourced their non-core functions to Indian BPOs and ITES firms who outsourced their jobs to third-party vendors in India. So there emerged a class of IT organizations, who were the third-party vendors to the IT and ITES companies in India.

11.3. Evolution of the IT Sector in India

To understand the evolution of the IT sector in India, its growth has to be studied in phases.

11.3.1. IT Growth in India Prior to the 1980s

Software as an industry in India was not in existence; IT as an industry in India started with the hardware products. This was a protected sector by the Indian government through licensing and high tariff rates. When the Indian government realized the potential of software sector to earn

Figure 11.1   Functioning of IT Organizations in India

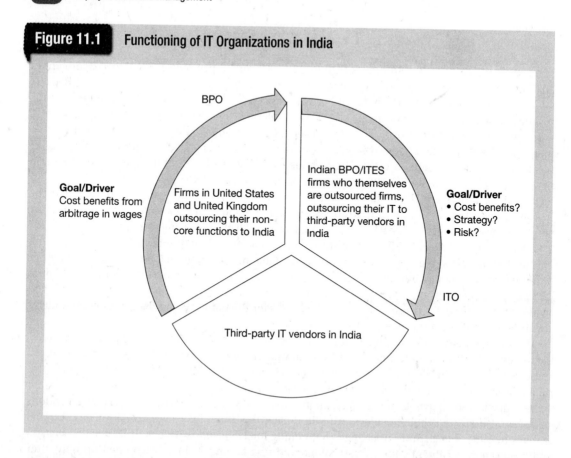

BPO

Goal/Driver
Cost benefits from
arbitrage in wages

Firms in United States
and United Kingdom
outsourcing their non-
core functions to India

Indian BPO/ITES
firms who themselves
are outsourced firms,
outsourcing their IT to
third-party vendors in
India

Goal/Driver
• Cost benefits?
• Strategy?
• Risk?

ITO

Third-party IT vendors in India

foreign exchange, it allowed the import of hardware and export of software through its new software export scheme formulated in 1972. TCS was the first company to be benefited out of this scheme in 1974.

11.3.2. IT Growth in India during 1980–1990

The government policies on export of software were not very encouraging to the organizations for it was dependent on the imports of hardware. Although during this period some companies had started exporting software, for example, TCS, Wipro, Infosys and so on, the results were not very encouraging. Moreover, there were no appropriate infrastructural facilities for software development. It was only in 1986 when the Indian government took decision to liberalize the IT sector and delicensed the imports of hardware and for exporters, things tended towards some favourable situations.

11.3.3. IT Growth in India during 1990–2000

During this period of trade liberalization, the market was opened up for foreign investors. This was a major change which helped the growth of the IT sector. Due to the liberalization, a flow of foreign investments came to India. MNCs in India introduced 'offshore model', 'onsite model' and 'global delivery model' (GDM) as part of their services. In this period, due to rapid growth in the IT sectors, the competition among the organizations was intensified. During this stage, with the change in the government policies, there were some substantial changes in Indian economy, including relaxation in the entry barriers. The software front also moved more towards standardization and productivity improvement. With time, metro cities such as Bangalore, Mumbai, Delhi, Chennai and Hyderabad became favourite destinations for all the big names such as HSBC, Dell, Microsoft, GE and Hewlett Packard (HP), and for several Indian multinational firms such as Infosys Technologies and Wipro to set up their offices in these cities. The infrastructure for the same was provided by the government including the state government with large floor space and great telecom facilities.

11.3.4. IT Growth in India during 2000–2010

This period witnessed a rapid growth of the IT sector in India. The business growth factors were the availability of cheap hardware, faster modes of communication and setting up of Software Technology Parks. The foreign exchange earnings of the software service companies drastically went up. This was also supported by the formation of special economic zones with the passing of the Special Economic Zones (SEZ) Act of 2005 which helped the organizations in importing duty-free hardware and income tax exemption on exports for 10 years. The result was an increase in the number of software companies. The Information Technology Act passed in 2000 gave a boost to e-commerce.

The government policies allowed foreign companies to have 100 per cent ownership without the need for an Indian partner, which helped large multinationals open their development centres in India, for example, Accenture, CISCO, Dell, GE, Oracle, Adobe, SAP, Philips, HP and Google.

11.3.5. IT Growth in India Post 2010

This was a period when Indian IT industry was accepted as the world's largest sourcing destination for IT industry. The rate of growth in the IT sector during 2016–2017 was approximately 12–14 per cent. Aspects such as online retailing, cloud computing and e-commerce contributed to the growth of the IT industry.

11.4. IT Industry's Contribution to the Economy

A phenomenal growth was witnessed in the Indian IT sector only in the post-economic liberalization period. The liberalized policy regime enabled fast technological advancement, mushrooming of computer science and technology education, readiness of a large pool of talent to the industry at a relatively lower cost and declined prices of computer hardware. All these factors together contributed significantly to the growth of this industry during approximately last three decades.

Indian IT industry has grown manifold since 1991. The industry has contributed significantly to the economy in terms of GDP (Figure 11.2), foreign exchange earnings and employments. Majority of the Fortune 500 and Global 2000 companies are sourcing IT-ITES from India. There are around 600 centres set up by Indian IT companies in 78 countries catering to the IT-related requirements of people in over 200 cities.

India is becoming one of the most preferred destinations for BPO as far as ITES are concerned. These services are boosting Indian economy and this is evident in their contributions to national GDP. Indian IT-ITES industry revenue was estimated at USD151 billion in FY2017–2018 as compared to USD141 billion in FY2016–2017, registering an increase of around 7 per cent. The overall growth of this sector over the last five years is given in the following table:

Year/ Description	2013–2014	2014–2015	2015–2016	2016–2017	2017–2018 (Estimated)	CAGR % (2013–2018)
Export	87.3	97.8	107.8	117.0	126.0	10.49
Domestic	19.0	21.0	21.7	24.0	25.5	5.42
Total	106.3	118.8	129.5	141.0	151.0	9.55

Source: NASSCOM SR-2018.

Figure 11.2 depicts the IT sector's per cent share to total GDP from 1991 to 2016.

Figure 11.2 IT Sector's Share in GDP (in %) of Total GDP

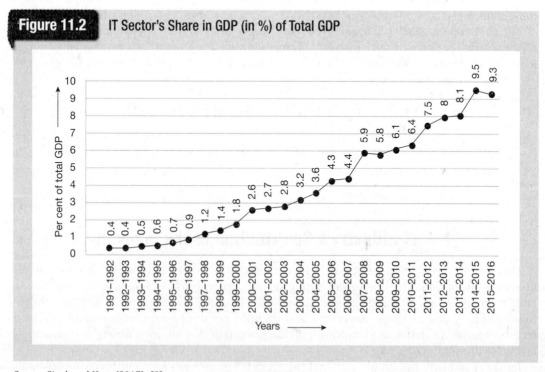

Source: Singh and Kaur (2017); [2].

11.5. Generation of Employment Opportunities and IT Labour Market

The rapid growth of IT industry in India has created a large number of jobs. The software companies, BPOs and other related business centres employ a large number of skilled and even unskilled people. The total employment in IT-ITES industry has been rising over the years and has reached around 36.88 lakh in 2015–2016. The IT industry has helped the economy in the following manner:

- The industry has raised the socio-economic level of a large number of families in India.
- It has increased employment in IT-ITES services which has helped other associated businesses such as security, housekeeping, catering, transportation and real estate.

Employment in IT-ITES Industry (in Millions)

Year	IT Services and Exports	BPO Exports	Domestic Market	Total Employment
2001–2002	0.17	0.11	0.25	0.52
2002–2003	0.21	0.18	0.29	0.67
2003–2004	0.3	0.22	0.32	0.83
2004–2005	0.39	0.32	0.35	1.06
2005–2006	0.51	0.42	0.38	1.29
2006–2007	0.69	0.55	0.38	1.62
2007–2008	0.86	0.7	0.45	2.01
2008–2009	0.92	0.79	0.5	2.21
2009–2010	0.99	0.78	0.52	2.29
2010–2011	1.15	0.83	0.56	2.54
2011–2012	1.15	0.83	0.56	2.54
2012–2013	1.29	0.83	0.6	2.77
2013–2014	1.6	0.989	0.699	3.288
2014–2015	1.74	1.03	0.745	3.515
2015–2016[a]	1.844	1.086	0.758	3.688

Source: NASSCOM https://meity.gov.in/content/employment
Note: [a]Estimated.

According to NASSCOM, in 2017, the IT sector added over 100,000 jobs. But the industry, one of India's top employment generators until a few years ago, laid off over 56,000 people between

2017 and 2018. In the past two years, TCS and Infosys, two of the country's largest IT companies, reduced their headcounts for the first time. But it is expected that after tepid job creation in 2017 and 2018, India's IT industry may be back in the market hunting for talents in 2019. This sector is expected to add around 250,000 new jobs in 2019.

The adoption of emerging technologies such as AI, machine learning and robotics for automation is driving the industry's growth. It is expected that the Indian IT companies will continue to spend on upskilling their employees and in 2019, this is estimated to increase by around 20 per cent, as viewed by the experts of the hiring companies. It is also projected that the jobs involving data analytics, machine learning and AI will continue to be in demand and will fetch higher salary bands. By 2020, job creation in the Indian IT sector is expected to surge to about 20 lakh new additions worldwide, of which around 13 per cent will be in India itself. A potentially strong area of employment will be data analytics, an increasingly crucial field across industries. The hiring experts project that the prominent roles in demand will be computer software developers, information security analysts, cloud engineers, network analysts and cyber security experts. There will be a 25 per cent rise in roles related to big data, business intelligence and analytics, whereas cloud computing opportunities will increase by 23 per cent. The start-ups will be strong contributors to generating employment during 2019–2022 because of their expanded adoption of AI, robotics, block chain and IoT.

11.6. Problems of the Employees of IT and ITES Organizations

Various surveys conducted have projected that there are a number of problems which the employees of an IT Industry face. The problems arise due to the fact that the IT industries are not following the general rules which have been formulated by the state and the central governments regarding the working hours and the other standards of employment. The IT industries have with no proper reasoning violated certain basic labour laws:

- The employees are working beyond the prescribed working hours without overtime payment. Many of the companies are flouting the weekly working hours norm set by the ILO. Employees working in the industry are forced to work for extra hours as managers pressurize their subordinates in the name of shrinking deadline of project.
- Many call centres and other ITES companies are forcing the employees to work frequently in night shifts without any extra payment or compensation of any nature. This is an utter violation of the law which very clearly specifies that a person cannot be allowed to work in night shifts for more than a prescribed period of time.
- Any employee raising his or her voice against such practice is blacklisted and victimized or even terminated.
- Any attempt by anyone to form a trade union is penalized by removing the employee from his or her job, which is a violation of the fundamental right to form a union under Article 19(1)(c) of the Indian Constitution.
- The IT and ITES industries are openly violating the law regarding the conditions and environment which are to be created by the industries for their employees.
- The IT and ITES industries try their best to exempt their employees from the definition of workers and deliberately declare them as supervisors by giving them attractive designation,

whereas they continue to do stereotyped workers job of data compilation or something of similar nature.

- Many of the IT and ITES industries do not give maternity benefits to women which have been provided by law to them.

11.7. Formation of Trade Unions by IT Employees in India

With more and more techies becoming jobless in various major IT companies, there emerged the need to set up dedicated IT employee unions in India. Such movements were visible in the cities such as Bangalore, Hyderabad and Kolkata. One of the early initiatives were the formation of the 'Union for Information Technology and Enabled Services (UNITES)' headquartered in Bangalore. UNITES is a part of global union UNI, which is a global union for skills and services having 12 lakh workers worldwide. The union strives to create a distinct and cogent link between employers and employees at all levels.

The question obvious to the context is 'whether the IT employees qualify for the formation and registration of a trade union'?

The first trade union dedicated to technology sector employees in India was registered on 7 November 2017. The Labour Department of Karnataka approved the application for registration of a trade union which exclusively caters to the interests of technology sector employees, under the provisions of the Trade Unions Act, 1926, and the Karnataka Trade Union Regulations, 1958.

As per available statistics, out of approximately 40 lakh employees across the country, Bangalore has approximately 15 lakh employees in the IT and ITES sectors and accordingly, the formation and registration of the first sector-specific employee trade union is a significant development in the technology industry [3].

The Indian labour laws, for example, the Trade Unions Act, 1926, and the ID Act, 1947, provide the right to form and join a trade union and engage in collective bargaining. In addition to the same, the following Constitutional provisions also provide the scope for such formation of trade unions.

Article 19(1)(c) of the Constitution of India, 1950, which envisages the fundamental right to 'freedom of speech and expression' also guarantees the citizens the right 'to form associations or unions' including trade unions. Accordingly, there is no prohibition or restriction on employees (including in the technology sector) to form trade unions within the establishment or joining external trade unions, subject to applicable laws. A registered trade union is deemed to be a body corporate, giving it the status of a legal entity that may, inter alia, acquire and hold property, enter into contracts and sue others. A registered trade union is also immune from certain contractual, criminal and civil proceedings.

Formation of trade unions was a general trend in the traditional sectors like the manufacturing sector. But of late, trade unions are trying to get a foothold in the Indian IT sector, though the success had been very little. With the registration of the trade union in the technology sector in Bangalore, the employees of IT organizations have formed and joined the trade union as well as voiced their concerns.

Following the footsteps of the 'UNITES headquartered in Bangalore', another unionized body the 'IT Professional's Forum' was formed under the aegis of UNI. The 'IT Professional's Forum' had following dual objectives of:

- Providing better working conditions for the employees of the IT and ITES
- Studying impact of social change and technology

While the Bangalore IT employees went ahead in the formation of trade unions, in West Bengal 'Information Technology Services Association' was set up under the patronage of CITU to safeguard welfare of all employees in the IT and ITES service sectors.

On 29 Dec 2014, F.I.T.E was launched when TCS was illegally terminating the employment of thousands of people. The executive body of F.I.T.E expressed, 'the forum was initiated with the understanding that we have the need for a body which unites IT employees and represents the fight for our rights'.

F.I.T.E announced its existence as a legally registered trade union in Maharashtra on 13 January 2018. The press release is as follows:

Date: 13 January 2018

F.I.T.E is extremely happy to announce that the forum has successfully achieved the status of a legally registered trade union in Maharashtra. We recognize this as a significant moment in the journey to collectivize and represent rights of IT workers in India. We express our gratitude to the trade unions that have laid the ground for such initiatives and have offered their support and solidarity. We look forward to continuing to work with our allies in the future and aim to strength this solidarity. [4]

Press Release

Date: 27.02.2019

Demands of IT/ITES/BPO/KPO Employees: –

On behalf of the IT/ITES employees, we demand the State governments and the Union government to hear out the concerns/issues faced by the IT employees before it turns out to be a big social crisis. We request the government to come forward to resolve the issues in the interest of the citizens and sustained growth of the IT industry in India. Our main demands are:

1. Constitute State level committee for IT employees including the Labour department, company representatives and the employees' representative forums like FITE in all States (similar to Maharashtra) to discuss the employees issues and enact appropriate measures to resolve them.
2. Industrial Employment Standing Order
   - Like any other industries, IT/ITES industrial Employment Standing order should be certified by the Labour Commissioner. The copy of the Standing order should be given to all the employees along with the appointment order.
   - The working hours, Notice Period, performance appraisal process, maternity leave, flexible working hours for women employees, and employees' grievance cell in the IT industry should be regulated and included in the Standing Order.
3. Job Security to be ensured for the IT/ITES employees
   - Illegal terminations, forced resignations or involuntary attrition are against the job protection given by Indian Labour Laws. Those illegal practices have to be stopped immediately.
   - Branding employees as poor performers and subsequently terminating their services should be stopped immediately.
   - The reason for every terminations or layoffs should be justified and notified to the state Labour Commissioner.
   - Companies should recognize employee forums in each premise/building/campus that would work closely with management for any employee related issues and policies.
4. Safety & Equality for Women employees
   - Set up 'Internal Complaints Committee (ICC)' as per the Sexual Harassment of Women at Workplace (Prevention, Prohibition, Redressal) Act, 2013 in all IT/ITES companies.
   - Maternity leave should be 26 weeks as per the Maternity Benefit Amendment Act, 2017
   - Crèche facility and work from home option as per the Act must be followed.

- Employers must educate their women about the maternity benefits available to them at the time of their appointment.
- Ensure equality to women employees in every business sphere like hiring, appraisal ratings, salary increment and promotions.

5. Set up special committee or tribunal of experts to investigate the suicide deaths of IT employees for the past two years and recommendations to avoid suicides in future.

Source: http://fite.org.in/2019/02/27/fite-met-dmk-representatives/

Prior to the above incidence, in 2013, the incident of the fresh HCL recruits forming a trade union to protest after the company delayed their joining dates at least five times officially is the evidence of the IT employees' eagerness under compelling context to form trade unions. Many of the professionals in Indian IT industry feel the need of organized trade unions which will progressively increase in other IT hubs such as Chennai, Delhi and Mumbai with time.

11.8. Application of the Labour Laws

Labour laws deal with the disputes or differences between the employer and employee, regarding wages, pension, insurance, condition of service of the employees and so on. *In India, labour laws come under the framework of industrial laws or employment laws* due to the fact that they deal mostly with the employment, non-employment, terms of employment and the condition of labour working in an industry. The Indian IT companies for a very long time were exempted from some of the basic rules and obligations which are applicable on the companies regarding employment of workers. For some time, some of the state governments in India exempted the IT companies from the application of 'Industrial Employment Standing Orders Act, 1946'. But of late, there is no such exemption provided by any state government.

11.8.1. IT Companies, Start-ups, KPOs, BPOs and so on in Karnataka to Now Comply with the Standing Orders Act

Although the Standing Orders Act is applicable to commercial establishments in Karnataka, IT and ITES companies in the state enjoyed a blanket exemption until the year 2011. For a brief period thereafter, labour authorities required IT/ITES companies to comply with the Standing Orders Act.

While some companies chose to comply at that stage, the general sentiment in the IT industry was that the Standing Orders Act was outdated, and not conducive to the functioning of the IT industry. On 25 January 2014, the Karnataka government renewed the exemption granted to IT/ITES companies from the Standing Orders Act on a conditional basis for another five years, that is, until 24 January 2019. This exemption also covered animation, gaming, computer graphics, telecom, start-ups, BPOs, KPOs, and other knowledge-based industries (all such organizations and IT/ITES companies are referred to as exempt establishments).

However, in order to avail the exemption, the exempted establishments had to comply with four preconditions, namely:

- Constituting an internal committee under the Sexual Harassment of Women at Workplace (Prevention, Prohibition and Redressal) Act, 2013

- Establishing a GRC
- Reporting disciplinary actions to the authorities
- Submitting to information demands from the authorities

With the expiry of this exemption on 24 January 2019, exempt establishments now have to comply with the Standing Orders Act, which means that they would need to draft and obtain certification of standing orders. In the absence of certified standing orders, the 'model' standing orders prescribed under the rules of the Standing Orders Act would apply to these establishments.

11.8.2. Commercial Establishments in Haryana Now Covered under the Payment of Wages Act and the Standing Orders Act

The Haryana Government has passed a notification dated 12 December 2018 (published on 25 December 2018), to extend the definition of 'industrial establishments' under the Payment of Wages Act to commercial establishments as well. While the provisions prohibiting deductions from wages applied earlier too, with this development, commercial establishments will now have to comply with all the requirements under this law, such as following timelines for payment of wages, obtaining prior approval from the government for imposing fines for misconduct, maintaining various records and registers and displaying notices.

Further, due to this notification, the Standing Orders Act will also now apply to commercial establishments in Haryana. Thus, within six months of the applicability, that is, by 25 June 2019, shops and commercial establishments in Haryana with 50 or more workmen would need to apply for certification of standing orders. They would also have to comply with all the other obligations under the Standing Orders Act (as discussed above).

A general misconception among the employers of IT industry was that the labour laws of the country do not apply to IT industries, but the same is not true. All the labour laws which are applicable to any other industry are also applicable to IT industry. The power to exempt any industry or group of industries have been vested on the respective state governments, where the organization is located. There had been also a common misconception that in the IT industry the Trade Unions Act, 1926, is not applicable and the employees cannot form trade unions. The fundamental right to form associations or unions is accorded to all citizens under Article 19(1)(c) of the Constitution of India and therefore, like all citizens, IT employees can form or join trade unions.

It has been very often debated by the employers that an IT employee is not a workman under any of the labour Acts in India. But whether a software professional/software engineer/IT employee can be termed an employee or a workman is entirely a question of fact connected with job role of the concerned employee. The answer to which depends on a number of factors such as 'the nature of work performed by the individual, his remuneration, the authority vested on him to take decision, the extent to which he is involved with the business of his company and power of supervision'. Considering all these aspects, it is necessary to understand how and to what extent some labour laws are applicable to the IT and ITES industry. The following is an analysis of the same.

11.8.3. The Trade Unions Act, 1926

'Trade union' under the Act is defined as '... any combination, whether temporary or permanent, formed primarily for the purpose of regulating the relations between workmen and employers or between workmen and workmen, or between employers and employers, or for imposing restrictive conditions on the conduct of any trade or business, and includes any federation of two or more trade unions'. By virtue of the right granted to all citizens under Article 19(1)(c) of the Constitution of India to form associations, even IT employees can form trade unions.

The Act does not make registration compulsory, registration is necessary to be entitled to the benefits provided under the Trade Unions Act, 1926, to the unions.

Under the provisions of the Trade Unions Act, 1926, any seven or more members of a trade union may apply in the prescribed manner to the Registrar of Trade Unions for registration of the union. A trade union after registration becomes a body corporate, gets perpetual succession and common seal, can acquire and hold both movable and immovable property, can enter into a contract and can even sue and be sued in its registered name. So there appears to be no bar in the application of the Trade Unions Act, 1926, to the IT employees.

11.8.4. Shops and Establishments Act (Bombay Shops and Establishments Act, 1948)

IT and ITES companies in a particular state are covered within the definition of 'commercial establishments' under the Shops and Establishments Act of the state. Various state rules have been framed considering the local conditions, deemed suitable for the employees, which are applicable to the employees. Few examples are as follows:

1. Chapter VI of the Bombay Shops and Establishments Act, 1948, covers work timings for young persons and women in a commercial establishment, which is also applicable to the employees of the IT organizations.
2. Section 33(3) of the Act states that no woman shall be required or allowed to work in an establishment after 9:30 PM. The same is also applicable to the employees of the IT organizations.
3. Schedule II of this Act under Exemption no. 476 (for Software and IT establishments) including Customer Service Care Centre operating through computer in the state of Maharashtra states that Section 33(3) shall be subject to the following:
   a. Special arrangement should be made for protection of female employees working before 6:00 AM and after 8:30 PM including transport.
   b. Female employees should be provided jobs jointly or in groups.
   c. Arrangement for rest rooms and lockers should be made for woman employees.

All the above provisions are also applicable to the IT organizations.

11.8.5. The Payment of Gratuity Act, 1972

The Payment of Gratuity Act applies to any establishment in which 10 or more persons are employed, or were employed on any day of the preceding 12 months. The provisions for the payment of gratuity as laid under the Act are:

It is usually paid at the time of retirement but it can be paid before provided certain conditions are met.

- A person is eligible to receive gratuity only if he has completed minimum five years of service with an organization. However, it can be paid before the completion of five years at the death of an employee or if he has become disabled due to accident or disease. After an employee renders continuous service for not less than five years, or on his superannuation, retirement or resignation, or on his death or disablement due to accident or disease, he/she is eligible for gratuity.

- To calculate how much gratuity is payable, the Payment of Gratuity Act, 1972, has divided non-government employees into two categories:
  - o Employees covered under the Act: The formula for computation of gratuity is (15 × last drawn salary × tenure of working) divided by 26.
  - o Employees not covered under the Act: There is no law that restricts an employer from paying gratuity to his employees even if the organization is not covered under the Act. The amount of gratuity payable to the employee can be calculated based on half month's salary for each completed year. Here also salary is inclusive of basic, DA and commission based on sales. The formula is as follows: (15 × last drawn salary × tenure of working) divided by 30.
- No gratuity payable to an employee or workman shall be liable to attachment in execution of any decree or order of any civil, revenue or criminal court (Section 13). In the event, gratuity is withheld by an employer or delayed; the aggrieved and dissatisfied employee may approach the labour commissioner and file a complaint against the employer.

All provisions of the Gratuity Act are equally applicable to the employees of the IT and ITES organizations.

11.8.6. The Employees' Provident Funds and Miscellaneous Provisions Act, 1952

The scheme is managed under the aegis of Employees' Provident Fund Organisation (EPFO). It covers every establishment in which 20 or more persons are employed and certain organizations are covered, subject to certain conditions and exemptions even if they employ less than 20 persons each.

As per the rules, in EPF, an employee whose 'pay' is more than ₹15,000 per month at the time of joining is not eligible and is called non-eligible employee. Employees drawing less than ₹15,000 per month have to mandatorily become members of the EPF. However, an employee who is drawing 'pay' above prescribed limit (at present ₹15,000) can become a member with permission of Assistant PF Commissioner, if he and his employer agree to the same.

11.8.6.1. Contribution by Employer and Employee

The contribution paid by the employer is 12 per cent of basic wages plus DA plus retaining allowance. An equal contribution is payable by the employee also. In the case of establishments which employ less than 20 employees or meet certain other conditions, as per the EPFO rules, the contribution rate for both employee and the employer is limited to 10 per cent.

For most employees of the private sector, it is the basic salary on which the contribution is calculated. Out of employer's contribution, 8.33 per cent will be diverted to Employees' Pension Scheme, but it is calculated on ₹15,000. So for every employee with basic pay equal to ₹15,000 or more, the diversion is ₹1,250 each month into EPS. If the basic pay is less than ₹15,000 then 8.33 per cent of that full amount will go into EPS. The balance will be retained in the EPF scheme.

On retirement, the employee will get his full share plus the balance of employer's share retained to his credit in EPF account.

Under the Act, the salary ceiling set for the applicability of the Act to employees is currently ₹6,500. Therefore, employees earning less than ₹15,000 are covered under the Act, whereas those earning more than the ceiling amount have an option to make an application with their company to exempt them from making provident fund contributions.

There is nothing in this Act which bars the IT and the ITES employees to contribute to the EPF till they are covered under the Act.

11.8.7. The Employees' Compensation Act, 1923

Employees Compensation Act, 1923, is one of the important social security legislations which aims to provide financial protection to employees and their dependents through compensation in case of any accidental injury that occurs during employment which results in either death or disablement of the worker. It was earlier known as the Workmen's Compensation Act, 1923, and has now been amended to cover employees within its preview. The Employees Compensation Act, 1923, aims at compensating workmen and employees for various injuries, even death, incurred during the course of their employment.

The Employees Compensation Act applies to the following entities:

- It applies to employees working in factories, mines, docks, construction establishments, plantations, oilfields and other establishments listed in Schedule II of the Employee's Compensation Act.
- It applies to persons recruited for working abroad and who are employed outside India as in Schedule II of the Act.
- It applies to a person recruited as the driver, helper, mechanic, cleaner or any other in connection with a motor vehicle and to a captain or other member of the crew of an aircraft.

The Employees of IT and ITES organizations will be covered under the category of 'other establishments' as specified above. So the Act is applicable to such employees.

11.8.8. The Employees' State Insurance Act, 1948

The ESI Act, 1948, provides for certain benefits to employees in case of sickness, maternity and employment injury and to make provision for certain other matters in relation thereto. All benefits are delivered by ESIs hospitals, clinics and approved independent medical practitioners. The ESI Act, 1948, applies to industries and establishments within a geographical area which has been notified by the appropriate government as an area covered by the Act. In case a commercial establishment has been brought under the purview of this Act by the appropriate government, the Act will cover employees whose compensation is up to ₹15,000.

In a commercial establishment, therefore, employees who are below the ₹15,000 cap shall be eligible to benefits under the ESI Act and those above shall be covered by the Employees Compensation Act, 1923. Since the ESI scheme applies to factories and other establishment's, namely road transport, hotels, restaurants, cinemas, newspaper, shops and educational/medical institutions including commercial establishments, wherein 10 or more persons are employed, the Act is equally applicable to IT and ITES organizations.

11.8.9. The Contract Labour (Regulation and Abolition) Act, 1970

The Contract Labour Act is applicable in case if the commercial establishment employs its personnel through a service provider for carrying out various jobs such as security, cleaning and loading/unloading. The registration of an establishment under this legislation is mandatory. In case the service provider employs 20 or more workers, registration of the contactor is also mandatory. The principle employer is responsible for payment of wages and all statutory compliances. This Act shall apply to housekeepers hired by the establishment for upkeeping of the premises and other menial duties.

The object of the Contract Labour (Regulation and Abolition) Act, 1970, is to prevent exploitation of contract labour. A workman is deemed to be employed as contract labour when he is hired in connection with the work of an establishment by or through a contractor. Contract workmen are indirect employees. The contract workmen are hired, supervised and remunerated by the contractor. The Act is equally applicable to the employees of the IT and ITES organizations.

11.8.10. The Payment of Bonus Act, 1965

The Payment of Bonus Act, 1965, regulates the amount of bonus paid to the persons employed in certain establishments based on their profits and productivity. The Act is applicable to the whole of India for all establishments employing 20 or more persons employed on any day during the year.

The objectives of the Bonus Act (Payment of Bonus Act) are as follows:

- To impose a legal responsibility upon an employer of every establishment covered by the Act to pay the bonus to employees in an establishment
- To designate the minimum and maximum percentage of bonus
- To prescribe the formula for calculating bonus
- To provide redressal mechanism

The Payment of Bonus Act is applicable to the following entities:

- It applies to any factory or establishment containing 20 or more workers employed on any day during the year.
- The Act does not apply to the non-profit-making organizations.
- It is not applicable to establishments such as LIC and hospitals which are excluded under Section 32.
- It is not applicable to establishments where employees have signed an agreement with the employer.
- It is not applicable to establishments exempted by the appropriate government like sick units.

In Maharashtra, the Payment of Bonus Act, 1965, applies to commercial establishments with 10 or more employees on any day during that accounting year. There is nothing in the Act which bars the IT and ITES organizations from the payment of bonus to its employees.

11.8.11. The Equal Remuneration Act, 1976

The Equal Remuneration Act, 1976, provides for payment of equal remuneration to men and women and help prevent gender discrimination. Article 39 of the Constitution of India envisages that the states will have a policy for securing equal pay for equal work for both men and women. To give effect to this constitutional provision, the Equal Remuneration Act, 1976, was introduced.

As per Section 1 of the Equal Remuneration Act, 1976, the Act is applicable to establishments only via notifications issued by the appropriate government. As per notification number S.O. 144 (E), dated 2 March 1977, 'Data processing and tabulating services' are covered under the ambit of the Act, thereby bringing IT and ITES industries under the Act. It also states the duty of employer to pay equal remuneration to men and women workers for work of a similar nature. The Act, thus, is applicable to IT and ITES organizations.

11.8.12. Industrial Employment (Standing Orders) Act, 1946

This Act requires employers in industrial establishments to formally define the conditions of employment of the employees under them and submit draft standing orders to certifying authority for its certification.

It applies to every industrial establishment wherein 100 (reduced to 50 by the central government in respect of the establishments for which it is the appropriate government) or more workmen are employed. The government can, however, apply the provisions of the Act to make it applicable to any industrial establishment employing less than 100 workmen.

The definition of 'industrial establishment' under the Act covers industrial establishments as defined under the Payment of Wages Act, 1936, and the Factories Act, 1948. The Act essentially covers 'workman' (as defined under the ID Act, 1947). In Maharashtra, the Act covers industrial establishments wherein 50 or more workmen are employed on any working day as well as all establishments covered under the Bombay Shops and Establishments Act, 1948, bringing under its ambit the IT and ITES industry.

11.8.13. The Minimum Wages Act, 1948

The Act provides for fixing of minimum rates of wages in certain employments. The appropriate government shall, in the manner provided, fix the minimum rates or wages payable to employees employed in an employment specified in Part I or Part II of the Schedule and in an employment added to either Part by notification under Section 27 of the Act. The Minimum Wages Act applies to commercial establishments. The Act applies to any person employed in a commercial establishment as defined in the Bombay Shops and Establishments Act, 1948. However, as the salary of employees in commercial establishment is normally quite high, compliance with the Act is usually not a problem.

11.8.14. The Maternity Benefit Act, 1961

The Maternity Benefit Act, 1961, exists for the benefit of working women who are pregnant, or have given birth or suffered a miscarriage.

The Maternity Benefit Act applies to any establishment in which 10 or more persons are employed, or were employed, on any day of the preceding 12 months. It is to be noted that the portion describing applicability of the Act uses the word 'persons' and not 'women', meaning that it is not necessary that there must be a minimum of 10 women in an establishment for the Act to apply, only 10 persons, including at least one woman. The Act regulates the employment of women in such establishments for certain periods before and after child birth. They will be entitled to maternity benefits as per the provisions of the Act. The Act equally applies to IT and ITES organizations.

11.8.15. The Sexual Harassment of Women at Workplace (Prevention, Prohibition and Redressal) Act, 2013

To solidify the Supreme Court's guidelines laid down in Vishaka versus State of Rajasthan case and to have a comprehensive legal framework for the protection of women at workplaces, the Sexual Harassment of Women at Workplace (Prevention, Prohibition and Redressal) Act, 2013, was brought into force from 9 December 2013. The Act ensures that women are protected against sexual harassment at all the workplaces, be it in public or private. The Act has made provisions for the creation of ICC at each office or branch of an organization employing at least 10 employees. The ICC shall comprise senior-level working women employed in company, two members from employees, one member from NGO or person familiar with issues relating to sexual harassment. As per the Act, the government must set up a 'local complaints committee' (LCC) at the district level to investigate complaints regarding sexual harassment from establishments where the ICC has not been constituted. The Act has laid down a detailed procedure for dealing with complaints and enquiries, protection of victims and prescribes punishment for sexual harassment and also punishes false complaints of harassment. The Act defines sexual harassment as sexually coloured remarks, demand or request for sexual favours, showing pornography, unwelcome physical, verbal, non-verbal sexual conduct and uninvited physical contact and advances. Non-compliance with this Act may invite a fine of up to ₹50,000 upon the employer and also cancellation of licence to carry out business activities.

IC.11.1. INDUSTRIAL CONTEXT FOR DISCUSSION

Termination of Employment in Software Development Companies and the Dilemma Concerning Applicable Chapter for Retrenchment under the ID

IT companies juggle with the applicability of various labour laws based on different interpretations concerning whether or not they are factories based on the manufacturing activity carried on by them and what are the compliances that need to be made. Key among the concerns of the HR teams of such companies while terminating employees is whether they should apply upon their company the label of an 'industrial establishment' and hence undertake measures under compliance driven Chapter VB comprising Section 25N of the ID Act or should they proceed, as per general practice, with the less onerous Chapter VA.

Whether a software development company is as an 'industrial establishment' has been a subject matter of debate over the past few years and while there are judicial precedents which indicate that the software development would fall outside the purview of Section 25N of the ID Act, the issue still is not settled.

Brief Legal Background

For the purposes of Chapter VB and the consequent applicability of retrenchment provisions under Section 25N, the term 'industrial establishment' has separately been defined under Section 25L of the ID Act. Accordingly, the term industrial establishment covers within its ambit, a factory (defined under the Factories Act, 1948), a mine (defined under the Mines Act, 1952) and a plantation (defined under the Plantations Labour Act, 1951). A factory under the Factories Act, 1948, ('FC Act') *inter alia* includes any premises including the precincts thereof where 10 or more workers are working and in any part of which a manufacturing process is being carried on with the aid of power. Explanation II to the aforesaid definition states that the mere fact that an Electronic Data Processing Unit or Computer Unit is installed in any premises or part thereof shall not be construed to be make it a factory if no manufacturing process is being carried on in such premises or part thereof. A manufacturing process in this regard has been defined under the FC Act to mean any process *inter alia* for the making altering, repairing, ornamenting, finishing, packing, oiling, washing, cleaning, breaking up, demolishing or otherwise treating or adapting any article or substance with a view to its use, sale, transport, delivery or disposal.

Judicial Precedents

The issue whether a software development company engages in a manufacturing process to be covered under the definition of factory has been taken up before various Indian Courts, as briefly discussed below[1]:

- **Madras High Court in Seelan Case:** The Division Bench of the Madras High Court in the matter of *Seelan Raj R and 14 Others vs. P. O., I Addl Labour Court and Ors.* ('Seelan Case') *inter alia* observed that: 'on a plain reading of Explanation II ... it becomes abundantly clear that an electronic data processing unit or computer unit installed in any premises or part thereof, and such activities may amount to manufacturing process, bringing within the ambit of "factory" as defined under the Section 2(m) of the Factories Act, yet Explanation II grants an exemption immunity to electronic data processing or computer unit from being within the purview of the welfare legislator namely the labour laws. *Thus, an establishment solely engaged as an electronic data processing unit or computer unit, though may be a factory, yet would be exempted from the application of labour laws by virtue of Explanation II and such establishment cannot be held as a factory'.*
- **Supreme Court in Seelan Case:** The Seelan Case was the subject matter of appeal in the Supreme Court in *Seelan Raj R and Ors vs. Presiding Officer 1st Additional Labour Court and Ors.* The Supreme Court referred to the background of the case—wherein the respondent company has been formed with the object of rendering computer services to its customers relating to collection and maintenance of information and develop company software application to suit special requirements of the customer and that subsequently it set up a data processing division.

---

[1] https://www.ilntoday.com/files/2018/05/LexCounsel52518.pdf. Accessed on 08 Aug 2019.

The data processing division was closed due to becoming unviable and the respondent company claimed that being a software manufacturer it was outside of the definition of the 'factory'. While the Labour Court held the company to be a factory the (single and) division bench of the Madras High Court held as above. Interestingly, the Supreme Court pointed to similar issues having been raised in the matter of *Tata Consultancy Services vs. State of Andhra Pradesh* ('TCS Case') which had been referred to a larger bench and for similar reasons referred this matter to a larger bench.

- **Supreme Court in TCS Case:** The Supreme Court in its judgment in 2004 in the TCS case limited itself to the determination that branded software was 'goods'. On other issues it stated that *'before the High Court certain other questions were raised. However, those have not been agitated or pressed before us'*. Thus, there was no determination concerning ID Act issues.
- **Mumbai High Court in Western Outdoor Case:** A single bench of the Mumbai High Court in *The Assistant Director vs M/S. Western Outdoor Interactive Pvt. Ltd.* ('Western Outdoor Case') in the context of the Employees State Insurance Act, 1948 ('ESI Act') while dealing with a company being a computer unit involved in software development and other activities not only distinguished the provisions of the ESI Act and ID Act with reference to definition of factory but also stated as below concerning the rationale expressed by Division Bench of Madras High Court: *'... with due respect, I endorse my disagreement with the view taken by the Division Bench of the Madras High Court on the point of Explanation-II of Section 2(m) of the Factories Act'*. It further observed that *'the issue of interpretation of "manufacturing process" in Explanation II of Section 2(m) of the Factories Act is not finally decided by the Supreme Court hence the issue is still res integra'*. Based on interpretation and provisions of the ESI Act the Court held that (a) creation of software or development of software itself is a manufacturing process, and (b) premises where computers are involved in manufacturing process would be considered a factory under the ESI Act.

Concluding Remarks

The above judgements reflect the fluid nature of interpretation which can be taken concerning whether IT industries can be considered as factories and to what extent such an interpretation would require these companies to now press ahead with compliances under Chapter VB of the ID Act.

Until the matter is settled by the Supreme Court, the issue would continue to be open to varied views on what is the best course to adopt and whether or not they should apply Section 25N of the ID Act to themselves and hence seek prior permission of the authorities for employee termination in addition to paying retrenchment compensation.

Source: http://www.mondaq.com/india/x/705568/Compliance/TERMINATION+OF+EMPLOYMENT+IN+SOFTWA RE+DEVELOPMENT+COMPANIES+AND+THE+DILEMMA+CONCERNING+APPLICABLE+CHAPTER+FOR+RETREN CHMENT+UNDER+THE+INDUSTRIAL+DISPUTES+ACT

Chapter Summary

1. The IT sector's contribution to India's GDP increased from 1.2 per cent in 1998 to 7.7 per cent in 2017 as per the NASSCOM report. The market size of India's IT and ITES industry grew to US$167 billion in 2017–2018. In the year 2019, the year-to-year growth of the industry is expected to be over by 13 per cent as per the NASSCOM report.

2. Firms in the United States, the United Kingdom and other developed countries outsourced their non-core functions to Indian BPOs and ITES firms who outsourced their jobs to third-party vendors in India. So there emerged a class of IT organizations, who were the third-party vendors to the IT and ITES companies in India.

3. A phenomenal growth was witnessed in the Indian IT organization only in the post-economic liberalization period. The liberalized policy regime enabled fast technological advancement, mushrooming of computer science and technology education, readiness of a large pool of talent to the industry at a relatively lower cost and declined prices of computer hardware. All these factors together contributed significantly to the growth of this industry during the last approximately three decades.

4. The total employment in IT-ITES industry has been rising over the years and reached around 36.88 lakh in 2015–2016. The IT industry has helped the economy in the following manner:
   a. The industry has raised the socio-economic level of a large number of families in India.
   b. It has increased employment in IT-ITES services which has helped other associated businesses such as security, housekeeping, catering, transportation and real estate.

5. With more and more techies becoming jobless in various major IT companies, there emerged the need to set up dedicated IT employee unions in India. Such movements were visible in the cities such as Bangalore, Hyderabad and Kolkata. One of the early initiatives was the formation of the 'UNITES' head quartered in Bangalore.

6. On 29 December 2014, the F.I.T.E was launched when TCS was illegally terminating the employment of thousands of people.

7. The Indian IT companies for a very long time were exempted from some of the basic rules and obligations which are applicable on the companies regarding employment of workers. For some time, some of the state governments in India exempted the IT companies from the application of 'Industrial Employment Standing Orders Act, 1946'. But of late, there is no such exemption provided by any state government.

8. The following labour Acts are applicable to IT and ITES organizations: The Trade Unions Act, 1926, Shops and Establishments Act, The Payment of Gratuity Act, 1972, The Employees' Provident Funds and Miscellaneous Provisions Act, 1952, The Employees' Compensation Act, 1923, The Employees' State Insurance Act, 1948, The Contract Labour (Regulation and Abolition) Act, 1970, The Payment of Bonus Act, 1965, Equal Remuneration Act, 1976, Industrial Employment (Standing Orders) Act, 1946, The Minimum Wages Act, 1948, The Maternity Benefit Act, 1961, The Sexual Harassment of Women at Workplace (Prevention, Prohibition and Redressal) Act, 2013.

Questions

1. Discuss the impacts of IT and ITES organizations and business on the Indian labour market.
2. Whether the labour laws are applicable to IT and the ITES organization in India. Discuss.
3. Efforts had been made to form and register trade unions by the employees of IT and ITES organizations in India. Discuss this situation in the light of the Trade Unions Act, 1926, and the constitutional provisions. Explain whether such steps are legally justified?
4. 'Hire and fire' had been the dictum of the IT and ITES organizations in India. What are its impacts on the employee and the organization?

References

1. Singh S. How the Indian IT services sector is seeking to make its biggest transformation, The Economic Times. 14 September 2017.
2. Singh, Ishmeet and Navjot, Kaur. Contribution of information technology in growth of Indian economy. *International Journal of Research – Granthaalayah*, 2017; 5:6, p 4.
3. Christopher N. IT employees get nod to set up trade union in Karnataka, The Economic Times. 9 November 2017. Available from https://economictimes.indiatimes.com/tech/ites/it-employees-get-nod-to-set-up-trade-union-in-karnataka/articleshow/61568071.cms
4. F.I.T.E. Formation of a Maharashtra state level tripartite committee [Press release]. 2019. Available from http://fite.org.in/2019/02/18/formation-tripartite-committee/

12 International Labour Organization

LEARNING OBJECTIVES

After reading this chapter, you will be able to:

❏ Understand the structure and the working of ILO
❏ Understand the way ILO influences its member states
❏ Understand the conventions and recommendations of ILO
❏ Understand the impact of ILO on Indian labour laws and procedures

12.1. Introduction

The ILO was founded in 1919 as part of the Treaty of Versailles. The mission of the ILO, as appears in various documents, is to promote social justice and internationally recognize human and labour rights based on the founding principle that social justice is essential to universal and lasting peace. Since 1946, the ILO is a specialized agency of the UNO. It is the only tripartite UNO agency that brings together governments, employers and workers' representatives from its 187 member states.

The Constitution of the ILO was drafted as early as 1919 by the Labour Commission, chaired by Samuel Gompers, head of the American Federation of Labour (AFL) in the United States. It was composed of representatives from nine countries: Belgium, Cuba, Czechoslovakia, France, Italy, Japan, Poland, the United Kingdom and the United States.

The founders of the ILO recognized the importance of social justice in securing security, humanitarian, political and economic considerations against a background of the exploitation of workers in the industrializing nations of that time. They felt the need for an increasing understanding of the world's economic interdependence and the need for cooperation to obtain similarity of working conditions in countries competing in the market. These ideas were translated in the Preamble to the Constitution of the ILO, which states:

- Whereas universal and lasting peace can be established only if it is based upon social justice;
- And whereas conditions of labour exist involving such injustice, hardship and privation to large numbers of people as to produce unrest so great that the peace and harmony of the world are imperiled; and an improvement of those conditions is urgently required;
- Whereas also the failure of any nation to adopt humane conditions of labour is an obstacle in the way of other nations which desire to improve the conditions in their own countries.

The above objectives for improvement, as listed in the Preamble, remain relevant even today. Aspects such as regulation of working time and labour supply, the prevention of unemployment and the provision of an adequate living wage, social protection of workers, children, young persons and women have been considered within the focus zone of ILO. The key principles which the Preamble recognizes are equal remuneration for work of equal value and freedom of association, and highlights, among others, the importance of vocational and technical education.

The ILO's basic goals and principles were enlarged after the Second World War in the Declaration of Philadelphia on 10 May 1944. The Declaration was adopted at the 26th Conference of the ILO in Philadelphia, United States.

12.2. The Philadelphia Charter

The Declaration of Philadelphia which came into being on 10 May 1944, stated the traditional objectives of the ILO and then branched out in two new directions. They are as follows:

- The centrality of human rights to social policy
- The need for international economic planning [1]

The declaration concerning the aims and purposes of the ILO was adopted at the 26th Conference of the ILO in Philadelphia, United States. It was drafted by the then acting ILO Director, Edward J. Phelan and C. Wilfred Jenks. In 1946, when the ILO's constitution was being revised by the General Conference convened in Montreal, the Declaration of Philadelphia was annexed to the constitution and forms an integral part of it by Article 1. The declaration focused on a series of key principles which includes:

- Labour is not a commodity (I, a).
- Freedom of expression and of association are essential to sustained progress (I, a).
- Poverty anywhere constitutes a danger to prosperity everywhere (I, c).
- The war against want requires...unrelenting vigor...(for) the promotion of the common welfare (I, d).
- All human beings, irrespective of race, creed or sex, have the right to pursue both their material well-being and their spiritual development in conditions of freedom and dignity, of economic security and equal opportunity (II, a).

ILO Declaration of Philadelphia

Declaration concerning the aims and purposes of the ILO
   The General Conference of the International Labour Organization, meeting in its Twenty-sixth Session in Philadelphia, hereby adopts, this tenth day of May in the year nineteen hundred and forty-four, the present Declaration of the aims and purposes of the ILO and of the principles which should inspire the policy of its Members.

I

The Conference reaffirms the fundamental principles on which the Organization is based and, in particular, that:

a. labour is not a commodity;
b. freedom of expression and of association are essential to sustained progress;
c. poverty anywhere constitutes a danger to prosperity everywhere;
d. the war against want requires to be carried on with unrelenting vigour within each nation, and by continuous and concerted international effort in which the representatives of workers and employers, enjoying equal status with those of governments, join with them in free discussion and democratic decision with a view to the promotion of the common welfare.

II

Believing that experience has fully demonstrated the truth of the statement in the Constitution of the ILO that lasting peace can be established only if it is based on social justice, the Conference affirms that:

a. all human beings, irrespective of race, creed or sex, have the right to pursue both their material well-being and their spiritual development in conditions of freedom and dignity, of economic security and equal opportunity;
b. the attainment of the conditions in which this shall be possible must constitute the central aim of national and international policy;
c. all national and international policies and measures, in particular those of an economic and financial character, should be judged in this light and accepted only in so far as they may be held to promote and not to hinder the achievement of this fundamental objective;
d. it is a responsibility of the ILO to examine and consider all international economic and financial policies and measures in the light of this fundamental objective;
e. in discharging the tasks entrusted to it the ILO, having considered all relevant economic and financial factors, may include in its decisions and recommendations any provisions which it considers appropriate.

III

The Conference recognizes the solemn obligation of the ILO to further among the nations of the world programmes which will achieve:

a. full employment and the raising of standards of living;
b. the employment of workers in the occupations in which they can have the satisfaction of giving the fullest measure of their skill and attainments and make their greatest contribution to the common well-being;
c. the provision, as a means to the attainment of this end and under adequate guarantees for all concerned, of facilities for training and the transfer of labour, including migration for employment and settlement;
d. policies in regard to wages and earnings, hours and other conditions of work calculated to ensure a just share of the fruits of progress to all, and a minimum living wage to all employed and in need of such protection;
e. the effective recognition of the right of collective bargaining, the cooperation of management and labour in the continuous improvement of productive efficiency, and the collaboration of workers and employers in the preparation and application of social and economic measures;
f. the extension of social security measures to provide a basic income to all in need of such protection and comprehensive medical care;
g. adequate protection for the life and health of workers in all occupations;
h. provision for child welfare and maternity protection;

i. the provision of adequate nutrition, housing and facilities for recreation and culture;
j. the assurance of equality of educational and vocational opportunity.

IV

Confident that the fuller and broader utilization of the world's productive resources necessary for the achievement of the objectives set forth in this Declaration can be secured by effective international and national action, including measures to expand production and consumption, to avoid severe economic fluctuations to promote the economic and social advancement of the less developed regions of the world, to assure greater stability in world prices of primary products, and to promote a high and steady volume of international trade, the Conference pledges the full cooperation of the ILO with such international bodies as may be entrusted with a share of the responsibility for this great task and for the promotion of the health, education and well-being of all peoples.

V

The conference affirms that the principles set forth in this Declaration are fully applicable to all peoples everywhere and that, while the manner of their application must be determined with due regard to the stage of social and economic development reached by each people, their progressive application to peoples who are still dependent, as well as to those who have already achieved self-government, is a matter of concern to the whole civilized world.

The ILO was the first agency associated with the newly formed UNO. On its 50th anniversary in 1969, it was awarded the Nobel Peace Prize. It became known worldwide in 1999 with their 'Decent Work Agenda'. The organization as part of its mission, aims to achieve 'decent work' for all by *promoting social dialogue, social protection and employment creation, as well as respect for international labour standards*. This agenda assured to provide opportunities for work which is productive and generates a fair income, security at the workplace and social protection for families, better prospects for personal development and social integration, freedom for people to express their concerns, organize and participate in the decisions that affect their lives and equality of opportunity and treatment for all women and men. The ILO also provides technical support to more than 100 countries to help to achieve these aims and objectives, with the support of development partners.

In short, the ILO is built on certain strong constitutional principles which ensure universal and lasting peace. The ILO's objectives are to establish social justice for the industrial society, such as the eight-hour working day, maternity protection, child-labour laws, and a range of policies which promote workplace safety and peaceful IR.

12.3. What the ILO Does?

The ILO has four principal strategic objectives:

- To promote and realize standards, and fundamental principles and rights at work.
- To create greater opportunities for women and men to secure decent employment.
- To enhance the coverage and effectiveness of social protection for all.
- To strengthen tripartism and social dialogue.

To achieve these objectives, the following initiatives are taken by the ILO:

1. Formulation of international policies and programmes to promote basic human rights, improve working and living conditions and enhance employment opportunities. The ILO's broad policies are set by the International Labour Conference (ILC), which meets once a year and brings together the organization's constituents. The Conference also adopts new international labour standards and approves the ILO's work plan and budget. Between sessions of the Conference, the ILO is guided by its Governing Body, which is composed of 28 government members, 14 employer members and 14 worker members.
2. To serve as guidelines for national authorities in putting the policies into action, the ILO creates the international labour standards, backed by a unique system to supervise the same.
3. An extensive programme of international technical cooperation, formulated and implemented in an active partnership with constituents, to help countries in making these policies effective in practice.
4. Training, education, research and publishing activities to help advance all of these efforts.

12.4. How the ILO Works?

The ILO accomplishes its work through three main bodies which comprise governments', employers' and workers' representatives.

12.4.1. International Labour Conference

The ILC is the body for setting the international labour standards and the broad policies of the ILO. It meets annually in Geneva. It is also called international parliament of labour. One of the most important tasks undertaken by the ILC is to create worldwide uniform standards of labour in 'the form of Conventions and Recommendations'. This Conference is also a forum for discussion of key social and labour questions related to the member countries.

The ILC is composed of four delegates. Two delegates represent the governments and two delegates represent (one each) the employers and the workers of the member states. Each delegate may be accompanied by advisers (also nominated by the government concerned), not exceeding two in number for each item on the agenda of the meeting. When questions specially affecting women are to be considered, at least one of the advisers needs to be a woman. Advisers can speak only on a request made by the delegate whom they accompany and by the special authorization of the President of the Conference, but are not allowed to vote. A delegate may authorize one of the advisers to act as deputy. Such adviser is allowed to speak as well as vote. Every delegate is entitled to vote individually on all matters that are taken into consideration.

The conference may be attended by representatives of non-governmental international organizations with which the ILO has entered into consultative relationship, such as the International Confederation of Free Trade Unions, the World Federation of Trade Unions and the International Federation of Christian Trade Unions.

The ILC, which is the supreme body of the organization, directs and supervises the work of the Governing Body and the International Labour Office. It also elects the members of the Governing Body and functions as a world parliament for labour.

12.4.2. Governing Body

The Governing Body functions under the direction of the ILC. This body appoints the director general of the International Labour Office, supervises its functioning, prepares the agenda to be placed before the ILO Conference and discharges such other duties as are assigned to it by the Conference. It takes decisions on the ILO policy and establishes the programme and the budget, which it then submits to the Conference for adoption. As such, the Governing Body is the executive council of the ILO. It meets three times a year in Geneva.

The earliest constitution of the Governing Body consisted of 24 members, which included 12 government, 6 employers' and 6 workers' representatives. Later, the proportion of government, employers' and workers' representatives was raised to 16:8:8 and subsequently to 40:10:10. At present, the Governing Body is composed of 56 members out of which 28 members are government members, 14 are employer members and 14 are worker members. There are also 66 deputy members which consist of 28 representations of government members, 19 representations of employers and 19 representations of workers. Out of the 28 titular government seats, 10 are permanently allotted to the 10 states which are of industrial importance. The present 10 permanent members are Brazil, China, France, India, Italy, Japan, the Russian Federation, the United Kingdom, the United States and Germany. The period of office of the Governing Body is three years. In case the elections of the Governing Body do not take place on the expiry of this period, the members elected for the previous term are to remain in office until such elections are held. The method of filling vacancies and of appointing substitutes and other similar questions are decided by the Governing Body, subject to the approval of the Conference.

The Governing Body is required to elect from its members a chairman and two vice chairmen so as to ensure representations of government, employers and workers. The procedure and the time of meetings are regulated by the Governing Body, but special meeting can be convened only on a written request made by at least 16 representatives of the Governing Body.

12.4.3. International Labour Office

The International Labour Office is the permanent secretariat of the ILO. It also works as the information centre and a publishing house for ILO. It is the focal point for ILO's overall activities, which it prepares under the scrutiny of the Governing Body and under the leadership of the director general.

The administrative head of the International Labour Office is its director general. The director general, subject to the instructions of the Governing Body, is 'responsible for the efficient conduct of the International Labour Office and for such other duties which may be assigned to him'. The director general as a part of his responsibility himself or his deputy is required to attend all meetings of the Governing Body. The staff members of the International Labour Office are appointed from different nations by the director general under regulations approved by the Governing Body and a certain percentage of them consists of women.

The functions of the International Labour Office include 'the collection and distribution of information on all subjects related to the international adjustment of the conditions of industrial life and labour, and particularly the examination of subjects which it is proposed to bring before the Conference[1] with a view to the conclusion of international Conventions, and the conduct of each special investigations as may be ordered by the Conference or the Governing Body'.

---

[1] The General Conference of Representatives of the Members of ILO. See Article 388 and 396 of ILO Official Bulletin Volume I (April 1919–August 1920), International Labour Office, Geneva, 1923.

The ILO conducts more than 1,000 technical cooperation programmes in more than 80 countries with the help of some 60 donor institutions worldwide. The ILO has decentralized the management of most activities to its regional, area and branch offices in more than 40 countries across Africa, Asia, Central and Eastern Europe, Latin America, the Middle East and the Pacific.

A notable feature of the ILO is its 'tripartite' nature. Within its structure and function, the ILO brings together governments, employer organizations and worker organizations to jointly shape policies and programmes that promote the concept of decent work for all.

12.5. Conventions and Recommendations

One of the principal functions of the ILO is to secure international minimum social and labour standards. These standards are embodied in resolutions in the form of conventions and recommendations, adopted by the ILC by at least two-thirds of the delegates present at the Conference through voting. The Conference decides whether these resolutions will take the form of a convention or a recommendation. Thus, conventions or recommendations are instruments for creating and establishing international minimum social and labour standards. These are often referred to as International Labour Code.

International labour standards are legal instruments drawn up by the ILO's constituents, that is, the body of governments, employers and workers, which set out basic principles and rights at work. Conventions and recommendations are drawn up by representatives of governments, employers and workers and are adopted at the ILO's annual ILC.

Such documents are either *conventions*, having legal binding, or *recommendations*, which serve as non-binding guidelines on the member states. In many cases, a convention lays down the basic principles to be implemented by ratifying countries, while a related recommendation supplements the convention by providing more detailed guidelines on how it could be applied. Recommendations can also be autonomous, that is, not linked to any convention.

If a convention is ratified, it generally comes into force for that country one year after the date of ratification. Ratifying countries commit themselves to applying the convention in law and practice and reporting on its application at regular intervals to the ILO. The ILO provides technical assistance, if necessary, in the matter. For violations of a convention or part thereof ratified by the member state, representation and complaint procedures can be initiated against such countries.

12.5.1. Fundamental Conventions

The ILO's Governing Body has identified eight conventions as 'fundamental', covering subjects that are considered as fundamental principles of rights at work. The eight fundamental conventions are:

1. Freedom of Association and Protection of the Right to Organise Convention, 1948 (No. 87)
2. Right to Organise and Collective Bargaining Convention, 1949 (No. 98)
3. Forced Labour Convention, 1930 (No. 29)
4. Abolition of Forced Labour Convention, 1957 (No. 105)
5. Minimum Age Convention, 1973 (No. 138)
6. Worst Forms of Child Labour Convention, 1999 (No. 182)

7. Equal Remuneration Convention, 1951 (No. 100)
8. Discrimination (Employment and Occupation) Convention, 1958 (No. 111)

12.5.2. Governance Conventions

The ILO's Governing Body has also designated another four conventions as 'priority' instruments, thereby encouraging member states to ratify them because of their importance for the functioning of the international labour standards system. The ILO Declaration on Social Justice for a Fair Globalization, in its follow-up, underlined the significance from the viewpoint of governance of these conventions. The four governance conventions are:

1. Labour Inspection Convention, 1947 (No. 81)
2. Employment Policy Convention, 1964 (No. 122)
3. Labour Inspection (Agriculture) Convention, 1969 (No. 129)
4. Tripartite Consultation (International Labour Standards) Convention, 1976 (No. 144)

One of the major responsibilities of ILO is to execute the international labour standards which implies drawing up, overseeing and assisting member states to ratify and implement those standards. These standards include the fundamental principles and rights at work, namely freedom from forced and child labour and discrimination, freedom of association and the right to collective bargaining. The 'Decent Work Agenda' is central to the ILO's operations. In addition to providing income, the Decent Work Agenda promotes the idea that work can pave the way for broader social and economic advancement, strengthening individuals, their families and communities. To achieve the Decent Work Agenda, it is organized around four interrelated and mutually reinforcing strategic objectives of the ILO. These are as follows:

- Creating jobs
- Guaranteeing rights at work
- Extending social protection
- Promoting social dialogue

The approach of India with regard to international labour standards has always been positive. The ILO instruments have provided guidelines and a useful framework for the evolution of legislative and administrative measures for the protection of labour. Since ratification of a convention imposes legal bindings and obligations on the country concerned, therefore India had been careful in ratifying the conventions. It has always been the practice that India ratifies a convention when it is fully satisfied that the laws and practices prevailing are in conformity with the relevant ILO convention.

12.6. Decent Work Agenda of the ILO

The ILO considers 'decent work' as a human right. The ILO Agenda 2030 places decent work for all and the ILO's mandate and purpose of social justice at the heart of policies for sustainable and inclusive growth and development. For that over 600 million new jobs need to be created by 2030. It is expected that it would keep pace with the growth of the working-age population. This implies that around 40 million jobs per year need to be created. The ILO further feels the need for improving the conditions for the 780 million men and women who are working but are paid wages below subsistence level. By putting job creation at the heart of economic policymaking and development plans, it is expected that people will have an opportunity for decent work as well as this would reduce the poverty levels and sustain an inclusive growth.

Decent work puts money in the pockets of individuals and families that they can spend in the local economy. Their purchasing power fuels the growth through multiplier effect and development of sustainable enterprises, especially smaller businesses, which in turn are able to hire more workers and improve their pay and conditions. It will also increase revenues earning for governments through more taxes.

The Universal Declaration of Human Right of the UN Charter from 1948 already stipulates the essence of good and decent work under Article 23, which is as follows:

- Everyone has the right to work, to free choice of employment, to just and favourable conditions of work and to protection against unemployment.
- Everyone, without discrimination, has the right to equal pay for equal work.
- Everyone who works has the right to just and favourable remuneration ensuring for himself and his family an existence worthy of human dignity and supplemented, if necessary, by other means of social protection.
- Everyone has the right to form and join trade unions for the protection of his interests.

ILO's basic goals of the decent work approach mean not only having an eye on the protection of these human rights but also implementing and expanding these rights with concrete regulations, and developing them together in dialogues between employers and trade unions. ILO's basic goals of decent work are as follows:

- Creating more and better employment opportunities
- Respecting and legally protecting workers' rights
- Building and expanding social security systems
- Promoting the social dialogue between employers and trade unions

So productive employment and decent work are key elements for achieving a fair globalization and poverty reduction. For this, the ILO has developed an agenda for the community of work looking at job creation, rights at work, social protection and social dialogue, with gender equality as a crosscutting objective.

During the UN General Assembly in September 2015, decent work and the four pillars of the Decent Work Agenda—employment creation, social protection, rights at work and social dialogue—became integral elements of the new 2030 Agenda for sustainable development. The 2030 Agenda calls for the promotion of sustained, inclusive and economic growth, full and productive employment and decent work, and will be a key area of engagement for the ILO and its constituents.

12.7. The International Labour Standards: An Overview

According to ILO's own wording, international labour standards are aimed at promoting decent and productive working conditions of freedom, equity, security and dignity. They are part of an international framework of governance designed to ensure that the global economy provides benefits for all.

The ILO labour standards are laid down in conventions, recommendations and protocols of the organization. Other important documents of relevance for international labour standards are ILO Declarations and Codes of Practice. At present, the ILO lists 189 conventions and 202 recommendations. A number of older conventions have been withdrawn or revised, but the corpus of international labour legislations through international labour standards is up to date. Conventions are legally binding, whereas the observation of recommendations is voluntary. Once a convention is adopted by the ILC, a minimum number of ratifications by ILO member states are required to put the convention into effect. Member states are obliged to submit the norm to their parliament or another competent national authority for ratification and enactment of the relevant legislation.

A ratified convention is subject to the ILO's supervisory system for ensuring that the convention is actually implemented and applied. The supervisory bodies include the independent committee of experts for the application of conventions and recommendations, and two tripartite committees of the ILC: the Committee on Freedom of Association and the Committee on the Application of Standards.

12.8. Obligation of Members after Adoption of International Labour Standards

The ILC is not a body with mandate to pass legislation that becomes binding on any member country. However, the written down norms of the ILO constitution make sure that conventions and recommendations adopted by the ILC are not regarded as mere points of pronouncements. As a part of the procedure, member governments report back to the ILO on the measures they have taken to bring the ILO convention or recommendation implementable in their countries.

Once a convention has been ratified and has come into force, every country that ratifies is obligated to take all necessary measures to make its provisions effective. By ratifying a convention, a country automatically agrees to report every year to the International Labour Office on how the convention is being applied in its territory. Such reports are much more than mere formality. Copies of each annual report prepared by a member government need to be sent to the country's most representative employers' and workers' organizations, and the report, as annually submitted to the ILO, has to state whether the government has received any comments from them on the practical implementation of the convention in question.

The object of such system of supervision is to enable the conference to determine the extent to which progress has been made in implementing the standards set forth in the conventions. On the basis of the intelligence it receives, the conference may, if it feels this to be necessary, make 'observations' to member governments, and suggest to them ways to overcome discrepancies between the provisions and existing practices.

The effectiveness of this supervisory machinery depends, naturally, on the cooperation of member governments in submitting their annual reports.

The ILO constitution provides two other procedures that may be followed to induce member governments to carry out the provisions of conventions that they have ratified. These are as follows:

1. The workers' or the employers' organizations may make representations to the International Labour Office if they believe that any government, even their own, has failed to live up to a

convention that it has ratified. If the member government fails to provide a satisfactory answer to the allegation, the Governing Body may decide to publish the allegation.

2. Any ILO member government may file a complaint against any other member for alleged non-compliance with a ratified convention. The ILO constitution provides that, in this situation, a commission of enquiry shall examine the matter, report on its findings and recommend such remedial steps as it thinks proper.

Recommendations adopted by the ILC, unlike the conventions, are not international treaties and are not subject to ratification. Hence, these recommendations can never be binding on a member government in the sense that the provisions of a ratified convention are binding. Nevertheless, the recommendations constitute an important part of the international labour code.

12.9. The ILO as a Promoter of Human Rights

The ILO has promoted the human rights from time to time as an integral part of its activity and responsibility. Some of the broad areas are discussed below.

12.9.1. Freedom of Association

The human rights are embodied in the ILO convention on Freedom of Association and Protection of the Right to Organise adopted in 1948, and convention on the Right to Organise and Collective Bargaining adopted in 1949.

These conventions lay down that all workers and employers shall possess the right to establish and join organizations of their own choice without having to obtain any authorization. Such organizations shall have the right to function freely and without interference from public authorities, but can be/ may be dissolved or suspended only by judicial procedure and not by administrative authority.

The relevant portion of the convention of 'Freedom of Association and Protection of the Right to Organise Convention, 1948 (No. 87)' are cited as follows.

C87: Freedom of Association

Article 2

Workers and employers, without distinction whatsoever, shall have the right to establish and, subject only to the rules of the organisation concerned, to join organisations of their own choosing without previous authorisation.

Article 3

1. Workers' and employers' organisations shall have the right to draw up their constitutions and rules, to elect their representatives in full freedom, to organise their administration and activities and to formulate their programmes.
2. The public authorities shall refrain from any interference which would restrict this right or impede the lawful exercise thereof.

Article 4

Workers' and employers' organisations shall not be liable to be dissolved or suspended by administrative authority.

Article 5

Workers' and employers' organisations shall have the right to establish and join federations and confederations and any such organisation, federation or confederation shall have the right to affiliate with international organisations of workers and employers.

Article 6

The provisions of Articles 2, 3 and 4 hereof apply to federations and confederations of workers' and employers' organisations.

Article 7

The acquisition of legal personality by workers' and employers' organisations, federations and confederations shall not be made subject to conditions of such a character as to restrict the application of the provisions of Articles 2, 3 and 4 hereof.

Article 8

1. In exercising the rights provided for in this Convention workers and employers and their respective organisations, like other persons or organised collectivities, shall respect the law of the land.
2. The law of the land shall not be such as to impair, nor shall it be so applied as to impair, the guarantees provided for in this Convention.

Article 9

1. The extent to which the guarantees provided for in this Convention shall apply to the armed forces and the police shall be determined by national laws or regulations.
2. In accordance with the principle set forth in paragraph 8 of Article 19 of the Constitution of the International Labour Organisation the ratification of this Convention by any Member shall not be deemed to affect any existing law, award, custom or agreement in virtue of which members of the armed forces or the police enjoy any right guaranteed by this Convention.

Source: https://www.ilo.org/dyn/normlex/en/f?p=NORMLEXPUB:12100:0::NO::P12100_ILO_CODE:C087

The convention of 'Right to Organize and Collective Bargaining Convention, 1949 (No. 98)', protects the workers against victimization. The relevant clauses are cited as follows.

C098: Right to Organize and Collective Bargaining Convention, 1949 (No. 98)

Article 1

1. Workers shall enjoy adequate protection against acts of anti-union discrimination in respect of their employment.
2. Such protection shall apply more particularly in respect of acts calculated to:
   a. make the employment of a worker subject to the condition that he shall not join a union or shall relinquish trade union membership;

b. cause the dismissal of or otherwise prejudice a worker by reason of union membership or because of participation in union activities outside working hours or, with the consent of the employer, within working hours.

Article 2

1. Workers' and employers' organisations shall enjoy adequate protection against any acts of interference by each other or each other's agents or members in their establishment, functioning or administration.
2. In particular, acts which are designed to promote the establishment of workers' organisations under the domination of employers or employers' organisations, or to support workers' organisations by financial or other means, with the object of placing such organisations under the control of employers or employers' organisations, shall be deemed to constitute acts of interference within the meaning of this Article.

Article 3

Machinery appropriate to national conditions shall be established, where necessary, for the purpose of ensuring respect for the right to organise as defined in the preceding Articles.

Article 4

Measures appropriate to national conditions shall be taken, where necessary, to encourage and promote the full development and utilisation of machinery for voluntary negotiation between employers or employers' organisations and workers' organisations, with a view to the regulation of terms and conditions of employment by means of collective agreements.

Source: https://www.ilo.org/dyn/normlex/en/f?p=NORMLEXPUB:12100:::NO:12100:P12100_ILO_CODE:C098:NO

These conventions provide that workers must be protected against discrimination on the grounds of union membership or activities; thus, a worker cannot be discharged only because he joined or is active in a union. By 2 May 2006, the first conventions were ratified by 145 countries and the second by 154 countries. The ILO is concerned with safeguarding the rights enumerated in these two conventions. It has made full use of its regular procedure to ascertain whether all member states have presented the conventions to the appropriate domestic authorities for ratification and to supervise the implementation of the conventions by states that have ratified them.

12.9.2. Forced Labour

Before the Second World War, ILO's efforts in regard to forced labour, including the adoption of the 1930 Convention on Forced Labour and the 1936 Convention on Recruiting of Indigenous Workers, were directed primarily towards stamping out abuses in non-self-governing territories. A convention adopted in 1939 prescribed that contracts for the employment of indigenous labour must always be made in writing, and an accompanying recommendation called for regulation of the maximum period of time for which an indigenous worker could bind himself under contract. Another convention adopted in 1939 required all penal sanctions exacted against indigenous labour for breach of contract to be progressively abolished 'as soon as possible'; when applicable to juvenile workers, the sanctions against breach of contract were to be abolished without delay.

After the Second World War, emphasis shifted from protection against exploitation in colonial areas to the abolition of systems of forced labour wherever they occur, as part of the promotion of human rights. The first step in this broader attack was an impartial enquiry into the nature and extent of forced labour, including prison labour, gang labour, labour service and the like. A joint UN–ILO committee studied the existence in the world of systems of forced or 'corrective' labour as a means of political coercion or as punishment for political views. In 1953, the committee reported that it had found two principal forms of forced labour existing in fully self-governing countries: one used mainly as a means of political coercion or political punishment and the other used mainly for economic reasons.

In 1957, the ILC, by a vote of 240 to 0, with one abstention, adopted the Convention on the Abolition of Forced Labour. The convention outlaws any form of forced or compulsory labour:

1. as a means of political coercion or education or as punishment for political or ideological views,
2. as a means of obtaining labor for economic development,
3. as a means of labor discipline,
4. as punishment for participation in strikes, or
5. as a means of racial, social, national, or religious discrimination.

The convention, one of the farthest-reaching adopted by the ILO, has been in force since 17 January 1959. The convention of 'Abolition of Forced Labour Convention, 1957 (No. 105)', protects the workers against victimization. The relevant clauses are cited as follows.

C105: Abolition of Forced Labour Convention, 1957 (No. 105)

Article 1

Each Member of the International Labour Organisation which ratifies this Convention undertakes to suppress and not to make use of any form of forced or compulsory labour:

1. as a means of political coercion or education or as a punishment for holding or expressing political views or views ideologically opposed to the established political, social or economic system;
2. as a method of mobilising and using labour for purposes of economic development;
3. as a means of labour discipline;
4. as a punishment for having participated in strikes;
5. as a means of racial, social, national or religious discrimination.

Article 2

Each Member of the International Labour Organisation which ratifies this Convention undertakes to take effective measures to secure the immediate and complete abolition of forced or compulsory labour as specified in Article 1 of this Convention.

Article 3

The formal ratifications of this Convention shall be communicated to the Director-General of the International Labour Office for registration.

Article 4

1. This Convention shall be binding only upon those Members of the International Labour Organisation whose ratifications have been registered with the Director-General.

2. It shall come into force twelve months after the date on which the ratifications of two Members have been registered with the Director-General.
3. Thereafter, this Convention shall come into force for any Member twelve months after the date on which its ratification has been registered.

Article 5

1. A Member which has ratified this Convention may denounce it after the expiration of ten years from the date on which the Convention first comes into force, by an act communicated to the Director-General of the International Labour Office for registration. Such denunciation shall not take effect until one year after the date on which it is registered.
2. Each Member which has ratified this Convention and which does not, within the year following the expiration of the period of ten years mentioned in the preceding paragraph, exercise the right of denunciation provided for in this Article, will be bound for another period of ten years and, thereafter, may denounce this Convention at the expiration of each period of ten years under the terms provided for in this Article.

Source: https://www.ilo.org/dyn/normlex/en/f?p=NORMLEXPUB:12100:::NO:12100:P12100_ILO_CODE:C105:NO

12.9.3. Discrimination in Employment and Occupation

The convention on discrimination in employment and occupation, adopted by the ILC in 1958 constitutes another effort to promote the principle of equal rights. The convention defines such discrimination as 'any distinction, exclusion or preference based on race, colour, sex, religion, political opinion, national extraction or social origin that impairs equal access to vocational training, employment and certain occupations, or equal terms and conditions of employment'.

However, norms provide that measures affecting a person justifiably suspected of being engaged in activities prejudicial to the security of the state are not to be deemed discrimination, provided such a person is guaranteed the right of appeal. Furthermore, special measures of protection or assistance required because of sex, age, disablement, family responsibility, or social or cultural status are not to be considered discriminatory, but workers' and employers' organizations must in certain cases be consulted on such measures.

Such goal is to be accomplished through cooperation with employers' and workers' organizations, through legislation and educational programmes. The convention was adopted by the ILO and has been in force since 15 January 1960. The convention of 'Discrimination (Employment and Occupation) Convention, 1958', protects the workers against victimization. The relevant clauses are cited as follows.

C111: Discrimination (Employment and Occupation) Convention, 1958 (No. 111)

Article 1

1. For the purpose of this Convention the term *discrimination* includes:
   a. any distinction, exclusion or preference made on the basis of race, colour, sex, religion, political opinion, national extraction or social origin, which has the effect of nullifying or impairing equality of opportunity or treatment in employment or occupation;

b. such other distinction, exclusion or preference which has the effect of nullifying or impairing equality of opportunity or treatment in employment or occupation as may be determined by the Member concerned after consultation with representative employers' and workers' organisations, where such exist, and with other appropriate bodies.

2. Any distinction, exclusion or preference in respect of a particular job based on the inherent requirements thereof shall not be deemed to be discrimination.

3. For the purpose of this Convention the terms *employment* and *occupation* include access to vocational training, access to employment and to particular occupations, and terms and conditions of employment.

Article 2

Each Member for which this Convention is in force undertakes to declare and pursue a national policy designed to promote, by methods appropriate to national conditions and practice, equality of opportunity and treatment in respect of employment and occupation, with a view to eliminating any discrimination in respect thereof.

Article 3

Each Member for which this Convention is in force undertakes, by methods appropriate to national conditions and practice:

1. to seek the co-operation of employers' and workers' organisations and other appropriate bodies in promoting the acceptance and observance of this policy;

2. to enact such legislation and to promote such educational programmes as may be calculated to secure the acceptance and observance of the policy;

3. to repeal any statutory provisions and modify any administrative instructions or practices which are inconsistent with the policy;

4. to pursue the policy in respect of employment under the direct control of a national authority;

5. to ensure observance of the policy in the activities of vocational guidance, vocational training and placement services under the direction of a national authority;

6. to indicate in its annual reports on the application of the Convention the action taken in pursuance of the policy and the results secured by such action.

Article 4

Any measures affecting an individual who is justifiably suspected of, or engaged in, activities prejudicial to the security of the State shall not be deemed to be discrimination, provided that the individual concerned shall have the right to appeal to a competent body established in accordance with national practice.

Article 5

1. Special measures of protection or assistance provided for in other Conventions or Recommendations adopted by the ILC shall not be deemed to be discrimination.

2. Any Member may, after consultation with representative employers' and workers' organisations, where such exist, determine that other special measures designed to meet the particular requirements of persons who, for reasons such as sex, age, disablement, family responsibilities or social or cultural status, are generally recognised to require special protection or assistance, shall not be deemed to be discrimination.

Source: https://www.ilo.org/dyn/normlex/en/f?p=NORMLEXPUB:12100:::NO:12100:P12100_ILO_CODE:C111:NO

12.9.4. ILO and Technical Assistance

Member states had the cooperation of the ILO in matters of 'technical assistance' since 1930 depending on integral feature of national development plans. Among these priorities are the development of HR, the raising of living standards and the promotion of full employment. As a part of its programme, the ILO works actively with the authorities to set up and put into effect concrete cooperative projects. Such tasks range from brief preliminary missions to major projects, such as the setting up of networks of vocational training or management development centres to the establishment of full-scale rural development programmes.

To many cooperative projects, the ILO also provides for study grants and organizes training courses and seminars. The supply of specialized equipment for certain services is another form of ILO aid, for example, equipment to set up vocational training centres. The ILO concentrates its efforts on activities that produce maximum long-term results, like the creation of institutions of various kinds or of training centres for trainers.

12.9.5. Unemployment and Underemployment

The ILO considers to help the member states in the struggle against unemployment which is one of its major responsibilities. Guided by international labour standards, and often with the practical aid of the ILO, many countries have taken steps to ease the load of unemployed mass. In 1964, the ILC recognized the need of an appropriate policy of reducing unemployment as well as for promotion and planning of employment needs to be integral part of the development effort.

The ILO launched the World Employment Programme in 1969, which was the starting point in ILO's efforts to help combat unemployment and underemployment. The World Employment Conference was held in 1976. The resulting declaration of principles and programme of action called the world's attention to the need for full employment and an adequate income for every inhabitant in the shortest possible time.

The ILO-developed concept of basic needs is paramount to the effort to get to the root of poverty. Basic needs include two elements:

- Certain minimum requirements of a family for private consumption—adequate food, shelter and clothing are obviously included, as would be certain household equipment and furniture.
- Essential services provided for the community at large, such as safe drinking water, sanitation, public transportation, and health and education facilities.

The programme of the 1976 Conference emphasized that strategies and national development plans and policies to include explicitly, as a priority objective, the promotion of employment and the satisfaction of the basic needs of each country's population. The people should participate in making the decisions that affect them through organizations of their own choice.

12.9.6. Development of Human Resources

Vocational training is one of the key elements of ILO's technical cooperation programme. Hundreds of projects have been implemented to strengthen the vocational training systems which are specific to different sectors of the economy, for example, agriculture, handicrafts, commerce, the hotel trade and tourism.

The ILO also cooperates in projects for management development and is active in the field of vocational rehabilitation. Its long-standing interest in handicapped people was expressed anew in 1983 with the adoption of a recommendation and a convention recognizing the importance that it attaches to the formulation and implementation of coherent national policies.

12.9.7. Social Institutions

The ILO fosters social justice in order to improve working and living conditions and to encourage balanced economic and social development. For that, there is a need for a social structure promoting large-scale participation and people involvement.

The ILO works in a standard setting having formative effect on social legislation and labour law throughout the world. The ILO also provide expert advice to various countries on request, on the measures needed to bring their legislation up to the level of international labour standards as well as to solve certain social problems. Many developing countries have sought ILO's help in establishing or codifying their labour and social legislations. In addition, the ILO facilitated for implementation of various training programmes and development of cooperative movements in various countries.

12.9.8. Training Programmes

As part of the training programmes, the ILO organizes seminars, study courses and technical discussions, often on a regional basis. An average of 50 courses of this type, including discussions on matters such as population and family planning are held each year in different parts of the world. There is also a publications programme, consisting of handbooks, booklets, bulletins and educational material, in addition to a film and filmstrip lending library.

12.9.9. Enterprise and Cooperative Development

Since its earliest days, the ILO has played an important role in developing the cooperative movement. Its range of activities in this field has grown with the introduction of the cooperative system in many developing countries. The governments of these countries recognize that cooperatives provide an instrument that can facilitate social and economic advancement. Above all, cooperatives are a key factor in rural development, for both production and marketing.

In 1991, a major programme to promote the establishment and effective operation of enterprises in the formal and informal sectors, in both rural and urban areas, was implemented. Projects in operation focus on four major areas: productivity and competitiveness, management systems and decent work, international labour standards and good management practices and socially responsible enterprise restructuring.

12.9.10. The Occupational Safety and Health Information Centre (CIS)

In 1976, the ILO launched the International Programme for the Improvement of Working Conditions and Environment (PIACT), aimed at giving governments', employers' and workers' organizations help in drawing up and implementing programmes for the improvement of working conditions and environment. The various means of action include standard-setting; technical cooperation, including the sending of multidisciplinary teams to member states at their request; tripartite meetings, particularly meetings of industrial committees, regional meetings, and meetings of experts; action-oriented research and studies; and gathering and dissemination of information, particularly through the CIS.

The objective of the CIS is to collect and disseminate world information that can contribute to the prevention of occupational accidents and diseases. The centre is assisted by more than 120 national centres representing all continents. The CIS also offers online compact disc and micro-computer databases.

In 1991, with the assistance of a grant from the German government, the International Programme on the Elimination of Child Labour (IPEC) was launched. More than 80 projects with government institutions, trade unions, employers' organizations and NGOs were implemented in at least 12 countries.

12.9.11. International Health Hazard Alert System

ILO's International Health Hazard Alert System, established in 1977, is a new approach to deal with newly discovered or suspected occupational hazards, which spread very quickly around the world. When a new hazard is discovered, an alert is sent out by the ILO to the participating countries for their assessment and reply. For example, the communication concerning possible health hazards in the use of carbonless copy papers was widely disseminated in several countries. In 1993, the Health Hazard Alert System circulated requests to member states for up-to-date information on major occupational health hazards and their prevention.

12.10. India and the ILO

India as a member country of ILO had been associated with the ILO even prior to its independence. India's association with the ILO has been studied in two phases, that is, the Colonial period and the period after Independence.

12.10.1. The Colonial Period

India was a founder member of the ILO, the only non-independent country to be so. In 1922, India became a permanent member of ILO's Governing Body. India had ratified 11 of the 28 conventions adopted on that date. The presentation of Indian employer and worker in the ILO was officially processed in India. In the initial years, employer delegates to the ILC came from the Associated Chambers of Commerce of India and Ceylon, formed in 1920. But in 1926, the Federation of Indian Chambers of Commerce and Industry was established, which also started sending employer delegates to the ILC [2].

Gandhiji as described by V. V. Giri was the founder of the modern trade union movement in India. He had influenced the ILO both through his activities and thoughts. According to Gandhiji, a model of trade unionism is based on responsibility, fair demands and social dialogue, and arbitration where necessary. These concepts were consistent with ILO's philosophy [3]; the

Ahmedabad TLA, created in 1920, pursued this philosophy under the leadership of Gandhiji. In 1928, the ILO opened a branch office in Delhi, the first branch in Asia.

N. M. Joshi, Indian worker representative in the ILO in its first conference and on many subsequent occasions, communicated with the ILO on various labour-related issues. In 1931, he also asked for and received ILO's advice on 'how to address the minimum rights of workers in the Indian Constitution', in preparation for the Constitutional Round Table in which he participated [4]. The Indian National Congress included in its demand for minimum rights of labour, which reflected several ILO priorities, including a living wage, limited hours of work, healthy conditions of work, protection against the economic consequences of old age, sickness and unemployment, freedom from serfdom, protection of women workers, prohibition of child labour and the right to form trade unions.

Atul Chatterjee, who was the High Commissioner of India in the United Kingdom from 1925 to 1931, took interest in ILO's affairs and chaired its conference in 1927. He was also in the Governing Body from 1932 to 1933. Various Indian labour legislations were also influenced by ILO's standards, as Menon has shown [5].

Harold Butler, who succeeded Thomas as director, visited India in 1938, the first by an ILO director, he concluded that the problems of Indian labour were different from European labour. He remarked,

> The Western mind is mainly preoccupied with questions of wage rates, working hours, unemployment, social insurance, protection against industrial accidents and disease, the safeguarding of women and children against exploitation, the organisation of factory inspection, relations between employer and worker, to which have been added in comparatively recent years the questions of housing, nutrition and vocational training. All these problems have made their appearance over the eastern horizon.... Nevertheless...it would be misleading to suggest that these problems, important as they are, dominate the social consciousness of the East. They necessarily yield priority to the fundamental and interlocking problems of population, poverty, illiteracy and disease. [6]

So many of the early ILO standards had separate provisions with lower requirements for China, India, Japan and some other countries, which varied according to the instrument. For instance, Convention 1 on hours of work specified a general limit of 48 hours per week, but 57 hours for Japan and 60 for India, and the situations of China, Persia and Siam were left for later consideration. During the discussions on Convention No. 33, 1932 (concerning the minimum working age in non-industrial employment), the workers demanded that Indian children have the same protection as children from other countries, but the employers and some governments argued for 'a principle of gradualness' [7]. Similar arguments were used about forced labour, even though ILO's Convention No. 29, 1930, did aim at its eventual elimination. The outcome was a dual framework, accepting lower standards in colonial territories, which became known as the 'native labour code'. It reflected, of course, that in the 1930s, the ILO was dominated by the colonial powers, and with the exception of India, the colonial territories were not directly represented in the ILO. There was always opposition to this differentiated approach, and it grew over time. Indian representatives in the ILO were vocal participants in this debate.

In 1941, Shanmukham Chetty, the Indian government delegate, said, 'we in the East often get a feeling that when European statesmen speak of democracy, self-determination and standards of living, they have mainly the white races of the world in their minds' [8]. Perhaps even more than by government delegates, the double standards were repeatedly criticized by Indian worker delegates, notably by Joshi, as Indian worker representative in the Governing Body from 1934 to 1944. The

Indian representatives kept up the pressure even when, as in the Philadelphia Conference in 1944, the Indian National Congress was not represented in the Government delegation. The native labour code was finally abandoned as decolonization began after the Second World War.

12.10.2. After Independence

Independence brought a radical change in the relationship between India and the ILO. The first ILO Asian Conference, held in New Delhi in 1947, discussed several major reports on aspects of development and institution building. As the first Prime Minister of India, Jawaharlal Nehru not only supported the ILO's stand on human rights but also called for the ILO to abandon its Eurocentric standpoint and embrace the problems faced by Asia. He called for greater activity in all areas of agricultural labour, and, above all, demanded assistance with industrialization, not out of generosity but as a moral obligation.

India's economic potential and the confidence of its government, which intended to establish the country as the leading power in Asia, generated pressure on the ILO to change. India's position was exceptional in that by the time it obtained independence it already had long experience of the ILO. Since the 1930s, India had increasingly used its position to establish itself as the mouthpiece of the colonial world within the international arena. At the same time, its special standing had allowed its representatives to gain a wealth of diplomatic experience before independence and to profit directly from the ILO's expertise in drafting legislation and political guidelines.

In 1957, Nehru addressed the ILO Regional Conference in Delhi. In this conference, his focus was concerned with overcoming labour–management conflict which he considered as a major constraint for development. For this, he looked at the ILO for cooperation.

India had adopted ILO's tripartism principle early on. In 1942, the Government of India set up a permanent Tripartite Labour Organization, which included a committee on conventions to examine ILO's standards, and an Indian Labour Conference modelled on the ILC [5].

The tripartite Indian Labour Conference continued to meet after Independence, and has now held 42 meetings. Naval Tata, who represented the Indian employers in the ILO for 40 years, carried over to the ILO the long Tata family tradition of social responsibility at the enterprise level. When he retired as President of the Employers' Federation of India in 1985, he summed up the results of his long experience in five points [9]. They are as follows:

1. The right to work should be recognized as a fundamental right.
2. The right to strike should also be recognized if the employer does not agree to voluntary arbitration.
3. Symmetrically, employers have the right to lockout.
4. State governments should be obliged to accept the verdict of national commissions on labour.
5. In case of violence, labour laws should cease to apply to those concerned.

During the two decades after the Second World War, there was a considerable expansion of ILO's technical cooperation programme. Some of the most important innovations in this programme occurred in India, especially around vocational training and occupational safety and health. ILO–India collaboration was particularly important in the case of the latter. The goal was to create national institutions with the technical capacity to research and oversee occupational safety and health policy, and successful programmes in India were subsequently emulated elsewhere [10].

In India's new economic strategy, productivity growth was seen as the key to successful industrialization. The ILO also helped India to set up the National Productivity Centre and supported the National Productivity Council. It also contributed in fields as diverse as occupational rehabilitation, wage policy, labour statistics and workers' education. But as national institutions were strengthened, calls for ILO's assistance diminished and the scope for technical cooperation narrowed after the 1960s.

India's view on labour standards was expressed on a number of occasions in the ILC. For instance, in 1971, Minister of Labour R. K. Khadilkar talked of standards 'becoming increasingly unrelated to the conditions prevailing in the developing regions of the world' and called on the ILO 'to meet the new challenges through programmes of practical action rather than through the elaborate enunciation of norms and standards'.

India had all through the beginning continued with the focus on development in the ILO's work. Indeed, the need for the ILO to address the problems of unorganized workers and the informal sector was a regular theme in the speeches of Indian labour ministers to the ILO [11]. But the ILO has always had difficulty reaching the informal sector. The dominant presence in ILO forums of employers' and workers' representatives from the modern sector, which in many countries represent only a fraction of the economy, tends to reinforce this tendency in the organization's work, and this remains true in India as elsewhere.

Since the 1980s, the ILO has continued to make a variety of contributions to thinking about India's development problems, with publications by ILO staff members on poverty, labour markets, social security, child labour, gender equality and a variety of other issues. At the same time, Indian economists such as Amartya Sen, Ashok Rudra, T. S. Papola and others have made major contributions to the ILO's work. There has therefore been a great deal of intellectual exchange. The following conventions have been ratified by India to date.

S. No.	No. and Title of Convention	Date of Ratification
1	No. 1 Hours of Work (Industry) Convention, 1919	14 July 1921
2	No. 2 Unemployment Convention, 1919	14 July 1921
3	No. 4 Night Work (Women) Convention, 1919	14 July 1921
4	No. 5 Minimum Age (Industry) Convention, 1919	9 September 1955
5	No. 6 Night Work of Young Persons (Industry) Convention, 1919	14 July 1921
6	No. 11 Right Of Association (Agriculture) Convention, 1921	11 May 1923
7	No. 14 Weekly Rest (Industry) Convention, 1921	11 May 1923
8	No. 15 Minimum Age (Trimmers And Stokers) Convention, 1921	20 November 1922
9	No. 16 Medical Examination of Young Persons (Sea) Convention, 1921	20 November 1922
10	No. 18 Workmen's Compensation (Occupational Diseases) Convention, 1925	30 September 1927
11	No. 19 Equality of Treatment (Accident Compensation) Convention, 1925	30 September 1927
12	No. 21 Inspection of Emigrants Convention, 1926	14 January 1928

S. No.	No. and Title of Convention	Date of Ratification
13	No. 22 Seamen's Articles of Agreement Convention, 1926	31 October 1932
14	No. 26 Minimum Wage-Fixing Machinery, Convention, 1928	10 January 1955
15	No. 27 Marking of Weight (Packages Transported By Vessels) Convention, 1929	7 September 1931
16	No. 29 Forced Labour Convention, 1930	30 November 1954
17	No. 32 Protection against Accidents (Dockers) Convention (Revised), 1932	10 February 1947
18	No. 41 Night Work (Women) Convention (Revised), 1934	22 November 1935
19	No. 42 Workmen's Compensation (Occupational Diseases) Convention (Revised), 1934	13 January 1964
20	No. 45 Underground Work (Women) Convention, 1935	25 March 1938
21	No. 80 Final Articles Revision Convention, 1946	17 November 1947
22	No. 81 Labour Inspection Convention, 1947	07 April 1949
23	No. 88 Employment Services Convention, 1948	24 June 1959
24	No. 89 Night Work (Women) Convention (Revised), 1948	27 February 1950
25	No. 90 Night Work of Young Persons (Industry) (Revised), 1948	27 February 1950
26	No. 100 Equal Remuneration Convention, 1951	25 September 1958
27	No. 107 Indigenous And Tribal Population Convention, 1957	29 September 1958
28	No. 111 Discrimination (Employment and Occupation) Convention, 1958	3 June 1960
29	No. 116 Final Articles Revision Convention, 1961	21 June 1962
30	No. 118 Equality of Treatment (Social Security) Convention, 1962	19 August 1964
31	No. 123 Minimum Age (Underground Work) Convention, 1965	20 March 1975
32	No. 115 Radiation Protection Convention, 1960	17 November 1975
33	No. 141 Rural Workers' Organisation Convention, 1975	18 August 1977
34	No. 144 Tripartite Consultation (International Labour Standards) Convention, 1976	27 February 1978
35	No. 136 Benzene Convention, 1971	11 June 1991
36	No. 160 Labour Statistics Convention, 1985	1 April 1992
37	No. 147 Merchant Shipping (Minimum Standards), 1976	26 September 1996
38	No. 122 Employment Policy Convention 1964	17 November 1998
39	No. 105 Abolition of Forced Labour, 1957	18 May 2000
40	No. 108 Seafarers' Identity Documents Convention, 1958	7 January 2005
41	No. 174 Prevention of Major Industrial Accidents, 1993	6 June 2008
42	No. 142 Human Resources Development, 1975	25 March 2009
43	No. 127 Maximum Weight, 1967	26 March 2010

S. No.	No. and Title of Convention	Date of Ratification
44	No. 185 Seafarers' Identity Documents Convention (Revised), 2003	9 October 2015
45	No. 186 Maritime Labour Convention, 2006 (MLC 2006)	9 October 2015
1 Protocol	P89 Protocol of 1990 to the Night Work (Women) Convention (Revised), 1948	
46	No. 138 The Minimum Age Convention, 1973	13 June 2017
47	No. 182 The Worst Forms of Child Labour Convention, 1999	13 June 2017

Source: https://www.ilo.org/dyn/normlex/en/f?p=1000:11200:0::NO:11200:P11200_COUNTRY_ID:102691 Accessed on 08-08-2019.

From time to time, India has adopted various ILO conventions, standards and recommendations. The first ILO office in Asia was set up in India even prior to its independence. The following table provides an idea of the various conventions, standards and recommendations adopted by India from time to time:

Decade	Labour/Social Developments in India	Developments in ILO	ILO–India Interaction
1919–1929	Growth of civil disobedience and protest 1920: Consolidation of trade union movement in AITUC 1920, 1926: Creation of Indian Chambers of Commerce 1926: Trade Unions Act 1929: Royal Commission on Labour	1919: ILO founded 1919: First Conference in Washington 1919–1929: 28 conventions adopted on major labour and social policy goals ILO research and statistics on production, employment, occupational safety and health, social protection	India is the only non-independent country founder member of ILO 1922: India becomes permanent member of Governing Body (GB) 1927: Atul Chatterjee chairs International Labour Conference (ILC) 1928: ILO office opens in Delhi India ratifies 11 of 28 conventions adopted
1930s	1930: Dandi Salt March Round Table Constitutional Conferences 1931: Congress Karachi platform and 1936 election manifesto stress fundamental rights	1934: The United States and USSR join ILO Development of dual standards for colonial territories in 'native labour code' ILO promotes Keynesian policies to counter Great Depression Expansion of work on social insurance	ILO helps specify rights at work in Congress programme ILO Geneva and Delhi offices help develop labour policy ILO GB chaired by Sir Atul Chatterjee (1932–1933): N. M. Joshi prominent as worker representative 1938: First visit to India by ILO Director

Decade	Labour/Social Developments in India	Developments in ILO	ILO–India Interaction
1940s	1942: Quit India Movement 1942: Tripartite Indian Labour Conference established on ILO model 1947: Industrial Disputes Act 1947: Independence and Partition Indian Constitution incorporates key labour and social rights	ILO in Canada during the Second World War 1944: Declaration of Philadelphia embeds universal rights 1946: ILO becomes specialized agency of UN 1948–1949: Conventions on freedom of association and collective bargaining adopted	1947: First ILO Asian Regional Conference held in Delhi Prime Minister Nehru endorses Declaration of Philadelphia 1948: First Indian Assistant Director General of ILO (Raghunath Rao) 1948–1949: Dharee Lal chairs GB
1950s	First Five-Year Plan built around public sector-driven industrialization Community development and zamindari abolition Reservations for Scheduled Castes (1953–1955: First Backward Castes Commission chaired by Kaka Kalelkar)	Adoption of further conventions on rights at work Development of ILO technical assistance programme Tensions due to the Cold War	1950: Jagjivan Ram chairs ILC Growth of technical cooperation on productivity, management development, wage policy India uses ILO forums to promote decolonization 1957: Fourth Asian Regional conference in Delhi India active in ILO governance (Naval Tata employer representative until the 1980s)
1960s	Bihar famine, shift in priority towards agriculture Start of Green Revolution 1967: National Commission on Labour	ILO action against apartheid Building of labour and social codes and institutions in newly independent countries Creation of International Institute for Labour Studies and Turin Training Centre 1969: ILO awarded the Nobel Peace Prize	ILO supports Indian institutions for occupational safety and health, manpower development Lower priority given to ratification of conventions 1961–1962: S. T. Merani chairs GB
1970s	1971: Garibi Hatao; strengthening of action against poverty 1975–1977: Emergency	World Employment Programme reorients ILO's action towards development goals 1976: World Employment Conference (unsuccessful) pressure for a new international economic order 1977: Multinationals Declaration adopted	1970: V. V. Giri addresses ILC; Nagendra Singh chairs (Maritime) ILC 1979: Ravindra Varma chairs ILC Indian economists involved in World Employment Programme Analytical/policy reports on labour markets, poverty, migration, industrialization, rural employment Labour and population programme starts

Decade	Labour/Social Developments in India	Developments in ILO	ILO–India Interaction
1980s	1982: Bombay textile strike Beginning of economic liberalization Economic growth accelerates National Rural Employment Programme, panchayati raj and local development	1984: World Labour Report launched neoliberal economic models undercut ILO action Promotion of freedom of association in Soviet bloc (Solidarnosc)	Asian Regional Team for Employment Promotion based in Delhi 1984–1985: B. G. Deshmukh chairs GB 1985: Rajiv Gandhi addresses ILC, calls for more attention to informal sector
1990s	Economic reforms and opening up of Indian economy 1991: National Commission on Rural Labour Political volatility Urbanization accelerates	Start of International Programme for Elimination of Child Labour UN Social Summit endorses ILO goals of employment and core labour standards 1998: Declaration on Fundamental Principles and Rights at Work 1999: Launch of Decent Work Agenda	India helps to prevent a social clause at WTO and keep international action on rights at work within ILO Indian representatives participate actively in process leading to adoption of 1998 Declaration
2000s	Indian economy globalizes High economic growth, slow formal sector employment growth, increase in inequality Growth of migration for work 2004–2009: National Commission on Enterprises in the Unorganized Sector	Global Programmes launched on employment and social security 2002–2004: World Commission on the Social Dimension of Globalization 2008: Declaration on Social Justice for a Fair Globalization	Development of action on child labour and HIV/AIDS ILO support to policies in India for entrepreneurship development, employment policies, reconstruction after disaster, hazard control, gender equality

Source: Rodgers G. India, the ILO and the quest for social justice since 1919. Econo. Pol. Wkly. 5 March 2011; 46(10).

India Ratifies both Fundamental ILO Conventions on Child Labour[2]

Geneva (ILO News): On 13 June 2017, the Government of India deposited with the International Labour Office the instruments of ratification of the two fundamental ILO Conventions concerning the elimination of child labour, the Minimum Age Convention, 1973 (No. 138) and the Worst Forms of Child Labour Convention, 1999 (No. 182).

[2] https://www.ilo.org/global/about-the-ilo/newsroom/news/WCMS_557295/lang--en/index.htm

India is the 170th ILO member State to ratify Convention No.138, which requires States party to set a minimum age under which no one shall be admitted to employment or work in any occupation, except for light work and artistic performances.

The second most populous country in the world is the 181st member State to ratify Convention No. 182. The latter calls for the prohibition and elimination of the worst forms of child labour, including slavery, forced labour and trafficking; the use of children in armed conflict; the use of a child for prostitution, pornography and in illicit activities (such as drug trafficking); and hazardous work.

India's Minister of Labour, Mr Bandaru Dattatreya, said that ratification of the two ILO Conventions reaffirmed his country's 'commitment to a child labour free society'.

He mentioned a series of measures in this regard, including the amendment to the Child Labour (Prohibition and Regulation) Act, 1986, which came into effect on 1 September 2016. This amendment now completely prohibits employment or work of children below 14 years in any occupation or process and also prohibits the employment of adolescents (14 to 18 years) in hazardous occupations and processes.

In addition, the Child Labour (Prohibition and Regulation) Central Rules, as recently amended, for the first time provide for a broad and specific framework for the prevention, prohibition, rescue and rehabilitation of child and adolescent workers.

Another prominent measure taken recently to meet the objective of a child labour free society is the strengthening of the National Child Labour project, which is a rehabilitative scheme providing bridge education and vocational training to adolescents.

'The momentum of the recent initiatives taken to eradicate child labour has to be maintained as elimination of child labour is also crucial for the attainment of Sustainable Development Goals by 2030', he concluded.

ILO Director-General Guy Ryder welcomed India among the member States party to the two fundamental Conventions. 'We all recognize the great progress India has made against child labour in recent years and the major role played by its convergence model of coherence between public policies and services, which was strongly supported by the ILO. Today, India's ratifications of Conventions 138 and 182 solidifies further—in treaty obligations—that commitment to the global fight against the scourge of child labour in all its forms. They also represent a positive step on the country's path towards full respect for fundamental rights at work'.

India's ratification confirms the status of Convention No. 182 as the most rapidly ratified ILO Convention.

'Universal ratification is within reach: as of today, only six member States remain to ratify this fundamental Convention. This reflects the overwhelming global consensus, as re-affirmed by the adoption of the sustainable development goals, and more particularly Goal 8-Target 8.7 (Sustainable Development Goal 8: Promote Inclusive and Sustainable Economic Growth, Employment and Decent Work for All), which aims at the complete eradication of child labour by 2025 and calls for immediate action to prohibit and eliminate its worst forms', the head of the ILO said.

Chapter Summary

1. ILO was founded in 1919 as part of the Treaty of Versailles with the mission to promote social justice and internationally recognized human and labour rights, based on the founding principle that social justice is essential to universal and lasting peace. The Constitution of the ILO was drafted as early as 1919.

2. The Declaration of Philadelphia which came into being on 10 May 1944, and was adopted at the 26th Conference of the ILO in Philadelphia stated the traditional objectives of the ILO and

then branched out in two new directions. They are: the centrality of human rights to social policy and the need for international economic planning.

3. ILO became known worldwide in 1999 with their 'Decent Work Agenda'. The organization as part of its mission, aims to achieve 'decent work' for all by *promoting social dialogue, social protection and employment creation, as well as respect for international labour standards*. This agenda assured to provide opportunities for work which is productive and generates a fair income, security at the workplace and social protection for families, better prospects for personal development and social integration, freedom for people to express their concerns, organize and participate in the decisions that affect their lives and equality of opportunity and treatment for all women and men.

4. ILO works through ILC, Governing Body and International Labour Office. One of the principal functions of the ILO is to secure international minimum social and labour standards. These standards are embodied in resolutions, in the form of conventions and recommendations, adopted by the ILC by at least two-thirds of the delegates present at the Conference through voting.

5. The ILO considers 'decent work' a human right. ILO agenda 2030 places decent work for all and ILO's mandate and purpose of social justice, at the heart of policies for sustainable and inclusive growth and development.

6. The ILO as a promoter of human rights through its conventions facilitates freedom of association, discourages forced labour and discrimination in employment and occupation. It also provides assistance to its member states in the form of technical assistance, managing unemployment and underemployment, developing HR, developing social institutions, imparting training programmes, facilitating enterprise and cooperative development, providing assistance through the CIS and providing International Health Hazard Alert System.

7. India as a member country of the ILO had been associated with the ILO even prior to its independence. The labour policies, labour laws have been highly impacted by the ILO. India has adopted 47 conventions by now.

Questions

1. What are the objectives of the ILO and how does it function?
2. What are convention and recommendations? What are the obligations of a member state after ratification of a convention?
3. Examine the various roles of the ILO.
4. Critically examine the influence of the ILO on the Indian labour policies and legislations.

References

1. Dufty NF. Organizational growth and goal structure: the case of the ILO. Int. Organ. 1972; 26(3):479–498.
2. Kaul NN. India and the International Labour Organisation. New Delhi: Metropolitan Book Co; 1956.
3. Chatterjee NN. Mahatma Gandhi and the industrial worker. Int. Labour Rev. 1970; 101(3):215–228.
4. Karmk VB. NMJosH: Servant of India. Bombay: United Asia Publications; 1972.
5. Menon VKR. The influence of international labour conventions on Indian labour legislation. Int. Labour Rev. 1956; 73:551–571.

6. ILO. Human Rights, Development and Decolonization: The International Labour Organization, 1940–70, London: Palgrave Macmillan Geneva: ILO; 1941. p. 33; quoted in Maul 2007.
7. ILO. Record of Proceedings, International Labour Conference, 16th Session, Geneva; 1932.
8. Nath A, Vithalani J. Horizons: the Tata-India century 1904–2004. Mumbai: India Book House; 2004.
9. Robert M, Parmeggiani L. Fifty years of international collaboration in occupational safety and health. Geneva: ILO; 1969.
10. Sangma PA, editor. India in ILO. Noida: National Labour Institute; 1994.

Index